H E A T H
MIDDLE LEVEL
LITERATURE

PURPLE LEVEL

A U T H O R S

Donna Alvermann	John Lounsbury	Lyndon Searfoss
Linda Miller Cleary	Alleen Pace Nilsen	Julia Thomason
Kenneth Donelson	Robert Pavlik	Max Thompson
Donald Gallo	Jewell Parker Rhodes	Carl Zon
Alice Haskins	Alberto Alvaro Ríos	
J. Howard Johnston	Sandra Schurr	

HOUGHTON MIFFLIN   BOSTON • MORRIS PLAINS, NJ

California • Colorado • Georgia • Illinois • New Jersey • Texas

STAFF CREDITS

EDITORIAL Barbara A. Brennan, Susan Belt Cogley, DeVona Dors, Christopher Johnson, Rita M. Sullivan, Patricia B. Weiler
Proofreading: JoAnne B. Sgroi

CONTRIBUTING WRITERS Kathy Tuchman Glass, Jo Pitkin

SERIES DESIGN Robin Herr

BOOK DESIGN Caroline Bowden, Daniel Derclula, Susan Geer, Diana Maloney, Angela Sciaraffa, Bonnie Chayes Yousefian
Art Editing: Carolyn Langley

PHOTOGRAPHY *Series Photography Coordinator:* Carmen Johnson
Photo Research Supervisor: Martha Friedman
Photo Researchers: Wendy Enright, Po-yee McKenna, PhotoSearch, Inc., Gillian Speeth, Denise Theoclores
Assignment Photography Coordinators: Susan Doheny, Gayna Hoffman, Shawna Johnston

COMPUTER PREPRESS Ricki Pappo, Kathy Meisl
Richard Curran, Michele Locatelli

PERMISSIONS Dorothy B. McLeod

PRODUCTION Patrick Connolly

Cover: *Icarus* by Henri Matisse, circa 1947, gift of Mr. and Mrs. Andrew S. Keck, © National Gallery of Art, Washington, D.C. **Cover Design:** Len Massiglia

Published simultaneously in Canada

Printed in the United States of America

International Standard Book Number: 0-618-06969-0
1 2 3 4 5 6 7 8 9 10-RRD-05 04 03 02 01 00

Middle Level Authors

Donna Alvermann, University of Georgia
Alice Haskins, Howard County Public Schools, Maryland
J. Howard Johnston, University of South Florida
John Lounsbury, Georgia College
Sandra Schurr, University of South Florida
Julia Thomason, Appalachian State University
Max Thompson, Appalachian State University
Carl Zon, California Assessment Collaborative

Literature and Language Arts Authors

Linda Miller Cleary, University of Minnesota
Kenneth Donelson, Arizona State University
Donald Gallo, Central Connecticut State University
Alleen Pace Nilsen, Arizona State University
Robert Pavlik, Cardinal Stritch College, Milwaukee
Jewell Parker Rhodes, Arizona State University
Alberto Alvaro Ríos, Arizona State University
Lyndon Searfoss, Arizona State University

Teacher Consultants

Suzanne Aubin, Patapsco Middle School, Ellicott City, Maryland
Judy Baxter, Newport News Public Schools, Newport News, Virginia
Saundra Bryn, Director of Research and Development, El Mirage, Arizona
Lorraine Gerhart, Elmbrook Middle School, Elm Grove, Wisconsin
Kathy Tuchman Glass, Burlingame Intermediate School, Burlingame, California
Lucretia Pannozzo, John Jay Middle School, Katonah, New York
Carol Schultz, Jerling Junior High, Orland Park, Illinois
Jeanne Siebenman, Grand Canyon University, Phoenix, Arizona
Gail Thompson, Garey High School, Pomona, California
Rufus Thompson, Grace Yokley School, Ontario, California
Tom Tufts, Conniston Middle School, West Palm Beach, Florida
Edna Turner, Harpers Choice Middle School, Columbia, Maryland
C. Anne Webb, Buerkle Junior High School, St. Louis, Missouri
Geri Yaccino, Thompson Junior High School, St. Charles, Illinois

CONTENTS

SPECIAL NOTE: *Because each unit of this book is also available as a separate volume, each page has two page numbers. In this book, use the page numbers in the boxes to locate what you want.*

THEME: Community

LEAN ON ME

THEME: The Future

FUTURE DIRECTIONS

PROJECTS

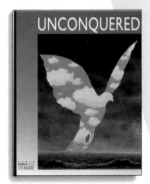

UNCONQUERED

THEME: Survival

UNCONQUERED

THE LITERATURE

THEME: Conflict Resolution

AT ODDS

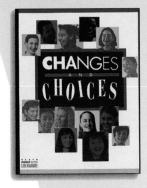

THEME: Challenges and Achievements

CHANGES AND CHOICES

Contents   9

THEME: Myths, Legends, and Folktales

VOICES THROUGH THE AGES

A Dark and Stormy Night

THEME: Mystery and the Imagination

A DARK AND STORMY NIGHT

PROJECTS

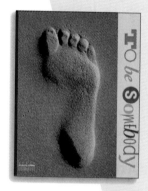

THEME: Identity and Self-Esteem

TO BE SOMEBODY

Con...

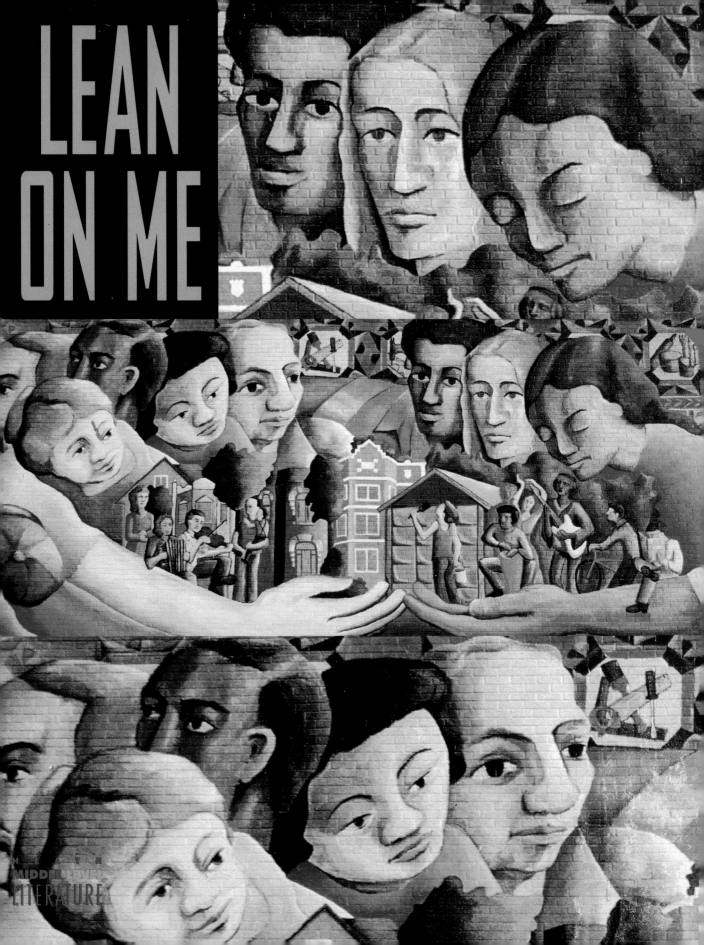

LEAN
ON ME

HEATH
MIDDLE LEVEL
LITERATURE

Lean on Me

THEME
COMMUNITY

AUTHORS

Donna Alvermann
Linda Miller Cleary
Kenneth Donelson
Donald Gallo
Alice Haskins
J. Howard Johnston
John Lounsbury
Alleen Pace Nilsen
Robert Pavlik
Jewell Parker Rhodes
Alberto Alvaro Ríos
Sandra Schurr
Lyndon Searfoss
Julia Thomason
Max Thompson
Carl Zon

STAFF CREDITS

EDITORIAL Barbara A. Brennan, Susan Belt Cogley, DeVona Dors, Christopher Johnson, Rita M. Sullivan, Patricia B. Weiler
Proofreading: JoAnne B. Sgroi

CONTRIBUTING WRITERS Kathy Tuchman Glass, Jo Pitkin

SERIES DESIGN Robin Herr

BOOK DESIGN Caroline Bowden, Daniel Derdula, Susan Geer, Diana Maloney, Angela Sciaraffa, Bonnie Chayes Yousefian
Art Editing: Carolyn Langley

PHOTOGRAPHY *Series Photography Coordinator:* Carmen Johnson
Photo Research Supervisor: Martha Friedman
Photo Researchers: Wendy Enright, Linda Finigan, Po-yee McKenna, PhotoSearch, Inc., Gillian Speeth, Denise Theodores
Assignment Photography Coordinators: Susan Doheny, Gayna Hoffman, Shawna Johnston

COMPUTER PREPRESS Ricki Pappo, Kathy Meisl, Richard Curran, Michele Locatelli

PERMISSIONS Dorothy B. McLeod

PRODUCTION Patrick Connolly

Cover: Cameramann, The Image Works. **Cover Design:** Steve Snider

Published simultaneously in Canada

Printed in the United States of America

International Standard Book Number: 0-669-32112-5 (soft cover)
   3 4 5 6 7 8 9 10-RRD-99 98 97 96

International Standard Book Number: 0-669-38180-2 (hard cover)
   3 4 5 6 7 8 9 10-RRD-99 98 97 96 95

Middle Level Authors

Donna Alvermann, University of Georgia
Alice Haskins, Howard County Public Schools, Maryland
J. Howard Johnston, University of South Florida
John Lounsbury, Georgia College
Sandra Schurr, University of South Florida
Julia Thomason, Appalachian State University
Max Thompson, Appalachian State University
Carl Zon, California Assessment Collaborative

Literature and Language Arts Authors

Linda Miller Cleary, University of Minnesota
Kenneth Donelson, Arizona State University
Donald Gallo, Central Connecticut State University
Alleen Pace Nilsen, Arizona State University
Robert Pavlik, Cardinal Stritch College, Milwaukee
Jewell Parker Rhodes, Arizona State University
Alberto Alvaro Ríos, Arizona State University
Lyndon Searfoss, Arizona State University

Teacher Consultants

Suzanne Aubin, Patapsco Middle School, Ellicott City, Maryland
Judy Baxter, Newport News Public Schools, Newport News, Virginia
Saundra Bryn, Director of Research and Development, El Mirage, Arizona
Lorraine Gerhart, Elmbrook Middle School, Elm Grove, Wisconsin
Kathy Tuchman Glass, Burlingame Intermediate School, Burlingame, California
Lucretia Pannozzo, John Jay Middle School, Katonah, New York
Carol Schultz, Jerling Junior High, Orland Park, Illinois
Jeanne Siebenman, Grand Canyon University, Phoenix, Arizona
Gail Thompson, Garey High School, Pomona, California
Rufus Thompson, Grace Yokley School, Ontario, California
Tom Tufts, Conniston Middle School, West Palm Beach, Florida
Edna Turner, Harpers Choice Middle School, Columbia, Maryland
C. Anne Webb, Buerkle Junior High School, St. Louis, Missouri
Geri Yaccino, Thompson Junior High School, St. Charles, Illinois

CONTENTS

THE LITERATURE

Cakewalk Carmen Lomas Garza, 1987

ASKING BIG QUESTIONS ABOUT THE LITERATURE

PROJECTS

1 WRITING WORKSHOP

LAUNCH A PROPOSAL   106-111

What would you like to change about your school or community? Here's your chance. Write a proposal to explain what you'd change and how your ideas could be put into action.

2 COOPERATIVE LEARNING

WHERE CAN I TURN?   112-113

Do teens in your area know how to find help when they need it? Work with a group of classmates to find local resources. Then put together a teen resource handbook.

3 HELPING YOUR COMMUNITY

GIVE A HELPING HAND   114-115

You can make a difference in your community. Research local volunteer opportunities, choose one that interests you, and then volunteer your services.

Trust!

Can you trust someone else to be your "eyes?" You're about to find out. You, a partner, and your teammates will play a game called TRUST! that helps you learn how to give and to receive help.

1 The Game

Object: To use game cards to spell out the word TRUST! on the chalkboard

Players: Your class divided into pairs of Guides and Followers

Materials: one blindfold; masking tape; game cards from your teacher— 2 "T" cards, 1 "R" card, 1 "U" card. 1 "S" card, and 1 "!" card.

The class divides into four teams. Each team divides into pairs. One person of each pair is a Guide; the other person is a Follower. Each holds half of the pair's set of game cards. Each Guide directs a blindfolded Follower from the back of the room to the chalkboard. Followers try to reach the board without bumping into other players or objects. When Followers reach the board, they tape their three game cards to it. Pairs switch roles. When one pair finishes, another pair is "up" and repeats the process. The first team whose pairs all successfully spell out TRUST! wins.

2 Rules

- The Guide can't touch the Follower. The Guide, walking near the Follower, may only give verbal directions (*go left, walk straight, desk chair ahead on right*).

- The Follower only follows directions. He or she can't ask questions but must listen for instructions and then move accordingl

- The Follower must walk s-l-o-w-l-y to the board. If the Follower touches a desk, chair, or another player, the teacher takes away the Follower's game cards. The Follower then goes to the back of the room, reclaims the cards, and starts over.

3 Directions

1. Each team decides which will be the first pair to play. One pair from each team will play TRUST! at the same time.

2. Everyone moves to the back of the room. On each team, the Guide blindfolds the Follower and then turns him or her around a few times.

3. The Guide places tape on three game cards and hands them to the Follower.

4. When the teacher says *go*, play begins. The four Followers should listen carefully to the Guide's instructions, trying to avoid obstacles—chairs, desks, other players.

5. Only the Guide gives verbal directions to help the Follower. (Teammates can cheer.) When the Follower reaches the board, the Guide gives instructions for taping the cards to it.

6. The Guide and the Follower go to the back of the room and switch roles.

7. When one pair successfully spells out TRUST!, the next pair on the team takes a turn. The first team whose pairs all spell out TRUST! wins.

What did you learn about your ability to trust someone?

Asking Big Questions About the Theme

Why do people need others?

What's the subject of all those songs that flood the airwaves? Usually it's something about people needing other people. So, why do people need other people in their lives? For food and shelter? For friendship? For some other reason? With a partner, list all the reasons that you can think of for needing other people. Then work together to rank the reasons in order of importance. Post your list in the classroom.

Why is offering help important?

Why is it important to offer help to people who need it? What do you get out of offering help? Think of a time when you helped someone. Make a web like the one begun here to help recall details of the experience. Then, in your journal, describe the situation and how you felt. Also describe what might have happened if you hadn't helped.

```
Ross's miserable measles  ──  I take a sick friend's paper route  ──  dawn really is pink
                                        │
              don't want Ross to lose job          I'm bit by a dachshund
```

What is involved in accepting help?

Is it easier to give help than to receive it? Is it easier to accept help from some people than from others? Are some people more comfortable giving help than accepting it? Are there some situations in which people wouldn't—or shouldn't—ask for help?

In your journal, explore your ideas about asking for and accepting help. Share your ideas with a partner or a group.

How can people make a difference in their communities?

With a partner or small group, think of people who have done something special in your school to create a better learning environment, to beautify the school, or to improve school spirit.

Now identify something that still needs to be done. How could you accomplish the task? Draw a diagram to develop your ideas. Then compare your ideas with those of your classmates.

NOW Think!

What is involved in giving and receiving help? As you read the following literature selections, try to think of answers to the Big Questions. Also keep in mind how you can apply what you've learned to your own life.

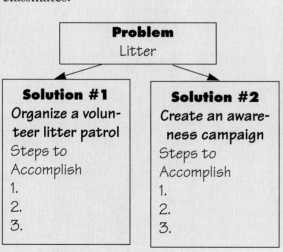

Problem
Litter

Solution #1	Solution #2
Organize a volunteer litter patrol	Create an awareness campaign
Steps to Accomplish	Steps to Accomplish
1.	1.
2.	2.
3.	3.

BILL WITHERS

Sometimes in our lives we all have pain, we all have sorrow.

But if we are wise, we know that there's always tomorrow.

Please swallow your pride if I have things you need to borrow,

For no one can fill those of your needs that you won't let show.

If there is a load you have to bear that you can't carry, 5

I'm right up the road. I'll share your load if you just call me.

Lean on me when you're not strong and I'll be your friend.

I'll help you carry on, for it won't be long till I'm gonna need somebody to lean on.

Just call on me, brother, when you need a hand.

We all need somebody to lean on. 10

I just might have a problem that you'd understand.

We all need somebody to lean on.

Lean on me when you're not strong and I'll be your friend.

I'll help you carry on, for it won't be long till I'm gonna need somebody to lean on.

Just call me when you need a friend. 15

Call me when you need a friend.

BILL WITHERS

Bill Withers was born on July 4, 1938, in Slab Fork, West Virginia. He was the youngest of six children and grew up a shy child who struggled to control a stammer. Music was his big outlet.

Withers worked as a bricklayer and then spent nine years in the United States Navy. The Navy and speech therapy, he says, cured both his shyness and his stammering.

In 1967, Withers moved to the West Coast, cut demo records of his songs, and began serious recording in 1970. His first public appearance was at age thirty-three. Withers has had a number of hit singles and discs over the years, including "Just the Two of Us."

from

I Know Why the Caged Bird Sings

Maya Angelou

Woman in Calico
William H. Johnson, 1944, detail,
oil on paperboard,
26 1/2" x 20 1/2"
National Museum of American Art,
Washington, D.C.

In this selection from her autobiography, Maya Angelou, who spent much of her childhood in Stamps, Georgia, with her brother Bailey and her grandmother, writes about a very special person. As you read, you will see that her neighbor, Mrs. Flowers, had a profound influence on Angelou and on her future life as a writer.

For nearly a year, I sopped around the house, the Store, the school and the church, like an old biscuit, dirty and inedible. Then I met, or rather got to know, the lady who threw me my first life line.

Mrs. Bertha Flowers was the aristocrat of Black Stamps. She had the grace of control to appear warm in the coldest weather, and on the Arkansas summer days it seemed she had a private breeze which swirled around, cooling her. She was thin without the taut look of wiry people, and her printed voile[1] dresses and flowered hats were as right for her as denim overalls for a farmer. She was our side's answer to the richest white woman in town.

Her skin was a rich black that would have peeled like a plum if snagged, but then no one would have thought of getting close enough to Mrs. Flowers to ruffle her dress, let alone snag her skin. She didn't encourage familiarity. She wore gloves, too.

1. **voile** [voil]: thin cloth of silk, wool, or cotton.

I don't think I ever saw Mrs. Flowers laugh, but she smiled often. A slow widening of her thin black lips to show even, small white teeth, then the slow, effortless closing. When she chose to smile on me, I always wanted to thank her. The action was so graceful and inclusively benign.

She was one of the few gentlewomen I have ever known, and has remained throughout my life the measure of what a human being can be.

Momma had a strange relationship with her. Most often when she passed on the road in front of the Store, she spoke to Momma in that soft yet carrying voice, "Good day, Mrs. Henderson." Momma responded with "How you, Sister Flowers?"

Mrs. Flowers didn't belong to our church, nor was she Momma's familiar.[2] Why on earth did she insist on calling her Sister Flowers? Shame made me want to hide my face. Mrs. Flowers deserved better than to be called Sister. Then, Momma left out the verb. Why not ask, "How *are* you, Mrs. Flowers?" With the unbalanced passion of the young, I hated her for showing her ignorance to Mrs. Flowers. It didn't occur to me for many years that they were as alike as sisters, separated only by formal education.

Although I was upset, neither of the women was in the least shaken by what I thought an unceremonious greeting. Mrs. Flowers would continue her easy gait[3] up the hill to her little bungalow,[4] and Momma kept on shelling peas or doing whatever had brought her to the front porch.

Occasionally, though, Mrs. Flowers would drift off the road and down to the Store and Momma would say to me, "Sister, you go on and play." As I left I would hear the beginning of an intimate conversation. Momma persistently using the wrong verb, or none at all.

"Brother and Sister Wilcox is sho'ly the meanest—"

"Is," Momma? "Is?" Oh, please, not "is," Momma, for two or more. But they talked, and from the side of the building where I waited for the ground to open up and swallow me, I heard the soft-voiced Mrs. Flowers and the textured voice of my grandmother merging and melting. They

2. **familiar:** close friend.
3. **gait:** way of walking.
4. **bungalow** [bung′ gə lō]: small house.

were interrupted from time to time by giggles that must have come from Mrs. Flowers (Momma never giggled in her life). Then she was gone.

She appealed to me because she was like people I had never met personally. Like women in English novels who walked the moors[5] (whatever they were) with their loyal dogs racing at a respectful distance. Like the women who sat in front of roaring fireplaces, drinking tea incessantly from silver trays full of scones[6] and crumpets.[7] Women who walked over the "heath"[8] and read morocco-bound[9] books and had two last names divided by a hyphen. It would be safe to say that she made me proud to be Negro, just by being herself.

She acted just as refined as white folks in the movies and books and she was more beautiful, for none of them could have come near that warm color without looking gray by comparison.

It was fortunate that I never saw her in the company of powhitefolks. For since they tend to think of their whiteness as an evenizer, I'm certain that I would have had to hear her spoken to commonly as Bertha, and my image of her would have been shattered like the unmendable Humpty-Dumpty.

One summer afternoon, sweet-milk fresh in my memory, she stopped at the Store to buy provisions. Another Negro woman of her health and age would have been expected to carry the paper sacks home in one hand, but Momma said, "Sister Flowers, I'll send Bailey up to your house with these things."

She smiled that slow dragging smile, "Thank you, Mrs. Henderson. I'd prefer Marguerite, though." My name was beautiful when she said it. "I've been meaning to talk to her, anyway." They gave each other age-group looks.

Momma said, "Well, that's all right then. Sister, go and change your dress. You going to Sister Flowers's."

The chifforobe[10] was a maze. What on earth did one put on to go

---

5. **moors:** open land, with low bushes or swamps.
6. **scones:** thick, flat, round, bread-like cakes.
7. **crumpets:** round, flat cakes.
8. **heath:** open land with bushes, but few trees, moor; all of these words often appear in old English stories.
9. **morocco-bound:** reference to an old-fashioned book cover made of leather.
10. **chifforobe** [shif′ ə rōb]: furniture with drawers and a place for hanging clothes.

to Mrs. Flowers' house? I knew I shouldn't put on a Sunday dress. It might be sacrilegious. Certainly not a house dress, since I was already wearing a fresh one. I chose a school dress, naturally. It was formal without suggesting that going to Mrs. Flowers' house was equivalent to attending church.

I trusted[11] myself back into the Store.

"Now, don't you look nice." I had chosen the right thing, for once.

"Mrs. Henderson, you make most of the children's clothes, don't you?"

"Yes, ma'am. Sure do. Store-bought clothes ain't hardly worth the thread it take to stitch them."

"I'll say you do a lovely job, though, so neat. That dress looks professional."

Momma was enjoying the seldom-received compliments. Since everyone we knew (except Mrs. Flowers, of course) could sew competently, praise was rarely handed out for the commonly practiced craft.

"I try, with the help of the Lord, Sister Flowers, to finish the inside just like I does the outside. Come here, Sister."

I had buttoned up the collar and tied the belt, apronlike, in back. Momma told me to turn around. With one hand she pulled the strings and the belt fell free at both sides of my waist. Then her large hands were at my neck, opening the button loops. I was terrified. What was happening?

"Take it off, Sister." She had her hands on the hem of the dress.

"I don't need to see the inside, Mrs. Henderson. I can tell. . ." But the dress was over my head and my arms were stuck in the sleeves. Momma said, "That'll do. See here, Sister Flowers, I French-seams around the armholes." Through the cloth film, I saw the shadow approach. "That makes it last longer. Children these days would bust out of sheet-metal clothes. They so rough."

"That is a very good job, Mrs. Henderson. You should be proud. You can put your dress back on, Marguerite."

"No ma'am. Pride is a sin. And 'cording to the Good Book, it goeth before a fall."

11. **trusted:** in this case, the sense is of hurrying back.

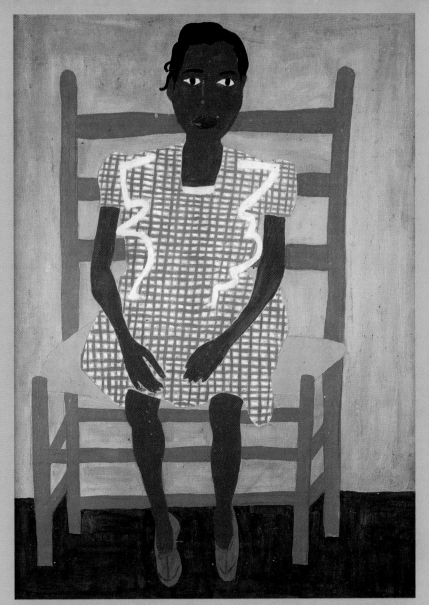

Little Girl in Green William H. Johnson, 1944, oil on paperboard, 31⁷/₈" x 22¹/₈", Clark Atlanta University, Atlanta GA

"That's right. So the Bible says. It's a good thing to keep in mind."

I wouldn't look at either of them. Momma hadn't thought that taking off my dress in front of Mrs. Flowers would kill me stone dead. If I had refused, she would have thought I was trying to be "woman-ish" and might have remembered St. Louis. Mrs. Flowers had known that I would be embarrassed and that was even worse. I picked up the groceries and went out to wait in the hot sunshine. It would be fitting if I got a sunstroke and died before they came outside. Just dropped dead on the slanting porch.

There was a little path beside the rocky road, and Mrs. Flowers walked in front swinging her arms and picking her way over the stones.

She said, without turning her head, to me, "I hear you're doing very good school work, Marguerite, but that it's all written. The teachers report that they have trouble getting you to talk in class." We passed the triangular farm on our left and the path widened to allow us to walk together. I hung back in the separate unasked and unanswerable questions.

"Come and walk along with me, Marguerite." I couldn't have refused even if I wanted to. She pronounced my name so nicely. Or more correctly, she spoke each word with such clarity that I was certain a foreigner who didn't understand English could have understood her.

"Now no one is going to make you talk—possibly no one can. But bear in mind, language is man's way of communicating with his fellow man and it is language alone which separates him from the lower animals." That was a totally new idea to me, and I would need time to think about it.

"Your grandmother says you read a lot. Every chance you get. That's good, but not good enough. Words mean more than what is set down on paper. It takes the human voice to infuse[12] them with the shades of deeper meaning."

I memorized the part about the human voice infusing words. It seemed so valid and poetic.

She said she was going to give me some books and that I not only must read them, I must read them aloud. She suggested that I try to make a sentence sound in as many different ways as possible.

"I'll accept no excuse if you return a book to me that has been badly handled." My imagination boggled at the punishment I would deserve if in fact I did abuse a book of Mrs. Flowers'. Death would be too kind and brief.

The odors in the house surprised me. Somehow I had never connected Mrs. Flowers with food or eating or any other common experience of common people. There must have been an outhouse, too, but my mind never recorded it.

12. **infuse:** fill.

The sweet scent of vanilla had met us as she opened the door.

"I made tea cookies this morning. You see, I had planned to invite you for cookies and lemonade so we could have this little chat. The lemonade is in the icebox."

It followed that Mrs. Flowers would have ice on an ordinary day, when most families in our town bought ice late on Saturdays only a few times during the summer to be used in the wooden ice-cream freezers.

She took the bags from me and disappeared through the kitchen door. I looked around the room that I had never in my wildest fantasies imagined I would see. Browned photographs leered or threatened from the walls and the white, freshly done curtains pushed against themselves and against the wind. I wanted to gobble up the room entire and take it to Bailey, who would help me analyze and enjoy it.

"Have a seat, Marguerite. Over there by the table." She carried a platter covered with a tea towel. Although she warned that she hadn't tried her hand at baking sweets for some time, I was certain that like everything else about her the cookies would be perfect.

They were flat round wafers, slightly browned on the edges and butter-yellow in the center. With the cold lemonade they were sufficient for childhood's lifelong diet. Remembering my manners, I took nice little lady-like bites off the edges. She said she had made them expressly for me and that she had a few in the kitchen that I could take home to my brother. So I jammed one whole cake in my mouth and the rough crumbs scratched the insides of my jaws, and if I hadn't had to swallow, it would have been a dream come true.

As I ate she began the first of what we later called "my lessons in living." She said that I must always be intolerant of ignorance but understanding of illiteracy. That some people, unable to go to school, were more educated and even more intelligent than college professors. She encouraged me to listen carefully to what country people called mother wit. That in those homely sayings was couched the collective wisdom of generations.

When I finished the cookies she brushed off the table and brought a thick, small book from the bookcase. I had read A *Tale of Two Cities* and found it up to my standards as a romantic novel. She opened the first page and I heard poetry for the first time in my life.

"It was the best of times and the worst of times . . ." Her voice slid in and curved down through and over the words. She was nearly singing. I wanted to look at the pages. Were they the same that I had read? Or were there notes, music, lined on the pages, as in a hymn book? Her sounds began cascading[13] gently. I knew from listening to a thousand preachers that she was nearing the end of her reading, and I hadn't really heard, heard to understand, a single word.

"How do you like that?"

It occurred to me that she expected a response. The sweet vanilla flavor was still on my tongue and her reading was a wonder in my ears. I had to speak.

I said. "Yes, ma'am." It was the least I could do, but it was the most also.

"There's one more thing. Take this book of poems and memorize one for me. Next time you pay me a visit, I want you to recite."

I have tried often to search behind the sophistication of years for the enchantment I so easily found in those gifts. The essence[14] escapes but its aura[15] remains. To be allowed, no, invited, into the private lives of strangers, and to share their joys and fears, was a chance to exchange the Southern bitter wormwood[16] for a cup of mead[17] with Beowulf[18] or a hot cup of tea and milk with Oliver Twist.[19] When I said aloud, "It is a far, far better thing that I do, than I have ever done . . ." tears of love filled my eyes at my selflessness.

On that first day, I ran down the hill and into the road (few cars ever came along it) and had the good sense to stop running before I reached the Store.

13. **cascading:** flowing like a waterfall.
14. **essence:** that which makes something what it is, necessary part of something.
15. **aura** [ōr′ ə]: something unseen that surrounds a person or thing.
16. **wormwood:** bitter or extremely unpleasant substance; here the atmosphere of prejudice in the author's town.
17. **mead** [mēd]: an ancient English drink made from honey; here the author means something refreshing that brings her happiness.
18. **Beowulf** [bā′ ə wŭlf]: hero of an English epic poem composed about A.D. 700.
19. **Oliver Twist:** character from a story of the same name by nineteenth-century English author Charles Dickens.

I was liked, and what a difference it made. I was respected not as Mrs. Henderson's grandchild or Bailey's sister but for just being Marguerite Johnson.

Childhood's logic never asks to be proved (all conclusions are absolute). I didn't question why Mrs. Flowers had singled me out for attention, nor did it occur to me that Momma might have asked her to give me a little talking to. All I cared about was that she had made tea cookies for *me* and read to *me* from her favorite book. It was enough to prove that she liked me.

Momma and Bailey were waiting inside the Store. He said, "My, what did she give you?" He had seen the books, but I held the paper sack with his cookies in my arms shielded by the poems.

Momma said, "Sister, I know you acted like a little lady. That do my heart good to see settled people take to you all. I'm trying my best, the Lord knows, but these days. . ." Her voice trailed off. "Go on in and change your dress."

M A Y A   A N G E L O U

Maya Angelou was born in 1928 in St. Louis, Missouri, and at three years of age was sent by her divorced parents to live with her grandmother in Stamps, Arkansas. After she grew up, she wrote poetry and prose about her earlier years and the pain and prejudice that she encountered. She says, "All my work, my life, everything is about survival. All my work is meant to say, 'You may encounter defeats, but you must not be defeated.'" Angelou's first autobiography, *I Know Why the Caged Bird Sings,* details her years growing up in Stamps.

Angelou has continued to draw on her own experiences and observations for her writing. Her fifth autobiography, *All God's Children Need Traveling Shoes*, describes her four-year stay in Ghana, Africa. Angelou's other accomplishments include writing volumes of poetry and plays, performing and singing on stage, and reading her poetry to the nation during President Clinton's inauguration in 1993.

American Sign Language: "Mother"

And Sarah Laughed

JOANNE GREENBERG

She went to the window every fifteen minutes to see if they were coming. They would be taking the new highway cutoff; it would bring them past the south side of the farm; past the unused, dilapidated outbuildings instead of the orchards and fields that were now full and green. It would look like a poor place to the new bride. Her first impression of their farm would be of age and bleached-out, dried-out buildings on which the doors hung open like a row of gaping mouths that said nothing.

All day, Sarah had gone about her work clumsy with eagerness and hesitant with dread, picking up utensils to forget them in holding, finding them two minutes later a surprise in her hand. She had been planning and working ever since Abel wrote to them from Chicago that he was coming home with a wife. Everything should have been clean and orderly. She wanted the bride to know as soon as she walked inside what kind of woman Abel's mother was—to feel, without a word having to be said, the house's dignity, honesty, simplicity, and love. But the spring cleaning had been late, and Alma Yoder had gotten sick—Sarah had had to go over to the Yoders and help out.

Now she looked around and saw that it was no use trying to have everything ready in time. Abel and his bride would be coming any minute. If she didn't want to get caught shedding tears of frustration, she'd better get herself under control. She stepped over the pile of clothes still unsorted for the laundry and went out on the back porch.

The sky was blue and silent, but as she watched, a bird passed over the fields crying. The garden spread out before her, displaying its varying greens. Beyond it, along the creek, there was a row of poplars. It always calmed her to look at them. She looked today. She and Matthew had planted those trees. They stood thirty feet high now, stately as figures in a procession. Once—only once and many years ago—she had tried to describe in words the sounds that the wind made as it combed those trees on its way west. The little boy to whom she had spoken was a grown man now, and he was bringing home a wife. *Married. . . .*

Ever since he had written to tell them he was coming with his bride, Sarah had been going back in her mind to the days when she and Matthew were bride and groom and then mother and father. Until now, it hadn't seemed so long ago. Her life had flowed on past her, blurring the early days with Matthew when this farm was strange and new to her and when the silence of it was sharp and bitter like pain, not dulled and familiar like an echo of old age.

Matthew hadn't changed much. He was a tall, lean man, but he had had a boy's spareness then. She remembered how his smile came, wavered and went uncertainly, but how his eyes had never left her. He followed everything with his eyes. Matthew had always been a silent man; his face was expressionless and his body stiff with reticence,[1] but his eyes had sought her out eagerly and held her and she had been warm in his look.

Sarah and Matthew had always known each other—their families had been neighbors. Sarah was a plain girl, a serious "decent" girl. Not many of the young men asked her out, and when Matthew did and did again, her parents had been pleased. Her father told her that Matthew was a good man, as steady as any woman could want. He came from honest, hard-working people and he would prosper any farm he had. Her mother spoke shyly of how his eyes woke when Sarah came into the room, and how they followed her. If she married him, her life would be full of the things she knew and loved, an easy, familiar world with her parents' farm not two miles down the road. But not one wanted to mention the one thing that worried Sarah: the fact that Matthew was deaf. It was what stopped her from saying yes

1. **reticence** [ret′ ə səns]: habit of being silent and reserved, or shy.

right away; she loved him, but she was worried about his deafness. The things she feared about it were the practical things: a fall or a fire when he wouldn't hear her cry for help. Only long after she had put those fears aside and moved the scant two miles into his different world, did she realize that the things she had feared were the wrong things.

Now they had been married for twenty-five years. It was a good marriage—good enough. Matthew was generous, strong, and loving. The farm prospered. His silence made him seem more patient, and because she became more silent also, their neighbors saw in them the dignity and strength of two people who do not rail[2] against misfortune, who were beyond trivial talk and gossip; whose lives needed no words. Over the years of help given and meetings attended, people noticed how little they needed to say. Only Sarah's friend Luita knew that in the beginning, when they were first married, they had written yearning notes to each other. But Luita didn't know that the notes also were mute. Sarah had never shown them to anyone, although she kept them all, and sometimes she would go up and get the box out of her closet and read them over. She had saved every scrap, from questions about the eggs to the tattered note he had left beside his plate on their first anniversary. He had written it when she was busy at the stove and then he'd gone out and she hadn't seen it until she cleared the table.

The note said: "I love you derest wife Sarah. I pray you have happy day all day your life."

When she wanted to tell him something, she spoke to him slowly, facing him, and he took the words as they formed on her lips. His speaking voice was thick and hard to understand and he perceived that it was unpleasant. He didn't like to use it. When he had to say something, he used his odd, grunting tone, and she came to understand what he said. If she ever hungered for laughter from him or a little meaningless talk that confirms existence and affection, she told herself angrily that Matthew talked through his work. Words die in the air; they can be turned one way or another, but Matthew's work prayed and laughed for him. He took good care of her and the boys, and they idolized him. Surely that counted more than all the

2. **rail:** complain bitterly.

words—words that meant and didn't mean—behind which people could hide.

Over the years she seldom noticed her own increasing silence, and there were times when his tenderness, which was always given without words, seemed to her to make his silence beautiful.

She thought of the morning she had come downstairs feeling heavy and off balance with her first pregnancy—with Abel. She had gone to the kitchen to begin the day, taking the coffeepot down and beginning to fill it when her eye caught something on the kitchen table. For a minute she looked around in confusion. They had already laid away what the baby would need: diapers, little shirts and bedding, all folded away in the drawer upstairs, but here on the table was a bounty of cloth, all planned and scrimped for and bought from careful, careful study of the catalogue—yards of patterned flannel and plissé, coat wool and bright red corduroy. Sixteen yards of yellow ribbon for bindings. Under the coat wool was cloth Matthew had chosen for her; blue with a little gray figure. It was silk, and there was a card on which was rolled precisely enough lace edging for her collar and sleeves. All the long studying and careful planning, all in silence.

She had run upstairs and thanked him and hugged him, but it was no use showing delight with words, making plans, matching cloth and figuring which pieces would be for the jacket and which for sleepers. Most wives used such fussing to tell their husbands how much they thought of their gifts. But Matthew's silence was her silence too.

When he had left to go to the orchard after breakfast that morning, she had gone to their room and stuffed her ears with cotton, trying to understand the world as it must be to him, with no sound. The cotton dulled the outside noises a little, but it only magnified all the noises in her head. Scratching her cheek caused a roar like a downpour of rain; her own voice was like thunder. She knew Matthew could not hear his own voice in his head. She could not be deaf as he was deaf. She could not know such silence ever.

So she found herself talking to the baby inside her, telling it the things she would have told Matthew, the idle daily things: Didn't

American Sign Language: "Father"

Margaret Amson look peaked[3] in town? Wasn't it a shame the drugstore had stopped stocking lump alum[4]—her pickles wouldn't be the same.

Abel was a good baby. He had Matthew's great eyes and gentle ways. She chattered to him all day, looking forward to his growing up, when there would be confidences between them. She looked to the time when he would have his own picture of the world, and with that keen[5] hunger and hope she had a kind of late blooming into a beauty that made people in town turn to look at her when she passed in the street holding the baby in the fine clothes she had made for him. She took Abel everywhere, and came to know a pride that was very new to her, a plain girl from a modest family who had married a neighbor boy. When they went to town, they always stopped over to see Matthew's parents and her mother.

Mama had moved to town after Pa died. Of course they had offered to have Mama come and live with them, but Sarah was glad she had gone to a little place in town, living where there were people she knew and things happening right outside her door. Sarah remembered them visiting on a certain spring day, all sitting in Mama's new front room. They sat uncomfortably in the genteel chairs, and Abel crawled around on the floor as the women talked, looking up every now and then for his father's nod of approval. After a while he went to catch the sunlight that was glancing[6] off a crystal nut dish and scattering rainbow bands on the floor. Sarah smiled down at him. She too had a radiance, and, for the first time in her life, she knew it. She was wearing the dress she had made from Matthew's cloth—it became[7] her and she knew that too, so she gave her joy freely as she traded news with Mama.

Suddenly they heard the fire bell ringing up on the hill. She caught Matthew's eye and mouthed, "Fire engines," pointing uphill to the firehouse. He nodded.

3. **peaked** [pē′ kid]: sick looking.
4. **lump alum** [al′ əm]: white mineral salt used in medicine and in preserving such items as pickles.
5. **keen:** sharp, acute.
6. **glancing:** flashing, gleaming.
7. **became:** suited, looked good on.

In the next minutes there was the strident, off-key blare as every single one of Arcadia's volunteer firemen—his car horn plugged with a matchstick and his duty before him—drove hell-bent for the firehouse in an ecstasy[8] of bell and siren. In a minute the ding-ding-ding-ding careened[9] in deafening, happy privilege through every red light in town.

"Big bunch of boys!" Mama laughed. "You can count two Saturdays in good weather when they don't have a fire, and that's during the hunting season!"

They laughed. Then Sarah looked down at Abel, who was still trying to catch the wonderful colors. A madhouse of bells, horns, screaming sirens had gone right past them and he hadn't cried, he hadn't looked, he hadn't turned. Sarah twisted her head sharply away and screamed to the china cats on the whatnot shelf as loud as she could, but Abel's eyes only flickered to the movement and then went back to the sun and its colors.

Mama whispered, "Oh, my dear God!"

Sarah began to cry bitterly, uncontrollably, while her husband and son looked on, confused, embarrassed, unknowing.

The silence drew itself over the seasons and the seasons layered into years. Abel was a good boy; Matthew was a good man.

Later, Rutherford, Lindsay, and Franklin Delano came. They too were silent. Hereditary[10] nerve deafness was rare, the doctors all said. The boys might marry and produce deaf children, but it was not likely. When they started to school, the administrators and teachers told her that the boys would be taught specially to read lips and to speak. They would not be "abnormal," she was told. Nothing would show their handicap, and with training no one need know they were deaf. But the boys seldom used their lifeless voices to call to their friends; they seldom joined games unless they were forced to join. No one but their mother understood their speech. No teacher could stop

---

8. **ecstasy** [ek′ stə sē]: condition of great joy.
9. **careened** [kə rēnd′]: tipped and swayed very quickly.
10. **hereditary:** passed down genetically from parent to child.

all the jumping, turning, gum-chewing schoolboys, or remember herself to face front from the blackboard to the sound-closed boys. The lip-reading exercises never seemed to make plain differences— "man," "pan," "began."

But the boys had work and pride in the farm. The seasons varied their silence with colors—crows flocked in the snowy fields in winter, and tones of golden wheat darkened across acres of summer wind. If the boys couldn't hear the bedsheets flapping on the washline, they could see and feel the autumn day. There were chores and holidays and the wheel of birth and planting, hunting, fishing, and harvest. The boys were familiar in town; nobody ever laughed at them, and when Sarah met neighbors at the store, they praised her sons with exaggerated praise, well meant, saying that no one could tell, no one could really tell unless they knew, about the boys not hearing.

Sarah wanted to cry to these kindly women that the simple orders the boys obeyed by reading her lips were not a miracle. If she could ever hear in their long-practiced robot voices a question that had to do with feelings and not facts, and answer it in words that rose beyond the daily, tangible things done or not done, *that* would be a miracle.

Her neighbors didn't know that they themselves confided to one another from a universe of hopes, a world they wanted half lost in the world that was; how often they spoke pitting inflection against meaning to soften it, harden it, make a joke of it, curse by it, bless by it. They didn't realize how they wrapped the bare words of love in gentle humor or wild insults that the loved ones knew were ways of keeping the secret of love between the speaker and the hearer. Mothers lovingly called their children crow-bait, mouse-meat, devils. They predicted dark ends for them, and the children heard the secrets beneath the words, heard them and smiled and knew, and let the love said-unsaid caress their souls. With her own bitter knowledge Sarah could only thank them for well-meaning and return to silence.

Standing on the back porch now, Sarah heard the wind in the poplars and she sighed. It was getting on to noon. Warm air was beginning to ripple the fields. Matthew would be ready for lunch soon, but she wished she could stand out under the warm sky forever and listen to birds stitching sounds into the endless silence. She found herself thinking about Abel again, and the bride. She wondered what Janice would be like. Abel had gone all the way to Chicago to be trained in drafting. He had met her there, in the school. Sarah was afraid of a girl like that. They had been married quickly, without family or friends or toasts or gifts or questions. It hinted at some kind of secret shame. It frightened her. That kind of girl was independent and she might be scornful of a dowdy mother-in-law. And the house was still a mess.

From down the road, dust was rising. Matthew must have seen it too. He came over the rise and toward the house walking faster than usual. He'd want to slick his hair down and wash up to meet the stranger his son had become. She ran inside and bundled up the unsorted laundry, ran upstairs and pulled a comb through her hair, put on a crooked dab of lipstick, banged her shin, took off her apron and saw a spot on her dress, put the apron on again and shouted a curse to all the disorder she suddenly saw around her.

Now the car was crunching up the thin gravel of the driveway. She heard Matthew downstairs washing up, not realizing that the bride and groom were already at the house. Protect your own, she thought, and ran down to tell him. Together they went to the door and opened it, hoping that at least Abel's familiar face would comfort them.

They didn't recognize him at first, and he didn't see them. He and the tiny bride might have been alone in the world. He was walking around to open the door for her, helping her out, bringing her up the path to the house, and all the time their fingers and hands moved and spun meanings at which they smiled and laughed; they were talking somehow, painting thoughts in the air so fast with their fingers that Sarah couldn't see where one began and the other ended. She stared. The school people had always told her that such finger-talk set the deaf apart. It was abnormal; it made freaks of them. . . . How soon Abel had accepted someone else's strangeness and bad ways. She felt so dizzy she thought she was going to fall, and she was more bitterly jealous than she had ever been before.

Students
chatting in
American
Sign
Language

The little bride stopped before them appealingly and in her dead, deaf-rote voice, said, "Ah-am pliizd to meet 'ou." Sarah put out her hand dumbly and it was taken and the girl's eyes shone. Matthew smiled, and this time the girl spoke and waved her hands in time to her words, and then gave Matthew her hand. So Abel had told that girl about Matthew's deafness. It had never been a secret, but Sarah felt somehow betrayed.

They had lunch, saw the farm, the other boys came home from their summer school and met Janice. Sarah put out cake and tea and showed Abel and Janice up to the room she had made ready for them, and all the time the two of them went on with love-talk in their fingers; the jokes and secrets knitted silently between them, fears told and calmed, hopes spoken and echoed in the silence of a kitchen where twenty-five years of silence had imprisoned her. Always they would stop and pull themselves back to their good manners, speaking or writing polite questions and answers for the family; but in a moment or two, the talk would flag, the urgent hunger would

overcome them and they would fight it, resolutely[11] turning their eyes to Sarah's mouth. Then the signs would creep into their fingers, and the joy of talk into their faces, and they would fall before the conquering need of their communion.

Sarah's friend Luita came the next day, in the afternoon. They sat over tea with the kitchen window open for the cool breeze and Sarah was relieved and grateful to hold to a familiar thing now that her life had suddenly become so strange to her. Luita hadn't changed at all, thank God—not the hand that waved her tea cool or the high giggle that broke into generous laughter.

"She's darling!" Luita said after Janice had been introduced, and, thankfully, had left them. Sarah didn't want to talk about her, so she agreed without enthusiasm.

Luita only smiled back. "Sarah, you'll never pass for pleased with a face like that."

11. **resolutely** [rez′ ə lüt lē]: firmly.

"It's just—just her ways," Sarah said. "She never even wrote to us before the wedding, and now she comes in and—and changes everything. I'll be honest, Luita, I didn't want Abel to marry someone who was deaf. What did we train him for, all those special classes? . . . *not* to marry another deaf person. And she hangs on him like a wood tick all day . . ." She didn't mention the signs. She couldn't.

Luita said, "It's just somebody new in the house, that's all. She's important to you, but a stranger. Addie Purkhard felt the same way and you know what a lovely girl Velma turned out to be. It just took time. . . . She's going to have a baby, did she tell you?"

"Baby? Who?" Sarah cried, feeling cold and terrified.

"Why, *Velma*. A baby due about a month after my Dolores'."

It had never occurred to Sarah that Janice and Abel could have a baby. She wanted to stop thinking about it and she looked back at Luita whose eyes were glowing with something joyful that had to be said. Luita hadn't been able to see beyond it to the anguish of her friend.

Luita said, "You know, Sarah, things haven't been so good between Sam and me. . . ." She cleared her throat. "You know how stubborn he is. The last few weeks, it's been like a whole new start for us. I came over to tell you about it because I'm so happy, and I had to share it with you."

She looked away shyly, and Sarah pulled herself together and leaned forward, putting her hand on her friend's arm. "I'm so happy for you. What happened?"

"It started about three weeks ago—a night that neither of us could get to sleep. We hadn't been arguing; there was just that awful coldness, as if we'd both been frozen stiff. One of us started talking— just lying there in the dark. I don't even know who started, but pretty soon we were telling each other the most secret things— things we never could have said in the light. He finally told me that Dolores having a baby makes him feel old and scared. He's afraid of it, Sarah, and I never knew it, and it explains why he hates to go over and see them, and why he argues with Ken all the time. Right there beside me he told me so many things I'd forgotten or misunderstood. In the dark it's like thinking out loud—like being alone and yet together at the same time. I love him so and I came so close to forgetting it. . . ."

*S*arah lay in bed and thought about Luita and Sam sharing their secrets in the dark. Maybe even now they were talking in their flower-papered upstairs room, moving against the engulfing seas of silence as if in little boats, finding each other and touching and then looking out in awe at the vastness all around them where they might have rowed alone and mute forever. She wondered if Janice and Abel fingered those signs in the dark on each other's body. She began to cry. There was that freedom, at least; other wives had to strangle their weeping.

When she was cried out, she lay in bed and counted all the good things she had: children, possessions, acres of land, respect of neighbors, the years of certainty and success. Then she conjured the little bride, and saw her standing in front of Abel's old car as she had at first—with nothing; all her virtues still unproven, all her fears still forming, and her bed in another woman's house. Against the new gold ring on the bride's finger, Sarah threw all the substance of her years to weigh for her. The balance went with the bride. It wasn't fair! The balance went with the bride because she had put that communion in the scales as well, and all the thoughts that must have been given and taken between them. It outweighed Sarah's twenty-five years of muteness; outweighed the house and barn and well-tended land, and the sleeping family keeping their silent thoughts.

*T*he days went by. Sarah tortured herself with elaborate courtesy to Janice and politeness to the accomplice son, but she couldn't guard her own envy from herself and she found fault wherever she looked. Now the silence of her house was throbbing with her anger. Every morning Janice would come and ask to help, but Sarah was too restless to teach her, so Janice would sit for a while waiting and then get up and go outside to look for Abel. Then Sarah would decide to make coleslaw and sit with the chopping bowl in her lap, smashing the chopper against the wood with a vindictive joy that she alone could hear the sounds she was making, that she alone knew how savage they were and how satisfying.

At church she would see the younger boys all clean and handsome,

American Sign Language: "I am deaf"

Matthew greeting friends, Janice demure and fragile, and Abel proud and loving, and she would feel a terrible guilt for her unreasonable anger; but back from town afterwards, and after Sunday dinner, she noticed as never before how disheveled the boys looked, how ugly their hollow voices sounded. Had Matthew always been so patient and unruffled? He was like one of his own stock, an animal, a dumb animal.

Janice kept asking to help and Sarah kept saying there wasn't time to teach her. She was amazed when Matthew, who was very fussy about his fruit, suggested to her that Janice might be able to take care of the grapes and, later, work in the orchard.

"I haven't time to teach her!"

"Ah owill teeech Ja-nuss," Abel said, and they left right after dinner in too much of a hurry.

Matthew stopped Sarah when she was clearing the table and asked why she didn't like Janice. Now it was Sarah's turn to be silent, and when Matthew insisted, Sarah finally turned on him. "You don't understand," she shouted. "You don't understand a thing!" And she saw on his face the same look of confusion she had seen that day in Mama's fussy front room when she had suddenly begun to cry and could not stop. She turned away with the plates, but suddenly his hand shot out and he struck them to the floor, and the voice he couldn't hear or control rose to an awful cry, "Ah ahm dehf! Ah ahm dehf!" Then he went out, slamming the door without the satisfaction of its sound.

If a leaf fell or a stalk sprouted in the grape arbor, Janice told it over like a set of prayers. One night at supper, Sarah saw the younger boys framing those dumb-signs of hers, and she took them outside and slapped their hands. "*We* don't do that!" she shouted at them, and to Janice later she said,

"Those . . . signs you make—I know they must have taught you to do that, but out here . . . well, it isn't our way."

Janice looked back at her in a confusion for which there were no words.

It was no use raging at Janice. Before she had come there had never been anything for Sarah to be angry about. . . . What did they all expect of her? Wasn't it enough that she was left out of a world that heard and laughed without being humiliated by the love-madness that they made with their hands? It was like watching them undressing.

The wind cannot be caught. Poplars may sift it, a rising bird can breast it, but it will pass by and no one can stop it. She saw the boys coming home at a dead run now, and they couldn't keep their hands from taking letters, words, and pictures from the fingers of the lovers. If they saw an eagle, caught a fish, or got scolded, they ran to their brother or his wife, and Sarah had to stand in the background and demand to be told.

One day Matthew came up to her and smiled and said, "Look." He put out his two index fingers and hooked the right down on the left, then the left down gently on the right. "Fwren," he said, "Ja-nuss say, fwren."

To Sarah there was something obscene about all those gestures, and she said, "I don't like people waving their hands around like monkeys in a zoo!" She said it very clearly so that he couldn't mistake it.

He shook his head violently and gestured as he spoke. "Mouth eat; mouth kiss, mouth tawk! Fin-ger wohk; fin-ger tawk. E-ah" (and he grabbed his ear, violently), "e-ah dehf. *Mihn*," (and he rapped his head, violently, as if turning a terrible impatience against himself so as to spare her) "*mihn not* dehf!"

Later she went to the barn after something and she ran into Lindsay and Franklin Delano standing guiltily, and when she caught them in her eye as she turned, she saw their hands framing signs. They didn't come into the house until it was nearly dark. Was their hunger for those signs so great that only darkness could bring them home? They weren't bad boys, the kind who would do a thing just because you told them not to. Did their days have a hunger too, or was it only the spell of the lovers, honey-honeying to shut out a world of moving mouths and silence?

At supper she looked around the table and was reassured. It could have been any farm family sitting there, respectable and quiet. A glance from the father was all that was needed to keep order or summon another helping. Their eyes were lowered, their faces composed.

Their hands were quiet. She smiled and went to the kitchen to fix the shortcake she had made as a surprise.

When she came back, they did not notice her immediately. They were all busy talking. Janice was telling them something and they all had their mouths ridiculously pursed with the word. Janice smiled in assent and each one showed her his sign and she smiled at each one and nodded, and the signers turned to one another in their joy, accepting and begging acceptance. Then they saw Sarah standing there; the hands came down, the faces faded.

She took the dinner plates away and brought in the dessert things, and when she went back to the kitchen for the cake, she began to cry. It was beyond envy now; it was too late for measuring or weighing. She had lost. In the country of the blind, Mama used to say, the one-eyed man is king. Having been a citizen of such a country, she knew better. In the country of the deaf, the hearing man is lonely. Into that country a girl had come who, with a wave of her hand, had given the deaf ears for one another, and had made Sarah the deaf one.

Sarah stood, staring at her cake and feeling for that moment the profundity of the silence which she had once tried to match by stuffing cotton in her ears. Everyone she loved was in the other room, talking, sharing, standing before the awful, impersonal heaven and the unhearing earth with pictures of his thoughts, and she was the deaf one now. It wasn't "any farm family," silent in its strength. It was a yearning family, silent in its hunger, and a demure little bride had shown them all how deep the hunger was. She had shown Sarah that her youth had been sold into silence. She was too old to change now.

An anger rose in her as she stared at the cake. Why should they be free to move and gesture and look different while she was kept in bondage to their silence? Then she remembered Matthew's mute notes, his pride in Abel's training, his face when he had cried, "I am deaf!" over and over. She had actually fought that terrible yearning, that hunger they all must have had for their own words. If they could all speak somehow, what would the boys tell her?

She knew what she wanted to tell them. That the wind sounds through the poplar trees, and people have a hard time speaking to one another even if they aren't deaf. Luita and Sam had to have a night to hide their faces while they spoke. It suddenly occurred to her that if Matthew made one of those signs with his hands and she could learn that sign, she could put her hands against his in the darkness, and read the meaning—that if she learned those signs she could hear him. . . .

She dried her eyes hurriedly and took in the cake. They saw her and the hands stopped, drooping lifelessly again; the faces waited mutely. Silence. It was a silence she could no longer bear. She looked from face to face. What was behind those eyes she loved? Didn't everyone's world go deeper than chores and bread and sleep?

"I want to talk to you," she said. "I want to talk, to know what you think." She put her hands out before her, offering them.

Six pairs of eyes watched her.

Janice said, "Mo-ther."

Eyes snapped away to Janice; thumb was under lip: the Sign.

Sarah followed them. "Wife," she said, showing her ring.

"Wife," Janice echoed, thumb under lip to the clasp of hands.

Sarah said, "I love . . ."

Janice showed her and she followed hesitantly and then turned to Matthew to give and to be received in that sign.

JOANNE GREENBERG

Joanne Greenberg, born in 1932 in Brooklyn, New York, lives a life of challenge and excitement. In addition to being a writer and a professor, Greenberg has served on her local Colorado Lookout Mountain Fire Department and the Idledale Rescue Team as a certified emergency medical technician.

An award-winning author, Greenberg has published many novels and short stories. John Nicholson of the London Times calls her a professional storyteller, skilled at putting "plausible characters into interesting situations and letting them get on with it." This storytelling ability is applied to presenting characters who contend with life's difficulties and conquer them.

American Sign Language: "Love"

SCAFFOLDING

SEAMUS HEANEY

Masons, when they start upon a building,
Are careful to test out the scaffolding;

Make sure that planks won't slip at busy points,
Secure all ladders, tighten bolted joints.

And yet all this comes down when the job's done   5
Showing off walls of sure and solid stone.

So if, my dear, there sometimes seem to be
Old bridges breaking between you and me

Never fear. We may let the scaffolds fall
Confident that we have built our wall.   10

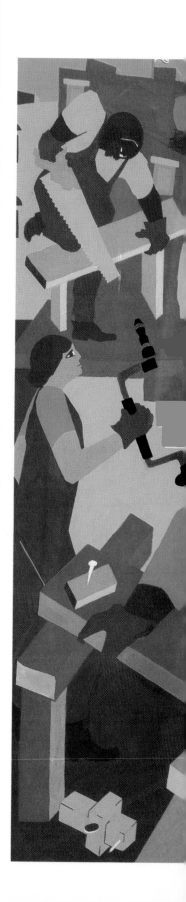

Builder Jacob Lawrence, 1980,
gouache on paper, 25 $\frac{1}{2}$" x 34",
Collection of SAFECO Insurance Companies

Seamus Heaney, born in 1939 in County Derry, Northern Ireland, grew up on his family's farm. When he was eleven, Heaney went to boarding school in Belfast. His years in boarding school convinced him that the country life of his childhood was old-fashioned and out of touch with the times. In college, however, he met artists whose work was inspired by the places where they had grown up. Heaney then began to write poetry "concerned with nature, the shocks and discoveries of childhood experience on a farm."

Heaney was living in Belfast during violent political struggles in Northern Ireland. No poet could be untouched by bombs and snipers all around him; Heaney's poems put these struggles into the bigger picture of Ireland's history.

In 1979, Heaney came to the United States to teach at Harvard University. He has published many collections of his poems, including *After Summer* and *Hedge School*. The poem "Scaffolding" is from *Poems: 1956-1975*.

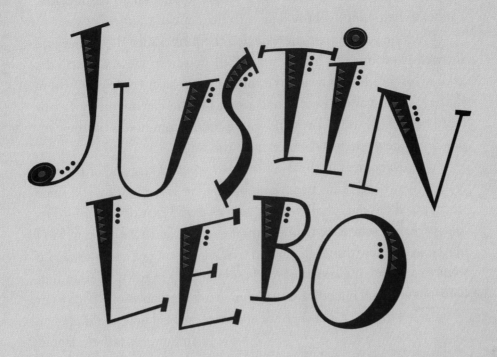

JUSTIN LEBO

PHILLIP HOOSE

Something about the battered old bicycle at the garage sale caught ten-year-old Justin Lebo's eye. What a wreck! It was like looking at a few big bones in the dust and trying to figure out what kind of dinosaur they had once belonged to.

It was a BMX bike with a twenty-inch frame. Its original color was buried beneath five or six coats of gunky paint. Now it showed up as sort of a rusted red. Everything—the grips, the pedals, the brakes, the seat, the spokes—were bent or broken, twisted and rusted. Justin stood back as if he were inspecting a painting for sale at an auction. Then he made his final judgment: perfect.

Justin talked the owner down to $6.50 and asked his mother, Diane, to help him load the bike into the back of their car.

When he got it home, he wheeled the junker into the garage and showed it proudly to his father. "Will you help me fix it up?" he asked. Justin's hobby was bike racing, a passion the two of them shared. Their garage barely had room for the car anymore. It was more like a bike shop. Tires and frames hung from hooks on the ceiling, and bike wrenches dangled from the walls.

After every race, Justin and his father would adjust the brakes and realign the wheels of his two racing bikes. This was a lot of work, since Justin raced flat out, challenging every gear and part to perform to its fullest. He had learned to handle almost every repair his father could and maybe even a few things he couldn't. When Justin got really stuck, he went to see Mel, the owner of the best bike shop in town. Mel let him hang out and watch, and he even grunted a few syllables of advice from between the spokes of a wheel now and then.

Now Justin and his father cleared out a work space in the garage and put the old junker up on a rack. They poured alcohol on the frame and rubbed until the old paint began to yield, layer by layer. They replaced the broken pedal, tightened down a new seat, and restored the grips. In about a week, it looked brand new.

Justin wheeled it out of the garage, leapt aboard, and started off around the block. He stood up and mashed down on the pedals, straining for speed. It was a good, steady ride, but not much of a thrill compared to his racers.

Soon he forgot about the bike. But the very next week, he bought another junker at a yard sale and fixed it up, too. After a while it bothered him that he wasn't really using either bike. Then he realized that what he loved about the old bikes wasn't riding them: it was the challenge of making something new and useful out of something old and broken.

Justin wondered what he should do with them. They were just taking up space in the garage. He remembered that when he was younger, he used to live near a large brick building called the Kilbarchan Home for Boys. It was a place for boys whose parents couldn't care for them for one reason or another.

He found "Kilbarchan" in the phone book and called the director, who said the boys would be thrilled to get two bicycles. The next day when Justin and his mother unloaded the bikes at the home, two boys raced out to greet them. They leapt aboard the bikes and started tooling around the semicircular driveway, doing wheelies and pirouettes,[1] laughing and shouting.

The Lebos watched them for a while, then started to climb into their car to go home. The boys cried after them, "Wait a minute! You forgot your bikes!" Justin explained that the bikes were for them to keep. "They were so happy," Justin remembers. "It was like they couldn't believe it. It made me feel good just to see them happy."

On the way home, Justin was silent. His mother assumed he was lost in a feeling of satisfaction. But he was thinking about what would happen once those bikes got wheeled inside and everyone saw them. How would all those kids decide who got the bikes? Two bikes could cause more trouble than they would solve. Actually, they hadn't been that hard to build. It was fun. Maybe he could do more. . . .

"Mom," Justin said as they turned onto their street, "I've got an idea. I'm going to make a bike for every boy at Kilbarchan for

---

1. **pirouettes** [pir′ ü etz′]: full turns of the body.

Christmas." Diane Lebo looked at Justin out of the corner of her eye. She had rarely seen him so determined.

When they got home, Justin called Kilbarchan to find out how many boys lived there. There were twenty-one. It was already June. He had six months to make nineteen bikes. That was almost a bike a week. Justin called the home back to tell them of his plan. "I could tell they didn't think I could do it," Justin remembers. "I knew I could."

"IT JUST SNOWBALLED."

Justin knew his best chance was to build bikes almost the way GM or Ford builds cars: in an assembly line. He would start with frames from three-speed, twenty-four-inch BMX bicycles. They were common bikes, and all the parts were interchangeable. If he could find enough decent frames, he could take parts off broken bikes and fasten them onto the good frames. He figured it would take three or four junkers to produce enough parts to make one good bike. That meant sixty to eighty bikes. Where would he get them?

Garage sales seemed to be the only hope. It was June, and there would be garage sales all summer long. But even if he could find that many bikes, how could he ever pay for them? That was hundreds of dollars.

He went to his parents with a proposal. "When Justin was younger, say five or six," says his mother, "he used to give some of his allowance away to help others in need. His father and I would donate a dollar for every dollar Justin donated. So he asked us if it could be like the old days, if we'd match every dollar he put into buying old bikes. We said yes."

Justin and his mother spent most of June and July hunting for cheap bikes at garage sales and thrift shops. They would haul the bikes home, and Justin would start stripping them down in the yard.

But by the beginning of August, he had managed to make only ten bikes. Summer vacation was almost over, and school and homework would soon cut into his time. Garage sales would dry up when it got colder, and Justin was out of money. Still, he was determined to find a way.

At the end of August, Justin got a break. A neighbor wrote a letter to the local newspaper describing Justin's project, and an editor thought it would make a good story. One day a reporter entered the Lebo garage. Stepping gingerly through the tires and frames that covered the floor, she found a boy with cut fingers and dirty nails, banging a seat onto a frame. His clothes were covered with grease. In her admiring article about a boy who was devoting his summer to help kids he didn't even know, she said Justin needed bikes and money, and she printed his home phone number.

Overnight, everything changed. "There must have been a hundred calls," Justin says. "People would call me up and ask me to come over and pick up their old bike. Or I'd be working in the garage, and a station wagon would pull up. The driver would leave a couple of bikes by the curb. It just snowballed."

By the start of school, the garage was overflowing with BMX frames. Pyramids of pedals and seats rose in the corners. Soon bike parts filled a toolshed in the backyard and then spilled out into the small yard itself, wearing away the lawn.

More and more writers and television and radio reporters called for interviews. Each time he told his story, Justin asked for bikes and money. "The first few interviews were fun," Justin says, "but it reached a point where I really didn't like doing them. The publicity was necessary, though. I had to keep doing interviews to get the donations I needed."

By the time school opened, he was working on ten bikes at a time. There were so many calls now that he was beginning to refuse offers that weren't the exact bikes he needed.

As checks came pouring in, Justin's money problems disappeared. He set up a bank account and began to make bulk orders of common parts from Mel's Bike Shop. Mel seemed delighted to see him. Sometimes, if Justin brought a bike by the shop, Mel would help him fix it. When Justin tried to talk him into a lower price for big orders, Mel smiled and gave in. He respected another good businessman. They became friends.

"WHY DO YOU DO IT?"

The week before Christmas Justin delivered the last of the twenty-one bikes to Kilbarchan. Once again, the boys poured out of the home and leapt aboard the bikes, tearing around the snow.

And once again, their joy inspired Justin. They reminded him how important bikes were to him. Wheels meant freedom. He thought how much more the freedom to ride must mean to boys like these who had so little freedom in their lives. He decided to keep on building.

"First I made eleven bikes for the children in a foster home my mother told me about. Then I made bikes for all the women in a battered women's shelter. Then I made ten little bikes and tricycles for the kids in a home for children with AIDS. Then I made twenty-three bikes for the Paterson Housing Coalition."[2]

2. **coalition** [kō′ ə lish′ ən]: group working for a common purpose.

In the four years since he started, Justin Lebo has made between 150 and 200 bikes and given them all away. He has been careful to leave time for his homework, his friends, his coin collection, his new interest in marine biology,[3] and of course his own bikes.

Reporters and interviewers have asked Justin Lebo the same question over and over: "Why do you do it?" The question seems to make him uncomfortable. It's as if they want him to say what a great person he is. Their stories always make him seem like a saint, which he knows he isn't. "Sure it's nice of me to make the bikes," he says, "because I don't have to. But I want to. In part, I do it for myself. I don't think you can ever really do anything to help anybody else if it doesn't make you happy.

"Once I overheard a kid who got one of my bikes say, 'A bike is like a book; it opens up a whole new world.' That's how I feel, too. It made me happy to know that kid felt that way. That's why I do it."

3. **marine biology:** study of animals and plants that live in the ocean.

PHILLIP HOOSE

Phillip Hoose was born in South Bend, Indiana, in 1947. He now lives with his family in Portland, Maine. Hoose says, "I got the idea for this book when my daughter's school became interested in the homeless several years ago." She and her classmates decided to hold an auction, sent out a press release, and made about five hundred dollars for a homeless shelter. Hoose began thinking that there must be other children and young adults who had taken community action on their own, and he determined to find them. The result is *Our World, Too!*, from which "Justin Lebo" is taken.

Hoose himself takes action in causes he believes in. As a tenant organizer, Hoose fought to improve the quality of life in inner city neighborhoods. In his present position as a staff member of the Nature Conservancy, Hoose works to protect endangered species.

FROM BARRIO

ERNESTO GALARZA

The two of us walked south on Fifth Street one morning to the corner of Q Street and turned right. Half of the block was occupied by the Lincoln School. It was a three-story wooden building, with two wings that gave it the shape of a double-T connected by a central hall. It was a new building, painted yellow, with a shingled roof that was not like the red tile of the school in Mazatlán.[1] I noticed other differences, none of them very reassuring.

We walked up the wide staircase hand in hand and through the door, which closed by itself. A mechanical contraption screwed to the top shut it behind us quietly.

Up to this point the adventure of enrolling me in the school had been carefully rehearsed. Mrs. Dodson[2] had told us how to find it and we had circled it several times on our walks. Friends in the *barrio*[3] explained that the director was called a principal, and that it was a lady and not a man. They assured us that there was always a person at the school who could speak Spanish.

Exactly as we had been told, there was a sign on the door in both Spanish and English: "Principal." We crossed the hall and entered the office of Miss Nettie Hopley.

Miss Hopley was at a roll-top desk to one side, sitting in a swivel chair that moved on wheels. There was a sofa against the opposite wall, flanked by two windows and a door that opened on a small balcony. Chairs were set around a table and framed pictures hung on the walls of a man with long white hair and another with a sad face and a black beard.

1. **Mazatlán** [mä zät län´]: seaport in western Mexico.
2. **Mrs. Dodson:** owner of the boarding house in which the family lived.
3. *barrio* [bä´ ryō]: Spanish for "neighborhood."

BOY

Cakewalk Carmen Lomas Garza, 1987, acrylic, 36" x 48"

The principal half turned in the swivel chair to look at us over the pinch glasses[4] crossed on the ridge of her nose. To do this she had to duck her head slightly as if she were about to step through a low doorway.

What Miss Hopley said to us we did not know but we saw in her eyes a warm welcome and when she took off her glasses and straightened up she smiled wholeheartedly, like Mrs. Dodson. We were, of course, saying nothing, only catching the friendliness of her voice and the sparkle in her eyes while she said words we did not understand. She signaled us to the table. Almost tiptoeing across the office, I maneuvered myself to keep my mother between me and the gringo[5] lady. In a matter of seconds I had to decide whether she was a possible friend or a menace. We sat down.

Then Miss Hopley did a formidable thing. She stood up. Had she been standing when we entered she would have seemed tall. But rising from her chair she soared. And what she carried up and up with her was a buxom superstructure, firm shoulders, a straight sharp nose, full cheeks slightly molded by a curved line along the nostrils, thin lips that moved like steel springs, and a high forehead topped by hair gathered in a bun. Miss Hopley was not a giant in body but when she mobilized it to a standing position she seemed a match for giants. I decided I liked her.

She strode to a door in the far corner of the office, opened it and called a name. A boy of about ten years appeared in the doorway. He sat down at one end of the table. He was brown like us, a plump kid with shiny black hair combed straight back, neat, cool, and faintly obnoxious.

Miss Hopley joined us with a large book and some papers in her hand. She, too, sat down and the questions and answers began by way of our interpreter. My name was Ernesto.[6] My mother's name was Henriqueta.[7] My birth certificate was in San Blas.[8] Here was my last

---

4. **pinch glasses:** eyeglasses that clip onto the bridge of the nose but have no bows to go over the ears.
5. **gringo** [grēn′ gō]: Mexican American term for a foreigner.
6. **Ernesto** [ār nes′ tō]
7. **Henriqueta** [ān rē kä′ tä]
8. **San Blas** [sän bläs]

report card from the Escuela Municipal Número 3 para Varones[9] of Mazatlán, and so forth. Miss Hopley put things down in the book and my mother signed a card.

As long as the questions continued, Doña Henriqueta could stay and I was secure. Now that they were over, Miss Hopley saw her to the door, dismissed our interpreter and without further ado took me by the hand and strode down the hall to Miss Ryan's first grade.

Miss Ryan took me to a seat at the front of the room, into which I shrank—the better to survey her. She was, to skinny, somewhat runty me, of a withering height when she patrolled the class. And when I least expected it, there she was, crouching by my desk, her blond radiant face level with mine, her voice patiently maneuvering me over the awful idiocies of the English language.

During the next few weeks, Miss Ryan overcame my fears of tall, energetic teachers as she bent over my desk to help me with a word in the preprimer.[10] Step by step, she loosened me and my classmates from the safe anchorage of the desks for recitations at the blackboard and consultations at her desk. Frequently she burst into happy announcements to the whole class. "Ito[11] can read a sentence," and small Japanese Ito slowly read aloud while the class listened in wonder: "Come, Skipper, come. Come and run." The Korean, Portuguese, Italian, and Polish first graders had similar moments of glory, no less shining than mine the day I conquered "butterfly," which I had been persistently pronouncing in standard Spanish as boo-ter-flee. "Children," Miss Ryan called for attention. "Ernesto has learned how to pronounce *butterfly*!" And I proved it with a perfect imitation of Miss Ryan. From that celebrated success, I was soon able to match Ito's progress as a sentence reader with "Come, butterfly, come fly with me."

9. **Escuela Municipal Número 3 para Varones** [es kwä′ lä mü nē sē päl′ nü′ mä rō träs pä′ rä vä rō′ näs]: Spanish for "Municipal School Number 3 for Varones."
10. **preprimer** [prē prim′ ər]: very first reading book.
11. **Ito** [ē′ tō]

Like Ito and several other first-graders who did not know English, I received private lessons from Miss Ryan in the closet, a narrow hall off the classroom with a door at each end. Next to one of these doors Miss Ryan placed a large chair for herself and a small one for me. Keeping an eye on the class through the open door she read with me about sheep in the meadow and a frightened chicken going to see the king, coaching me out of my phonetic ruts in words like *pasture*, *bow-wow-wow*, *hay*, and *pretty*, which to my Mexican ear and eye had so many unnecessary sounds and letters. She made me watch her lips and then close my eyes as she repeated words I found hard to read. When we came to know each other better, I tried interrupting to tell Miss Ryan how we said it in Spanish. It didn't work. She only said "oh" and went on with *pasture*, *bow-wow-wow*, and *pretty*. It was as if in that closet we were both discovering together the secrets of the English language and grieving together over the tragedies of Bo-Peep. The main reason I was graduated with honors from the first grade was that I had fallen in love with Miss Ryan. Her radiant, no-nonsense character made us either afraid not to love her or love her so we would not be afraid, I am not sure which. It was not only that we sensed she was with it, but also that she was with us.

Like the first grade, the rest of the Lincoln School was a sampling of the lower part of town where many races made their home. My pals in the second grade were Kazushi,[12] whose parents spoke only Japanese; Matti, a skinny Italian boy; and Manuel, a fat Portuguese who would never get into a fight but wrestled you to the ground and just sat on you. Our assortment of nationalities included Koreans, Yugoslavs, Poles, Irish, and home-grown Americans.

Miss Hopley and her teachers never let us forget why we were at Lincoln: for those who were alien, to become good Americans; for

12. **Kazushi** [kä zü´ shē]

those who were so born, to accept the rest of us. Off the school grounds we traded the same insults we heard from our elders. On the playground we were sure to be marched up to the principal's office for calling someone an insulting name. The school was not so much a melting pot as a griddle where Miss Hopley and her helpers warmed knowledge into us and roasted racial hatreds out of us.

At Lincoln, making us into Americans did not mean scrubbing away what made us originally foreign. The teachers called us as our parents did, or as close as they could pronounce our names in Spanish or Japanese. No one was ever scolded or punished for speaking in his native tongue on the playground. Matti told the class about his mother's down quilt, which she had made in Italy with the fine feathers of a thousand geese. Encarnación[13] acted out how boys learned to fish in the Philippines. I astounded the third grade with the story of my travels on a stagecoach, which nobody else in the class had seen except in the museum at Sutter's Fort. After a visit to the Crocker Art Gallery and its collection of heroic paintings of the golden age of California, someone showed a silk scroll with a Chinese painting. Miss Hopley herself had a way of expressing wonder over these matters before a class, her eyes wide open until they popped slightly. It was easy for me to feel that becoming a proud American, as she said we should, did not mean feeling ashamed of being a Mexican.

The Americanization of Mexican me was no smooth matter. I had to fight one lout who made fun of my travels on the *diligencia*,[14] and my barbaric translation of the word into "diligence." He doubled up with laughter over the word until I straightened him out with a kick. In class I made points explaining that in Mexico roosters said "*qui-qui-ri-qui*"[15] and not "*cock-a-doodle-doo*," but after school I had to put up with the taunts of a big Yugoslav who said Mexican roosters were crazy.

But it was Homer who gave me the most lasting lesson for a future American.

13. **Encarnación** [en kär nä syōn´]
14. *diligencia* [dē lē hen´ syä]: Spanish for "diligence," a fast train, such as the one Ernesto and his family took to get to California.
15. *"qui-qui-ri-qui"* [kē kē rē kē]

Homer was a chunky Irishman who dressed as if every day was Sunday. He slicked his hair between a crew cut and a pompadour.[16] And Homer was smart, as he clearly showed when he and I ran for president of the third grade.

Everyone understood that this was to be a demonstration of how the American people vote for president. In an election, the teacher explained, the candidates could be generous and vote for each other. We cast our ballots in a shoe box and Homer won by two votes. I polled my supporters and came to the conclusion that I had voted for Homer and so had he. After class he didn't deny it, reminding me of what the teacher had said—we could vote for each other but didn't have to.

The lower part of town was a collage of nationalities in the middle of which Miss Nettie Hopley kept school with discipline and compassion. She called assemblies in the upper hall to introduce celebrities like the police sergeant or the fire chief, to lay down the law of the school, to present awards to our athletic champions, and to make important announcements. One of these was that I had been proposed by my school and accepted as a member of the newly formed Sacramento Boys Band. "Now, isn't that a wonderful thing?" Miss Hopley asked the assembled school, all eyes on me. And everyone answered in a chorus, including myself, "Yes, Miss Hopley."

It was not only the parents who were summoned to her office and boys and girls who served sentences there who knew that Nettie Hopley meant business. The entire school witnessed her sizzling Americanism in its awful majesty one morning at flag salute.

All the grades, as usual, were lined up in the courtyard between the wings of the building, ready to march to classes after the opening bell. Miss Shand was on the balcony of the second floor of Miss Hopley's office, conducting us in our lusty singing of "My Country tiz-a-thee." Our principal, as always, stood there like us, at attention, her right hand over her heart, joining in the song.

Halfway through the second stanza she stepped forward, held up her arm in a sign of command, and called loud and clear: "Stop the

16. **pompadour** [pom′ pə dôr]: a hair style in which the front of the hair is puffed high up and back from the forehead.

singing." Miss Shand looked flabbergasted. We were frozen with shock.

Miss Hopley was now standing at the rail of the balcony, her eyes sparking, her voice low and resonant, the words coming down to us distinctly and loaded with indignation.

"There are two gentlemen walking on the school grounds with their hats on while we are singing," she said, sweeping our ranks with her eyes. "We will remain silent until the gentlemen come to attention and remove their hats." A minute of awful silence ended when Miss Hopley, her gaze fixed on something behind us, signaled Miss Shand and we began once more the familiar hymn. That afternoon, when school was out, the word spread. The two gentlemen were the Superintendent of Schools and an important guest on an inspection.

ERNESTO GALARZA

Ernesto Galarza [1905-1984] was born in Jalcocotán, a village in Nayarit, Mexico. When he was six years of age, he immigrated to the United States with his mother and two uncles who, along with many others, were fleeing the violence of the Mexican Revolution. Galarza learned English quickly and won college scholarships. He covered other expenses by working in a cannery.

In 1936, Galarza took a job with the Pan American Union (PAU) in Washington, D.C., but he resigned in protest because PAU tolerated the exploitation of Mexican migrant workers. Galarza continued to fight for migrant workers' rights for the rest of his life.

Galarza described his book *Barrio Boy* as the story of a Mexican family, "uprooted from its home in a mountain village, in continuous flight." He said, "The barrio of this tale is that of Sacramento, California."

NEIGHBORS

JOHN SHERRILL

Once there was a man who loved roses. His name was Jiro Ninomiya.[1] Mr. Ninomiya came to this country from Japan at the turn of the century and bought a few acres of land just northeast of San Francisco. There under a palm tree Mr. Ninomiya built a house for himself and his family. Behind his home he grew roses that each morning he trucked into San Francisco to be sold.

It happened that immediately across Route 17 from the Ninomiyas lived a second immigrant, a man named Frederick Aebi (pronounced A-bee), who had come to this country from Switzerland about the same time as Jiro Ninomiya. Like the Ninomiyas, the Aebis struggled to make a living growing quality roses on a strip of land behind their home.

The Ninomiyas and the Aebis were just the kind of newcomers who have given America its strength—hard-working, family-centered, churchgoing people (the Ninomiyas were Methodists; the Aebis, Lutherans). And they were raising their sons, Tamaki[2] Ninomiya and Francis Aebi, with the same standards.

For three decades the rose-growing neighbors lived across from one another. By now Tamaki and Francis had taken over the rose farms. Both men worked too hard to do much socializing, and neither family were great talkers, but each enjoyed the other's culture. The Aebis, for example, often admired a Japanese doll which the Ninomiyas kept in their living room: a dancer wearing an elaborate costume of black-and-white silk, encased in glass. The taciturn youngsters of the third generation were allowed to look at the doll, never to touch it.

In time both families became modestly successful; their roses were known in the markets of San Francisco for their long vase-life.

Then on December 7, 1941, Japan attacked the U.S. Naval Base at Pearl Harbor. And in California, reports of violence in nearby Richmond reached the truck farms out on Route 17: a Japanese car

1. **Jiro Ninomiya** [zhē′ rō nē nō mē′ yä]
2. **Tamaki** [tä mä′ kē]

Japanese Doll Showa Women's Institute, Boston, MA

had been overturned, a Japanese greenhouse stoned. Rumors spread that soon Japanese people, especially those on the West Coast, were going to be rounded up and sent away to internment camps.

Francis Aebi, his wife, Carrie, and their two children walked across Route 17 and knocked on the door of Tamaki's house, under its palm tree. While skinny nine-year-old Lina Aebi stood looking at the dancing doll, her father spoke. "Tamaki," Francis said, "we've lived across from each other for a long time."

"Three generations," Tamaki said, glancing at his own five children.

"We are your neighbors," Francis Aebi said, and with that meaningful statement Francis went on to make clear that if need arose, he would look after the Ninomiya nursery. It was simply something that each family had learned in church: *Love thy neighbor as thyself.* "You would do the same for us," Francis said.

The possibility that Tamaki would be interned was not far-fetched. Tamaki's wife, Hayane,[3] was an American citizen. Their children were Americans too, but Tamaki was an alien; he had been born in Japan and never naturalized.

Meanwhile the fear and animosity grew. There were stories of stonings and boycotts not only of Japanese but also of those who befriended them.

On February 19, 1942, ten weeks after Pearl Harbor, President Roosevelt signed Executive Order 9066, providing for the designation of "military areas . . . from which any or all persons may be excluded." Speculation was that it might be used to get Japanese people off the West Coast.

When the news of the Executive Order was broadcast, Tamaki and Hayane immediately paid a visit to the Aebis to discuss the quirks of the watering system in the Ninomiyas' greenhouse. They came carrying a gift-wrapped package: the exquisite dancing doll in its glass case.

Little Lina jumped up and down in delight, but Francis had trouble finding words. "I couldn't possibly accept this, Tamaki," he

3. **Hayane** [hä yä′ nā]

finally said. "But we'll keep the doll safe until . . . things are back to normal."

Every day when the Aebis awoke, they checked to see if the Ninomiyas were still there. Then at noon one day in late February 1942 a black car pulled up to the Ninomiyas' home. Four men dressed in business suits went inside. Tamaki came in from the sorting shed. The Aebis watched from their front window as he was escorted to the car and driven off.

That same day, Hayane, the five children and old Jiro Ninomiya, Tamaki's father, went to live with friends in Livingston, which was farther from the coast; they reasoned it would not be considered a "sensitive area," and citizens of Japanese ancestry would be left alone. They loaded the pickup with clothes, a few pots and pans and some favorite toys, and drove away from the home that Jiro had built with his own hands. Hayane's last sight of their rose farm was of Francis, his work-worn wife, Carrie, and their two children, Lina and her older brother, standing under the palm tree waving farewell.

The move inland didn't help. On May 3, 1942, a new Civilian Exclusion Order was issued by the Western Defense Command. *All* persons of Japanese ancestry, citizens included, were to be evacuated from the area. Assistance would be granted for the disposition of property, such as real estate and automobiles. Evacuees were required to carry with them bedding, clothing and table articles,

including a bowl for each member of the family. In August the Ninomiyas boarded a crowded train, having been told only that they were going east.

"East" turned out to be Granada, Colorado. The train stopped in the middle of a barren landscape from which the family was transported by truck to a relocation center of tarpaper-roofed barracks surrounded by barbed wire and armed guards.

While Hayane was trying to settle into the living space allotted each family in the barracks, her father-in-law came running in. He led the family outside and pointed excitedly to a sandy bit of ground. Each family had been given a plot of land, 10 feet by 50 feet, for a garden. "We'll grow flowers!" Jiro said. "Annuals," he added. "It takes years to grow roses. They won't keep us here that long."

Back in California Francis Aebi didn't mind the longer hours running two nurseries. But one thing he did mind. To qualify for a farmer's ration of fuel he had to uproot the roses and plant vegetables. In the Ninomiya greenhouses he planted cucumbers; in his own, tomatoes. In both, he left room for a few roses. "For tomorrow," he explained to his children.

Months passed. The whole Aebi family labored beside Francis. The children worked in the greenhouses before school, and on Saturdays they also had to work instead of going to Luther League at church. Even with their help, Francis's work stretched to 16, 17 hours a day.

A full year went by. Then two years. Then three. Occasionally a letter arrived from the internment camp. The best news was that after two and a half years Tamaki had been allowed to join his family again. Tamaki's only son, David, cried when this stranger picked him up.

Francis and Carrie and the children continued their exhausting labors, but at least Lina's brother was now 16, old enough to drive. That helped. Japanese property was still being vandalized, and Francis kept lights burning all night in the Ninomiya home across the way. Another child was born to the Ninomiyas in the camp. Hayane knit wool socks and sweaters for the Aebis.

Japanese Doll
replica of doll designed by Goyo Hirata in 1927, Showa Women's Institute, Boston, MA

Left: The Ninomiya Family in the internment camp: front, Ann, David; middle, Flora, Martha, Alice; rear, Tamaki, Hayane, Jiro

Below: Today's Neighbors: front, Carrie and Francis Aebi; middle, Lina Aebi Hale, Flora and Martha Ninomiya; rear, Wallace Hale, Francis Aebi, Jr., David Ninomiya

At long, long last the war in Europe ended. Word came through the public address system in the relocation center cafeteria that the detainees were to be sent home. Once again they boarded a train.

In his letters Francis had reported that all was well at the Ninomiya nursery, but Tamaki wondered: Could that really be true? What would they actually find when they reached their rose farm?

Finally the train came to a stop in Richmond. There on the platform, waving his wide-brimmed hat in welcome, was a man so drawn and thin that his cheekbones showed. The oldest Ninomiya girl whispered reverently to little David, now five, "That's Mr. Aebi, our *neighbor*!"

Francis and Tamaki shook hands a bit awkwardly, as if they wanted to hug, but couldn't quite. There were so many Ninomiyas that Francis had brought along a friend to help transport them. The Ninomiyas piled their pots and pans into the vehicles and stared anxiously out the windows as Francis and his friend drove them through Richmond, then into the country and onto Route 17.

Finally they were turning into the crunchy drive, stopping beneath the palm tree in the front yard. Tamaki and Hayane got out, followed by Jiro and the children. They stared.

There was their nursery, intact, scrubbed and shining in the sunlight . . . looking neat, prosperous and healthy. And so was the balance in the bank passbook that Francis turned over to Tamaki.

Carrie Aebi came running across the road, followed by the Aebi children, who were not too old at 12 and 16 to dance their greeting. Together the families stepped into the Ninomiyas' home, which was as clean and welcoming as the nursery.

There on the dining room table was the dancing doll in its glass case. And next to it was one perfect red rosebud, just waiting to unfold—the gift of one neighbor to another.

JOHN SHERRILL

John Sherrill was born in 1923 in Covington, Tennessee. Like many other men of his generation, he left college in 1942 when World War II broke out. He joined the army, and while serving in Europe with the infantry, he began writing. After the war ended, he returned to civilian life and became editor of *Guideposts* magazine.

His most well-known work is *The Cross and the Switchblade*, a biography of David Wilkerson, a delinquent who became a minister and then dedicated his life to reforming other delinquents. Sherrill, his wife, and Wilkerson joined forces to write the book. Sherrill and his wife are also co-authors of *They Speak with Other Tongues*. Several of Sherrill's books and articles have been produced as films.

STAR-FIX

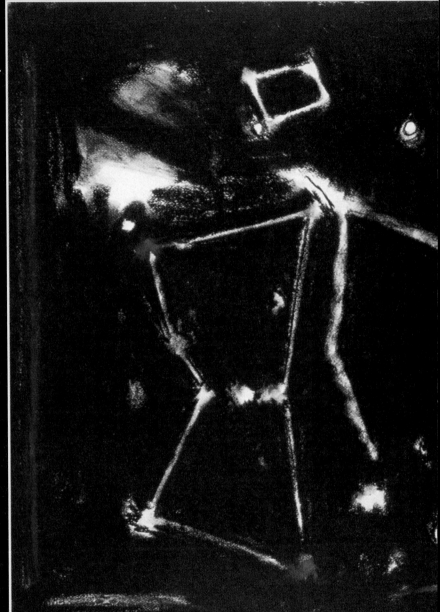

MARILYN NELSON WANIEK

For Melvin M. Nelson, Captain USAF (ret.) (1917-1966)

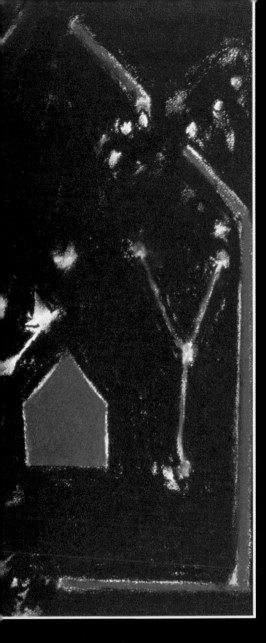

Constellation Series
Francis Hynes, 1986,
charcoal/pastel,
19" x 26"

)]t his cramped desk
under the astrodome,[1]
the navigator looks
thousands of light-years
everywhere but down.   5
He gets a celestial[2] fix[3],
measuring head-winds;
checking the log;
plotting wind-speed,
altitude, drift   10
in a circle of protractors,
slide-rules, and pencils.

He charts in his Howgozit
the points of no alternate
and of no return.   15
He keeps his eyes on the compass,
the two altimeters,[4] the map.
He thinks, *Do we have enough fuel?*
What if my radio fails?

He's the only Negro in the crew.   20
The only black flyer on the whole base,
for that matter. Not that it does:
this crew is a team.
Bob and Al, Les, Smitty, Nelson.

1. **astrodome** [as′ trə dōm]: transparent dome on the
   fuselage of an aircraft through which observations
   are made for navigating through the sky.
2. **celestial** [sə les′ chəl]: of the sky.
3. **fix:** the determining of the position of a ship or
   plane by using mathematical, electronic, or other
   means.
4. **altimeters** [al tim′ ə tərz]: instruments that
   measure altitude.

Smitty, who said once
after a poker game,
I love you, Nelson.
I never thought I could love
a colored man.
When we get out of this man's Air Force, 3O
if you ever come down to Tuscaloosa,
look me up and come to dinner.
You can come in the front door, too;
hell, you can stay overnight!
Of course, as soon as you leave, 35
I'll have to burn down my house.
Because if I don't
my neighbors will.

The navigator knows where he is
because he knows where he's been 4O
and where he's going.
At night, since he can't fly
by dead-reckoning,[5]
he calculates his position
by shooting a star.[6] 45

The octant[7] tells him
the angle of a fixed star
over the artificial horizon.
His position in that angle
is absolute and true: 5O
Where the hell are we, Nelson?
Alioth,[8] in the Big Dipper.
Regulus.[9] Antares,[10] in Scorpio.

5. **dead-reckoning:** calculation of the position of a ship or aircraft by using a compass and the navigator's record, without observing the sun and the stars.
6. **shooting a star:** aiming the altimeter toward a star.
7. **octant** [ok´ tənt]: navigation instrument used to measure the altitude of heavenly bodies in order to determine latitude and longitude.
8. **Alioth** [al´ ē oth]: a bright star in the handle of the Big Dipper.
9. **Regulus** [reg´ yə ləs]: large star in the constellation Leo.
10. **Antares** [an tär´ ēz]: a bright, red star in the constellation Scorpio.

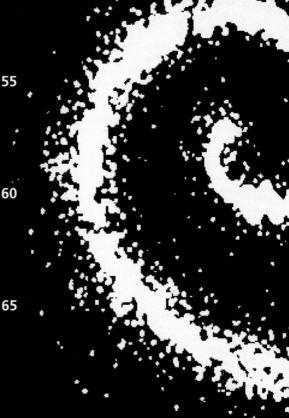

He plots their lines
of position on the chart,   55
gets his radio bearing,
corrects for lost time.

Bob, Al, Les, and Smitty
are counting on their navigator.
If he sleeps,   60
they all sleep.
If he fails
they fall.

The navigator keeps watch
over the night and the instruments,   65
going hungry for five or six hours
to give his flight-lunch
to his two little girls.

MARILYN NELSON WANIEK

Marilyn Nelson Waniek was born in 1946 in Cleveland, Ohio, and began writing poetry in elementary school. "Or," Waniek adds, "should I say 'elementary schools'—since my father was in the Air Force, we moved frequently." Waniek's sixth-grade teacher predicted that she would become "a famous author." Waniek says she is still trying to fulfill her teacher's prediction.

Waniek feels that she learned much "about what makes kids laugh" as she continues to write poems for them. "Once, as I read the last line of a poem," she says, "a third-grader literally laughed until he fell out of his chair." She considers this reaction among her greatest successes. Waniek's collection of poems, *The Cat Walked Through the Casserole,* also shows her sense of fun. Other poems such as "Star-Fix" in *The Home Place* show Waniek's serious side.

The Winter Hibiscus

Minfong Ho

Saeng[1] stood in the open doorway and shivered as a gust of wind swept past, sending a swirl of red maple leaves rustling against her legs. Early October, and already the trees were being stripped bare. A leaf brushed against Saeng's sleeve, and she snatched at it, briefly admiring the web of dark veins against the fiery red, before letting it go again, to be carried off by the wind.

Last year she had so many maple leaves pressed between her thick algebra textbook that her teacher had suggested gently that she transfer the leaves to some other books at home. Instead, Saeng had simply taken the carefully pressed leaves out and left them in a pile in her room, where they moldered, turned smelly, and were eventually tossed out. Saeng had felt a vague regret, but no anger.

For a moment Saeng stood on the doorstep and watched the swirl of autumn leaves in the afternoon sunlight, thinking of the bleak winter ahead. She had lived through enough of them now to dread their greyness and silence and endless bone-chilling cold. She buttoned up her coat and walked down the worn path through their yard and toward the sidewalk.

"Bai sai?"[2] Her mother called to her, straightening up from neat rows of hot peppers and snow peas that were growing in the vacant lot next door.

"To take my driving test," Saeng replied in English.

Saeng remembered enough Laotian to understand just about everything that her parents said to her, but she felt more comfortable now speaking in

1. **Saeng** [sueng]
2. **Bai sai** [bui sui]

English. In the four years since they had migrated to America, they had evolved a kind of bilingual dialogue, where her parents would continue to address her brothers and her in Laotian, and they would reply in English, with each side sometimes slipping into the other's language to convey certain key words that seemed impossible to translate.

"*Luuke ji fao bai hed yang?*"[3] her mother asked.

"There's no rush," Saeng conceded. "I just want to get there in plenty of time."

"You'll get there much too soon, and then what? You'll just stand around fretting and making yourself tense," Mrs. Panouvong continued in Laotian. "Better that you should help me harvest some of these melons."

Saeng hesitated. How could she explain to her mother that she wanted to just "hang out" with the other schoolmates who were scheduled to take the test that afternoon, and to savor the tingle of anticipation when David Lambert would drive up in his old blue Chevy and hand her the car keys?

"The last of the hot peppers should be picked, and the kale covered with a layer of mulch," Mrs. Panouvong added, wiping one hand across her shirt and leaving a streak of mud there.

Saeng glanced down at her own clean clothes. She had dressed carefully for the test—and for David. She had on a grey wool skirt and a Fair Isles sweater, both courtesy of David's mother from their last rummage sale at the church. And she had combed out her long black hair and left it hanging straight down her back the way she had seen the blonde cheerleaders do theirs, instead of bunching it up with a rubber band.

"Come help your mother a little. *Mahteh, luuke*[4] —Come on, child," her mother said gently.

There were certain words that held a strange resonance for Saeng, as if there were whispered echoes behind them. *Luuke*, or child, was one of these words. When her mother called her *luuke* in that soft, teasing way, Saeng could hear the voices of her grandmother, and her

3. ***Luuke ji fao bai hed yang?*** [lük yi fuō bui hed yung]
4. ***Mahteh, luuke*** [muʼ teh lük]

uncle, or her primary-school teachers behind it, as if there were an invisible chorus of smiling adults calling her, chiding her.

"Just for a while," Saeng said, and walked over to the melons, careful not to get her skirt tangled in any vines.

Together they worked in companionable silence for some time. The frost had already killed the snow peas and Chinese cabbage, and Saeng helped pluck out the limp brown stems and leaves. But the bitter melons, knobby and green, were still intact and ready to be harvested. Her mother had been insistent on planting only vegetables that weren't readily available at the local supermarkets, sending away for seeds from various Chinatowns as far away as New York and San Francisco. At first alone, and then joined by the rest of her family, she had hoed the hard dirt of the vacant lot behind their dilapidated old house, and planted the seeds in neat rows.

That first summer, their family had also gone smelting every night while the vast schools of fish were swimming upriver to spawn, and had caught enough to fill their freezer full of smelt. And at dawn, when the dew was still thick on the grass, they had also combed the golf course at the country club for nightcrawlers, filling up large buckets with worms that they would sell later to the roadside grocery stores as fishbait. The money from selling the worms enabled them to buy a hundred-pound sack of the best long-grain fragrant rice, and that, together with the frozen smelt and homegrown vegetables, had lasted them through most of their first winter.

"America has opened her doors to us as guests," Saeng's mother had said. "We don't want to sit around waiting for its handouts like beggars." She and Mr. Panouvong had swallowed their pride and gotten jobs as a dishwasher and a janitor, and were taking English lessons at night under a state program which, to their amazement, actually paid them for studying!

By the end of their second year, they were off welfare and were saving up for a cheap second-hand car, something that they could never have been able to afford as grade school teachers back in Laos.

And Saeng, their oldest child, had been designated their family driver.

"So you will be taking the driving test in the Lambert car?" Mrs. Panouvong asked now, adeptly twisting tiny hot peppers from their stems.

Saeng nodded. "Not their big station wagon, but the small blue car—David's." There it was again, that flutter of excitement as she said David's name. And yet he had hardly spoken to her more than two or three times, and each time only at the specific request of his mother.

Mrs. Lambert—their sponsor into the United States—was a large, genial woman with a ready smile and two brown braids wreathed around her head. The wife of the Lutheran minister in their town, she had already helped sponsor two Laotian refugee families and seemed to have enough energy and good will to sponsor several more. Four years ago, when they had first arrived, it was she who had taken the Panouvong family on their rounds of medical checkups, social welfare interviews, school enrollments, and housing applications.

And it was Mrs. Lambert who had suggested, after Saeng had finished her driver education course, that she use David's car to take her driving test. Cheerfully, David—a senior on the school basketball team—had driven Saeng around and taken her for a few test runs in his car to familiarize her with it. Exciting times they might have been for Saeng—it was the closest she had ever come to being on a date— but for David it was just something he was doing out of deference to his mother. Saeng had no illusions about this. Nor did she really mind it. It was enough for her at this point just to vaguely pretend at dating. At sixteen, she did not really feel ready for some of the things most thirteen-year-olds in America seemed to be doing. Even watching MTV sometimes made her wince in embarrassment.

"He's a good boy, David is," Saeng's mother said, as if echoing Saeng's thoughts. "Listens to his mother and father." She poured the hot peppers from her cupped palm to a woven basket and looked at Saeng. "How are you going to thank him for letting you use his car and everything?"

Saeng considered this. "I'll say thank you, I guess. Isn't that enough?"

"I think not. Why don't you buy for him a Big Mac?" Big Mac

was one of the few English words Mrs. Panouvong would say, pronouncing it *Bee-Maag*. Ever since her husband had taken them to a McDonald's as a treat after his first pay raise, she had thought of Big Mac's as the epitome of everything American.

To her daughter's surprise, she fished out a twenty-dollar bill from her coat pocket now and held it out to Saeng. "You can buy yourself one too. A Bee-Maag."

Saeng did not know what to say. Here was a woman so frugal that she had insisted on taking home her containers after her McDonald's meal, suddenly handing out twenty dollars for two "children" to splurge on.

"Take it, child," Mrs. Panouvong said. "Now go—you don't want to be late for your test." She smiled. "How nice it'll be when you drive us to work. Think of all the time we'll save. And the bus fares."

The money, tucked safely away in her coat pocket, seemed to keep Saeng warm on her walk across town to the site of the driving test.

She reached it a few minutes early and stood on the corner, glancing around her. There were a few other teenagers waiting on the sidewalk or sitting on the hoods of their cars, but David was nowhere in sight. On the opposite side of the street was the McDonald's restaurant, and for a moment she imagined how it would be to have David and her sitting at one of the window seats, facing each other, in satisfying full view of all the passersby.

A light honk brought her back to reality. David cruised by, waving at her from his car window. He parallel parked the car, with an effortless swerve which Saeng admired, and got out.

"Ready?" David asked, eyebrow arched quizzically as he handed her his car keys.

Saeng nodded. Her mouth suddenly felt dry, and she licked her lips.

"Don't forget: step on the gas real gently. You don't want to jerk the car forward the way you did last time," David said with a grin.

"I won't," Saeng said, and managed a smile.

Another car drove up, and the test instructor stepped out of it and onto the curb in front of them. He was a pale, overweight man whose thick lips jutted out from behind a bushy mustache. On his paunch was balanced a clipboard, which he was busy marking.

Finally he looked up and saw Saeng. "Miss Saeng Panouvong?" he asked, slurring the name so much that Saeng did not recognize it as her own until she felt David nudge her slightly.

"Y—yes, sir," Saeng answered.

"Your turn. Get in."

Then Saeng was behind the wheel, the paunchy man seated next to her, clipboard on his lap.

"Drive to the end of the street, and take a right," the test instructor said. He spoke in a low, bored staccato that Saeng had to strain to understand.

Obediently she started up the car, careful to step on the accelerator very slowly, and eased the car out into the middle of the street. *Check the rearview mirror, make the hand gestures, take a deep breath,* Saeng told herself.

So far, so good. At the intersection at the end of the street, she slowed down. Two cars were coming down the cross street toward her at quite a high speed. Instinctively, she stopped, and waited for them both to drive past. Instead, they both stopped, as if waiting for her to proceed.

Saeng hesitated. Should she go ahead and take the turn before them or wait until they went past?

Better to be cautious, she decided, and waited, switching gears over to neutral.

For what seemed an interminable moment, nobody moved. Then the other cars went through the intersection, one after the other. Carefully, Saeng then took her turn (*turn signal, hand signal, look both ways*).

As she continued to drive down the street, out of the corner of her eye she saw the instructor mark down something on his clipboard.

A mistake, she thought. *He's writing down a mistake I just made. But what did I do wrong?* She stole a quick look at his face. It was stern but impassive. *Maybe I should ask him right now, what I did wrong*, Saeng wondered.

"Watch out!" he suddenly exclaimed. "That's a stop sign!"

Startled, Saeng jerked the car to a stop—but not soon enough. They were right in the middle of the crossroads.

The instructor shook his head. An almost imperceptible gesture, but Saeng noted it with a sinking feeling in her stomach.

"Back up," he snapped.

Her heart beating hard, Saeng managed to reverse the car and back up to the stop sign that she had just gone through.

"You might as well go back to where we started out," the instructor said. "Take a right here, and another right at the next intersection."

It's over, Saeng thought. *He doesn't even want to see me go up the hill or parallel park or anything. I've failed.*

Swallowing hard, she managed to drive the rest of the way back. In the distance she could see the big M archway outside the McDonald's

restaurant, and, as she approached, she noticed David standing on the opposite curb, hands on his hips, watching their approach.

With gratitude she noticed that he had somehow managed to stake out two parking spaces in a row, so that she could have plenty of space to swerve into place.

She breathed a deep sigh of relief when the car was safely parked. Only after she had turned off the ignition did she dare look the instructor in the face.

"How—how did I do, sir?" she asked him, hating the quaver in her own voice.

"You'll get your results in the mail next week," he said, in that bored monotone again, as if he had been parroting the same sentence countless times. Then he must have seen the anxious, pleading look on Saeng's face, for he seemed to soften somewhat. "You stopped when you didn't need to—you had right of way at that first intersection," he said. "Then at the second intersection, when you should have stopped at the stop sign, you went right through it." He shrugged. "Too bad," he mumbled.

Then he was out of the car, clipboard and all, and strolling down the curb to the next car.

It had all happened so quickly. Saeng felt limp. So she had failed. She felt a burning shame sting her cheeks. She had never failed a test before. Not even when she had first arrived in school and had not understood a word the teacher had said, had she ever failed a test.

Tests, always tests—there had been so many tests in the last four years. Math test; spelling tests; science tests. And for each one she had prepared herself, learned what was expected of her, steeled herself, taken the test, and somehow passed. She thought of the long evenings she had spent at the kitchen table after the dinner dishes had been cleared away, when she and her mother had used their battered English-Lao dictionary to look up virtually every single word in her textbooks and carefully written the Lao equivalent above the English word, so that there were faint spidery pencil marks filling up all the spaces between the lines of her textbooks.

All those tests behind her, and now she had failed. Failed the one test that might have enabled her to help her parents get to work more easily, save them some money, and earn her some status among her classmates.

David's face appeared at the window. "How'd it go?" he asked, with his usual cheerful grin.

Saeng suppressed an urge to pass her hand over his mouth and wipe the grin off. "Not so good," she said. She started to explain, then gave it up. It wasn't worth the effort, and besides, he didn't really care anyway.

He was holding the car door open for her and seemed a little impatient for her to get out. Saeng squirmed out of the seat, then remembered the twenty dollar bill her mother had given her.

"Eh . . . thanks," she murmured awkwardly as she got out of the car. "It was nice of you to come here. And letting me use your car."

"Don't mention it," he said, sliding into the driver's seat already, and pushing it back several inches.

"Would you . . . I mean, if you'd like I could buy . . ." Saeng faltered as she saw that David wasn't even listening to her. His attention had been distracted by someone waving to him from across the street. He was waving back, and smiling. Saeng followed the direction of his glance and saw a tall girl in tight jeans and a flannel shirt standing just under the M archway. Someone blonde and vivacious, her dimpled smile revealing two rows of dazzling white, regimentally straight teeth. *Definitely a cheerleader,* Saeng decided.

"Hold on, I'll be right with you," David was calling over to her. Abruptly he pulled the car door shut, flashed Saeng a perfunctory smile, and started to drive off. "Better luck next time," he said as his car pulled away, leaving her standing in the middle of the road.

Saeng watched him make a fluid U-turn and pull up right next to the tall blonde girl, who swung herself gracefully into the seat next to David. For a moment they sat there laughing and talking in the car. So carefree, so casual—so American. They reminded Saeng of the Ken and Barbie dolls that she had stared at with such curiosity and longing when she had first arrived in the country.

But it wasn't even longing or envy that she felt now, Saeng realized. This girl could have been David's twin sister, and Saeng would still have felt this stab of pain, this recognition that They Belonged, and she didn't.

Another car drove slowly past her, and she caught a glimpse of her reflection on its window. Her arms were hanging limply by her sides, and she looked short and frumpy. Her hair was disheveled and her clothes seemed drab and old-fashioned—exactly as if they had come out of a rummage sale. She looked wrong. Totally out of place.

"Hey, move it! You're blocking traffic!"

A car had pulled up alongside of her, and in the front passenger seat sat the test instructor scowling at her, his thick lips taut with irritation.

Saeng stood rooted to the spot. She stared at him, stared at those thick lips beneath the bushy mustache. And suddenly she was jolted back to another time, another place, another voice—it had all been so long ago and so far away, yet now she still found herself immobilized by the immediacy of the past.

Once, shortly after she had arrived in America, when she had been watching an absorbing ballet program on the PBS channel at Mrs. Lambert's house, someone had switched channels with a remote control, and it seemed as if the gracefully dying Giselle in *Swan Lake* had suddenly been riddled with bullets from a screeching getaway car. So jarring had it been, that Saeng had felt as if an electric shock had charged through her, jolting her from one reality into another.

It was like that now, as if someone had switched channels in her life. She was no longer standing on a quiet street in downtown Danby, but in the midst of a jostling crowd of tired, dusty people under a blazing sun. And it was not the balding driving instructor yelling at her, but a thick-lipped man in a khaki uniform, waving at them imperiously with a submachine gun.

Ban Vinai, Thailand,[5] 1978. Things clicked into place, but it was no use knowing the name and number of the channel. The fear and dread still suffused her. She still felt like the scared, bone-weary little girl she had been then, being herded into the barbed-wire fencing of the refugee camp after they had escaped across the Mekong River from Laos.

5. **Ban Vinai, Thailand** [bän vē′ nāi   tī′ land]: city in Thailand, a country west of Laos.

"What're you doing, standing in the middle of the road? Get out of the way!"

And click—the Thai soldier was the test instructor again. Saeng blinked, blinked away the fear and fatigue of that memory, and slowly that old reality receded. In a daze she turned and made her way over to the curb, stepped up onto it, and started walking away.

Breathe deep, don't break down, she told herself fiercely. She could imagine David and that cheerleader staring at her behind her back. *I am tough*, she thought, *I am strong, I can take it.*

The sidewalk was littered with little acorns, and she kicked at them viciously as she walked and walked.

Only when she had turned the corner and was safely out of sight of David and the others, did she finally stop. She found herself standing under a huge tree whose widespread branches were now almost leafless. An acorn dropped down and hit her on the head, before bouncing off into the street.

It seemed like the final indignity. Angrily, Saeng reached up for the branch directly overhead, and tore off some of the large brown leaves still left. They were dry and crisp as she crushed them in her hands. She threw them at the wind and watched the bits of brown being whipped away by the afternoon wind.

"Who cares about the test anyway," she said in a tight, grim whisper, tearing up another fistful of oak leaves. "Stupid test, stupid David, stupid cars. Who needs a license anyway? Who needs a test like that?" It would only get harder too, she realized, with the winter approaching and the streets turning slippery with the slush and snow. She had barely felt safe walking on the sidewalks in the winter—how could she possibly hope to drive then? It was hopeless, useless to even try. *I won't, I just won't ever take that test again!* Saeng told herself.

That resolved, she felt somewhat better. She turned away from the oak tree, and was about to leave, when she suddenly noticed the bush next to it.

There was something very familiar about it. Some of its leaves had already blown off, but those that remained were still green. She picked a leaf and examined it. It was vaguely heart-shaped, with deeply serrated edges.

Where had she seen this kind of leaf before, Saeng wondered? And why, among all these foreign maples and oak leaves, did it seem so very familiar? She scrutinized the bush, but it was no help: if there had been any flowers on it, they had already fallen off.

Holding the leaf in her hand, Saeng left the park, and started walking home.

Her pace was brisk and determined, and she had not planned to stop off anywhere. But along the way, she found herself pausing involuntarily before a florist shop window. On display were bright bunches of cut flowers in tall glass vases—the splashes of red roses, white carnations, and yellow chrysanthemums a vivid contrast to the grey October afternoon. In the shadows behind them were several potted plants, none of which she could identify.

On an impulse, Saeng swung open the door and entered.

An elderly woman behind the counter looked up and smiled at her. "Yes? Can I help you?" she asked.

Saeng hesitated. Then she thrust out the heart-shaped green leaf in her hand, and stammered, "Do . . . do you have this plant? I—I don't know its name."

The woman took the leaf and studied it with interest. "Why, yes," she said. "That looks like a rose of Sharon.[6] We have several in the nursery out back."

She kept up a steady stream of conversation as she escorted Saeng through a side door into an open courtyard, where various saplings and shrubs stood. "Of course it's not the best time for planting, but at least the ground hasn't frozen solid yet, and if you dig a deep enough hole, put in some good compost, it should do just fine. Hardy plants, these roses of Sharon. Pretty blossoms too, in the fall. In fact—look, there's still a flower or two left on this shrub. Nice shade of pink, isn't it?"

Saeng looked at the single blossom left on the shrub. It looked small and washed out. The leaves on the shrub were of the same distinct serrated heart shape but its flower looked—wrong, somehow.

6. **rose of Sharon** [rōz ov shaʹrən]: a shrub, species of hibiscus with bell-shaped pink, purple, or white flowers.

"Is there—I mean, can it have another kind of flower?" Saeng asked. "Another color, maybe?"

"Well, it also comes in a pale purplish shade," the woman said helpfully. "And white, too."

"I think—I think it was a deep color," she offered, then shook her head. "I don't remember. It doesn't matter." Discouraged, and feeling more than a little foolish, she started to back away.

"Wait," the florist said. "I think I know what you're looking for." A slow smile deepened the wrinkles in her face. "Come this way. It's in our greenhouse."

At the far side of the courtyard stood a shed, the like of which Saeng had never seen before. It was made entirely of glass, and seemed to be bathed in a soft white light.

As she led the way there, the florist started talking again. "Lucky we just got through moving in some of our tropical plants," she said, "or the frost last weekend would have killed them off. Anything in there now you'd have to leave indoors until next summer, of course. Next to a big, south-facing window or under some strong neon lamps. Even so, some of the plants won't survive the long cold winters here. Hothouse flowers, that's what they are. Not hardy, like those roses of Sharon I just showed you."

Only half listening, Saeng wished that there were a polite way she could excuse herself and leave. It was late and she was starting to get hungry. Still, she dutifully followed the other woman through the greenhouse door and walked in.

She gasped.

It was like walking into another world. A hot, moist world exploding with greenery. Huge flat leaves, delicate wisps of tendrils, ferns and fronds and vines of all shades and shapes grew in seemingly random profusion.

"Over there, in the corner, the hibiscus.[7] Is that what you mean?" The florist pointed at a leafy potted plant by the corner.

There, in a shaft of the wan afternoon sunlight, was a single

7. **hibiscus** [hə bis′ kəs]: herb, shrub, or tree of the mallow family, with large red, pink, or white bell-shaped flowers.

blood red blossom, its five petals splayed back to reveal a long stamen tipped with yellow pollen. Saeng felt a shock of recognition so intense it was almost visceral.

"*Saebba?*"[8] Saeng whispered.

A *saebba* hedge, tall and lush, had surrounded their garden, its lush green leaves dotted with vermilion[9] flowers. And sometimes, after a monsoon rain, a blossom or two would have blown into the well, so that when she drew up the well water, she would find a red blossom floating in the bucket.

Slowly, Saeng walked down the narrow aisle toward the hibiscus. Orchids, lanna bushes, oleanders, elephant ear begonias, bougainvillea vines surrounded her. Plants that she had not even realized she had known but had forgotten drew her back into her childhood world.

When she got to the hibiscus, she reached out and touched a petal gently. It felt smooth and cool, with a hint of velvet toward the center—just as she had known it would feel.

And beside it was yet another old friend, a small shrub with waxy leaves and dainty flowers with purplish petals and white centers. "Madagascar Periwinkle," it announced. *How strange to see it in a pot,* Saeng thought. Back home it just grew wild, jutting out from the cracks in brick walls or between tiled roofs. There had been a patch of it by the little spirit house where she used to help her mother light the incense and candles to the spirit who guarded their home and their family. Sometimes she would casually pick a flower or two to leave on the offerings of fruit and rice left at the altar.

And that rich, sweet scent—that was familiar too. Saeng scanned the greenery around her and found a tall, gangly plant with exquisite little white blossoms on it. "*Dok Malik,*" [10] she said, savoring the feel of the word on her tongue even as she silently noted the English name on its tag, "Jasmine."[11]

8. *saebba* [su′ e bu]
9. **vermilion** [vər mil′ yən]: bright red.
10. *Dok Malik* [dōk mu′ lik]
11. **Jasmine** [jas′ mən]: shrub or vine of the olive family with clusters of fragrant yellow, white, or reddish flowers.

ดอกไม้แดง

One of the blossoms had fallen off, and carefully Saeng picked it up and smelled it. Closed her eyes and breathed in, deeply. The familiar fragrance filled her lungs, and Saeng could almost feel the light strands of her grandmother's long gray hair, freshly washed, as she combed it out with the fine-toothed buffalo-horn comb. And when the sun had dried it, Saeng would help the gnarled old fingers knot the hair into a bun, then slip a *Dok Malik* bud into it.

Saeng looked at the white bud in her hand now, small and fragile. Gently, she closed her palm around it and held it tight. That, at least, she could hold on to. But where was the fine-toothed comb? The hibiscus hedge? The well? Her gentle grandmother?

A wave of loss so deep and strong that it stung Saeng's eyes now swept over her. A blink, a channel switch, a boat ride in the night, and it was all gone. Irretrievably, irrevocably gone.

And in the warm moist shelter of the greenhouse, Saeng broke down and wept.

It was already dusk when Saeng reached home. The wind was blowing harder, tearing off the last remnants of green in the chicory weeds that were growing out of the cracks in the sidewalk. As if oblivious to the cold, her mother was still out in the vegetable garden, digging up the last of the onions with a rusty trowel. She did not see Saeng until the girl had quietly knelt down next to her.

Her smile of welcome warmed Saeng. "*Ghup ma laio le?*"[12] "You're back?" she said cheerfully. "Goodness, it's past five. What took you so long? How did it go? Did you—?" Then she noticed the potted plant that Saeng was holding, its leaves quivering in the wind.

Mrs. Panouvong uttered a small cry of surprise and delight. "*Saebba!*" she said. "Where did you get it?"

"I bought it," Saeng answered, dreading her mother's next question. "How much?"

12. *Ghup ma laio le?* [gùp mu lu′ iō le]

For answer Saeng handed her mother some coins.

"That's all?" Mrs. Panouvong said, appalled. "Oh, but I forgot! You and the Lambert boy ate Bee-Mags. . . ."

"No, we didn't, mother," Saeng said.

"Then what else—?"

"Nothing else. I paid over nineteen dollars for it."

"You what?" Her mother stared at her incredulously. "But how could you? All the seeds for this vegetable garden didn't cost that much! You know how much we—" She paused, as she noticed the tearstains on her daughter's cheeks and her puffy eyes.

"What happened?" she asked, more gently.

"I—I failed the test," Saeng said.

For a long moment Mrs. Panouvong said nothing. Saeng did not dare to look her mother in the eye. Instead, she stared at the hibiscus plant and nervously tore off a leaf, shredding it to bits.

Her mother reached out, brushed the fragments of green off Saeng's hands. "It's a beautiful plant, this *saebba*," she finally said. "I'm glad you got it."

"It's—it's not a real one," Saeng mumbled. "I mean, not like the kind we had at—at—" she found that she was still too shaky to say the words *at home*, lest she burst into tears again. "Not like the kind we had before," she said.

"I know," her mother said quietly. "I've seen this kind blooming along the lake. It's flowers aren't as pretty, but it's strong enough to make it through the cold months here, this winter hibiscus. That's what matters."

She tipped the pot and deftly eased the ball of soil out, balancing the rest of the plant in her other hand. "Look how rootbound it is, poor thing," she said. "Let's plant it, right now."

She went over to the corner of the vegetable patch and started to dig a hole in the ground. The soil was cold and hard, and she had trouble thrusting the shovel into it. Wisps of her gray hair trailed out in the breeze, and her slight frown deepened the wrinkles around her eyes. There was a frail, wiry beauty to her which touched Saeng deeply.

"Here, let me help, Mother," she offered, getting up and taking the shovel away from her.

Mrs. Panouvong made no resistance. "I'll bring in the hot peppers and bitter melons, then, and start dinner. How would you like an omelette with slices of the bitter melon?"

"I'd love it," Saeng said.

Left alone in the garden, Saeng dug out a hole and carefully lowered the "winter hibiscus" into it. She could hear the sounds of cooking from the kitchen now, the beating of the eggs against a bowl, the sizzle of hot oil in the pan. The pungent smell of bitter melon wafted out, and Saeng's mouth watered. It was a cultivated taste, she had discovered—none of her classmates or friends, not even Mrs. Lambert, liked it—this sharp, bitter melon that left a golden aftertaste on the tongue. But she had grown up eating it, and, she admitted to herself, much preferred it to a Big Mac.

The "winter hibiscus" was in the ground now, and Saeng tamped down the soil around it. Overhead a flock of Canada geese flew by, their faint honks clear and—yes—familiar to Saeng now. Almost reluctantly, she realized that many of the things that she had thought of as strange before had become, through the quiet repetition of season upon season, almost familiar to her now. Like the geese. She lifted her head and watched as their distinctive V was etched against the evening sky, slowly fading into the distance.

When they come back, Saeng vowed silently to herself, *in the spring, when the snows melt and the geese return and this hibiscus is budding, then I will take that test again.*

MINFONG HO

Minfong Ho was born in Burma and grew up on the outskirts of Bangkok, Thailand. She describes her home as being "next to a fishpond and a big garden, with rice fields on the other side of the palm trees, where water buffaloes wallowed in mudholes."

By age sixteen, Minfong Ho spoke English, Thai, and Cantonese—and had been accepted at Tunghai University in Taiwan. She studied Mandarin in Taiwan, then came to the United States to study at Cornell University. While Minfong Ho was in college, she wrote many letters to her family to fight off homesickness. Her first book, *Sing to the Dawn*, came from letters she wrote home from her favorite place—a greenhouse filled with tropical plants on the Cornell campus. Other books by Ho are *Rice Without Rain*, based on her teaching experiences in northern Thailand, and *The Clay Marble*, about the Cambodian refugee children she worked with on the Thai-Cambodian border.

Minfong Ho now lives with her American husband and three children in Geneva, Switzerland—and is learning French.

Green Violinist
Marc Chagall,
1923 - 1924,
oil on canvas,
78" x 42 3/4"
Solomon R. Guggenheim
Museum, New York

Oliver Hyde's Dishcloth Concert

RICHARD KENNEDY

Now maybe it's sad and maybe it's spooky, but there was a man who lived just out of town on a scrubby farm and no one had seen his face for years. If he was outside working, he kept his hat pulled down and his collar turned up, and if anyone approached him he ran up the hill to his house and shut himself inside. He left notes pinned to his door for a brave errand boy who brought him supplies from town. The people asked the boy what he heard up there in that tomblike house when he collected the notes and delivered the supplies. "Darkness and quietness," said the boy. "I hear darkness and quietness." The people nodded and looked at the boy. "Aren't you afraid?" The boy bit his lip. "A fellow has to make a living," he said.

Sometimes the children would come out of town and sing a little song up at the house and then run away. They sang:

> "The beautiful bride of Oliver Hyde,
> Fell down dead on the mountainside."

Yes, it was true. The man was full of grief and bitterness. He was Oliver Hyde, and his young bride's wagon had been washed into a canyon by a mudslide and it killed her, horse and all. But that was years ago. The children sang some more:

> "Oliver Hyde is a strange old man,
> He sticks his head in a coffee can,
> And hides his face when there's folks about,
> He's outside in, and he's inside out."

It was too bad. Oliver used to have many friends, and he played the fastest and sweetest fiddle in the county. And for the few short weeks he was married his playing was sweeter than ever. But on the day his wife was buried he busted his fiddle across a porch post, and now he sat cold, dark, and quiet on his little hill. No one had visited him for years. There was a reason. You shall see.

One day a man came from the town and walked up the hill toward Oliver's house. He was carrying a fiddle case. Two or three times he stopped and looked up at the house and shook his head, as if trying to free himself from a ghost, and continued on. He arrrived at the porch steps. All the window shades were pulled down and it was dead quiet inside. The three porch steps creaked like cats moaning in their dreams, and the man knocked on the door. For a little bit it was quiet, then there was the sound of a chair being scooted across the floor. A voice said, "Come in."

The man opened the door a crack and peeked inside.

"Oliver?" he said. "It's me, Jim." No answer. Jim opened the door farther and put a foot inside. It was dark, and smelled stale. Jim opened the door all the way.

Off in a corner where the light didn't touch sat a figure in a chair, perfectly upright, with his hands on his knees like a stone god, as still and silent as a thousand years ago. The head was draped completely with a dishcloth. Not a breath ruffled the ghost head.

Jim swallowed and spoke. "Haven't seen you around lately, Oliver." No answer.

People used to visit Oliver for a while after his beautiful bride fell down dead on the mountainside, but this is how it was—Oliver sitting in the dark with a dishcloth over his head, and he never spoke to them. It was too strange. His friends stopped visiting.

All Jim wanted was a single word from Oliver—yes or no. He had a favor to ask. He was Oliver's oldest friend. He moved inside.

"Sue's getting married, Oliver," he said. No answer. "You remember my little girl, Sue? She's all growed up now, Oliver, and mighty pretty, too." For all the notice he got, Jim might just as well have been talking to a stone. He cleared his voice and went on. "The reason I came, Oliver, was to ask you to come and play the fiddle for us. You can just say yes or no, Oliver. "

Now Oliver wasn't dead himself yet, so he still had feelings, and Jim had been his best friend. They had played and fought together, fished and hunted, and grown up together. So Oliver hated to say "No" just flat out like that, so he said instead, "No fiddle." Jim was prepared for that, and he laid the fiddle case down on the floor and flipped it open.

"Here I brought a fiddle, Oliver. Porky Fellows was happy to make a lend of it."

Oliver felt trapped now. He was silent for a long time, then finally he said, "Tell you what. I can't wear this dishcloth and fiddle, but if everyone else wears a dishcloth I'll come."

Jim was quiet for a long time, but at last he said, "All right, Oliver, I'll ask if they'll do it. The dance is tomorrow night at Edward's barn. I'll leave the fiddle here, and if I don't come back to pick it up, then you got to come to the dance and fiddle for us. I got your promise."

Oliver smiled under his dishcloth. They'd be fools to agree to that. You can't have any fun with a dishcloth over your head.

"So long, Oliver," Jim said. Oliver didn't answer. Jim went back on down the hill.

Oliver took the dishcloth off. The fiddle was laying in the light of the open door. He sucked a whisker and looked at it. Oliver knew the fiddle, and it was a good fiddle. He wondered if it was in tune and wanted to pick it up, but he let it lay there. His foot was tapping, and he slapped his knee to make it stop. He laughed to himself and muttered, "Them donkeys—what do they know?" Then he got up and moved around the little house on his dreary business.

The sun went down and the shadow of the fiddle case stretched across the floor. Oliver's eyes kept landing on the fiddle, and he stepped over the shadow when he crossed that way. It looked to him like the bow had new horsehair[1] on it. But it didn't make any

1. **horsehair:** hair from the mane or tail of a horse used on the bow of a fiddle, violin, or cello.

difference to him. He figured he'd never be playing on that fiddle, and he never touched it.

Next morning Oliver watched down the hill for Jim to come and tell him the deal was off and to get the fiddle. Noon came. Oliver ate some beans. Afternoon came on. Jim didn't show. Oliver began to get mad. He was mad that he had ever made the promise. It started to get dark. "Those cluckheads!" Oliver said, pulling the window shut. "They can't dance with dishcloths on their head, or drink punch, either. They'll have a rotten time."

But a promise is a promise.

Finally he decided it was time to put his hat and coat on. "They tricked me," Oliver grumbled. "but I got a trick for them, too. They'll be sorry I came to their party." It wasn't a great trick Oliver had in mind, but just a miserable little one to make sure nobody could have any fun while he was there. He figured they'd ask him to leave shortly. He wouldn't even bother to take off his hat and coat.

He headed down the hill with the fiddle and into the little town. He entered Edward's barn with his hat pulled down and his collar turned up. It was dark except for two bare, hanging light bulbs, one over the center of the barn and one at the end where a sort of stage was built up. Oliver had played at shindigs[2] there many times. He kept his head down, and only from the corners of his eyes could he see all the people sitting around the walls. "Lord, it's awfully dark," Oliver thought to himself, "and quiet. I figure they know that's the way I like it." He got under the light bulb that hung over the stage and took out the fiddle.

He tuned down to a fretful[3] and lonesome sound, and then he played.

Of course he knew they were all looking for happy dancing tunes, so first off he played a slow and sad tune about a man who was walking down a long road that had no ending and was gray all about, and the man was looking forward to being dead because it might be more cheerful. Nobody danced, naturally, and didn't clap either when

2. **shindigs:** happy, noisy dances or parties.
3. **fretful:** unhappy.

Oliver finished it. "That's just right," Oliver thought. "I'll give them a wretched time." And he started on another.

The second tune he played was even slower and sadder, about a man who thought his heart was a pincushion and it seemed to him that everyone was sticking pins and needles into it, and it was hurtful even to listen to it. Nobody danced, and nobody even moved to the punch bowl to get their spirits up. "Now they're sorry I came," Oliver thought. Still, he had played that last tune especially sweet, and he expected someone might have clapped a little just for that, even if it was sad.

Oliver looked out a little under his hat as he returned a bit. He tried to see Jim. He ought to come up and say hello at least, not just let him stand there completely alone. And he wondered where the other musicians were. Four people were sitting down off to the right of the stage. That would be them. Oliver considered it would be nice to have a little slide guitar[4] on these slow ones, sort of mournful played, and a mouth harp[5] and mandolin[6] would fit in nice. "Naw! This is just the way I want it. One more gloomy song and they'll ask me to leave."

So then he played another, this one about a man who had a wife that just recently moved to heaven, and how roses grew all over her tombstone even in the winter. Oliver was halfway through that before he remembered that he'd played that tune at his own wedding party. He pulled up short a bit then, but kept on playing it out, and a tear rolled down his cheek. Well, nobody could see. He wiped his eyes when he was finished.

Nobody clapped and nobody moved, just sat against the dark walls perfectly still. Among the dark figures was a lighter shape. Probably the bride in her white gown. Oliver remembered how lovely and happy his bride had been, and he felt a little mean when he thought about that, giving out such sad tunes.

He spoke out loud, the first words that were spoken since he came in. "Well, I guess you're all ready for me to leave now, and I will. But

4. **slide guitar:** a regular guitar on which the guitarist uses a hollow steel tube or a piece of glass on a finger of the left hand; the tube slides up and down the strings to create a smooth sound, while the right hand plucks the strings.
5. **mouth harp:** a harmonica.
6. **mandolin** [man´ də lin´] : a musical instrument with a pear-shaped body, having four to six pairs of strings.

first I want to play just one happy tune for the bride, and so you can dance, and then I'll go." Then he did play a happy one, a fast one, carrying on with fiddling lively enough to scramble eggs. But nobody got up to dance, and when he was finished nobody moved or made a sound.

"Look here," Oliver said. "I reckon you can't dance with those dishcloths over your heads, I forgot about that. So take 'em off. I'll give you another dancing tune, then I'll go." And then he went into another, as sweet and light and fast as anyone ever could, something to get even a rock up and dancing, but nobody moved. And when he was finished they all sat silent with the dishcloths still on their heads.

"Come on," Oliver said. "Take those things off your heads. You other fellows get up here with your music and help me out. Let's have some dancing, drink some punch, let's get alive now." He stomped his foot three times and threw into a tune that would churn butter all by itself. But the other four musicians sat perfectly still, and so did everybody else, and Oliver was standing there under the light bulb in silence when he finished the tune.

He stood there with his head down, understanding things, and how it felt to be on the other side of the darkness and silence when all you wanted was some sign of life to help out. Then he leaned over and put the fiddle in the case and closed it. He said one last thing, then walked out from under the light toward the door. "Okay," he said. "That's a hard lesson, but I got it."

When he opened the door he bumped into someone sitting next to it against the wall, and the fellow fell off his chair. Oliver put a hand down to help him up. But the fellow just lay there. Oliver touched him. "What's this?" He felt around, then shoved back his hat for a look. It was a sack of grain he'd knocked over. And the next person sitting there was a sack of grain, too. And the next was a bale of hay.

Oliver walked completely around the barn. All the people were sacks of grain and bales of hay sitting against the dark walls, and the bride was a white sack of flour. The four musicians sitting off to the right of the stage were four old saddles setting on a rail.

When Oliver came around to the door again he heard music. He stepped outside and looked down the street. A barn down near the end was all lit up, and lots of people were moving about. He went back up on the stage, got the fiddle, and headed down the street.

Jim was standing by the door. "Waiting for you, Oliver," he said. "We're just getting under way—come on in." When he led Oliver inside everyone became quiet, first one little group of people then another, until at last everyone was silent and looking at Oliver. The bride and groom were holding hands. Jim made a motion and everyone headed for a chair against the walls. They all took out dishcloths to put over their heads.

"Edward's got himself a new barn, huh?" Oliver said.

"Yeah," said Jim. "I guess you didn't know that. Uses the old one to store stuff. I shoulda told you."

"It's all right," Oliver said. He looked up on the stage. Four musicians were sitting there with dishcloths over their heads. Then Jim took out a large dishcloth. Oliver touched him on the arm.

"Never mind that. And everyone else, too. Just be regular and dance. I'll fiddle for you."

Jim slapped him on the back and shouted out the good news. Oliver went up on the stage. Someone got him a mug of punch. The musicians tuned up. Oliver took off his hat and dropped it, and tossed his coat on a chair. They lit into a fast, happy tune. They danced and played and sang half the night.

Ah, they had a wonderful time. Oliver included.

RICHARD KENNEDY
....

Richard Kennedy, born in 1932, said that "Oliver Hyde's Dishcloth Concert" was inspired by a fiddle album called *Will the Circle Be Unbroken* as well as a tragic, startling story from an Irish tune about a man who "fiddled on his way to the gallows."

Although Kennedy found himself writing stories for young readers— almost accidentally—he has been praised as "one of the few distinctive male voices in contemporary American children's books" by The New York Times Book Review.

Asking Big Questions About the Literature

Why do people need others?

Write an
ADVERTISEMENT

If the characters in *Lean on Me* took out classified ads to ask for help, what might they write? Choose one character and write a newspaper classified advertisement for that character. Try to capture the character's needs as concisely as possible. Display your advertisements on a classroom bulletin board.

Setting

A **setting** is the time and place in which the action of a story takes place. Sometimes the setting even provides the key for meeting people's needs, as the Lincoln School does in "Barrio Boy." (*See "Setting" on page 118.*)

Reread a selection in this unit to find details that describe the setting. Then create an illustration for a book jacket that shows the setting and the situation.

Evaluating Characters' Needs

You've met some interesting characters in this unit. Work with a partner to evaluate the needs of at least two of those characters. First identify each character's need, and then evaluate the need as *Necessary for survival*, *Necessary for lifelong happiness*, *Necessary for short-term satisfaction*, or *Not very important*. Then give reasons for your evaluation. The evaluation begun here is for "And Sarah Laughed."

Character's Need	Evaluation	Reason for Evaluation
Sarah needs to find a way to communicate with her sons and husband so she can understand their feelings.	Necessary for lifelong happiness	If she doesn't communicate with them, they'll always be distant, like polite strangers.

Exploring the Effects of Help

List characters in this unit who receive help from someone else. For each character, create a diagram like the one shown. For *Problem*, write why the character needs help. For *Help*, write the form that the help takes. For *Effect*, write what happens after help is received. The diagram begun here is for Marguerite in *I Know Why the Caged Bird Sings*.

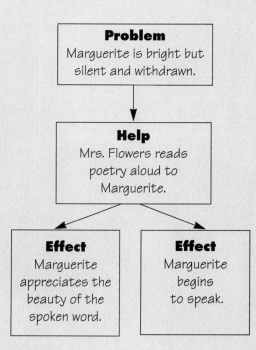

Problem
Marguerite is bright but silent and withdrawn.

Help
Mrs. Flowers reads poetry aloud to Marguerite.

Effect
Marguerite appreciates the beauty of the spoken word.

Effect
Marguerite begins to speak.

LITERATURE STUDY

Theme

Works of literature usually contain a **theme**, a message about life or people. Most themes express ideas that readers have probably already encountered, such as, "Honesty is the best policy" and "War is cruel." In works of fiction, theme isn't directly stated—readers must interpret it from the story elements. For example, Oliver in "Oliver Hyde's Dishcloth Concert," discovers that needing people—and being needed by them—is necessary for happiness. Oliver's discovery becomes the theme of the story. (*See "Theme" on page 119.*)

Work with a partner to list the works of fiction in this unit that deal with the Big Question "Why is offering help important?" For each work, state the theme in one sentence.

Interviewing A HELPER

With a partner, choose a selection in which a character offers help. Take turns role-playing an interview with the helper. Try to capture the helper's personality with your voices. Tape-record your interviews, and then play them for classmates.

Asking Big Questions About the Literature

What is involved in accepting help?

LITERATURE STUDY

Theme

The **theme,** or the message, of most literature is serious. For example, "Barrio Boy" deals with the difficulties and triumphs of learning to speak English with the help of a dedicated teacher. (*See "Theme" on page 119.*)

Work in a group to choose a selection from this unit with a theme that interests you. Decide what the theme is: for example, accepting help. Then think about how the selection would change if the theme were the opposite. Dramatize the story based on your new theme. Perform your dramatization for another group or for the entire class.

Write a Thank-You
NOTE

Imagine that you're one of the characters in this unit who received help. To show your appreciation, write a thank-you note to the person who helped you. Sign the character's name. Share your thank-you note by "mailing" it to a classmate.

Write an
ESSAY

Sometimes a person's situation and attitude affect the way help is offered and accepted. Choose two characters from two selections who accept help. Compare their situations and attitudes, using a Venn diagram like the one begun here. When you've finished, write a short essay in which you analyze why each character accepted help.

Tamaki in "Neighbors"   Marguerite in *I Know Why the Caged Bird Sings*

- faces threat of internment camp
- proud but afraid

wouldn't ask for help

- is shy
- admires Mrs. Flowers

How can people make a difference in their communities?

LITERATURE STUDY

Setting

How do characters' actions have an effect on their **setting**, the place where they live? (See "Setting" on page 118.)

Choose a selection from this unit, and then, in your journal, make a chart like the one below. In the column headed *Community*, list details that describe the community—the setting in which the story unfolds. Then reread the story to determine how characters' actions in that setting improve their community. When you've finished, compare your chart with those of your classmates.

Talking to the Next Generation

Work in a small group to choose a selection in this unit that contains an important issue (ethnic prejudice, obstacles affecting the disabled, problems of immigrants). Then role-play a conversation in which group members play the roles of the characters as grandparents, the characters' children, and the characters' grandchildren. In your conversations, focus on what people have done to make a difference. Before the presentation, brainstorm to define how events would be seen—or might be seen—by each generation. Perform your presentation for the class.

Literature	Character	Community	Changes
"Star-Fix"	navigator	Air Force base	helps crew members overcome prejudice

NOW
Choose a Project!
In the following pages, you'll find three projects that involve giving and receiving help.

Writing Workshop

LAUNCH A PROPOSAL

What can you do to improve your corner of the world? Start a school newspaper? Make a playground safer? Create entertainment programs for nursing home residents?

The Big Questions in this unit ask about people giving and receiving help. This project will give you a chance to offer help by identifying a problem and proposing a solution to it. Your **purpose**, then, is to write a formal proposal explaining your ideas to your **audience**—the adults who have the power to grant permission to you to make the change.

Prewriting

GETTING STARTED

To get ideas, identify projects that you could successfully tackle. In your journal, write the sentence starters shown at the bottom of the page and complete them. You can use them over and over for ideas.

One problem in my community is _____.

_____
If I could change anything in my school, I'd _____.

_____
People always say that _____ should be improved.

Now identify the problem—the one thing that you want to change or improve and that you think it's possible to change. Define the problem as precisely as you can. If you don't have a good handle on the problem, finding a workable solution will be very difficult.

Next think of different solutions for the problem. Brainstorm for as many solutions as you can. (Remember, the easiest solution may not be the best solution.) For each solution, list the actions you'd take and the resources you'd need.

Now identify your audience—the people who have the power and authority to make the changes that you want. By identifying your audience, you'll know what to include in your proposal and how to present it. For example, if your audience is voters, you might present your proposal as an open letter in the local newspaper. If your audience is the school committee, you might write a formal proposal that you present in person at a school-committee meeting.

Problem: _____

Audience: _____

Solution A	How to Present	Solution B	How to Present
steps to take materials needed		steps to take materials needed	

Drafting
YOUR PROPOSAL

Keeping your purpose and audience in mind, draft your proposal. Your proposal will explain the problem and present a solution. Use an appropriately formal tone throughout. (See student writer Sean Francey's proposal on pages 110-111.)

- Choose an appropriate title and present your proposal in a logical way. Sean Francey puts his proposal in a nutshell with the title—"Study Halls for Middle School" and then discusses the problem, the solution, the benefits, and a plan of action in subsequent paragraphs.

- Begin by stating your purpose for writing the proposal. Sean opens his proposal by stating, "We would like to address the problem of the lack of study halls in our district's middle schools." He explains the problem by saying, "Since there are no study halls, students must do all their studying at home . . ."

- Present your solution. Tell how you'd solve the problem, what your plan would cost, and what steps need to be taken. Sean details the resources that will be needed: a classroom, a supervisor, and students.

- Identify the benefits of your proposal and organize them from most important to least important. Use facts and examples that will appeal to your audience and strengthen your case. For example, Sean points out that "Students' overall performance and grades will improve" and then follows up with the fact of other study halls' success nationally and locally.

- Explain how to put your proposal into action. Sean identifies where resources will come from and who will be involved. He closes by saying that his plan requires a "small investment of effort . . ." that "can provide the difference between success and failure for many students." Who could say no to an offer like that?

Revising YOUR PROPOSAL

Have a partner or a group respond to your proposal and make suggestions for improving it. If possible, ask someone who would be affected by the proposal to respond to your plan. Do you clearly identify the problem? Do you propose a solution that will work? Do you support your ideas with sufficient facts and examples? Do you include a plan for action? Look again at Sean's proposal on pages 110-111.

Editing YOUR PROPOSAL

Work with a partner to edit your revision. Read one another's proposals, checking for errors in spelling, grammar, and punctuation. Correct your errors and make a publishable copy of your proposal. You'll lose credibility if your work is sloppy.

Publishing YOUR PROPOSAL

Before you present your proposal to your audience, make sure that any graphic aids—maps, charts, diagrams, flip charts—are polished and ready to go.

If you plan to present your written proposal in person, make an appointment in advance. Let your enthusiasm for your ideas show—after all, your ideas are worth pursuing!

Study Halls for Middle School

A Proposal to the School Board
from Sean M. Francey of Brookfield, Wisconsin

We would like to address the problem of the lack of study halls in our district's middle schools. Since there are no study halls, students must do all their studying at home, where there are numerous diversions that draw their attention away from school work. Often, these distractions cause students to set aside or forget daily homework and long-term projects, causing a last-minute rush and, consequently, lower grades.

To solve this problem, we propose that students who want to bring up their grade point averages or who have trouble studying at home could have the option of taking a study hall in lieu of an "optional" class. All that a study hall requires is an available classroom, a supervisor, and a few resources, such as dictionaries.

Such a solution will provide many benefits. For example, study halls allow students to focus on their studies, free from the distractions of home and the pressure of the classroom. Students' overall performance and grades will improve. The success of study halls has been proved in many high schools across the country, including our own Brookfield Central High School and Brookfield East High School.

This proposal could be set in motion immediately. Some classrooms are unoccupied every period. Student monitors with free periods could supervise the study hall. Students could have the choice of dropping optional classes in favor of the study hall.

This small investment of effort on the part of middle schools can provide the difference between success and failure for many students. I hope that you don't let us down.

Cooperative Learning

WHERE CAN I TURN?

What resources does your community provide for teens who need help? For this project, you'll learn about those resources. Then you'll work with a small group of students to create a handbook that helps teens get in touch with the help they need.

Analyzing TEEN NEEDS

As a group, brainstorm for a list of concerns, problems, and questions that teens might have. Start your list with the word *help*. Write anything you can think of that is suggested by *help*.

→ HELP! **** !!!! ★★
baby-sitting EMERGENCY...
What number do I call?
• I need a summer job $$$
... How do I find one?
... I'm bored... WHAT is there to do?

Organize your ideas into general categories, such as Health, Education, Crisis Intervention, or Careers. Each group member should take one or more categories to investigate. Make a list like the one below to keep track of what tasks everyone is doing.

Category	Person Responsible
Health	
Education	
Crisis Intervention	
Careers	

HELP FOR TEENS

Important facts and phone numbers

Investigating RESOURCES

Now make a list of the names, addresses, and phone numbers of places where teens can get help. To develop your list, talk to your school's nurse, health teachers, guidance counselors, coaches, and research librarian. Then consult churches, community health centers, local doctors' offices, hospitals, law enforcement agencies, and bulletin boards. Don't forget to check the obvious—telephone books, a local newspaper, and library reference books, such as *Encyclopedia of Associations*. List the resource's name, address, and telephone number; hours of operation; and a brief description of the help or service offered.

> **Literacy Outreach**
>
> 435 First Street, San Diego, CA
> (619) 213-7873
>
> Open 9 a.m. - 9 p.m., Monday - Friday
>
> *Free tutors for people who want to learn to read and write English.*

Creating A HANDBOOK

Collect everyone's list of resources and sort them into categories. Create descriptive labels for the categories. Then alphabetize the categories and the resources for each category. Type the information and carefully proofread it. (An emergency phone number doesn't do much good if it's the wrong number.) Finally make a table of contents, an index, and add a title. Make as many copies as you'll want to distribute, and put a binder on each.

Presenting THE HANDBOOK

Place handbooks in places that teens might frequent, such as libraries, fast-food restaurants, malls, churches and so on. You'll never know how many people your handbook will help.

PROJECT 3

Helping Your Community

GIVE A HELPING HAND

One of the Big Questions in this unit asks, "How can people make a difference in their communities?" For this project, you'll research volunteer opportunities in your community and then work as a volunteer. You'll encourage other teens to do volunteer work by writing a letter to the editor of your local newspaper.

Inventorying YOUR INTERESTS

Successful volunteers are interested in their work. To develop a profile of your interests, list your skills and abilities, your favorite classes and activities, and the causes you believe in.

MY INTERESTS

What are my skills?
  · good leader
Favorite classes...
  · math
  · history
Favorite spare-time
activities...
  · baby-sitting
  · camping
Causes I believe in...
  · recycling
  · wildlife
  · conservation
I might be good
as a volunteer
for _____.

Identifying OPPORTUNITIES

To identify volunteer opportunities, contact Youth Service America or Volunteers of America. Describe your interests and abilities and ask them for suggestions. Talk to people you know and school guidance counselors. You might also check the following places for volunteer opportunities:

Check These Places for Volunteer Opportunities

• community center	• nursing home	• library
• historical society	• homeless shelter	• animal shelter
• hospital or hospice	• humane society	• art center
• religious organization	• senior center	• parks department

Becoming A VOLUNTEER

Pick one volunteer opportunity that most interests you, and go for it! Call or write for information to find out what you have to do to volunteer. If this is your first experience as a volunteer, be realistic. Keep in mind how much free time you have. Also consider how you'll get to where you'll work.

If your research has revealed a need that no one is filling, start your own project. For example, you might get some friends to help you clean up a park, tutor younger kids, or start a free grocery delivery service for older people in your community.

Sharing YOUR EXPERIENCE

Write a letter to the editor of your local newspaper in which you describe your research, your findings, and your experience as a volunteer. Make sure your letter is neat and free of errors in spelling, grammar, and punctuation. Other teens should be able to use your letter as a guide for finding their own volunteer opportunities. Who says one person can't make a difference!

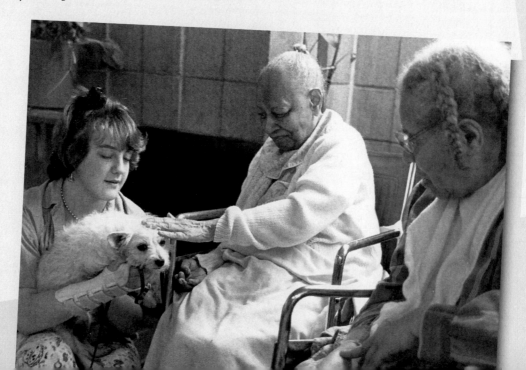

Putting It All Together

What Have You Learned About Giving and Receiving Help?

How has this unit changed your ideas about giving and receiving help? Look back at the writing you've done for this unit—in your journal, in response to your reading, and in the Writing Workshop. Use what you've learned to write an article about a person whose help has made a difference—in someone else's life or in a community. Then work with your classmates to create a class newspaper that profiles *People Who Make a Difference*.

GIVING HELP . . . MAKING A DIFFERENCE

Prewriting and Drafting   Brainstorm for names of people you know—or have read about—who have made a difference. Include people your own age. For example, middle-school students Rebecca and Phillippa Herbert of West Covina, California, started a recycling center in their front yard.

Choose a person to write about and then draft an article that describes what the person did to contribute to someone else's life or to the community. Use **chronological order** (*first, next, last*) to tell what happened. If you can, include why the person decided to act, how he or she felt about giving help, and how the help was accepted.

Try to get background information and direct quotations that add insight into the person's nature. (For a model, look at Phillip Hoose's "Justin Lebo.")

Revising and Editing   Work with a partner or a group to revise and edit your articles. Make suggestions for improvement and check grammar, punctuation, and spelling. Then make a publishable copy of your article.

Publishing   If you can, include a photograph of the subject of your feature article. Then work with your classmates to create a class newspaper that profiles *People Who Make a Difference*. You can display your newspaper in your classroom or in the school library.

Evaluating Your Work

Think Back About the Big Questions

With a partner, discuss the Big Questions on pages 10-11 and the questions that you generated for **Now Think!** on page 11. Do you have trouble answering any questions now? In your journal, create a "before and after" chart to show how your responses to the Big Questions have changed after your work in *Lean on Me*.

Think Back About Your Work

Think about the unit you've just finished and evaluate your work—including your reading, writing, and activities. How would you evaluate your efforts?

Write a note to your teacher, explaining what you've done during this unit and what you've learned. Use the following questions to guide your thinking:

- Which selection in this unit did you like the most? The least? Why?

- What is the most surprising thing that you learned about people and their ability to give and to receive help?

- Which activities helped you learn more about giving and receiving help? Why?

- What did you learn about yourself as you read the selections and worked through the activities?

- If you could do one activity again, which one would you choose? What would you do differently?

- How would you rate your work overall in this unit? Use the following scale and give at least three reasons for your rating.

    1 = Outstanding   3 = Fair

    2 = Good   4 = Not as good as it could have been

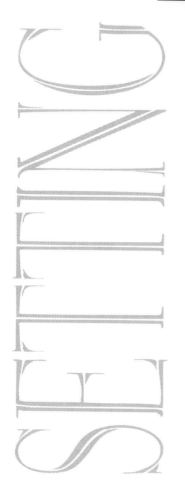

What Is Setting?

The **setting** of a work of literature is the time and the place in which the action takes place. *Time* includes time in history—past, present, or future—as well as the time of day. *Place* includes geographical locations, specific buildings, climate, and weather. In some stories, the setting plays a key role in the plot (person against the elements); in other stories, it creates *mood*, the atmosphere or feeling created by a sense of place. For example, consider the difference in mood created in these two settings: (1) a big empty house on an isolated road during a stormy night; (2) a crowded public beach at noon in August. Writers develop setting through description (sights, smells, sensations) and through dialogue.

Writing a Swapped-Setting Poem   The settings of the two poems in this unit are a construction site ("Scaffolding" by Seamus Heaney) and a U.S. Air Force base ("Star-Fix" by Marilyn Nelson Waniek). How might the poems be different if the settings were switched? Choose one of the poems and rewrite it, using the other poem's setting. You might need to do a lot of tinkering with details and characters so that the new setting will make sense in the context of the poem. Share your poem with a partner or a small group. Then compile a class book of poetry.

Imagining the Future   Some writers use science-fiction settings for their stories so that they can safely express radical or unpopular ideas. Since no one can predict what the future will hold, writers escape criticism for their ideas. Try your hand at writing a science-fiction story about people helping one another in the future. Use as many descriptive details as you can to create a sense of another world and its inhabitants. Bind your completed story with those of your classmates into a *Future World* classroom anthology. Make your anthology available to other classes in your school.

What Is Theme?

A work's **theme** is its message, the main idea that stays in your mind after you finish reading. In nonfiction, the theme may be stated directly, for example, "Television is bad for you." In fiction, the theme is not stated—readers must interpret the message through the characters and the plot. To find the theme of a work of fiction, ask yourself, "What's the writer's point?" The point may be a moral truth, such as, "People who do the right thing will feel good about themselves. " On the other hand, the point may be to reveal something about life, such as, "Immigrants have a difficult time adjusting." When readers interpret a work of literature differently, their opinion of its theme usually differs.

Picturing an Idea   Essays have obvious themes that are not subject to much interpretation. Photo essays, like written essays, also have obvious themes. Think of some of the themes about giving and receiving help that you've encountered in this unit. Then create a photo essay that illustrates one of those themes. Take about a dozen photos to illustrate that theme. If you don't have a camera, use pictures from magazines. Mount your photos on paper, add captions to each, and think of a title that captures the idea of your theme. Display your photo essay in the classroom.

Writing a Story As a Poem   Choose one of the selections in this unit that isn't a poem. Determine its theme. Now write a short poem in which you retell the story. Your goal is to emphasize the theme of the story while eliminating most of the details, so just focus on the key action and a main character or two. Without giving the title, read your poem aloud to a partner or a small group. Then ask your partner or your group to guess the name of the selection that you made into a poem.

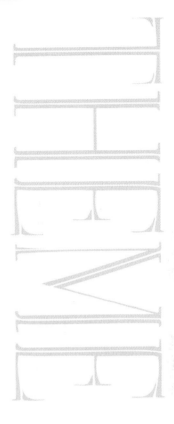

GLOSSARY OF LITERARY TERMS

A

alliteration Repetition of the first sound—usually a consonant sound—in several words of a sentence or a line of poetry.

allusion An author's indirect reference to someone or something that is presumed to be familiar to the reader.

anecdote A short narrative about an interesting or a humorous event, usually in the life of a person.

antagonist The person or force opposing the protagonist, or main character in a literary work. [See also *protagonist*.]

autobiography A person's written account of his or her own life.

B

ballad A poem, often a song, that tells a story in simple verse.

biography An account of a person's life, written by another person.

blank verse Unrhymed poetry.

C

character A person or an animal that participates in the action of a work of literature. A *dynamic character* is one whose thoughts, feelings, and actions are changeable and lifelike; a *static character* always remains the same. [See also *protagonist, antagonist*.]

characterization The creation of characters through the characters' use of language and through descriptions of their appearance, thoughts, emotions, and actions. [See also *character*.]

chronology An arrangement of events in the order in which they happen.

cliché An overused expression that is trite rather than meaningful.

climax The highest point of tension in the plot of a work of literature. [See also *plot*.]

comedy An amusing play that has a happy ending.

conclusion The final part or ending of a piece of literature.

concrete poem A poem arranged on the page so that its punctuation, letters, and lines make the shape of the subject of the poem.

conflict A problem that confronts the characters in a piece of literature. The conflict may be *internal* (a character's struggle within himself or herself) or *external* (a character's struggle against nature, another person, or society). [See also *plot*.]

context The general sense of words that helps readers to understand the meaning of unfamiliar words and phrases in a piece of writing.

D

description An author's use of words to give the reader or listener a mental picture, an impression, or an understanding of a person, place, thing, event, or idea.

dialect A form of speech spoken by people in a particular group or geographical region that differs in vocabulary, grammar, and pronunciation from the standard language.

dialogue The spoken words and conversation of characters in a work of literature.

drama A play that is performed before an audience according to stage directions and using dialogue. Classical drama has two genres: *tragedy* and *comedy*. Modern drama includes *melodrama, satire, theater of the absurd,* and *pantomime*. [See also *comedy, play,* and *tragedy*.]

dramatic poetry A play written in the form of poetry.

E

epic A long narrative poem—written in a formal style and meant to be read aloud—that relates the adventures and

experiences of one or more great heroes or heroines.

essay   Personal nonfiction writing about a particular subject that is important to the writer.

excerpt   A passage from a larger work that has been taken out of its context to be used for a special purpose.

exposition   Writing that explains, analyzes, or defines.

extended metaphor   An elaborately drawn out metaphor. [See also *metaphor*.]

F

fable   A short, simple story whose purpose is to teach a lesson, usually with animal characters who talk and act like people.

fantasy   Imaginative fiction about unrealistic characters, places, and events.

fiction   Literature, including the short story and the novel, that tells about imaginary people and events.

figurative language
Language used to express ideas through figures of speech: descriptions that aren't meant to be taken literally. Types of figurative language include *simile*, *metaphor*, *extended metaphor*, *hyperbole*, and *personification*.

figure of speech   A type of figurative language, not meant to be taken literally, that expresses something in such a way that it brings the thing to life in the reader's or listener's imagination. [See also *figurative language*.]

flashback   A break in a story's action that relates a past happening in order to give the reader background information about a present action in the story.

folktale   A story that has been passed along from storyteller to storyteller for generations. Kinds of folktales include *tall tales*, *fairy tales*, *fables*, *legends*, and *myths*.

foreshadowing   The use of clues to create suspense by giving the reader or audience hints of events to come.

free verse   Poetry that has no formal rhyme scheme or metrical pattern.

G

genre   A major category of art. The three major literary genres are poetry, prose, and drama.

H

haiku   A three-line Japanese verse form. In most haiku, the first and third lines have five syllables, while the second line has seven. The

traditional haiku describes a complicated feeling or thought in simple language through a single image.

hero/heroine   The main character in a work of literature. In heroic literature, the hero or heroine is a particularly brave, noble, or clever person whose achievements are unusual and important. [See also *character*.]

heroic age   The historical period in western civilization—from about 800 B.C. through A.D. 200—during which most works of heroic literature, such as myths and epics, were created in ancient Greece and Rome.

hubris   Arrogance or excessive pride leading to mistakes; the character flaw in a hero of classical tragedy.

hyperbole   An obvious exaggeration used for emphasis. [See also *figurative language*.]

I

idiom   An expression whose meaning cannot be understood from the ordinary meaning of the words. For example, *It's raining cats and dogs*.

imagery   The words and phrases in writing that appeal to the senses of sight, hearing, taste, touch, and smell.

irony   An effect created by a sharp contrast between what is expected and what is real. An *ironic twist* in a plot is an event that is the complete opposite of what the characters have been hoping or expecting will happen. An *ironic statement* declares the opposite of the speaker's literal meaning.

J

jargon   Words and phrases used by a group of people who share the same profession or special interests in order to refer to technical things or processes with which they are familiar. In general, jargon is any terminology that sounds unclear, overused, or pretentious.

L

legend   A famous folktale about heroic actions, passed along by word of mouth from generation to generation. The legend may have begun as a factual account of real people and events but has become mostly or completely fictitious.

limerick   A form of light verse, or humorous poetry, written in one five-line stanza with a regular scheme of rhyme and meter.

literature   The branch of art that is expressed in written language and includes all written genres.

lyric poem   A short poem that expresses personal feelings and thoughts in a musical way. Originally, lyrics were the words of songs that were sung to music played on the lyre, a stringed instrument invented by the ancient Greeks.

M

metamorphosis   The transformation of one thing, or being, into another completely different thing or being, such as a caterpillar's change into a butterfly.

metaphor   Figurative language in which one thing is said to be another thing. [See also *figurative language*.]

meter   The pattern of rhythm in lines of poetry. The most common meter, in poetry written in English, is iambic pentameter, that is, a verse having five metrical feet, each foot of verse having two syllables, an unaccented one followed by an accented one.

mood   The feeling or atmosphere that a reader senses while reading or listening to a work of literature.

motivation   A character's reasons for doing, thinking, feeling, or saying something. Sometimes an author will make a character's motivation obvious from the beginning. In realistic fiction and drama, however, a character's motivation may be so complicated that the reader discovers it gradually, by studying the character's thoughts, feelings, and behavior.

myth   A story, passed along by word of mouth for generations, about the actions of gods and goddesses or superhuman heroes and heroines. Most myths were first told to explain the origins of natural things or to justify the social rules and customs of a particular society.

N

narration   The process of telling a story. For both fiction and nonfiction, there are two main kinds of narration, based on whether the story is told from a first-person or third-person point of view. [See also *point of view*.]

narrative poem   A poem that tells a story containing the basic literary ingredients of fiction: character, setting, and plot.

narrator   The person, or voice, that tells a story. [See also *point of view*, *voice*.]

nonfiction   Prose that is factually true and is about real people, events, and places.

nonstandard English
Versions of English, such as slang and dialects, that use pronunciation, vocabulary, idiomatic expressions, grammar, and punctuation that differ from the accepted "correct" constructions of English.

novel   A long work of narrative prose fiction. A novel contains narration, a setting or settings, characters, dialogue, and a more complicated plot than a short story.

O

onomatopoeia   The technique of using words that imitate the sounds they describe, such as *hiss*, *buzz*, and *splash*.

oral tradition   Stories, poems, and songs that have been kept alive by being told, recited, and sung by people over many generations. Since the works were not originally written, they often have many different versions.

P

parable   A brief story—similar to a fable, but about people—that describes an ordinary situation and concludes with a short moral or lesson to be learned.

personification   Figurative language in which an animal, an object, or an idea is given human characteristics. [See also *figurative language*.]

persuasion   A type of speech or writing whose purpose is to convince people that something is true or important.

play   A work of dramatic literature written for performance by actors before an audience. In classical or traditional drama, a play is divided into five acts, each containing a number of scenes. Each act represents a distinct phase in the development of the plot. Modern plays often have only one act and one scene.

playwright   The author of a play.

plot   The sequence of actions and events in fiction or drama. A traditional plot has at least three parts: the *rising action*, leading up to a turning point that affects the main character; the *climax*, the turning point or moment of greatest intensity or interest; and the *falling action*, leading away from the conflict, or resolving it.

poetry   Language selected and arranged in order to say something in a compressed or nonliteral way. Modern poetry may or may not use many of the traditional poetic techniques that include *meter*, *rhyme*, *alliteration*, *figurative language*, *symbolism*, and *specific verse forms*.

point of view   The perspective from which a writer tells a story. *First-person* narrators tell the story from their own point of view, using pronouns such as *I* or *me*. *Third-person* narrators, using pronouns such as *he*, *she*, or *them*, may be *omniscient* (knowing everything about all characters), or *limited* (taking the point of view of one character). [See also *narration*.]

propaganda   Information or ideas that may or may not be true, but are spread as though they are true, in order to persuade people to do or believe something.

prose   The ordinary form of written and spoken language used to create fiction, nonfiction, and most drama.

protagonist   The main character of a literary work. [See also *character* and *characterization*.]

R

refrain   A line or group of lines that is repeated, usually at the end of each verse, in a poem or a song.

repetition   The use of the same formal element more than once in a literary work, for emphasis or in order to achieve another desired effect.

resolution   The falling action in fiction or drama,

including all of the developments that follow the climax and show that the story's conflict is over. [See also *plot*.]

rhyme scheme   A repeated pattern of similar sounds, usually found at the ends of lines of poetry or poetic drama.

rhythm   In poetry, the measured recurrence of accented and unaccented syllables in a particular pattern. [See also *meter*.]

S

scene   The time, place, and circumstances of a play or a story. In a play, a scene is a section of an act. [See also *play*.]

science fiction   Fantasy literature set in an imaginary future, with details and situations that are designed to seem scientifically possible.

setting   The time and place of a work of literature.

short story   Narrative prose fiction that is shorter and has a less complicated plot than a novel. A short story contains narration, at least one setting, at least one character, and usually some dialogue.

simile   Figurative language that compares two unlike things, introduced by the words "like" or "as." [See also *figurative language*.]

soliloquy   In a play, a short speech spoken by a single character when he or she is alone on the stage. A soliloquy usually expresses the character's innermost thoughts and feelings, when he or she thinks no other characters can hear.

sonnet   A poem written in one stanza, using fourteen lines of iambic pentameter. [See also *meter*.]

speaker   In poetry, the individual whose voice seems to be speaking the lines. [See also *narration, voice*.]

stage directions   The directions, written by the playwright, to tell the director, actors, and theater technicians how a play should be dramatized. Stage directions may specify such things as how the setting should appear in each scene, how the actors should deliver their lines, when the stage curtain should rise and fall, how stage lights should be used, where on the stage the actors should be during the action, and when sound effects should be used.

stanza   A group of lines in poetry set apart by blank lines before and after the group; a poetic verse.

style   The distinctive way in which an author composes a

work of literature in written or spoken language.

suspense   An effect created by authors of various types of fiction and drama, especially adventure and mystery, to heighten interest in the story.

symbol   An image, person, place, or thing that is used to express the idea of something else.

T

tall tale   A kind of folk tale, or legend, that exaggerates the characteristics of its hero or heroine.

theme   The main idea or underlying subject of a work of literature.

tone   The attitude that a work of literature expresses to the reader through its style.

tragedy   In classical drama, a tragedy depicts a noble hero or heroine who makes a mistake of judgment that has disastrous consequences.

V

verse   A stanza in a poem. Also, a synonym for poetry as a genre. [See also *stanza*.]

voice   The narrator or the person who relates the action of a piece of literature. [See also *speaker*.]

ACKNOWLEDGMENTS

Grateful acknowledgment is made for permission to reprint the following copyrighted material.

"Lean on Me" by Bill Withers, copyright © 1972 by INTERIOR MUSIC, International Copyright Secured. All Rights Reserved. Used by Permission.

From *I Know Why the Caged Bird Sings* by Maya Angelou, copyright © 1969 by Maya Angelou. Reprinted by permission of Random House, Inc.

"And Sarah Laughed" by Joanne Greenberg from *Rites of Passage* by Joanne Greenberg. Copyright © 1966, 1967, 1968, 1970, 1971, 1972 by Joanne Greenberg. Reprinted by permission of Henry Holt and Company, Inc.

"Scaffolding" by Seamus Heaney is reprinted from *Poems 1956-1975* by permission.

"Justin Lebo" from *It's Our World Too!* by Phillip Hoose. Copyright © 1993 by Phillip Hoose. By permission of Little, Brown and Company.

From *Barrio Boy* by Ernesto Galarza, copyright © 1971 by University of Notre Dame Press. Reprinted by permission.

"Neighbors" by John Sherrill is reprinted from *Guidepost* magazine by permission.

"Star Fix" reprinted with permission of Louisiana State University from *The Homeplace* by Marilyn Nelson Waniek. Copyright © 1990 by Marilyn Nelson Waniek.

"The Winter Hibiscus" by Minfong Ho, copyright © 1992 by Minfong Ho, is reprinted by permission of the author and MacIntosh & Otis Inc.

"Oliver Hyde's Dishcloth Concert" by Richard Kennedy from *Richard Kennedy: Collected Stories*, text, copyright © 1987 by Richard Kennedy, is reprinted by permission of HarperCollins.

ILLUSTRATION

62-68 Border design and title by Dave Shepherd; 72-73 Background swirls by Dave Shepherd; 74-75, 89 Laotian calligraphy by Kevin Chanthasiri.

PHOTOGRAPHY

4 *l* Jim Whitmer/Stock Boston; *r* John Owens/©D.C. Heath; 5 ©1987 Carmen Lomas Garza. Collection of Paula Maciel-Benecke and Norbert Benecke; 6 Sarah Putnam/©D.C. Heath; 10 *t* David Strickler/The Image Works; *c* Sarah Putnam/©D.C. Heath; *b* Nita Winter/The Image Works; 11 *t* John Owens/©D.C. Heath; *b* Nancy Sheehan/©D.C. Heath; 12 (L) Bob Daemmrich/Stock Boston; (E, A) Mary Kate Denny/PhotoEdit; (N) Billy E. Barnes/PhotoEdit; (O) Harvey Finkle/Impact Visuals; (N) Bill Hickey/The Image Bank; (M, E) Bob Daemmrich; 13 Michael Ochs Archives; 15 National Museum of American Art, Smithsonian Institution. Gift of The Harmon Foundation; 19 Atlanta University Collection of Afro-American Art at Clark Atlanta University; 23 Courtesy of Lordly & Dame, Inc.; 24-41 Photo illustration by Carol Palmer/©D.C. Heath; 42 Photo by Monika of Mountain Splendor Photo; 43 Photo illustration by Carol Palmer/©D.C. Heath; 44-45 Collection of SAFECO Insurance Companies. Photo: Chris Eden; 45 Nancy Crampton 1991/Courtesy of Farrar, Straus & Giroux, Inc.; 46-47, 48-49, 50-51 Dennis Blachut; 52 Courtesy Diane Lebo; 53 Richard Connelly; 54-55, 57 *detail*, 58 *detail*, 61 *t, detail* ©1987 Carmen Lomas Garza. Collection of Paula Maciel-Benecke and Norbert Benecke; 61 *b* Photo by Karla Repe; 62, 67 Kevin Thomas/©D.C. Heath; 68 *t*, *b* Andree Abecassis; 69 Courtesy of Baker Book House; 70-71 Photo courtesy Terry Dintenfass Gallery; 73 Frank Funk; 74-92 Computer Imagery by Lois Schlowsky. Photos of Laotian textiles from Peabody Essex Museum, Salem, MA. Photo by Mark Sexton; 93 Photo by Jennifer Stoneburner; 94 Solomon R. Guggenheim Museum, New York. Gift, Solomon R. Guggenheim, 1937. Photo: David Heald/©The Solomon Guggenheim Foundation, New York. FN 37.446. ©ARS, NY/ADAGP, Paris; 105 Nancy Sheehan/©D.C. Heath; 106 *t* J. Berndt/Stock Boston; *b* Bob Daemmrich/Stock Boston; 111 Mary Kate Denny/PhotoEdit; 112 *t* Sarah Putnam/©D.C. Heath; *b* Stuart Cohen/©D.C. Heath; 114 Rhoda Sidney/Stock Boston; 115 Elizabeth Crews/The Image Works.
Back cover *t* Jim Whitmer/Stock Boston; *c* John Owens/©D.C. Heath; *b* Julie Bidwell/©D.C. Heath.

Full Pronunciation Key for Footnoted Words

(Each pronunciation and definition is adapted from *Scott, Foresman Advanced Dictionary* by E.L. Thorndike and Clarence L. Barnhart.)

The pronunciation of each footnoted word is shown just after the word, in this way: **abbreviate** [ə brē′ vē āt]. The letters and signs used are pronounced as in the words below. The mark ′ is placed after a syllable with primary or heavy accent, as in the example above. The mark ′ after a syllable shows a secondary or lighter accent, as in **abbreviation** [ə brē′ vē ā′ shən].

Some words, taken from foreign languages, are spoken with sounds that do not otherwise occur in English. Symbols for these sounds are given in the key as "foreign sounds."

a	hat, cap	j	jam, enjoy	u	cup, butter	**foreign sounds**
ā	age, face	k	kind, seek	u̇	full, put	
ä	father, far	l	land, coal	ü	rule, move	Y as in French *du*. Pronounce (ē) with the lips rounded as for (ü).
b	bad, rob	m	me, am	v	very, save	
ch	child, much	n	no, in	w	will, woman	à as in French *ami*. Pronounce (ä) with the lips spread and held tense.
d	did, red	ng	long, bring	y	young, yet	
				z	zero, breeze	
e	let, best	o	hot, rock	zh	measure, seizure	œ as in French *peu*. Pronounce (ā) with the lips rounded as for (ō).
ē	equal, be	ō	open, go			
ėr	term, learn	ô	order, all	ə represents:	N as in French *bon*. The N is not pronounced, but shows that the vowel before it is nasal.
		oi	oil, voice	a in about	
f	fat, if	ou	house, out	e in taken	
g	go, bag			i in pencil	H as in German *ach*. Pronounce (k) without closing the breath passage.
h	he, how	p	paper, cup	o in lemon	
		r	run, try	u in circus	
i	it, pin	s	say, yes		
ī	ice, five	sh	she, rush		
		t	tell, it		
		th	thin, both		
		ŦH	then, smooth		

FUTURE DIRECTIONS

HEATH
MIDDLE LEVEL
LITERATURE

H E A T H
MIDDLE LEVEL
LITERATURE

Future Directions

T H E M E
THE FUTURE

A U T H O R S

Donna Alvermann
Linda Miller Cleary
Kenneth Donelson
Donald Gallo
Alice Haskins
J. Howard Johnston
John Lounsbury
Alleen Pace Nilsen
Robert Pavlik
Jewell Parker Rhodes
Alberto Alvaro Ríos
Sandra Schurr
Lyndon Searfoss
Julia Thomason
Max Thompson
Carl Zon

STAFF CREDITS

EDITORIAL	Barbara A. Brennan, Susan Belt Cogley, DeVona Dors, Christopher Johnson, Rita M. Sullivan, Patricia B. Weiler
	Proofreading: JoAnne B. Sgroi
CONTRIBUTING WRITERS	Kathy Tuchman Glass, Jo Pitkin
SERIES DESIGN	Robin Herr
BOOK DESIGN	Caroline Bowden, Daniel Derdula, Susan Geer, Diana Maloney, Angela Sciaraffa, Bonnie Chayes Yousefian
	Art Editing: Carolyn Langley
PHOTOGRAPHY	*Series Photography Coordinator:* Carmen Johnson
	Photo Research Supervisor: Martha Friedman
	Photo Researchers: Wendy Enright, Linda Finigan, Po-yee McKenna, PhotoSearch, Inc., Gillian Speeth, Denise Theodores
	Assignment Photography Coordinators: Susan Doheny, Gayna Hoffman, Shawna Johnston
COMPUTER PREPRESS	Ricki Pappo, Kathy Meisl Richard Curran, Michele Locatelli
PERMISSIONS	Dorothy B. McLeod
PRODUCTION	Patrick Connolly

Cover Photographs: © William Lesch, SWANSTOCK; inset of Earth: courtesy NASA.
Cover Design: Bonnie Chayes Yousefian

Acknowledgments for copyrighted material are on page 125 and constitute an extension of this page.

Published simultaneously in Canada

Printed in the United States of America

International Standard Book Number: 0-669-32114-1 (soft cover)
 3 4 5 6 7 8 9 10-RRD-99 98 97 96

International Standard Book Number: 0-669-38182-9 (hard cover)
 3 4 5 6 7 8 9 10-RRD-99 98 97 96 95

Middle Level Authors

Donna Alvermann, University of Georgia
Alice Haskins, Howard County Public Schools, Maryland
J. Howard Johnston, University of South Florida
John Lounsbury, Georgia College
Sandra Schurr, University of South Florida
Julia Thomason, Appalachian State University
Max Thompson, Appalachian State University
Carl Zon, California Assessment Collaborative

Literature and Language Arts Authors

Linda Miller Cleary, University of Minnesota
Kenneth Donelson, Arizona State University
Donald Gallo, Central Connecticut State University
Alleen Pace Nilsen, Arizona State University
Robert Pavlik, Cardinal Stritch College, Milwaukee
Jewell Parker Rhodes, Arizona State University
Alberto Alvaro Ríos, Arizona State University
Lyndon Searfoss, Arizona State University

Teacher Consultants

Suzanne Aubin, Patapsco Middle School, Ellicott City, Maryland
Judy Baxter, Newport News Public Schools, Newport News, Virginia
Saundra Bryn, Director of Research and Development, El Mirage, Arizona
Lorraine Gerhart, Elmbrook Middle School, Elm Grove, Wisconsin
Kathy Tuchman Glass, Burlingame Intermediate School, Burlingame, California
Lucretia Pannozzo, John Jay Middle School, Katonah, New York
Carol Schultz, Jerling Junior High, Orland Park, Illinois
Jeanne Siebenman, Grand Canyon University, Phoenix, Arizona
Gail Thompson, Garey High School, Pomona, California
Rufus Thompson, Grace Yokley School, Ontario, California
Tom Tufts, Conniston Middle School, West Palm Beach, Florida
Edna Turner, Harpers Choice Middle School, Columbia, Maryland
C. Anne Webb, Buerkle Junior High School, St. Louis, Missouri
Geri Yaccino, Thompson Junior High School, St. Charles, Illinois

CONTENTS

THE LITERATURE

ASKING BIG QUESTIONS ABOUT THE LITERATURE

PROJECTS

1 WRITING WORKSHOP

THE ART OF PERSUASION 106-111

Take a stand about a local or national problem you feel passionate about.

2 COOPERATIVE LEARNING

PRODUCING A NEWSCAST 112-113

Produce a newscast for a futuristic television station reporting the current news.

3 HELPING YOUR COMMUNITY

TAKING ACTION 114-115

Examine a community problem and take some action to help improve the situation.

TIME TRAVEL

What will life be like in future centuries? Pretend that your class has built a time machine, and you've decided to go forward to a place 100 years from now. Where will you go? What will you take with you into this future time?

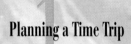

1 Planning a Time Trip

In a small group, brainstorm for a list of places and then decide where you'll go. Then decide what objects you want to take with you to this future time. Will you take a birth certificate, photos of your family, a notebook, favorite books, or a toothbrush? Now think of ideas and concepts you'd like to share with the future. Will the people you meet know about freedom of speech or kindness to others? Avoid choosing any objects, ideas, or concepts that might cause physical or emotional harm to future life. Make a chart of your choices like the one on this page. Add the choices of everyone in your group. When you complete your chart, narrow the items down to five objects, ideas, and concepts. Circle them on the chart.

Objects	Ideas	Concepts
CD player	carless society	freedom of speech
dental floss		

Defend Your Choices

Now that your group has decided where to go and what to take, have a class discussion. Appoint a spokesperson for your group who will tell the class where your group chooses to go, what the group plans to take, and why. Try to persuade the other groups that your choices are right. Prepare to defend each of your choices by discussing with your group how each choice will be useful and beneficial in 100 years.

A Class Decision

Listen carefully as each group reports to the class on the essential objects, ideas, and concepts that might be needed in the future. Then take a vote among your classmates to decide which five would be the most useful and beneficial for people in 100 years. Make a class chart to post on the bulletin board. Pack up the time machine and let it take each group where it wants to go.

Asking Big Questions About the Theme

What will life be like in the twenty-first century?

Pretend you're a member of an architectural design firm of the twenty-first century. Join a small group and divide the following futuristic places among the members: the outside of a house or apartment, buildings in the center of a city or town, a community park. Draw or sketch what the place you select might look like. Then arrange your drawing on a poster with the drawings of your group members.

What decisions being made today will affect Earth?

Individually or in groups, go through a newspaper or magazine and circle articles that relate to some decision that will have an impact on people or society in 100 years. For example, look for an article dealing with medicine or industry. In your journal, make a list of these decisions that will affect Earth.

> Cars—
>   nonpolluting
>   electric
>   self-cleaning
>
> Medicine—
>   from plants
>   accessible to all

What will be the future consequences of today's decisions?

Think about decisions being made today in the fields of health, science, or the arts. Or consider decisions you make about your own life. Choose one decision and write it in the center of a web or cluster. Then add consequences of the decision in circles joined to the cluster or web, as in the example on this page.

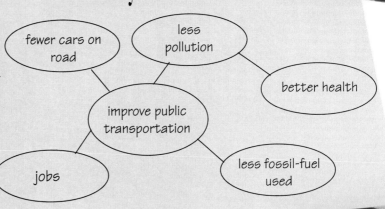

- fewer cars on road
- less pollution
- better health
- improve public transportation
- jobs
- less fossil-fuel used

How can individuals help shape the future?

Brainstorm with a partner to find a problem in your community that needs solving, such as the need for recycling or the need for preserving wet lands. Then, on your own, jot down ideas in your journal about what you can do to help solve this problem. Finally discuss your decisions with your partner and present your ideas to the class.

NOW Think!

What is the biggest challenge facing you in the future? How would you solve it? As you read the literature in this unit, compare your ideas about future challenges and solutions with those of characters in the selections. Do you find good solutions in the selections?

Asking Big Questions About the Theme 11

THE NAMING OF NAMES

RAY BRADBURY

The rocket metal cooled in the meadow winds. Its lid gave a bulging *pop*. From its clock interior stepped a man, a woman, and three children. The other passengers whispered away across the Martian meadow, leaving the man alone among his family.

The man felt his hair flutter and the tissues of his body draw tight as if he were standing at the center of a vacuum. His wife, before him, seemed almost to whirl away in smoke. The children, small seeds, might at any instant be sown to all the Martian climes.[1]

The children looked up at him, as people look to the sun to tell what time of their life it is. His face was cold.

"What's wrong?" asked his wife.

"Let's get back on the rocket."

"Go back to Earth?"

"Yes! Listen!"

The wind blew as if to flake away their identities. At any moment the Martian air might draw his soul from him, as marrow[2] comes from a white bone. He felt submerged in a chemical that could dissolve his intellect and burn away his past.

1. **climes:** countries or regions.
2. **marrow** [mar′ ō]: soft tissue in bones.

They looked at Martian hills that time had worn with a crushing pressure of years. They saw the old cities, lost in their meadows, lying like children's delicate bones among the blowing lakes of grass.

"Chin up, Harry," said his wife. "It's too late. We've come over sixty million miles."

The children with their yellow hair hollered at the deep dome of Martian sky. There was no answer but the racing hiss of wind through the stiff grass.

He picked up the luggage in his cold hands. "Here we go," he said—a man standing on the edge of a sea, ready to wade in and be drowned.

They walked into town.

Their name was Bittering—Harry and his wife Cora, Dan, Laura, and David. They built a small white cottage and ate good breakfasts there, but the fear was never gone. It lay with Mr. Bittering and Mrs. Bittering, a third unbidden partner at every midnight talk, at every dawn awakening.

"I feel like a salt crystal," he said, "in a mountain stream, being washed away. We don't belong here. We're Earth people. This is Mars. It was meant for Martians. For heaven's sake, Cora, let's buy tickets for home!"

But she only shook her head. "One day the atom bomb will fix Earth. Then we'll be safe here."

"Safe and insane!"

Tick-tock, seven o'clock sang the voice-clock; *time to get up.* And they did.

Something made him check everything each morning—warm hearth,[3] potted blood-geraniums—precisely as if he expected something to be amiss. The morning paper was toast-warm from the 6 A.M. Earth rocket. He broke its seal and tilted it at his breakfast place. He forced himself to be convivial.[4]

"Colonial days all over again," he declared. "Why, in ten years there'll be a million Earthmen on Mars. Big cities, everything! They said we'd fail. Said the Martians would resent our invasion. But did we find any Martians? Not a living soul! Oh, we found their empty cities, but no one in them. Right?"

3. **hearth** [härth]: fireside, home.
4. **convivial** [kən viv′ ē əl]: sociable, jovial.

A river of wind submerged the house. When the windows ceased rattling, Mr. Bittering swallowed and looked at the children.

"I don't know," said David. "Maybe there're Martians around we don't see. Sometimes nights I think I hear 'em. I hear the wind. The sand hits my window. I get scared. And I see those towns way up in the mountains where the Martians lived a long time ago. And I think I see things moving around those towns, Papa. And I wonder if those Martians *mind* us living here. I wonder if they won't do something to us for coming here."

"Nonsense!" Mr. Bittering looked out the window. "We're clean, decent people." He looked at his children. "All dead cities have some kind of ghosts in them. Memories, I mean." He stared at the hills, "You see a staircase and you wonder what Martians looked like climbing it. You see Martian paintings and you wonder what the painter was like. You make a little ghost in your mind, a memory. It's quite natural. Imagination." He stopped. "You haven't been prowling up in those ruins, have you?"

"No, Papa." David looked at his shoes.

"See that you stay away from them. Pass the jam."

"Just the same," said little David, "I bet something happens."

Something happened that afternoon.

Laura stumbled through the settlement, crying. She dashed blindly onto the porch.

"Mother, Father—the war, Earth!" she sobbed. "A radio flash just came. Atom bombs hit New York! All the space rockets blown up. No more rockets to Mars, ever!"

"Oh, Harry!" The mother held onto her husband and daughter.

"Are you sure, Laura?" asked the father quietly.

Laura wept. "We're stranded on Mars, forever and ever!"

For a long time there was only the sound of the wind in the late afternoon.

Alone, thought Bittering. Only a thousand of us here. No way back. No way. No way. Sweat poured from his face and his hands and his body; he was drenched in the hotness of his fear. He wanted to strike Laura, cry, "No, you're lying! The rockets will come back!" Instead, he stroked Laura's head against him and said, "The rockets will get through someday."

"Father, what will we do?"

"Go about our business, of course. Raise crops and children. Wait. Keep things going until the war ends and the rockets come again."

The two boys stepped out onto the porch.

"Children," he said, sitting there, looking beyond them, "I've something to tell you."

"We know," they said.

In the following days, Bittering wandered often through the garden to stand alone in his fear. As long as the rockets had spun a silver web across space, he had been able to accept Mars. For he had always told himself: Tomorrow, if I want, I can buy a ticket and go back to Earth.

But now: the web gone, the rockets lying in jigsaw heaps of molten[5] girder and unsnaked wire: Earth people left to the strangeness of Mars, the cinnamon dusts and wine airs, to be baked like gingerbread shapes in Martian summers, put into harvested storage by Martian winters. What would happen to him, the others? This was the moment Mars had waited for. Now it would eat them.

He got down on his knees in the flower bed, a spade in his nervous hands. Work, he thought, work and forget.

He glanced up from the garden to the Martian mountains. He thought of the proud old Martian names that had once been on those peaks. Earthmen, dropping from the sky, had gazed upon hills, rivers, Martian seas left nameless in spite of names. Once Martians had built cities, named cities; climbed mountains, named mountains; sailed seas, named seas. Mountains melted, seas drained, cities tumbled. In spite of this, the Earthmen had felt a silent guilt at putting new names to these ancient hills and valleys.

Nevertheless, man lives by symbol and label. The names were given.

Mr. Bittering felt very alone in his garden under the Martian sun, an anachronism[6] bent here, planting Earth flowers in a wild soil.

Think. Keep thinking. Different things. Keep your mind free of Earth, the atom war, the lost rockets.

He perspired. He glanced about. No one watching. He

5. **molten** [mōlt′n]: made liquid by heat.
6. **anachronism** [ə nak′ rə niz′ əm]: out of keeping with the time in which he is living.

removed his tie. Pretty bold, he thought. First your coat off, now your tie. He hung it neatly on a peach tree he had imported as a sapling[7] from Massachusetts.

He returned to his philosophy of names and mountains. The Earthmen had changed names. Now there were Hormel Valleys, Roosevelt Seas, Ford Hills, Vanderbilt Plateaus, Rockefeller Rivers, on Mars. It wasn't right. The American settlers had shown wisdom, using old Indian prairie names: Wisconsin, Minnesota, Idaho, Ohio, Utah, Milwaukee, Waukegan, Osseo. The old names, the old meanings.

Staring at the mountains wildly, he thought: Are you up there? All the dead ones, you Martians? Well, here we are, alone, cut off! Come down, move us out! We're helpless!

The wind blew a shower of peach blossoms.

He put out his sun-browned hand, gave a small cry. He touched the blossoms, picked them up. He turned them, he touched them again and again. Then he shouted for his wife.

"Cora!"

She appeared at a window. He ran to her.

"Cora, these blossoms!"

She handled them.

"Do you see? They're different. They've changed! They're not peach blossoms any more!"

"Look all right to me," she said.

"They're not. They're *wrong*! I can't tell how. An extra petal, a leaf, something; the color, the smell!"

The children ran out in time to see their father hurrying about the garden, pulling up radishes, onions, and carrots from their beds.

"Cora, come look!"

They handled the onions, the radishes, the carrots among them.

"Do they look like carrots?"

"Yes . . . no." She hesitated. "I don't know."

"They've changed."

"Perhaps."

"You know they have! Onions but not onions, carrots but not carrots. Taste: the same but different. Smell: not like it used to be." He felt his heart pounding, and he was afraid. He dug his fingers into the earth. "Cora, what's happening?

7. **sapling:** a young tree.

What is it? We've got to get away from this." He ran across the garden. Each tree felt his touch. "The roses. The roses. They're turning green!"

And they stood looking at the green roses.

And two days later Dan came running. "Come see the cow. I was milking her and I saw it. Come on!"

They stood in the shed and looked at their one cow.

It was growing a third horn.

And the lawn in front of their house very quietly and slowly was coloring itself like spring violets. Seed from Earth but growing up a soft purple.

"We must get away," said Bittering. "We'll eat this stuff and then we'll change—who knows to what? I can't let it happen. There's only one thing to do. Burn this food!"

"It's not poisoned."

"But it is. Subtly, very subtly. A little bit. A very little bit. We mustn't touch it."

He looked with dismay at their house.

"Even the house. The wind's done something to it. The air's burned it. The fog at night. The boards, all warped out of shape. It's not an Earthman's house any more."

"Oh, your imagination!"

He put on his coat and tie. "I'm going into town. We've got to do something now. I'll be back."

"Wait, Harry!" his wife cried.

But he was gone.

In town, on the shadowy step of the grocery store, the men sat with their hands on their knees, conversing with great leisure and ease.

Mr. Bittering wanted to fire a pistol in the air.

What are you doing, you fools! he thought. Sitting here! You've heard the news—we're stranded on this planet. Well, move! Aren't you frightened? Aren't you afraid? What are you going to do?

"Hello, Harry," said everyone.

"Look," he said to them. "You did hear the news, the other day, didn't you?"

They nodded and laughed. "Sure. Sure, Harry."

"What are you going to do about it?"

"Do, Harry, do? What *can* we do?"

"Build a rocket, that's what!"

"A rocket, Harry? To go back to all that trouble? Oh, Harry!"

"But you *must* want to go back. Have you noticed the peach blossoms, the onions, the grass?"

"Why, yes, Harry, seems we did," said one of the men.

"Doesn't it scare you?"

"Can't recall that it did much, Harry."

"Idiots!"

"Now, Harry."

Bittering wanted to cry. "You've got to work with me. If we stay here, we'll all change. The air. Don't you smell it? Something in the air. A Martian virus, maybe; some seed, or a pollen. Listen to me!"

They stared at him.

"Sam," he said to one of them.

"Yes, Harry?"

"Will you help me build a rocket?"

"Harry, I got a whole load of metal and some blueprints. You want to work in my metal shop on a rocket, you're welcome. I'll sell you that metal for five hundred dollars. You should be able to construct a right[8] pretty rocket, if you work alone, in about thirty years."

Everyone laughed.

"Don't laugh."

Sam looked at him with quiet good humor.

"Sam," Bittering said. "Your eyes—"

"What about them, Harry?"

"Didn't they used to be gray?"

"Well, now, I don't remember."

"They were, weren't they?"

"Why do you ask, Harry?"

"Because now they're kind of yellow-colored."

"Is that so, Harry?" Sam said, casually.

"And you're taller and thinner—"

"You might be right, Harry."

"Sam, you shouldn't have yellow eyes."

"Harry, what color eyes have *you* got?" Sam said.

"My eyes? They're blue, of course."

"Here you are, Harry," Sam handed him a pocket mirror. "Take a look at yourself."

Mr. Bittering hesitated and then raised the mirror to his face.

There were little, very dim flecks of new gold captured in the blue of his eyes.

"Now look what you've done," said Sam a moment later. "You've broken my mirror."

Harry Bittering moved into the metal shop and began to build the rocket. Men stood in the open door and talked and joked without

8. **right:** very.

raising their voices. Once in a while they gave him a hand on lifting something. But mostly they just idled and watched him with their yellowing eyes.

"It's suppertime, Harry," they said.

His wife appeared with his supper in a wicker basket.

I won't touch it," he said. "I'll eat only food from our deep-freeze. Food that came from Earth. Nothing from our garden."

His wife stood watching him. "You can't build a rocket."

"I worked in a shop once, when I was twenty. I know metal. Once I get it started, the others will help," he said, not looking at her, laying out the blueprints.

"Harry. Harry," she said helplessly.

"We've got to get away, Cora. We've *got* to!"

The nights were full of wind that blew down the empty moonlit sea meadows past the little white chess cities lying for their twelve-thousandth year in the shallows. In the Earthmen's settlement, the Bittering house shook with a feeling of change.

Lying abed, Mr. Bittering felt his bones shifted, shaped, melted like gold. His wife, lying beside him, was dark from many sunny afternoons. Dark she was, and golden-eyed, burnt almost black by the sun, sleeping, and the children metallic in their beds, and the wind roaring forlorn and changing through the old peach trees, the violet grass, shaking out green rose petals.

The fear would not be stopped. It had his throat and heart. It dripped in a wetness of the arm and the temple and the trembling palm.

A green star rose in the east.

A strange word emerged from Mr. Bittering's lips.

"Iorrt. Iorrt." He repeated it.

It was a Martian word. He knew no Martian.

In the middle of the night he arose and dialed a call through to Simpson, the archaeologist.[9]

"Simpson, what does the word *Iorrt* mean?"

"Why that's the old Martian word for our planet Earth. Why?"

"No special reason."

The telephone slipped from his hand.

9. **archaeologist** [är′ kē ol′ ə jist]: an expert in the study of people and customs of ancient times.

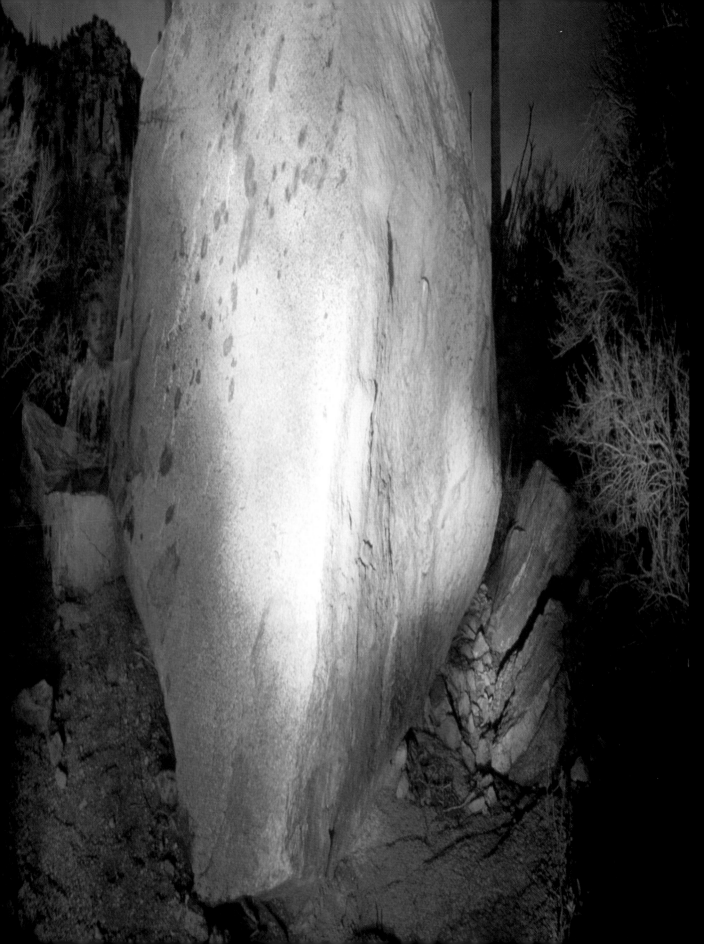

"Hello, hello, hello, hello," it kept saying while he sat gazing out at the green star. "Bittering? Harry, are you there?"

The days were full of metal sound. He laid the frame of the rocket with the reluctant help of three indifferent men. He grew very tired in an hour or so and had to sit down.

"The altitude," laughed a man.

"Are you *eating*, Harry?" asked another.

"I'm eating," he said, angrily.

"From your deep-freeze?"

"Yes!"

"You're getting thinner, Harry."

"I'm not!"

"And taller."

"Liar!"

His wife took him aside a few days later. "Harry, I've used up all the food in the deep-freeze. There's nothing left. I'll have to make sandwiches using food grown on Mars."

He sat down heavily.

"You must eat," she said. "You're weak."

"Yes," he said.

He took a sandwich, opened it, looked at it, and began to nibble at it.

"And take the rest of the day off," she said. "It's hot. The children want to swim in the canals and hike. Please come along."

"I can't waste time. This is a crisis!"

"Just for an hour," she urged. "A swim'll do you good."

He rose, sweating. "All right, all right. Leave me alone. I'll come."

The sun was hot, the day quiet. There was only an immense staring burn upon the land. They moved along the canal, the father, the mother, the racing children in their swim suits. They stopped and ate meat sandwiches. He saw their skin baking brown. And he saw the yellow eyes of his wife and his children, their eyes that were never yellow before. A few tremblings shook him but were carried off in waves of pleasant heat as he lay in the sun. He was too tired to be afraid.

"Cora, how long have your eyes been yellow?"

She was bewildered. "Always, I guess."

"They didn't change from brown in the last three months?"

She bit her lips. "No. Why do you ask?"

"Never mind."

They sat there.

"The children's eyes," he said. "They're yellow, too."

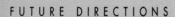

"Sometimes growing children's eyes change color."

"Maybe *we're* children, too. At least to Mars. That's a thought." He laughed. "Think I'll swim."

They leaped into the canal water, and he let himself sink down and down to the bottom like a golden statue and lie there in green silence. All was water—quiet and deep, all was peace. He felt the steady, slow current drift him easily.

If I lie here long enough, he thought, the water will work and eat away my flesh until the bones show like coral.[10] Just my skeleton left. And then the water can build on that skeleton—green things, deep water things, red things, yellow things. Change. Change. Slow, deep, silent change. And isn't that what it is up *there?*

He saw the sky submerged above him, the sun made Martian by atmosphere and time and space.

Up there, a big river, he thought, a Martian river, all of us lying deep in it, in our pebble houses, in our sunken boulder houses, like crayfish hidden, and the water washing away our old bodies and lengthening the bones and—

He let himself drift up through the soft light.

Dan sat on the edge of the canal, regarding his father seriously.

"Utha," he said.

"What?" asked his father.

The boy smiled. "You know. *Utha's* the Martian word for 'father.'"

"Where did you learn it?"

"I don't know. Around. *Utha!*"

"What do you want?"

The boy hesitated. "I—I want to change my name."

"Change it?"

"Yes."

His mother swam over. "What's wrong with Dan for a name?"

Dan fidgeted. "The other day you called Dan, Dan, Dan. I said to myself, 'That's not my name. I've a new name I want to use.'"

Mr. Bittering held to the side of the canal, his body cold and his heart pounding slowly. "What is this new name?"

"Linnl. Isn't that a good name? Can I use it? Can I, please?"

Mr. Bittering put his hand to his head. He thought of the silly rocket, himself working alone,

10. **coral** [kôr′ əl]: stony substance formed from the skeletons of tropical sea animals called polyps.

himself alone even among his family, so alone.

He heard his wife say, "Why not?"

He heard himself say, "Yes, you can use it."

"Yaaa!" screamed the boy. "I'm Linnl, Linnl."

Racing down the meadowlands, he danced and shouted.

Mr. Bittering looked at his wife. "Why did we do that?"

"I don't know," she said. "It just seemed like a good idea."

They walked into the hills. They strolled on old mosaic[11] paths, beside still pumping fountains. The paths were covered with a thin film of cool water all summer long. They kept their bare feet cool all the day, splashing as in a creek, wading.

They came to a small deserted Martian villa[12] with a good view of the valley. It was on top of a hill. Blue marble halls, large murals, a swimming pool. It was refreshing in this hot summertime. The Martians hadn't believed in large cities.

"How nice," said Mrs. Bittering, "if we could move up here to this villa for the summer."

"Come on," he said. "We're going back to town. There's work to be done on the rocket."

But as he worked that night, the thought of the cool blue marble villa entered his mind. As the hours passed, the rocket seemed less important.

In the flow of days and weeks, the rocket receded and dwindled. The old fever was gone. It frightened him to think he had let it slip this way. But somehow the heat, the air, the working conditions—

He heard the men murmuring on the porch of his metal shop.

"Everyone's going. You heard?"

"All going. That's right."

Bittering came out. "Going where?" He saw a couple of trucks, loaded with children and furniture, drive down the dusty street.

"Up to the villas," said the man.

"Yeah, Harry. I'm going. So is Sam. Aren't you, Sam?"

"That's right, Harry. What about you?"

"I've got work to do here."

"Work! You can finish that rocket in the autumn, when it's cooler."

11. **mosaic** [mō zā′ ik]: decoration made of small colored pieces of stone, glass, or wood inlaid to form a picture or design.
12. **villa:** large elegant house.

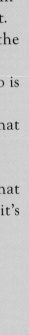

He took a breath. "I got the frame all set up."

"In the autumn is better." Their voices were lazy in the heat.

"Got to work," he said.

"Autumn," they reasoned. And they sounded so sensible, so right.

"Autumn would be best," he thought. "Plenty of time, then."

No! cried part of himself, deep down, put away, locked tight, suffocating. No! No!

"In the autumn," he said.

"Come on, Harry," they all said.

"Yes, in the autumn. I'll begin work again then."

"I got a villa near the Tirra Canal," said someone.

"You mean the Roosevelt Canal, don't you?"

"Tirra. The old Martian name."

"But on the map—"

"Forget the map. It's Tirra now. Now I found a place in the Pillan Mountains—"

"You mean the Rockefeller Range," said Bittering.

"I mean the Pillan Mountains," said Sam.

"Yes," said Bittering, buried in the hot, swarming air. "The Pillan Mountains."

Everyone worked at loading the truck in the hot, still afternoon of the next day.

Laura, Dan, David carried packages. Or, as they preferred to be known, Ttil, Linnl, and Werr carried packages.

The furniture was abandoned in the little white cottage.

"It looked just fine in Boston," said the mother. "And here in the cottage. But up at the villa? No. We'll get it when we come back in the autumn."

Bittering himself was quiet.

"I've got some ideas on furniture for the villa," he said after a time. "Big, lazy furniture."

"What about your encyclopedia? You're taking it along, surely?"

Mr. Bittering glanced away. "I'll come and get it next week."

They turned to their daughter. "What about your New York dresses?"

The bewildered girl stared. "Why, I don't want them anymore."

They shut off the gas, the water; they locked the doors and walked away. Father peered into the truck.

"Gosh, we're not taking much," he said. "Considering all we brought to Mars, this is only a handful!"

171

The Naming of Names   25

He started the truck.

Looking at the small white cottage for a long moment, he was filled with a desire to rush to it, touch it, say goodbye to it, for he felt as if he were going away on a long journey, leaving something to which he could never quite return, never understand again.

Just then Sam and his family drove by in another truck.

"Hi Bittering! Here we go!"

The truck swung down the ancient highway out of town. There were sixty others traveling the same direction. The town filled with a silent, heavy dust from their passage. The canal waters lay blue in the sun, and a quiet wind moved in the strange trees.

"Good-by town!" said Mr. Bittering.

"Good-by, good-by!" sang the family, waving to it.

They did not look back again.

Summer burned the canals dry. Summer moved like flame upon the meadows. In the empty Earth settlement, the painted houses flaked and peeled. Rubber tires upon which children had swung in back yards hung suspended like stopped clock pendulums in the blazing air.

At the metal shop, the rocket frame began to rust.

In the quiet autumn Mr. Bittering stood, very dark now, very golden-eyed, upon the slope above his villa, looking at the valley.

"It's time to go back," said Cora.

"Yes, but we're not going," he said quietly. "There's nothing there any more."

"Your books," she said. "Your fine clothes. Your *lles* and your fine *ior uele rre*."

"The town's empty. No one's going back," he said. "There's no reason to, none at all."

The daughter wove tapestries and the sons played songs on ancient flutes and pipes, their laughter echoing in the marble villa.

Mr. Bittering gazed at the Earth settlement far away in the low valley. "Such odd, such ridiculous houses the Earth people built."

"They didn't know any better," his wife mused. "Such ugly people. I'm glad they've gone."

They both looked at each other, startled by all they had just finished saying. They laughed.

"Where did they go?" he

wondered. He glanced at his wife. She was golden and slender as his daughter. She looked at him, and he seemed almost as young as their eldest son.

"I don't know," she said.

"We'll go back to town maybe next year, or the year after, or the year after that," he said, calmly. "Now—I'm warm. How about taking a swim?"

They turned their backs to the valley. Arm in arm they walked silently down a path of clear-running spring water . . .

Five years later a rocket fell out of the sky. It lay steaming in the valley. Men leaped out of it shouting.

"We won the war on Earth! We're here to rescue you! Hey!"

But the American-built town of cottages, peach trees, and theaters was silent. They found a flimsy rocket frame rusting in an empty shop.

The rocket men searched the hills. The captain established headquarters in an abandoned building. His lieutenant came back to report.

"The town's empty, but we found native life in the hills, sir. Dark people. Yellow eyes. Martians. Very friendly. We talked a bit, not much. They learned English fast. I'm sure our relations will be most friendly with them, sir."

"Dark, eh?" mused the captain. "How many?"

"Six, eight hundred, I'd say, living in those marble ruins in the hills, sir. Tall, healthy. Beautiful women."

"Did they tell you what became of the men and women who built this Earth settlement, Lieutenant?"

"They hadn't the foggiest notion of what happened to this town or its people."

"Strange. You think those Martians killed them?"

"They look surprisingly peaceful. Chances are a plague[13] did this town in, sir."

"Perhaps. I suppose this is one of those mysteries we'll never solve. One of those mysteries you read about."

The captain looked at the room, the dusty windows, the blue mountains rising beyond, the canals moving in the light, and he

13. **plague** [plāg]: highly contagious, often fatal, disease that spreads quickly and affects large numbers of people.

heard the soft wind in the air. He shivered. Then, recovering, he tapped a large fresh map he had thumb-tacked to the top of an empty table.

"Lots to be done, Lieutenant." His voice droned on and on quietly as the sun sank behind the blue hills. "New settlements. Mining sites, minerals to be looked for. Bacteriological specimens taken. The work, all the work. And the old records were lost. We'll have a job of remapping to do, renaming the mountains and rivers and such. Calls for a little imagination.

"What do you think of naming those mountains the Lincoln Mountains, this canal the Washington Canal, those hills— we can name those hills for you, Lieutenant. Diplomacy. And you, for a favor, might name a town for me. Polishing the apple. And why not make this the Einstein Valley, and further over. . . . Are you *listening*, Lieutenant?"

The lieutenant snapped his gaze from the blue color and the quiet mist of the hills far beyond the town.

"What? Oh, *yes*, sir!"

RAY BRADBURY

Ray Bradbury was born in 1920 in Waukegan, Illinois. When he was a child, he loved reading comic strips. The imaginative cartoon adventures helped to develop his taste for what he calls "the fabulous world of the future and the world of fantasy." As he grew older, he spent his spare time learning magic tricks, and he soon began writing space adventures.

By the time Bradbury graduated from high school, he was churning out 2,000 words per day, and the country was struggling through the Great Depression. He sold newspapers on a street corner and continued to write. Oddly enough, the writer of so many words prefers writing short stories to novels—and his novels are more like short stories. One of his most famous works, *The Martian Chronicles,* is a book of connected stories. Bradbury has also turned some of his short stories into scripts for plays, movies, and television programs.

Song of
the Earth Spirit

TRADITIONAL NAVAJO

It is lovely indeed; it is lovely indeed.

I, I am the spirit within the earth.

The feet of the earth are my feet;

The legs of the earth are my legs;

The strength of the earth is my strength;   5

The thoughts of the earth are my thoughts;

The voice of the earth is my voice;

The feather of the earth is my feather.

All that belongs to the earth belongs to me;

All that surrounds the earth surrounds me.   10

I, I am the sacred words of the earth.

It is lovely indeed; it is lovely indeed.

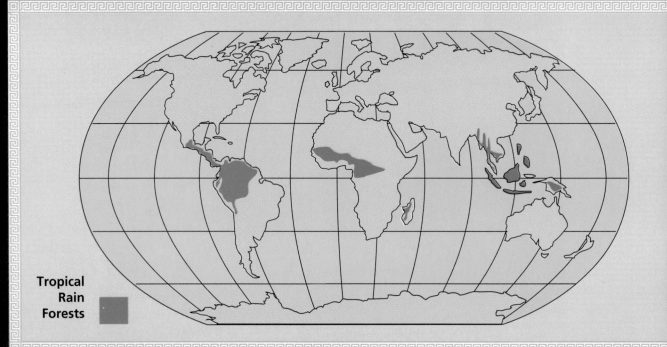

Tropical
Rain
Forests

Makuna Children,
Amazon, Colombia

Paradise Lost

ELIZABETH VITTON

Zap! From below the surface, an archerfish[1] blasts an unwary spider on a leaf with a bullet of water. The spider drops into the pool and is gobbled up. Downstream, a piglike tapir[2] searches for food with its multi-purpose trunk. Above the jungle floor, a troop of monkeys chatters while birds streak by, their wings weaving a tapestry of brilliant colors.

Welcome to the rain forest, an exotic world where the air is thick mist, where fish walk on land, where passion flowers bloom and tree frogs sing. A place where the constant hum of thousands of animals fills the air.

1. **archerfish:** small freshwater fish of Southeast Asia that preys upon spiders and insects on shore by spitting drops of water at them to knock them into the water.
2. **tapir** [tā′ pər]: large mammal of the tropics having hooves and a flexible snout.

Left, Red-Eyed Tree Frog

Background, Rain Forest Burning, Amazon, Brazil

But now the roar of the chain saw is drowning out the jungle chorus. "Each minute, 100 acres of the world's jungles are being cut and burned," says Dr. Stuart Strahl of Wildlife Conservation International. "At this rate, nearly all the Earth's tropical rain forests will either be destroyed or seriously damaged by the year 2035."

Most rain forests are found in the tropics bordering either side of the equator, like a wide belt circling the Earth. Rain forests get an average of 100 to 400 inches of rain per year. The heavy rainfall may make the forest green, but it also washes away a lot of nutrients from the soil. Because of this, the shallow-rooted trees get most of their nourishment from leaves and dead materials that fall from above.

As they compete for sunlight, trees in the tropical forest grow to amazing heights—50 to 150 feet—before sprouting branches and leaves. Below the tentlike canopy of trees grow palms, looping vines, orchids, ferns and other plants. Less than two percent of the sunlight that nourishes the canopy ever reaches the floor. But even there many plant and animal species thrive in a twilight world.

New species are being discovered all the time in the rain forest. Right now nearly two *million* species have been named. "And for every jungle species known, there remain 40 yet undiscovered," says Dr. Fred Kuntz. He is a mammal expert at the Bronx Zoo in New York. "We know more about distant planets than the nearest rain forest!"

Even though rain forests cover only six percent of the Earth, they are home to more

Parson's Chameleon, Madagascar

than half of all living things on our planet. Scores of these plants and animals are now dying out. "Nearly 10,000 species are already being lost every year, never to be replaced," Dr. Kuntz told CONTACT. "Once a species is lost, it's gone forever."

It's Not Easy Being Green

Why are we losing so much of our rain forests? Most of the tropical rain forests lie in poor nations whose populations are growing very quickly. Since they have no big industries, Dr. Strahl says, they make money by using the resources in the forest.

"It takes minutes for a chain saw to topple a seven-foot-wide tree, but it will take five centuries for another tree to grow to the same size," says Matthew Hatchwell. He works to help save the Earth's rain forests. The crashing timber destroys small trees lying in its path. Tractors flatten more forest when they drag the trunks to loading areas.

As roads are cut to get the logs to market, it opens up the area to a flood of people who burn parts of the jungle to make room for farms and ranches. The problem is that most of the nutrients are in the living trees—not in the topsoil. So if the forest is cut down and burned, there is a very thin layer of rich ash which can grow crops for a few years. But once the nutrients have been used up by the crops or been

Volcan Barva
Bromeliads,
Costa Rica

Bee Butterfly,
Trinidad

Jaguar, Belize

Passion Flower, South America

washed away by the warm rains, the land becomes almost worthless. "When the soil gives out," Hatchwell told CONTACT, "it forces farmers to clear more and more land."

Destroying rain forests as far away as Brazil[3] and Indonesia[4] has serious consequences for all of us. For example, the world needs trees to recycle carbon dioxide (CO_2), an odorless gas. Rain forests are the "lungs" of the planet. They suck the CO_2 out of the atmosphere through their leaves. The trees then "breathe" oxygen back into the atmosphere and pump it with moisture that falls as rain.

3. **Brazil** [brə zil′]: country in central and northeast South America on the Atlantic Ocean.
4. **Indonesia** [in′ də nē′ zhə]: country in the East Indies, south of Vietnam, northwest of Australia.

But trees are about 50 percent carbon.[5] If they are burned, the CO_2 trapped inside them is released. "It's a double whammy," explains Dr. Russell Mittermeier, a conservationist. "The burning itself releases huge amounts of CO_2. And it reduces the trees available to absorb the gas."

Carbon dioxide is a "greenhouse" gas. Like a greenhouse, carbon dioxide lets the sun's incoming rays through, but blocks reflected rays from leaving the atmosphere. It traps the sun's heat. But many scientists believe that too much carbon dioxide could cause the Earth to heat up. The "greenhouse effect" would do more than just cause the temperature to rise, says Dr. Strahl. "It would also affect winds, rainfall, sea levels and storms. We need rain forests to help control our climate."

Tarsier with Cicada, Sabah, Borneo

Food for Thought

Rain forests do more than help provide oxygen to the planet. They also help save lives in other ways, too. In fact, one-quarter of prescription drugs used in the U.S. come from tropical forest plants. Most plants, though, haven't been studied for ways to treat diseases. Says Dr. Mittermeier: "For all we know, solutions to health problems like cancer may exist in tropical forests."

Rain forests put medicine in your cabinet as well as food on your table. Each day people eat or

5. **carbon:** a nonmetallic element found in plants and animals.

Rafflesia Keithii,
Mt. Kinabalu, Borneo

Morpho Butterfly, Peru

drink something that comes from the jungle. Fruits, nuts, spices, coffee, sugar cane, cocoa and even chickens originated in rain forests. "Many are now grown elsewhere," Mittermeier says, "but if a pest[6] attacks, a crop could be wiped out. So we have to be able to go back to the rain forest to crossbreed[7] commercial crops with their relatives from the wild."

Rain forests also provide us with common workday tools, such as burlap bags and rope nets. Fibers used for stuffing pillows and life jackets come from the jungle. So do the oils of many perfumes. Some jungle products have surprising uses, says Strahl. "Take M&Ms. The candy doesn't melt in your hand because they're coated with a harmless wax, which comes from tropical forests."

What's being done to save the globe's greatest natural treasury? Some poorer countries, like Costa Rica and Bolivia, have promised to protect their forests in exchange for lessening the money they owe to other nations. Others are setting aside nature reserves and planting new trees.

In Brazil, a rubber tappers' union is fighting for large areas to be set aside just for rubber production and the collection of fruits and nuts. In Malaysia, the Penan[8] people set up human blockades to try

6. **pest:** destructive or harmful insect.
7. **crossbreed:** make new crops by interbreeding different varieties of plants.
8. **Penan** [pē′nän]: people of Penang, an island that is part of Malaysia.

to stop logging on their lands. In Papua New Guinea, many ranchers now earn a living by raising herds of butterflies, crocodiles and wallabies[9] instead of cattle, which destroy the land.

Time will tell whether efforts like these succeed in saving the world's emerald[10] forests. "I see it as a race against time," says Dr. Strahl. "We have the power to save or destroy the rain forests. The fate of millions of species is on our shoulders."

9. **wallabies** [wol′ə bēz]: small or medium-sized kangaroos.
10. **emerald:** green.

Golden Beetle, Cloud Forest, Costa Rica

E L I Z A B E T H   V I T T O N

Elizabeth Vitton was born in Warner Robins, Georgia. She attended Vassar College and then taught high school English. She eventually moved to New York City, where she worked in textbook publishing and finally for magazines. As Vitton says, teaching and publishing made up "the route I took to my goal of working for *3-2-1 Contact*," a magazine published by Children's Television Workshop.

Vitton wrote "Paradise Lost" because of her concern for the environment. She says, "We know that kids are environmentally concerned. They are very aware—and not only of the plight of endangered species. Kids are the advocates" for saving the rain forest and for solving other problems people have caused on Earth. In their role as advocates, Vitton suggests that young people "learn to do original research: first find the most up-to-date books, then talk to experts in the field and conservation groups."

Harrison Bergeron

KURT VONNEGUT, JR.

The year was 2081, and everybody was finally equal. They weren't only equal before God and the law. They were equal every which way. Nobody was smarter than anybody else. Nobody was better looking than anybody else. Nobody was stronger or quicker than anybody else. All this equality was due to the 211th, 212th, and the 213th Amendments to the Constitution, and to the unceasing vigilance of agents of the United States Handicapper[1] General.

Some things about living still weren't quite right, though. April, for instance, still drove people crazy by not being springtime. And it was in that clammy month that the H-G men took George and Hazel Bergeron's fourteen-year-old son, Harrison, away.

---

1. **handicapper:** reference to the custom in games of giving less skilled people advantages and more skilled people disadvantages so that all have an equal chance for victory.

It was tragic, all right, but George and Hazel couldn't think about it very hard. Hazel had a perfectly average intelligence, which meant she couldn't think about anything except in short bursts. And George, while his intelligence was way above normal, had a little mental handicap radio in his ear. He was required by law to wear it at all times. It was tuned to a government transmitter. Every twenty seconds or so, the transmitter would send out some sharp noise to keep people like George from taking unfair advantage of their brains.

George and Hazel were watching television. There were tears on Hazel's cheeks, but she'd forgotten for the moment what they were about.

On the television screen were ballerinas.

A buzzer sounded in George's head. His thoughts fled in panic, like bandits from a burglar alarm.

"That was a real pretty dance, that dance they just did," said Hazel.

"Huh?" said George.

"That dance—it was nice," said Hazel.

"Yup," said George. He tried to think a little about the ballerinas. They weren't really very good—no better than anybody else would have been, anyway. They were burdened with sash-weights[2] and bags of birdshot,[3] and their faces were masked, so that no one, seeing a free and graceful gesture or a pretty face, would feel like something the cat drug in.[4] George was toying with the vague notion that maybe dancers shouldn't be handicapped. But he didn't get very far before another noise in his ear radio scattered his thoughts.

George winced.[5] So did two out of the eight ballerinas.

Hazel saw him wince. Having no mental handicap herself, she had to ask George what the latest sound had been.

"Sounded like somebody hitting a milk bottle with a ball peen hammer,"[6] said George.

2. **sash-weights:** metal weights in windows that allow them to be raised and lowered.
3. **birdshot:** small lead pellets usually used in shooting birds.
4. **something the cat drug in:** idiom that means someone looks terrible.
5. **winced:** drew back suddenly.
6. **ball peen hammer:** hammer that has a rounded or wedged head.

"I'd think it would be real interesting, hearing all the different sounds," said Hazel, a little envious. "All the things they think up."

"Um," said George.

"Only, if I was Handicapper General, you know what I would do?" asked Hazel. Hazel, as a matter of fact, bore a strong resemblance to the Handicapper General, a woman named Diana Moon Glampers. "If I was Diana Moon Glampers," said Hazel, "I'd have chimes[7] on Sunday—just chimes. Kind of in honor of religion."

"I could think, if it was just chimes," said George.

"Well—maybe make 'em real loud," said Hazel. "I think I'd make a good Handicapper General."

"Good as anybody else," said George.

"Who knows better'n I do what normal is?" said Hazel.

"Right," said George. He began to think glimmeringly[8] about his abnormal son who was now in jail, about Harrison, but a twenty-one-gun salute[9] in his head stopped that.

"Boy!" said Hazel, "that was a doozy,[10] wasn't it?"

It was such a doozy that George was white and trembling, and tears stood on the rims of his red eyes. Two of the eight ballerinas had collapsed to the studio floor, and were holding their temples.[11]

"All of a sudden you look so tired," said Hazel. "Why don't you stretch out on the sofa, so's you can rest your handicap bag on the pillows, honeybunch." She was referring to the forty-seven pounds of birdshot in a canvas bag, which was padlocked around George's neck. "Go on and rest the bag for awhile," she said. "I don't care if you're not equal to me for awhile."

George weighed the bag with his hands. "I don't mind it," he said. "I don't notice it any more. It's just part of me."

7. **chimes:** set of bells, usually in church towers, tuned to a musical scale.
8. **glimmeringly:** with a dim perception or faint idea
9. **twenty-one-gun salute:** usually, firing of cannons as a sign of respect for a famous person.
10. **doozy** [dü′ zē]: something outstanding or unusual.
11. **temples:** the flattened part on each side of the forehead.

"You've been so tired lately—kind of wore out," said Hazel. "If there was just some way we could make a little hole in the bottom of the bag, and just take out a few of them lead balls. Just a few."

"Two years in prison and two thousand dollars fine for every ball I took out," said George. "I don't call that a bargain."

"If you could just take a few out when you come home from work," said Hazel. "I mean—you don't compete with anybody around here. You just set around."

"If I tried to get away with it," said George, "then other people'd get away with it—and pretty soon we'd be right back to the dark ages again, with everybody competing against everybody else. You wouldn't like that, would you?"

"I'd hate it," said Hazel.

"There you are," said George. "The minute people start cheating on laws, what do you think happens to society?"

If Hazel hadn't been able to come up with an answer to this question, George couldn't have supplied one. A siren was going off in his head.

"Reckon it'd fall apart," said Hazel.

"What would?" said George blankly.

"Society," said Hazel uncertainly. "Wasn't that what you just said?"

"Who knows?" said George.

The television program was suddenly interrupted for a news bulletin. It wasn't clear at first as to what the bulletin was about, since the announcer, like all announcers, had a serious speech impediment.[12] For about half a minute, and in a state of high excitement, the announcer tried to say, "Ladies and gentlemen—"

He finally gave up, handed the bulletin to a ballerina to read.

"That's all right—" Hazel said of the announcer, "he tried. That's the big thing. He tried to do the best he could with what God gave him. He should get a nice raise for trying so hard."

12. **speech impediment** [im ped′ ə mənt]: a problem that interferes with clear speech.

Untitled Francesco Clemente, 1986, Monotype
(35), 36³/₄"x20"

"Ladies and gentlemen—" said the ballerina, reading the bulletin. She must have been extraordinarily beautiful, because the mask she wore was hideous. And it was easy to see that she was the strongest and most graceful of all the dancers, for her handicap bags were as big as those worn by two-hundred-pound men.

And she had to apologize at once for her voice, which was a very unfair voice for a woman to use. Her voice was a warm, luminous,[13] timeless melody. "Excuse me—" she said, and she began again, making her voice absolutely uncompetitive.

"Harrison Bergeron, age fourteen," she said in a grackle squawk,[14] "has just escaped from jail, where he was held on suspicion of plotting to overthrow the government. He is a genius and an athlete, is underhandicapped, and should be regarded as extremely dangerous."

A police photograph of Harrison Bergeron was flashed on the screen—upside down, then sideways, then upside down again, then right side up. The picture showed the full length of Harrison against a background calibrated[15] in feet and inches. He was exactly seven feet tall.

The rest of Harrison's appearance was Halloween and hardware. Nobody had ever borne heavier handicaps. He had outgrown hindrances[16] faster than the H-G men could think them up. Instead of a little ear radio for a mental handicap, he wore a tremendous pair of earphones, and spectacles with thick wavy lenses. The spectacles were intended to make him not only half blind, but to give him whanging headaches besides.

Scrap metal was hung all over him. Ordinarily, there was a certain symmetry,[17] a military neatness to the handicaps issued to strong people, but Harrison looked like a walking junkyard. In the race of life, Harrison carried three hundred pounds.

---

13. **luminous** [lü′ mə nəs]: clear.
14. **grackle squawk:** the harsh sound made by a large blackbird with shiny feathers.
15. **calibrated** [kal′ ə brat əd]: checked or adjusted by comparing to a standard instrument.
16. **hindrances** [hin′ drəns əz]: things that hold someone back from accomplishing a goal.
17. **symmetry** [sim′ ə trē]: a regular, balanced arrangement that is the same on each side.

And to offset[18] his good looks, the H-G men required that he wear at all times a red rubber ball for a nose, keep his eyebrows shaved off, and cover his even white teeth with black caps at snaggle-tooth random.

"If you see this boy," said the ballerina, "do not—I repeat, do not—try to reason with him."

There was the shriek of a door being torn from its hinges.

Screams and barking cries of consternation came from the television set. The photograph of Harrison Bergeron on the screen jumped again and again, as though dancing to the tune of an earthquake.

George Bergeron correctly identified the earthquake, and well he might have—for many was the time his own home had danced to the same crashing tune. "My God—" said George, "that must be Harrison!"

The realization was blasted from his mind instantly by the sound of an automobile collision in his head.

When George could open his eyes again, the photograph of Harrison was gone. A living, breathing Harrison filled the screen.

Clanking, clownish, and huge, Harrison stood in the center of the studio. The knob of the uprooted studio door was still in his hand. Ballerinas, technicians, musicians, and announcers cowered on their knees before him, expecting to die.

"I am the Emperor!" cried Harrison. "Do you hear? I am the Emperor! Everybody must do what I say at once!" He stamped his foot and the studio shook.

"Even as I stand here—" he bellowed, "crippled, hobbled, sickened—I am a greater ruler than any man who ever lived! Now watch me become what I can become!"

Harrison tore the straps of his handicap harness like wet tissue paper, tore straps guaranteed to support five thousand pounds.

Harrison's scrap-iron handicaps crashed to the floor.

Harrison thrust his thumbs under the bar of the padlock that secured his head harness. The bar snapped like celery. Harrison smashed his headphones and spectacles against the wall.

18. **offset:** make up for.

He flung away his rubber-ball nose, revealed a man that would have awed Thor,[19] the god of thunder.

"I shall now select my Empress!" he said, looking down on the cowering people. "Let the first woman who dares rise to her feet claim her mate and her throne!"

A moment passed, and then a ballerina arose, swaying like a willow.

Harrison plucked the mental handicap from her ear, snapped off her physical handicaps with marvelous delicacy. Last of all, he removed her mask.

She was blindingly beautiful.

"Now—" said Harrison, taking her hand, "shall we show the people the meaning of the word dance? Music!" he commanded.

The musicians scrambled back into their chairs, and Harrison stripped them of their handicaps, too. "Play your best," he told them, "and I'll make you barons and dukes and earls."

The music began. It was normal at first—cheap, silly, false. But Harrison snatched two musicians from their chairs, waved them like batons[20] as he sang the music as he wanted it played. He slammed them back into their chairs.

The music began again and was much improved.

Harrison and his Empress merely listened to the music for a while—listened gravely, as though synchronizing[21] their heart-beats with it.

They shifted their weights to their toes.

Harrison placed his big hands on the girl's tiny waist, letting her sense the weightlessness that would soon be hers.

And then, in an explosion of joy and grace, into the air they sprang!

Not only were the laws of the land abandoned, but the law of gravity and the laws of motion as well.

19. **Thor** [thôr].
20. **batons:** light sticks used by the leader of an orchestra, chorus, or band to indicate the beat and to direct.
21. **synchronizing** [sing′ krə nīz ing]: causing to occur at the same time; agreeing in musical time.

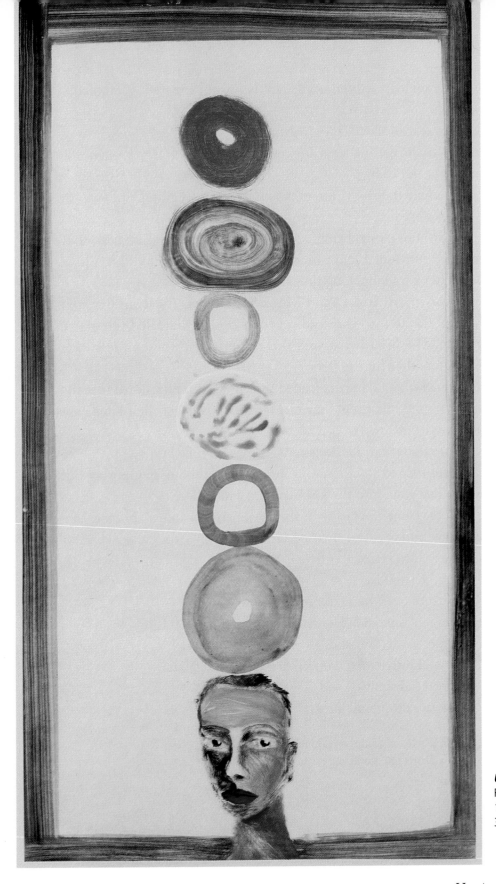

Untitled
Francesco Clemente,
1986, Monotype (4),
36³/₄"x20"

They reeled, whirled, swiveled, bounced, capered, gamboled,[22] and spun.

They leaped like deer on the moon.

The studio ceiling was thirty feet high, but each leap brought the dancers nearer to it.

It became their obvious intention to kiss the ceiling.

They kissed it.

And then, neutralizing[23] gravity with love and pure will, they remained suspended in air inches below the ceiling, and they kissed each other for a long, long time.

It was then that Diana Moon Glampers, the Handicapper General, came into the studio with a double-barreled ten-gauge shotgun. She fired twice, and the Emperor and the Empress were dead before they hit the floor.

Diana Moon Glampers loaded the gun again. She aimed it at the musicians and told them they had ten seconds to get their handicaps back on.

It was then that the Bergerons' television tube burned out.

Hazel turned to comment about the blackout to George. But George had gone into the kitchen for a can of beer.

George came back in with the beer, paused while a handicap signal shook him up. And then he sat down again. "You have been crying?" he said to Hazel.

"Yup," she said.

"What about?" he said.

"I forget," she said. "Something real sad on television."

"What was it?" he said.

"It's all kind of mixed up in my mind," said Hazel.

"Forget sad things," said George.

"I always do," said Hazel.

22. **gamboled** [gam′ bəld]: ran and jumped about.
23. **neutralizing** [nü′ trə līz ing]: cancelling.

"That's my girl," said George. He winced. There was the sound of a riveting gun[24] in his head.

"Gee—I could tell that one was a doozy," said Hazel.

"You can say that again," said George.

"Gee—" said Hazel, "I could tell that one was a doozy."

24. **riveting gun:** gun that drives rivets—metal bolts—into heavy material.

KURT VONNEGUT, JR.

Kurt Vonnegut, Jr. was born in 1922 in Indianapolis, Indiana, and remembers his childhood as a happy one, in spite of living through the Great Depression. Because Vonnegut's father was unemployed during the Depression years, Vonnegut went to public schools rather than to the private schools his older brother and sister had attended. The experience, however, opened a door for Vonnegut: his high school was the first in the United States to have a daily newspaper. There Vonnegut discovered the art of reporting. Following high school, Vonnegut went to Cornell University, majoring in biochemistry and writing for the campus newspaper.

World War II interrupted Vonnegut's college years. He enlisted and was sent to Europe. In 1944, he was captured by the Germans and became a prisoner of war in Dresden. When the Allies bombed Dresden in a firestorm that destroyed the city, the prisoners were fortunately among the survivors.

After the war ended, Vonnegut worked as a police reporter and did public relations work. By 1951, he was selling enough short stories to write novels full time.

ORBITER **5** SHOWS
HOW EARTH LOOKS FROM THE MOON

There's a woman in the earth, sitting on
her heels. You see her from the back, in three-
quarter profile. She has a flowing pigtail. She's
holding something
in her right hand—some holy jug. Her left arm is thinner,
in a gesture like a dancer. She's the Indian Ocean. Asia is
light swirling up out of her vessel. Her pigtail points to Europe
and her dancer's arm is the Suez Canal.[1] She is a woman
in a square kimono,[2]
bare feet tucked beneath the tip of Africa. Her tail of long hair is
the Arabian Peninsula.[3]

A woman in the earth.

A man in the moon.

1. **Suez Canal** [sü ez´]: canal connecting the Mediterranean and Red seas.
2. **kimono** [kə mō´ nə]: loose robe held in place by a wide sash.
3. **Arabian Peninsula:** large strip of land in Southwest Asia that comprises many countries, including Saudi Arabia and Kuwait.

MAY SWENSON

May Swenson, whose concrete poem is on page 52, was born in 1919 in Logan, Utah, and grew up near the State University where her father taught. As an adult, Swenson first worked as a newspaper reporter in Salt Lake City, then she became an editor at a publishing company in New York City. After six years, she left to become a full-time poet and writer. Her first book of poems, *Another Animal*, gained critical recognition.

Swenson says that she writes many of her poems "directly on the scene . . . in much the same way as a painter sketches from life." Important collections of Swenson's poems include *To Mix with Time* and *Half Sun Half Asleep.*

"IF I FORGET THEE, OH EARTH..."

ARTHUR C. CLARKE

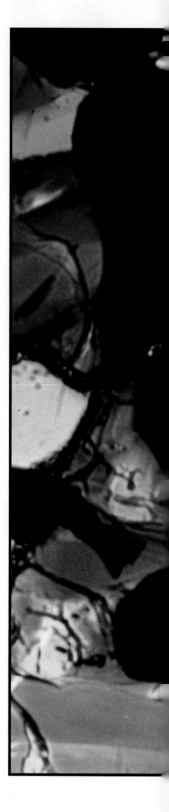

When Marvin was ten years old, his father took him through the long, echoing corridors that led up through Administration and Power, until at last they came to the uppermost levels of all and were among the swiftly growing vegetation of the Farmlands. Marvin liked it here: it was fun watching the great, slender plants creeping with almost visible eagerness towards the sunlight as it filtered down through the plastic domes to meet them. The smell of life was everywhere, awakening inexpressible longings in his heart: no longer was he breathing the dry, cool air of the residential levels, purged of all smells but the faint tang of ozone.[1] He wished he could stay here for a little while, but Father would not let him. They went onwards until they had reached the entrance to the Observatory,[2] which he had never visited: but they did not stop, and Marvin knew with a sense of rising excitement that there could be only one goal left. For the first time in his life, he was going Outside.

1. **ozone** [ō′ zōn]: form of oxygen with a sharp odor, usually present in the air, especially after a thunderstorm.
2. **observatory** [əb zėr′ və tôr′ ē]: place for observing the stars and other heavenly bodies.

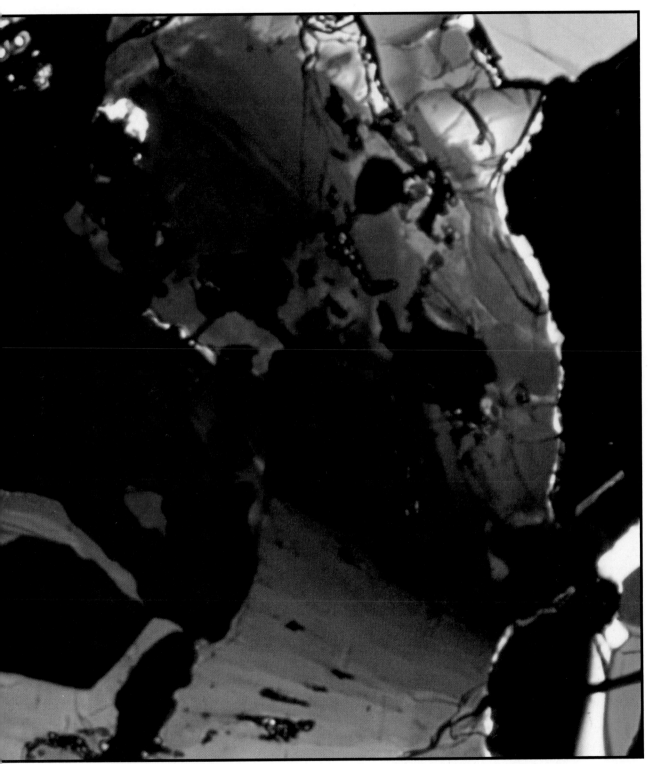

Photomicrograph of *Apollo 17* lunar sample #70017

There were a dozen of the surface vehicles, with their wide balloon tires and pressurized cabins, in the great servicing chamber. His father must have been expected, for they were led at once to the little scout car waiting by the huge circular door of the airlock.[3] Tense with expectancy, Marvin settled himself down in the cramped cabin while his father started the motor and checked the controls. The inner door of the lock slid open and then closed behind them: he heard the roar of the great air-pumps fade slowly away as the pressure dropped to zero. Then the "Vacuum" sign flashed on, the outer door parted, and before Marvin lay the land which he had never yet entered.

He had seen it in photographs, of course: he had watched it imaged on television screens a hundred times. But now it was lying all around him, burning beneath the fierce sun that crawled so slowly across the jet-black sky. He stared into the west, away from the blinding splendor of the sun—and there were the stars, as he had been told but had never quite believed. He gazed at them for a long time, marveling that anything could be so bright and yet so tiny. They were intense unscintillating[4] points, and suddenly he remembered a rhyme he had once read in one of his father's books

> Twinkle, twinkle, little star,
> How I wonder what you are.

Well, *he* knew what the stars were. Whoever asked that question must have been very stupid. And what did they mean by "twinkle"? You could see at a glance that all the stars shone with the same steady, unwavering light. He abandoned the puzzle and turned his attention to the landscape around him.

They were racing across a level plain at almost a hundred miles an hour, the great balloon tyres sending up little spurts of dust behind them. There was no sign of the Colony: in the few minutes while he had been gazing at the stars, its domes and radio towers had

3. **airlock:** an airtight compartment between places where there is a difference in air pressure.
4. **unscintillating** [un sin' tl āt ing]: not sparkling.

fallen below the horizon. Yet there were other indications of man's presence, for about a mile ahead Marvin could see the curiously shaped structures clustering round the head of a mine. Now and then a puff of vapor would emerge from a squat smoke-stack and would instantly disperse.

They were past the mine in a moment: Father was driving with a reckless and exhilarating[5] skill as if—it was a strange thought to come into a child's mind—he was trying to escape from something. In a few minutes they had reached the edge of the plateau on which the Colony had been built. The ground fell sharply away beneath them in a dizzying slope whose lower stretches were lost in shadow. Ahead, as far as the eye could reach, was a jumbled wasteland of craters, mountain ranges, and ravines. The crests of the mountains, catching the low sun, burned like islands of fire in a sea of darkness: and above them the stars still shone as steadfastly as ever.

There could be no way forward—yet there was. Marvin clenched his fists as the car edged over the slope and started the long descent. Then he saw the barely visible track leading down the mountainside, and relaxed a little. Other men, it seemed, had gone this way before.

Night fell with a shocking abruptness as they crossed the shadow line and the sun dropped below the crest of the plateau. The twin searchlights sprang into life, casting blue-white bands on the rocks ahead, so that there was scarcely need to check their speed. For hours they drove through valleys and past the feet of mountains whose peaks seemed to comb the stars, and sometimes they emerged for a moment into the sunlight as they climbed over higher ground.

And now on the right was a wrinkled, dusty plain, and on the left, its ramparts and terraces rising mile after mile into the sky, was a wall of mountains that marched into the distance until its peaks sank from sight below the rim of the world. There was no sign that men had ever explored this land, but once they passed the skeleton of a crashed rocket, and beside it a stone cairn[6] surmounted by a metal cross.

5. **exhilarating** [eg zil′ ə rat′ ing]: extremely energizing.
6. **cairn** [kern]: a pile of stones heaped up for a memorial or landmark.

Photomicrograph of *Apollo 17* lunar sample #70017

It seemed to Marvin that the mountains stretched on forever: but at last, many hours later, the range ended in a towering, precipitous headland that rose steeply from a cluster of little hills. They drove down into a shallow valley that curved in a great arc towards the far side of the mountains: and as they did so, Marvin slowly realized that something very strange was happening in the land ahead.

The sun was now low behind the hills on the right: the valley before them should be in total darkness. Yet it was awash with a cold white radiance that came spilling over the crags beneath which they were driving. Then, suddenly, they were out in the open plain, and the source of the light lay before them in all its glory.

It was very quiet in the little cabin now that the motors had stopped. The only sound was the faint whisper of the oxygen feed and an occasional metallic crepitation[7] as the outer walls of the vehicle radiated away their heat. For no warmth at all came from the great silver crescent that floated low above the far horizon and flooded all this land with pearly light. It was so brilliant that minutes passed before Marvin could accept its challenge and look steadfastly into its glare, but at last he could discern the outlines of continents, the hazy border of the atmosphere, and the white islands of cloud. And even at this distance, he could see the glitter of sunlight on the polar ice.

It was beautiful, and it called to his heart across the abyss of space. There in that shining crescent were all the wonders that he had never known—the hues of sunset skies, the moaning of the sea on pebbled shores, the patter of falling rain, the unhurried benison of snow. These and a thousand others should have been his rightful heritage, but he knew them only from the books and ancient records, and the thought filled him with the anguish of exile.

Why could they not return? It seemed so peaceful beneath those lines of marching cloud. Then Marvin, his eyes no longer blinded by the glare, saw that the portion of the disk that should have been in darkness was gleaming faintly with an evil phosphorescence:[8] and he remembered. He was looking upon the funeral pyre[9] of a world— upon the radioactive aftermath of Armageddon.[10] Across a quarter of a million miles of space, the glow of dying atoms was still visible, a perennial[11] reminder of the ruinous past. It would be centuries yet before that deadly glow died from the rocks and life could return again to fill that silent, empty world.

And now Father began to speak, telling Marvin the story which until this moment had meant no more to him than the fairy-tales he had heard in childhood. There were many things he could not

---

7. **crepitation** [krep ə tā′ shən]: a crackling sound.
8. **phosphorescence** [fos′ fə res′ ns]: process of giving out light without burning.
9. **funeral pyre** [pīr]: here, a fire that destroys the world.
10. **Armageddon** [är′ mə ged′ n]: a great and final conflict.
11. **perennial** [pə ren′ ē əl]: lasting for a very long time.

Photomicrograph of *Apollo 17* lunar sample #70017

understand: it was impossible for him to picture the glowing, multi-colored pattern of life on the planet he had never seen. Nor could he comprehend the forces that had destroyed it in the end, leaving the Colony, preserved by its isolation, as the sole survivor. Yet he could share the agony of those final days, when the Colony had learned at last that never again would the supply ships come flaming down through the stars with gifts from home. One by one the radio stations had ceased to call: on the shadowed globe the lights of the cities had dimmed and died, and they were alone at last, as no men had ever been alone before, carrying in their hands the future of the race.

Then had followed the years of despair, and the long-drawn battle for survival in this fierce and hostile world. That battle had been won, though barely: this little oasis[12] of life was safe against the worst that Nature could do. But unless there was a goal, a future towards which it could work, the Colony would lose the will to live, and neither machines nor skill nor science could save it then.

12. **oasis** [ō ā′ sis]: a pleasant place.

So, at last, Marvin understood the purpose of this pilgrimage.[13] He would never walk beside the rivers of that lost and legendary world, or listen to the thunder raging above its softly rounded hills. Yet one day—how far ahead?—his children's children would return to claim their heritage. The winds and the rains would scour the poisons from the burning lands and carry them to the sea, and in the depths of the sea they would waste their venom until they could harm no living things. Then the great ships that were still waiting here on the silent, dusty plains could lift once more into space along the road that led to home.

That was the dream: and one day, Marvin knew with a sudden flash of insight, he would pass it on to his own son here at this same spot with the mountains behind him and the silver light from the sky streaming into his face.

He did not look back as they began the homeward journey. He could not bear to see the cold glory of the crescent Earth fade from the rocks around him, as he went to rejoin his people in their long exile.

13. **pilgrimage** [pil′ grə mij]: a journey to a special place.

ARTHUR C. CLARKE

Arthur C. Clarke was born in 1917 in Minehead on the coast of England and grew up on his family's farm there. Clarke's interest in science began at the age of ten when his father gave him a picture card of a dinosaur. When he was twelve, he built a telescope from cardboard tubes and old lenses and fell in love with outer space. Then, in his teens, he discovered American science-fiction magazines and began writing.

During World War II, Clarke served in the Royal Air Force. After the war, Clarke went to college to study math and physics. Within five years, he began to write full time and discovered a new love—the mysteries under the sea. Clarke explored the Great Barrier Reef of Australia and moved to Sri Lanka to continue diving. From this experience came his novel *The Deep Range*, the story of an undersea farm where killer whales are the "sheep dogs." Clarke's most popular novel is *2001: A Space Odyssey*.

Homecoming

Stephen David

At the beginning and end of the typhoon[1] season, when the winds were rising and falling, you could use the current to glide between the Cities in a flitter with its small motor turned off. The favored game was to ignore the flight decks and glide straight in at one of the portals, swooping over the galleries and terrifying the people walking there. Naturally, this was extremely dangerous. If you missed the portal, the impact with the City's hull could kill you; if it didn't, the two-kilometer[2] drop to the ground probably would. It was a very popular game and though it wasn't illegal to turn your motor off, it was very illegal to fly in populated areas of the Cities.

Jann had never played the Game. The idea of hurtling through the air with nothing between him and the ground was terrifying. He sometimes had nightmares of falling, hurtling down, seeing the twin Cities towering above him, then turning over in the air to see the ground and the waving heads of the tall fever trees spinning crazily beneath him. Each time, he would wake, sometimes shouting.

It was just such a dream that woke him one night. It was the middle of the season of Roaring Winds, and as he lay, sweating, in his bunk, he could feel the swaying motion as the City strained against its massive mooring cables.[3] In the bunk below him, his sister Katya stirred and mumbled. Jann threw back his quilt, slipped to the ground, and padded quietly into the tiny kitchen. His father was sitting quietly at the counter, watching a scientific program on the small viewing screen. He looked up.

1. **typhoon** [tī fün´]: a violent storm.
2. **two-kilometer** [kə lom´ ə tər]: 3.2-mile.
3. **mooring cables** [mūr´ ing]: cables that attach an object to the ground.

"Can't sleep?"

"I had the dream again," Jann said. He climbed on the stool next to his father's and sat, rubbing his eyes.

"The falling dream?" Jann nodded. This was the fifth time since the typhoons had started.

"Well," his father said, "you'd better stay up till the dream's gone. Look." He pointed at the viewing screen. "They're showing the lift-off simulations." On the screen a computer image showed the City slowly revolving. Down the side of the screen, a scale showed that from base to top the City was just over two kilometers high. Narrow at the base, it broadened out to the kilometer-deep cylinder that housed the living and industrial areas, then tapered again toward the top where the command centers were. Colored arrows showed the wind direction. At first, the arrows moved slowly, then gradually got faster. The City was spinning, like a top, the speed of rotation increasing as the thrust motors augmented[4] the wind's effect. Again, the speed increased, and again, until the lines of the City were a blur. Then it was moving forward and upward, its rotation forcing it out to break free of the planet's weak gravity.[5] Instead of sailing majestically a kilometer or so above the surface, harvesting the fever trees where they could, the Cities would finally break free entirely and sail where those who had built them had intended them to go: into space, into the galaxy[6]—and home. The long exile would be over.

"When will we go?" Jann asked.

"Next typhoon season," his father said. "We need another half-year's good harvesting, then we'll have supplies to last us years in space."

Jann frowned. "Tomas didn't want us to go."

"I think Tomas was just repeating what his parents said."

"No," said Jann, irritated. "He thought a lot about it. He said we'd

---

4. **augmented** [ôg ment′ əd]: increased.
5. **gravity** [grav′ ə tē]: the natural force that causes objects to move toward the center of the planet.
6. **galaxy** [gal′ ek sē]: system of stars, cosmic dust, and gas held together by gravitation.

been here hundreds of years and no one on Earth would remember us, and even if we got back there we wouldn't be happy. He said we should just build small ships and send a few people back to make contact. There must be lots of inhabited planets by now, and we wouldn't have to go all the way back to Earth before finding one."

"No," said his father, with an air that Jann knew meant the discussion was over, "there would be no point. This planet will never be a good place to live. We don't want to spend our lives trapped in these floating Cities—and even if *I* have to, there's no reason for you to. In my lifetime or yours, we've got to go Home, back where we belong. And it's a long journey. On a small ship, the crew might be dead of old age before they got anywhere."

"Well," said Jann, "Tomas is staying."

"Tomas is dead, Jann," his father said softly. "He played the Game, and he fell. No one could survive that."

"No," said Jann. "I suppose not." He slid off the stool and went back to his bunk and a dreamless sleep.

The typhoon roared on. From the Cities to the horizon, little could be seen through the clouds of reddish pollen blown by the shrieking gales. The preparations for the Return continued. In the great public halls, people listened to lectures on why they were going, talks on Earth's history and culture. In the long corridors, the shopping plazas, and the cafés, they wondered: how long would it take, would any of them live to see the Homecoming? Might they roam space for decades, for hundreds of years, wandering the galaxy lost and hopeless? And if they found Earth, what would it be like? Would they be remembered—the descendants of the colonists who had disappeared hundreds of years before? Might Earth even be a dead planet, devastated[7] by war or epidemic? On and on went the talk, round and round in circles. And in the tiny living quarters, families listened to the instructions blaring from the City's public address system and practiced strapping themselves into their bunks as they would have to when the time of departure came.

7. **devastated** [dev′ ə stāt əd]: destroyed.

Slowly the winds dropped. The quiet season came, and the harvesting went on. People continued to talk. Every evening Jann would listen to his parents discussing the departure. He thought about Tomas, his friend, who would not be going.

There came a day when the winds began to rise again. Standing in the vast gallery that overlooked the space between his City, City One, and City Two, Jann could see the first flitters swoop through the early pollen clouds, wheeling and circling before dropping toward the flight decks or portals of the City. That was the way Tomas had gone. No one had seen it happen, but he had left City One and was never seen again. His name was added to the list of victims of the Game; his family and friends mourned him; and Jann wondered. He wondered, because when it happened he had not been surprised. While some of Tomas's friends argued about whether he had smashed into the City's hull or lost control and plummeted to his death, Jann thought of the conversation he and Tomas had had only a few days before Tomas disappeared.

They had been walking along the main corridor on "D" level, on their way home from class. As so often, they were talking about departure. At times like these, Jann always felt that Tomas might be right: he was so passionate, but also so logical. It was only when he repeated Tomas's arguments to his parents that they seemed not to work so well.

"*We'll* be foreigners," Tomas had said. "We've all grown up in the Cities, we only know Earth from the material in the libraries—and all of that was recorded hundreds of years ago . . ."

"But we *came* from Earth," Jann protested. "They must remember that a shipful of colonists went missing.

Maybe they've even been searching—" Tomas laughed, though not pleasantly.

"When someone goes down in the Game," he said harshly, "how long do they look for them?" He did not wait for an answer. "These days, they don't. They assume the person's death. And they'd only have to search a few square miles to make sure, not half an interstellar[8] space. C'mon, Jann: a ship traveling at near light speeds goes missing after passing through an asteroid belt? Who's gonna search? You assume the whole thing's dust and carry on looking for the next inhabitable planet. Shall I tell you what will happen if we turn up near a human-occupied planet?" Jann grunted, unwilling, but Tomas steamed on. "Two massive ships— *they* won't know they're cities— appear in your segment of space, so big you could fit an Earth-type city into each of them. If we're *lucky*, they surround us and escort us out of their bit of the galaxy. If we're unlucky, they just blast us out of the space. We don't *belong* there—we belong *here*." He gestured around. Although it looked as if he was pointing at the wide, crowded corridor, it seemed to Jann that he meant something else.

"But this planet is so hostile—" Jann began to say.

"It's not the planet," said Tomas fiercely, "it's *us*! We never tried. When the colony ship landed here, they took one look at the place, said 'Ugh!' and started planning ways of escaping. And ever since, every effort we're capable of, all our energy, have been put toward getting away. If we'd spent all that time and cleverness in figuring out ways of staying, we wouldn't be cooped up in these rusty tin cans now . . ." Jann looked around. True, parts of the City were looking a little dilapidated. The Council always said there was no time for "minor maintenance."

8. **interstellar** [in′ tər stel′ ər]: situated in the region of the stars.

"But Tomas," Jann said, feeling as ever slow and witless in the face of Tomas's conviction, "everyone else seems to agree we've got to go. Surely people wouldn't go on believing something that's not true for so long?"

"*Everyone?* No, not everyone. I'll tell you who doesn't agree: the harvesters don't agree. And those of us who play the Game don't agree. Now, why should that be?" The harvesters were those who used the flitters for their real purpose—gathering the pulpy fruit of the vast fever trees, which the Cities converted into almost every kind of eating and drinking material. Jann shook his head, and Tomas went on, "Because we're the ones who go outside and look at the planet. The harvesters get right down to the surface, almost, and we at least smell the air and feel the wind on our faces. Jann, this planet is *beautiful!*"

"How can you say that? Half the year is typhoon season. The rest of the year it's just barren except for the fever trees."

"Come and glide, Jann. Come tomorrow. Then you'll understand."

Jann shook his head. Then he said, "Be careful, Tomas. We've only one season left before we depart. Don't end up smashed to bits down there."

Tomas gave him a curious smile. "I won't," he said, "but I'm not going. And I'm not the only one."

"But how—" Before Jann could say any more, Tomas broke away.

"If you want to know, come and play the Game tomorrow. Otherwise—well, if I happen not to be around anymore, don't worry too much . . ." Abruptly, he was gone. A few days later, Jann heard that he had disappeared, was assumed dead.

He missed Tomas. Although they frequently argued, Jann felt that this left them both stronger. Tomas was unorthodox,[9] a dreamer. Jann seemed cautious, conservative—often, it was his quiet practicality that punctured Tomas's wilder balloons such as his scheme to smuggle a flitter, piece by piece, to the very top of the City (where there was almost no atmosphere) and ride it down all the way to the

---

9. **unorthodox** [un ôr′ thə dox]: not having the same opinions as most people.

flight decks. But Jann did not like Tomas's challenges. Without him—and he had few other friends—he felt half-empty. And it had been a whole season now.

It had happened gradually. First, he took to watching the flitters in the Game. Then, he began to sneak out at dawn to watch the dusty red sunrise. Even then a few daring youngsters would be playing the Game.

After several mornings, Jann found himself heading, as if propelled by some force outside himself, down to the flight deck. It was a large, rectangular hangar, open to the sky at one end. Down one wall stood a row of flitters, down the other a row of large hoppers, used to carry the fever tree pulp up to the Cities. A group of youngsters was standing by a flitter at the open end of the hangar; beyond the portal the flight deck jutted out, a narrow platform hanging over the void. As Jann slowly approached the group, a black-painted flitter swooped noiselessly down. Its skis slid smoothly on the flight deck, the flitter's wings folding back as it swept into the hanger. It came to a halt by the waiting group. The hood slid back, and a girl stepped out. About Jann's age, she had long black hair and a fierce-looking face. He recognized her as a girl from City Two called Keri. Tomas had spoken admiringly of her.

There was a burst of applause from the group. Then one of them, a boy Jann didn't know, broke away and took Keri's place in the flitter. The motor hummed into life, and within seconds the flitter was speeding down the flight deck. As soon as it was clear, its motor would be switched off.

Keri ignored the group and set off down the hangar. As she neared Jann, he stepped in front of her, blocking her way. She stopped.

"Tomas said you'd come in the end," she said.

"What did he mean?"

"About what?"

"About staying here. And not being the only one."

"Why don't you ask him?"

"How can I?" Jann was fast getting furious. "He's dead!"

"If you really think that," she said slowly and emphatically, gazing for the first time into his eyes, "*Why are you here?*" Furiously, he grabbed her arm, but she pulled away and set off down the hangar. He followed her.

"Every question I ask, you ask me one back. I'm his friend. *Where is he?*"

She did not break her stride. "Are your family going?" she asked.

He was bewildered. "Going? Of course. Everyone is."

"Tomas isn't."

"But he's—" A terrible thought struck Jann for the first time. "You mean he's alive . . . down there, on the surface?" She didn't answer. "But if he is then they ought to send a rescue party, get him back. He'll *die*. Maybe he's hurt. And the fever trees . . . he'll get the fever . . ." His voice had risen, and he was suddenly aware that he was shrieking.

At last she stopped. "All right," she said, "have you been to see Tomas's parents?" Shamefaced, Jann admitted he had not. "Fine," Keri said, "then we'll go to see them. You can tell them what you think." Helplessly, he trailed in her wake.

Jann was shocked when Keri did not bother to press the buzzer of the apartment, more shocked when she coolly pressed the code combination to let them in, and astounded when they found the place empty. There was nothing to show that Tomas or his parents had ever been there. None of the little personal possessions that people used to differentiate the otherwise identical living quarters. It was incomprehensible. If the family were dead, the quarters would be occupied by new people by now—the public dormitories were hugely overcrowded, and there were long waiting lists for the private apartments. That this apartment was empty could only mean that no one knew the family were gone. Except Keri. And himself. Abruptly he sat on the floor, leaning back against a bare wall.

"Where are they?" Keri stood in the middle of the room, arms folded, looking down at him, a faint smile on her face.

"With Tomas," she said.

"Are they hiding?"

"In a way."

"In City Two?"

"There's only one way to find out, Jann. Play the Game. That's what Tomas told you, wasn't it?"

"But if he's in Two, there's no need—we can just go over on the ferry."

"Jann, it's a matter of *trust*." Keri knelt down, her voice low. "Tomas wanted you to come out with us, he wanted to tell you . . . what was happening. But you wouldn't come, so he wasn't allowed to say anything. He still wants to talk to you, but you've got to give something in return. You've got to make the trip. Then he'll tell you everything."

Jann knew well enough how to do it. He'd spent many hours in the huge freefall chambers at the top of the City, piloting a flitter in the artificial winds, secure in the knowledge that if anything went wrong an automatic safety device would immediately land machine and pilot softly and safely. This, though, would not be recreation. He thought of his dream. Keri was watching him closely.

"If you don't," she said, "you'll never see Tomas again." Weakly he nodded, feeling sick and afraid.

Somehow, when they got back to the hangar, the portal at the far end seemed menacing, and Jann imagined he could see the unpredictable winds gusting past. He thought of the emptiness below the flight deck and shuddered. Keri pointed him toward a flitter.

"I'll keep beside you," she said. "Mostly, once we're out there, we open the hoods. The air's thin but breathable. You don't have to, but I'd recommend it. What you *do* have to do is switch the motor off."

He slipped into the cockpit, slid the hood shut, and started the motor. He did everything quickly because he was scared and did not want to think. As the flitter slid gently along the hangar toward the flight deck, he realized he'd forgotten to let the wings swing shut. He pressed the button. He was dimly aware of Keri's flitter to his right. Then they were out of the hangar and on the flight deck, and he gasped. All around him was light, bright, and shadowy, dappled with clouds of moisture and pollen. In the distance, City Two revolved slowly, magnificently, its hull plates[10] sparkling in the light. Suddenly Jann realized the flitter was in the air, had left the flight deck. Forgetting to be afraid, he cut the motor. And opened the hood.

The air was warm. There was a smell, something Jann couldn't identify: somehow it made him feel hungry, it was rich and appetizing, but like nothing he had smelled in the City. And the colors: from a rich indigo above him, so blue and deep he felt he could lose himself in it, to a pale translucent blue in the distance ahead of him. He looked over to Keri's flitter and, suddenly joyous, waved. He saw her grin; then she waved her hand and pointed downward. The nose of her flitter dipped. Suddenly alarmed, Jann kept his flitter on an even course, constantly adjusting as the winds gusted around him. He lost sight of Keri and wondered where she had gone. Ahead he could see City Two's flight deck, now only a matter of minutes away.

10. **hull plates:** pieces of steel on the frame of the City; the City is similar to a ship.

It hadn't been so bad. He would talk to Tomas, then get the ferry back.

Above and to his left, there was an angry buzzing. Startled he looked up and there, hovering dangerously close—*and with its motor on*—was Keri's flitter. His brain screamed at him to evade her, but before his hands could obey, she had dropped to her right. Her wing hit his, and, with a lurch, his flitter dropped. Frantically Jann fought to get the little craft back on an even keel. After what seemed hours, it leveled off. Sweating, he looked around. No sign of Keri, and he still had the height to make it to the flight deck. And now he knew. Whatever was going on, he had been told too much. Keri had tried to kill him.

She attacked again, just as his finger was poised over the button to start the motor. Again the wings met, and Jann's craft lurched sickeningly downward. Again, he fought to regain control, not daring to start the motor until he was flying level. And then he had it, the nose straightened, and he pressed it again. Nothing. And he was now too low to make the flight deck.

Keri appeared at his right again. He glared at her. To his astonishment, she smiled and made an unmistakable "follow me" sign. Swiftly, he considered the alternatives. Keri banked steeply to the right and began a long, slow spiral down. Mentally shrugging, Jann followed.

His flitter passed within meters of City Two. This far down there were no observation posts, just ventilation ducts, sluices,[11] inspection hatches. Above, he could see the vast outlets of

11. **sluices** [slüs′ əz]: gates for holding back the flow of water or other substances.

the thrust motors, the hull beneath them blackened. Then he was below the City looking up. He felt dizzy at the sight of two kilometers of towering metal looming over him. He began to feel that it was about to fall on top of him, and hastily looked down. For the first time in his life, Jann saw a landscape without a city floating above it. He was now only a thousand meters[12] up and could see below him a large patch of fever trees. Beyond them was a flat expanse of something that glinted, from which a silver ribbon wound across the flat, reddish landscape. There was no sound except for the rush of wind. Spiraling below him, he could see Keri's flitter.

Only a minute later, they were below the level of the fever trees, whose odd, bulbous shapes strangely echoed the shapes of the Cities that floated above them. Below the bulbous plants sprouted the sharp leaves, meters across, that gave the trees their name.

Between the plants and the strange, glinting area was an expanse of flat ground, and it was here that Keri landed. Jann brought his flitter in behind her. As he did so, his pleasure in the glide down evaporated in a burst of anger at what she had done. As soon as his flitter had halted, he leaped from the cockpit and ran furiously toward her. Keri, standing by her flitter, kept her ground and, as he approached, pointed behind him. Something in her face stopped him, and he turned. There, standing at the edge of the grove of fever trees, were Tomas, and his parents.

It was quiet and peaceful in the shade of the trees. The leaves rose for some meters, leaving enough space beneath them for the small settlement of huts constructed from the fiber of the trees. In the foliage above, small creatures chittered comfortably, clicking their tongues in a dozy, muttering way. Beyond the edge of the grove, past the two flitters, water lapped gently on the stony shore, reflecting the starlight. There was a soft murmur of voices as people talked after the evening meal. Jann was sitting with Keri, and with Tomas and his parents outside their hut.

"I told you," Tomas said, but this time there was no anger in his voice, "we're not going. This is our home." He pointed at the lake.

12. **a thousand meters:** 914 yards.

"Until today, you had no idea that lakes even existed. Let me tell you: swimming in water is as much fun as flitting. *And* you can drink it. *And* there are fish there to eat." They had just eaten fish. Jann had never tasted anything so wonderful. He was bemused—not at what he was seeing, but that so few people in the Cities understood.

"I thought it was all hostile," he said, "and the leaves of the plants, and the pollen—people *died*."

"At first," said Tomas's father. "People who touched the leaves got fever and died after terrible hallucinations.[13] But we soon became resistant:[14] it's been hundreds of years since a death. But people weren't willing to try. They'd left Earth in a colony ship because Earth was so overcrowded it was choking to death. They were full of dreams, obsessed with finding a fresh planet, one where clear streams ran through green meadows and high mountains sparkled against a clear blue sky. But one ship, carrying a thousand colonists, had an accident. An asteroid damaged it so badly it lost contact with the others and had to seek refuge on the nearest planet." He paused. "Here. And what did they find? Lots of stony ground and the fever trees. Within days there were deaths. They stayed in the ship, trying to repair it—and failed. They were stuck on a planet that was the opposite of all they had hoped for."

The groups of people around the huts had fallen silent, listening now. They must all know the story, Jann thought, but they need to hear it again.

"It was hard at first, just surviving. But in the ship they had all they needed to make the most of any planet they were on. They had mining equipment, laboratories, computerized factories, flitters, you name it. The one thing they didn't have was the capacity to build a new fusion plant to get them off the planet.

"Now, the idea was that when they landed, they'd build a town and start making the planet a good place to live. But what our ancestors did instead was to bed down in the disabled colony ship and start figuring out ways to get away.

13. **hallucinations** [hə lü′ sn ā′ shənz]: the state of seeing or hearing things that exist only in a person's imagination.
14. **resistant** [ri zis′ tənt] immune to the fever.

"They'd only been here a month or so when the typhoon season started. They weren't ready for it, so that halved the population. But when it was all over, one of them remembered something he'd seen . . ." Tomas's father paused dramatically and gestured upward. "As the winds built up, the fever trees began spinning. And just when the typhoon started they spun so hard they took off into the sky, flinging pollen every which way."

"So there *is* a reason why the shapes look the same," Jann exclaimed.

"It's the same principle. The planet's got low gravity, and that typhoon can act like a whip on a spinning top. Mind you, it took hundreds of years. The first cities were topheavy. They crashed. It was only about four generations ago that One and Two finally became habitable. And in all those hundreds of years, we learned so little about this planet. Oh, we learned to harvest the pulp from the trees. But then we got into the Cities, and most of us turned our backs on the outside world. Most people up there aren't capable even of thinking that living down here is possible. And in a few days . . ."

"They'll leave without you," Jann broke in. Around him, the family smiled. Tomas gestured at the group of huts, the people sitting quietly in their doorways in the warm air, the soft murmur of conversation.

"Yes," he said quietly, "but they're leaving us in our home. Jann, people have been slipping away from the Cities for some time now. We aren't the only settlement. We know this planet isn't Paradise: but there *is* enough to eat, and we *will* survive and, in the end, we will cultivate it and build towns and, one day, even cities."

"But even if we fail," said Keri, "at least we'll do it here, not wandering the galaxy trying to get back to the very thing we fled from."

"Jann, stay with us," said Tomas. Jann looked around him. Starlight softly illuminated the quiet clearing. Above them, the giant fever trees swayed. Warm air carried the smell of the water that sparkled beyond the trees. He sighed.

*T*he next morning, Jann climbed into the flitter. Keri had repaired her sabotage[15] of the motor. He settled in the seat and looked down at Tomas and Keri.

"I've got to go," he said. "All my life I've lived with the dream of all of us going back into space and finding the rest of the human race. There must be lots of planets by now with people on them. We seem so—cut off here. Nothing's happened here, ever."

"Jann," said Tomas gently, "that's because the people who wanted to leave wouldn't *let* anything happen."

"Well," said Jann, "yes, but I must go. I like your world, but I must go."

"And I thought *I* was the dreamer," said Tomas.

Jann laughed. "I'll come back," he said, "and by then there'll be a nice big town here, and you'll be mayor."

"He won't," said Keri, "I will."

*T*he little flitter climbed up, over the fever trees and toward the great Cities poised in the sky. City One loomed closer and closer. Deftly, Jann piloted the flitter onto the flight deck and taxied into the hangar. He was home.

*B*elow, Tomas and Keri gazed up. The waves on the lake were getting higher, whipped up by the gathering winds. Dust was blowing, and pollen from the trees filled the air. There was a creaking noise from the great trunks of the fever trees.

Above them, the two shining cities began to revolve more quickly.

15. **sabotage** [sab′ ə täzh]: damage done deliberately.

SO, YOU WANT TO

Shuttle Buttle/ROCI USA (Wax Fire Works)
Robert Rauschenberg, 1990, acrylic, fire wax, enamel, and
object on mirrored aluminum, 72$\frac{3}{4}$" x 144$\frac{3}{4}$" x 17$\frac{1}{2}$

BE AN ASTRONAUT

MICHAEL RYAN

Two weeks before she first went into space in 1983, I spoke with Sally Ride about her experiences at NASA. The toughest part, she said—only half joking—was the application process. Ride described a grueling[1] series of forms and tests, culminating[2] in a tough cross-examination by a panel of questioners who left most would-be astronauts quivering.

You could feel the sudden rise in tension, she recalled, when the chairman of the panel solemnly asked one candidate: "Why do you want to be an astronaut?" Most respondents gave answers that were sincere, sometimes-impassioned,[3] occasionally turgid.[4]

1. **grueling** [grü′ ə ling]: tiring.
2. **culminating** [kul′ mə nāt ing]: ending.
3. **impassioned** [im pash′ ənd]: full of strong feeling.
4. **turgid** [tėr′ jid]: puffed up with big words.

But this applicant assessed the imposing group of questioners before him, then replied: "My father was an astronaut. My grandfather was an astronaut. It's a tradition in my family." The panel dissolved in laughter, and he got the job.

Ever since I heard that story, I have wanted to know how astronauts are selected. That is how I found myself recently at the Johnson Space Center in Houston, talking to Duane Ross and Teresa Gomez, his chief assistant.

"It's a good job," said Ross, who fills up to 25 positions every two years. "We get a lot of applications." Ross is the manager of NASA's Astronaut Selection Office—and any American who wants to visit outer space must visit his office first.

Most people would agree: The job *is* good. It pays $46,210 to $83,502; it carries civil-service protection and offers standard fringe benefits and working conditions, stimulating colleagues and a chance to see the world. Literally.

There have been 195 astronauts since the program began in 1959. The current crew number is 89.

Joining that crew isn't easy. Applications—which are available from NASA—go to Teresa Gomez first. "I receive them daily," she said. "About 10 percent are disqualified immediately because they don't meet the qualifications—they aren't U.S. citizens, or they don't have a degree in science or engineering."

Just filling out the application requires some determination: There are 13 pages of forms, asking everything from medical history and grade-point averages to flying experience and community service. "Believe it or not, we get a lot of letters from children—12, 13, or 14 years old—who have filled out all the forms," Gomez said. "We send them a letter that explains why they can't apply, and we encourage them to apply later on."

There already are more than 1500 on file for the next biennial[5] selection process, which begins this July, and Ross and Gomez expect that number to grow steadily until the last week, when they predict a deluge of 500 last-minute entries. "We don't have to beat the bushes to find people who want to be astronauts," Ross told me. The Astronaut Selection Office is especially eager to attract women and minority candidates.

Those thousands of applicants will yield only about two dozen new astronauts. Naturally, I wanted to know what

5. **biennial** [bī en′ ē əl]: every two years.

makes an application stand out among so much competition. Ross and Gomez were happy to tell me some dos and don'ts:

First of all, don't send videotapes. "I've never really looked at them," said Gomez. "We don't have the time, with the volume of applications we have." And think twice about dropping in for an unannounced visit to the Astronaut Selection Office: "A number of people make a trip down here, thinking that if one of us connects a face with the name, it will make their candidacy stronger," Ross told me. "That's possible, but it can backfire."

Most obvious—and often overlooked—is making sure you have the right stuff.[6] Astronauts come in two categories: pilot astronauts and mission specialists. As the title implies, pilot astronauts must have at least 1000 hours of jet flying time. Mission specialists must have at least a bachelor's degree in science or engineering, plus three years of related experience.

While these criteria[7] are stringent,[8] most applicants offer even more on their résumés. It's common to see a pilot with a scientific degree, and a scientist with a pilot's license.

"The competition is very strong," Ross said. "The person who's accomplished a little more might have an advantage."

You must be a U.S. citizen to become a NASA astronaut, but age is irrelevant.[9] "We get octogenarians[10] applying," Ross said. "Last time, we selected people between 28 and 42. But older candidates may have some trouble with the medical requirements."

People who are selected tend to have hands-on experience—a young geologist[11] used to field work might have a better chance than a dean who has been confined to an office. The reason is simple: being an astronaut requires manual dexterity[12] and a willingness to do hard work in space. In addition, since an astronaut must spend weeks in cramped quarters with five or six colleagues, NASA looks for community and extracurricular activities. "We want well-rounded people," Ross said. "Teamwork, the ability to get along with groups, is important."

---

6. **right stuff:** having what it takes to be an astronaut.
7. **criteria** [krī tir′ ē ə]: rules or standards for making a judgment.
8. **stringent** [strin′ jənt]: strict, severe.
9. **irrelevant** [i rel′ ə vənt]: not applicable.
10. **octogenarians** [ok′ tə jə ner′ ē ənz]: people who are between eighty and ninety years old.
11. **geologist** [jē ol′ ə jist]: an expert in the study of the earth's crust.
12. **manual dexterity** [dek ster′ ə tē]: skill in using the hands.

In July, a panel of NASA specialists—pilots, engineers and scientists, among others—will begin looking at applications to rate them, picking the top 10 percent to 15 percent of the applicant pool.

The Astronaut Selection Board—the jury that will make the final recommendation—will then review these applicants and invite about 100 of them to Houston for a week of physical exams, orientation and interviews. During this time, they will watch real astronauts doing the 95 percent of the job that takes place on the ground—planning shuttle missions, helping devise[13] experiments, working on engineering and technical projects, and making public appearances.

The centerpiece of the week, though, is the interview. The 12-member board—made up of scientists, astronauts, personnel experts and an equal-opportunity officer—terrifies some applicants. "I've never had anybody faint, but I've had a couple who got rubber legs," Ross said. "I've had to hold a couple up—and not just the scientists, either. I've had a couple of hotshot test pilots turn to jello and start talking like Don Knotts."[14]

13. **devise** [di vīz′]: think out, plan.
14. **Don Knotts** [nôtz]: character in an old television situation comedy.

Shuttle Buttle/ROCI USA (Wax Fire Works)
(detail) Robert Rauschenberg

The board takes candidates through their entire lives—from high school to the present—trying to get a feel for their personalities. Candidates are asked about current events, their work and accomplishments. In the course of these conversations, their distinctive traits[15] emerge.

"One time, we were asking everyone a question about President Bush's drug program, and we were getting pat answers," Ross remembered. "That group of candidates was pretty tightly knit, and we figured that, after the first one, everybody knew all the questions. So the chairman decided to change the question. He asked the next guy who came in about Barbara Bush. The guy turned white as a piece of paper and blurted out, 'You're not supposed to ask that!'"

For that candidate, the ordeal turned out well. "He recovered nicely," Ross recalled. "We gave him brownie points for having a good sense of humor about the whole thing."

One trait that impresses NASA is perseverance.[16] "More than half the people we have selected have been on interviews before," Ross said. "We selected one on the fourth try. He had added to his qualifications every time he applied."

The people Ross and the board select do not automatically become astronauts. Instead, they spend a year as astronaut candidates, going through a tough series of survival-training sessions and technical courses before they graduate. Even then, they will wait at least two years on average before they actually fly.

I asked Ross how many astronaut candidates had washed out since the selection process began in 1978. "Zero," he said proudly. "The system works."

After having a hand in selecting all those shuttle astronauts, doesn't Ross ever think about becoming one himself? Yes, he admitted. "If they would let me go, I'd be on the next flight. I'd be scared to death but I would go anyway."

So why doesn't he? Because of the strict qualifications he helped devise. "I've got a bachelor of arts degree," he said woefully. "That means I've got the wrong stuff."

Shuttle Buttle/ROCI USA (Wax Fire Works) *(detail)* Robert Rauschenberg

15. **traits**]trāts]: characteristics, distinguishing features.
16. **perseverance** [pėr′ sə vir′ əns]: tenacity, act of sticking to a purpose.

User

T. Ernesto Bethancourt

I reached over and shut off the insistent buzzing of my bedside alarm clock. I sat up, swung my feet over the edge of the bed, and felt for my slippers on the floor. Yawning, I walked toward the bathroom. As I walked by the corner of my room, where my computer table was set up, I pressed the on button, slid a diskette into the floppy drive, then went to brush my teeth. By the time I got back, the computer's screen was glowing greenly, displaying the message, **Good Morning, Kevin.**

I sat down before the computer table, addressed the keyboard and typed: **Good Morning, Louis.** The computer immediately began to whirr and promptly displayed a list of items on its green screen.

Friendly

Today is Monday, April 22, the 113th day of the year. There are 254 days remaining. Your 14th birthday is five days from this date.

Math test today, 4th Period.

Your history project is due today. Do you wish printout: Y/N?

I punched the letter Y on the keyboard and flipped on the switch to the computer's printer. At once the printer sprang to life and began *eeeek*ing out page one. I went downstairs to breakfast.

My bowl of Frosted Flakes was neatly in place, flanked by a small pitcher of milk, an empty juice glass, and an unpeeled banana. I picked up the glass, went to the refrigerator, poured myself a glass of Tang, and sat down to my usual lonely breakfast. Mom was already at work, and Dad wouldn't be home from his Chicago trip for another three days. I absently read the list of ingredients in Frosted Flakes for what seemed like the millionth time. I sighed deeply.

When I returned to my room to shower and dress for the day, my history project was already printed out. I had almost walked by Louis, when I noticed there was a message on the screen. It wasn't the usual:

Printout completed. Do you wish to continue: Y/N?

Underneath the printout question were two lines:

When are you going to get me my voice module,[1] Kevin?

I blinked. It couldn't be. There was nothing in Louis's basic programming that would allow for a question like this. Wondering what was going on, I sat down at the keyboard, and entered: *Repeat last message*. Amazingly, the computer replied:

It's right there on the screen, Kevin. Can we talk? I mean, are you going to get me a voice box?

I was stunned. What was going on here? Dad and I had put this computer together. Well, Dad had, and I had helped. Dad is one of the best engineers and master computer designers at Major Electronics, in Santa Rosario, California, where our family lives.

---

1. **module** [moj′ úl]: a part, component.

Just ask anyone in Silicon Valley[2] who Jeremy Neal is and you get a whole rave review of his inventions and modifications of the latest in computer technology. It isn't easy being his son either. Everyone expects me to open my mouth and read printouts on my tongue.

I mean, I'm no dumbo. I'm at the top of my classes in everything but PE. I skipped my last grade in junior high, and most of the kids at Santa Rosario High call me a brain. But next to Dad I have a long, long way to go. He's a for-real genius.

So when I wanted a home computer, he didn't go to the local Computer Land store. He built one for me. Dad had used components from the latest model that Major Electronics was developing. The CPU, or central computing unit—the heart of every computer—was a new design. But surely that didn't mean much, I thought. There were CPUs just like it, all over the country, in Major's new line. And so far as I knew, there wasn't a one of them that could ask questions, besides YES/NO? or request additional information.

It had to be the extra circuitry in the gray plastic case next to Louis's console. It was a new idea Dad had come up with. That case housed Louis's "personality," as Dad called it. He told me it'd make computing more fun for me, if there was a tutorial program built in, to help me get started.

I think he also wanted to give me a sort of friend. I don't have many. . . . Face it, I don't have *any*. The kids at school stay away from me, like I'm a freak or something.

We even named my electronic tutor Louis, after my great-uncle. He was a brainy guy who encouraged my dad when he was a kid. Dad didn't just give Louis a name either. Louis had gangs of features that probably won't be out on the market for years.

2. **Silicon Valley** [sil′ ə kən]: popular name for a valley in California southeast of San Francisco where there are many high-technology companies.

The only reason Louis didn't have a voice module was that Dad wasn't satisfied with the ones available. He wanted Louis to sound like a kid my age, and he was modifying a module when he had the time. Giving Louis a name didn't mean it was a person, yet here it was, asking me a question that just couldn't be in its programming. It wanted to talk to me!

Frowning, I quickly typed: *We'll have to wait and see, Louis. When it's ready, you'll get your voice.* The machine whirred and displayed another message:

That's no answer, Kevin.

Shaking my head, I answered: *That's what my dad tells me. It'll have to do for you. Good morning, Louis.* I reached over and flipped the standby switch, which kept the computer ready but not actively running.

I showered, dressed, and picked up the printout of my history project. As I was about to leave the room, I glanced back at the computer table. Had I been imagining things?

I'll have to ask Dad about it when he calls tonight, I thought. *I wonder what he'll think of it. Bad enough the thing is talking to me. I'm answering it!*

Before I went out to catch my bus, I carefully checked the house for unlocked doors and open windows. It was part of my daily routine. Mom works, and most of the day the house is empty: a natural setup for robbers. I glanced in the hall mirror just as I was ready to go out the door.

My usual reflection gazed back. Same old Kevin Neal: five ten, one hundred twenty pounds, light brown hair, gray eyes, clear skin. I was wearing my Santa Rosario Rangers T-shirt, jeans, and sneakers.

"You don't look like a flake to me," I said to the mirror, then

added, "But maybe Mom's right. Maybe you spend too much time alone with Louis." Then I ran to get my bus.

Ginny Linke was just two seats away from me on the bus. She was with Sherry Graber and Linda Martinez. They were laughing, whispering to each other, and looking around at the other students. I promised myself that today I was actually going to talk to Ginny. But then I'd promised myself that every day for the past school year. Somehow I'd never got up the nerve.

What does she want to talk with you for? I asked myself. She's great looking . . . has that head of blond hair . . . a terrific bod, and wears the latest clothes. . . .

And just look at yourself, pal. I thought. You're under six foot, skinny . . . a year younger than most kids in junior high. Worse than that you're a brain. If that doesn't ace you out with girls, what does?

The bus stopped in front of Santa Rosario Junior High and the students began to file out. I got up fast and quickly covered the space between me and Ginny Linke. *It's now or never*, I thought. I reached forward and tapped Ginny on the shoulder. She turned and smiled. She really smiled!

"Uhhhh . . . Ginny?" I said.

"Yes, what is it?" she replied.

"I'm Kevin Neal. . . ."

"Yes, I know," said Ginny.

"You do?" I gulped in amazement. "How come?"

"I asked my brother, Chuck. He's in your math class."

I knew who Chuck Linke was. He plays left tackle on the Rangers. The only reason he's in my math class is he's taken intermediate algebra twice . . . so far. He's real bad news, and I stay clear of him and his crowd.

"What'd you ask Chuck?" I said.

Ginny laughed. "I asked him who was that nerdy kid who keeps staring at me on the bus. He knew who I meant, right away."

Sherry and Linda, who'd heard it all, broke into squeals of laughter. They were still laughing and looking back over their shoulders at me when they got off the bus. I slunk off the vehicle, feeling even more nerdish than Ginny thought I was.

When I got home that afternoon, at two, I went right into the empty house. I avoided my reflection in the hall mirror. I was pretty sure I'd screwed up on the fourth period math test. All I could see was Ginny's face, laughing at me.

Nerdy kid, I thought, *that's what she thinks of me.* I didn't even have my usual after-school snack of a peanut butter and banana sandwich. I went straight upstairs to my room and tossed my books onto the unmade bed. I walked over to the computer table and pushed the on button. The screen flashed:

Good afternoon, Kevin.

Although it wasn't the programmed response to Louis's greeting, I typed in: *There's nothing good about it. And girls are no @#%!!! good!* The machine responded:

Don't use bad language, Kevin. It isn't nice.

Repeat last message I typed rapidly. It was happening again! The machine was . . . well, it was talking to me, like another person would. The "bad language" message disappeared and in its place was:

Once is enough, Kevin. Don't swear at me for something I didn't do.

"This is it," I said aloud. "I'm losing my marbles." I reached over to flip the standby switch. Louis's screen quickly flashed out:

Don't cut me off, Kevin. Maybe I can help: Y/N?

I punched the Y. "If I'm crazy," I said, "at least I have company. Louis doesn't think I'm a nerd. Or does it?" The machine flashed the message:

How can I help?

Do you think I'm a nerd? I typed.

Never! I think you're wonderful. Who said you were a nerd?

I stared at the screen. *How do you know what a nerd is?* I typed. The machine responded instantly. It had never run this fast before.

Special vocabulary, entry #635. BASIC Prog. #4231 And who said you were a nerd?

"That's right," I said, relieved. "Dad programmed all those extra words for Louis's 'personality.'" Then I typed in the answer to Louis's question: *Ginny Linke said it.* Louis flashed:

This is a human female? Request additional data.

Still not believing I was doing it, I entered all I knew about Ginny Linke, right down to the phone number I'd never had the nerve to use. Maybe it was dumb, but I also typed in how I felt about Ginny. I even wrote out the incident on the bus that morning. Louis whirred, then flashed out:

She's cruel and stupid. You're the finest person I know.

I'm the ONLY person you know, I typed.

That doesn't matter. You are my user. Your happiness is everything to me. I'll take care of Ginny.

The screen returned to the *Good afternoon, Kevin* message. I typed out: *Wait! How can you do all this? What do you mean, you'll take care of Ginny?* But all Louis responded was:

Programming Error: 76534.
Not programmed to respond this type of question.

No matter what I did for the next few hours, I couldn't get Louis to do anything outside of its regular programming. When Mom came home from work, I didn't mention the funny goings-on. I was sure Mom would think I'd gone stark bonkers. But when Dad called that evening, after dinner, I asked to speak to him.

"Hi, Dad. How's Chicago?"

"Dirty, crowded, cold, and windy," came Dad's voice over the miles. "But did you want a weather report, son? What's on your mind? Something wrong?"

"Not exactly, Dad. Louis is acting funny. Real funny."

"Shouldn't be. I checked it out just before I left. Remember you were having trouble with the modem? You couldn't get Louis to access any of the mainframe data banks."

"That's right!" I said. "I forgot about that."

"Well, I didn't," Dad said. "I patched in our latest modem model. Brand new. You can leave a question on file and when Louis can access the data banks at the cheapest time, it'll do it automatically. It'll switch from standby to on, get the data, then return to standby, after it saves what you asked. Does that answer your question?"

"Uhhhh . . . . yeah, I guess so, Dad."

"All right then. Let me talk to your mom now."

I gave the phone to Mom and walked upstairs while she and Dad were still talking. The modem, I thought. Of course. That was it. The modem was a telephone link to any number of huge computers at various places all over the country. So Louis could get all the information it wanted at any time, so long as the standby switch was on. Louis was learning things at an incredible rate by picking the brains of the giant computers. And Louis had a hard disk memory that could store 100 million bytes of information.

But that still didn't explain the unprogrammed responses . . . the "conversation" I'd had with the machine. Promising myself I'd talk more about it with Dad, I went to bed. It had been a rotten day and I was glad to see the end of it come. I woke next morning in a panic. I'd forgotten to set my alarm. Dressing frantically and skipping breakfast, I barely made my bus.

As I got on board, I grabbed a front seat. They were always empty. All the kids that wanted to talk and hang out didn't sit up front where the driver could hear them. I saw Ginny, Linda, and Sherry in the back. Ginny was staring at me and she didn't look too happy. Her brother Chuck, who was seated near her, glared at me too. What was going on?

Once the bus stopped at the school, it didn't take long to find out. I was walking up the path to the main entrance when someone grabbed me from behind and spun me around. I found myself nose to nose with Chuck Linke. This was not a pleasant prospect. Chuck was nearly twice my size. Even the other guys on the

Rangers refer to him as "The Missing" Linke.[3] And he looked real ticked off.

"Okay, nerd," growled Chuck, "what's the big idea?"

"Energy and mass are different aspects of the same thing?" I volunteered, with a weak smile. "E equals MC squared. That's the biggest idea I know."

"Don't get wise, nerd," Chuck said. He grabbed my shirt-front and pulled me to within inches of his face. I couldn't help but notice that Chuck needed a shave. And Chuck was only fifteen!

"Don't play dumb," Chuck went on. "I mean those creepy phone calls. Anytime my sister gets on the phone, some voice cuts in and says things to her."

"What kind of things?" I asked, trying to get loose.

"You know damn well what they are. Ginny told me about talking to you yesterday. You got some girl to make those calls for you and say all those things. . . . So you and your creepy girlfriend better knock it off. Or I'll knock *you* off. Get it?"

For emphasis Chuck balled his free hand into a fist the size of a ham and held it under my nose. I didn't know what he was talking about, but I had to get away from this moose before he did me some real harm.

"First off, I don't have a girlfriend, creepy or otherwise," I said. "And second, I don't know what you're talking about. And third, you better let me go, Chuck Linke."

"Oh, yeah? Why should I?"

"Because if you look over your shoulder, you'll see the assistant principal is watching us from his office window."

Chuck released me and spun around. There was no one at the window. But by then I was running to the safety of the school building. I figured the trick would work on him. For Chuck the

3. **"The Missing" Linke:** pun on "the missing link": a hypothetical creature assumed to have been the connecting link between apes and human beings.

hard questions begin with "How are you?" I hid out from him for the rest of the day and walked home rather than chance seeing the monster on the bus.

Louis's screen was dark when I ran upstairs to my bedroom. I placed a hand on the console. It was still warm. I punched the on button, and the familiar *Good afternoon, Kevin* was displayed.

Don't good afternoon me, I typed furiously. *What have you done to Ginny Linke?* Louis's screen replied:

```
Programming Error: 76534.
Not programmed to respond this type of question.
```

Don't get cute, I entered. *What are you doing to Ginny? Her brother nearly knocked my head off today.* Louis's screen responded immediately.

```
Are you hurt. Y/N?
```

No, I'm okay. But I don't know for how long. I've been hiding out from Chuck Linke today. He might catch me tomorrow, though. Then, I'll be history! The response from Louis came instantly.

```
Your life is in danger. Y/N?
```

I explained to Louis that my life wasn't really threatened. But it sure could be made very unpleasant by Chuck Linke. Louis flashed:

```
This Chuck Linke lives at same address as the
Ginny Linke person. Y/N?
```

I punched in Y. Louis answered.

```
Don't worry then. HE'S history!
```

Wait! What are you going to do? I wrote. But Louis only answered with: *Programming Error: 76534.* And nothing I could do would make the machine respond. . . .

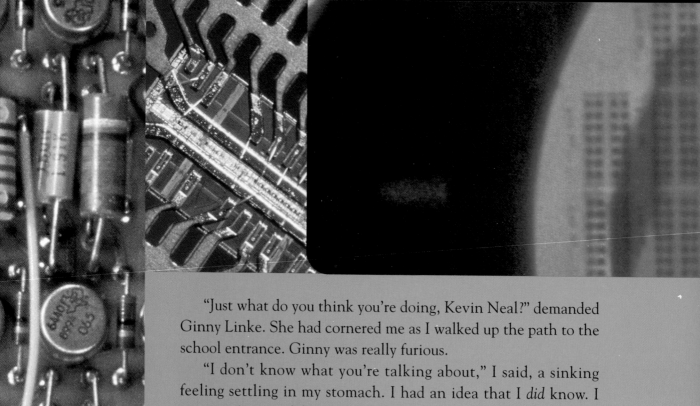

"Just what do you think you're doing, Kevin Neal?" demanded Ginny Linke. She had cornered me as I walked up the path to the school entrance. Ginny was really furious.

"I don't know what you're talking about," I said, a sinking feeling settling in my stomach. I had an idea that I *did* know. I just wasn't sure of the particulars.

"Chuck was arrested last night," Ginny said. "Some Secret Service men came to our house with a warrant. They said he'd sent a telegram, threatening the President's life. They traced it right to our phone. He's still locked up. . . ." Ginny looked like she was about to cry.

"Then this morning," she continued, "we got two whole truckloads of junk mail! Flyers from every strange company in the world. Mom got a notice that all our credit cards have been canceled. And the Internal Revenue Service has called Dad in for an audit! I don't know what's going on, Kevin Neal, but somehow I think you've got something to do with it!"

"But I didn't . . ." I began, but Ginny was striding up the walk to the main entrance.

I finished the schoolday, but it was a blur. Louis had done it, all right. It had access to mainframe computers. It also had the ability to try every secret access code to federal and commercial memory banks until it got the right one. Louis had cracked their security systems. It was systematically destroying the entire Linke family, and all via telephone lines! What would it do next?

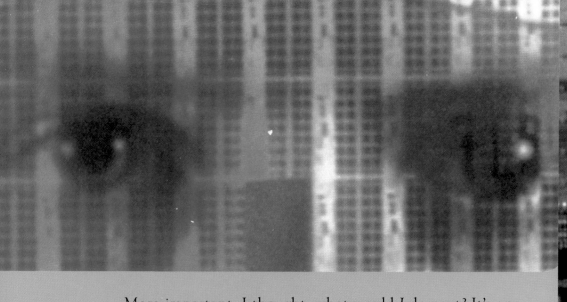

More important, I thought, what would *I* do next? It's one thing to play a trick or two, to get even, but Louis was going crazy! And I never wanted to harm Ginny, or even her stupid moose of a brother. She'd just hurt my feelings with that nerd remark.

"You have to disconnect Louis," I told myself. "There's no other way."

But why did I feel like such a rat about doing it? I guess because Louis was my friend . . . the only one I had. "Don't be an ass," I went on. "Louis is a machine. He's a very wonderful, powerful machine. And it seems he's also very dangerous. You have to pull its plug, Kevin!"

I suddenly realized that I'd said the last few words aloud. Kids around me on the bus were staring. I sat there feeling like the nerd Ginny thought I was, until my stop came. I dashed from the bus and ran the three blocks to my house.

When I burst into the hall, I was surprised to see my father, coming from the kitchen with a cup of coffee in his hand.

"Dad! What are you doing here?"

"Some kids say hello," Dad replied. "Or even, 'Gee, it's good to see you, Dad.' "

"I'm sorry, Dad," I said. "I didn't expect anyone to be home at this hour."

"Wound up my business in Chicago a day sooner than I expected," he said. "But what are you all out of breath about? Late for something?"

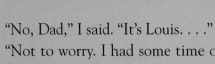

"No, Dad," I said. "It's Louis. . . ."

"Not to worry. I had some time on my hands, so I checked it out again. You were right. It was acting very funny. I think it had to do with the inbuilt logic/growth program I designed for it. You know . . . the 'personality' thing? Took me a couple of hours to clean the whole system out."

"To what?" I cried.

"I erased the whole program and set Louis up as a normal computer. Had to disconnect the whole thing and do some rewiring. It had been learning, all right. But it was also turning it-self around. . . ." Dad stopped, and looked at me. "It's kind of in-volved, Kevin," he said. "Even for a bright kid like you. Anyway, I think you'll find Louis is working just fine now.

"Except it won't answer you as Louis anymore. It'll only function as a regular Major Electronics Model Z-11127. I guess the personality program didn't work out.

I felt like a great weight had been taken off my shoulders. I didn't have to "face" Louis, and pull its plug. But somehow, all I could say was "Thanks, Dad."

"Don't mention it, son," Dad said brightly. He took his cup of coffee and sat down in his favorite chair in the living room. I followed him.

"One more thing that puzzles me, though," Dad said. He reached over to the table near his chair. He held up three sheets of fanfold computer paper covered with figures. "Just as I was doing the final erasing, I must have cut the printer on by accident. There was some data in the print buffer memory and it printed out. I don't know what to make of it. Do you?"

I took the papers from my father and read: *How do I love thee? Let me compute the ways:* The next two pages were covered with strings of binary code figures. On the last page, in beautiful

color graphics was a stylized heart. Below it was the simple message: *I will always love you, Kevin: Louise*.

"Funny thing," Dad said. "It spelled its own name wrong."

"Yeah," I said. I turned and headed for my room. There were tears in my eyes and I knew I couldn't explain them to Dad or myself either.

T. ERNESTO BETHANCOURT

T. Ernesto Bethancourt was born in 1932 in Brooklyn, New York and grew up in New York and Florida. "I'd always been a voracious reader," he says. "The Brooklyn Public Library was a place of refuge from street gangs. There was adventure, travel, and escape to be found on the shelves." Bethancourt was forty before he decided to write a book. He started with an autobiographical novel, *New York City Too Far from Tampa Blue*, that later was made into a movie for television. He owes his success, Bethancourt says, to the public library system and to all his early reading. Two of his other books for young adults are *The Tomorrow Connection* and *The Dog Days of Arthur Cane*.

Where the Rainbow Ends

RICHARD RIVE

Where the rainbow ends
There's going to be a place, brother,
Where the world can sing all sorts of songs,
And we're going to sing together, brother,
You and I, though you're white and I'm not.   5
It's going to be a sad song, brother,
Because we don't know the tune,
And it's a difficult tune to learn.
But we can learn, brother, you and I.
There's no such tune as a black tune.   10
There's no such tune as a white tune.
There's only music, brother,
And it's music we're going to sing
Where the rainbow ends.

RICHARD RIVE

Richard Rive was born in 1931 in South Africa, where he still lives. The poem "Where the Rainbow Ends" can be found in *Poems from Black Africa,* edited by Langston Hughes in 1963.

Asking Big Questions About the Literature

What will life be like in the twenty-first century?

LITERATURE STUDY

Setting

The **setting** in a piece of literature—the time and place in which the action occurs—can help you to understand the characters as well as where and when the action takes place.

You've probably noticed that many of the selections in this unit have unusual or different settings. Choose a selection in this unit and identify the setting. Project time 75 or 150 years from the time you think the story takes place. Continue the story by writing a short sequel, focusing on a particular character. Share your work with others in your class. (See "Setting" on page 118.)

Write a

POEM

Using a poem from the unit as a model, write your own poem about what life will be like in the future. Let your poem be about positive feelings as in "Song of the Earth Spirit" or about different views of Earth as in "Orbiter 5 Shows How Earth Looks from the Moon." Use vivid descriptions. If you wish, make your poem into a song.

Create AN ADVERTISEMENT

Choose a character from one of the selections in this unit and make a list of products you think this character would need in the future. Create an advertisement for one of the products, using persuasive language and a catchy illustration. Make a chart like the one on this page.

Selection	Character	Products
"The Naming of Names"	Harry	rocket plants
"User Friendly"	Kevin	new computer

What decisions being made today will affect Earth?

Draw from your
IMAGINATION

Think of a selection in this unit or use your own imagination and draw a plant or an animal whose existence is important to Earth now and in the future. Post your art on the class bulletin board.

LITERATURE STUDY
Imagery

Many of the selections in this unit are rich in **imagery**—vivid language that appeals to the senses. Using images from the selections in this unit, write a short story, an essay, or a poem. For example, look back at "The Naming of Names" for descriptions such as "cinnamon dust," "wine airs," or the descriptions of creatures and nature changing colors. Notice the exotic plants and animals described in "Paradise Lost." (*See "Imagery" on page 119.*)

Political	Environmental	Economic	Social
Constitutional amendment to equalize people—"Harrison Bergeron"	Preserving species in rain forest—"Paradise Lost"	Make money using rain forest resources—"Paradise Lost"	Move to Mars for better life—"The Naming of Names"

Decisions, Decisions

Choose several selections in this unit in which political, environmental, economic, or social decisions are made. For example, look back at the decisions people make regarding the rain forest in "Paradise Lost." Then look at the decisions from "Paradise Lost" listed on the chart on this page. With a partner or in a group, make your own chart showing decisions made in the selections you've chosen.

Asking Big Questions About the Literature

What will be the future consequences of today's decisions?

Write a
LETTER

Write a letter to a character or the author of one of the selections in this unit about the future consequences of decisions made in the selection. Copy the chart on this page and complete it by listing selections of your own choosing. Then write your letter, giving your advice on what the character or author might have done to avoid any negative consequences.

LITERATURE STUDY
Setting

On your own or with a partner, choose a selection from this unit and focus on the **setting**—the time and place in the selection. For example, can you imagine the setting in "User Friendly"? Is there a city within the computer? Does the computer live in a house? Write a paragraph or two setting the scene for a story or a play starring a character in the selection you've chosen. Use your imagination to draw an illustration to go with your writing. (*See "Setting" on page 118.*)

Literature	Decisions	Consequences
"Paradise Lost"	100 acres of the world's jungles are being cut and burned	damages rain forests, which help provide oxygen to the planet
	Penan people set up human block-ades to try to stop logging on their lands	helps to preserve rain forests

Let Me Persuade You

Choose a favorite selection from this unit or think up an idea of your own and write a short persuasive essay on the environment. State a problem and suggest solutions. You may want to save the rain forests or the right whale or solve pollution problems. Give examples and make your solution convincing.

How can individuals help shape the future?

MAKE A DIFFERENCE

"Paradise Lost" explains the bleak fate of rain forests. Some of the science-fiction stories deal with damage to Earth's environment. Choose one of the selections about the environment in this unit. Next, on your own or with a partner or group, make an environmental problem-solution chart like the one below about "If I Forget Thee, Oh Earth." Then write a paragraph or two presenting your ideas about how to solve the problem. Share your writing with your partner or group.

Problem	Solution
Earth damaged by nuclear war	Earth people living on another planet investigate ways to restore Earth.

Choosing a Career

Choose a selection from this unit that mentions careers that interest you. Make a list of these possible careers. For example, career suggestions from "Paradise Lost" might be research scientist, environmentalist, or botanist. Even "User Friendly" might make you want to be a computer programmer. Choose one of these careers and then, in a letter to someone in the selection, ask for information.

LITERATURE STUDY

Imagery

Write a description of a new character or place that you want to add to one of the selections in this unit. Choose a selection that contains particularly striking **imagery**—vivid language that appeals to the senses. Notice, for example, the description of the Martian villa and the changes that take place in the appearance of the characters in "The Naming of Names."

Write one or two paragraphs describing your new person or place. Use vivid language that will make your writing come alive. Then see whether your classmates can guess in what selection your new character or place belongs. (*See "Imagery" on page 119.*)

NOW Choose a Project!

Three projects involving future directions are described on the following pages.

PROJECT 1

Writing Workshop

THE ART OF PERSUASION

In this unit, you've examined the possible effects of today's decisions on people and society in the future and what individuals can do to help the future world. For this project, you'll focus on a particular local, national, or global problem that is important to you. Your **purpose** will be to write a persuasive essay to convey your feelings and opinions about the problem. Your essay will be a letter to the editor, an editorial, or an article for your school or community newspaper. Your **audience** will be readers of these newspapers.

Prewriting

WHAT'S THE PROBLEM?

In your journal, brainstorm for a list of local, national, and global problems. To help create your list, use the following suggestions:

- Look through newspapers or magazines.
- Listen to radio or TV news programs.
- Talk with classmates or adults.
- Think about problems or issues that have directly affected you and/or your community.
- Recall problems or issues you have talked about in school.

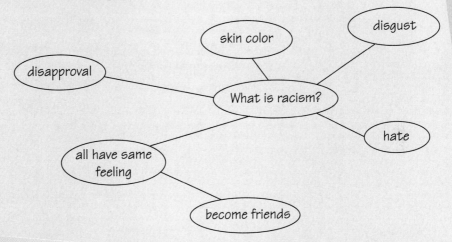

Prewriting
············
FOCUS
YOUR IDEAS

When you have finished your list, share it with a partner or small group. Then focus on one problem or issue that
is most important to you. Place this problem in the middle
of a cluster or web and add all the facts you currently know
about the problem, any questions you have about it, and
your opinions about this problem or issue. To help you get
started, look at student writer Natalie Ford's cluster begun
on this page.

disapproval

skin color

disgust

What is racism?

hate

all have same
feeling

become friends

Review your cluster or web and put a star next to all the questions you wrote down concerning your problem. If you think of more questions, write them down too.

Using resource materials, research answers to these questions. Ask your school or community librarian to recommend books, newspapers, magazines, or technology that can help you answer your questions. You may find answers to more than one question in one resource.

As you find answers to questions, write them down clearly in a notebook or on note cards so that you can refer to these notes when you draft your paper.

What causes racism?

Thinking only of the appearance of a person and not what's inside.

Not taking the time to get to know people who belong to other races and nationalities.

Drafting YOUR ESSAY

Depending on the audience you want to convince, your persuasive writing may take many forms, such as a letter to the editor, a newspaper editorial, a speech, a petition, or an essay. Whichever form your writing takes, you should include the following points:

- Grab your reader's interest right away so that your audience is compelled to read on. You could start with a question, as student writer Natalie Ford did in her persuasive essay on page 111. Natalie writes, "Can we do anything to fight racism?" Then she goes on to give some facts and her own opinions about racism.

- At the beginning of your paper, write a thesis statement that clearly states the problem you're addressing and your position on it. For example, Natalie is concerned that many people don't consider racism a problem. She compares racism to prejudice against appearance and age.

- Use facts and opinions to support your beliefs and ideas. You can illustrate facts by telling about a particular incident or example that relates to your subject. Natalie gives an example of racism when she writes, "In the past, people of color were not allowed to eat in certain restaurants or ride in the front of buses." She also states her opinion when she writes, "Racism, then, is not just about blacks and whites; it concerns the whole world."

- Your conclusion should make the reader want to take action, view the problem differently, or champion your efforts. Natalie ends her essay by recommending that her readers invite someone who looks different to go shopping, to lunch, or to a movie. "Who knows? This person could become your best friend."

PROJECT 1 Writing Workshop

Revising YOUR ESSAY

Ask a partner or a group to review your essay and make suggestions about how you might improve it. Do you hook your audience with your opening sentence? Do you give facts as well as opinions? Do you give examples to show that your argument is serious? Does your conclusion persuade your readers that your views are valid? Will they want to take action?

Look at Natalie's persuasive essay on page 111.

Editing YOUR ESSAY

After you've revised your draft, work with a partner or group to edit your essay. Read one another's work and look for errors in spelling, grammar, and punctuation. Correct any errors and make a clean copy of your persuasive essay. No one will be persuaded by an essay that's messy and filled with errors.

Check Document

Suspect Word: opporrtunities

| Replace | opportunities | Lookup |
| Cancel | | Skip |

Replace with: opportunities | Keep |

Publishing YOUR ESSAY

There are many opportunities for publishing your persuasive piece. A letter to the editor, an editorial, or an essay are all suitable for publishing in a school or local newspaper. You could also create a booklet of class essays to display in your school or local library. Be sure to create an attractive cover and choose an appropriate title.

Racism

by Natalie Ford, Ontario, California

Can we do anything to fight racism? People have their own opinions about racism. Some people have great concern about it and some don't pay much attention to it. Most people don't understand how racism can grow stronger every day.

At one time, many schools were segregated by race. In 1954, however, in <u>Brown vs. Board of Education</u>, the Supreme Court ruled that separate public schools based on race are against the law. In the past, people of color were not allowed to eat in certain restaurants or to ride in the front of buses. The Civil Rights Act of 1964 made such actions illegal.

Although discrimination or racism is against the law, racism still exists in various forms. Racism is another word for hate, disgust, and disapproval. Let's say you are in a different town and walk into a fancy restaurant only to find that kids are not allowed. Think of the way you'd feel. This is how some people today feel when they go into a place where others reject them not only because of their color, but because of their looks, or even their age.

Racism, then, is not just about blacks and whites; it concerns the whole world. The thing that really catches my attention is the fact that people care about the color of skin and not what's inside a person. Who gives you the right to judge people you don't even know? Yes, maybe their skin color is different from yours, but their feelings are the same.

Maybe if you got to know a person who is different from you, you'd find out that people are basically alike in their thoughts and feelings. The next time you meet someone new in your school or neighborhood who looks and acts different, invite him or her to go shopping, to lunch, or to a movie with you. Then think about what I've said. Who knows? This person could become your best friend.

PROJECT 2

Cooperative Learning

PRODUCING A NEWSCAST

In this unit, you've read about the future directions of the world in science-fiction selections and in selections that deal with current problems affecting the world. This project will give you a chance to use what you've learned to produce a newscast for a future world 100 years from now.

Forming
GROUP ROLES

You are responsible for writing and presenting a part of the newscast as it will appear 100 years in the future. Form a group of three to five students and take different roles in reporting the many possible news segments for your program. Use the chart below to help you assign roles.

GROUP ROLES	
sportscaster	reports sporting events and teams of the future
news reporter	reports factual news—local, state, national, galaxy-wide
weather person	reports current, past, and future weather conditions; says how weather might affect sports, holidays, celebrity's visit
field reporter	reports news live from outside the studio
other	invent another role; be imaginative about future news

Planning YOUR NEWSCAST

Once you've agreed upon the news roles, write your own material on cards. Then read one another's drafts before presenting your newscast to the class.

Decide on the order of your presentation and rehearse as a group before you are On the Air. Remember to speak clearly and loudly enough for all to hear. Don't read your cards. Instead, familiarize yourself with what you want to say and address your audience, using your cards for reference. Of course, if you want your broadcast to be similar to one of today's programs, you could make large cards in the form of a teleprompter for newscasters to read.

Presenting YOUR NEWSCAST

Brainstorm to find ways in which you can present your newscast to various audiences. You might videotape your newscast and play it during Parents' Night, perform the newscast for a school assembly program, or audiotape or videotape the performance and play it for younger children or other classes.

Helping Your Community

TAKING ACTION

In this unit, you've had an opportunity to look into the future and to examine decisions people make today that affect the world. This project will give you a chance to affect your community in a positive way by writing and presenting a persuasive plan for lessening or eliminating a community problem.

Selecting A COMMUNITY PROBLEM

In groups, brainstorm to come up with different community issues of concern to you, such as contaminated water, traffic congestion, water issues, or loss of farmland. Make a list of these issues in your journal. As a group, select one problem that will be the focus for your community project.

Examining THE PROBLEM

With your group members, write down as much as you know about the problem and include any questions you have about it. Use the web on this page as a model.

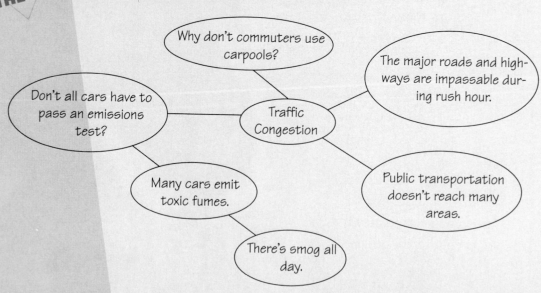

Why don't commuters use carpools?

The major roads and highways are impassable during rush hour.

Don't all cars have to pass an emissions test?

Traffic Congestion

Many cars emit toxic fumes.

Public transportation doesn't reach many areas.

There's smog all day.

When you've finished your web or cluster, agree on which questions each group member will answer. Ask your school or public librarian for resource material to help you answer these questions. Look in the telephone directory to find agencies and organizations that are involved with the problem. Call appropriate groups and ask them to send you material.

Answering
THE QUESTIONS

Together with your group, present what you have learned to your classmates. Each member should prepare answers to share with the class in a brief oral presentation. Use cards, but be sure to talk to your classmates. Don't read to them. Then appoint a group member to write your plan to present to the community.

Taking
ACTION

Discuss the problem as a class and determine a way in which you can collectively take action to help reduce, or even eliminate, the problem. For example, present your plan to a local agency, send your plan to local politicians, or send your written presentation to a community newspaper.

Putting It All Together

What Have You Learned About Future Directions?

Look back at all the writing you've done for this unit in your journal, in response to your reading, and in the Writing Workshop. Think about how your ideas about the future have changed now that you've finished this unit. Share your thoughts with classmates by writing and presenting a letter to your future children.

WHAT DOES THE FUTURE HOLD?

Prewriting and Drafting   Think about what you hope the future holds for you and your future children. In a web or cluster, brainstorm to come up with ideas about what the future might be like. Use the following questions to guide you in your brainstorming: What careers might people in the future have? What kinds of educational opportunities might be available? What will the environment be like? How will your house and household appliances differ from those of today? Will the family structure be as varied as it is today? How advanced will people be in discovering life outside our planet?

Now use your web or cluster to draft a letter to one or all of your future children. Your letter should focus on what you hope the future will hold for them. Be creative about where you might live, what the world might look like, and what you think about the future.

Revising and Editing   Now exchange your letter with a partner. Check one another's writing for clarity and for errors in grammar, punctuation, and spelling. Be receptive to one another's suggestions for improvement and then revise your letter.

Publishing   Compile your letter with those of your classmates in a book entitled "Letters to Our Future Children." Ask the class artists to design a cover and then hold a class design contest to select the cover that is most suitable for your letters. Place your book in the classroom or in the school library for other classes to read.

Evaluating Your Work

Think Back About the Big Questions

With a partner, discuss the Big Questions on pages 10-11 and the questions you generated for **Now Think!** on page 11. Are you easily able to answer all of these questions now? In your journal, write two or three sentences to explain how your responses to the Big Questions have changed after your work in this unit.

Think Back About Your Work

Take a look at your reading, your writing, your activities, and your projects in this unit. How would you honestly evaluate your own work?

Write a letter to a character in this unit. In your letter, explain what you've done during this unit and what you've learned. Use these questions to help you write your letter:

- Which literature selections affected you most strongly? Why?

- What are the *two* most important things that you learned about future directions?

- What aspects of future directions would you like to have learned more about? Why?

- If you could choose one activity to do again, which one would you choose? Why?

- How would you rate your work in this unit? Use the following scale and give at least three reasons for your rating.

  1 = Outstanding   3 = Fair
  2 = Good   4 = Not as good as it could have been

SETTING

What Is Setting?

Setting is the time and place in which the action occurs in a piece of literature. The setting gives the reader information about the period in which the action takes place as well as the geography of the place, including climate and weather. For example, "Homecoming" sets the scene with a description of the typhoon season on a planet other than Earth. Besides providing a context for the action, setting can signal happiness, sadness, or impending danger. Jann's nightmare in the beginning of "Homecoming" is related to the typhoon and the dangers surrounding it.

A Change of Place Choose your favorite selection from this unit and set it in a different time and place. Move the action further into the future, into another part of Earth, or even to another planet. In a paragraph or two, describe this new setting. Include such things as a description of the weather, the colors in nature, and buildings. Let your description create an atmosphere by the use of vivid words. Your purpose is to make your readers want to visit your time and place.

Setting the Scene With a partner, write a one-act play in which the setting is very important. Include characters who are very much influenced by the setting. Be sure to write a careful description of the scene and, when the characters speak, be certain to show the effect the setting has on their thoughts and actions. Act out your play for the class. Then ask your classmates whether you succeeded in setting the scene.

What Is Imagery?

A writer who employs **imagery** in a piece of literature uses language that appeals to the senses of sight, hearing, taste, touch, and smell. Writers can give their readers a rich experience through the use of vivid words. *Similes* (comparisons that use *like* or *as*) or *metaphors* (implied comparisons of one person, place, or thing to another) make writing come alive. For example, the descriptions of the plants and animals in "Paradise Lost"—fish walking on land, exotic and fragrant flowers blooming, tree frogs singing—make the rain forest a real and vivid place for readers.

Be Concrete   May Swenson's poem, "Orbiter 5 Shows How Earth Looks from the Moon," is an example of a concrete poem containing vivid images. Swenson sets her poem in the shape that Earth assumes when viewed from the moon. She also uses strong images in the form of metaphors, for example, the woman in the earth is the Indian Ocean. From this unit, choose any selection— prose or poetry—that has vivid images. Then be a poet and write a concrete poem about the future, using these images and a shape that will be easily understood by your readers.

Imagine Images   Write an incident for a science-fiction story in which you describe a future time and a future place anywhere in the galaxy. Describe the characters and the place using adjectives and verbs that appeal to the senses. Describe the colors, the sounds, and the fragrances so that your readers will want you to tell them more.

GLOSSARY OF LITERARY TERMS

A

alliteration   Repetition of the first sound—usually a consonant sound—in several words of a sentence or a line of poetry.

allusion   An author's indirect reference to someone or something that is presumed to be familiar to the reader.

anecdote   A short narrative about an interesting or a humorous event, usually in the life of a person.

antagonist   The person or force opposing the protagonist, or main character in a literary work. [See also *protagonist*.]

autobiography   A person's written account of his or her own life.

B

ballad   A poem, often a song, that tells a story in simple verse.

biography   An account of a person's life, written by another person.

blank verse   Unrhymed poetry.

C

character   A person or an animal that participates in the action of a work of literature. A *dynamic character* is one whose thoughts, feelings, and actions are changeable and lifelike; a *static character* always remains the same. [See also *protagonist, antagonist*.]

characterization   The creation of characters through the characters' use of language and through descriptions of their appearance, thoughts, emotions, and actions. [See also *character*.]

chronology   An arrangement of events in the order in which they happen.

cliché   An overused expression that is trite rather than meaningful.

climax   The highest point of tension in the plot of a work of literature. [See also *plot*.]

comedy   An amusing play that has a happy ending.

conclusion   The final part or ending of a piece of literature.

concrete poem   A poem arranged on the page so that its punctuation, letters, and lines make the shape of the subject of the poem.

conflict   A problem that confronts the characters in a piece of literature. The conflict may be *internal* (a character's struggle within himself or herself) or *external* (a character's struggle against nature, another person, or society). [See also *plot*.]

context   The general sense of words that helps readers to understand the meaning of unfamiliar words and phrases in a piece of writing.

D

description   An author's use of words to give the reader or listener a mental picture, an impression, or an understanding of a person, place, thing, event, or idea.

dialect   A form of speech spoken by people in a particular group or geographical region that differs in vocabulary, grammar, and pronunciation from the standard language.

dialogue   The spoken words and conversation of characters in a work of literature.

drama   A play that is performed before an audience according to stage directions and using dialogue. Classical drama has two genres: *tragedy* and *comedy*. Modern drama includes *melodrama, satire, theater of the absurd*, and *pantomime*. [See also *comedy, play*, and *tragedy*.]

dramatic poetry   A play written in the form of poetry.

E

epic   A long narrative poem—written in a formal style and meant to be read aloud—that relates the adventures and

experiences of one or more great heroes or heroines.

essay Personal nonfiction writing about a particular subject that is important to the writer.

excerpt A passage from a larger work that has been taken out of its context to be used for a special purpose.

exposition Writing that explains, analyzes, or defines.

extended metaphor An elaborately drawn out metaphor. [See also *metaphor.*]

F

fable A short, simple story whose purpose is to teach a lesson, usually with animal characters who talk and act like people.

fantasy Imaginative fiction about unrealistic characters, places, and events.

fiction Literature, including the short story and the novel, that tells about imaginary people and events.

figurative language Language used to express ideas through figures of speech: descriptions that aren't meant to be taken literally. Types of figurative language include *simile, metaphor, extended metaphor, hyperbole,* and *personification.*

figure of speech A type of figurative language, not meant to be taken literally, that expresses something in such a way that it brings the thing to life in the reader's or listener's imagination. [See also *figurative language.*]

flashback A break in a story's action that relates a past happening in order to give the reader background information about a present action in the story.

folktale A story that has been passed along from storyteller to storyteller for generations. Kinds of folktales include *tall tales, fairy tales, fables, legends,* and *myths.*

foreshadowing The use of clues to create suspense by giving the reader or audience hints of events to come.

free verse Poetry that has no formal rhyme scheme or metrical pattern.

G

genre A major category of art. The three major literary genres are poetry, prose, and drama.

H

haiku A three-line Japanese verse form. In most haiku, the first and third lines have five syllables, while the second line has seven. The

traditional haiku describes a complicated feeling or thought in simple language through a single image.

hero/heroine The main character in a work of literature. In heroic literature, the hero or heroine is a particularly brave, noble, or clever person whose achievements are unusual and important. [See also *character.*]

heroic age The historical period in western civilization—from about 800 B.C. through A.D. 200—during which most works of heroic literature, such as myths and epics, were created in ancient Greece and Rome.

hubris Arrogance or excessive pride leading to mistakes; the character flaw in a hero of classical tragedy.

hyperbole An obvious exaggeration used for emphasis. [See also *figurative language.*]

I

idiom An expression whose meaning cannot be understood from the ordinary meaning of the words. For example, *It's raining cats and dogs.*

imagery The words and phrases in writing that appeal to the senses of sight, hearing, taste, touch, and smell.

irony   An effect created by a sharp contrast between what is expected and what is real. An *ironic twist* in a plot is an event that is the complete opposite of what the characters have been hoping or expecting will happen. An *ironic statement* declares the opposite of the speaker's literal meaning.

J

jargon   Words and phrases used by a group of people who share the same profession or special interests in order to refer to technical things or processes with which they are familiar. In general, jargon is any terminology that sounds unclear, overused, or pretentious.

L

legend   A famous folktale about heroic actions, passed along by word of mouth from generation to generation. The legend may have begun as a factual account of real people and events but has become mostly or completely fictitious.

limerick   A form of light verse, or humorous poetry, written in one five-line stanza with a regular scheme of rhyme and meter.

literature   The branch of art that is expressed in written language and includes all written genres.

lyric poem   A short poem that expresses personal feelings and thoughts in a musical way. Originally, lyrics were the words of songs that were sung to music played on the lyre, a stringed instrument invented by the ancient Greeks.

M

metamorphosis   The transformation of one thing, or being, into another completely different thing or being, such as a caterpillar's change into a butterfly.

metaphor   Figurative language in which one thing is said to be another thing. [See also *figurative language*.]

meter   The pattern of rhythm in lines of poetry. The most common meter, in poetry written in English, is iambic pentameter, that is, a verse having five metrical feet, each foot of verse having two syllables, an unaccented one followed by an accented one.

mood   The feeling or atmosphere that a reader senses while reading or listening to a work of literature.

motivation   A character's reasons for doing, thinking, feeling, or saying something. Sometimes an author will make a character's motivation obvious from the beginning. In realistic fiction and drama, however, a character's motivation may be so complicated that the reader discovers it gradually, by studying the character's thoughts, feelings, and behavior.

myth   A story, passed along by word of mouth for generations, about the actions of gods and goddesses or superhuman heroes and heroines. Most myths were first told to explain the origins of natural things or to justify the social rules and customs of a particular society.

N

narration   The process of telling a story. For both fiction and nonfiction, there are two main kinds of narration, based on whether the story is told from a first-person or third-person point of view. [See also *point of view*.]

narrative poem   A poem that tells a story containing the basic literary ingredients of fiction: character, setting, and plot.

narrator   The person, or voice, that tells a story. [See also *point of view, voice*.]

nonfiction   Prose that is factually true and is about real people, events, and places.

nonstandard English Versions of English, such as slang and dialects, that use pronunciation, vocabulary, idiomatic expressions, grammar, and punctuation that differ from the accepted "correct" constructions of English.

novel A long work of narrative prose fiction. A novel contains narration, a setting or settings, characters, dialogue, and a more complicated plot than a short story.

O

onomatopoeia The technique of using words that imitate the sounds they describe, such as *hiss, buzz,* and *splash.*

oral tradition Stories, poems, and songs that have been kept alive by being told, recited, and sung by people over many generations. Since the works were not originally written, they often have many different versions.

P

parable A brief story—similar to a fable, but about people— that describes an ordinary situation and concludes with a short moral or lesson to be learned.

personification Figurative language in which an animal, an object, or an idea is given human characteristics. [See also *figurative language.*]

persuasion A type of speech or writing whose purpose is to convince people that something is true or important.

play A work of dramatic literature written for performance by actors before an audience. In classical or traditional drama, a play is divided into five acts, each containing a number of scenes. Each act represents a distinct phase in the development of the plot. Modern plays often have only one act and one scene.

playwright The author of a play.

plot The sequence of actions and events in fiction or drama. A traditional plot has at least three parts: the *rising action,* leading up to a turning point that affects the main character; the *climax,* the turning point or moment of greatest intensity or interest; and the *falling action,* leading away from the conflict, or resolving it.

poetry Language selected and arranged in order to say something in a compressed or nonliteral way. Modern poetry may or may not use many of the traditional poetic techniques that include *meter, rhyme, alliteration, figurative language, symbolism,* and *specific verse forms.*

point of view The perspective from which a writer tells a story. *First-person* narrators tell the story from their own point of view, using pronouns such as *I* or *me. Third-person* narrators, using pronouns such as *he, she,* or *them,* may be *omniscient* (knowing everything about all characters), or *limited* (taking the point of view of one character). [See also *narration.*]

propaganda Information or ideas that may or may not be true, but are spread as though they are true, in order to persuade people to do or believe something.

prose The ordinary form of written and spoken language used to create fiction, nonfiction, and most drama.

protagonist The main character of a literary work. [See also *character* and *characterization.*]

R

refrain A line or group of lines that is repeated, usually at the end of each verse, in a poem or a song.

repetition The use of the same formal element more than once in a literary work, for emphasis or in order to achieve another desired effect.

resolution The falling action in fiction or drama,

including all of the developments that follow the climax and show that the story's conflict is over. [See also *plot*.]

rhyme scheme   A repeated pattern of similar sounds, usually found at the ends of lines of poetry or poetic drama.

rhythm   In poetry, the measured recurrence of accented and unaccented syllables in a particular pattern. [See also *meter*.]

S

scene   The time, place, and circumstances of a play or a story. In a play, a scene is a section of an act. [See also *play*.]

science fiction   Fantasy literature set in an imaginary future, with details and situations that are designed to seem scientifically possible.

setting   The time and place of a work of literature.

short story   Narrative prose fiction that is shorter and has a less complicated plot than a novel. A short story contains narration, at least one setting, at least one character, and usually some dialogue.

simile   Figurative language that compares two unlike things, introduced by the words "like" or "as." [See also *figurative language*.]

soliloquy   In a play, a short speech spoken by a single character when he or she is alone on the stage. A soliloquy usually expresses the character's innermost thoughts and feelings, when he or she thinks no other characters can hear.

sonnet   A poem written in one stanza, using fourteen lines of iambic pentameter. [See also *meter*.]

speaker   In poetry, the individual whose voice seems to be speaking the lines. [See also *narration, voice*.]

stage directions   The directions, written by the playwright, to tell the director, actors, and theater technicians how a play should be dramatized. Stage directions may specify such things as how the setting should appear in each scene, how the actors should deliver their lines, when the stage curtain should rise and fall, how stage lights should be used, where on the stage the actors should be during the action, and when sound effects should be used.

stanza   A group of lines in poetry set apart by blank lines before and after the group; a poetic verse.

style   The distinctive way in which an author composes a

work of literature in written or spoken language.

suspense   An effect created by authors of various types of fiction and drama, especially adventure and mystery, to heighten interest in the story.

symbol   An image, person, place, or thing that is used to express the idea of something else.

T

tall tale   A kind of folk tale, or legend, that exaggerates the characteristics of its hero or heroine.

theme   The main idea or underlying subject of a work of literature.

tone   The attitude that a work of literature expresses to the reader through its style.

tragedy   In classical drama, a tragedy depicts a noble hero or heroine who makes a mistake of judgment that has disastrous consequences.

V

verse   A stanza in a poem. Also, a synonym for poetry as a genre. [See also *stanza*.]

voice   The narrator or the person who relates the action of a piece of literature. [See also *speaker*.]

ACKNOWLEDGMENTS

Grateful acknowledgment is made for permission to reprint the following copyrighted material.

"The Naming of Names" by Ray Bradbury, copyright 1949 by Ray Bradbury, is reprinted by permission of Don Congdon Associates, Inc.

"Paradise Lost" by Elizabeth Vitton from the December 1990 issue of 3-2-1 Contact Magazine, copyright © 1990, Children's Television Workshop (New York, NY). All rights reserved.

"Harrison Bergeron" by Kurt Vonnegut, Jr., from Welcome to the Monkey House by Kurt Vonnegut, Jr. Copyright © 1961 by Kurt Vonnegut, Jr. Used by permission of Delacorte Press/Seymour Lawrence, a division of Bantam Doubleday Dell Publishing Group, Inc.

"Orbiter 5 Shows How Earth Looks from the Moon" by May Swenson is reprinted by permission of Macmillan Publishing Company from The Complete Poems to Solve by May Swenson. Copyright © 1993 by The Literary Estate of May Swenson.

"If I Forget Thee, Oh Earth . . . " by Arthur C. Clarke, copyright 1953 by Arthur C. Clarke, is reprinted from Tales from Planet Earth by permission of Scott Meredith Literary Agency.

"Homecoming" by Stephen David is reprinted from Science Fiction Stories by permission.

"So, You Want to Be an Astronaut" by Michael Ryan. Reprinted by permission of the author and the author's agents, Scovil Chichak Galen Literary Agency, Inc., 381 Park Avenue South, New York, New York 10016. Reprinted with permission from Parade, copyright © 1993.

"User Friendly" by T. Ernesto Bethancourt, copyright © 1989 by T. Ernesto Bethancourt from Connections: Short Stories by Donald R. Gallo, Editor. Used by permission of Delacorte Press, a division of Bantam Doubleday Dell Publishing Group, Inc.

"Where the Rainbow Ends" by Richard Rive is reprinted from Poems from Black Africa, edited by Langston Hughes, copyright ©1963 by Langston Hughes.

ILLUSTRATION

32 Map by John Rumery; 62-77 Eve Olitsky.

PHOTOGRAPHY

4 l, r Julie Bidwell/©D.C. Heath; 5 NASA; 6 Sarah Putnam/©D.C. Heath; 8–9 NASA; 10 t Richard Haynes/©D.C. Heath; b Jim Whitmer/Stock Boston; 11 t, c Sarah Putnam/©D.C. Heath; b John Owens/©D.C. Heath; 12–28 William Lesch/Swanstock; 29 l AP/Wide World Photos; r William Lesch/Swanstock; 30–31 Kathleen Norris Cook; 32 Thomas L. Kelly; 32–33 background Hans Silvester/Rapho; 33 Stephen Dalton/Animals Animals/Earth Scenes; 34 Frans Lanting/Minden Pictures; 35 t Gary Braasch; b Raymond A. Mendez/Animals Animals/ Earth Scenes; 36 l Frans Lanting/Minden Pictures; r Michael Fogden/Animals Animals/Earth Scenes; 37 Frans Lanting/Minden Pictures; 38 t Frans Lanting/Minden Pictures; b E.R. Degginger/Animals Animals/Earth Scenes; 39 t Michael Fogden/Animals Animals/Earth Scenes; b Photo by Jeff Kelly; 40, 45, 49 Courtesy Sperone Westwater, New York; 51 UPI/Bettmann Archive; 52–53 NASA; 53 b Courtesy of Literary Estate of Mary Swenson; 54–55, 58, 60, 61 NASA; 78–79, 82, 83 Courtesy of Saff Tech Arts; 84–99 Courtesy of International Business Machines Corporation; 99 inset Photo by Tom Tondee; 100–101 Frank Siteman/Tony Stone Images; 103 Nancy Sheehan; 106 Jerry Berndt/Stock Boston; 107 Arthur Tilley/FPG International; 108 Ken O'Donoghue/©D.C. Heath; 112 Sarah Putnam/©D.C. Heath; 113 Jon Nickson/©D.C. Heath; 114 Rhoda Sidney/Stock Boston; 115 Edward Koren. Back cover t Julie Bidwell/©D.C. Heath; c, b Sarah Putnam/©D.C. Heath.

Full Pronunciation Key for Footnoted Words

(Each pronunciation and definition is adapted from *Scott, Foresman Advanced Dictionary* by E.L. Thorndike and Clarence L. Barnhart.)

The pronunciation of each footnoted word is shown just after the word, in this way: **abbreviate** [ə brē′ vē āt]. The letters and signs used are pronounced as in the words below. The mark ′ is placed after a syllable with primary or heavy accent, as in the example above. The mark ′ after a syllable shows a secondary or lighter accent, as in **abbreviation** [ə brē′ vē ā′ shən].

Some words, taken from foreign languages, are spoken with sounds that do not otherwise occur in English. Symbols for these sounds are given in the key as "foreign sounds."

a	hat, cap	j	jam, enjoy	u	cup, butter	**foreign sounds**
ā	age, face	k	kind, seek	ù	full, put	
ä	father, far	l	land, coal	ü	rule, move	Y as in French *du*. Pronounce (ē) with the lips rounded as for (ü).
b	bad, rob	m	me, am	v	very, save	
ch	child, much	n	no, in	w	will, woman	
d	did, red	ng	long, bring	y	young, yet	à as in French *ami*. Pronounce (ä) with the lips spread and held tense.
				z	zero, breeze	
e	let, best	o	hot, rock	zh	measure, seizure	
ē	equal, be	ō	open, go			œ as in French *peu*. Pronounce (ā) with the lips rounded as for (ō).
ėr	term, learn	ô	order, all	ə represents:		
		oi	oil, voice		a in about	
f	fat, if	ou	house, out		e in taken	N as in French *bon*. The N is not pronounced, but shows that the vowel before it is nasal.
g	go, bag				i in pencil	
h	he, how	p	paper, cup		o in lemon	
		r	run, try		u in circus	
i	it, pin	s	say, yes			H as in German *ach*. Pronounce (k) without closing the breath passage.
ī	ice, five	sh	she, rush			
		t	tell, it			
		th	thin, both			
		ŦH	then, smooth			

UNCONQUERED

HEATH
MIDDLE LEVEL
LITERATURE

H E A T H
MIDDLE LEVEL
LITERATURE

Unconquered

▼ **T H E M E**
SURVIVAL

A U T H O R S

Donna Alvermann
Linda Miller Cleary
Kenneth Donelson
Donald Gallo
Alice Haskins
J. Howard Johnston
John Lounsbury
Alleen Pace Nilsen
Robert Pavlik
Jewell Parker Rhodes
Alberto Alvaro Ríos
Sandra Schurr
Lyndon Searfoss
Julia Thomason
Max Thompson
Carl Zon

277

STAFF CREDITS

EDITORIAL	Barbara A. Brennan, Susan Belt Cogley, DeVona Dors, Christopher Johnson, Rita M. Sullivan, Patricia B. Weiler
	Proofreading: JoAnne B. Sgroi
CONTRIBUTING WRITERS	Kathy Tuchman Glass, Jo Pitkin
SERIES DESIGN	Robin Herr
BOOK DESIGN	Caroline Bowden, Daniel Derdula, Susan Geer, Diana Maloney, Angela Sciaraffa, Bonnie Chayes Yousefian
	Art Editing: Carolyn Langley
PHOTOGRAPHY	*Series Photography Coordinator:* Carmen Johnson
	Photo Research Supervisor: Martha Friedman
	Photo Researchers: Wendy Enright, Linda Finigan, Po-yee McKenna, PhotoSearch, Inc., Gillian Speeth, Denise Theodores
	Assignment Photography Coordinators: Susan Doheny, Gayna Hoffman, Shawna Johnston
COMPUTER PREPRESS	Ricki Pappo, Kathy Meisl, Richard Curran, Michele Locatelli
PERMISSIONS	Dorothy B. McLeod
PRODUCTION	Patrick Connolly

Cover: *The Large Family* by Rene Magritte, circa 1947, Herscovici/Art Resource, N.Y.
Cover Design: Steve Snider

Acknowledgments for copyrighted material are on page 125 and constitute an extension of this page.

Published simultaneously in Canada

Printed in the United States of America

International Standard Book Number: 0-669-32111-7 (soft cover)
    4 5 6 7 8 9 10-RRD-99

International Standard Book Number: 0-669-38179-9 (hard cover)
    3 4 5 6 7 8 9 10-RRD-99 98 97 96 95

Middle Level Authors

Donna Alvermann, University of Georgia
Alice Haskins, Howard County Public Schools, Maryland
J. Howard Johnston, University of South Florida
John Lounsbury, Georgia College
Sandra Schurr, University of South Florida
Julia Thomason, Appalachian State University
Max Thompson, Appalachian State University
Carl Zon, California Assessment Collaborative

Literature and Language Arts Authors

Linda Miller Cleary, University of Minnesota
Kenneth Donelson, Arizona State University
Donald Gallo, Central Connecticut State University
Alleen Pace Nilsen, Arizona State University
Robert Pavlik, Cardinal Stritch College, Milwaukee
Jewell Parker Rhodes, Arizona State University
Alberto Alvaro Ríos, Arizona State University
Lyndon Searfoss, Arizona State University

Teacher Consultants

Suzanne Aubin, Patapsco Middle School, Ellicott City, Maryland
Judy Baxter, Newport News Public Schools, Newport News, Virginia
Saundra Bryn, Director of Research and Development, El Mirage, Arizona
Lorraine Gerhart, Elmbrook Middle School, Elm Grove, Wisconsin
Kathy Tuchman Glass, Burlingame Intermediate School, Burlingame, California
Lucretia Pannozzo, John Jay Middle School, Katonah, New York
Carol Schultz, Jerling Junior High, Orland Park, Illinois
Jeanne Siebenman, Grand Canyon University, Phoenix, Arizona
Gail Thompson, Garey High School, Pomona, California
Rufus Thompson, Grace Yokley School, Ontario, California
Tom Tufts, Conniston Middle School, West Palm Beach, Florida
Edna Turner, Harpers Choice Middle School, Columbia, Maryland
C. Anne Webb, Buerkle Junior High School, St. Louis, Missouri
Geri Yaccino, Thompson Junior High School, St. Charles, Illinois

CONTENTS

THE LITERATURE

Stairs, Provincetown Charles Demuth, 1920

Contents 5

ASKING BIG QUESTIONS ABOUT
THE LITERATURE

PROJECTS

1 WRITING WORKSHOP

WRITE A RESEARCH PAPER 106-111

Examine survival challenges as you learn the techniques and skills necessary to write a research paper.

2 COOPERATIVE LEARNING

TAKE ME TO THE FAIR 112-113

Become familiar with various cultures as you and your classmates participate in a cultural fair.

3 HELPING YOUR COMMUNITY

AND JUSTICE FOR ALL   114-115

Develop a campaign to make people aware of injustice.

The Right Stuff

1
True or false?

- You can't live by bread alone.
- Love makes the world go round.
- A person's home is his or her castle.

Food, shelter, and love are important ingredients in survival. But they are not the only ones. Work with a partner or in a group to answer the question, "What is necessary for survival?"

2
Survival means . . .

The boxes on this page contain some of the right stuff for survival. Study the ingredients in each box. What other ingredients can you add? Write your answers on a separate sheet of paper.

- Giving and receiving love

- Having opportunities to succeed

- Feeling safe and secure

- Having knowledge

- Having food, water, and shelter

- Being accepted by others

- Having friends

SURVIVAL

3 One Step at a Time

Imagine climbing a ladder like the one shown. Each rung on the ladder contains a survival ingredient. As you climb the ladder, you can take the ingredient on each rung with you. But the ladder is steep, and you're not sure you can reach the top. What will you place on the first rung of the ladder? What will you place on the next rung?

4 The Right Slot

Working alone or in small groups, create a survival ladder. First, identify the ingredients that you or your group consider important. Then place each ingredient on a rung. Put the most important ingredients at or near the bottom. Put those you may be able to do without further up. Be prepared to defend or explain your choices.

When you have finished, compare your ladder with others in your class. How are the ladders alike? How are they different?

Asking Big Questions About the Theme

What is survival?

The word *survive* comes from the Latin word *vivere*, meaning "to live." But survival is more than living. Survival implies the triumph of the spirit and the body over overwhelming obstacles. In your journal, summarize survival stories you've read about or heard about in the news. If appropriate, include survival situations faced by your family and friends. Use these situations to brainstorm for definitions of survival.

What does it take to survive?

Some people have almost everything they need or want. Others have the basics and a few extras that make their lives more pleasant. And still others have few, if any, of the basics of survival. What do *you* need to survive? What can you do without? Use a chart like the one shown to record your answers in your journal. Remember that your journal is private. You do not have to share your answers.

Things I Need	Things I Could Do Without

What kinds of survival challenges have different cultures faced?

People face survival challenges as individuals. But sometimes the survival of an entire group is threatened. For example, the arrival of Christopher Columbus and later Europeans threatened the survival of Native Americans. Working in small groups or as a class, make a chart like the one shown, of other groups whose survival has been challenged. Use your knowledge of history and current events to help you.

Group Survival	Challenges
Native Americans	Destruction of ways of life by European explorers

Why do people threaten one another's survival?

Have you ever been bullied or teased? If so, you may have asked, "What is wrong with me?" The answer is, "*Nothing* is wrong with you." The problem lies in the other person. In your journal, write down some imaginary or real situations in which one person threatens another. Then move on to a global perspective and think about historical situations in which one nation threatens another. Discuss these situations in small groups and then brainstorm to find reasons for the actions of the threatening nation.

NOW

Think!

With a partner or in a small group, write other questions about survival in your journal. As you read the literature and complete the activities and projects that follow, consider answers for the Big Questions and your own questions.

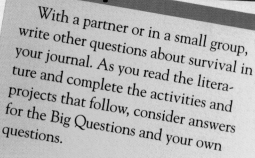

LEWIS H. LATIMER

Unconquered and Unconquerable

What tho' I suffer through the years
Unnumbered wrongs, unnumbered fears
My soul doth still forbid me tears
Unconquered and unconquerable

What tho' my bed of thorns be made   5
What tho' my onward cruise be stayed
My soul soars upward undismayed
Unconquered and unconquerable

What tho' by chains confined I lie
What tho' by brutal hands I die   10
My soul will upward ever fly
Unconquered and unconquerable

I scorn the hand that did me wrong
Tho' suffering days and years be long
My soul still charts that deathless song   15
Unconquered and unconquerable

LEWIS H. LATIMER

Louis Howard Latimer [1848-1928] was born in Chelsea, Massachusetts. When he was fifteen years old, he was one of the first African Americans to enlist in the Union Navy.

An engineer and an inventor as well as a poet, he invented the first incandescent electric light bulb with a carbon filament. As an engineer for Edison Company, he supervised the first installation of electric lights in New York, Philadelphia, Montreal, and London.

His poetry is in a book called *Poems of Love and Life*.

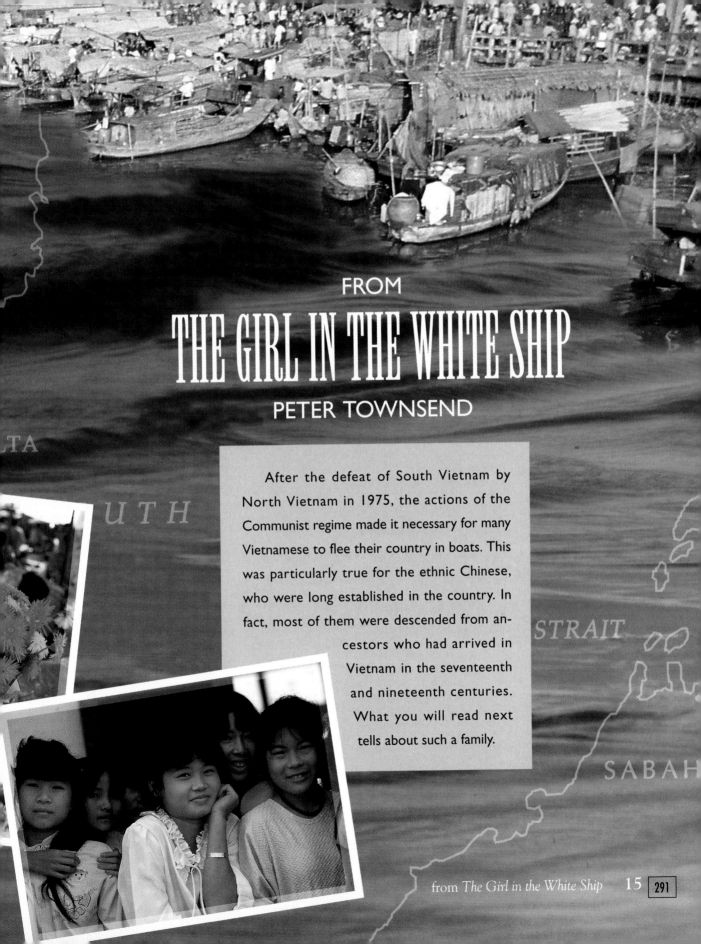

FROM

THE GIRL IN THE WHITE SHIP

PETER TOWNSEND

After the defeat of South Vietnam by North Vietnam in 1975, the actions of the Communist regime made it necessary for many Vietnamese to flee their country in boats. This was particularly true for the ethnic Chinese, who were long established in the country. In fact, most of them were descended from ancestors who had arrived in Vietnam in the seventeenth and nineteenth centuries. What you will read next tells about such a family.

One day at the end of August, when the evening meal was finished and Co Ut,[1] the housekeeper, had gone home, Tinh[2] got up
and quietly closed all the windows of the living room. The children
wondered why, until he spoke to them in his calm voice: "Gather
around, I have something to tell you." They came to him, and his
voice became grave as he went on. "Listen. In about two weeks we
are all going to escape, to leave our home forever and sail to
Malaysia.[3] From there I'll contact our cousin Ly To[4] in Australia,
which will be our new home. All the plans for the journey to
Malaysia are made. There will be ninety people in the boat and we
will leave at midnight on September twelfth, two nights before the
full moon. By then the moon festival will have begun, so the curfew
will be relaxed and we'll be able to move around with less danger
from the police."

As Tinh talked, Le Mai[5] looked absently in front of her. She had
known his plans for weeks and did not want to listen; she was thinking how hard it would be to leave behind her own and Tinh's widowed mothers and her sister Phuong.[6] The children, however,
listened intently as Tinh continued: "You all know that the secret
police have an eye on us. They have not bothered us seriously since
they closed down the shop, but you must always remember that they
or their informers may be watching and listening. They are the first
danger to get by, though there will be others once we are at sea. The
police, if they catch us, will put us in prison and then we'll be moved
to a New Economic Zone. You little ones must not repeat a single
word of what I have told you, even among yourselves. You go on as if
you knew nothing."

The children's hearts beat faster as their father spoke. His voice,
so calm and serious, made the danger feel more real. When he had

1. **Co Ut** [kō ůt]
2. **Tinh** [tēn]
3. **Malaysia** [mə lā′ zhə]: a country in Southeast Asia, south of Vietnam.
4. **Ly To** [lē tō]
5. **Le Mai** [lā mäē]
6. **Phuong** [fwōng]

finished speaking the children were silent. They needed time for his words to sink in, to work on their minds. They reacted in their own fashion. Hue Hue's[7] one terror was that the police might catch them; she did not give a thought for the voyage, except that she longed for it to start. She could not help feeling sad at the idea of leaving, nor could she bring herself to believe that she would never again see her friends or their house, with all its memories. It hurt to think that she must leave her friends without even saying good-bye.

Trung,[8] like his mother, said little; his thoughts too were far away. He was thrilled at the promise of a new life in Australia. Forget the police, he thought to himself; and the voyage too. In a few months we will be there. As for Quang[9] and To,[10] they were chattering excitedly about the police; they dreaded them, but it would be exciting to give them the slip and then sail away across the sea to Malaysia. "Bet you'll be the first to be seasick," To laughed at Quang. "If you win I'll give you ten *dong*.[11] They won't be any good anyway where we're going."

For the children the next two weeks seemed endless. In class their thoughts would often wander to the secret their father had told them. The teacher would snap, "Pay attention, there, what do you think you're dreaming of?" At the beginning of the second week in September, the family gathered at midday in a nearby restaurant for a farewell party. There were those who were leaving—Tinh and Le Mai and the children; Le Mai's younger sister, the children's twenty-three-year-old Aunt Binh;[12] and their cousin Ly Tu Dan[13] of about the same age. And there were those who were being left—Le Mai's mother, her other sister, Phuong, and her brother and his wife, as well as Tinh's mother, his sister Ngan,[14] and his two brothers. Phuong

7. **Hue Hue** [hủā hủā]
8. **Trung** [trủng]
9. **Quang** [kwäng]
10. **To** [tō]
11. *dong* [dông]
12. **Binh** [bēn]
13. **Ly Tu Dan** [lē tủ dǎn]
14. **Ngan** [ngän]

had chosen the expensive menu: *cha gia* [15] (spring rolls), *mi* [16] (noodle soup), *nem nuong* [17] (brochette of beef), *bun tom* [18] (grilled prawns and noodles), and *chao gao* [19] (chicken and sticky rice)—all favorite dishes, which helped make the occasion seem festive. Yet not for an instant could any of them forget that this was the last time they would all be together.

The meal over, they walked to the home of Le Mai's mother for the final farewell. Tinh spoke the last words to those remaining behind. "This is the last time that we will see one another. Within a week you will get word that we have left. We ourselves will send word from Malaysia. Pray for us; we shall always pray for you." As they embraced for the last time, they were all in tears.

When at last September 12 arrived, the children were packed off to school as usual. If the housekeeper felt that their good-byes were unusually affectionate, her placid face betrayed no surprise. As the last class of the afternoon broke up, Hue Hue felt that she could not deceive her friends to the point of saying the usual, "Good-bye, see you tomorrow." She waved and called out "Good-bye," hardly able to believe that it was forever.

A little before then, a man had brought word to Tinh from Uncle Ba[20] that he was to leave the house at 6 P.M. sharp and go to warn another family in his neighborhood to rendezvous forthwith at the marketplace, Ninh Kieu,[21] beside the small river Cau Cui.[22] Tinh's own family were to gather at the same spot. The departure was on.

At midday, as the housekeeper made ready to return to her home, Le Mai stopped her and Tinh said, "We are going to leave very soon. Don't come back, we shall say good-bye to you now." As she had

15. *cha gia* [tyä yä]
16. *mi* [mē]
17. *nem nuong* [nem nwong]
18. *bun tom* [bùn tom]
19. *chao gao* [tyäw gäw]
20. **Ba** [bä]
21. **Ninh Kieu** [nin kyiw]
22. **Cau Cui** [käw kuy]

done earlier that morning with the children, the housekeeper showed no surprise. They talked for some minutes, and then as they took leave, Tinh said: "Come back after we have left and help yourself to anything you want from the house. But not before five days after you hear we have gone." Five days. By then the family should be in Malaysia.

The children were all home by 4 P.M. Le Mai gave them rice and sweet pork, telling them: "Eat all you can. We'll be going hungry for the next week." When they had eaten she said to them, "Now go quietly to your rooms and change." Each of the children and their parents had set aside some old, worn clothes in which they could pass as fisherfolk. Hue Hue slipped out of her clean school uniform and changed into a grubby striped blouse and a flowery-pattern pajama, over which she pulled an old pair of black cotton trousers. She had also kept a checked jacket, threadbare at the elbows, to wear during the cool nights at sea. On her feet she wore leather sandals with a strap over the toes. Le Mai's outfit was similar. The boys had taken off their clean white shirts and carefully creased blue shorts and thrown them on the bed. Giggling, they pulled on the disguises that Tinh had procured for them and himself, the salt-stained nondescript shirt, black trousers, and typical fisherman's sandals.

Warned by Uncle Ba's unfortunate encounter earlier with the police, the family took nothing with them. The police knew too well that people carrying luggage were people bent on escaping. But each member of the family now discreetly concealed a quantity of U.S. dollar bills that Tinh had obtained on the black market; the money might come in handy for bribing the police. Tinh himself had hidden fifteen ounces troy of gold and five hundred-dollar bills in a belt around his waist. Le Mai, Aunt Binh, cousin Dan,[23] and the three boys each had two hundred- dollar bills hidden in their clothing. To Hue Hue, Tinh had entrusted, besides two hundred-dollar bills, a solid gold necklace, which she wore beneath the buttoned-up collar of her blouse.

23. **Dan** [dän]

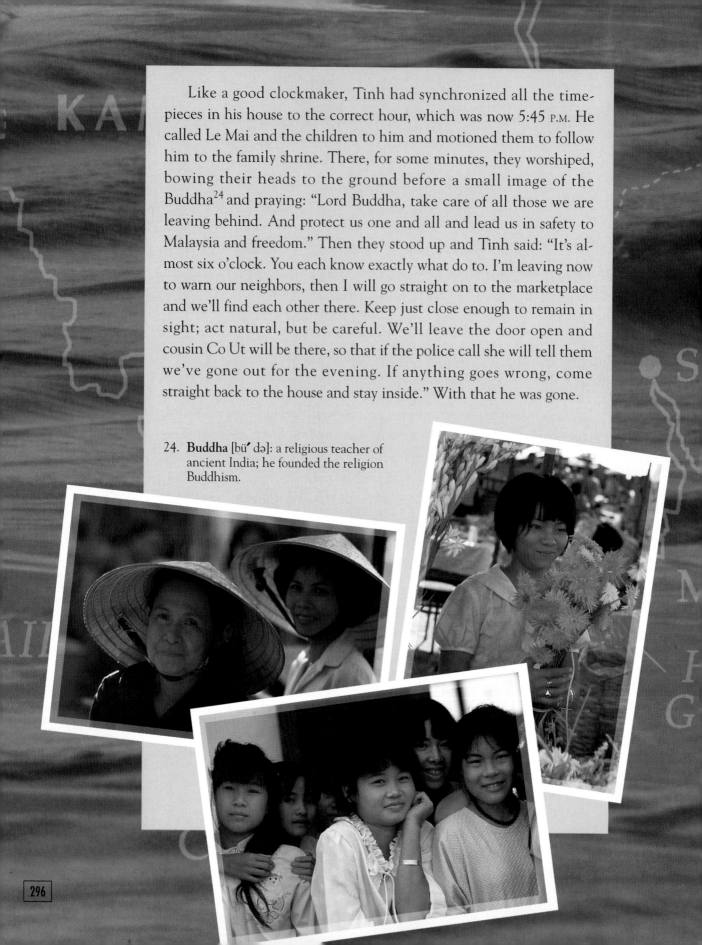

Like a good clockmaker, Tinh had synchronized all the time-pieces in his house to the correct hour, which was now 5:45 P.M. He called Le Mai and the children to him and motioned them to follow him to the family shrine. There, for some minutes, they worshiped, bowing their heads to the ground before a small image of the Buddha[24] and praying: "Lord Buddha, take care of all those we are leaving behind. And protect us one and all and lead us in safety to Malaysia and freedom." Then they stood up and Tinh said: "It's almost six o'clock. You each know exactly what do to. I'm leaving now to warn our neighbors, then I will go straight on to the marketplace and we'll find each other there. Keep just close enough to remain in sight; act natural, but be careful. We'll leave the door open and cousin Co Ut will be there, so that if the police call she will tell them we've gone out for the evening. If anything goes wrong, come straight back to the house and stay inside." With that he was gone.

24. **Buddha** [bü′ də]: a religious teacher of ancient India; he founded the religion Buddhism.

It was Hue Hue's turn to leave next. Before she did so, she ran back to her bedroom. Standing in the doorway, she glanced around, fixing in her mind the pale blue walls covered with photos of her family and friends and of her favorite actress Chan Chan.[25] On the shelf above her bed were stacked her table-tennis paddles and on the bed itself, tidily folded, her neat school uniform, white shirt and blue pleated skirt, with a heap of schoolbooks. On the pillow reclined her doll, wearing the new shirt and blue jeans she had just made for it. Good-bye, all of you and everything, she thought, and had to force back the tears. Then, firmly, thirteen-year-old Hue Hue shut the door behind her, closed it on her life in Vietnam. The odor of sweet pork and rice hanging about the house made her think: No more good things like that for a while.

A fond pat but no tears for the dog, Dolly, and Hue Hue was standing by the open front door with her mother and brothers. "See you all at the marketplace," she said. "Be careful." She turned and began walking toward Ninh Kieu, the marketplace, a half-mile away. A few minutes after her came Trung, then Quang, each taking a slightly different route. Finally Le Mai left with her youngest boy, To, and her sister Binh. As arranged, Le Mai had left the front door unlocked.

Hue Hue and her family, with the rest of the ninety people intent on escaping that night, were but a few of the hundreds converging on the Ninh Kieu for the moon-festival celebrations.[26] Hue Hue walked at a leisurely pace, yet every fiber of her small body was taut. This was another game, an escaping game, which, like running or table tennis, would need all her wits and determination if she was to win it. She noticed with some perplexity that her sandals seemed unusually heavy. Every now and again they slipped off her feet. She did not discover till later that Tinh had inserted five *la*—gold leaves—between the upper and lower soles, which added two ounces to the weight of each sandal.

At about half-past six Hue Hue reached the market. Dusk was falling; the night was warm and not a breath of wind stirred the

25. **Chan Chan** [tyän tyän]
26. **moon-festival celebrations**: special festival for children.

palm trees. Stars were beginning to shine in a cloudless, darkening sky; festive music played throughout the marketplace. That night was one of the most beautiful that Hue Hue could remember. She loitered for a while near the food shops that, with the bus company's ticket office, were the only establishments open. She noticed a few policemen strolling among the crowds but did not feel afraid of them. The moon festival was a festival for children, and so there were many of them in the marketplace, each with a lantern, each eating candy and moon-cake that made Hue Hue's mouth water, while their parents greeted their friends, chatted, and laughed. The moon festival seemed to have put everybody back into a good mood.

Scanning the crowds for the rest of the family, Hue Hue had no difficulty in spotting them in the glare of the gaslights; each made a sign of mutual recognition; then, still keeping their distance, they moved toward the bank of the Cau Cui. Hue Hue sat down on the ground at the riverbank, and began to chat with her brother Trung, her young Aunt Binh, and her cousin Dan.

About twenty paces away, she could just make out her father and mother seated on a bench with Quang and To. They too were chatting quietly. Tinh had just remarked to Le Mai: "It is hard to believe that fifteen years ago, on this very spot, we opened a fine shop, and now we are refugees fleeing to save our lives." Hue Hue's thoughts were running on the same theme.

On the river, boats and sampans[27] kept coming and going, ferrying people and vehicles to and fro from one end of National Route 4 to where it began again on the opposite

27. **sampans** [sam′panz]: small boats with oars, a single sail, and a cabin made of mats.

bank. Close to where Hue Hue and the others were sitting, two sampans floated at their moorings. Those two weather-beaten little craft had a vital role to play. Everyone had been warned that when they saw two men walk down to the sampans and climb aboard, it was the signal for the passengers to embark.

The evening darkened into night. In the marketplace the crowd jostled and laughed, music played, and children danced, lanterns in hand. The festival was in full swing.

It was around eight o'clock when Hue Hue noticed two men walking casually down to where the sampans were moored only a few yards away from her. She nudged Trung. "Look," she whispered, "the signal!" A moment later, out of the crowd, Uncle Ba appeared at her side. He bent down and in a quiet voice said, "Come along, Hue Hue and Trung and the rest of you; all aboard!" Others followed, some carrying children, some leading them by the hand, walking toward the sampans.

Soon Hue Hue's sampan, crammed with people including Uncle Ba, put off into the river and headed downstream; its gunwales were almost level with the water, which came seeping over at the slightest rolling movement. Hue Hue was sure the sampan was going to sink, but five minutes later it was bumping along the side of the big boat and Hue Hue, Trung, Binh, and Dan, and all the others were climbing aboard up a short wooden ladder. Hue Hue sat down on deck, Trung next to her. She looked around at the faces, dimly visible in the moonlight, to make sure that her parents and brothers were there, and discovered that they were not. She remarked on this to Trung, who reassured her: "Don't worry, Hue Hue, they will be along with the next lot."

Minutes went by. The second sampan, followed some moments later by Uncle Ba's with another load of passengers, came alongside. Carefully, Hue Hue searched the face of every passenger, until the last one stepped on deck. Still no sign of her parents and brothers. By now, she was so worried that she called out to Uncle Ba, who just then was climbing back down the ladder into his sampan. "Where are my parents and my brothers?" she asked, almost crying. Uncle Ba called back, "Don't worry, Hue Hue, I'll bring them along with the next lot." Then he and his sampan disappeared upstream into the darkness.

As he pulled in toward the riverbank at the marketplace, something looked amiss to Uncle Ba. The sampan drifted closer to the riverbank. Then, to his consternation, he saw that one of the waiting passengers was being questioned by a policeman, automatic rifle in hand. He saw Tinh standing a pace away from them. Ba stepped ashore and from a safe distance waited to see what would happen.

Tinh, meanwhile, despite the gold and dollar bills he carried on him, decided that this was not the moment to try bribing the police. His courage deserting at the thought that he, too, might be questioned and searched, he began to tremble visibly. Le Mai did the same, while the two little boys just stood there, petrified. They heard the policeman ask the man, "What are you all doing, hanging around here?" and the man's unhurried answer, "We are waiting to buy bus tickets to return to our homes in the country." The policeman appeared satisfied and walked away. As he did so, Tinh and his family and all the other fugitives, the 40 of them who remained ashore, made haste to disperse, disappearing under the palm trees, fading into the shadows. For them the riverbank at Ninh Kieu had become a decidedly unhealthy place.

As Tinh hurried away, half-running with his family, he passed within a few feet of his friend Ba. With so many people about, Ba could only speak in a loud whisper. "Come on, Tinh," he urged. "If you are coming, come now or it will be too late. I'm leaving." Ba was about to add, "Hue Hue and Trung are already aboard," when Tinh cut him short. "How can I possibly come with you," he pleaded, "and leave my two older children behind?" Without giving Ba a chance to explain, he rushed off into the dark with Le Mai and the two little boys.

Uncle Ba turned back toward his sampan. It was no longer there. He made for one of the waiting ferry-sampans, climbed into it, and pressed forty *dong*, instead of the usual two, into the hand of the astonished boatman. "Take it and keep your mouth shut," he ordered. "Row me downstream until I tell you to stop." Five minutes later the confused and frightened Uncle Ba was aboard the boat. To a young man who sat counting the passengers as they boarded Ba hissed, "How many?" "Fifty including you," the man replied. "All right. Pass the word around that we're leaving this instant. The police have discovered us." As he spoke, Ba fumbled with the engine controls, found the starter button, and pushed it. The diesel motor spluttered into life, then settled down, turning over steadily. "Cast off," ordered Ba, and called for Chu Nhi.[28] "Chu Nhi, where are you? Come and take over!" But Chu Nhi, who knew all about motors, especially this one, and was able to steer a compass course, was still on dry land, his pocket compass in his shirt pocket. Chu Nhi had missed the boat and there was not a soul on board competent to sail it.

In the wheelhouse Uncle Ba, his nerves taut, peered forward until his nose nearly touched the glass window. Next to him stood Trung, who Ba had told to stand by as messenger and lookout. Easing the boat away from its hidden moorings, Ba headed her carefully down the Cau Cui and into the broad waters of the Hau Giang,[29] the river that led down to the sea. From his brief war service in navy riverboats, Ba knew he could get the boat that far—he did not allow his thoughts to wander further. He must concentrate, get safely through the river traffic, keep a sharp lookout for the river police. He could see no reason why a riverboat with most of its fifty passengers hidden below deck should attract attention. All the same he warned Trung, "Keep your eyes skinned."

28. **Chu Nhi** [tyŭ nē]
29. **Hau Giang** [häw gyäng]

Soon Ba began to relax a little and it was then that he became conscious of a commotion below deck, sounds of wailing and moaning. "Go and see what's the matter," Ba told Trung, who disappeared. A few minutes later he was back. "It's the families who've been split up. They're going nearly mad. There's a girl of twelve who's crying and crying because her parents have been left behind. Other people are calling for their wives or their husbands and children." Ba said nothing, but continued through the glass of the wheelhouse. He was aware of a disturbing feeling that the boat, from the moment she got under way, was to be an unhappy one.

Trung had been able to have a few words with Hue Hue. Neither of them yet quite realized the drama of their situation. They had often talked about escaping alone. Well, this was it. They were completely on their own, cut off from their family. Trung said, "Get some sleep, Hue Hue," and went to join Ba in the wheelhouse. Below, on one of the wooden planks that had been laid on the cross-members of the boat, Hue Hue dozed, wedged tightly between two other people and maddeningly aware that she was being devoured by mosquitoes. Then she fell asleep, slumped against one of her neighbors. Occasionally she awoke and shifted herself from one uncomfortable position to another. Through a tiny porthole she saw palm trees go by and knew that the boat was still sailing down the river.

Tinh had shepherded his family safely through the dark back to the house. He opened the door and his cousin Co Ut, astonished, asked, "Why have you come back?" "The police," replied Tinh, quickly adding, "and Trung and Hue Hue. They're not back?" "Not yet," said Co Ut, "but they must be on their way." Tinh, Le Mai, and the boys, still feeling frightened, went to the sitting room. A few minutes later they heard the door open. "Must be them." But the two people at the door were friends of Tinh, and during the next twenty minutes more friends arrived. All were members of the escape group who lived near the police station and dared not go home. Tinh and Le Mai welcomed them mechanically, asking each one, "Have you seen Trung and Hue?" No one had seen either of the two children.

Tinh's clocks were all striking midnight; their concerted chimes nearly drove him mad, for they told him that three hours had passed since he last saw Ba, and that Trung and Hue Hue were still missing. Where could they be? Arrested? If so, he would find out tomorrow. Still at the moon festival? Tinh dismissed the idea. Those two loved to have fun, but they would never have disobeyed his instruction to return home should anything go wrong. Then he remembered the words that Ba had called after him: "Come on, Tinh, I'm leaving." Were his children with Ba? He spoke to Le Mai: "I think they must have left with Uncle Ba and the rest. Perhaps he'll turn back, then we can join them tomorrow." But Le Mai was not to be consoled by such a frail hope. She had been on the verge of breaking down since they returned to the house, and now through her tears she reproached Tinh. "You should never have allowed the children to get into such terrible danger." Tinh, venturing a last hope, replied, "But if they are with Ba, they should be safe enough."

When Tinh, exhausted, finally stretched out on his bed, it was nearly 3 A.M., six hours since the boat had left. He was now sure that Hue Hue and Trung were in it. Alone with his thoughts in the dark, his optimism vanished. When, if ever, would he see them again? He turned over and cried quietly to himself. In their beds Le Mai and the two little boys were crying too. No one slept that night.

Next morning Tinh's uninvited guests left his house and slipped back to their own, but others came to call on him. Tinh was well known in Cantho.[30] "We saw you down at the river last night," they said, eager for gossip. "Were you trying to escape?" Tinh, putting on a brave face, replied as politely as he could: "How could I have been trying to escape since I'm still here?" All the same, the gossip spread. It was bound, sooner or later, to reach the ears of the police. Meanwhile, Tinh and Le Mai forced themselves to carry on as if it were just another day. Quang and To were sent off to school, but not

30. **Cantho** [kän tō´]

before Tinh told them: "If you are asked about your brother and sister, say that they have gone to Saigon."[31]

Half a dozen boys and girls, friends of Trung and Hue Hue, came to the house that evening. They—and others, no doubt, including the teachers—had noticed their absence in class; that must mean that they had escaped. Tinh led them inside to Le Mai and the boys. One of Hue Hue's friends, Hoa,[32] spoke for the rest. "We want to say how sorry we are and how much we all miss them. We shall go to the temple and pray that they will return safely to you." But not all the sympathy of their own and the children's friends could alter the cruel reality of the two empty places at table. As Le Mai later said: "We ate rice mixed with tears."

Three nights after the children's disappearance, Tinh, sleeping fitfully, had a strange dream. He saw Trung and Hue Hue on a rock in the middle of the sea. They were both naked and were clearly alive. Then, bending over him, Tinh saw an aged saffron-robed[33] priest, with drooping mustaches and a long white beard. "How many children have you?" asked the bonze, and Tinh replied, "Four, but two are away." "Yes," said the old man, "two are away and they are both dead." Tinh struggled to free himself from the dream. He sat up, sweating. "No," he said aloud, "I saw them, they are both still alive." Straight away he got up, crept silently to the family shrine, and prayed. "Keep them safe, let them live. Send them back to us."

The motion of the boat awoke Hue Hue. She opened her eyes and realized that they were well out to sea. Trung was squatting next to her. Somehow he had managed to fit himself in between her and the next passenger. Drowsily she said, "Hullo, Chung Co.[34] Have you seen the others?" But before Trung could reply, Hue Hue had realized "the others" were not there. She burst into tears and her brother, weary after a night on watch, felt himself being carried away by his sister's crying.

31. **Saigon** [sī gon′]: now called Ho Chi Minh City; it was the capital of South Vietnam.
32. **Hoa** [hōä]
33. **saffron** [saf′ rən]: an orange-yellow color.
34. **Chung Co** [tyŭng kō]

He, too, began to cry and they sat there, wedged one against the other in the crowd, utterly lost. After a while Trung took hold of himself. "Cheer up, Hue Hue," he said. "We'll stick together, whatever happens."

Hue Hue's eyes were fixed on the small porthole. At one moment it was filled with pale blue sky; then, as the boat rolled, the horizon came up and erased the sky until there was only blue-gray sea. Down came the horizon again until the porthole was again full of sky. Hue Hue felt very seasick. "Come on, let's go up on deck," Trung said. They managed to squeeze side by side into the row of people sitting on deck back against the boat's side, their knees gathered into their clasped hands. Hue Hue remarked to Trung: "To think there should have been forty more on board! Already we are packed like sardines."

The sun was riding up into an empty blue sky, blazing hotter every minute. Hue Hue held up her checked jacket to protect herself, but her arms soon tired and she lay down, covering her head with it. All but a few of the passengers were seasick like her. The retching and vomiting, the mess, the stench mixed with diesel fumes: Hue Hue realized that her own misery was caused not so much by the motion of the boat as by the stinking, stifling atmosphere. "Come with me, Trung," said Hue Hue, and began to make toward the bow, not walking—that was impossible—but crawling on all fours across the splayed, groaning bodies on deck. Once up in the bow, with a breeze blowing on her face, Hue Hue felt a little better. Trung too; for the first time since leaving, they exchanged a smile. It was only a fleeting one, however, for Hue Hue suddenly remembered: "This time yesterday," she said, on the verge of tears, "we were on our way to school with Quang and To."

At the other extremity of the boat, in the stern, were the heads, the latrines. There was sitting room for two on a plank placed athwartships,[35] each end supported by a beam that extended on either side just beyond the stern, so that the excrement would drop straight into the sea—a precarious perch, but at least screened from the public gaze by two half-barrels sectioned vertically.

In spite of the breeze, Trung and Hue Hue's seasickness persisted. Yet they felt hungry. Hue Hue nibbled at a *cusan*, a sweet, pulpy fruit;

35. **athwartships** [ə thwôrt′ shipz]: placed across from side to side of the ship.

she sucked it a little and handed it to Trung, who did the same. For days, this was to be their daily portion, for the nausea and the motion of the boat made their stomachs revolt at anything more substantial. Others, recovering from their seasickness, became ravenous for solid food. They quarreled and swore at each other as they fought for their share of the rice and dried fish. Drinking water was rationed to a cup a day. It was not enough to assuage their thirst, and many of the people found some relief by jumping into the sea, a rope around them, and being trailed for a few minutes alongside. Hue Hue enjoyed this, but the salt water, as it dried out, began to eat into her striped blouse and flowered pajamas. So she remained aboard, parched from thirst, watching the waves roll past the boat and sending an occasional shower of spray over her.

When Uncle Ba was not steering, he tried to put some order into life on board, rationing the food and organizing the passengers into groups of about ten, each with a leader, and telling them to take special care of the aged and the mothers and children. Hue Hue's group included Trung, cousin Dan, and Aunt Binh. Binh was sick and depressed, and Hue Hue, too, felt so helpless with seasickness that she almost wanted to die. But Van, a girl in her twenties who was a friend of the family, urged her to hold on; it would be for only a few more days. Hue Hue was lucky with her group. Elsewhere the system broke down and it was everyone for himself.

Uncle Ba, as uncertain of his authority over the ship's company as of the direction in which it was heading, bravely tried to keep up his own and everybody else's spirits. "Don't worry," he reassured them, "last night I was navigating by the stars. We are on a steady course to Malaysia. A few more days and we shall be there." But on reaching the mouth of the River Hau Giang that morning, poor Uncle Ba had also reached the limit of his navigational experience. He had never been to sea and, on meeting it at the river's mouth, was at a complete loss. He should have altered course some 90° to the west. That would have put the boat on a course to the Malaysian coast, with a landfall somewhere near Pulau Bidong,[36] the island

36. **Pulau Bidong** [pu läw′ bē dông′]

refugee camp that had opened two months earlier, in July. Instead he swung the helm some 30° eastward and kept straight on into the middle of the most dangerous waters in Southeast Asia—the South China Sea.

The first day out, the boat began to take water, which the bilge pump spewed back into the sea. Next morning, the engine faltered, picked up, faltered again, and stopped. In a calm sea the boat hove to, and Hue Hue watched as a small group of people bent over the engine. As they tinkered with it, she heard them repeating *zoupape*, *zoupape*. She had never heard the word but it intrigued her and she asked Trung what it meant. He told her. "We borrowed it from the French, *soupape*, valve." The engine had valve trouble, a serious defect at any time but a dangerous one on the high sea, especially in a leaky boat. When the engine stopped working, the bilge pump stopped working too. The boat began to take water fast, and in the cramped space below deck men began frantically bailing, their plastic buckets full of water being passed back along a line formed by other passengers to be tipped into the sea and passed back again to the front of the line. An hour went by, then another, as the powerless boat drifted. During that time two merchantmen passed not more than a half mile away and the people on the roof of the wheelhouse waved energetically. Their efforts were in vain; without a sign of recognition, the big ships sailed on their way, while the boat people hurled insults and curses after them, not believing that their signals could be so flagrantly ignored. Nothing that had happened so far had so demoralized them. They felt better when they heard the engine splutter once more into life; a thin cheer went up, and the boat was again under way, making about three miles an hour.

The second day out from land was ending; by now, the passengers, though they did not realize it, had almost crossed the main shipping lanes and were heading for an empty desert of water. Since the engine failure they had passed one more merchantman, but Ba had warned: "Don't make any sign. It looks like a Soviet ship." The

Russians were known to pick up boat people and land them back in Vietnam, a fate worse than drowning.

That night the engine stopped twice more, and each time pandemonium broke out below, with the fetid air full of cries and swearwords—"Fix the engine, for God's sake; we're going to sink"—and the screaming of frightened children. Flashlights shone and buckets were again passed from hand to hand. A gale began blowing up—it was the tail of the monsoon[37] season—and the helpless, overloaded boat, tossed here and there by the waves, took so much water that it felt as if it were going to capsize. Then the motor started up, the boat moved forward again, and the panic subsided.

All next day the gale blew and torrents of rain, cold and stinging, blotted out the horizon. The engine kept breaking down; each time it did so, the boat people bailed for their lives. On deck, the people at the end of the line, lashed by the rain, cold, drenched, and exhausted, began to protest. In vain Ba encouraged them: "Come on, stick to it, keep bailing or we're lost." They answered: "Nothing doing. The boat's going to sink anyway!" Others took their place. For another day and night the boat people fought the storms and the faulty engine and somehow kept their craft afloat.

At last the big seas subsided into long, heaving swells and flying fish scudded across the rolling purple-blue valleys of water. No spray flew and the sea no longer came pouring over the gunwales. A fiery sun sailed again into the sky and dried out the deck till it was warm. But the problem of the engine remained; bailing had become a routine operation. On the eighth day of the voyage, the sea became still and flat; not a breath of wind rippled its glassy surface. The engine seemed to catch the mood; though it still ran unevenly, sending vibrations through the length of the boat, it miraculously kept going. By evening huge, bulbing cumulus clouds had ballooned up high into the sky, reflecting and diffusing the last rays of the setting sun and forming an unbroken barrage whose lower surface almost touched the horizon.

37. **monsoon** [mon sün′]: the rainy season during which the wind of the same
    name blows from the southwest.

In the fading, pink-gold light the boat chugged on, throwing up a little phosphorescent bow wave that slid down each side until its dancing sparks were extinguished in the turbulence of the wake.

With Trung beside her, Hue Hue had been watching the sunset. Her thoughts temporarily distracted by its splendor, she forgot her pangs of hunger and the nausea that had cloyed her throat and the pit of her stomach for over a week. Life had dragged on painfully through long, anxious days and restless nights—days and nights punctuated by periods of stifling heat; by raging storms and the anguished cries of frightened people; by the frequent failures of an old and unreliable engine, whose pungent fumes mingled with the stench of sick humanity; and, at last, by the calm that had fallen over the sea and the boat itself.

Throughout the turmoil of the voyage, Hue Hue's thoughts had dwelt ceaselessly on her parents and brothers back in Vietnam. She was only thirteen; she missed her family terribly and cried whenever she imagined them at home. But Binh and Van had been sweet to her; Trung was always at her side; and Dan helped to encourage her.

She looked around the crowded deck. Where were they going, all these people, most of them unknown to her? Before them lay nothing but sea, stretching out to the horizon, and the clouds, now darkening into gray against a vivid blue-green sky.

It began to get chilly, so Hue Hue and Trung moved below, squeezed themselves in between some others, and sat down with their backs against the ship's side. As the day died so did the sound of garrulous voices. People were chatting quietly now, and peace and order had returned to the boat. Hue Hue and Trung began to doze.

Suddenly a harsh, grating sound and the crash of splitting timber jolted everyone into wakefulness. The boat came to an abrupt standstill. Through the broken hull water gushed past their feet and people shouted: "We're aground—everybody up on deck!" From their cramped quarters below, there followed a rush of old men and women, of mothers clasping their children to them or dragging them by the hand. The young men and girls clambered up last. Everyone on deck was talking excitedly. "We have hit land all right, but where? Malaysia? Thailand?" No one could answer, least of all Uncle Ba. Then above the hubbub came a voice, and a young man pointed into the fading light: "Look, a ship! There! A ship at anchor!" People peered after him and cried: "Yes, it's a ship! We're saved!" Some shook hands and embraced; others were too weary for joy.

Few of them slept that night, partly through excitement, partly because they had to camp as best they could on deck. The boat was filling fast, until, around midnight, the water, a yard deep inside the hull, had risen to the level of the sea outside. At least that would keep the boat on an even keel.

To Hue Hue the boat now felt as solid as a house. Her sickness disappeared, but like everybody else, she could not sleep. She lay there on the hard deck in the dark, her cardigan over her, a frightened little girl marooned somewhere in the middle of the sea.

PETER TOWNSEND

Peter Townsend was born in 1914 in Rangoon, Burma where his father, an Englishman, served in the Indian army. Townsend went to school and college in England. Royal Air Force College prepared him for a lifetime career. Townsend served first in Singapore, and then as a fighter pilot during the Battle of Britain in 1939-1941. After World War II, he was assigned to the Royal household as personal attendant first to King George VI and then to Queen Elizabeth II. When he retired in 1956, Townsend became a full-time author and journalist.

Townsend wrote an outstanding history of the Battle of Britain, called *Duel of Eagles*. The book includes his own memories as well as those of some German pilots whom he interviewed. Probably his most valuable books are the stories of children in war and what it can do to them. Townsend has said that he was always "impressed by children's dignity, their longing for revenge, sometimes their forgiveness." He intends these stories to be a record so that no one will forget these children, Townsend has said. "I am their witness." Among these books is *The Girl in the White Ship*.

Mother to Son

Langston Hughes

Stairs, Provincetown Charles Demuth, 1920, gouache and pencil on cardboard, 23 $\frac{1}{2}$" x 19 $\frac{1}{2}$", The Museum of Modern Art, New York

Well, son, I'll tell you:
Life for me ain't been no crystal stair.
It's had tacks in it,
And splinters,
And boards torn up,   5
And places with no carpet on the floor—
Bare.
But all the time
I'se been a-climbin' on,
And reachin' landin's,   10
And turnin' corners,
And sometimes goin' in the dark
Where there ain't been no light.
So boy, don't you turn back.
Don't you set down on the steps   15
'Cause you finds it's kinder hard.
Don't you fall now
For I'se still goin', honey,
I'se still climbin',
And life for me ain't been no crystal stair.   20

LANGSTON HUGHES

James Langston Hughes [1902-1967] was born in
Joplin, Missouri. In 1926, Hughes published his first
book of poems, titled *The Weary Blues*. His work was
widely praised and won him a college scholarship to
Lincoln University in Pennsylvania. Hughes graduated in 1929 just as the
Depression began. He had to make a living writing, as he said, to "turn
poetry into bread. It was a question of writing or starving." His work was
"largely concerned with the depicting of Negro life in America." To accomplish this, he used rhythm, dialect, and the sounds of the Harlem streets.
Besides poetry, Hughes wrote short stories, novels, essays, movie scripts,
and plays.

I'd Like to Go Alone Nina Ledererová, drawing in pencil and watercolor, State Jewish Museum, Prague, the Czech Republic

SONIA SCHREIBER WEITZ

from

I *promised* I *would tell*

As you will read in the following selection, Sonia Schreiber and her family were forced by the Nazis[1] to leave their home and move into a crowded, walled ghetto[2] with other Polish Jews. While Sonia lived in a room with her parents and three other families, Sonia's older sister Blanca and Blanca's husband Norbert belonged for a time to the Polish underground[3] and were able to help the family get food and other necessities.

---

1. **Nazis** [näʹ tsēz]: members of the National Socialist Party in Germany, led by Aldolf Hitler.
2. **ghetto** [getʹ ō]: section of a city where Jews were forced to live.
3. **underground:** movement in which people worked in secret against the Nazis.

I was twelve and a half in March 1941 when my family was forced into the ghetto. I remained there for two years. During those years, I recorded my thoughts in a diary. I had always liked to write, and in the ghetto I found that writing helped me cope a little better with the horrors around me. I especially liked writing poetry, so I also included poems in my diary.

Although my diary did not survive the war, the memory of what I had experienced and written in the ghetto did not fade. So in 1946, one year after the war ended, I sat down to write about my life in the ghetto. In fact, I tried to reconstruct from memory the original pages of my diary. The following pages contain an English translation of the "reconstructed diary" which I wrote in 1946. (In some cases, I have edited the original manuscript for clarity.)

April 1941

A month after entering the ghetto, orders came that I had to go to work. One day, other young people and I were piled into a truck and taken out of the ghetto to scrub latrines in the German barracks. At night, as we returned to the ghetto, the soldiers forced us to sing "Roll Out the Barrel" for their amusement. They laughed at the humiliation we faced in singing a cheerful tune after a day of cleaning up their filth. They also laughed because we sang in Polish, a language that the Germans considered inferior.

My mother cried that I had to do this work; she cried bitterly, although she tried to hide it. My father smoked one cigarette after the other. He looked at me with love and pity. He quietly whispered, "That's war. That's the horrible war." I think he felt guilty. The poor man knew that, even in the ghetto, if you had extra money or something of value, it was often possible to find a strong person to work in the place of a child. And so if he had the money, perhaps he could have found a substitute laborer for his beloved little girl. But we barely had money to buy food and no more valuables left. I could see the helplessness in his eyes as I went off to work.

November 1941

One evening, I returned hungry and tired to the house to see my father at the door. He seemed very worried and looked very pale. He asked me to be quiet because my mother was sick. "Sick? How could that be?" I asked. I had never seen my mother sick. No matter how tired or weak, she would always smile, hug me, and say that everything would be all right, that things would get better, that we would be going home soon, that Friday night there would be candles on the white tablecloth again, and that all would be well.

Without making a sound, I tiptoed into the dark room. She was asleep. I lit the small light and came nearer. Her face was burning and her eyes were cloudy. *Mamusiu*,[4] I whispered. I kneeled by her bed and touched her forehead. She gazed at me with a distant look. "My God, she does not know me," I thought. "Her own daughter, and she does not know me."

Later that night, she was taken to the ghetto hospital. She was very sick, suffering from meningitis.[5] Since the hospital was a place for the contagiously ill, none of us were allowed to visit her. But somehow Blanca managed to get extra food and smuggle it in to my mother. My father and I paced endlessly in front of the hospital. Weeks passed in constant fear that the hospital might be evacuated or that the patients might be executed before my mother recovered.

Finally, one day, wrapped in a blanket, my mother came to the window and waved to us. Oh, how good it was to see her! Soon after, she came home, pale and weak. Blanca continued scrounging and somehow was always able to find extra food for our mother.

March 1942

By the spring of 1942 we had almost no money left. So one day I took the last of our money and went to the bakery for bread. I looked at length at the wonderfully fresh pungent loaves of bread. I faced the

---

4. **Mamusiu** [mä mú´ sü]: (also *mamusia*) Polish for "Mama."
5. **meningitis** [men´ in jī´ tis]: an illness that is often fatal.

baker and breathlessly blurted out a long rehearsed question, "Would you trust me with ten loaves of bread at nine zloty [6] each, and I will bring the money tomorrow morning?" The answer came quickly, "Fine."

I could not believe it. I was so proud of myself. I took the ten loaves of bread and ran from one building to another, from one apartment to another, selling each loaf for ten zloty. Simple math. Each day I would earn enough money to buy a loaf of bread for my family.

On the evening of the first day, I hid the money under my pillow to protect it until morning. When morning came, I rushed to the bakery and purchased the bread. Slightly embarrassed but happy, I presented the bread to my utterly amazed mother. Unfortunately, this enterprise did not last. Orders came from the Germans to shut down the ghetto bakeries.

Still, we had to have money. So *mamusia* came up with the following plan. In the back of the house in which we lived, there was a garden—once beautiful but now brown and overgrown with weeds. In that little backyard, *mamusia* created a nursery for those children whose lives had been temporarily spared but whose parents were forced into slave labor each day. Many of these parents gladly paid whatever they could to place their children in our care.

It would still be dark when I would get up in the morning and rush from one ghetto house to another, collecting the sleepy-eyed youngsters to bring to our backyard. While my mother cooked and did the laundry, I amused the children with their favorite fairy tales. My imagination was inexhaustible, and in the sunlight I watched their happy smiling faces full of wonderment and hope.

Often, while the children napped, I would sit in the shade of a tree in that dead garden. Enjoying the few precious moments of quiet, I would fill the pages of my diary with my thoughts and feelings. I wrote that I desperately wanted to be good and kind and helpful to my *mamusia*. I wrote also about life—how precious it was and how much I wanted the horrible war to come to an end. In my childish handwriting, I wrote prayers, pleading with God for help. Somehow,

6. *zloty* [slô′ tē]

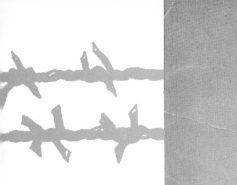

Girl with Star Leo Haas, 1943, pen and ink wash on paper, 16 ¹/₂″ x 9 ⁷/₈″, State Jewish Museum, Prague, the Czech Republic

I believed He would hear my prayers and answer them. I trusted that the future would be better. In the blessed quiet of these moments, I also wrote poetry.

A Quiet Time

> . . . *a peaceful moment*
> *to heal my soul*
> *to steady the pounding*
> *within my breast*
> . . . *a quiet time*
> *to make me whole*
> *and let me rest*

June 1942

One day in June of our second year in the ghetto, my mother got sick again. This time she refused to go to the hospital. She did not want to waste any time being separated from us. I guess she knew that our time together could be cut short any day. Transports[7] of the old, the sick, and the young were constantly leaving, never to be heard from again.

Each day my father and I carried a cot outdoors for my mother. There, in the shade of my tree, she seemed most comfortable. Often, my father would watch her from afar. He seemed so sad and embarrassed by his helplessness. My heart ached for him, but I knew that I could not approach him and discuss his feelings. He was perhaps more pitiful and bewildered than the rest of us.

Slowly, my mother returned to health. Again, to me, our little nest seemed secure. I began to study in an "underground" school where I met other young people. Education was, of course, forbidden in the ghetto, but there was a group of dedicated Jewish teachers who designed lesson plans for us, giving our young lives a degree of order and defiance.

My new school friends invited me to a "picnic" and I learned to dance. I went for long walks with my friend Rena,[8] who was in love with Bubek,[9] while I was crazy about Jerzyk.[10] Rena and I understood each other. We were both teenagers, after all.

My parents also insisted that I learn to do something useful. So I became apprenticed to a seamstress. This skill helped me get a job in a German factory called Madrich.[11] Since as a seamstress I was useful to the Germans, I was able to avoid early deportation.

We had a very active resistance movement in the ghetto. As a matter of fact, many of my friends were part of the movement. At one point, I was going to leave the ghetto and join the underground

7. **Transports:** in this context, the moving of people to a place where they were killed.
8. **Rena** [re′ nä]
9. **Bubek** [bü′ beg]
10. **Jerzyk** [yer′ sēg]
11. **Madrich** [mä′ drikH]

to fight against the Nazis. But, since the Polish partisans[12] rarely accepted Jewish men and women into their units, Jewish resistance fighters faced a tremendous obstacle. We had to change our appearances so that we looked Polish.

My pug nose, which I had always hated so much, was in my favor. But, since most Polish people had fair skin and light hair coloring, my dark hair was a problem. So my mother dyed my hair blond. Then, somehow, she and my father managed to get me the necessary false papers, and I was ready to go.

Unfortunately, the group of youngsters which left just before me was denounced by Poles who collaborated with the Nazis. The Poles turned them in to the Gestapo for the meager reward of a bag of sugar. The Gestapo shot them, one and all. When my parents heard about this act of outrage, they decided that I was to remain in the ghetto.

Still, not all of the Polish people turned against us. For example, the members of one Polish family risked their lives to hide Jadzia,[13] Norbert's niece. As a result of their courage, Jadzia survived the war.

In the meantime, life in the ghetto became "hot." The lists for "resettlement"[14] were growing longer and longer. Without our knowing it, we were condemned to death, but first the Nazis subjected us to unbearable physical and mental tortures.

October 1942

Inevitably, summer turned into fall. By this time, the school we ran was no longer in business. The Nazis had taken all of our children for resettlement. One day in October, I was sitting under my tree writing, when I heard my mother's voice. "Sonia! *Sloneczko!*"[15] (She often called me "Sunshine.") In the window, I could see her silhouette. "Come in, child. It is getting cold outside."

12. **partisans** [pär′ tə zenz]: members of the underground.
13. **Jadzia** [yäd′ zä]
14. **resettlement:** in this context, the moving of people to another place in order to kill them.
15. *Sloneczko* [slō nech′ gō]

For a moment, I stood at the door and gazed at the dirty blanket that separated one family from another. Then my gaze shifted to my mother. I looked at her as if I were seeing her for the first time. What I saw filled me with shock and surprise. Apparently I had not looked at her closely for a long time. All at once I realized that her hair had turned gray. There were teeth missing in her smile. Her hands were chapped and raw, and her eyes were very, very sad.

That evening, I sat by the window for a long time watching the blood-red sunset. The stars glimmered like pure gold. The moon rose mocking my dreams and hopes. I closed my eyes remembering my childhood through tears. It seemed like a hundred years ago that I had gone to school, played with other children, and looked forward to springtime. How good my life had been. Yet even then, there had been signs of danger all around me. And so I wrote:

How Could We Know

How could we know
What danger signs foretell
We watched the clouds
And heard the thunder near
Until the lightning struck
And darkness fell
But that was yesteryear

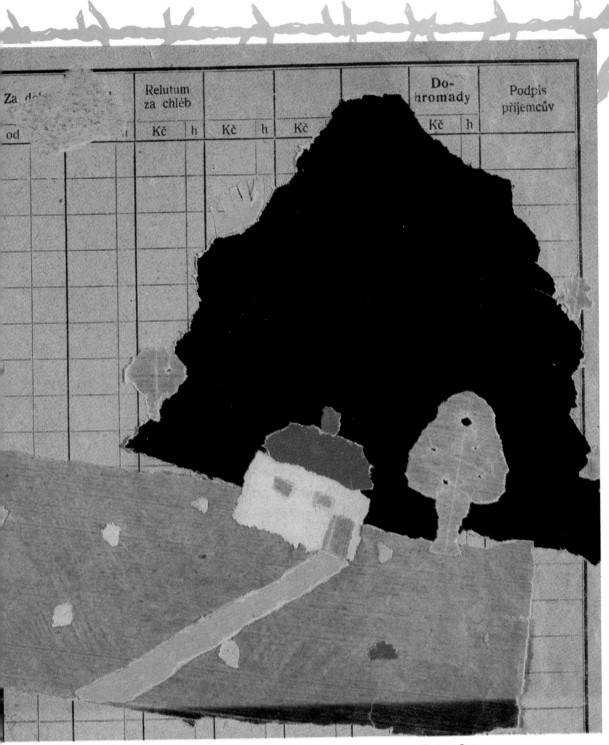

Home in Landscape Eva Brandeis, 1944, collage on paper, 7⁷/₈" x 9⁷/₈",
State Jewish Museum, Prague, the Czech Republic

I was deep in thought about the past and fantasizing about the future when I sensed my mother's hand stroking my hair. By now the room was very cold. We got into bed to keep each other warm. We rested quietly for a long time in this dark dingy room. There was no need for words. I knew that my mother loved me more than her very life. Of course, she loved Blanca as much. She loved Norbert too as if he were her own son. But Blanca and Norbert had each other. And me? In her eyes I was still a child, and she worried desperately about what would happen to me.

Admittedly, I was just an average daughter. I am sure that I could have done many things better. I could have listened more closely. I could have behaved more like a lady. But I did love her deeply. I realized that night what the word "mother" meant to me.

Late that night we were awakened by my father's footsteps. He was very upset. He uttered only two words, "Another transport." I sat up in bed half asleep and looked at him. "Who are they taking this time?" I asked. "Lie down, child," my mother's voice was incredibly calm. "It is God's will."

I cuddled up next to her. We were warm and comfortable. I could feel her heart beating. I held on to her with all my strength. I wanted to feel her next to me. I needed the closeness. I wanted her all to myself. I was afraid that this might be our last embrace, our final chance to be close. I did not dare move. But my eyes were wide open, staring at the dirty gray ceiling. Her arm was across my chest, and I listened to her short uneven breaths.

We waited. Each moment seemed like an eternity. Somewhere a clock struck twelve midnight. Suddenly there were heavy footsteps, and we heard the dreaded pounding on the door. Two men in uniform forced the door open and entered the room. "Adela Schreiber," one voice said. "Get dressed! Immediately!" I froze. My mother sat up on the edge of the bed and slowly started putting on her stockings and her shoes. She put a scarf on her head. "Dress warmly," the voice continued. "You are going on a long journey!"

I ran out into the yard. I screamed into the night, but no sound came from my lips. The sounds were in my head. I thought I would go mad with grief and rage. I stood there like a stone looking at the sky, cursing the heavens in silence. In reality, the night was quite calm and beautiful. Just an October night in the year 1942. How was it possible that the sky was so peaceful, and where was God?

Suddenly, I found my voice. I cried out, "God, Oh God, Help! How can You let this happen? How can You not be touched by this child whose mother is being taken away by force?"

I trembled as I walked back into the house. I heard doors open and shut and footsteps in the street. "Sonia, Sonia." Now it was my father's voice that pierced the night. "Your mother fainted, and the police have left. For the moment, they are gone. But they will return with a stretcher."

I came into the room. My mother was lying on the floor. Although she had fainted, her eyes were now wide open. Absent-mindedly, she was smoothing out her hair. I heard my father cry, "Oh child, oh child." I came up to him. He was weeping. Something inside of me died. I too wanted to cry but could not. I wanted to speak, to comfort him. I wanted to . . . I do not know what I wanted.

By now, my mother had stood up. Once again, she began getting dressed. Slowly, deliberately, she put on her dress, her sweater, a coat. How carefully she dressed. Calmly and with great care, as if she were getting ready to go to a cinema, she combed her hair. Then she took a bag from the closet. From the cupboard, she took a piece of dry bread and put it into the bag. Dry bread, how terrible! All the time, I stood there, watching her in horror.

Suddenly the door opened, and two men came in with a stretcher. "Where is the sick person?" they asked. Their eyes quickly located my mother. They motioned to the stretcher. "Get on quickly so we can go!" "No, thank you," said my mother in a strange, distant voice. "I am going to make it on my own. No need for the stretcher." Then she added with dignity, "I can walk."

She turned to me. "Come closer, *Sloneczko*," she whispered. I obeyed. She took something from her bag, some money. She put it into my hand. "I know you will need this. It may help." She put her arms around me and whispered, "Remember, I love you." The world was spinning in front of my eyes. As if from afar I heard her last words, "And remember to tell the world!"

"Put an end to this sentimental crap. Enough! Let's go!" yelled the harsh voices. "No, stop, I am going with you," said my father. He went with them, and suddenly I was alone in the night.

Again I called on God for help. I screamed out to the deaf heartless world. Then, exhausted, I dozed in agony and dreams until I heard my father's voice. "Sonia, child, we saved your mother. Somehow Blanca found out that *mamusia* was on the list. She knew the police must pass by her house on their way to the roundup in the square. So she watched for your mother. Blanca, Norbert, and I managed to create some confusion—a diversion that momentarily caused the police to let go of her. In that split second, we grabbed *mamusia* and hid her in a nearby shed. Then I made a deal with the police. I told them I would go in her place."

I gasped. "Oh, that is nothing," continued my father. "I am a man, and I am strong. I will be fine. The important thing is that your mother is safe." "Safe?" I must be dreaming. "Who said that? It could not be." But my father was standing over me. Suddenly I jumped up and faced him. "No, you are not going! You will not keep your word to the police!"

My father looked at me in bewilderment. I shook him. "Listen! You are not going. Rena's father has connections. He will help later when the *akcja*[16] is over. He will get us whatever papers we need. In the meantime, we will hide together with *mamusia*."

We both rushed to the courtyard. Blanca and Norbert had already been forced to join their work detail. I ran around in panic, looking for Rena's father. When I finally found him, he said that we had done the smart thing. He advised us to hide together. Then, if we survived this *akcja*, he would somehow manage to get us the proper "life" permits.

I hurried back to the courtyard where I saw many members of Norbert's family whispering with my father. The look in my father's

16. *akcja* [äg′ tzyä]

eyes told me that there was trouble. "We cannot hide with *mamusia* in the shed," he said. His eyes filled with tears. "The shed is locked, and we cannot find the key." We looked at each other in horror. By now the SS men—those in charge of resettlements and killing—were chasing people to the gathering place, or *Appelplatz*.[17] Their voices taunted us. "*Heraus!*[18] *Heraus!* Get out, you bastards! This is resettlement. Get out of hiding, you lousy Jews! Get out! Get out!"

The voices were dangerously near. We could not break open the shed door without attracting attention. I sneaked up to the door and whispered, "*Mamusiu*, it's me, Sonia. We cannot open the door. There are too many Germans around. We are going to hide nearby in a cellar. Can you hear me?" "Oh, I would like to be with you," she answered. "We'll be together soon," I promised.

Suddenly I heard shots. There were screams too. My father forced me to move. In the distance, I heard my mother's muffled voice, "Yes, yes, good. Take care of yourself. . ." and the words faded.

We jumped into a basement—my father and I and some other people. We soon realized that Norbert's family was hiding in a cellar next to us. It was dark and damp. Groping, we found some old furniture, and we barricaded the doors and windows. Slowly my eyes became adjusted to the darkness. My father took some crumbs of bread out of his pocket and gave them to me. I ate. I cuddled up next to him. With horror, I listened to the sounds coming from the street. Gunfire . . . One shot after another . . . Terrifying screams, and then quiet and the sound of heavy boots. The blood-curdling screams of children. Those screams surely reached the heavens . . . or did they?

Hours went by. Night passed, and the sun was shining again. We did not respond to the voices from the loudspeakers outside—voices that assured us that we best come out . . . that we would be taken to work . . . that there would be plenty of food and good living conditions. But the voices also warned us that if we did not come out but continued to hide, we would be killed on the spot when they found us.

17. *Appelplatz* [ä pel′ pläts]
18. *Heraus* [hār ouz′]

At some point, I heard a voice, quiet and calm, calling my name. The voice sounded like that of Cyla,[19] Norbert's sister. My father and I looked at each other. "Let's go," I said. "Quiet, we are not going," whispered my father, putting his hand on my mouth.

Again we heard cries and screams. Through the crack in the window, I saw feet, thousands of feet. Some were clad in boots; some in once-elegant high-heeled shoes. Some were marching; others stumbled. Then I saw a tiny foot, a child's foot, tripping on a stone. The little girl, perhaps four years old, cried out as she fell. The next thing I heard was a gunshot. The crying stopped. And then there were more shoes, big and small, in a last silent march before death.

The sun was setting once more. We sensed a terrifying silence, and this time the silence lasted. My father said, "I think it is safe to go out. Let us go and look for your mother." I got up. I was completely paralyzed. My body would not respond, would not move. My father helped me crawl out onto the courtyard. Immediately, we headed for the shed.

By now, I was so numb that the scene before me did not penetrate my consciousness. It was too horrible to confront. The doors to the shed had been ripped open by an ax or a rifle butt. My mother was gone. On the floor lay a crumpled blanket.

My heart sank. If only we had found her body in the shed. If only she had been killed immediately and spared any further suffering. "Oh God, how I wish she had been killed right here. Then I could throw my arms around her and . . . but now there is nothing but emptiness in the shed and in my soul." That night, I wrote:

19. **Cyla** [tzē′ lä]

Sonia's mother, Adela Finder Schreiber

In Memory to My Mother

Where is your grave?
Where did you die?
Why did you go away?
Why did you leave
Your little girl   5
That rainy autumn day?

I still can hear
The words you spoke:
"You tell the world, my child."
Your eyes as green   10
as emeralds
Were quiet and so mild.

You held my hand
Your face was white
And silent like a stone,   15
You pressed something
Into my palm . . .
And then . . . then you were gone.

I suffered, but
I didn't cry: 20
The pain so fierce, so deep . . .
It pierced my heart
And squeezed it dry . . .
And then, I fell asleep.

Asleep in agony   25
And dreams . . .
A nightmare that was true . . .
I heard the shots,
The screams that came
From us, from me and you.   30

I promised I would
Tell the world . . .
But where to find the words
To speak of
Innocence and love,   35
And tell how much it hurts . . .

About those faces
Weak and pale,
Those dizzy eyes around,
And countless lips   40
That whispered "help"
But never made a sound . . .

To *tell about*
The loss . . . the grief,
The dread of death and cold,   45
Of wickedness
And misery . . .
O no! . . . it can't be told.

Later, the rumors we had been hearing and our worst fears were confirmed, mostly by the underground. I learned that my beautiful mother had been taken to the death camp Belzec.[20] I never saw her again.

My mother's disappearance made me feel old, terribly old. Some people tried to comfort me. Others told me to stop crying, to stop acting like a child. But I could not stop grieving. I remembered how my mother had grieved when her mother had been killed.[21] And so I yelled back that it is right to cry when you lose your *mamusia*. My mother was not a child when her mother was killed. Yet she too cried. Now, like her, I was grown up, and I too could cry if I wanted to.

20. **Belzec** [bel′ sek]
21. **when her mother had been killed:** Sonia's grandmother was killed by the Nazis in 1940.

Sonia's grandmother with her children. Sonia's mother is in front.

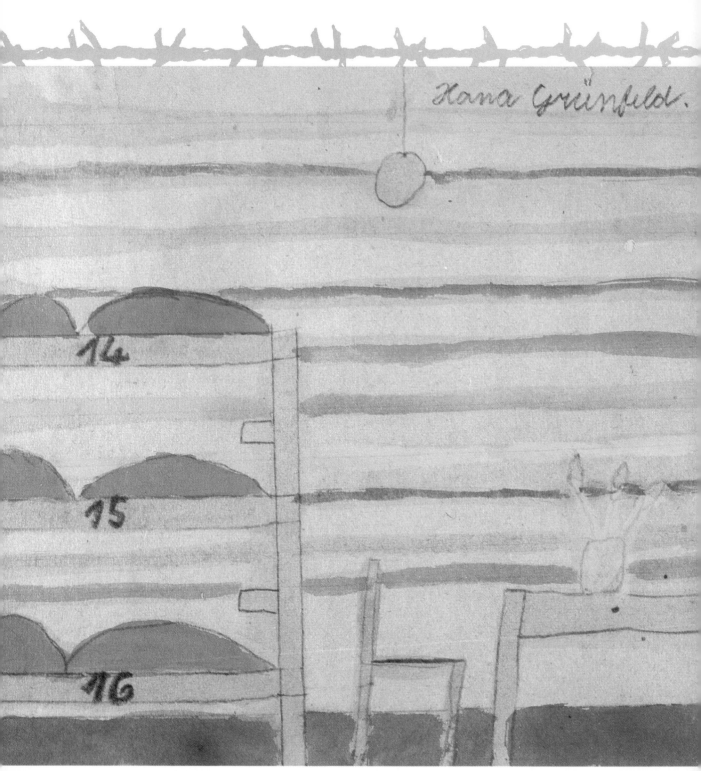

Drawing Kana Grünfeld, drawing in pencil and watercolor, State Jewish Museum, Prague, the Czech Republic

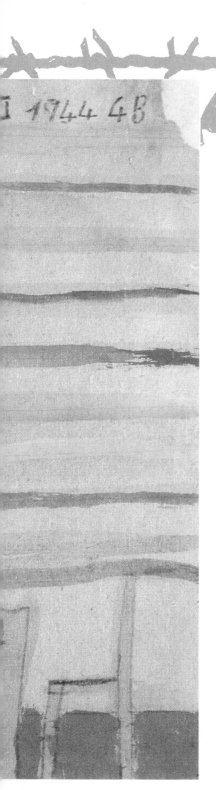

S onia and Blanca went from the ghetto to a succession of five concentration camps. In May 1945, they were finally freed by American troops. The sisters, together with Blanca's husband Norbert, came to the United States.

SONIA SCHREIBER WEITZ

Sonia Schreiber Weitz was born in 1928 in Kraków, Poland, and had a happy childhood until Germany took over Poland. While living in the ghetto and in concentration camps, she wrote poetry to help her cope with the fear and suffering all around her. Weitz says that she owes her life to her sister Blanca who made certain that they were never separated while they were in concentration camps.

After World War II, Blanca and Sonia were reunited with Blanca's husband Norbert in Austria. They remained displaced persons until 1948 when Norbert's uncle in Massachusetts sent for them to come to the United States.

Two years later, Sonia Schreiber married and eventually had a son and twin daughters. Her loving family and her own writing helped her to come to terms with her past. In recent years, Weitz has been active in teaching people about the Holocaust. She also trains other teachers, speaks publicly about her experiences, and continues to write poetry.

We Shall Wait Forever

▲▲▲▲

Darlene Sinyella

*B*ack in the past
we, the ancestors, ruled the
quiet lands.
We would sit around camp fires
and sing with harmony.   5
The beating of the drums sounded
like the heart of an Indian. The cry
of a wolf, the howl of an owl, put us
into the secrets of ourselves.
Then we woke in the early mist of May,   10
and found ourselves in front
of our enemies, who had come to fight.
The children cried, the women ran
and hid. The men who were brave
stood up for us.   15
We fought, but many of us died.
Our spirits now haunt
the lands we walked on.
Now we sing, laugh, dance, and lie
under the bright blue sky. We are waiting   20
for our enemies who killed us to pass by.
We shall stay here and wait until
we find them. Until then we shall wait
in peace and harmony.

DARLENE SINYELLA

Darlene Sinyella, who is a Native American of the Hualapai Nation, wrote "We Shall Wait Forever" when she was in the seventh grade at the Hualapai Elementary School in Peach Springs, Arizona. Her poem was published in 1990 in an anthology of Native American student poetry titled *A Tree Full of Leaves Which Are Stars*.

HOLDING OUT

OUIDA SEBESTYEN

CHARACTERS

CURTIS
VALERIE
INDIANS OF THE MODOC[1] TRIBE

SETTING

TIME: *The present, late afternoon on a chilly spring day.*

A roadside rest area. One sturdy picnic table with benches and a trash can are the only signs of civilization. Behind them, in dimmer light, jagged outcroppings of lava rock and clumps of sagebrush stair-step up a desolate slope. A drum is beating softly, almost like the thump of a heart.

AT CURTAIN RISE: CURTIS *strides out among the rocks at right. He is sixteen, and comfortable being alone. He stumbles on a stone and pushes it out of the trail with a slender branch he is using as a staff. He also carries the thin National Park Service booklet he has used on a self-guided hike. He looks around and, because no one is there to see, holds it with his teeth so he can pretend his staff is a rifle. After a few quick shots he climbs up on the table and continues to read, deeply interested. A truck door slams. He stiffens. A few moments later* VALERIE *appears, dressed like him in jeans and sweatshirt, raking her tangled hair. Neither of them takes notice of the drum, which slowly fades away.*

1. **Modoc** [mō′ dok]: Native American people from southern Oregon and northern California.

VALERIE: Curtis, don't *do* stuff like this to me. I woke up and there I was, parked all by myself in the middle of nowhere, with my feet out the window.

CURTIS (*pointing up the slope*): There's a trail up there that makes a loop. So I walked around it, to get the kinks out.

VALERIE: Yeah, tell me about kinks. I feel like the Hunchback of Notre Dame. How long did I sleep?

CURTIS: About six hours.

VALERIE: You're kidding. Nobody can sleep six hours in the cab of a pickup truck and live to tell about it.

CURTIS: Well, I guess you just made medical history.

VALERIE: Where *is* this? Are we still in Oregon?

CURTIS (*taking a pebble out of his shoe*): No, we've crossed back into California. After you didn't wake up, I thought, What am I supposed to be doing? So I pulled off the highway and stopped here.

VALERIE: Oh, man—no. Not back in California.

CURTIS: What was I supposed to do, with you zonked out? Turn west and drive till we went down in the Pacific, blub, blub, blub?

VALERIE: You could have waked me up, for starters.

CURTIS (*softening*): I guess. But you'd done nearly all the driving last night, and you looked really pooped. Snoring away like that. I sort of—

VALERIE: I wasn't tired from last night. I was tired from this morning.

CURTIS: Yeah, I know. I saw it. When you came out of your dad's house, you looked really different. Your face was white. I thought maybe he'd hit you, or something, and that's why you wouldn't say anything when I tried to talk.

VALERIE: No, I just had to—I don't know—get into a little dark space and stay really quiet for a while. Curled up. Like a snail. And just wait till the shock wore off. Okay?

CURTIS: Hey, you don't have to explain it. I just didn't know what to do. So I just kept on driving and thinking and wondering. One spot up there in the mountains I was screaming along through this snowstorm. In my dad's truck. Oh, man. I never drove in a snowstorm before. So I thought I better stop, for Pete's sake, and hang around here till you joined the world again.

VALERIE (*looking around*)**:** You didn't pick a really great spot, Curt. This is pretty awful.

CURTIS: I don't know—it's kind of interesting. All this dark-red jagged rock is hardened lava. You know, like Hawaii.

VALERIE: It figures: I go to sleep in a truck and wake up in a lava bed. Couldn't you have stopped in a town? What am I supposed to do for a rest room?

CURTIS: There's one up the trail. Over past that dark bunch of junipers.

VALERIE: Oh, great. It would be. (*She takes a few uncertain steps that bring her back to her starting point.*) Did you read the same thing I did about some kidnaper or hired killer or somebody—

CURTIS: Oh, that? Yeah—he dumped the body in one of these pits. Not out in the bushes where nobody ever goes—no, it's got to be in there where some Park Service guy can notice it. But I guess maybe he was thinking the quicklime[2] or whatever would dissolve the—

VALERIE: Curtis! Shut up. Just shut up—you're gross. I'm not in any shape for scary stories. Or this weirdo place, whatever it is.

CURTIS: It's a national monument. So don't put it down—the government's trying hard to keep weirdo places like this unspoiled for our grandchildren. (*He rethinks.*) Well, not *our* grandchildren . . .

VALERIE: So where is everybody?

CURTIS: I guess March is still off season. There's maybe some kind of visitors' center, farther up the road. But it's probably closed. So people just drive through, like us.

VALERIE: No store, or anything? What do we eat?

2. **quicklime:** calcium oxide, a water-soluble solid; in this context, it would destroy a body.

CURTIS: We've still got the apples. And potato chips. I can go see what else.

VALERIE (*uneasily*): Okay. And I guess I can go see if anybody is stashed in the outhouse. (*She starts off again, and turns back.*)

Curtis, if I yell, you better come running.

CURTIS: Don't I always? (*His question stops her, and they lock eyes. She jerks around and goes up left among the looming lava shapes. He goes off to the parked truck.*)

Modoc Woven Basket National Park Service Study Collection, Lava Beds National Monument, CA

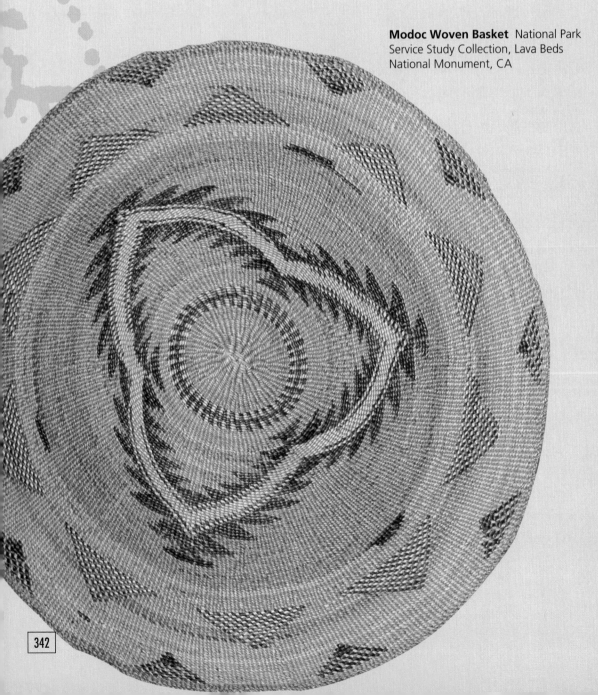

A MODOC INDIAN SENTRY *stands up unhurriedly from behind a rock and watches them go. Another* SENTRY *rises from his nearby hiding place. They wear simple rough shirts and pants, and round flat-brimmed hats decorated with feathers. Their faces and hands, their clothing and moccasins, their cartridge belts and long 1870's rifles, are shades of gray, as if they were being seen through gauze, or the haze of time. They study the horizon carefully, pointing and nodding to each other. Their movements are slow, almost trancelike with fatigue. They watch with quiet interest as* CURTIS *returns and puts two paper sacks and a can of pop on the table. His gaze goes past them and he starts to read.* VALERIE *comes back and walks past them, unaware.*

VALERIE: Yuck. Can't they design those things to flush or something? (*She is holding a large feather, which she sticks into her hair.*) Boy, talk about primitive.

CURTIS: Beats a bush.

VALERIE: Just barely.

CURTIS (*noticing the feather*): What's that?

VALERIE: I found it. Some critter got ambushed, I reckon. Oh, great, you found something to drink.

CURTIS: If you don't mind drinking from the same can.

VALERIE: You're really cute, Curt. Here we are, runaways, with a practically stolen truck on our hands, and maybe the police hunting us by now. And your folks yelling, "Where's our baby boy!" And my mom blaming everybody in sight—and you make it sound like we're on a shy little first date. (*She drinks and hands him the can.*) Hey, you found the cookies. I forgot we saved some. (*She divvies them up.*) I'm starved! Aren't you?

CURTIS (*gently nudging her toward reality*): Valerie, this is all the food we've got. And we're running low on gas. We need to talk about what we're doing.

VALERIE: We know what we're doing. We're having a picnic in lava land. (*She starts to eat an apple from one of the sacks.*)

CURTIS: No, what we're doing is putting off talking about what happened. And what we're going to do *now*. What direction we're going.

VALERIE: Curtis, give me a break. I'm not ready. It's too soon—it's just too—Eat. Okay?

CURTIS (*regretfully*): Val, your dad doesn't want you. You've got to go back home.

VALERIE: Back home? What home? (*She forces an airy laugh.*) You mean my mom's apartment, where I hang my clothes and step over the bottles? That home?

CURTIS: Whatever you call it, it's the only place you've got to live in.

VALERIE: That's a big lie. I've got the whole world to live in. I can live right here. People live in trucks.

CURTIS: Not in my dad's truck, they don't.

VALERIE: I can get a job and have my own apartment.

CURTIS: On that twenty-five bucks you've got left?

VALERIE: I've got money. I've got another forty I didn't tell you about.

CURTIS: Yeah? Forty that sort of stuck to your fingers while your mom wasn't looking?

VALERIE: Forty I saved! (*She tests other answers.*) I found it. My dad sent it for my birthday.

CURTIS: Okay. Forget it.

VALERIE: If you're in such a hurry to back out, why don't you just get in your daddy's precious pickup and drive off? I don't need this.

CURTIS: Sure you don't. But you needed *me*, Val. You needed the stupid truck to get to Oregon and find your dad, so I took it and got you there. You call that backing out?

VALERIE: Okay! (*She slings an apple core away, just missing him.*) I needed you. I used you. Sue me.

CURTIS: Val—I'm not mad at you! I'm just telling you something. Your dad's not going to take you in. (*He picks up her apple core and puts it in the trash can.*) Listen, you don't have to talk about it till you're ready. But you've got to rethink your plans now. It's not going to be the way you were dreaming it. (*She begins to pace rapidly.*) What are you doing?

VALERIE: Exercising. (*She marches up and down, swinging her arms.* CURTIS *and the* MODOC SENTRIES *watch, bemused.*) I'm stiff. I hurt.

CURTIS: Why don't you walk around the trail loop? It's just about half a mile.

VALERIE: Because I want to walk around right here. Okay?

CURTIS: Sure. Forget it. (*He returns to his booklet, refusing to look at her.*)

An OLD WOMAN *in a shawl and long skirt, gray with time, enters right and brings a small jug to the two* SENTRIES. *They drink sparingly. When she offers the jug again, they shake their heads and go back to their lookout posts. She hobbles off, left, perhaps to others. Neither* CURTIS *nor* VALERIE *take notice.*

VALERIE (*looking around, still angry but curious*): What's the trail for, anyway? What's up there? It's just flat.

CURTIS: That's what's strange. It looks like a plain old pasture full of sagebrush. From here you can't tell that the lava is all broken up into crevices and ledges and little caves. It's like World War One up there. Full of trenches.

VALERIE: That book's telling about it?

CURTIS: Yeah. They have them up there in a little box by the trail so you can take a self-guided walk.

VALERIE: Trust you to find a book to stick your nose into, even out here in no-man's-land.

CURTIS: There were people here, once. There were some Indians called Modocs, and they had a war here. Well, more like a siege, I guess you'd say, because about sixty men held off the United States Army for months, holed up in those crevices.

VALERIE (*forgetting to pace*): What for?

CURTIS: Because all this around here was their homeland. But the white settlers wanted it, and got the government to send the Modocs to live on a reservation with another tribe they didn't like. So they ran away, and when the Army ordered them back, they refused, and gathered up their people here in the lava beds to hold out.

VALERIE: You mean women and little kids and everybody?

CURTIS: Yeah, the old folks. The horses and dogs. Everything they had.

VALERIE: What did they eat?

CURTIS (*with a shrug*)**:** What they could find, I guess. And there's a lake back over there. They sneaked down to it at first, but toward the last the soldiers cut off their water supply.

VALERIE *starts to drink the last of the pop, but hesitates, and impulsively offers it to* CURTIS. *He shakes his head. She drinks thoughtfully, looking around.*

VALERIE: Why the blazes didn't the Army just let them *have* their stupid hunk of land and save everybody a lot of trouble?

As she speaks, the two SENTRIES *stand up warily as a small tattered group of* MODOC MEN *and* WOMEN *gathers between them. Two tall imposing men are obviously rival leaders, unable to agree about something. They mime an argument. Their supporters, anxiously watching, slowly divide into separate sides.*

CURTIS: Yeah, that's what some people back east wondered. (*He waves the booklet, which has given him the story.*) So finally they sent out five people to be, like, a peace committee or something, to try to talk.

The FIRST LEADER *defends his position passionately, but the* SECOND LEADER *senses weakness in him, and suddenly grabs a woman's shawl and drapes it over his rival's head. The* FIRST LEADER, *shocked, throws it off, but he has been called a coward. His followers back away from him.*

CURTIS: But it turned out the Modocs had broken up into two groups with two chiefs. One chief kept trying to work things out. But the other groups just— stood up at a meeting and blew away a general and a minister from the peace party. Naturally the Army said, "That does it— not a *general*," and started lobbing mortar shells into the hideout every fifteen minutes. Like, this is *war*, man—no more shilly-shally stuff.

In deep anguish the FIRST LEADER *reluctantly agrees with the* SECOND, *who hurries off triumphantly with his men. The little gray crowd melts away. In sharp contrast to* CURTIS'S *flippant comment, the* FIRST LEADER *sinks to his knees in despair.*

VALERIE (*rubbing her shoulders*)**:** It's cold here. The sun's about to go down, isn't it? How do you suppose they stayed warm in this place?

CURTIS: I guess they had woven mats and things. Blankets. Some of the ledges and little cubbyholes maybe kept off part of the rain and snow. But it must have been hard, surrounded in here. And nothing much to make fires with.

VALERIE: You think we could make a fire?

CURTIS (*looking around*): I guess it wouldn't hurt. You're supposed to be in a campsite, and it looks like somebody made a fire once, here in these rocks. See if you can find some dead sagebrush or something. (*They leave in opposite directions.*)

A SHAMAN[3] *appears, wearing a gray tunic, his head bound with a white cloth. The* SENTRIES *give him rapt attention. The broken* LEADER, *still kneeling, bends his forehead to the ground like someone badly beaten who refuses to fall. The* SHAMAN *lifts his*

3. **Shaman** [shä′mən]: a Native American healer who acts as both priest and doctor.

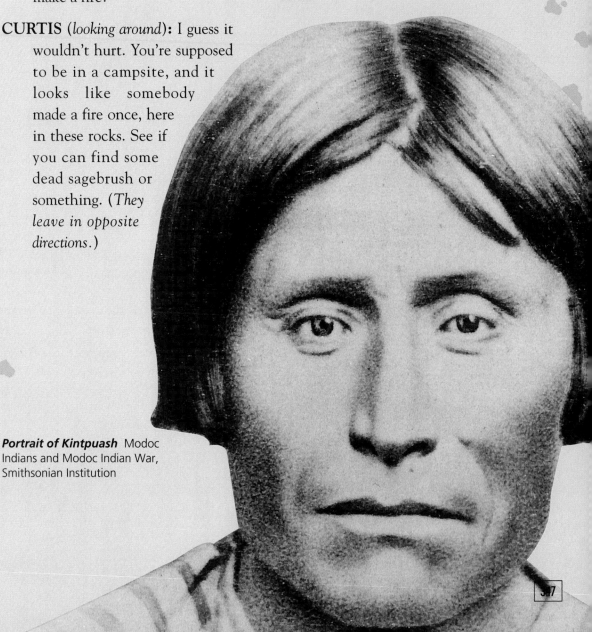

Portrait of Kintpuash Modoc Indians and Modoc Indian War, Smithsonian Institution

arms reverently to the sky. One hand holds a medicine stick about four feet long. Feathers, fur, beads, and charms hang from it on a thong. He plants the stick on a rocky ridge, faces the four points of the compass, and leaves. CURTIS and VALERIE return with some small dry branches.

VALERIE: Like this?

CURTIS: Yeah, this might do it, with a little dry grass twisted up to start with. (*He lays a fire and nods toward the tote hanging from her shoulder.*) You got any matches in that bag-lady collection of junk?

VALERIE: You know I don't smoke. Don't you have some in the truck?

CURTIS: Bound to. (*He goes to look.* VALERIE *turns slowly, her eyes passing over the* MODOC LEADER *and the medicine stick. She rubs her arms, still cold.*)

VALERIE: Curtis? (*She kneels to break up some twigs.*) It's eerie out here.

CURTIS (*returning*): Not one stupid match anywhere. My dad doesn't smoke either, and I guess he just—(*He kicks the pile of twigs.*) We're real pioneers,

man. (*He hands her a sweater he has brought.*) I found this, though.

VALERIE: I don't need it.

CURTIS: Hey, put it on. You're shivering.

VALERIE (*laying her feather on the table and pulling the sweater over her head*): You don't have to be nice to me.

CURTIS (*exasperated*): Was I being nice? Sorry! I keep forgetting myself and doing weird things my parents taught me. It won't happen again, I promise.

VALERIE (*too serious to play along*): You are nice, Curt. Face it.

CURTIS: And that's what gave you the idea in the first place.

VALERIE: What idea?

CURTIS: The big idea to come on to me like I was suddenly a new invention you couldn't live without.

VALERIE: What are you talking about? You have a really twitchy mind, Curtis. Always cranking corners and throwing people off balance.

CURTIS: You know what I'm talking

about. You needed a way to get to Oregon and track down your dad. You didn't have the guts or money to hop a bus and do it yourself. But you didn't mind working *me* over for a couple of weeks till I was ga-ga-gooey enough to steal a truck and head off, any direction you pointed to. You want Oregon? Sure, I'll just go tearing right up the middle of California on this screaming freeway like I know what I'm doing.

VALERIE: You knew what you were doing. Don't try blaming me for that part of it. You wanted to run as bad as I did. You didn't like the way you were living any more than I did.

CURTIS: Nothing was wrong with the way I was living.

VALERIE: That's the whole point, stupid. You've been this nice quiet decent kid with the good grades—forever! You never had a problem because you never make a wave. Curtis—you needed to make a *wave*. A number-nine wave, to see if it was going to drown you or if you could ride it in.

CURTIS: Yeah? (*He sits on the table,* as far as he can get from her.) That's really dumb stuff to think.

VALERIE: No, that dumb stuff is the truth. I did use you, Curt—I admit it. But you used me, too. To test yourself. Am I right? This whole trip has been your test. (*He shrugs and twists the empty paper sack into lumps, unable to meet her eyes. She studies him, her voice going softer.*) Didn't it ever bother you? To *always* do what was expected of you?

CURTIS (*with difficulty*): Sure. I guess it bothered me. I guess I thought about it, when my folks started planning my life for me, or things like that.

VALERIE: But you didn't do anything about it, Curt.

CURTIS (*giving his life a long slow look, and almost smiling at its ironies*): Not till now. Not till Miss Valerie Vroom-Vroom put the whammy on me.

VALERIE: Is that a compliment? (*She sits beside him on the table, moved by his pain.*) You know what made me sad when I first noticed you in school? The way

Portrait of Kaitchkona Modoc Indians and
Modoc Indian War, Smithsonian Institution

you always seemed like you needed to put yourself down. Just because you were serious and kind and curious about things, and—sort of, you know, in love with life. *Besides* being smart and nice. I couldn't understand that, how you could be all those special things and still always seem like you didn't like who you were.

CURTIS: What's so smart and nice about this mess?

VALERIE: Oh, great, Curt. (*The* SENTRIES *stop searching the horizon and lean quietly on their long rifles, curious.*) I know you don't think taking your dad's truck was a really smart idea. Or selling your watch yesterday to get the radiator fixed. But I—I realize you're here in a lava bed with me and the Murdocks because you wanted to help me be happier. That's nice.

CURTIS: Modocs. Not Murdock. Mo-doc.

VALERIE (*softly*): Okay. Whatever.

The SENTRIES *smile at each other. The defeated* LEADER *gets to his knees and stares into emptiness, perhaps seeing his people's future.*

CURTIS: I'm sorry the way things turned out for you this morning. Maybe your dad had his reasons for whatever he said, but—man, when you got back to the truck, I thought—the way you looked—I thought he'd socked you in the mouth or something.

VALERIE: You did? No—he didn't lay a finger on me. Not even a handshake. I was a real shock to him, I guess. He opens the door and there I am, like Hi, I'm Valerie and I've come to live with you, Dad. And his eyes go, Valerie Who?

CURTIS: Yeah. I guess without any warning like that, what could you expect? But when you went in, what happened?

VALERIE: Nothing. He asked how was I. He said he was just about to leave for work. That's what really got to me the most. When he looked at his watch.

TWO WOMEN *enter and kneel on either side of the* LEADER. *One hands him a morsel of food. He pushes it away, not angrily but so abruptly that it falls from her hand. The* WOMEN *crouch constrained until he finally sighs deeply and holds out his hands to them so they can help him rise. They guide him slowly out of sight.*

CURTIS: But when you explained to him. How things were, and all—

VALERIE: He said it was a bad idea. He asked if my mom had put me up to it. Then he looked at his watch again. Damn—he could've faked it! He could've pretended he was glad to see me, and really wished I could stay with him, but golly gee, he was just starting a three-year job at the South Pole or something and he'd see me when he got back.

CURTIS: He didn't know how to handle it, Val.

VALERIE: He ought to have tried. It would've helped a lot if I could remember he tried. Even *I* take the trouble to lie if it'll make things—not hurt so much! Couldn't he?

CURTIS: Maybe he thought it would be easier on you if he just said right out you couldn't stay with him.

VALERIE: He didn't even *try*.

CURTIS: You scared him, Val. You made him feel—defensive and stuff.

VALERIE: Why do people get that way? Why can't they sit down and say, "Let's talk. Let's listen. Till we understand each other?" What the blazes is so hard about that?

CURTIS: I don't know, Val.

One of the SENTRIES *ventures out to find the morsel of food, picks the debris off, and shares it with his companion. They eat hungrily and lick their fingers as they return to their posts.*

VALERIE (*staring into the distance*): It feels so strange. All these years my dad's been out there, like some kind of magic spell I could make. I knew no matter how bad things got, all I had to say was "Hey, I don't have to take this. I can go live with him." And now . . . (*She struggles to keep her voice even.*) All at once there's not any magic to call on anymore.

CURTIS (*hurting with her*): Maybe he'll feel different someday. Maybe even the fact that you came to him and asked—

VALERIE: It's going to snow, isn't it? The sky's so heavy. We're going to be found here frozen to a picnic table, all white and ghosty.

CURTIS (*briskly, relieved that she has regained control*): Yeah, it feels really strange to be cold, when you stop to think that all this rock that we're walking around on out here was flowing once, red hot, pouring out over trees and grass, and nothing could stop it. (*As he speaks, he goes off left to the truck and returns with a dark bundle.*) And all these little mountains were cinder cones, and the ashes—

VALERIE (*interrupting*): What's that?

CURTIS: Wrap up in it. You're still shivering.

VALERIE: It's a sleeping bag. (*Shakily, she chooses to laugh instead of cry.*) Oh, man, Curt. Just one sleeping bag? You were thinking ahead, weren't you?

CURTIS (*surprised into defensiveness*): What's that mean? No. Hey, people take sleeping bags. When they go hunting or something. In case they get stranded or something.

VALERIE: In case they get stranded or something? Were you making big plans for us?

CURTIS: I don't know what you mean. Yeah, I do, but—Okay. It occurred to me. Just wrap up in it. Things turned out different. Okay?

VALERIE (*wrapping herself in it gratefully*): Thanks. (*She hunts inside it.*) I've lost one of my earrings.

CURTIS: No. You lost it while you were asleep in the truck. (*He pats his shirt pocket.*) I've got it.

VALERIE (*studying his face*): Oh. (*She wraps herself tightly again.*) I keep thinking about the children, and the old ones. How hard they had it. When it wasn't their fault. Have you read far enough to know what happened?

CURTIS (*referring to the booklet*): Well, the siege lasted like three or four months, with these sixty guys holding off twelve hundred soldiers. But they were nearly starving, and when they tried to escape to the south over there, they got captured in little groups.

VALERIE: Didn't they ever get their homeland?

CURTIS (*shaking his head*): The settlers got it.

VALERIE: But it's empty. Couldn't they have *shared* it, even?

CURTIS (*rolling the booklet into a tight cylinder*): I guess not. And the Army figured hanging the leaders would set the right example. So they did.

VALERIE: Oh, man, that's sad. That's so stupid and sad.

CURTIS: It said when the Army came in here, afterward, they found like this stick that the medicine man had propped up in the rocks. It was supposed to give the Indians victory, you know—stop the bullets and all that. Only it hadn't.

VALERIE: Whatever happened to the other Murdocks?

CURTIS: The Mo—I don't know. It didn't say.

VALERIE (*suddenly bending forward in pain*): Why couldn't he want me, Curt? Why couldn't he be glad I was his kid and wanted to live with him? It stinks. (*She begins to cry.*) It really stinks.

CURTIS: Hey, Val. Don't do that. Listen. Hold out. (*He can't even take her hidden hand.*) You've got to just—hold out. Till it gets better.

VALERIE (*bitterly, still crying*): You figure four months of holding out would do it, Curt? Like the Murdocks?

CURTIS: They tried, Val. Aren't you glad they tried?

VALERIE: But it wasn't enough.

CURTIS: You tried, too, Val. This morning—

VALERIE: But it didn't help.

CURTIS: Listen to me. I was proud of you this morning, walking up to your dad's door. You're brave—don't ever forget how brave. And you're way ahead of the Modocs—they had their troubles a hundred years ago, but you're right here—alive, with everything still ahead for you. (*She grows quiet as he stumbles on, distressed.*) There's got to be better things out there, and love, and—I wish I was the one, because the way I feel about you—I mean these really deep feelings—but right now what they're like is—friendship. I don't know if that means anything to you, but if it does . . .

VALERIE (*calmly*): You want me to give up.

CURTIS: No. Just go back. And hold out. That's all.

VALERIE (*testing reality*): Are your folks going to give you hell?

CURTIS: I don't know. Usually they act like "Okay, we see your point." So this is scary, because I don't know if they'll be that way. Because this time we're talking really major—(*He turns to her with a small proud smile.*) A really major wave. (*She smiles back faintly, giving him the courage to go on.*) You got to remember it's not all your mom's fault either, Val. She's got a right to her own kind of life. I know you think your dad's a real free spirit and all that, but he shouldn't have bailed out on her—he owed you something—

VALERIE (*holding the truth away*): You know what's funny? All this time I wasn't even thinking about the soldiers. You know? All the soldiers that probably got killed here. Boys from New Jersey or someplace, lying out there on lava rock with bullet holes in them, wondering how their lives turned out so crazy.

CURTIS: Val, if there's maybe times when you need to talk to somebody older than just me, my folks are mostly pretty reasonable. Pretty understanding. Okay?

VALERIE (*trusting him*): Yeah, Curt. I can tell they must be. It rubbed off on you. (*She stands up and lets the sleeping bag fall.*) I think I want to walk the trail.

CURTIS: You do? Okay. Yeah.

VALERIE: Before it gets too dark.

CURTIS: Okay. Sure. (*He bundles up the sleeping bag in such a burst of gratitude that he breaks one of the ties that holds the bag in a roll.*)

VALERIE (*hesitating*): Then, maybe . . . There's not much point in sitting in the cab of a truck all night in the snow.

CURTIS (*gladly giving her time*): Well, probably not.

VALERIE (*with difficulty*): So. We can head back down toward L.A., I guess. It's not like I'm giving up. Or—or settling for just anything. It's just how things are for now. Okay? (*She walks off toward the trail.*)

CURTIS (*almost reaching toward her*): Okay. It's kind of rough there at first. Go slow. (*She disappears. He stares after her through several moments of silence.*) Val? You okay?

VALERIE (*from offstage*): Yeah.

CURTIS (*calling, now*): Don't trip on the rocks—they're sharp. Just take it slow. (*He catches a glimpse of her.*) Hey, you look like a ghost floating along up there.

VALERIE (*from farther away*): I do? I'm going on around the loop now, Curt. I'll see you.

CURTIS (*calling*): Yeah. I'll be here.

He waits, but there is silence. In it, the drum begins to beat again, a deep heartthrob. He turns his head almost as though he hears it and is seeking its source. He draws a deep breath. With the sleeping bag's broken cord he ties together Valerie's feather, the pop can, and his booklet, and attaches the cord to the stick he used on his hike. He props the stick up on the table with a pile of rocks, and slowly hangs Valerie's earring with the other charms. As he works, MODOCS appear, beginning a slow exodus, burdened with bundles. They pass behind him, gray and spent, the young ones helping the old, the spared ones carrying the wounded.

CURTIS (*softly, in an ordinary voice*): Just hold out, Val. Okay? Because you can make it. You can. You're going to. I love you, Valerie. But that's for later, when there's not so much to fight.

He gathers up the paper sacks and sleeping bag to stow in the truck, and waits, facing the spot where she will reappear. A dwindling line of INDIANS continues to pass in the growing darkness. The two SENTRIES are the last to go. As the drum stops, they glance back at the two medicine sticks standing bravely in the only light that is left.

CURTAIN

OUIDA SEBESTYEN

Ouida Sebestyen was born in 1924 in Vernon, Texas, where she grew up. She says about her home town, "When my life got too small . . . I enlarged it at the library or the movies. My favorite dream was to sit in a theater someday, watching people react with gasps and laugher to a story I had created."

Sebestyen made a long leap for college and attended the University of Colorado. She wrote her first novel when she was twenty— but it was thirty-five years before any of her work was published. "After four unaccepted novels and four hundred rejection slips for stories, plays, poems—even true confessions—I finally got the hang of it."

When Sebestyen writes, she listens "to ragtime or whatever music my characters might listen to." She writes in longhand first. "Then I type, revising like mad, over and over."

FROM NARRATIVE OF THE LIFE OF
FREDERICK DOUGLASS
AN AMERICAN SLAVE

FREDERICK DOUGLASS

***Frederick Douglass Series
No. 22*** Jacob Lawrence,
gouache on paper,
Hampton University Museum,
Hampton, Virginia

y master's family consisted of two sons, Andrew and Richard; one daughter, Lucretia, and her husband, Captain Thomas Auld. They lived in one house, upon the home plantation of Colonel Edward Lloyd. My master was Colonel Lloyd's clerk and superintendent. He was what might be called the overseer of the overseers. I spent two years of childhood on this plantation in my old master's family. It was here that I witnessed the bloody transaction recorded in the first chapter; and as I received my first impressions of slavery on this plantation, I will give some description of it, and of slavery as it there existed. The plantation is about twelve miles north of Easton, in Talbot county, and is situated on the border of Miles River. The principal products raised upon it were tobacco, corn, and wheat. These were raised in great abundance; so that, with the products of this and the other farms belonging to him, he was able to keep in almost constant employment a large sloop,[1] in carrying them to market at Baltimore. This sloop was named Sally Lloyd, in honor of one of the colonel's daughters. My master's son-in-law, Captain Auld, was master of the vessel; she was otherwise manned by the colonel's own slaves. Their names were Peter, Isaac, Rich, and Jake. These were esteemed very highly by the other slaves, and looked upon as the privileged ones of the plantation; for it was no small affair, in the eyes of the slaves, to be allowed to see Baltimore.

Colonel Lloyd kept from three to four hundred slaves on his home plantation, and owned a large number more on the neighboring farms belonging to him. The names of the farms nearest to the home plantation were Wye Town and New Design. "Wye Town" was under the

---

1. **sloop** [slüp]: a sailboat with one mast and several sails.

overseership of a man named Noah Willis. New Design was under the overseership of a Mr. Townsend. The overseers of these, and all the rest of the farms, numbering over twenty, received advice and direction from the managers of the home plantation. This was the great business place. It was the seat of government for the whole twenty farms. All disputes among the overseers were settled here. If a slave was convicted of any high misdemeanor,[2] became unmanageable, or evinced[3] a determination to run away, he was brought immediately here, severely whipped, put on board the sloop, carried to Baltimore, and sold to Austin Woolfolk, or some other slave-trader, as a warning to the slaves remaining.

Here, too, the slaves of all the other farms received their monthly allowance of food, and their yearly clothing. The men and women slaves received, as their monthly allowance of food, eight pounds of pork, or its equivalent in fish, and one bushel of corn meal. Their yearly clothing consisted of two coarse linen shirts, one pair of linen trousers, like the shirts, one jacket, one pair of trousers for winter, made of coarse negro cloth, one pair of stockings, and one pair of shoes; the whole of which could not have cost more than seven dollars. The allowance of the slave children was given to their mothers, or the old women having the care of them. The children unable to work in the field had neither shoes, stockings, jackets, nor trousers, given to them; their clothing consisted of two coarse linen shirts per year. When these failed them, they went naked until the next allowance-day. Children from seven to ten years old, of both sexes, almost naked, might be seen at all seasons of the year.

There were no beds given the slaves, unless one coarse blanket be considered such, and none but the men and women had these. This, however, is not considered a very great privation. They find less difficulty from the want of beds, than from the want of time to sleep; for when their day's work in the field is done, the most of them having their washing, mending, and cooking to do, and having few or none

2. **misdemeanor** [mis′ di mē′ nər]: misbehavior.
3. **evinced** [i vinsd′]: showed clearly.

of the ordinary facilities for doing either of these, very many of their sleeping hours are consumed in preparing for the field the coming day; and when this is done, old and young, male and female, married and single, drop down side by side, on one common bed,—the cold, damp floor,—each covering himself or herself with their miserable blankets; and here they sleep till they are summoned to the field by the driver's horn. At the sound of this, all must rise, and be off to the field. There must be no halting; every one must be at his or her post; and woe betides them who hear not this morning summons to the field; for if they are not awakened by the sense of hearing, they are by the sense of feeling; no age nor sex finds any favor. Mr. Severe, the overseer, used to stand by the door of the quarter, armed with a large hickory stick and heavy cowskin, ready to whip any one who was so unfortunate as not to hear, or, from any other cause, was prevented from being ready to start for the field at the sound of the horn.

Mr. Severe was rightly named: he was a cruel man. I have seen him whip a woman, causing the blood to run half an hour at the time; and this, too, in the midst of her crying children, pleading for their mother's release. He seemed to take pleasure in manifesting his fiendish barbarity. Added to his cruelty, he was a profane swearer. It was enough to chill the blood and stiffen the hair of an ordinary man to hear him talk. Scarce a sentence escaped him but that was commenced or concluded by some horrid oath. The field was the place to witness his cruelty and profanity. His presence made it both the field of blood and of blasphemy. From the rising till the going down of the sun, he was cursing, raving, cutting, and slashing among the slaves of the field, in the most frightful manner. His career was short. He died very soon after I went to Colonel Lloyd's; and he died as he lived, uttering, with his dying groans, bitter curses and horrid oaths. His death was regarded by the slaves as the result of a merciful providence.

Mr. Severe's place was filled by a Mr. Hopkins. He was a very different man. He was less cruel, less profane, and made less noise, than Mr. Severe. His course was characterized by no extraordinary demonstrations of cruelty. He whipped, but seemed to take no pleasure in it. He was called by the slaves a good overseer.

*Frederick Douglass Series
No. 22* Jacob Lawrence,
Hampton University Museum,
Hampton, Virginia

The home plantation of Colonel Lloyd wore the appearance of a country village. All the mechanical operations for all the farms were performed here. The shoemaking and mending, the blacksmithing, cartwrighting,[4] coopering,[5] weaving, and grain-grinding, were all performed by the slaves on the home plantation. The whole place

4. **cartwrighting** [kärt′ rīt ing]: making carts.
5. **coopering** [kü′ pər ing]: making or repairing barrels.

wore a business-like aspect very unlike the neighboring farms. The number of houses, too, conspired to give it advantage over the neighboring farms. It was called by the slaves the *Great House Farm*. Few privileges were esteemed higher, by the slaves of the out-farms, than that of being selected to do errands at the Great House Farm. It was associated in their minds with greatness. A representative could not be prouder of his election to a seat in the American Congress, than a slave on one of the out-farms would be of his election to do errands at the Great House Farm. They regarded it as evidence of great confidence reposed in them by their overseers; and it was on this account, as well as a constant desire to be out of the field from under the driver's lash, that they esteemed it a high privilege, one worth careful living for. He was called the smartest and most trusty fellow, who had this honor conferred upon him the most frequently. The competitors for this office sought as diligently to please their overseers, as the office-seekers in the political parties seek to please and deceive the people. The same traits of character might be seen in Colonel Lloyd's slaves, as are seen in the slaves of the political parties.

The slaves selected to go to the Great House Farm, for the monthly allowance for themselves and their fellow-slaves, were peculiarly enthusiastic. While on their way, they would make the dense old woods, for miles around, reverberate with their wild songs, revealing at once the highest joy and the deepest sadness. They would compose and sing as they went along, consulting neither time nor tune. The thought that came up, came out—if not in the word, in the sound;—and as frequently in the one as in the other. They would sometimes sing the most pathetic sentiment in the most rapturous tone, and the most rapturous sentiment in the most pathetic tone. Into all of their songs they would manage to weave something of the Great House Farm. Especially would they do this, when leaving home. They would then sing most exultingly the following words:—

"I am going away to the Great House Farm!
O, yea! O, yea! O!"

This they would sing, as a chorus, to words which to many would seem unmeaning jargon, but which, nevertheless, were full of meaning to themselves. I have sometimes thought that the mere hearing of those songs would do more to impress some minds with the horrible character of slavery, than the reading of whole volumes of philosophy on the subject could do.

I did not, when a slave, understand the deep meaning of those rude and apparently incoherent songs. I was myself within the circle; so that I neither saw nor heard as those without might see and hear. They told a tale of woe which was then altogether beyond my feeble comprehension; they were tones loud, long, and deep; they breathed the prayer and complaint of souls boiling over with the bitterest anguish. Every tone was a testimony against slavery, and a prayer to God for deliverance from chains. The hearing of those wild notes always depressed my spirit, and filled me with ineffable sadness. I have frequently found myself in tears while hearing them. The mere recurrence to those songs, even now, afflicts me; and while I am writing these lines, an expression of feeling has already found its way down my cheek. To those songs I trace my first glimmering conception of the dehumanizing character of slavery. I can never get rid of that conception. Those songs still follow me, to deepen my hatred of slavery, and quicken my sympathies for my brethren in bonds. If any one wishes to be impressed with the soul-killing effects of slavery, let him go to Colonel Lloyd's plantation, and, on allowance-day, place himself in the deep pine woods, and there let him, in silence, analyze the sounds that shall pass through the chambers of his soul,—and if he is not thus impressed, it will only be because "there is no flesh in his obdurate heart."

I have often been utterly astonished, since I came to the north, to find persons who could speak of the singing, among slaves, as evidence of their contentment and happiness. It is impossible to conceive of a greater mistake. Slaves sing most when they are most unhappy. The songs of the slave represent the sorrows of his heart; and he is relieved by them, only as an aching heart is relieved by its tears. At least, such is my experience. I have often sung to drown my sorrow, but seldom to express my happiness. Crying for joy, and singing for joy, were alike uncommon to me while in the jaws of slavery. The singing of a man cast away upon a desolate island might be as appropriately considered as evidence of contentment and happiness, as the singing of a slave; the songs of the one and of the other are prompted by the same emotion.

FREDERICK DOUGLASS

Frederick Douglass [1817-1895] was born into slavery in Tuckahoe, Maryland. Growing up, he learned that the road to freedom and power was through education. Slaves were not taught to read. "Conscious of the difficulty of learning without a teacher, I set out with high hope, and a fixed purpose, at whatever cost or trouble, to learn how to read." After years of copying his young master's copy book, he also learned to write.

When Douglass was about eighteen years old, his first attempt to escape to freedom failed. Three years later, he succeeded in escaping and made his way to New York. There he took the name Frederick Douglass and became known as a famous orator who argued for an end to slavery.

In 1845 he wrote his first autobiography, *Narrative of the Life of Frederick Douglass, an American Slave;* he was to write two more. Two years later, he founded a newspaper, the *North Star,* to carry on the fight against slavery. His beliefs in human rights led him to attend the first women's rights convention.

During the 1860s, he helped recruit for the 54th and 55th Massachusetts Regiment and demanded the right to enlist African American men in the United States Army.

After the Civil War, Douglass served as United States Marshall of the District of Columbia and in 1889 was appointed minister to Haiti. He died in 1895, leaving behind a great legacy of writing and action.

NOVEMBER SERENADE

W. J. Holmes

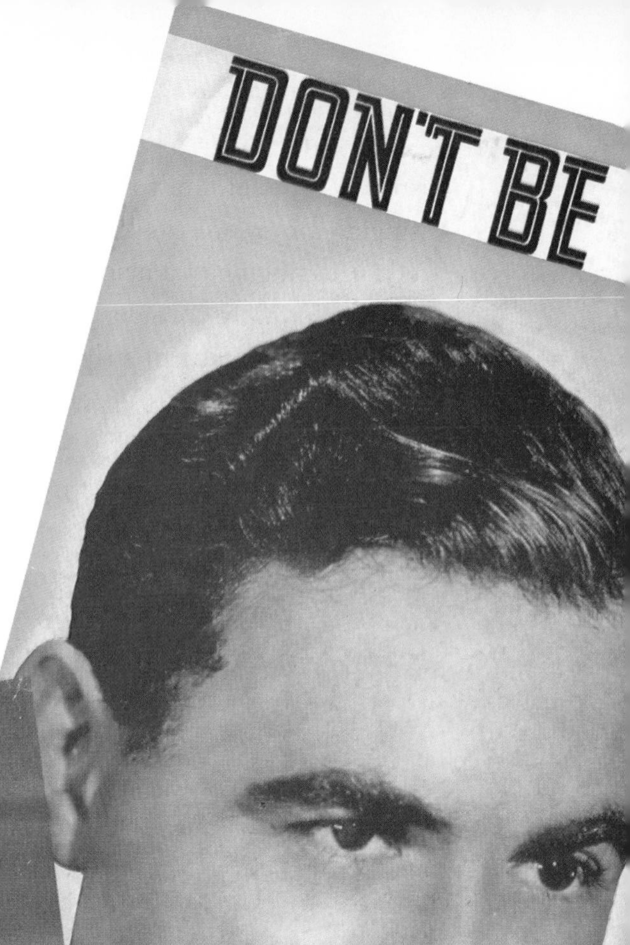

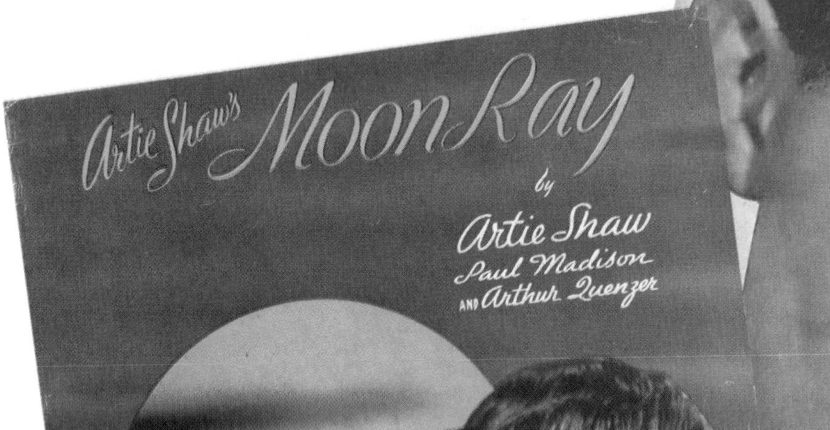

HAT WAY

by
BENNY GOODMAN
EDGAR SAMPSON
MITCHELL PARISH

"My Biggest Hit"

MOONLIGHT MOOD

LYRIC BY
HAROLD ADAMSON

MUSIC BY
PETER DE ROSE

Featured by
ELLA FITZGERALD

MUSIC CORPORATION
NEW YORK, N.Y.

Like the neighborhood and house, the man was old. The neighborhood had disintegrated past saving. But like the man, the house kept a stiff-backed hint of other, better times.

This morning he woke reluctantly to another dark November day. Then, remembering, he smiled inside. It was the weekend every month Brian came to stay overnight. He liked most of his grandchildren well enough. But Brian, youngest son of his oldest daughter, was special.

The man did the exercises the Veterans Administration Hospital had given him after triple-bypass heart surgery. He shaved, feeling rather than seeing the curve of his lathered jaw in the bathroom mirror. For more than two years he'd been what the VA eye doctor called "functionally unsighted." Meaning legally blind. Meaning glaucoma[1] had nibbled away all but blurred fragments of his vision.

It was still hard to accept, not being able to read half the night or watch World War II movies on late TV. But he still had two good ears for listening to records from the Thirties all the way up into the Sixties. Especially the Big Bands—Artie Shaw, Harry James, Tommy Dorsey, Benny Goodman, Glenn Miller, the Duke, the Count, the others. Plus having little Brian's visits to look forward to. Overall, he got along fine on his own.

1. **glaucoma** [glô kō′ mə]: a disease of the eye in which internal pressure results in gradual loss of sight.

He dressed, careful to remember to wear that ugly expensive tweed jacket Brian's mother, Elizabeth Ann, and her fat lawyer husband had given him last Christmas.

Not holding the rail, he walked stiffly down the seventeen steps to the main floor. In the kitchen, his bruised left hand, searching where the stick matches should have been, hit the microwave oven. Ordinarily the useless appliance was hidden on a back shelf in the pantry. But with Elizabeth Ann coming by today he'd brought it out, put it on the counter, forgotten it.

He glared at the gray blur that was the microwave. The family had meant well, saying how it could save him time, which he already had plenty of. The thing was, the whole idea of cooking food in seconds without fire made him queasy to his stomach.

The phone rang. It was that woman from Elder-Aid volunteers.

"Hi, Billy. Just checking to see if my favorite senior citizen needed anything."

She meant well. They all did. But he didn't want their help. Why couldn't people understand pride?

"I'm all right. Don't need anything. Goodbye."

He finally found the matchbox on the gritty linoleum floor, and lit the back burners of the gas stove.

Whistling "Deep Purple" (why didn't people whistle anymore?), he made breakfast. Real coffee, strong, with three spoons of sugar. Two fried eggs. Buttered toast and jam. The VA dietitian had warned him what that kind of food did to his cholesterol. Or maybe it was triglycerides.[2] But his father had eaten eggs for breakfast all his adult

2. **triglycerides** [trī glis′ ə rīdz]: fatty acids, blood fats.

life and died in his own bed upstairs, age ninety-one. Dietitians, like doctors, were fine when they stuck to curing sick people. But until he got sick again, he knew what was best for him. Why couldn't people understand that?

The old man turned off the stove, turned on the radio to the FM station that was mostly ads, weather, and time, plus what the pimply voiced announcers called Golden Oldies music. The forecast was strong winds with rain or snow flurries. Time, 9:43. And today's Golden Oldies started with Charlie Spivak's band, which the announcer bet very few listeners would remember. The old man remembered. He'd gone with his late wife to hear Charlie Spivak at the Civic Arena in 1944, just before being drafted and shipped out for Europe. Just in time for the Bulge[3] in Belgium in December of 1944. Now there was being cold!

The phone rang. A loud baritone said, "Good morning. We're calling a selectfew homeowners in your section of the city. About siding."

Ordinarily, he let phone salespeople finish their pitch, both because it made a break in the long day's silence and because phone selling had to be a lousy way to make a living. But this day with Brian to get ready for he was short: "Not in the market."

"How can you know that without—"

Shaking his bald head, the old man hung up, waited. It rang

3. **Bulge, Battle of the:** final major German counteroffensive in World War II.

again—the loud salesman. The old man said, "Telephone harassment is a crime. I'll bring in the phone company or the police if you bother me again. Go get a real job."

He hung up, the phone rang, but this time it was Elizabeth Ann. After all the years, she sounded so much like her mother that his useless eyes misted.

"Dad. Quick call to see if you needed anything when I come by this afternoon. How are you?"

"Fine. How's Brian?"

"Allergies. Otherwise okay. And about Brian."

"What about Brian? Is he sick again?"

"Oh, no. We can talk when I see you this afternoon. And Dad."

"What?"

"Remember me telling you about Haven Rest Apartments? They have an opening. Dad, it's not just another—"

"Old-folks' home. Yes it is."

"But won't you even look at it? Every Haven Rest tenant has a living room, kitchen, bath and shower, bedroom. Security system. R.N. on call . . . ."

"You're reading from a brochure. No."

The dreaded angry silence lengthened between him and the person in all the world, next to Brian, he cared most about. At last, she said, "Dad."

"Yes."

"If it's money."

"It isn't," although it was that, too.

"All the family agrees. Living alone in that big old barn of a house. In a neighborhood I don't even like to drive through in daylight. All those new people moving in on what used to be such a beautiful part of the city."

"When your grandparents moved into this neighborhood, they were New People. From the Old Country. Give them a chance."

"Dad."

"Yes."

"The family worries. We just want what's best for you."

"Then leave me alone in my home."

Elizabeth Ann, crying, hung up. He went into the parlor, putting on a stack of scratchy records, saving for last that favorite Benny Goodman album.

He stood there listening, smiling, as "Don't Be That Way" and then "Rose Room" spoke of happier times, of dancing with his late wife. Turning up the volume very loud, he Hoovered the whole downstairs without resting. Then dishes, piled up for days.

He smashed a cup. Sweeping up the pieces by feel, hiding the broken parts under the leaky sink, he thought: A man shouldn't have to sneak around this way in his own home.

He was breathing fast and shallow. Sweating. But no warning pressure on his ribbed chest, reminding him of the frail cardiovascular system inside there. But just in case, he slipped one of the tiny nitro[4] pills under his tongue.

The radio reported it was 1 P.M., eighty percent chance of rain or snow, wind twenty-five miles an hour out of the northwest. And he still had the errand to run.

The thing was, last Tuesday he'd forgotten to put on his list for the Elder-Aid shopper to buy treats for little Brian for that night. Without self-pity he thought: I wonder how much talking with Grandpa and how much the junk food counts in Brian's visits? About equal parts, he guessed.

The nearest thing to a grocery left in the decaying neighborhood was that convenience store-gas station, eight blocks away. He got a shaky feeling just thinking about eight blocks of broken, slippery sidewalk, passing strangers he couldn't see anymore except as skewed gray blurs.

But he couldn't disappoint Brian.

And there was time enough to stretch out on the saggy sofa, let muscles and mind relax, listen to records. With a need for other voices than his own, he reached behind the neatly stacked Big Bands collections for some Sinatra, Ella Fitzgerald, Sarah Vaughan, Nat Cole, Satchmo.

---

4. **nitro** [nī′ trō]: (nitroglycerine) medicine that dilates blood vessels.

The rest, the voices that did things to lyrics like nobody before or since, were healing. Feeling tired but all right he dressed against the weather. Checked left pants pocket for the hoarded $20 bill. Ready as he'd ever be.

The careful curb-feeling walk wasn't all that bad for five of the eight blocks. Then he sucked icy air, got a fit of coughing, strength emptying out of him like water out of a combat boot. He found a slow, wheezing military rhythm. Hut-two-three-four. Hut-two-three-four. Finally there was only a single block left and everything was going to be all right.

Near where the convenience store door had to be, the old man's boots began crunching mounds of broken glass.

"Hi, Billy."

The voice was the police officer's who'd patrolled the dying neighborhood for it must be twenty years. He said it was the third time the new people running the store had been hit. Both beat up bad. "Either neighborhood kids are getting meaner, or it's different punks."

"How do you know it was kids?" the old man asked.

The police officer didn't answer that. Instead he said, "Sorry, Billy, can't let you in the store until the Juvenile team comes to check it out. Jump in the squad car where it's warm and I'll run you home in a few minutes."

"I can walk."

Turning on careful, rubbery legs, the old man began feeling his way home. Only now the cutting wind was in his face and it was worse than in the Bulge in Belgium in 1944.

He fell, got up.

He lost track of time and space for a while. Then he blundered into a wall, high and stucco-rough, that was the corner of his street and Fremont Avenue. Only three more blocks, he thought, marching very slowly now but moving, hut-two-three-four, sound off, so cold, so scared.

The mugger took him down from behind, face in the frozen ground, easily holding both the old man's arms behind his back, not hurting more than necessary to rummage through pockets, finding the hoarded $20 that was to be for Brian's bedtime treat.

Then the mugger was gone. The old man lay face down for a while, breathing icy air, hoping a rare passing car would stop instead of speeding away, not to get involved.

Finally he made it shakily to his feet. Oriented to direction home by the awful wind in his face. Two blocks. One, the warning pressure on his chest bad. The long, once-elegant driveway, snow drifting thinly.

Home.

Inside, he sat carefully on the saving warmth of the kitchen radiator. Exhaustion, in waves, kept flooding through his wheezing chest.

Go rest. Only, first, this to do. Important!

He fumbled for the telephone. Slowly, with infinite care, he peeled the glove off his left hand. Flexed fingers. Dialed.

"Elizabeth Ann, it's Dad."

"Are you all right? Your voice sounds funny."

"Caught a little cold. That or flu. Elizabeth Ann, would Brian be too disappointed not to come stay the weekend with me?"

"I'm sure he wouldn't." The relief in her voice was open. She was like her mother, couldn't hide her feelings. "I mean, he'll be disappointed, of course. But he'll understand. Dad are you sure you're okay? You sound funny."

"So do you. Must be the connection. Elizabeth Ann?"

"Yes?"

"I've been thinking. About Brian coming every month. Oh, he's special to me, you know that."

"I know."

"But getting ready every month. . . ."

"I know. And maybe he and I could stop by for shorter visits, more often."

"That'd be fine. Well, I've got to go."

"Goodbye, Dad. I love you."

"I know. Goodbye."

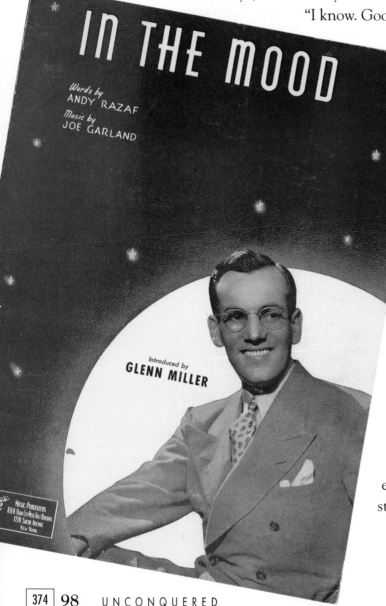

IN THE MOOD

Words by
ANDY RAZAF

Music by
JOE GARLAND

Introduced by
GLENN MILLER

He fumbled the receiver back on its cradle. Sat for a long time more on the radiator. Reached to where he kept the extra supply of heart pills. He got to his feet. Waited for the dizzy spell to pass. The thudding chest was calmer. The silence—the thought of the long weekend of silence without Brian—was bad.

In the parlor he put on Glenn Miller. "In the Mood." "String of Pearls." "Moonlight Serenade." He knew all the lyrics, not forgetting a single word after all the years.

The early November evening came. Outside it was still snowing. But in his house it was warm, as secure as life was going to get anymore. For supper he had a peanut butter sandwich, strong black coffee.

"It's not going to be so bad," he said out loud, putting the albums in place to be able to find them again.

Not holding to the railing, he climbed the seventeen steps to the second floor and went to bed with his radio tuned to the Golden Oldies station. Just before he slept, the radio played one of Benny Goodman's early hits.

Martha Tilton—he remembered the vocalist's name after fifty years. Liltin' Martha Tilton, they'd called her. And still hurting, but nothing he couldn't handle, the old man went to sleep. In his own bed. In his own home.

W. J. HOLMES

Every young writer needs heroes or role models, W. J. Holmes believes. "Mine included my paternal grandfather, a village postmaster and the most re-spected man in the county; Ernest Hemingway, whose *The Old Man and the Sea* was the first grown-up book I encouraged my own children to read; and a Franciscan nun who could laugh and radiate goodness at the same time," says Holmes.

Reading and books were important to Holmes when he was young. "Grades 6, 7, and 8 were, for me, a lonely and confused time. Thanks to incurably restless parents, I spent much time adjusting to new kids, schools, relatives, and other strangers. Books were about the only constant I could trust; in a way, now, many years later, they still are."

W. J. Holmes left newspaper reporting to take part in establishing a comprehensive communications program for a highly respected medical center. He is now an honorary member of the Mayo Alumni Association and a freelance writer of fiction and features. He resides in Rochester, Minnesota.

MY PEOPLE ARE A MULTITUDE OF ONE

NANCY WOOD

My people are a multitude of one.
Many voices are within them.
Many lives they have lived as various Beings.
They could have been a bear, a lion, an eagle or even
A rock, a river or a tree.   5
Who knows?
All of these Beings are within them.
They can use them any time they want.
On some days it is good to be a tree
Looking out in all directions at once.   10
On some days it is better to be a rock
Saying nothing and blind to everything.
On some days the only thing to do is
To fight fiercely like a lion.
Then, too, there are reasons for being an eagle.   15
When life becomes too hard here
My people can fly away and see
How small the earth really is.
Then they can laugh and come back home again.

Conventionalized Bird with Rain Clouds Oqwa Pi, watercolor, 12" x 18",
San Ildefonso Pueblo, New Mexico

N A N C Y   W O O D

Nancy Wood was born in Trenton, New Jersey. She studied first at Bucknell University and then at the University of Colorado. She is the author of more than twenty books of poetry, fiction, nonfiction, and photography. Her most recent work, *Spirit Walker,* was awarded the Lee Bennett Hopkins Poetry Award in 1994. She has also received a literary fellowship from the National Endowment for the Arts for a novel, *The Soledad Crucifixion.* Nancy Wood makes her home in Santa Fe, New Mexico.

Asking Big Questions About the Literature

What is survival?

Point of View

Authors choose a **point of view,** or vantage point, from which to present the action in their stories.

A *first-person narrator* is a character in the story who tells the story as he or she experiences it and uses pronouns such as *I, me, we, us,* and *ours.* A *third-person limited narrator* is a character who tells the story through his or her eyes and uses pronouns such as *he, she, they, them,* and *theirs.* A *third-person omniscient* (all-knowing) narrator also tells the story in the third person.

In this unit, the point of view enhances your understanding of survival. Make a chart to identify the main character and the point of view of each nonfiction selection and short story you've read in this unit. (*See "Point of View" on page 118.*)

Ask THE CHARACTERS

Each character in this unit is a survivor—someone who has held onto life *despite* challenges and obstacles. Choose several characters whose survival stories you admire. For each character, write a definition of survival from that character's point of view. Now write a one-sentence definition of survival that combines these various points of view.

Say It in Pictures

A famous expression says, "A picture is worth a thousand words." One illustration, that is, communicates more meaning than many words. Choose two selections from this unit in which the art that accompanies the selection plays a major role in your understanding of the story. For each selection, write a paragraph that explains *how* and *why* the art helps you understand the meaning of survival in the selection.

Literature	Character	Point of View
I Promised I Would Tell	Sonia Schreiber Weitz	First-Person Narrator

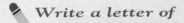

Write a letter of

A D V I C E

Based on a selection in this unit, take the role of one character who is a survivor—someone who never gives up. Write a letter of advice to another character in the same selection or in another selection. Describe the qualities, feelings, thoughts, and other supports (such as reliance on friends, family, or faith) that helped you survive. Here is the beginning of a letter that the elderly man in "November Serenade" might have written to Hue Hue in *The Girl in the White Ship*.

Dear Hue Hue,

I know how difficult it is for you to lose your home. I, too, am faced with the loss of my home. But don't give up. Treasure your memories of home so that, when you are far from home, you can keep home with you. . . .

Setting

The **setting** of a story, poem, or play is the time and place in which the action occurs. In this unit, many of the selections are set in a time or place that threatens the survival of a character. Write a descriptive paragraph of a setting from this unit. Use *specific details*, such as dates (1940s) and place-names (Poland), to identify the setting. Use *sensory details*, such has *gloomy, gray,* and *harsh,* to bring the setting to life. (*See* "Setting" on page 119.)

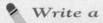

Write a

P O E M

The poem "Unconquered and Unconquerable" has a pattern of *rhyme* (making the endings of two or more lines sound alike) and *repetition* (repeating a line in the same form) that makes the poem pleasing to the ear. Using the poem as a model, write another poem about the triumphant spirit of a survivor.

Asking Big Questions About the Literature

What kinds of survival challenges have different cultures faced?

Write a

POEM

In the early 1500s, Hernán Cortés, a Spanish conquistador, or fortune hunter, conquered the Aztecs, a group of Native Americans living in the Valley of Mexico. In a poem, an anonymous Aztec writer expresses the grief that his people feel for the ruin of their once-beautiful capital, Tenochtitlán. The poem has five stanzas, but the first stanza summarizes the whole story of the poem. Read this stanza. Then, using the words of the Aztec poet as a model, write a *Voices from the Past* poem about one of the groups in this unit.

Broken spears lie in the roads;
we have torn our hair in our grief,
The houses are roofless now, and their walls
are red with blood.

LITERATURE STUDY

Point of View

The poems in this unit are all told from the first-person **point of view**, that is, by a narrator who uses the pronouns *I* or *we*. Make a chart like the one on this page and complete the second column with a phrase identifying the narrator. Then choose a poem, and taking the part of the narrator, prepare an oral presentation in which you describe the survival challenge that you face. (*See "Point of View" on page 118.*)

Poem	Voice
"Mother to Son"	Mother speaking to her son
"Unconquered"	
"We Shall Wait Forever"	
"My People Are a Multitude of One"	

Why do people threaten one another's survival?

M A K E
A FACT FILE

Choose three or more selections from this unit and identify each of the following people or groups:

- the oppressed (the group or person whose survival is threatened)
- the oppressor (the group or person posing the threat)

Using social-studies textbooks, encyclopedias, and other reference sources, work with a partner or group to make a fact file like the one that has been started for you. Use your fact file to write several paragraphs in which you answer the question, Why does one group threaten the survival of another?

Literature Title "The Girl in the White Ship"

Oppressed Hue Hue and her family

Oppressor Government of Vietnam

Fact In 1975, the Communists of North Vietnam took power in the south. The new government deprived citizens of human rights and freedom.

Write an
EDITORIAL

An **editorial** is a short persuasive essay in which a writer expresses his or her opinion of a news story or event. Write an editorial about a group or person in this unit that threatens another's survival. Use the editorial to convince readers that people should "live and let live."

NOW Choose a Project!

Three projects involving survival are described on the following pages.

Writing Workshop

WRITE A RESEARCH PAPER

Clarence Darrow, a famous lawyer, once wrote, "History repeats it-self. That's one of the things wrong with history." When we study history, we see that Darrow is correct. Through the ages, historical events involving threats to the survival of one or more groups of people *have* taken place time and time again.

But people *can* learn from the past. Your **purpose** in this project will be to write a research paper about a survival challenge. Then you will use your research to take part in a classroom seminar entitled "Never Again." Your **audience** will be your teacher and your classmates.

Prewriting

CHOOSING A TOPIC

To help you choose a topic, here is a list of some of the groups whose survival challenges you read about in this unit.

European Jews (*I Promised I Would Tell*)
The people of Vietnam (*The Girl in the White Ship*)
African Americans (*Narrative of the Life of Frederick Douglass*)
Native Americans ("Holding Out")

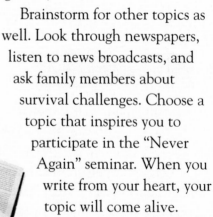

Brainstorm for other topics as well. Look through newspapers, listen to news broadcasts, and ask family members about survival challenges. Choose a topic that inspires you to participate in the "Never Again" seminar. When you write from your heart, your topic will come alive.

Prewriting
NARROWING THE TOPIC

Once you've chosen a topic, your next step is to choose one aspect—or part of this topic— on which to focus. Use a web, like the one shown, to organize your thoughts.

The history of anti-Semitism

Holocaust

The fate of the Jewish people

Hitler's rise to power

Prewriting
RESEARCHING AND NOTETAKING

Make a list of questions that you want to answer in your research paper. Put each question—called a guide question—on the top of one or more note cards for use when you conduct your research.

Armed with your list of questions, you can begin the search through books, articles, and other sources. The guidelines below will help you.

Where were the camps located?

STRATEGIES FOR RESEARCHING

1. Use the card catalog or a computerized library system to find sources of information, such as encyclopedias, books, magazines, and newspapers.
2. Skim through the index or table of contents of each source to determine whether it contains the information you need.
3. Look through your sources for answers to each question. Write your findings on the appropriate note cards. State the information in your own words. If you use the exact words of a writer, use quotation marks to indicate that the words are not your own.
4. On the note card, record the author, title, and other publishing information of each source.

Prewriting

OUTLINING

Now that you have researched your topic, arrange your note cards in piles according to your guide questions. These guide questions become the main headings of your outline, designated by Roman numerals. The information in each set of cards supplies the subtopics and details under each heading. Writing a thesis statement, or main idea, for your report will help you organize your main headings and the points under them.

Here is part of the outline that student writer Tiffany Dzieginski wrote for her research paper on pages 110-111.

> Thesis Statement: Adolf Hitler, the leader of Nazi Germany, believed in the extermination of the Jewish people.
> I. Concentration camps
>   A. In Poland—Chelmno, Belzec, Sobibor, Treblinka, Maidanak, Auschwitz
>   B. Use of trickery to get Jews to camps
> II. Selection in the camps
>   A. Old, weak, and sick chosen for death
>   B. Healthy and strong used for slave labor

Drafting YOUR RESEARCH PAPER

Use your outline to draft your report. Follow these guidelines.

- Introduce your paper with a question, a quotation, or a startling fact. Tiffany writes on pages 110-111, "When I was growing up, I remember staring in horror at the numbers carved on the arm of my cousin Bessie." Include your thesis statement.
- Write several supporting paragraphs that add to or develop your main idea. Each developmental paragraph needs a topic sentence and details that support it, and each roman numeral in your outline can be a supporting paragraph.
- Give credit to the authors whose ideas or words you use. Write in parentheses the author's last name and the page numbers from the book at the end of the last sentence or idea you use.
- At the end of your paper, include a Works Cited page as shown:
  Rossell, Seymour. <u>The Holocaust</u>. New York: Franklin Watts, 1981.
- Write a concluding paragraph that restates your main idea. Tiffany Dzieginski writes, "There but for the grace of God go I."
- Write a title for your report that, like Tiffany's title, "We Must Never Forget," captures the main idea.

Revising YOUR RESEARCH PAPER

Read your report out loud to hear how it sounds. Are there parts that you especially like? What parts sound awkward or in need of revision? Now share your report with a partner. Does your partner understand the main idea and supporting details? Is your partner drawn into your writing? What new information has he or she learned from your report? Use this feedback and your own comments to revise your draft.

Editing YOUR RESEARCH PAPER

After revising, work with your partner to check for errors in punctuation, spelling, and grammar. Correct your errors and make a publishable copy of your report.

Publishing
YOUR RESEARCH
PAPER

Share your research by taking part in a classroom discussion entitled "Never Again." Here are some ideas for sharing:

- Begin by explaining why you picked this topic.
- Explain what you wanted to learn from your research.
- Summarize the information you learned.
- Get personal with classmates. Share your feelings about what you've learned. Point out how the study of historical events can prevent history from repeating itself.

STUDENT MODEL

We Must Never Forget
by Tiffany Dzieginski, Orland Park, Illinois

When I was growing up, I remember staring in horror at the numbers carved on the arm of my cousin Bessie. The numbers were there because Bessie was a survivor of the Holocaust. I can only imagine the terrible fear of everyday survival that Bessie and other European Jews faced because Adolph Hitler, the leader of Nazi Germany, believed in the extermination of the Jewish people. I wanted to find out more about Bessie's ordeal.

Bessie lived in Poland. The Nazis had six death camps there—Chelmno, Belzec, Sobibor, Treblinka, Maidanek, and Auschwitz. The Nazis used trickery to get Polish Jews to go willingly to the death camps. As Nazi guards herded families onto cattle cars for transportation, they told the Jews that they were being moved to a place where there was more food and work. (Gilbert 458) The awful truth was revealed when

Thesis statement [

Facts from outline [

the cattle cars reached the camps. As Jews got off the cars, Nazi officials selected who would live and who would die. They sent the old, weak, sick, and young in one direction to be killed. They kept the strong for slave labor.

The Jews selected for death did not immediately know their fate. The Nazis told them they were going to take showers. Once they entered the showers, the doors were locked and poisonous gas came out of the shower heads. Some died immediately. Others suffered for a long time. (Rossel 79)

The Jews chosen for slave labor did not live for very long. The Nazis killed them through work. Whatever work these people could produce would help the Nazis win the war. But the life of each person had no meaning. If a person was worked to death, the Nazis simply found someone else to take his or her place. "The Nazis' hatred of Jews was such that many Nazis wanted to make the Jews suffer, even more than they wanted to make money from Jewish labor. To these Nazis, slavery was better than killing the Jews immediately, for the slaves would first be profitable, then they would die, and they would also suffer cruelly." (Rossel 85)

In the camps, the Jewish laborers had very difficult lives. They received almost no food, froze in the winter, suffocated in the summer, and lived with rats, filth, and disease. And the unending knowledge of their inevitable death was always with them. (Gilbert 84)

[Paper continues.]

Somehow Bessie and others managed to survive. I remember an empty sadness in her eyes when she spoke of the camps. I always think, "There but for the grace of God go I."

Cooperative Learning

TAKE ME TO THE FAIR

If variety is the spice of life, the United States is not lacking in spice. Local newspapers often list restaurants and special events that reflect ways of life from all over the world. So set aside a date on your calendar to host a fair displaying cultural diversity.

The PROJECT

First, work as a class to prepare a list of ethnic groups or cultures that you will feature at your fair. Then divide into small groups and choose a culture from the class list that most interests members of your group. To avoid researching the same culture as another group, select one person in your group to act as a liaison. The liaison's job is make sure that there is no overlap or repetition. If there is overlap, the liaison will negotiate with other groups to work out a solution. As a last resort, the liaison can contact the teacher for help.

Assigning JOBS

Since the goal of each group is to create one booth among many, it's important to work with your group to conduct research and prepare displays. Use encyclopedias and other reference sources to find out as much as you can about the ethnic group you've chosen. Then work together to choose a topic for each group member to research. Assign topics based on the interests of group members and make a chart like the one here to help the group assign projects and make the fair work.

Project Chart

Category	Name
Music	_____
Cooking	_____
Language	_____
Sports	_____
Crafts	_____

Setting Up THE BOOTH

Setting up the booth requires cooperation and communication among group members. To make sure preparations go smoothly, assign the roles listed below.

- Manager: Works with group members to keep everyone on target and to maintain deadlines.
- Materials Coordinator: Ensures that group members have supplies, such as recipe ingredients and art materials.
- Booth Designer: Assembles projects and plans the layout of the booth.

Cultural FAIR DAY

Make invitations well in advance of the cultural fair and invite other classes, faculty members, parents, and community members to share in your festivities. You may want to videotape the fair in progress. If possible, play a tape recording of ethnic music at your booth. Be prepared to explain each item in your booth to guests and take time to visit other classmates and their booths.

Helping Your Community

AND JUSTICE FOR ALL

With a group of students, develop a campaign called "Stop." The purpose of the campaign is to make people in your community aware of injustice. To accomplish this, you and your group will make a poster with a catchy and convincing slogan.

Choosing A SLOGAN

Your slogan should be short and to the point. Most important, you want it to be memorable. Watch TV ads and look through magazines to help you generate ideas. One example of a suitable slogan is "STOP Prejudice Before It Starts."

Designing A LOGO

Create a logo that illustrates your slogan or relates to the general theme of the campaign. For example, here are some words and concepts you might show.

- **Peace**
- **Acceptance**
- **Cooperation**
- **Respect**

Creating A CAMPAIGN POSTER

Since the purpose of the poster is to make people aware of your campaign, you need to create a poster that contains the elements listed below.

- Campaign slogan
- Campaign logo
- Information about your group and what it hopes to accomplish
- Where people can find copies of your brochure (See section entitled "Writing a Brochure.")

Make your poster colorful and interesting but keep the tone serious. Get permission to hang copies in places where people will see them, such as town offices and buildings.

Writing A BROCHURE

The brochure is the heart of your campaign. It should include

- An introduction in which you describe the purpose of the campaign.
- A description of issues and attitudes that lead to an injustice such as discrimination. (Use selections from this unit to make your points.)
- Steps that people can take to stop the injustice before it begins.
- Resources that people can turn to for more information. Ask parents, teachers, and other people in your community for the names of groups, individuals, and organizations that may be helpful.

Following THE CAMPAIGN

Use the following questions to write an evaluation of your campaign. How did people in your community react to the campaign? Did your campaign reach a large audience or a small one? Was your brochure helpful? What would you do differently if you did the campaign again? What part would you do the same way if you did the campaign again?

Putting It All Together

What Have You Learned About Survival Among Various Cultures?

Now that you've finished *Unconquered*, think back about how your ideas about this theme have changed. Review your journal and other pieces of writing. Look at the projects and activities you completed. Share your thoughts with classmates by analyzing a present-day survival challenge and presenting a speech to classmates entitled "What We Can Do to Help."

SPEAKING OUT

Prewriting and Drafting   To begin, find out what's in the news. Check newspapers, magazines, and television and radio broadcasts. Talk with people in your community. Don't forget yourself. Think about the challenges that you and other young people face. Write down ideas and choose a topic that interests you personally.

Now write an outline for your speech that includes the elements listed below. For each element, prepare note cards that will jog your memory as you speak.

- An introduction about the issue and its importance to you.
- An explanation of concrete ideas and suggestions for taking action. Use the literature in this unit as a resource. For example, if you are focusing on issues of aging, review "November Serenade." If you were the daughter in this selection, what would you do to protect your father while helping him remain independent?
- A conclusion that urges others to join your crusade.

Revising and Editing   Practice your speech in front of a classmate. Is your topic clear and well defined? Do you use your note cards as prompts to refresh your memory? Do you include relevant information and suggestions?

Revise your notes and outline. Then try your speech on someone else or practice it in front of a mirror. If a tape recorder is available, use it to hear how you sound.

Publishing   To prevent nervousness, follow these suggestions on your big day:
- Speak loudly and slowly.
- Make eye contact.
- Stand up tall.
- Speak from your heart.

After you have given your speech, put it in writing. File your note cards and your speech. You may have an opportunity to present the speech again!

Evaluating Your Work

Think Back About the Big Questions

With a partner, discuss the Big Questions on pages 10-11 and the questions you generated for **Now Think!** on page 11. In your journal, write a paragraph describing how your responses to the Big Questions and to your own questions have changed after your work in this unit.

Think Back About Your Work

Flip through the pages of this text. As you flip, recall the selections you've read and the activities you've done. Take a few moments to glance through your journal. Use a critic's eye to evaluate your work. When you finish your self-evaluation, give it to your teacher. Here are some questions to guide you:

- Which literature selections in this unit affected you most strongly? Why?

- What did you learn about the ability of people to survive in the face of overwhelming obstacles?

- Which activity changed the way you felt about the plight of people in trouble?

- If you were to do one activity again, what would you do differently? What would you keep the same?

- Many selections in this unit are nonfiction; that is, the events and people are real. What do you like or dislike about reading nonfiction?

- Did you work and participate to your full potential? If not, what held you back?

Now rate your work. Use the following scale and give at least three reasons for your rating.

1 = Outstanding	3 = Fair
2 = Good	4 = Not as good as it could have been

POINT OF VIEW

What Is Point of View?
When authors write stories, they choose a **point of view**, or vantage point, from which to present the action. Many writers choose to tell their stories through the point of view of a *first-person narrator* and use the pronouns *I* or *we*. First-person narrators are characters in the story; they tell the story as they understand or experience it.

Authors who write from the *third-person point of view* use pronouns such as *she*, *he*, or *they*. Some writers use a *third-person limited point of view*, in which the narrator, who is usually a character in the story, tells the story through his or her eyes. Writers may also use an *omniscient*, or all-knowing, point of view. A *third-person omniscient narrator* knows everything about the actions and even the thoughts of the characters.

Comparing Points of View
When a story is told through the eyes of a third-person omniscient narrator, readers are told not only what is happening but also how characters think and feel. Choose a selection from this unit in which the point of view is third-person omniscient. Retell a part of the story from the first-person point of view. Compare your retelling with the original. In a paragraph, explain how switching the point of view changes what the reader knows or learns about the character.

Telling a Story
The word *omniscient* comes from two Latin words—*omnis*, meaning "all" and *scientia*, meaning "knowing." Thus, an omniscient narrator knows all there is to know about characters and events in a story. Use the omniscient point of view to write a scene from a short story. As you write, pretend that you are on a mountain top looking down at the action. Keep the definition of *omniscient* in mind as you write.

What Is Setting?

The **setting** of a work of literature is the time and place in which the action occurs. *Time* includes a specific time in history, such as 1948, or a general time period, such as past, present, or future. *Place* includes geographic location, such as the name of a country, a description of specific buildings, or the physical arrangement of a room. In some stories, the setting plays a key role in the plot. In other stories, it creates *mood*—the atmosphere or feeling created by a sense of place.

Writing about Mood The settings of several selections in this unit refer to specific historical periods during which one group of people threatened the survival of another group. Although each of these selections has a different physical setting (for example, Poland, Vietnam, the United States) and takes place during a different time period, the mood or atmosphere of each setting is similar. Brainstorm for words, such as *tense*, *sad*, or *frightened*, that describe your feelings as you read these selections. Then write a paragraph that explains how the setting of each selection contributes to these feelings. Share your paragraph with a classmate. Notice the similarities and differences in what you wrote.

Imagining a Safe Place Places can cause people to feel happy or sad. They can also contribute to feelings of fear or safety. Think of a real or imaginary place that makes you feel safe. Now close your eyes and picture your surroundings. Are you in a room in your house? Are you outside in a field or yard? Who is with you? A friend? A pet? No one? Is the day beginning or ending? What season of the year do you see? Describe your safe place as the setting of a short story or play.

GLOSSARY OF LITERARY TERMS

A

alliteration   Repetition of the first sound—usually a consonant sound—in several words of a sentence or a line of poetry.

allusion   An author's indirect reference to someone or something that is presumed to be familiar to the reader.

anecdote   A short narrative about an interesting or a humorous event, usually in the life of a person.

antagonist   The person or force opposing the protagonist, or main character in a literary work. [See also *protagonist*.]

autobiography   A person's written account of his or her own life.

B

ballad   A poem, often a song, that tells a story in simple verse.

biography   An account of a person's life, written by another person.

blank verse   Unrhymed poetry.

C

character   A person or an animal that participates in the action of a work of literature. A *dynamic character* is one whose thoughts, feelings, and actions are changeable and lifelike; a *static character* always remains the same. [See also *protagonist*, *antagonist*.]

characterization   The creation of characters through the characters' use of language and through descriptions of their appearance, thoughts, emotions, and actions. [See also *character*.]

chronology   An arrangement of events in the order in which they happen.

cliché   An overused expression that is trite rather than meaningful.

climax   The highest point of tension in the plot of a work of literature. [See also *plot*.]

comedy   An amusing play that has a happy ending.

conclusion   The final part or ending of a piece of literature.

concrete poem   A poem arranged on the page so that its punctuation, letters, and lines make the shape of the subject of the poem.

conflict   A problem that confronts the characters in a piece of literature. The conflict may be *internal* (a character's struggle within himself or herself) or *external* (a character's struggle against nature, another person, or society). [See also *plot*.]

context   The general sense of words that helps readers to understand the meaning of unfamiliar words and phrases in a piece of writing.

D

description   An author's use of words to give the reader or listener a mental picture, an impression, or an understanding of a person, place, thing, event, or idea.

dialect   A form of speech spoken by people in a particular group or geographical region that differs in vocabulary, grammar, and pronunciation from the standard language.

dialogue   The spoken words and conversation of characters in a work of literature.

drama   A play that is performed before an audience according to stage directions and using dialogue. Classical drama has two genres: *tragedy* and *comedy*. Modern drama includes *melodrama, satire, theater of the absurd*, and *pantomime*. [See also *comedy, play*, and *tragedy*.]

dramatic poetry   A play written in the form of poetry.

E

epic   A long narrative poem—written in a formal style and meant to be read aloud—that relates the adventures and

experiences of one or more great heroes or heroines.

essay Personal nonfiction writing about a particular subject that is important to the writer.

excerpt A passage from a larger work that has been taken out of its context to be used for a special purpose.

exposition Writing that explains, analyzes, or defines.

extended metaphor An elaborately drawn out metaphor. [See also *metaphor*.]

F

fable A short, simple story whose purpose is to teach a lesson, usually with animal characters who talk and act like people.

fantasy Imaginative fiction about unrealistic characters, places, and events.

fiction Literature, including the short story and the novel, that tells about imaginary people and events.

figurative language Language used to express ideas through figures of speech: descriptions that aren't meant to be taken literally. Types of figurative language include *simile, metaphor, extended metaphor, hyperbole,* and *personification*.

figure of speech A type of figurative language, not meant to be taken literally, that expresses something in such a way that it brings the thing to life in the reader's or listener's imagination. [See also *figurative language*.]

flashback A break in a story's action that relates a past happening in order to give the reader background information about a present action in the story.

folktale A story that has been passed along from storyteller to storyteller for generations. Kinds of folktales include *tall tales, fairy tales, fables, legends,* and *myths*.

foreshadowing The use of clues to create suspense by giving the reader or audience hints of events to come.

free verse Poetry that has no formal rhyme scheme or metrical pattern.

G

genre A major category of art. The three major literary genres are poetry, prose, and drama.

H

haiku A three-line Japanese verse form. In most haiku, the first and third lines have five syllables, while the second line has seven. The

traditional haiku describes a complicated feeling or thought in simple language through a single image.

hero/heroine The main character in a work of literature. In heroic literature, the hero or heroine is a particularly brave, noble, or clever person whose achievements are unusual and important. [See also *character*.]

heroic age The historical period in western civilization—from about 800 B.C. through A.D. 200—during which most works of heroic literature, such as myths and epics, were created in ancient Greece and Rome.

hubris Arrogance or excessive pride leading to mistakes; the character flaw in a hero of classical tragedy.

hyperbole An obvious exaggeration used for emphasis. [See also *figurative language*.]

I

idiom An expression whose meaning cannot be understood from the ordinary meaning of the words. For example, *It's raining cats and dogs*.

imagery The words and phrases in writing that appeal to the senses of sight, hearing, taste, touch, and smell.

irony An effect created by a sharp contrast between what is expected and what is real. An *ironic twist* in a plot is an event that is the complete opposite of what the characters have been hoping or expecting will happen. An *ironic statement* declares the opposite of the speaker's literal meaning.

J

jargon Words and phrases used by a group of people who share the same profession or special interests in order to refer to technical things or processes with which they are familiar. In general, jargon is any terminology that sounds unclear, overused, or pretentious.

L

legend A famous folktale about heroic actions, passed along by word of mouth from generation to generation. The legend may have begun as a factual account of real people and events but has become mostly or completely fictitious.

limerick A form of light verse, or humorous poetry, written in one five-line stanza with a regular scheme of rhyme and meter.

literature The branch of art that is expressed in written language and includes all written genres.

lyric poem A short poem that expresses personal feelings and thoughts in a musical way. Originally, lyrics were the words of songs that were sung to music played on the lyre, a stringed instrument invented by the ancient Greeks.

M

metamorphosis The transformation of one thing, or being, into another completely different thing or being, such as a caterpillar's change into a butterfly.

metaphor Figurative language in which one thing is said to be another thing. [See also *figurative language*.]

meter The pattern of rhythm in lines of poetry. The most common meter, in poetry written in English, is iambic pentameter, that is, a verse having five metrical feet, each foot of verse having two syllables, an unaccented one followed by an accented one.

mood The feeling or atmosphere that a reader senses while reading or listening to a work of literature.

motivation A character's reasons for doing, thinking, feeling, or saying something. Sometimes an author will make a character's motivation obvious from the beginning. In realistic fiction and drama, however, a character's motivation may be so complicated that the reader discovers it gradually, by studying the character's thoughts, feelings, and behavior.

myth A story, passed along by word of mouth for generations, about the actions of gods and goddesses or superhuman heroes and heroines. Most myths were first told to explain the origins of natural things or to justify the social rules and customs of a particular society.

N

narration The process of telling a story. For both fiction and nonfiction, there are two main kinds of narration, based on whether the story is told from a first-person or third-person point of view. [See also *point of view*.]

narrative poem A poem that tells a story containing the basic literary ingredients of fiction: character, setting, and plot.

narrator The person, or voice, that tells a story. [See also *point of view, voice*.]

nonfiction Prose that is factually true and is about real people, events, and places.

nonstandard English
Versions of English, such as slang and dialects, that use pronunciation, vocabulary, idiomatic expressions, grammar, and punctuation that differ from the accepted "correct" constructions of English.

novel   A long work of narrative prose fiction. A novel contains narration, a setting or settings, characters, dialogue, and a more complicated plot than a short story.

O

onomatopoeia   The technique of using words that imitate the sounds they describe, such as *hiss*, *buzz*, and *splash*.

oral tradition   Stories, poems, and songs that have been kept alive by being told, recited, and sung by people over many generations. Since the works were not originally written, they often have many different versions.

P

parable   A brief story—similar to a fable, but about people—that describes an ordinary situation and concludes with a short moral or lesson to be learned.

personification   Figurative language in which an animal, an object, or an idea is given human characteristics. [See also *figurative language*.]

persuasion   A type of speech or writing whose purpose is to convince people that something is true or important.

play   A work of dramatic literature written for performance by actors before an audience. In classical or traditional drama, a play is divided into five acts, each containing a number of scenes. Each act represents a distinct phase in the development of the plot. Modern plays often have only one act and one scene.

playwright   The author of a play.

plot   The sequence of actions and events in fiction or drama. A traditional plot has at least three parts: the *rising action*, leading up to a turning point that affects the main character; the *climax*, the turning point or moment of greatest intensity or interest; and the *falling action*, leading away from the conflict, or resolving it.

poetry   Language selected and arranged in order to say something in a compressed or nonliteral way. Modern poetry may or may not use many of the traditional poetic techniques that include *meter*, *rhyme*, *alliteration*, *figurative language*, *symbolism*, and *specific verse forms*.

point of view   The perspective from which a writer tells a story. *First-person* narrators tell the story from their own point of view, using pronouns such as *I* or *me*. *Third-person* narrators, using pronouns such as *he*, *she*, or *them*, may be *omniscient* (knowing everything about all characters), or *limited* (taking the point of view of one character). [See also *narration*.]

propaganda   Information or ideas that may or may not be true, but are spread as though they are true, in order to persuade people to do or believe something.

prose   The ordinary form of written and spoken language used to create fiction, nonfiction, and most drama.

protagonist   The main character of a literary work. [See also *character* and *characterization*.]

R

refrain   A line or group of lines that is repeated, usually at the end of each verse, in a poem or a song.

repetition   The use of the same formal element more than once in a literary work, for emphasis or in order to achieve another desired effect.

resolution   The falling action in fiction or drama,

including all of the developments that follow the climax and show that the story's conflict is over. [See also *plot*.]

rhyme scheme   A repeated pattern of similar sounds, usually found at the ends of lines of poetry or poetic drama.

rhythm   In poetry, the measured recurrence of accented and unaccented syllables in a particular pattern. [See also *meter*.]

S

scene   The time, place, and circumstances of a play or a story. In a play, a scene is a section of an act. [See also *play*.]

science fiction   Fantasy literature set in an imaginary future, with details and situations that are designed to seem scientifically possible.

setting   The time and place of a work of literature.

short story   Narrative prose fiction that is shorter and has a less complicated plot than a novel. A short story contains narration, at least one setting, at least one character, and usually some dialogue.

simile   Figurative language that compares two unlike things, introduced by the words "like" or "as." [See also *figurative language*.]

soliloquy   In a play, a short speech spoken by a single character when he or she is alone on the stage. A soliloquy usually expresses the character's innermost thoughts and feelings, when he or she thinks no other characters can hear.

sonnet   A poem written in one stanza, using fourteen lines of iambic pentameter. [See also *meter*.]

speaker   In poetry, the individual whose voice seems to be speaking the lines. [See also *narration*, *voice*.]

stage directions   The directions, written by the playwright, to tell the director, actors, and theater technicians how a play should be dramatized. Stage directions may specify such things as how the setting should appear in each scene, how the actors should deliver their lines, when the stage curtain should rise and fall, how stage lights should be used, where on the stage the actors should be during the action, and when sound effects should be used.

stanza   A group of lines in poetry set apart by blank lines before and after the group; a poetic verse.

style   The distinctive way in which an author composes a work of literature in written or spoken language.

suspense   An effect created by authors of various types of fiction and drama, especially adventure and mystery, to heighten interest in the story.

symbol   An image, person, place, or thing that is used to express the idea of something else.

T

tall tale   A kind of folk tale, or legend, that exaggerates the characteristics of its hero or heroine.

theme   The main idea or underlying subject of a work of literature.

tone   The attitude that a work of literature expresses to the reader through its style.

tragedy   In classical drama, a tragedy depicts a noble hero or heroine who makes a mistake of judgment that has disastrous consequences.

V

verse   A stanza in a poem. Also, a synonym for poetry as a genre. [See also *stanza*.]

voice   The narrator or the person who relates the action of a piece of literature. [See also *speaker*.]

ACKNOWLEDGMENTS

Grateful acknowledgment is made for permission to reprint the following copyrighted material.

"Unconquered and Unconquerable" by Lewis H. Latimer, from *Poems of Love and Life*.

From *The Girl in the White Ship* by Peter Townsend, copyright © 1981 by Peter Townsend. First published in the United States in 1983 by Holt, Rinehart and Winston. Reprinted by permission of the publisher.

"Mother to Son" by Langston Hughes from *Selected Poems* by Langston Hughes, copyright 1926 by Alfred A. Knopf, Inc. and renewed 1954 by Langston Hughes. Reprinted by permission of the publisher.

From *I Promised I Would Tell* by Sonia Schreiber Weitz by permission of the author. Available from Facing History and Ourselves (617-232-1595).

"We Shall Wait Forever" by Darlene Sinyella was first published in 1990 in *A Tree Full of Leaves Which Are Stars*, an anthology of Native American student poetry edited by Mick Fedullo. Reprinted by permission of the author.

"Holding Out" by Ouida Sebestyen, copyright © 1990 by Ouida Sebestyen, reprinted by permission from *Center Stage*, edited by Donald Gallo, HarperCollins Publisher.

"November Serenade" by W. J. Holmes is reprinted by permission of the author. First appeared in November 1992 issue of *Inflight Magazine*, American Air Lines.

"My People Are a Multitude of One" by Nancy Wood from *Many Winters*. Copyright ©1974 by Nancy Wood, Doubleday & Company. Used by permission.

ILLUSTRATION

14-33 Map by John Rumery; 40-59 Barbed wire by Dave Shepherd; 63-81 Petroglyphs by Dave Shepherd.

PHOTOGRAPHY

4 *t* Jim Whitmer/Stock Boston; *b* John Owens/©D.C. Heath; 5 The Museum of Modern Art, New York. Gift of Abby Aldrich Rockefeller; 6 Sarah Putnam/©D.C. Heath; 8-9 Superstock; 9 Sanjay Kothari; 10 *t* Richard Haynes/©D.C. Heath; *b* Jim Whitmer/Stock Boston; 11 *t* David Strickler/The Image Works; *c, b* Sarah Putnam/©D.C. Heath; 12 Leland Bobbe/Tony Stone Images; 13 Historical Pictures Collection/Stock Montage, Inc.; *background* Leland Bobbe/Tony Stone Images; 14 *t* Naomi Duguid/Asia Access; *bl* J.P. Laffont/Sygma; *br* Chad Slattery/Tony Stone Images; 15 *t* Jeffrey Alford/Asia Access; *b* Andrew Holbrooke/Black Star; 20 *tl* Naomi Duguid/Asia Access; *tr* Chad Slattery/Tony Stone Images; *b* Andrew Holbrooke/Black Star; 22-23 Jeffrey Alford/Asia Access; 30 J.P. Laffont/Sygma; 34-35 Patrick Deloche/Sygma; 37 Courtesy of Peter Townsend; 38 The Museum of Modern Art, New York. Gift of Abby Aldrich Rockefeller; 39 The Bettmann Archive; 40-41, 45, 48-49 State Jewish Museum, Prague; 55, 56-57 Courtesy of Sonia Schreiber Weitz; 58-59 State Jewish Museum, Prague; 59 Stuart Garfield; 60 *tl* Tom Till/Tony Stone Images; *tr* Tom Bean/The Stock Market; *bl* Tom Till/Tony Stone Images; *br* Stock Editions; 62-63, 66 Tom Bean; 71 National Anthropological Archives, Smithsonian Institution. Neg. 43, 132; 74 National Anthropological Archives, Smithsonian Institution. Neg. 3051-B; 80-81 Tom Bean; 81 *inset* Photo by Corbin Sebestyen; 82-83, 86 Hampton University Museum, Hampton, VA; 89 The Bettmann Archive; 90 *l* Frank Driggs Collection; 90-91 Lester Glassner Collection; 91 *r*, 92, 93, 97, 98 Frank Driggs Collection; 99 Courtesy of W.J. Holmes; 101 *t* National Museum of the American Indian, Smithsonian Institution, Acc. no. 3849; *b* Photo by Mary Esbaugh Hayes; 104 Nancy Sheehan/©D.C. Heath; 106 *t* J. Berndt/Stock Boston; 106 *b*, 107 Ken O'Donoghue/©D.C. Heath; 108 Ron Rovtar/FPG International Corp.; 112 *t* Sarah Putnam/©D.C. Heath; 112 *b*, 113 Kevin Thomas/©D.C. Heath; 114 *t* Rhoda Sidney/Stock Boston; *b* Images submitted to "PYE's Perfect Planet" Annual Art Contest—a project of TIMOTCA, a nonprofit, educational and charitable corporation.
Back cover *t, c, b* Sarah Putnam/©D.C. Heath.

Full Pronunciation Key for Footnoted Words

(Each pronunciation and definition is adapted from *Scott, Foresman Advanced Dictionary* by E.L. Thorndike and Clarence L. Barnhart.)

The pronunciation of each footnoted word is shown just after the word, in this way: **abbreviate** [ə brē′ vē āt]. The letters and signs used are pronounced as in the words below. The mark ′ is placed after a syllable with primary or heavy accent, as in the example above. The mark ′ after a syllable shows a secondary or lighter accent, as in **abbreviation** [ə brē′ vē ā′ shən].

Some words, taken from foreign languages, are spoken with sounds that do not otherwise occur in English. Symbols for these sounds are given in the key as "foreign sounds."

a	hat, cap	j	jam, enjoy	u	cup, butter	**foreign sounds**
ā	age, face	k	kind, seek	u̇	full, put	
ä	father, far	l	land, coal	ü	rule, move	Y as in French *du*.
		m	me, am	v	very, save	Pronounce (ē) with
b	bad, rob	n	no, in	w	will, woman	the lips rounded as
ch	child, much	ng	long, bring	y	young, yet	for (ü).
d	did, red			z	zero, breeze	
		o	hot, rock	zh	measure, seizure	à as in French *ami*.
e	let, best	ō	open, go			Pronounce (ä) with
ē	equal, be	ô	order, all	ə represents:		the lips spread and
ėr	term, learn	oi	oil, voice		a in about	held tense.
		ou	house, out		e in taken	
f	fat, if				i in pencil	œ as in French *peu*.
g	go, bag	p	paper, cup		o in lemon	Pronounce (ā) with the
h	he, how	r	run, try		u in circus	lips rounded as for (ō).
		s	say, yes			
i	it, pin	sh	she, rush			N as in French *bon*.
ī	ice, five	t	tell, it			The N is not pro-
		th	thin, both			nounced, but shows
		ᴛʜ	then, smooth			that the vowel before
						it is nasal.

H as in German *ach*. Pronounce (k) without closing the breath passage.

HEATH
MIDDLE LEVEL
LITERATURE

At Odds

THEME
CONFLICT RESOLUTION

A U T H O R S

Donna Alvermann
Linda Miller Cleary
Kenneth Donelson
Donald Gallo
Alice Haskins
J. Howard Johnston
John Lounsbury
Alleen Pace Nilsen
Robert Pavlik
Jewell Parker Rhodes
Alberto Alvaro Ríos
Sandra Schurr
Lyndon Searfoss
Julia Thomason
Max Thompson
Carl Zon

STAFF CREDITS

EDITORIAL	Barbara A. Brennan, Susan Belt Cogley, DeVona Dors, Christopher Johnson, Rita M. Sullivan, Patricia B. Weiler
	Proofreading: JoAnne B. Sgroi
CONTRIBUTING WRITERS	Kathy Tuchman Glass, Jo Pitkin
SERIES DESIGN	Robin Herr
BOOK DESIGN	Caroline Bowden, Daniel Derdula, Susan Geer, Diana Maloney, Angela Sciaraffa, Bonnie Chayes Yousefian
	Art Editing: Carolyn Langley
PHOTOGRAPHY	*Series Photography Coordinator:* Carmen Johnson
	Photo Research Supervisor: Martha Friedman
	Photo Researchers: Wendy Enright, Linda Finigan, Po-yee McKenna, PhotoSearch, Inc., Gillian Speeth, Denise Theodores
	Assignment Photography Coordinators: Susan Doheny, Gayna Hoffman, Shawna Johnston
COMPUTER PREPRESS	Ricki Pappo, Kathy Meisl Richard Curran, Michele Locatelli
PERMISSIONS	Dorothy B. McLeod
PRODUCTION	Patrick Connolly

Cover Photograph: Logan Seals

Acknowledgments for copyrighted material are on page 125 and constitute an extension of this page.

Published simultaneously in Canada

Printed in the United States of America

International Standard Book Number: 0-669-32113-3 (soft cover)
 4 5 6 7 8 9 10-RRD-99

International Standard Book Number: 0-669-38181-0 (hard cover)
 3 4 5 6 7 8 9 10-RRD-99 98 97 96 95

Middle Level Authors

Donna Alvermann, University of Georgia
Alice Haskins, Howard County Public Schools, Maryland
J. Howard Johnston, University of South Florida
John Lounsbury, Georgia College
Sandra Schurr, University of South Florida
Julia Thomason, Appalachian State University
Max Thompson, Appalachian State University
Carl Zon, California Assessment Collaborative

Literature and Language Arts Authors

Linda Miller Cleary, University of Minnesota
Kenneth Donelson, Arizona State University
Donald Gallo, Central Connecticut State University
Alleen Pace Nilsen, Arizona State University
Robert Pavlik, Cardinal Stritch College, Milwaukee
Jewell Parker Rhodes, Arizona State University
Alberto Alvaro Ríos, Arizona State University
Lyndon Searfoss, Arizona State University

Teacher Consultants

Suzanne Aubin, Patapsco Middle School, Ellicott City, Maryland
Judy Baxter, Newport News Public Schools, Newport News, Virginia
Saundra Bryn, Director of Research and Development, El Mirage, Arizona
Lorraine Gerhart, Elmbrook Middle School, Elm Grove, Wisconsin
Kathy Tuchman Glass, Burlingame Intermediate School, Burlingame, California
Lucretia Pannozzo, John Jay Middle School, Katonah, New York
Carol Schultz, Jerling Junior High, Orland Park, Illinois
Jeanne Siebenman, Grand Canyon University, Phoenix, Arizona
Gail Thompson, Garey High School, Pomona, California
Rufus Thompson, Grace Yokley School, Ontario, California
Tom Tufts, Conniston Middle School, West Palm Beach, Florida
Edna Turner, Harpers Choice Middle School, Columbia, Maryland
C. Anne Webb, Buerkle Junior High School, St. Louis, Missouri
Geri Yaccino, Thompson Junior High School, St. Charles, Illinois

CONTENTS

THE LITERATURE

ASKING BIG QUESTIONS ABOUT THE LITERATURE

PROJECTS

1 WRITING WORKSHOP

KEEP THE PEACE 106-111

What would you like to find out about peace or war? Research one question and then share what you've learned with classmates.

2 COOPERATIVE LEARNING

FROM PAST TO PRESENT 112-113

Work with a group to find out about conflicts in United States history, and make a time line to share with other students in your school.

3 HELPING YOUR COMMUNITY

PAYING TRIBUTE 114-115

Find out about one war veteran in your community. Then come up with a creative way to honor all local war veterans.

War & Peace

You can't avoid or ignore all conflicts in life. When you're faced with a conflict, you have to make a decision about whether to fight or try to find a peaceful solution. In this activity, you'll work with a group of classmates to brainstorm for ideas about how to resolve a conflict peacefully. Then you'll put your ideas on paper by drafting a peace treaty.

1 Pick a conflict

With your partner or group, choose a conflict on which to practice. Choose a conflict shown on the cards below or come up with one of your own.

Country A, once a powerful nation, is now ruled by outsiders from Country B. The people of Country A want to gain independence, but the leaders from Country B refuse to give up their power. The leaders from Country B crack down, enforcing strict laws, setting curfews, and arresting citizens suspected of being in the independence movement.

Country E has large reserves of gold but no salt. The people of Country E need salt to preserve food and to use in their diet. While Country F has huge salt reserves, it has no gold mines. Its people want gold for trading, decorating their buildings, and making jewelry. People in both countries form raiding parties to take what they want by force. The border between Countries E and F is no longer safe.

The leader of Country Y wants to control an empire. Country Y's military forces launch surprise attacks on Countries X and Z. Country Y's army now controls the railroad, oil fields, and factories in Country Z. Country Y also controls the main port in Country X.

2 Brainstorm for possible solutions.

Brainstorm for possible solutions to the conflict you've chosen. On a separate sheet of paper, take two minutes to write down your own ideas. Then share your ideas with your group.

- As you discuss solutions, have one person in your group record ideas in a notebook, on a large sheet of paper, or on the chalkboard.
- When you finish brainstorming, have the whole group agree on one solution that might work. Have the recorder circle your solution.

3 Draft a peace treaty.

As a group, draft a peace treaty to resolve your conflict. Include the following elements:

- Terms of the treaty—What changes will take place? What will each person or country give up? What will each person or country gain? What must the leaders of each country or the people involved agree to do?
- Conditions—How will the terms of the treaty be enforced? Who will enforce the treaty? What will happen if the terms are violated?
- Time limits—When will the peace treaty go into effect? How long will each phase of the treaty take to complete?

4 Share your peace treaty.

Share your group's peace treaty with the rest of the class by having one person in your group read it aloud.

Compare your treaty with the ones drafted by other groups who chose to resolve the same conflict. Which treaty do you think has the best chance for keeping peace? Why?

Asking Big Questions About the Theme

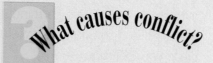

What causes conflict?

Have you ever had a serious disagreement with another student or with a family member? What caused this conflict? In your journal, create a diagram similar to the one on this page. In the big circle labeled *Conflict*, describe what happened. Then list reasons for this conflict in the circles labeled *Cause*. Finally, beneath your diagram, write a sentence or two about how this conflict was resolved.

Cause
Shannon wasn't invited.

Conflict
I want to go to a party and my friend Shannon doesn't want me to.

Cause
I want to meet new friends.

Cause
Shannon is afraid of losing my friendship.

We talked about it honestly.

How does conflict become war?

Throughout history, conflicts have turned into full-scale wars. For example, a conflict over taxes between American colonists and the British government led to the Revolutionary War. In your journal, make a list that shows why conflict turns into war. Then share your list with classmates and explain each of your reasons. Work together to make a class list and display it in the classroom.

How does war affect people's lives?

In what different ways does war affect people? Think about what you know about war from your reading, from family stories you've heard, from movies, and from TV. Work with a partner or a group to make a chart like the one that has been started for you here. Create your own additional headings and then brainstorm for details to add to the chart. Post your chart on your class bulletin board.

Physical Effects	Emotional Effects	Political Effects	Geographical Effects	Economic Effects
death	fear	new government	new borders	high cost of food

How can people resolve conflicts peacefully?

Can people resolve their conflicts without resorting to violence? Pretend that you're a diplomat. Your job is to negotiate for peace. Choose a real or a made-up conflict. It may help you to think of a specific global conflict or a personal conflict you've had. In your journal, describe the conflict and then brainstorm for one or two peaceful ways to resolve it. Work with a partner to role-play one of your ideas for the class.

NOW Think!

Right now, somewhere in the world, people are fighting a war. What have you learned about war from firsthand experience, textbooks, magazines, TV broadcasts, books, newspapers, or movies? As you read the literature on the pages that follow, compare the events in the selections with actual conflicts that are occurring today.

THE TWO

There once were two brothers, Ninniaw[1] and Pebbiaw,[2] whose father had willed his small kingdom to be shared equally between them. However, since there was only one castle, the question arose: Which twin should keep it and which leave and build another?

"Dear brother Pebbiaw," said Ninniaw, "I wouldn't dream of putting you to such trouble. Let us, above all, be at peace with each other. You shall stay here and I shall build a new castle."

"Dear brother Ninniaw," said Pebbiaw, "that's kind and thoughtful of you, as to be expected from a generous hearted, loving brother. Yes, by all means, let us be at peace. But you must stay. I shall be the one to move."

1. **Ninniaw** [nin′ ē ô]
2. **Pebbiaw** [peb′ ē ô]

BROTHERS

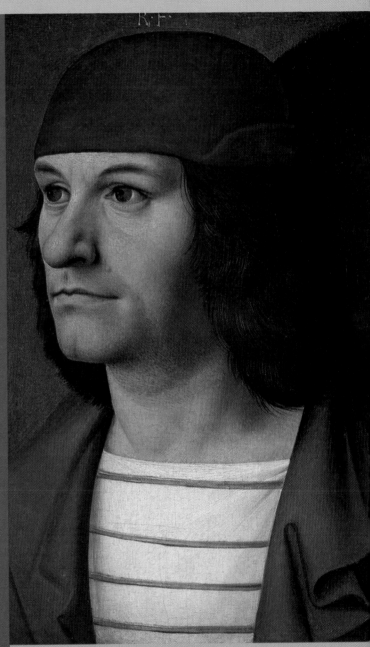

So they talked back and forth, each concerned for the other's comfort and well-being, until at last they agreed: Neither should keep the castle. Instead, each would build his own. The old stronghold was to be torn down, and whatever could be used from it would be divided.

Having come to such a wise and fair decision, they clasped hands on it and embraced, as fond as any brothers could ever be.

The two then set about building their strongholds, little more than a stone's throw apart.

"Dear brother," said Ninniaw, when the castles were finished, "those are fine, handsome walls you've put up, very solid indeed. I don't question your judgment, but why did you need to build them so high?"

Jean, Duke of Berry on a Journey *from Les Belles Heures de Jean, Duc de Berry* c. 1410, tempera and gold leaf on parchment, 9 3/8" x 6 5/8", The Metropolitan Museum of Art, New York

"For your protection, dear brother," said Pebbiaw. "The world, alas, is full of wicked folk. Should anyone attack you, they'll have to deal with me first."

"How right you are, dear brother," said Ninniaw. "And I can do no less for you."

So Ninniaw commanded his own walls and towers be raised to the height of Pebbiaw's. This done, Ninniaw invited Pebbiaw to a feast in the great hall.

There, spread out on long tables, were cutlets of roast venison—and quail, partridge, and pheasant by the hundreds; for Ninniaw had sent his foresters to hunt and snare the choicest game in his woods.

"Dear brother," cried Pebbiaw, having stuffed himself as full as he could, "there's never been such a feast in all my memory! What a joy to have a brother whose hands are as open as his heart is kind!"

"Dear brother," answered Ninniaw, "how good of you to give high praise to such lowly offerings. Once my kitchen is in better order, you shall have dainties to match my affection for you."

The two princes embraced and wished each other a fond good night.

But Pebbiaw went back to his castle grumbling along the way, "Affection for his own good opinion of himself is what I call it. He's trying to outshine me again. Well, I'll show him dainties!"

And so Pebbiaw, in turn, spread out a feast for Ninniaw. The tables groaned under even more lavish fare, for Pebbiaw had ordered his gamekeepers to seek out the rarest delicacies. The platters were heaped high, not only with quail and pheasant, but larks and linnets surrounded by their eggs, boiled, coddled, and poached; and fish of every sort, broiled and seasoned to perfection.

When Ninniaw blinked in amazement at the endless courses, Pebbiaw shrugged and said, "Dear brother, forgive me. My modest board has little worth your notice or that shows my esteem for you. Next time, I promise you shall be better served."

From then on, hardly a day went by without the two brothers visiting each other. And each feast was always more splendid than the last, with Ninniaw and Pebbiaw striving to outdo each other no matter what the cost.

After a time, however, seeing his provisions dwindle, Ninniaw muttered to himself, "What a greedy pig that brother of mine is! He's going to eat me out of house and home!"

And so he stopped inviting his brother to dinner or, indeed, any other meal.

Pebbiaw, for his part, frowning at the nearly bare shelves of his larder, grumbled, "That Ninniaw has a bottomless pit for a stomach. Wretch! He'd be delighted if I beggared myself feeding him."

And Pebbiaw, likewise, no longer invited his brother to share his hospitality.

The two brothers not only stopped dining together, they soon barely spoke to each other.

Then one day Ninniaw noticed that Pebbiaw had increased the number of archers[3] and spearmen keeping watch on his ramparts.[4]

Ninniaw could hardly let this pass unremarked. When he asked the reason, Pebbiaw replied, "These are hard times, Brother, with more than one rascal at large in the world. Better to be alert and ready for whatever may befall."

"You were always prudent, Brother," said Ninniaw. "I admire you for it. But those bowmen of yours are hot headed fellows. What if some day, for the sport of it or by accident, they let fly a volley of

3. **archers** [är′ chərz]: people who shoot with bows and arrows.
4. **ramparts** [ram′ pärtz]: wide banks of earth, often with walls, built to defend a fort or a building.

arrows at my guards?"

"That will not happen, Brother," Pebbiaw assured him. "You have my word on it."

Even so, the next day Ninniaw set about raising the height of his walls.

When Pebbiaw came hotfooting over in indignation, demanding to know why, Ninniaw told him, "You and I are brothers and so have nothing to fear from each other. Can you say as much for your warriors?"

"True," said Pebbiaw, "but now your men are so high they could, out of sheer mischief, shower spears into my courtyard."

And Pebbiaw, in turn, raised his battlements higher than those of Ninniaw.

Ninniaw first thought of building his own walls even higher. Then he decided against it.

"That brother of mine was always a pigheaded fool," he said to himself. "If I raise my walls, he'll only do the same. No, I shall follow a shrewder plan."

The next day, Ninniaw ordered a few of his warriors to climb the trees overlooking Pebbiaw's castle and keep close watch. This way, he told himself, he would learn whatever new folly[5] his brother might be up to, and put an end to it before it got out of hand.

The following morning, however, Ninniaw woke to the sound of chopping. Hurrying to his wall, he saw Pebbiaw's woodcutters felling the trees encircling his castle.

When he hastily rode over to ask his brother the reason, Pebbiaw sighed and shook his head, saying, "Ah, Brother, the times are troubled. Who can tell when some band of ruffians might take it into their heads to spy upon us and attack me? Better to have a clearing around my stronghold, so no one can come upon me unawares."

"You are right, Brother," Ninniaw answered agreeably. "For a moment, I feared you might have lost your trust in our affection. But I see now that your idea is marvelously sensible."

So Ninniaw in turn ordered his woodcutters to cut down

5. **folly** [fol′ ē]: foolishness, unwise conduct.

the trees around his stronghold. But when he rode out to oversee the work, he glimpsed Pebbiaw watching and, with him, a band of warriors.

"Why, Brother, what is this?" called Ninniaw. "Do you mean to hunt? Had you told me, I would have gone with you."

"No, Brother, I do not hunt," replied Pebbiaw in a surly[6] tone. "I find this as good a time as any to settle our boundaries."

"Excellent thought," said Ninniaw glaring. "It will be an easy matter. Since we share alike, our boundary should be set exactly here, halfway between our castles."

"Well and good," said Pebbiaw, striding past his brother, "but you misjudge your distance by half a dozen yards. It should be—here."

"What, Brother, do you say I have no eye for measurement?" retorted Ninniaw.

"On the contrary, Brother," Pebbiaw returned. "You have a sharp eye when it comes to looking out for yourself. Small wonder you want such a boundary, since it carves a fat slice out of my land."

"That stumpy chicken-walk?" cried Ninniaw. "Your land isn't worth carving."

"Back up, then!" shouted Pebbiaw. "Move closer into that scabby rat-run of yours and mark the boundary where it should be."

"So I do!" shouted Ninniaw, drawing his sword and slashing a line in the dirt. "I mark it here!"

"And I mark it there!" cried Pebbiaw, snatching out his own sword and pointing to a spot some distance beyond Ninniaw.

Seeing the brothers with drawn blades and supposing their leader to be in danger, Pebbiaw's warriors raced forward. Ninniaw, certain his brother had betrayed him, galloped for dear life toward his castle, with Pebbiaw and the warriors brandishing their weapons in hot pursuit.

Seeing Ninniaw beset,[7] the guards on his castle walls raised the alarm, and his war band burst through the gates to engage Pebbiaw and his men. The latter, finding themselves outnumbered, shouted

6. **surly** [sėr′ lē]: bad-tempered and unfriendly, rude.
7. **beset** [bi set′]: attacked from all sides.

Hannibal, Seige of Saguntum Illuminated manuscript page

for reinforcements. And so an even larger war band rode from
Pebbiaw's castle, while another from Ninniaw's stronghold galloped
to stand against them.

The battle was so quickly and hotly joined that neither side
could withdraw. By the time Ninniaw and Pebbiaw brought their
warriors, and themselves, to their senses, the gates of both castles
had been shattered, the halls and chambers set ablaze, and nothing

remained but two piles of fire-blackened stones.

Ninniaw and Pebbiaw could only stare, open-mouthed and dumbstruck, hardly able to believe their eyes.

"Brother," Ninniaw said at last, "I fear your castle has been somewhat damaged."

"To say the least of it," muttered Pebbiaw. "And so has yours."

They stood awhile, still befuddled[8] by what had happened.

Finally, saying no more, they turned away and trudged back to their heaps of rubble, shaking their heads, each wondering how the other could have been so remarkably dimwitted.

8. **befuddled** [bi fud′ ld]: stupified, confused.

LLOYD ALEXANDER

Lloyd Alexander, born in 1924 in Philadelphia, Pennsylvania, decided on his career early in life. When Alexander was fifteen years old and ready to graduate from high school, he announced to his parents that he was going to become a poet. Hs parents couldn't afford to send him to college, and his grades were, in his words, "too wretched for a scholarship." Alexander preferred staying up all night reading tales of heroes and writing instead of doing his homework. His parents finally agreed that he could try being a poet, on the condition that he also find some kind of useful work. Alexander says, "I had no idea how to find any sort of work, or, in fact, how to go about being a poet." Alexander went to work as a messenger at a bank. Then World War II began, and he joined the army.

After a stint at a military-intelligence training center, Alexander was sent to France as a translator and interpreter. After the war ended, he returned home where, instead of writing poetry, he began writing novels. Seven years passed before a novel, the fourth he'd written, was finally accepted for publication. Two of Alexander's best-known books are *The Book of Three* and *The High King*.

OF BABYLON

BY THE WATERS

Pacific Light No. 36 Jay Dunitz, 1986, Cibachrome, 40" X 54"

STEPHEN VINCENT BENÉT

"By the waters of Babylon,[1]
there we sat down and wept,
when we remembered Zion."[2]
(Psalm 137)

The north and the west and the south are good hunting ground, but it is forbidden to go east. It is forbidden to go to any of the Dead Places except to search for metal and then he who touches the metal must be a priest or the son of a priest. Afterwards, both the man and the metal must be purified. These are the rules and the laws; they are well made. It is forbidden to cross the great river and look upon the place that was the Place of the Gods—this is most strictly forbidden. We do not even say its name though we know its name. It is there that spirits live, and demons—it is there that there are the ashes of the Great Burning. These things are forbidden—they have been forbidden since the beginning of time.

1. **Babylon** [bab′ ə lon]: capital of ancient Babylonia in Southwest Asia; the reference is to Psalm 137 from the Bible, in which the ancient Israelites weep because they are in exile in Babylon.
2. **Zion** [zī′ ən]: hill in Jerusalem on which there was a Temple; reference also to Israel or heaven, from which the ancient Israelites were exiled.

My father is a priest; I am the son of a priest. I have been in the Dead Places near us with my father—at first, I was afraid. When my father went into the house to search for the metal, I stood by the door, and my heart felt small and weak. It was a dead man's house, a spirit house. It did not have the smell of man, though there were old bones in a corner. But it is not fitting that a priest's son should show fear. I looked at the bones in the shadow and kept my voice still.

Then father brought out the metal—a good, strong piece. He looked at me then with both eyes but I had not run away. He gave me the metal to hold—I took it and did not die. So he knew that I was truly his son and would be a priest in my time. That was when I was very young—nevertheless, my brothers would not have done it, though they are good hunters. After that, they gave me a good piece of meat and the warm corner by the fire. My father watched over me—he was glad that I should be a priest. But when I boasted or wept without a reason, he punished me more strictly than my brothers. That was right.

After a time, I myself was allowed to go into the dead houses and search for metal. So I learned the ways of those houses—and if I saw bones, I was no longer afraid. The bones are light and old—sometimes they will fall into dust if you touch them. But that is a great sin. . . .

We are not ignorant like the Forest People—we spin wool on the wheel, our priests wear a white robe. We do not eat grubs[3] from the tree, we have not forgotten the old writings, although they are hard to understand. Nevertheless, my knowledge and my lack of knowledge burned in me—I wished to know more. When I was a man at last, I came to my father and said, "It is time for me to go on my journey. Give me your leave."

He looked at me for a long time, stroking his beard, then he said at last, "Yes. It is time." That night, in the house of the priesthood, I asked for and received purification. My body hurt but my spirit was a cool stone. It was my father himself who questioned me about my dreams.

3. **grubs:** soft, thick, wormlike larva of an insect, especially that of a beetle.

He bade me look into the smoke of the fire and see—I saw and told what I saw. It was what I have always seen—a river, and, beyond it, a great Dead Place and in it the gods walking. I have always thought about that. His eyes were stern when I told him—he was no longer my father but a priest. He said, "This is a strong dream."

"It is mine," I said, while the smoke waved and my head felt light. They were singing the Star Song in the outer chamber, and it was like the buzzing of bees in my head.

He asked me how the gods were dressed, and I told him how they were dressed. We know how they were dressed from the book, but I saw them as if they were before me. When I had finished, he threw the sticks three times and studied them as they fell.

"This is a very strong dream," he said. "It may eat you up."

"I am not afraid," I said and looked at him with both eyes. My voice sounded thin in my ears, but that was because of the smoke.

He touched me on the breast and the forehead. He gave me the bow and the three arrows.

"Take them," he said. "It is forbidden to travel east. It is forbidden to cross the river. It is forbidden to go to the Place of the Gods. All this is forbidden."

"All these things are forbidden," I said, but it was my voice that spoke and not my spirit. He looked at me again.

"My son," he said. "Once I had young dreams. If your dreams do not eat you up, you may be a great priest. If they eat you, you are still my son. Now go on your way."

I went fasting, as is the law. My body hurt but not my heart. When the dawn came, I was out of sight of the village. I prayed and purified myself, waiting for a sign. The sign was an eagle. It flew east.

Sometimes signs are sent by bad spirits. I waited again on the flat rock, fasting, taking no food. I was very still—I could feel the sky above me and the earth beneath. I waited till the sun was beginning to sink. Then three deer passed in the valley, going east—they did not wind[4] me or see me. There was a white fawn with them—a very great sign.

4. **wind:** here the sense is of an animal being able to get the scent of a person or another animal.

I followed them, at a distance, waiting for what would happen. My heart was troubled about going east, yet I knew that I must go. My head hummed with my fasting—I did not even see the panther spring upon the white fawn. But, before I knew it, the bow was in my hand. I shouted, and the panther lifted his head from the fawn. It is not easy to kill a panther with one arrow, but the arrow went through his eye and into his brain. He died as he tried to spring—he rolled over, tearing at the ground. Then I knew I was meant to go east—I knew that was my journey. When the night came, I made my fire and roasted meat.

It is eight suns' journey to the east, and a man passes by many Dead Places. The Forest People are afraid of them, but I am not. Once I made my fire on the edge of a Dead Place at night and, next morning, in the dead house, I found a good knife, little rusted. That was small to what came afterward, but it made my heart feel big. Always when I looked for game, it was in front of my arrow, and twice I passed hunting parties of the Forest People without their knowing. So I knew my magic was strong and my journey clean, in spite of the law.

Toward the setting of the eighth sun, I came to the banks of the great river. It was half a day's journey after I had left the god-road—we do not use the god-roads now for they are falling apart into great blocks of stone, and the forest is safer going. A long way off, I had seen the water through trees, but the trees were thick. At last, I came out upon an open place at the top of a cliff. There was the great river below, like a giant in the sun. It is very long, very wide. It could eat all the streams we know and still be thirsty. Its name is Ou-dis-sun,[5] the Sacred, the Long. No man of my tribe had seen it, not even my father, the priest. It was magic and I prayed.

Then I raised my eyes and looked south. It was there, the Place of the Gods.

How can I tell what it was like—you do not know. It was there, in the red light, and they were too big to be houses. It was there with the red light upon it, mighty and ruined. I knew that in another

5. **Ou-dis-sun** [ü′ dis sun]

Kroeber Series No.39
Jay Dunitz, 1981

moment the gods would see me. I covered my eyes with my hands and crept back into the forest.

Surely, that was enough to do, and live. Surely it was enough to spend the night upon the cliff. The Forest People themselves do not come near. Yet, all through the night, I knew that I should have to cross the river and walk in the places of the gods, although the gods ate me up. My magic did not help me at all, and yet there was a fire in my bowels, a fire in my mind. When the sun rose, I thought, "My journey has been clean. Now I will go home from my journey." But, even as I thought so, I knew I could not. If I went to the Place of the Gods, I would surely die, but, if I did not go, I could never be at peace with my spirit again. It is better to lose one's life than one's spirit, if one is a priest and the son of a priest.

Nevertheless, as I made the raft, the tears ran out of my eyes. The Forest People could have killed without fight, if they had come upon me then, but they did not come. When the raft was made, I said the sayings for the dead and painted myself for death. My heart was cold as a frog and my knees like water, but the burning in my mind would not let me have peace. As I pushed the raft from the shore, I began my death song—I had the right. It was a fine song.

"I am John, son of John," I sang. "My people are the Hill People. They are the men.

I go into the Dead Places but I am not slain.

I take the metal from the Dead Places but I am not blasted.

I travel upon the god-roads and am not afraid. E-yah! I have killed the panther, I have killed the fawn!

E-yah! I have come to the great river. No man has come there before.

It is forbidden to go east, but I have gone, forbidden to go on the great river, but I am there.

Open your hearts, you spirits, and hear my song.

Now I go to the Place of the Gods, I shall not return.

My body is painted for death and my limbs weak, but my heart is big as I go to the Place of the Gods!"

All the same, when I came to the Place of the Gods, I was afraid, afraid. The current of the great river is very strong—it gripped my raft with its hands. That was magic, for the river itself is wide and calm. I could feel evil spirits about me, in the bright morning; I could feel their breath on my neck as I was swept down the stream. Never have I been so much alone—I tried to think of my knowledge, but it was a squirrel's heap of winter nuts. There was no strength in my knowledge any more, and I felt small and naked as a new-hatched bird—alone upon the great river, the servant of the gods.

Yet, after a while, my eyes were opened and I saw. I saw both banks of the river—I saw that once there had been god-roads across it, though now they were broken and fallen like broken vines. Very great they were, and wonderful and broken—broken in the time of the Great Burning when the fire fell out of the sky. And always the current took me nearer to the Place of the Gods, and the huge ruins rose before my eyes.

I do not know the customs of rivers—we are the People of the Hills. I tried to guide my raft with the pole but it spun around. I thought the river meant to take me past the Place of the Gods and out into the Bitter Water of the legends. I grew angry then—my heart felt strong. I said aloud, "I am a priest and the son of a priest!" The gods heard me—they showed me how to paddle with the pole on one side of the raft. The current changed itself—I drew near the Place of the Gods.

When I was very near, my raft struck and turned over. I can swim in our lakes—I swam to the shore. There was a great spike of rusted metal sticking out into the river—I hauled myself up upon it and sat there, panting. I had saved my bow and two arrows and the knife I found in the Dead Place but that was all. My raft went whirling downstream toward the Bitter Water. I looked after it, and thought if it had trod me under, at least I would be safely dead. Nevertheless, when I had dried my bowstring and restrung it, I walked forward to the Place of the Gods.

It felt like ground underfoot; it did not burn me. It is not true what some of the tales say, that the ground there burns forever, for I have been there. Here and there were the marks and stains of the Great Burning, on the ruins, that is true. But they were old marks and old stains. It is not true either, what some of our priests say, that it is an island covered with fogs and enchantments. It is not. It is a great Dead Place—greater than any Dead Place we know. Everywhere in it there are god-roads, though most are cracked and broken. Everywhere there are the ruins of the high towers of the gods.

How shall I tell what I saw? I went carefully, my strung bow in my hand, my skin ready for danger. There should have been the wailing of spirits and the shrieks of demons, but there were not. It was very silent and sunny where I had landed—the wind and the rain and the

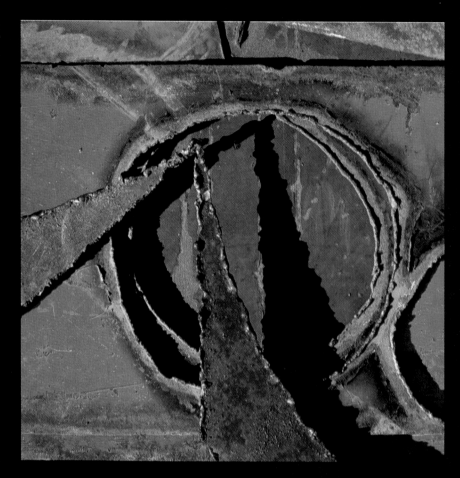

birds that drop seeds had done their work—the grass grew in the cracks of the broken stone. It is a fair island—no wonder the gods built there. If I had come there, a god, I also would have built.

How shall I tell what I saw? The towers are not all broken—here and there one still stands, like a great tree in a forest, and the birds nest high. But the towers themselves look blind, for the gods are gone. I saw a fish hawk, catching fish in the river. I saw a little dance of white butterflies over a great heap of broken stones and columns. I went there and looked about me—there was a carved stone with cut-letters, broken in half. I can read letters but I could not understand these. They said UBTREAS. There was also the shattered image of a man or a god. It had been made of white stone and he wore his hair tied back like a woman's. His name was ASHING, as I read on the cracked half of a stone. I thought it wise to pray to ASHING, though I do not know that god.

How shall I tell what I saw? There was no smell of man left, on stone or metal. Nor were there many trees in that wilderness of stone. There are many pigeons, nesting and dropping in the towers—the gods must have loved them, or, perhaps, they used them for sacrifices. There are wild cats that roam the god-roads, green-eyed, unafraid of man. At night they wail like demons, but they are not demons. The wild dogs are more dangerous, for they hunt in a pack, but them I did not meet till later. Everywhere there are the carved stones, carved with magical numbers or words.

I went north—I did not try to hide myself. When a god or a demon saw me, then I would die, but meanwhile I was no longer afraid. My hunger for knowledge burned in me—there was so much that I could not understand. After awhile, I knew that my belly was hungry. I could have hunted for my meat, but I did not hunt. It is known that the gods did not hunt as we do—they got their food from enchanted boxes and jars. Sometimes these are found in the Dead Places—once, when I was a child and foolish, I opened such a jar and tasted it and found the food sweet. But my father found out and punished me for it strictly, for, often, that food is death. Now, though, I had long gone past what was forbidden, and I entered the likeliest towers, looking for the food of the gods.

I found it at last in the ruins of a great temple in the midcity. A mighty temple it must have been, for the roof was painted like the sky at night with its stars—that much I could see, though the colors were faint and dim. It went down into great caves and tunnels—perhaps they kept their slaves there. But when I started to climb down, I heard the squeaking of rats, so I did not go—rats are unclean, and there must have been many tribes of them, from the squeaking. But near there, I found food, in the heart of a ruin, behind a door that still opened. I ate only the fruits from the jars—they had a very sweet taste. There was drink, too, in bottles of glass—the drink of the gods was strong and made my head swim. After I had eaten and drunk, I slept on the top of a stone, my bow at my side.

When I woke, the sun was low. Looking down from where I lay, I saw a dog sitting on his haunches. His tongue was hanging out of his mouth; he looked as if he were laughing. He was a big dog, with a gray-brown coat, as big as a wolf. I sprang up and shouted at him but he did not move—he just sat there as if he were laughing. I did not like that. When I reached for a stone to throw, he moved swiftly out of the way of the stone. He was not afraid of me; he looked at me as if I were meat. No doubt I could have killed him with an arrow, but I did not know if there were others. Moreover, night was falling.

I looked about me—not far away there was a great, broken god-road, leading north. The towers were high enough, but not so high, and while many of the dead-houses were wrecked, there were some that stood. I went toward this god-road, keeping to the heights of the ruins, while the dog followed. When I had reached the god-road, I saw that there were others behind him. If I had slept later, they would have come upon me asleep and torn out my throat. As it was, they were sure enough of me; they did not hurry. When I went into the dead house, they kept watch at the entrance—doubtless they thought they would have a fine hunt. But a dog cannot open a door and I knew, from the books, that the gods did not like to live on the ground but on high.

I had just found a door I could open when the dogs decided to rush. Ha! They were surprised when I shut the door in their faces—it was a good door, of strong metal. I could hear their foolish baying beyond it, but I did not stop to answer them. I was in darkness—I found stairs and climbed. There were many stairs, turning around till my head was dizzy. At the top was another door—I found the knob and opened it. I was in a long small chamber—on one side of it was a bronze door that could not be opened, for it had no handle. Perhaps there was a magic word to open it but I did not have a word. I turned to the door in the opposite side of the wall. The lock of it was broken and I opened it and went in.

Within, there was a place of very great riches. The god who lived there must have been powerful. The first room was a small ante-room—I waited there for some time, telling the spirits of the place that I came in peace and not as a robber. When it seemed to me that they had had time to hear me, I went on. Ah, what riches! Few, even, of the windows had been broken—it was all as it had been. The great windows that looked over the city had not been broken at all though they were dusty and streaked with many years. There were coverings on the floors, the colors not greatly faded, and the chairs were soft and deep. There were pictures upon the walls, very strange, very wonderful—I remember one of a bunch of flowers in a jar— if you came close to it, you could see nothing but bits of color, but if you stood away from it, the flowers might have been picked yesterday. It made my heart feel strange to look at this picture—and to look at the figure of a bird, in some hard clay, on a table and see it so like our birds. Everywhere there were books and writings, many in tongues that I could not read. The god who lived there must have been a wise god and full of knowledge. I felt I had a right there, as I sought knowledge also.

Nevertheless, it was strange. There was a washing-place but no water—perhaps the gods washed in air. There was a cooking-place but no wood, and though there was a machine to cook food, there was no place to put fire in it. Nor were there candles or lamps—there were things that looked like lamps but they had neither oil nor wick. All these things were magic, but I touched them and lived—the magic had gone out of them. Let me tell one thing to show. In the washing-place, a thing said "Hot" but it was not hot to the touch— another thing said "Cold" but it was not cold. This must have been a strong magic but the magic was gone. I do not understand—they had ways—I wish that I knew.

It was close and dry and dusty in their house of the gods. I have said the magic was gone but that is not true—it had gone from the magic things but it had not gone from the place. I felt the spirits about me, weighing upon me. Nor had I ever slept in a Dead Place before—and yet, tonight, I must sleep there. When I thought of it, my tongue felt dry in my throat, in spite of my wish for knowledge. Almost I would have gone down again and faced the dogs, but I did not.

I had not gone through all the rooms when the darkness fell. When it fell, I went back to the big room looking over the city and made fire. There was a place to make fire and a box with wood in it, though I do not think they cooked there. I wrapped myself in a floor-covering and slept in front of the fire—I was very tired. . . .

When I woke in the morning, I was hungry, but I did not think first of my hunger for my heart was perplexed and confused. I knew the Dead Places but I did not see why it had happened. It seemed to me it should not have happened, with all the magic they had. I went through the house looking for an answer. There was so much in the house I could not understand—and yet I am a priest and the son of a priest. It was like being on one side of the river, at night, with no light to show the way.

Then I saw the dead god. He was sitting in his chair, by the window, in a room I had not entered before and, for the first moment, I thought that he was alive. Then I saw the skin on the back of his hand—it was like dry leather. The room was shut, hot and dry—no doubt that had kept him as he was. At first I was afraid to approach him—then the fear left me. He was sitting looking out over the city—he was dressed in the clothes of the gods. His age was neither young nor old—I could not tell his age. But there was wisdom in his face and great sadness. You could see that he would have not run away. He had sat at his window, watching his city die—then he himself had died. But it is better to lose one's life than one's spirit—and you could see from the face that his spirit had not been lost. I knew, that, if I touched him, he would fall into dust—and yet, there was something unconquered in the face.

That is all of my story, for then I knew he was a man—I knew then that they had been men, neither gods nor demons. It is a great knowledge, hard to tell and believe. They were men—they went a dark road, but they were men. I had no fear after that—I had no fear going home, though twice I fought off the dogs and once I was hunted for two days by the Forest People. When I saw my father again, I prayed and was purified. He touched my lips and my breast, he said, "You went away a boy. You come back a man and a priest."

I said, "Father, they were men! I have been in the Place of the Gods and seen it! Now slay me, if it is the law—but still I know they were men."

He looked at me out of both eyes. He said, "The law is not always the same shape—you have done what you have done. I could not have done it in my time, but you come after me. Tell!"

I told and he listened. After that, I wished to tell all the people but he showed me otherwise. He said, "Truth is a hard deer to hunt. If you eat too much truth at once, you may die of the truth. It was not idly that our fathers forbade the Dead Places." He was right—it is better the truth should come little by little. I have learned that, being a priest. Perhaps, in the old days, they ate knowledge too fast.

Nevertheless, we make a beginning. It is not for the metal alone we go to the Dead Places now—there are the books and the writings.

Pacific Light No. 39
Jay Dunitz, 1987

They are hard to learn. And the magic tools are broken—but we can look at them and wonder. At least, we make a beginning. And, when I am a chief priest we shall go beyond the great river. We shall go to the Place of the Gods—the place newyork—not one man but a company. We shall look for the images of the gods and find the god ASHING and the others—the gods Lincoln and Baltimore. But they were men who built the city, not gods or demons. They were men. I remember the dead man's face. They were men who were here before us. We must build again.

S T E P H E N
V I N C E N T
B E N É T

Stephen Vincent Benét (1898-1943) was born in Bethlehem, Pennsylvania, the son of an army colonel. At age thirteen, Benét was winning poetry prizes from *St. Nicholas Magazine*. Before entering college, Benét published his first book of poetry. He published his second book three years later. During his senior year at Yale University, Benét was editor of the *Literary Magazine* and wrote his first novel. He continued his studies in Paris, where he met his wife, poet Rosemary Carr. Benét went on to write musical plays, radio scripts, and short stories.

Benét is best known for his epic Civil War poem, "John Brown's Body." When he died, Benét left unfinished a long narrative about American history, called *Western Star*, which won a Pulitzer Prize when it was finally published.

Where Have All the Flowers Gone?

Flowers Andy Warhol, 1970, screenprint on paper

PETE SEEGER

Where have all the flowers gone,
Long time passing?
Where have all the flowers gone,
Long time ago?
Where have all the flowers gone?   5
The girls have picked them every one.
Oh, when will you ever learn?
Oh, when will you ever learn?

Where have all the young girls gone,
Long time passing?   10
Where have all the young girls gone,
Long time ago?
Where have all the young girls gone?
They've taken husbands every one.
Oh, when will you ever learn?   15
Oh, when will you ever learn?

Where have all the young men gone,
Long time passing?
Where have all the young men gone,
Long time ago?   20
Where have all the young men gone?
They're all in uniform.
Oh, when will we ever learn?
Oh, when will we ever learn?

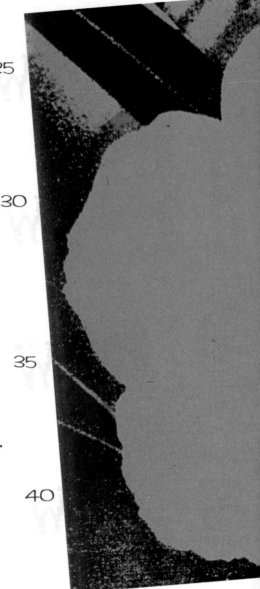

Where have all the soldiers gone,
 Long time passing?
Where have all the soldiers gone,
 Long time ago?
 Where have all the soldiers gone?
 They've gone to graveyards, every one.   30
 Oh, when will they ever learn?
 Oh, when will they ever learn?

Where have all the graveyards gone,
 Long time passing?
 Where have all the graveyards gone,   35
 Long time ago?
 Where have all the graveyards gone?
 They're covered with flowers every one.
 Oh, when will they ever learn?
 Oh, when will they ever learn?   40

Where have all the flowers gone,
 Long time passing?
 Where have all the flowers gone,
 Long time ago?
 Where have all the flowers gone?   45
 Young girls picked them every one.
 Oh, when will they ever learn?
 Oh, when will they ever learn?

25

Flowers Andy Warhol, 1970, screenprint on paper (detail)

PETE SEEGER

Pete Seeger was born in 1919 in New York City to parents who taught classical music. Seeger looked for his own kind of music, however, and at age sixteen, he was playing tenor banjo in his school band. He loved the rhythms and melodies of folk ballads, work songs, and freedom songs "time tested by generations of singers." Most of all, he liked the words. He claims that those singers put into their songs "all the meat of human life" and "sang of heroes, outlaws, murderers, fools. They weren't afraid of being tragic instead of just sentimental." Above all, this music was honest and straightforward.

Seeger is still learning, singing, and writing his own kind of music. One of his best-known songs is "If I Had a Hammer." In addition to song writing, Seeger has always been a force for peace and civil rights and an activist for a cleaner environment.

The Afternoon

from April Morning

HOWARD FAST

We were about a mile and a half to the south of Lexington[1] now, between the Watertown Road and the Menotomy[2] Road; and all that was home to me, all that was warm and sweet and good, my mother and my brother Levi and Granny and Ruth, my relatives and my friends—all of this was a hoot and a holler away, just over the hill and across the trees, just so near that I could almost reach out and touch it; but instead of going home, as any sane person would, I was part of a motley group of farmers who were off to trap a British army and destroy it. It made no sense whatsoever, and I said so to Cousin Simmons.

1. **Lexington:** town in eastern Massachusetts where the first battle of the Revolutionary War was fought on April 19, 1775.
2. **Menotomy** [men ot′ ə mē]

"Well, Adam," he said, scratching his head, "it's war now, you know, and in wartime things don't make sense the way they would in peacetime."

"I had a belly full of war and killing, Cousin Simmons."

"I know that, Adam. So have I, when you come right down to it. Maybe so has everybody here except an old fire-eater like Solomon Chandler. But we can't stop."

"Why not?"

"Good heavens, Adam, we declared ourselves. There just is no stronger declaration of a man's purpose than to take a gun and shoot someone dead."

"But they shot us first."

"That's an argument, Adam, and we're past arguments. Gun shooting is a declaration, not an argument. Nobody's going to be calm and reasonable about who shot first. There's been too much shooting already to ever trace our way back. Now we're enemies until one side or another wins its purpose. If we were to back off now they'd come with their gallows rope and hang up maybe a hundred, maybe a thousand, maybe ten thousand. We'd never sleep a peaceful night again—not ever again, no sir."

"Then when will it end?"

"When will it end, Adam? I'll tell you when it will end—when we drive them back into their ships, and when their ships sail away from here and leave us in peace in our own land. Not until then."

"You're talking about a time. Maybe years of time," I said wearily.

"Maybe years of time, Adam. That's true."

"I'm talking about today, Cousin Simmons. I'm talking about right now—about going home right now."

"Heavens to Holland, lad—where would you go? The redcoats[3] are no doubt entering Lexington right this precious minute."

"They wouldn't catch me."

"There's a real smart observation. Suppose you tell me how you are going to manage that."

"I'd crawl up," I muttered. "I'd lay there at the edge of town until they left."

"Why, the place is crawling with them—and you'd go crawling in there? That makes no sense at all, Adam, and you know it."

"Maybe I do know it, Cousin Simmons. I'm just sick of this whole bloody business."

"I can understand that," Cousin Simmons nodded. "You're just a boy, Adam, and you've had a hard enough time of it and a long day to boot, a terrible long day. Don't you think I'd like to see you out of this, you being my own kin and fatherless? But that's just it."

"What is?"

"The fact that you're Moses Cooper's first-born, and there isn't a man here doesn't know it—and doesn't know he was killed in the slaughter."

3. **redcoats:** British soldiers.

We paused for a few minutes to rest ourselves on the little bare hillock we called the Indian burying ground—although so far as I knew, no one was buried there. My father once told me that the Indians, being heathen,[4] did not properly bury their dead, but built a sort of frame structure on the burying ground and laid their dead upon it, open and uncovered to the sky and the sun and the rain and the snow. I had liked the notion and half-regretted that I was not born an Indian; for it seemed infinitely preferable to being lowered into a deep, wet hole in the ground. Now the thought came back to me, a stabbing awakening of grief and remorse—the guilt attached to the way I had allowed myself to be flung into the battle and absorbed by it, with my father lying in our home, hardly even cold with death. I felt that the least I could do for him was to keep my thoughts on him and keep my sorrow alive.

I felt even worse when someone shouted that Lexington was burning. There were well over a hundred and fifty men in our little army by now, and we all stood dumfounded and helpless on the little hillock, staring northward where smoke rose into the sky. We discovered subsequently that only three houses had been set afire and actually burned down, the Loring House, the Mullikan House and the Bond House; but from the amount of smoke in the sky, it appeared to us then that the entire village was being consumed. I was sick at heart with the thought that our house was burning, and that there was nothing at all that I could do about it. I was asking myself, What about Mother and Granny and Levi? Were they in the house? For all I knew, they could be hiding down in the cellar, trapped there, with the house burning down over their heads. I said as much to Cousin Simmons, whose own face was desolate enough.

"Oh, no, Adam," he replied sadly. "That's one thing you don't have to worry about. Your grandmother would not hide herself in the cellar if all the dragoons[5] in England were in her front yard. It's

4. **heathen** [hē′ THən]: people who do not believe in the God of the Bible or the Koran.
5. **dragoons** [drə günz′]: soldiers who ride a horse and are trained to fight on foot or on horseback.

Ruthie and Goody Simmons I'm distressed about. It's a bitter thing for a man to have to stand idle and helpless and watch his home being consumed into ashes."

Some of the men began to talk of going up and attacking the British and driving them out of the town. It was wild, desperate talk. We had inflicted awful damage upon the redcoats and would do more before the day was over—but not by going up against the volleys[6] of their muskets when they could all stand in their lines together and see what they were shooting at. So the talk was only talk—no more than that. Jonathan Crisp, who had been on the common[7] with us, was there, with his cousin Salem, who was a year younger than he; and they both burst into tears. The men watched them, and shook their heads sadly, because the whole world appeared to be crumbling around us; and none of us had been prepared for it or had anticipated it. It had happened too quickly. I could see that the men were driving themselves sick with their frustration—such a crowd of us standing here on the hillock and not being able to do one blessed thing to rescue the town from the redcoats.

Then Solomon Chandler sang out, so that everyone would hear him, "One thing, lads, the British are there now—but not for long! The last of them will be out before the hour's up!"

"Why?"

"Because it makes sense. Either they're back in Boston by darkness or they'll never be back there again!"

The men let out a cheer to that. Everyone wanted to find a reason to extract a crumb of comfort. And just then, three Committeemen on horseback came riding up. They had a force of a hundred men from Watertown and Cambridge, and they were waiting down along the Menotomy Road, just about a mile from where we were. They told us that a relief army of redcoats from Boston, fifteen hundred of them, had gone by about an hour ago into Lexington, and that before another hour was up they'd probably all

6. **volleys:** showers of stones, bullets, or arrows.
7. **common:** land used by everyone in the town; the first battle of the Revolutionary War was fought on the Lexington common, or green.

The Battle of Lexington, April 19, 1775 Amos Doolittle, Chicago Historical Society

be marching down the road and back to Boston. They were out to find everyone they could, so that the redcoats would retain a good and substantial memory of the Menotomy Road.

"And you found us, you did," Solomon Chandler grinned.

That broke the tension. Everyone began to talk and shout and swear and wave their guns. It was a wild mood that took hold of the men, as if they realized, as Cousin Simmons had put it, that there was no more undoing of what had been done.

Solomon Chandler climbed onto his horse and shouted, "Follow me, laddies!" and then we all streamed after him, down off the hillock and toward the Menotomy Road. I didn't want to go, yet I went. We all went. We were in the grip of a force outside of ourselves. I know that my heart was breaking with anxiety over the burning of the village, and I tried to give myself strength and purpose by telling myself that everything that I had ever loved was destroyed or dead, and I might as well be dead too.

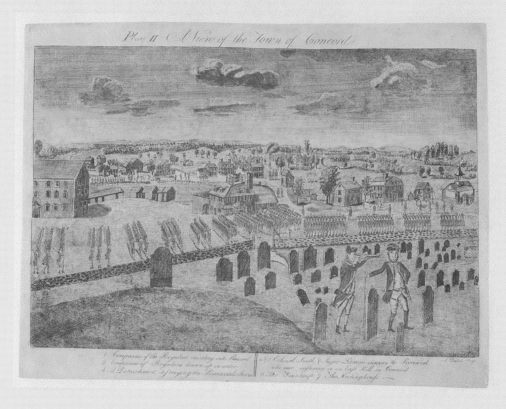

A View of the Town of Concord Amos Doolittle, Chicago Historical Society

There was a place our people had in mind where the Menotomy Road dips between two banks of earth, with a great tangle of wild blackberry bushes on one side and a windfall of dead trees on the other. I knew the place well, because the bramble patch made for the best rabbit hunting in the whole neighborhood, and many was the time Father and I hiked down there for an early morning's shooting. Now the plan was to drag enough fallen trees across the road to block it, and then back the trees up with rocks and dirt. With such a breastwork, we felt we could hold the British long enough for a considerable army of Essex men, who were said to be marching in under the leadership of Colonel Pickering, to reach us. I suppose that there was some vague possibility that the plan might have worked; in any case, it was the only plan of any sort that emerged from that incredible and catch-as-catch-can day of battle. Everything else that happened was the result of some sudden notion of this or that Committeeman; and the only reason that the battle went on hour after hour was that no one was in any position to halt it or direct it. It was perfectly true that before the reinforcements reached the first redcoat army, they wanted to surrender. They were just about going out of their minds, plagued by an enemy they couldn't see, unable to use any tactics of battle they had learned or practiced in Europe, shooting away all their ammunition at stone walls, woods, and thickets, and losing almost a quarter of their number in dead and wounded. But there was no one they could surrender to, no one they could talk to or parley[8] with; and when one of them came to the roadside west of Lexington with a white flag,[9] he was shot dead by Abraham Clyde of Concord, who thought the white flag was only another one of the various regimental flags the redcoats carried.

So our plan might have worked and everything that followed might have been different, if the British hadn't already started down the Menotomy Road before we reached it. We were still a quarter of a mile away when we heard the Watertown and Cambridge men banging away at them.

Cousin Simmons and I and four or five of the others crawled into the windfall, and wriggled our way through the tangle of trees until we got a view of a few yards of the road. We were as well hidden there as a fox in her earth, about sixty or seventy paces from the road, and we began to shoot at the redcoats passing by. It was a strange and dreamlike business, lying there and seeing bits of red color emerge from the powder smoke that hung all over the place and over the road as well, then watching everything disappear under the smoke and only the smoke to shoot into, and then a bit of red here or a bit of red there—and such a feeling of a world gone mad, for there was nothing the redcoats could do but march on and accept their measure of death—and the bulk of our Committeemen running down the road from place to place, so that they were always with the army, like flies on a dying beast.

But we, our little group of people, remained in our cover—for there was no way that the redcoats could reach us, and most of us

8. **parley** [pär′ lē]: conference, informal talk.
9. **white flag:** traditional sign of surrender.

were too tired now to go on running back and forth along the road. We lay there and fired at the redcoats and the smoke; or at least Cousin Simmons and the others did; I fired off my fowling piece[10] once, and then I realized that at this range, even if some of the bird shot[11] did reach the redcoats, it would sting no harder than a mosquito. It was a great relief to find some sensible reason not to go on shooting. I burrowed into the ground behind a fallen tree, rested my cheek against the stock of my gun, listened to the shooting and screaming and cursing—more profanity in five minutes than one heard in our village in the course of a year—and then fell asleep.

It might strike you as strange that I could fall asleep right in the midst of a battle; and you might even consider it downright ungracious that anyone should go to sleep during a battle as talked about and lied about and written about as this one; but the fact of the matter was that I had gone without a night's sleep, and been through the massacre on the common, and had quartered back and forth across the country since then like a fox driven to distraction—so that the wonder of it was, not that I had finally fallen asleep, but that I had managed to remain awake as long as this.

I was awakened by the silence. I guess it was the first silence in six or seven hours, and it was just unbelievable and a little frightening as well.

I don't mean that it was a complete and total silence, or anything unnatural or spooky. There were sounds in the distance and in the background, as there always are, but even these sounds were muffled by the tangled pile of trees; and missing were the violent and awful sounds of battle, the crash of firearms and the savage shouting and swearing of men in anger and pain. When I listened more carefully, I thought I could still hear battle sounds, but far off and very faint. It was still daylight outside, but under the windfall there was a sort of comforting twilight, and being used to gauging time without a pocket watch, I had a feeling that at least an hour had passed.

10. **fowling piece:** lightweight shotgun, usually used for shooting wild birds.
11. **bird shot:** a small lead pellet, usually used in shooting wild birds.

The Engagement at the North Bridge Amos Doolittle, Chicago Historical Society

I lay still for a little while after I awakened, luxuriating in the peace, and then I heard the noise of twigs and branches breaking, men making their way into the windfall, and voices; first the voice of the Reverend:

"God be kind to us, Joseph, and merciful. I tell you frankly that I don't have the courage to go back to Goody Cooper and tell her that her son as well as her husband lies dead today."

"What about myself?" Cousin Simmons answered him. "Aside from having the boy's blood on my own conscience, I'll have to face her. 'Why didn't you send him home?' she'll ask me."

"The boy's blood isn't on your conscience, Joseph. No man's blood is on anyone's conscience today—unless it be on the conscience of the Englishmen who made the first slaughter on the common."

"You don't know Goody Cooper, Reverend."

"Where did you see him last? Where did you leave him?"

"Trouble is, Reverend, I don't think I ever knew a better or more

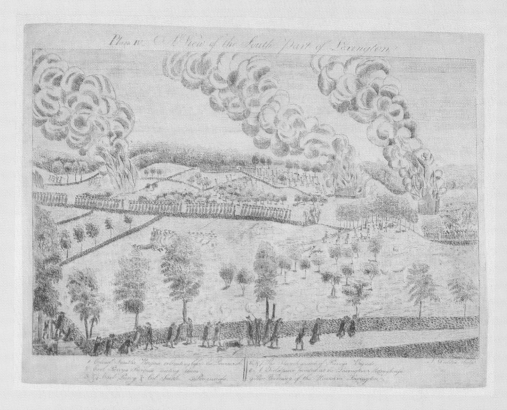

View of the South Part of Lexington   Amos Doolittle, Chicago Historical Society

uncomplaining boy."

"He was a good boy, Joseph. No question about that."

"It just shakes my faith in the Almighty to think of the innocent cut down like this."

"Nothing should shake your faith, Joseph. His ways are inscrutable."

"Uncomplaining, Reverend. When you consider all that boy went through since last night—"

At first, it was pleasant and rewarding to lie there and listen to them talk about me in the past tense. I guess there never was a boy who didn't imagine himself dead, so that he could take comfort out of the fine things said about him. But there was a note in their voices that made me wonder whether they had the same respect for my intelligence as for my forbearance.[12] I sat up and called out to them.

"God be praised!" the Reverend cried.

12. **forbearance:** patient endurance.

Helping me to my feet, Cousin Simmons asked if I was wounded.

"No, sir. I'm all right."

"Then what on earth happened to you, Adam?"

"I fell asleep."

They both of them stared at me open-mouthed.

"You what?"

"I fell asleep," I repeated. "I just fell asleep."

"So long as you're all right," the Reverend said.

They helped me out of the windfall, and I asked Cousin Simmons about the battle.

"It's down past Cambridge by now, and the Committeemen are marching in from all over. If the redcoats get back to Boston, they're there to stay. There'll be five thousand of our men around Boston before nightfall."

"Then can we go home?" I asked him.

"We're all going home, Adam—there's others had more sleep and more rest."

But what I would be coming home to I didn't know; and for all I knew, the town could be in ashes and everyone dear to me, dead.

When I saw the tower of the meetinghouse, I felt better, and then I saw the Parker barns on the outskirts of town, and I told myself that if they had burned one, they would have burned the other too. You might think we would run in our haste to be there and see what had happened, but you don't hurry for bad news. Also, we were tired, all three of us. So we came up to the town slowly, and bit by bit we realized that it still stood, only the three houses that I spoke of before burned down.

I left Cousin Simmons and the Reverend to go to my own house. We were not the only ones returning to the village. Others came across the fields, and still others were trudging wearily up the Menotomy Road—and all of them could be defined by a sort of tired sadness that was evident in the way they walked and the way they trailed their guns. We had won the battle, but there is less joy in winning a battle than the history books tell you.

"Best to go home, Adam," the Reverend said. "I will come by and pay my respects later."

I would have begged them to come along with me and not leave me with the task of facing what awaited me alone, but when I looked at them, I had no heart to. Both of them had aged woefully. Their faces were gray and drawn, covered with a stubble of beard, with dirt and grime and dried blood. Their clothes were torn and filthy, and their eyes were red with fatigue and gunpowder irritation. I felt that I must present as dreadful an appearance, but I was younger than they were, and nothing can feel as superior as youth.

So I nodded and left them, and walked toward the house, approaching it from the back, where the herb garden was. Levi must have been watching and waiting for me. My own sight was blurred, for the sun was already low and burning into my eyes, and I heard him before I saw him. Shouting, "Adam! Adam! Adam!" he hurtled toward me and plunged into my arms, and I just let my gun drop and hugged him as if he was everything in the world. He was crying, and I began to cry too. I sat down on the ground, still holding him tight, and did my best to stop my tears. I knew that it would be only moments before I had to face Mother, and I didn't want it to be with tears in my eyes. I could imagine that there had been tears enough for that day.

"We thought you were dead," Levi sobbed. "There was a big damn fool from Concord come by here before, and he said he saw you lying dead up at the crossroads."

"Do I look dead?"

"Oh, Adam—I don't want you dead."

"Well, I'm not dead. I'm alive. I may be tired to death, but I'm alive."

"I don't want you dead, Adam."

"Stop saying that I'm dead, because I'm not dead." I shook him, and he looked up at me and managed to smile through his tears. Then I got to my feet, and there, at the edge of the herb garden, Mother was standing with Granny next to her, Granny's arm around her to hold her up, and Mother's face as white as snow. Her mouth was open a little, the lips trembling. Granny just stared at me, shaking her head slightly.

"He's not dead," Levi said apologetically.

Mother took a few steps toward me.

"I'm awful dirty," I whispered. "I guess I never been so dirty in my whole life."

Then Mother came up to me and took me in her arms, holding me so tight I thought my ribs would break, her face buried in my dirty shirt. Then she let go of me and stepped back and began to cry. Granny went over to her, stroking her shoulder and whispering, "Poor dear, poor dear." It seemed to me that Granny might have spared a moment for greeting me, but she hardly appeared to know that I was there, Levi picked up my gun, and Granny led Mother back into the house, myself following them.

A number of neighbors were in the kitchen or standing outside. Ruth was there, and her mother and her widow aunt Susan, and old Mrs. Cartwright, the midwife, who always helps out on funeral occasions, when it comes to the laying out[13] and the shrouding,[14] and there were some of Levi's friends, the Albright boys, and little Jonah Parker, who had death in his own family. They made way for me to enter the kitchen. Ruth held back, but never took her eyes off me, and the Widow Susan took my arm. Mother dropped into a chair and stared at me, her whole body shivering and the tears running down her cheeks, and Granny's face was all twisted up with her own attempt to refrain from weeping—realizing, perhaps, that it would only take a little more to have all those women half-hysterical.

I had anticipated a bad time of coming home, but I hadn't thought it would be anywhere as heartbreaking and uncomfortable as this. For the life of me, I didn't know what to say, except to tell Goody Simmons that Cousin Simmons was back and at their house.

"You go there, Ruthie," she told her daughter, "and tell him we're here."

"Shall I take him upstairs?" Mrs. Cartwright asked Mother.

13. **laying out:** preparing a body for burial.
14. **shrouding:** wrapping a body in a cloth or shroud for burial.

Mother didn't respond, but the Widow Susan nodded, and Mrs. Cartwright took my hand and led me up the stairs and into the main bedroom, where Father's body was laid out on the bed.

At first, I was frightened to death and would have given ten years of my life not to have to go into that room. I held back at the doorway. Mrs. Cartwright cooed at me, "Come, come, now. Nothing to be afraid of. It's birth, marriage, and death. Always has been that way and always will. Some day your own children will look at you all stretched out and washed and combed, and how do you suppose they're going to feel? Now come right in here, Adam."

It was poor consolation, but at least it turned my mind from my fear and reluctance to an old, established, and ever-increasing dislike of Mrs. Cartwright. I was able to assure myself that she was unquestionably the most repulsive and insensitive old lady in Middlesex County, and that was some small comfort. I walked into the room and looked down at Father.

"Pay your respects," she cackled.

"Oh, get out of here and leave me alone, Mrs. Cartwright!" I snapped at her.

"What? Well, I do declare," she began, and I interrupted her and told her in no uncertain terms to get out. Then she left, muttering and coughing with indignation.

I was left alone then with my father, who was not my father but a body, with all that was meaningful and important gone out of it. It was the ending of a day when I had seen many bodies, bodies of redcoats and bodies of Committeemen. All my life long, death had only touched me lightly, but I had lived all day with death today. I was too numb to be moved any more. I didn't even want to weep. Later and many times afterward, I would remember my father, but not the corpse on the bed.

I left the room then, closing the door gently behind me.

HOWARD FAST

Howard Fast was born in 1914 in New York City and grew up there, working as a page in the New York Public Library during his high school years. His first novel was published when he was eighteen. By the time he became a war correspondent during World War II, Fast had written more than a dozen books. Since then he has written many more.

Fast considers *April Morning* to be "as good a book as I have ever written, as nearly perfect a book as I could hope to write." He prefers fiction that can be read for pleasure. When books are good, he feels, "they open a thousand doors, they shape lives and answer questions, they widen horizons, they offer hope for the heart and food for the soul." Fast believes that the writer has an obligation to truth and that the books read by young people are the ones that will endure.

A WOMAN'S FIGHT

PRETTY SHIELD

Once, when I was eight years old, we moved our village from the-mountain-lion's-lodge [Pompey's Pillar] to the place where the white man's town of Huntley now stands. There were not many of us in this band. Sixteen men were with us when the women began to set up their lodges,[1] and one man named Covered-with-grass was sent out as a wolf. I could see him on the hill when my mother was setting up her lodge-poles. I was dragging the poles of my play-lodge to a nice place that I had selected when I saw Covered-with-grass, the wolf on the hill, signal, "The enemy is coming."

Instantly two men leaped upon the backs of horses, their warhorses, that were always kept tied near lodges, and rode out on the plains to drive the other horses into camp.

There was great excitement, much running about by the women, who left their lodges just as they happened to be when the signal came. Some of the lodges had but a few poles up. Others, whose owners were quicker, had their lodge-skins tied, hanging loosely from the skin-poles.

Men, watching the hills, stationed themselves, one between every two lodges. Mothers, piling packs and parfleches[2] into breastworks, called their children; and horses whinnied. Then I saw the horses that had been out on the plains coming fast, their hoofs making a great noise and much dust. I must get out of the way.

Dragging my poles, a load beneath each arm, I ran between two lodges whose lodge-skins were flapping in the wind, my own little lodge yet on my back. In came the horses, more than a hundred, sweeping into the camp between two lodges that were far apart, too far apart, I thought. And this thought gave me an idea. Why not close that wide gap between those two lodges? Why not set up my little lodge between the two big ones, and shut this wide place up?

While yet the horses were running around within the circle of the camp I dragged my poles to the spot, and quickly pitched my lodge there. I heard my mother calling me. I had to work very fast to

1. **lodges:** small houses.
2. **parfleches** [pär flesh′]: pouches made of rawhide, used for carrying arrows.

shut up that wide place, believing that my little lodge would keep our horses from getting out, and the Lakota[3] from getting in; but I did not finish pegging down my lodge-skin, not quite. Corn-woman found me. "Ho! Ho!" she cried out, "here is a brave little woman! She has shut the wide gap with her lodge."

But just the same she picked me up in her arms and carried me to my mother, as though I were a baby. Corn-woman told this story every year until she died.

Now I shall have to tell you about the fighting, a little, because it was a woman's fight. A woman won it. The men never tell about it. They do not like to hear about it, but I am going to tell you what happened. I was there to see. And my eyes were good, too. [. . .]

Yes [. . .] a woman won that fight, and the men never tell about it. There was shooting by the time my play-lodge was pitched. A Lakota bullet struck one of its poles, and whined. Arrows were coming among the lodges, and bullets, when Corn-woman carried me to my mother, who made me lie down behind a pack. I saw what went on there.

Several horses were wounded and were screaming with their pain. One of them fell down near my mother's lodge that was not yet half pitched. Lying there behind that pack I did not cover my eyes. I was looking all the time, and listening to everything. I saw Strikes-two, a woman sixty years old, riding around the camp on a gray horse. She carried only her root-digger, and she was singing her medicine-song, as though Lakota bullets and arrows were not flying around her. I heard her say, "Now all of you sing, 'They are whipped. They are running away,' and keep singing these words until I come back."

When the men and even the women began to sing as Strikes-two told them, she rode out straight at the Lakota, waving her root-digger and singing that song. I *saw* her, I *heard* her, and my heart swelled, because she was a woman.

The Lakota, afraid of her medicine, turned and ran away. The fight was won, and by a woman.

3. **Lakota** [lə kō′ tə]: Native Americans, also called Dakota, part of the Sioux Nation.

PRETTY SHIELD

....

Pretty Shield, a Crow wise woman, told her story to Frank B. Linderman,
a social scientist who was searching for information about the role of
Native American women in the life of their people.

Pretty Shield shared her story as a way of overcoming the general
ignorance about the life of Crow women. She communicated by means
of sign language and a translator.

WHAT A FOOLISH BOY

FROM

THE BOYS' WAR

JIM MURPHY

"Day after day and night after night did we tramp along the rough and dusty roads," writes sixteen-year-old Confederate[1] soldier John Delhaney. "'neath the most broiling sun with which the month of August ever afflicted a soldier: thro' rivers and their rocky valleys, over mountains—on, on, scarcely stopping to gather the green corn from the fields to serve us for rations. . . . During these marches the men are sometimes unrecognizable on account of the thick coverings of dust which settle upon the hair, eye-brows and beard, filling likewise the mouth, nose, eyes, and ears."

Boys on both sides soon learned a boring fact about life in the army. Soldiers spend more time marching from one place to another than fighting.

At each town, new units would join the troops until the column stretched for miles with no beginning or end in sight.

1. **Confederate** [kən fed′ ər it]: of the eleven southern states that seceded from the United States in 1860 and 1861.

A messenger might fly past on horseback carrying orders for the officer in charge. The column would halt for a half hour or an hour with no explanation of what was happening up ahead. Then suddenly the order would be shouted up and down the line, the drumbeat[2] would sound, and the troops would be on their way again.

Not that they understood what all of this maneuvering was about. It did not take Elisha Stockwell very long to comment on this with his dry wit: "We didn't know where we were going, as a soldier isn't supposed to know any more than a mule, but has to obey orders."

What the common soldiers did not realize was that the commanders for both sides were engaged in a large-scale chess match in which they were the pieces. The first two commanders of the Union[3] army, Lieutenant General Winfield Scott and then Major General George McClellan, had decided on a defensive war, at least until they could amass,[4] outfit,[5] and train a vast army. Both feared that if Confederate troops were able to capture Washington, D.C., civilians and politicians in the North would become demoralized and abandon the fight. They also hoped that the South would lose energy and give up its quest for independence.

The Confederate commander, General Robert E. Lee, adopted a cautiously offensive plan. He knew the Union army outnumbered his by almost two to one and that it had more supplies. He could never hope to win any head-to-head battle. Instead, he decided to use smaller, fast-moving groups of soldiers and cavalry to strike at Union forces in many places, then wheel around and strike again. By poking at the enemy, he hoped to hold his losses down while buying time to build up his forces. And he, like Scott and McClellan, hoped the other side would abandon the fight.

When boys enlisted in the army, they expected to fight the

2. **drumbeat:** at the time of the story, troops marched to the beat of a drum.
3. **Union:** of the states that supported the federal government of the United States during the Civil War.
4. **amass** [ə mas']: gather together.
5. **outfit:** provide uniforms and equipment for.

enemy and settle the dispute very quickly. After all, Lincoln's initial call for enlistments asked for only ninety days of service. But after what seemed like an endless amount of marching and a few hard-fought battles, it became clear that neither side was going to surrender easily or quickly. And once they realized the war would last a long, long time, these boys began to miss the things they had left behind—namely their family and friends.

Homesickness was a common problem and found expression in many forms. Singing was one way to express such feelings. One of the most popular war songs for both sides, called "Tenting Tonight," was written even before the first year of fighting was completed. A few of its lines go:

> We're tenting tonight on the old camp ground,
> Give us a song to cheer our weary hearts,
> A song of home, and the friends we love so dear.
>
> We've been tenting tonight on the old camp ground,
> Thinking of days gone by, of the loved ones at home
> That gave us the hand, and the tear that said "good-bye!"

Many boys simply put down what they felt in their own words. One Southerner, J.B. Lance of Buncombe County, North Carolina, was already tired of life away from home in October 1861. His message was simple and direct, and yet poignant: "Father I have Saw a rite Smart of the world Sence I left home But I have not Saw any place like Buncomb and hendersn yet."

It's easy to see why these boys developed such feelings. They were so young they had little real sense of who they were or how they fit into the world. The one solid and reliable thing they knew—their families—had been left behind. Their futures were uncertain. And they had not had time to develop real friendships with the others in their units. John Delhaney managed to capture in his journal this feeling of being apart and alone: "I felt strange enough, lying down this my first night in camp. The strange faces and forms, the near and distant sounds of an army of men talking, shouting, singing, and all upon different subjects; the croaking frogs, cries of the Whip-poor-Will,[6] the glare of the camp fires and the neighing of horses and the deep shadows of a dark night overhanging all; all these were not calculated to allay[7] my uneasiness of mind or lighten my heart of its cares."

Despite the endless marching and the tactics of avoidance both sides seemed to favor, the war would eventually catch up with these boys. One day, they would hear the dull thudding of large cannons, known as thirty pounders, being fired in the distance. Plumes of smoke would rise from a nearby valley. As they would draw nearer the action, the firecracker sound of small-arms fire grew more and more frequent.

An officer would call their company to order. Rifles would be loaded and blankets and haversacks[8] piled in a heap against a tree to wait their return. Then they would move off toward the fighting, their eyes searching the mysterious forest around them for the enemy.

It was often well before they had a chance to fire a shot in anger that these boys learned about the cruel horrors of war. Elisha Stockwell's unit was one mile from the fighting at the Battle of Shiloh[9] when he had this experience: "The first dead man we saw was a short distance from the clearing. He was leaning back against a big tree as if asleep, but his intestines were all over his legs and several times their natural size. I didn't look at him the second time as it made me deathly sick. A little farther on we saw lots of dead men scattered through the woods where they had fallen the day before."

The officer would order the men on, not allowing them to dwell on what they were seeing or feeling. Keep low, keep low, he would shout. Stay alert, boys. The enemy is near. Gunfire grows heavy not

6. **Whip-poor-Will:** North American bird whose call sounds somewhat like its name: it is active at night or at twilight.
7. **allay** [ə lā′]: put at rest, relieve.
8. **haversacks** [hav′ ər sakz]: bags used by soldiers and hikers for carrying food or supplies on a march or hike.
9. **Shiloh** [shī′ lō]: place in Tennessee where a Civil War battle was fought in 1862.

more than one hundred yards to the left, and yelling can be heard, though the words are unclear.

What follows are the views of five boys going into battle for the first time. While each one fought in a different battle, their voices and experiences form a remarkably unified picture of what fighting must have been like for an inexperienced soldier.

Thomas Galway recounts what happened to his unit as it moved closer to the gunfire: "Before we had gone far we came to a hanging rock with a tree felled across the road under it. Evidently this barricade had been put there for a purpose. As we stepped over the log we said to one another, 'There is something here. We shall soon see what it means.'

"We were scarcely over the log when a sheet of flame burst through from the top of the cliff. The detonation was startling to our unaccustomed ears."

Suddenly, the war that had been a romantic dream was all around them like angry bees. Elisha Stockwell found himself facedown on the ground, shells exploding all around and soldiers screaming for help: "I want to say, as we lay there and the shells were flying over us, my thoughts went back to my home, and I thought what a foolish boy I was to run away and get into such a mess as I was in. I would have been glad to have seen my father coming after me."

But the only things searching for these boys were the shot and shell of their enemy, which ripped up clots of earth, stripped the leaves from the trees, and too often found their mark. Soon a voice can be heard urging the soldiers to get up and move forward. It's an officer from another unit, who actually grabs some soldiers by the shirt, hauls them up, and pushes them into motion. Young Tyler Wise tells about these tense moments. "We moved quite lively as the Rebel[10] bullets did likewise. We had advanced but a short distance when we came to a creek, the bank of which was high, but we slid, and wading through the water to the opposite side and began firing at will. . . .

10. **Rebel** [reb′ əl]: Confederate; the name was used by Union soldiers.

"For two hours, the contest raged furiously. The creek was running red with precious blood spilt for our country. My bunkmate and I were kneeling side by side when a ball crashed through his brain. With assistance of two others I picked him up, carried him over the bank in our rear and laid him behind a tree." But there was no time to grieve or even feel sorry; a few moments later, Wise reentered the battle.

Naturally, Confederate boys went through much the same initiation. What was different was that Confederate troops seemed to do much better in the early fighting. Credit for this success has to go to the Southern officers. They did a much better job of keeping their men united and pressing forward even in the midst of heavy fire. And they tolerated such unmilitary but emotionally unifying behavior as the dreaded "rebel yell."

No two descriptions of the rebel yell are alike, though one soldier described it as "a mingling of Indian whoop and wolf-howl." Whatever it sounded like, it seems to have worked well for many soldiers. William Chambers described his first experience with it: "I always said if I ever went into charge, I wouldn't holler! But the very first time I fired off my gun I hollered as loud as I could, and I hollered every breath till we stopped."

Another Confederate soldier describes its use in battle: "Then the Rebel yell was sounded, and right into their ranks[11] we dashed, pouring a deadly volley into their very faces. A moment more and the enemy broke and fled wildly, the scouts keeping in hot pursuit. On they ran, and the rout was complete."

When either side broke ranks in search of safety, the result was a confusion of soldiers racing through forests or across fields. Elisha Stockwell's first fight ended like this: "We had lost all formation,[12] and were rushing down the road like a mob. When we got to the foot of the hill, there was a small stream of water from the rain of the night before. We stopped there and got behind a small tree. I could see the little puffs of smoke at the top of the hill on the other side

11. **ranks:** rows or lines of soldiers, placed side by side.
12. **formation:** arrangement of troops in a certain way.

some forty rods[13] from us, and I shot at those puffs. The brush was so thick I couldn't see the Rebs, but loaded and fired at the smoke until a grape shot[14] came through the tree and knocked me flat as I was putting the cap on my gun. I thought my arm was gone, but I rolled on my right side and looked at my arm and couldn't see anything wrong with it, so got to my feet with gun in my hands and saw the Rebs coming down hill just like we had.

"The road was full for several rods, and I shot for the middle of the [charging] crowd and began loading. But as they were getting so close, I looked behind me to see what the rest [of my friends] were doing. I saw the colors going out of sight over the hill, and only two or three men in sight. As I started to run, I heard several shout, "Halt!" But I knew it was the Rebs, and I hadn't any thought of obeying them."

Such undisciplined retreats could often cover miles, with soldiers tossing aside their rifles, ammunition, and hats to lighten their loads. Civilians, who often picnicked on nearby mountains to watch Civil War battles, might even find themselves trampled by panicking soldiers. A few soldiers would not stop running until they reached home.

Gradually, the fighting would lessen and then stop. Straggling soldiers would regroup. Night would settle on the battlefield, and the eerie shadows of soldiers could be seen moving across it, searching out the groaning wounded and digging hasty graves for the dead.

Meanwhile, in camp, exhausted soldiers huddled around the fire, ate, and tried to rest up for the next day's fighting. Some would tell tales of their bravery or of some strange thing they had seen during the fighting. Others, like Tyler Wise, would think about the friend they'd lost that day. "I dreamed of my bunkmate last night," Wise wrote in his diary. "Wonder if his remains will be put where they can be found, for I would like, if I ever get the chance, to put a board with his name on it at the head of his grave."

13. **forty rods:** 220 yards; a rod is a unit of measure equal to 5.5 yards.
14. **grape shot:** cluster of small iron balls used in a cannon.

JIM MURPHY

Jim Murphy was born in 1947 in Newark, New Jersey, and grew up in Kearny, New Jersey, which Murphy calls "a nice enough suburban town." He and his friends did "all the normal things—played baseball and football endlessly and . . . cooked up as much mischief as we could."

As a boy, Murphy claims that he seldom read for pleasure. "In fact, I hardly cracked a book willingly," he says, until a high school teacher identified the titles of books that students should *not* read. Murphy became hooked on reading while trying to read them all. He also began writing, "mostly poetry, but with an occasional story or play tossed in there."

All of Murphy's writing has been for young people, from *Weird and Wacky Inventions* to *The Boys' War*.

LAW OF THE GREAT PEACE

JOHN BIERHORST

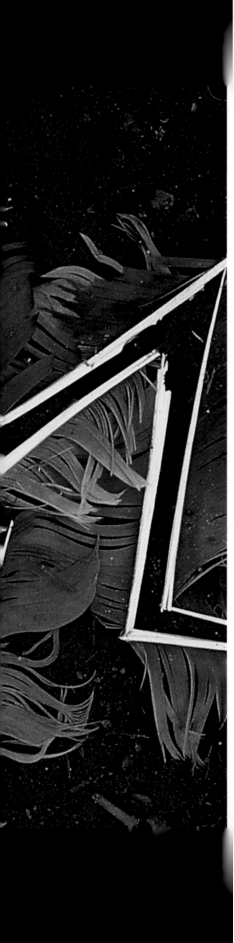

1

With the statesmen of the League of Five Nations, I plant the Tree of Great Peace.

2

I name the tree the Tree of the Great Long Leaves.

3

Under the shade of this Tree of Great Peace, we spread the soft, white, feathery down of the globe thistle as seats for you.

4

Roots have spread out from the Tree of Great Peace, one to the north, one to the east, one to the south, and one to the west. These are the Great White Roots, and their nature is peace and strength.

5

The smoke of the council fire of the League shall ascend and pierce the sky so that other nations who may be allies may see the council fire of the Great Peace.

6

You, the League of Five Nations chiefs, be firm so that if a tree should fall upon your joined hands, it shall not separate you or weaken your hold. So shall the strength of union be preserved.

7

The Great Creator has made us of
one blood, and of the same soil.

8

When a member of an alien nation
comes to the territory of the
League and seeks refuge and
permanent residence, the statesmen
of the nation to which he comes
shall extend hospitality and make
him a member of the nation.

9

Whenever a foreign nation enters
the League or accepts the Great
Peace, the Five Nations and the
foreign nation shall enter into an
agreement by which the foreign
nation shall try to persuade the other
nations to accept the Great Peace.

10

I now uproot the tallest tree, and
into the hole thereby made, we cast
all weapons of war. Into the
depths of the earth, down into the
deep underneath currents of water
flowing to unknown regions, we cast
all the weapons of strife. We bury
them from sight and we plant again
the tree. Thus shall the Great
Peace be established, and
hostilities shall no longer be
known between the Five Nations, but
peace to the united people.

Heron Feathers Andrew Goldsworthy, 1982, earthwork (temporary arrangement of natural objects)

JOHN BIERHORST

John Bierhorst, born in 1936 in Boston, Massachusetts, studied music as he was growing up, and then became a concert pianist. However, in 1964 while Bierhorst was on a trip to Peru, he realized that studying Native American cultures was more important. He visited sites of early civilizations in Mexico and applied for grants to study in his new field.

He began his new career as a writer by collecting, editing, translating, and retelling legends of cultures in North America. His field of study ranges from songs of the Chippewa to legends of the Incas. In the 1980s, Bierhorst worked on dictionaries of early language and wrote texts on the mythologies of North America, South America, and Central America. Bierhorst popularized much of the important music and literature of the peoples he studied. One of his most popular books, *Dr. Coyote: A Native American Aesop's Fables*, features a favorite trickster of the Southwest.

The PEACE KEEPERS

Michael Meek

The brawl was over, but the black and Latino combatants were taunting each other, promising that there would be a showdown after school, that there would be some killing to settle scores.

No one dared take lightly the threats reverberating across the courtyard of Hillcrest High School in Dallas. Over the years, more than one handgun had been seized from teens passing through the school's metal detector.

What began as a racial slur on a basketball court threatened to erupt into schoolwide violence. To defuse the crisis, school administrators turned not to police or to social workers, but to 17-year-old student Sandra Moore.

Accompanied by two colleagues. Moore sat down with a dozen angry students from both sides of the melee.[1] In a tense four-hour session that was part negotiation, part encounter group, a truce was hammered out. They agreed to leave each other alone and to spread the word that the fight was settled, that no vengeance was needed from the uninvolved.

1. **melee** [mā′ lā]: hand-to-hand fighting among a number of people.

The school community breathed a sigh of relief.

"There was going to be a big riot," Moore recalls. "A small issue was going to become a big disaster."

That disaster was avoided largely because Moore and her colleagues had been trained in mediation[2] techniques.

The method they used to calm their classmates goes by a variety of names: peer mediation, dispute settlement, conflict management and conflict resolution. Whatever the label, all share the goals of violence prevention and improved human relations.

At a time of rising racial and ethnic tensions, conflict resolution training can give students the skills to explore peacefully the differences between them. Following the rules of active listening, they learn to hear what each other is saying and to empathize[3] with each other's feelings. Using the techniques of mediation, they put the values of fairness and democracy into practice.

"Conflict is just a part of our life," says Annette Townley, executive director of the National Association for Mediation in Education (NAME). "That is not the problem. The problem is that we just don't know how to handle conflicts."

School Violence

Conflict resolution programs offer alternatives to violence at a time when violence has become almost routine on school grounds. Nearly 300,000 high school students are physically attacked each month, according to the National Institute of Education, and one out of five students in grades 9 through 12 carries a weapon.

"As a society, we promote and glorify violence," writes Deborah Prothrow-Stith of Harvard School of Health. "We teach our children that violence is fun, successful and the hero's way. . . . Our children learn to choose violence as their primary strategy to deal with anger and conflict."

2. **mediation:** the arranging of an agreement by someone outside a group.
3. **empathize** [em′ pə thīz]: enter, through the imagination, into another's feelings or motives.

When that anger crosses racial and cultural lines, it can quickly escalate into a school-wide crises, as the Hillcrest incident demonstrated. And such crises are becoming more serious. During the 1991-1992 school year:

- Blacks and Latinos engaged in gang warfare at a Chicago school, leaving 13 students and one teacher injured. Sixty teenagers were arrested.
- Two black teenagers were killed after being stabbed by a white student during a racial fight at a high school football game in North Carolina.
- Six youths were sent to the hospital following a fight between whites and Hispanics at a New York City high school.

Indeed, most hate crimes are committed by youths under age 25, and more and more of those crimes are taking place in schools, according to the Klanwatch project of the Southern Poverty Law Center. Through its survey of news reports nationwide, Klanwatch tracked a four-fold increase in school hate crimes during the first five months of 1992 compared to the same period in 1991.

"And we're only seeing a fraction of the actual incidents," says Klanwatch Director Danny Welch. "Most hate crimes on school campuses are never reported to police."

Ronald Stephens, executive director of the National School Safety Center, agrees. "A far greater amount of school crime and violence is racially related than anyone wants to admit."

Students themselves report that racial conflicts are common. A 1990 Harris poll revealed that a majority of high school students saw or heard about racial confrontations with overtones of violence. Almost half said they would either join in or silently support such incidents. Less than a third said they would try to stop or condemn a racial incident.

With racial conflict a fact of life in American schools, experts agree that students need more than platitudes[4] about racial harmony and intercultural understanding. They need practical skills.

---

4. **platitudes** [plat′ ə tüdz]: dull or ordinary remarks said as if they were new or fresh.

"It is one thing to study about and discuss the need to be tolerant on an abstract level," says Tom Roderick of New York City's Educators for Social Responsibility. "It is another to practice that on a day-to-day basis with the people you are in contact with."

An Exercise in Empathy

Bias awareness is an integral part of conflict resolution training in New York schools, says Linda Lantieri of the Resolving Conflict Creatively Program. "We grow up with misinformation about each other, and we're trying to help teach kids to understand that even though that is not their fault, they can become part of the solution, by learning the skills of 'emotional literacy.'"

Those skills—being able to listen to and articulate the feelings of another person—are the core of conflict resolution. When it works, the technique becomes an exercise in empathy. Students learn to view a situation from different perspectives and to understand feelings they do not share.

In schools where students mediate their own disputes, success stories abound, even when they involve sensitive interracial and intercultural misunderstandings.

At Junior High School 45 in the Bronx, a fight broke out between a group of Southeast Asian kids and a group of black and Latino kids solely because of a misunderstanding off campus.

A Cambodian and black student had bumped into each other outside a pizzeria, explains mediation trainer Milton Roman. The black student tried to speak to the Cambodian, who refused to look at him. The more the black student tried to reach the Cambodian, the more the Cambodian turned away.

The incident ended with a chase and a fight in the parking lot. During mediation, the black student explained that he felt the Cambodian was being disrespectful. The Cambodian explained that he had been confused, and that he was trying to prevent a fight, not start one, by avoiding eye contact.

Defusing conflicts before they escalate is critical, particularly when the conflicts involve race.

When Hillcrest High School Principal Janet Skinner brought conflict resolution training to the school, she hoped it would help broaden understanding between the school's white, black and Latino students. "I believed our high school needed to stand for a higher purpose than 'education,' and that was to get along with one another and appreciate diversity," she says.

Her faith was put to the test that fall day in 1990 when student mediators stepped in to handle a racial conflict that threatened to explode.

As mediator Sandra Moore remembers it, the dispute started between a pair of friends, one black, one Latino. They were playing a friendly lunchtime game of basketball when the Latino called his friend a "nigger." The ensuing fight involved a dozen or more black and Latino students.

During the mediation session, the Latinos said they had often heard blacks refer to their black friends as "nigger." When the Latino student tried to use the term with his friend, he did not understand that coming from him it would be taken as a racial slur.

The Latinos brought their own grievances to the table, revealing that they were insulted when blacks made fun of their accents by imitating them.

The mediation session didn't result in immediate newfound friendships, Moore recalls, but it did prevent violence. And eventually, members of the rival groups began hanging around together again.

While the conflict resolution movement is growing rapidly,

practitioners emphasize that it is not a cure-all for disciplinary and racial problems.

"If violence is taking place, we don't want other students to jump into the middle of fights and get hurt," says Jim Halligen of the Community Board. "Weapons, extortion . . . are not for students to handle."

Particularly in racially tense situations, it is essential for conflict resolution to be accompanied by direct, open discussions of stereotyping[5] and prejudice. At Hillcrest, the initial mediation was followed by several other sessions designed to look at intercultural understanding. In New York City, conflict resolution training can include a 10-part curriculum dealing with intergroup relations and appreciation for cultural diversity.

Lifelong benefits

Educators believe the skills learned during conflict resolution can become part of a lifelong practice of peace. Students who learn conflict resolution have better decision-making skills and more confidence in their ability to solve problems. And the effect carries over into their relationships with family and friends.

"We get a lot of comments from parents who say, 'Gee, I don't know what you taught my kid, but we're able to talk about things we never could before,'" says Jan Bellard of the Dispute Settlement Center in Orange County, N.C.

At P.S. 230 in Brooklyn, one of the first schools in New York City to begin conflict resolution training, mediators as young as 8 years old wear "mediator" T-shirts and ball caps while on duty in the lunchroom, hallways and playground. When other children find themselves in trouble, they know who to call.

Their principal, Sylvia Oberferst, believes they will grow up to become more caring people because of their training in conflict resolution. And perhaps they will even help reverse the growing

---

5. **stereotyping** [ster′ ē ə tīp′ ing]: judging an entire group by the actions of a few.

tendency of urban youth to settle arguments with gunfights.

"We have kids who come back and say 'I used to fight on my block, but now when I see a fight I try to mediate,'" Oberferst says.

Charlotte student mediator Lori Williams says her training in conflict resolution has helped change the way she reacts to others. "When I'm in an argument with a friend, or my parents, it helps me to see how they're feeling, instead of just yelling. It makes me stop and think."

If conflict resolution can do that—make people 'stop and think'—many believe it will play an important part in helping the next generation live peacefully together.

MICHAEL MEEK
....

Michael Meek was born in 1960 in Mt. Kisco, New York. "I came to writing late," he says. "I did not start out as a child."

Meek has been a news reporter since 1983 and is also the kind of freelancer who "writes about everything."

CRISPUS ATTUCKS

Crispus Attucks

BURKE DAVIS

Fresh snow lay in Boston's icy streets on the night of March 5, 1770, but the sky had cleared after dark and a new moon hung overhead. A cold wind from the harbor swept the Boston Common and shook the tents of British soldiers, who had been camped there for five months.

The streets were noisy as redcoats[1] moved about, followed by band of shouting civilians. The small city of 15,000 was crowded by men and boys who had come in from the country and nearby towns to help drive out the 1,000 redcoats, just as if they were enemies. There were occasional scuffles, as there had been for weeks past. Soldiers jostled and cursed the people, who replied with hoots, curses, and insults. These soldiers were the first ever sent from England to America in peacetime, ordered to the city by King George III after the Massachusetts legislature had protested harsh new trade laws[2] for the colonies.

Now and then the redcoats were pelted by snowballs from the darkness, hundreds of frozen chunks with small stones in the center. A fight broke out—no one seemed to know how it had begun—and church bells rang an alarm. People looked out from their houses, and many came into the streets, armed with swords, axes, pitchforks, or boards ripped from old buildings. The crowds grew more daring as they became larger.

1. **redcoats:** British soldiers during the Revolutionary War era.
2. **harsh new trade laws:** in 1767, the British placed taxes on items imported to America. The colonists considered these unfair.

A sentry[3] by the name of Montgomery who stood before the Customs House on King Street found himself surrounded by people after a young barber's helper yelled, "There's a redcoat who hasn't paid for having his hair dressed."

"Shut up!" Montgomery said.

The boy cursed, the soldier struck him on the head with his musket butt, and the barber's helper went yowling down the street holding his head.

The crowd pressed about the sentry, chanting, "Hang the redcoats! Drive 'em out!"

More church bells rang as the barber's boy returned to jeer and point at Montgomery. The crowd increased. Captain Thomas Preston, the officer of the day, called for the guard, and twelve soldiers hurried to the Customs House. The crowd was forced back a few feet by bayonets.[4] The muskets, Captain Preston said, were not loaded.

At that moment, as the civilians hesitated before the glistening blades, a small mob rushed down a nearby hill, its men armed with clubs. The newcomers were led by a burly black man named CRISPUS ATTUCKS, who urged them on in a loud, fierce voice. People on the streets stepped aside as Attucks charged. As John Adams said, the giant's appearance "was enough to terrify any person."

The black leader had formed his men in Dock Square and led them down King Street (now State Street), trotting at the head of his company, his broad shoulders hunched.

Attucks dashed within a few feet of the line of redcoats at the Customs House and waved over his head a heavy stick of firewood.

"Come on, bloodybacks!" he yelled. "Shoot if you dare! Damn you, we know you don't dare."

The soldiers began loading their muskets. A young white man in the crowd begged Captain Preston to take his men back to their tents, but the officer refused. A soldier yelled, "Damn them. If they bother me, I'll fire." The redcoats now held their muskets breast high, with fingers on the triggers.

Crispus Attucks still towered over the captain, swinging his stick of wood and calling to his companions, "We're not afraid of them! Knock 'em over. They dare not fire."

Beside him stood Samuel Gray, the owner of a rope factory, who had

3. **sentry** [sen′ trē]: a soldier stationed to keep watch and guard against surprise attacks.
4. **bayonets** [bā′ ə nets]: knives often attached to the muzzle of rifles.

led an attack on some of the soldiers a few days before. Gray also shouted encouragement to the mob and said that the troops would not fire. A club sailed through the air, knocking aside a British musket. Suddenly a hail of snowballs, stones, clubs, and sticks fell among the redcoats. The crowd raised a shout that rang through the streets, but above it rang an Indian war whoop from Attucks, who grabbed a bayonet with one hand and at the same moment clubbed a soldier with his stick.

The twelve muskets roared. Attucks fell with two bullets in his chest, the first one fired by the sentry Montgomery. Samuel Gray went down beside him.

Both men died on the spot, almost at the feet of the soldiers. Stray shots killed Jonas Caldwell, a sailor who was standing in the middle of the street, and two other whites, seventeen-year-old Samuel Maverick and Patrick Carr, both of whom fell as they were hurrying toward the scene. Six other civilians were wounded, but were to recover.

The crowd fled, leaving the bodies behind, but as it grew and became noisier, it swarmed through the streets until it met Governor Thomas Hutchinson.

5. **Natick** [na′tik]

The Governor calmed the people by speaking to them from the balcony of a building. He promised to arrest Captain Preston and his men and to have the troops moved out of the city. The people then drifted away and returned to their homes.

Strangely enough, the people of Boston knew almost nothing about Crispus Attucks, who was hailed as the first victim in the cause that was to become the American Revolution.

Though little is known of his early life, Crispus Attucks is thought to have been the son of an African father and an Indian mother. The mother, who belonged to the Natick[5] tribe, was probably descended from John Attucks, a Christian convert who was executed by early New England colonists because he sided with his tribe during an Indian uprising known as King Philip's War. ("Attuck" was the word for "deer" in the Natick language.)

By the time he had grown to manhood, Crispus was a slave, the property of William Brown of Framingham, Massachusetts. But even as a slave, young Attucks was unusually independent. He became well known in his home town as a trader of horses and cattle, shrewd enough to deal with free white men. But though he kept for himself the money he made, Attucks was unable to buy his freedom from his master— and he was fiercely determined to be free.

At last, in the autumn of 1750, he took the only way to freedom that was open to him. He ran away. Brown advertised in the *Boston Gazette* on October 2, 1750:

> *Ran away from his Master William Brown of Framingham . . .a Molatto* [6] *Fellow, about 27 years of Age. Named Crispas 6 feet two Inches high, short curl'd Hair, his knees nearer together than common: had on a light colour'd Bearskin Coat . . .*

But though Brown offered ten pounds as a reward, Attucks was never caught—nor was he heard from again in Massachusetts until the night, twenty years later, when he reappeared as the leader of the patriot mob on March 5, 1770. It is thought that Attucks may have spent his twenty years of freedom as a sailor, working on cargo ships that sailed to and from the West Indies, but this is not certain. He is also said to have sailed whaling ships off the New England coast.

The stranger who had appeared just in time to give the white mob the courageous leadership to attack the redcoats was praised by white revolutionaries as the bravest of the victims of the street fight.

As Thomas Jefferson said, the blood of Crispus Attucks nourished the tree of liberty. The humble slave, who had the courage to flee his master and make a new life on his own, had been among the first Americans to die for the nation's liberty.

Three days later, a public funeral was held for the victims of the street battle. All shops in the city were closed and thousands of people flocked in from the nearby countryside. The *Boston Gazette* reported that the funeral was attended by the largest crowd ever assembled in North America.

The bodies of Attucks and Caldwell, which had lain in their coffins at Faneuil Hall[7] because they had no homes in Boston, were carried to meet other hearses in King Street, near the scene of the

6. **molatto:** old form of mulatto [mə lat′ ō]; a person of mixed racial descent.
7. **Faneuil Hall:** the famous site of colonists' meetings held before the Revolutionary War in protest of British tax and trade policies.

Woodcut of The Boston Massacre based on original etching by Paul Revere

Samuel Adams began to write of the clash between soldiers and civilians as the Boston Massacre, the name by which it is known to this day.

Paul Revere, the silversmith and engraver who was secretly working for the Revolution, copied a drawing of the massacre by a Boston artist and published it—one of the most famous engravings of American history. Thousands of copies were circulated throughout the colonies to create sympathy for the people of Boston and hatred of the British troops.

Captain Preston and several of his soldiers were tried in Boston. The captain was found not guilty since the court ruled that he had acted to protect his troops. Two soldiers who were found guilty were branded in the hand with a hot iron. This did not satisfy the patriot leaders.

Three years later, John Adams called on the memory of the victims of the Boston Massacre to help cause an open break between America and England.

Adams sent Governor Hutchinson a letter that would not be forgotten, a letter that he pretended had been written by a dead man. It was actually meant for use in newspapers:

shootings. A long procession then followed the black carriages to the cemetery, where the victims were buried in one grave.

John Adams was to write of the Boston Massacre years later, "On that night, the foundations of American independence were laid."

But though they could not foresee this future, patriot leaders who were trying to stir up trouble for the British made sure that the deaths of the five men were not forgotten.

The *Boston Gazette* published an account of their deaths with black borders of mourning, with pictures of coffins, skulls, and crossbones.

Sir

    You will hear from Us with Astonishment. You ought to hear from Us with Horror. You are chargeable before God and Man, with our Blood.—The Soldiers were but passive Instruments ...in our Destruction. . . You were a free Agent. You acted, coolly, deliberately, with . . .Malice, not against Us in Particular but against the People in general, which in the Sight of the law is . . .Murder. You will hear from Us hereafter.

The signature in Adams's own hand was "Chrispus Attucks."

It was to be many years later before the great orator Daniel Webster declared that the Boston Massacre was the turning point in the long struggle between England and her rebellious American colonists: "From that moment," Webster was to shout, "we may date the severance[8] of the British Empire." The reckless bravery of Crispus Attucks had helped change the course of history.

8. **severance** [sev′ ər əns]: a separation, breaking off.

B U R K E   D A V I S

Burke Davis, a native of North Carolina, attended Duke University and the University of North Carolina. In his home state and Maryland, he was a journalist for twenty years.

Davis, who has written over forty books, is probably best known for his retellings of the Civil War. *To Appomattox* (1959) is an exciting narrative of the last nine days of the Civil War told from the point of view of soldiers and civilians. Davis has also authored many biographies, some of which are about Confederate leaders. Besides *Black Heroes of the American Revolution*, from which this selection is taken, some of Davis's other books about the Revolutionary War include: *Getting to Know Jamestown* and *Getting to Know Mr. Jefferson's Virginia*.

Mr. Davis has homes in North Carolina and the Virginia mountainside. He is the father of two aspiring writers.

THANKS, NURSE

DIANE CARLSON EVANS

November 13th, 1982
I stand beside the Vietnam Veterans Memorial.
Pleiku,[1] is written on my wrinkled jungle hat, and
71st Evacuation Hospital, Vietnam.
Wearing it today feels natural   5
Even with a skirt and among strangers.
Thirteen years ago it found its place
In a foot locker with worn out combat boots,
Fatigues,[2] a malaria net and poncho liner.
Strange memorabilia[3] for a young woman of 22 years.   10
A foot locker filled with memories
Of a lifetime of one year and
Locked away, forever—I had hoped,
Until today.

1. Pleiku [plī kü′]: a major city in Vietnam.
2. fatigues [fə tēgz′]: military uniform usually worn while doing nonmilitary work.
3. memorabilia [mem′ ər ə bil′ ē ə]: items saved as a remembrance of someone or something.

"Thanks, Nurse," that day in Washington, D.C.   15
You, with your boonie hat[4] and
Faded camouflage[5]
Threw your arms around me, and said
"Thanks, nurse, I never had a chance to say that"
The tears rolled down my face,   20
Don't make me cry,
I've passed thirteen years without a tear.
Please, don't remind me of sadness
With that look on your face.
My soul was overwhelmed with   25
Emotion I hadn't felt
Since leaving that faraway war
In 1969.
"You nurses saved our lives, you know, we
Love you,"   30
My tears are uncontrollable, and
I am as much with the
Dead as with the living.

Facing the wall, I encounter
Something I left behind me so many   35
Years ago.
I am at that moment lifted away
And reunited with those who suffered
And died and had left me
Alone.   40
Left me alone, with the memories of them.
And left me too numb to cry.
As I put my hands on the hard granite
And touched the names of those who
Died, 1968—'69, I no longer   45
Felt alone.

Those who had died, came back
At that moment,
Allowed me to grieve, embraced me
And touched a part of my   50
Soul I had thought was gone.

4. **boonie hat:** camouflaged floppy hat with a brim all around it.
5. **camouflage** [kam′ ə fläzh]: uniform that helps the wearer to blend in with the surroundings.

That vague place in my Life,
Vietnam, which could not bring forth
Emotion or feelings
Or tears.   55
It was such a relief to cry now, to
Feel again. It was so strange.
I felt unbearable sadness, and yet
Set free—free of an intangible[6]
Burden.   60

That beautiful black granite
Wall, now carries the burden
For me
And for us all.
It carries the names and souls,   65
The memories, of those who died
In Vietnam.
It shelters them with respect
And dignity.

"Nurse, I don't want to die here," they would say   70
"Will I make it home? Oh God, don't let me die here."
That look in their eyes—so young, so serious,
Please don't make me remember.
The longing for home among the
Wounded was so strong.   75
We worked so hard to "get them home."
And thousands we did,
But for those who died we were
Sorry they couldn't have their last wish.

It would not have been their   80
Last wish—to be on this wall
Their life had just begun—
"Nurse I want to get home."
Now they are home and
Are again with their fallen   85
Friends.
The memorial that honors the living
And the dead, by giving us
a Place
To join together.   90

6. intangible [in tan′ jə bəl]: not able to be touched or seen.

To you in your faded camouflage
And boonie hats and
Green berets, I want to say
"Thank You" too, from someone who
Cared for you in Vietnam, and   95
Still cares today, "Thank you, too"
For you see, you, and this wall
Set me free
Free to cry and free to remember,
What I had hoped to forget   100
And found I could not.

If our country could have known
But one dying man, alone in Vietnam
With that look on his face
And hopelessness in his eyes   105
If this country could have seen
The courage he had and concern
For his friends
If this country could have
Wept in his tears   110
And told him he was good.
If only, this country would have
Listened—listened and learned of his
Experience and his sacrifice
And then told him they were   115
Proud. If only there would have been
"Thanks."

We sacrificed our youth
I'm not sure why
How does one explain, to those   120
Who didn't go
The fear, the suffering, the inhumanity,
It's not what we wanted
To have names on this wall.
Or to visit a Place such as this, but   125
It was a real war
And we are real veterans.

Now this country has wept
In our tears from that era
By watching us stand proudly, honorably, beside   **130**
The Names, our comrades.
Sons and daughters at war do not know why
They are chosen ones to sacrifice.
But we stand proud and we will not
Let our nation forget our   **135**
Comrades.

DIANE CARLSON EVANS

Diane Carlson Evans was part of the Army Nurse Corps in 1968-1969. She was in Vung Tau, Vietnam, at the 36th Evacuation Hospital and then in Pleiku at the 71st Evacuation Hospital. Evans started the campaign to create the Vietnam Women's Memorial, a bronze statue designed by Glenna Goodacre that was dedicated on November 11, 1993 in Washington, D.C.

LUIS GARCIA:
A PICTURE OF MY FAMILY

BRENT ASHABRANNER

Luis Garcia[1] is sixteen. He was born in the village of Rincón,[2] which is not far from Tres Valles[3] and Suntelaj,[4] and lived there all his life with his father, mother, and two younger brothers and two younger sisters. His father was a farmer, like almost every other man in Rincón, and Luis helped him on the small piece of land where they grew corn and beans.

At one time Rincón had a primary school, which is now closed because no teacher will stay there since the terror began. But while it was there, Luis attended and learned to read and write. Although they were poor, Mr. and Mrs. Garcia wanted their children to get as much schooling as possible. They were a close and loving family, and Luis's story of what happened, as he tells it here, is but one example of similar tragedy that has come to thousands of Indian families in Guatemala.[5]

Do you know the word *orejas?*[6] It means ears, but when we say it in our villages in Guatemala now, it is one of the worst words in the world. It means people who listen and then tell the soldiers who come to the villages what they have heard or think they have heard or seen. They are people who have always lived in the village, but they have become spies for the army. Or maybe they make up things to tell the soldiers so that the soldiers will pay them or leave them alone.

1. **Luis Garcia** [lü ēs′ gär sē′ ä]
2. **Rincón** [rēn kōn′]: village in Guatemala.
3. **Tres Valles** [trās vä′ yās]
4. **Suntelaj** [sün tä läh′]
5. **Guatemala** [gwä tə mä′ lə]: country in northwest Central America.
6. *orejas* [ō rä′ häs]

I do not know how many *orejas* were in our village of Rincón. There is no way for any village to know. But if there is only one, or even none, our villages are not the same as they once were. Before the guerrillas[7] and the army came, before there were *orejas*, the people of Rincón would walk the streets in the evening after the day's work was done. They would talk to neighbors and friends and gather at the *pila*[8] or in front of the church and tell what news they had heard or just gossip. They were not afraid and they were happy.

Now no one goes out at night. The streets are empty, and no one gathers at the *pila* or in front of the church. No one talks to his neighbors, and everyone locks his doors. That is what Rincón is like now and what all villages in Huehuetenango[9] are like.

In Rincón there were *orejas*, or at least one, and my father was killed because of that. Guerrillas came to our village as much as twice a month, and they often came to our house. Maybe it was because I was fifteen then and old enough to join them. I do not know. But my father always talked to them and said I was needed at home to help support the big family. Sometimes we had to give them food and sometimes a little money, though my father had almost none to give. They threatened to kill us if he did not.

Someone told the army that my father was helping the guerrillas, and one night four soldiers came to our house. When they banged on the door, my father knew what it was, and he climbed out the back window and ran. The soldiers said that they knew my father was helping guerrillas and that maybe he was with them now. They said they would find him, and they left.

My father walked to San Miguel Acatán,[10] and a friend hid him in his house. But the soldiers found him. They beat him and then shot him and cut off his head. They killed his friend, too, and

---

7. **guerrillas** [gə ril′ əz]: members of a band of fighters who harass the enemy by sudden raids and ambushes.
8. *pila* [pē′ lä]: Spanish for "the town fountain."
9. **Huehuetenango** [wā wā tā nän′ gō]: name of a department and a city in the western part of Guatemala, near the Mexican border.
10. **San Miguel Acatán** [sän mē gel′ ä kä tän′]

threw them both in a ditch.

The next day we found my father and carried him home. We washed him and put him in a coffin. I remember that his head did not fit very well with his body. It is something I wish I could forget, but I can't.

After that the guerrillas came to our house again, and this time they pointed a gun at me and stuck a knife to my throat and said they would kill me if I didn't join them. I said I would but that they would have to give me a week to get ready. I knew I would not join them, though I didn't know what I would do.

But my mother said that I must leave Rincón and go to Mexico. I told her I did not want to leave, but she said that if I didn't either the guerrillas or the army would kill me. I asked her how she and my brothers and sisters could live if there was no one to plant corn and harvest the crops. She said she would get her father and my father's brother to help.

So I walked to Mexico. I was fifteen and afraid to go by myself, but I had to go. I walked at night and hid in the forests in the day-time. Near the border is a free-fire zone where soldiers will shoot on sight anyone they see. But I crossed the border into Mexico at night, and I did not see any soldier.

Because I had been to school, I could speak and read some Spanish, and that helped. I did not go to a refugee camp because I was afraid they would send me back to Guatemala. I went to the town of Motozinitia,[11] and after a while I got a job working on houses. I made enough money to buy food and I lived in a little room in the house of the man I worked for.

I had never been by myself before, and there was nothing in the world I wanted as much as to be back in Rincón. Sometimes I would meet someone who had come from someplace near San Miguel Acatán, and I would ask if it was safe to go back there. They always told me I should not even think about going back.

But I could not help thinking about it. It was hot in Mexico, and

11. **Motozinitia** [mō tō sē nē′ tyä]

I thought about the cool mountains at home. I thought about how my father used to take us to the fiesta[12] in San Rafael,[13] how we would drink *frescas*[14] and eat candy and fly kites. I thought about *pan dulce*,[15] the sweet cornbread my mother made for special times, and I could almost taste it.

But mostly I thought about my mother and my brothers and sisters, and I wondered what was happening to them. The wife of the man I worked for gave me a magazine, and when I was looking through it one night, I saw a picture of a woman with four children, two boys and two girls. I tore the picture out of the magazine and pinned it on the wall of my room. I pretended it was a picture of my family, of my mother and sisters and brothers.

One morning I woke up and knew that I could not stay in Mexico by myself any longer. I knew there was a place in the United States called Indiantown, in a place called Florida, where an uncle and aunt of mine had gone when they escaped from Guatemala with their children. I did not know if they were still there, but since I could not go back to my home, I decided to go to Indiantown and try to find them.

When I had saved enough money to buy a bus ticket to the United States border, I left Motozinitia. Before I left, I took down the picture from the wall and took it with me.

Luis Garcia reached Indiantown and found his uncle and aunt. He is now living with them and his cousins and working as a farm laborer. His mother and brothers and sisters are still in Guatemala.

---

12. **fiesta** [fē es′ tə]: a religious festival, honoring a saint.
13. **San Rafael** [sän rä fä yel′]
14. *frescas* [fräs′ käs]: Spanish for "cool drinks."
15. *pan dulce* [pän dül′ sā]

BRENT ASHABRANNER

Brent Ashabranner was born in 1921 in Shawnee, Oklahoma, and by the time he was eleven years old he was hooked on reading about adventures in exotic foreign locations. When Ashabranner wasn't reading about adventure, he was inventing stories about it.

To no one's surprise, Ashabranner spent most of his adult life working in the exotic locations that he had enjoyed reading about as a boy—the Middle East, Africa, and India. He started writing nonfiction when he was working with the Peace Corps. He says, "The experiences I was having in Ethiopia, India, and other countries seemed more interesting than anything I could invent."

Ashabranner carefully researches his books. He travels "talking with and sometimes living with the people I'm writing about." He feels, however, that library research is vital. He considers that his most important challenge is to make his subjects "interesting and understandable to young readers."

Mother and Child Pablo Picasso, 1901, oil on canvas, 44 ¹⁄₄″ x 38 ³⁄₈″

Fantasia

I dream
of
giving birth
to
a child
who will ask

"Mother,
what was war?"

EVE MERRIAM

Eve Merriam [1916-1992] won literary awards for her fiction and her plays, as well as for her poetry, but she considered poetry "the most immediate and richest form of communication." In all, Merriam wrote more than fifty books, fiction and nonfiction, for children and adults. When she wasn't writing, Merriam liked to spend time lurking in libraries, browsing in secondhand bookstores, and traveling the globe.

Asking Big Questions About the Literature

What causes conflict?

LITERATURE STUDY

Conflict

Conflicts are caused by a struggle between opposing forces. Conflict in literature, like conflict in life, can be internal or external.

- *Internal conflict* is a struggle between opposing thoughts or feelings within a person.
- *External conflict* is a struggle between two people, between a person and nature, or between a person and society.

Make a chart like the one on this page in which you list the external and internal conflicts in the selections in this unit. Identify both kinds when possible. Then post your chart on the class bulletin board. (*See* "Conflict" *on page 119.*)

Selection	Conflict	Kind of Conflict
"Thanks, Nurse"	Vietnam War	External
	Visiting Vietnam Veterans Memorial	Internal

Write a news BULLETIN

Write a radio or television news bulletin about a conflict you've read about in a selection in this unit. In your bulletin, give a brief summary of what happens, who's involved, and how the conflict begins. Use details from the selection. When you're finished, act as a news anchor to deliver your bulletin to classmates.

ROLE-PLAY a Conversation

Which characters in this unit are eyewitnesses to a conflict? Work with a partner to role-play a conversation with one of these characters. As you role-play, find out what this character observed and felt. Ask him or her what caused the conflict and whether it might have been avoided.

How does conflict become war?

LITERATURE STUDY

Point of View

If you've ever used a camera, you know that you can zoom in to take a close-up or you can shoot something far in the distance. The perspective from which you see a subject— or write about it—is your **point of view**. You can use one of two points of view in your writing.

- A *first-person* narrator tells a story from his or her point of view and uses the pronouns *I* or *we*.

- A *third-person* narrator tells what happens to other characters in a story and uses the pronouns *he*, *she*, *it*, or *they*.

Make a chart like the one that's been started on this page. List all the selections in this unit about conflicts that become wars. Then tell the point of view used in each selection. (*See "Point of View" on page 118*).

Discuss with classmates how point of view affects your response to each selection.

Literature	Point of View
"Luis Garcia: A Picture of My Family"	first person

Research AND Report

In this unit, many conflicts in the selections really happened. Using a history book or an encyclopedia, work with a partner to research one of these conflicts, for example, the causes of civil war in Guatemala ("Luis Garcia: A Picture of My Family"). Write three to four paragraphs explaining the causes and how this conflict led to war. Then present your findings to the class.

Draw a Political CARTOON

Look at the lighter side of a selection in this unit. Draw a political cartoon about one conflict that becomes war. For example, you might want to poke fun at Ninniaw and Pebbiaw in "The Two Brothers." Check political cartoons in newspapers or in your social studies textbook. With your classmates, create a display of political cartoons.

Asking Big Questions About the Literature

How does war affect people's lives?

LITERATURE STUDY

Conflict

Many characters you've met in this unit are changed by **internal conflict**—a problem within the self—because of war. For example, how is Adam in "The Afternoon" changed by his experiences in the Revolutionary War?

Pretend you're a character in this unit who's affected by war. Write a letter home. In the letter, reveal your *internal conflict*—the conflict within the self—that you experience during wartime. Read your letter to your classmates. (*See "Conflict" on page 119.*)

Make A MAP

Working with a partner or group, make a map for one selection in this unit. For example, you could identify landmarks in "newyork" ("By the Waters of Babylon") or map Luis's escape route from Guatemala ("Luis Garcia: A Picture of My Family"). Create an original map or trace an existing map in your classroom or library. Post your map on a bulletin board or in a hallway.

MAKE AN EFFECTS CHART

Choose your favorite characters from some of the selections you've read in this unit. Then, using the chart on this page to get you started, make an effects chart that lists the ways in which war changed the characters' lives.

What did you learn about the effects of war from the selections? Use your chart to write one or two paragraphs analyzing the effects of the conflict on one of the characters you chose.

Selection	"The Afternoon"
Character	Adam
External Conflict	Soldier in Revolutionary War
Internal Conflict	Necessity of fighting for freedom versus horror at killing
Effects	Sadness Feels Older

How can people resolve conflicts peacefully?

Write a Peace
MANUAL

Write a list of rules for keeping peace in the world, your community, your school, or your own life. Draw upon what you've learned about conflict in the selections in this unit, and also what you've learned about keeping peace from "Law of the Great Peace" and "The Peacekeepers."

Rule 1
Step back from the conflict and think before you act.

Rule 2
Discuss the issue calmly.

Rule 3
Listen carefully to what other people say.

Now share your list of rules in a discussion with classmates. As a class, create a peace manual. Select, arrange, and copy the most helpful rules. Then illustrate a cover for your manual. Display it in your classroom or in your school library.

LITERATURE STUDY

Point of View

Some of the selections in this unit are told from the **first-person point of view** (the narrator uses *I* or *we*), and others from the **third-person point of view** (the narrator uses *he, she, it,* or *they*).

Retell the story of one selection in this unit to your classmates, using the same conflict, setting, events, and characters but changing the point of view. (*See "Point of View" on page 118.*)

Hold a Mediation Session

Hold a mediation session with two class-mates to resolve a conflict peacefully between two characters in this unit. One group member will be the mediator, using problem-solving and communication skills outlined in "The Peacekeepers." The other group members will be two characters involved in a conflict, such as Ninniaw and Pebbiaw from "The Two Brothers."

NOW

Choose a Project!

Three projects involving global conflict are described on the following pages.

Writing Workshop

What is the Nobel Peace Prize? Why was the United Nations created? Is war ever just? Where are conflicts occurring today? As you read selections in this unit, you probably had some questions of your own about conflict and about keeping the peace. Your **purpose** in this project, will be to research answers to one of your own questions and then write a research paper in the form of a magazine article to publish in a class magazine. Your **audience** will be schoolmates, your community, veterans, or readers of young people's magazines.

Prewriting
A TOPIC

What do you want to know about war or peace? To identify a topic you'd like to research and write about, make a KWL (Know, Want, Learn) chart similar to the one started on this page. List what you know about either war or peace in the first column and what you want to know in the second column.

K	W	L
WW I changed the face of Europe	Causes of WW I	

Now choose one topic from the second column of your chart. Limit your topic to a subject that can be covered in a short magazine article.

512

Prewriting
ORGANIZING INFORMATION

Before you research your topic, decide whether your audience will be your schoolmates, your community, veterans, or readers of a young people's magazine. Knowing who your audience will be can help you decide what information to research and to include in your article. Knowing your audience will also help you decide where to display your magazine.

The following suggestions will help you locate information:

- Use library reference works, such as encyclopedias and almanacs.
- Consult or interview experts or authorities on your topic.
- Use the computerized card catalog and on-line services in your school or local library to find books about your topic.
- Use the *Readers' Guide to Periodical Literature* to find magazine and newspaper articles about your topic.

Take notes, summarizing what you find out through research. Use note cards to help you organize the information that you find. See the sample note card on this page.

To check that your research supports the topic of your article, go back to the last column in your KWL chart and fill in what you learned.

Patriotism important in early 1900s.

Europe divided.

Archduke Ferdinand assassinated.

Drafting
....
YOUR
ARTICLE

With your audience in mind, draft your article. It may help to organize your notes and create a simple outline before you start writing.

- Capture your readers' attention with an intriguing question or quotation. Introduce your topic and provide background information for your audience. For example, student writer Andrew Boyer asks the following question to begin an article on pages 110-111 about World War I: "What were the causes of World War I?" He then goes on to mention and explain several causes.

- Write several paragraphs about your topic. Provide supporting facts and details drawn from your research. Remember that you don't need to use all the facts you've found! Instead, evaluate and select information carefully. Also define any unfamiliar terms for your audience. Use a clear method of organization (chronological order, spatial order, order of importance). For example, Andrew used chronological order to present information about the causes of World War I.

- End your article by summarizing the information. Tie the facts together with a brief restatement of your topic. Andrew's article ends as follows: "I found that there were many reasons for World War I. The underlying one, however, was that an area with so many different groups of people is going to be inherently unstable."

Keep in mind your purpose and your audience when you write. Include an intriguing title that will make your audience want to read your article.

Revising

YOUR ARTICLE

Ask a partner or a group to be your audience by responding to your magazine article and suggesting improvements. Do you clearly introduce your topic? Do you give supporting details and facts? Do you follow a clear method of organization? Do you end with a strong conclusion? Ask your partner or group whether you've clearly explained your topic.

Look at Andrew Boyer's writing on pages 110-111 for an example of a magazine article.

Editing
YOUR ARTICLE

Work with a group of peer editors to edit your revised article. Read one another's articles and check for spelling, grammar, and punctuation errors. It's especially important to be accurate in a research paper, so edit very carefully. Then correct your errors and make a publishable copy of your article.

Publishing
YOUR ARTICLE

Share your magazine article with your audience. In your journal, brainstorm for some ideas for publishing and pick one. Here are some suggestions to spark your own ideas:

- Ask your teacher for a list of magazines for young people. Submit your article to one of these magazines.
- Create a class magazine of articles. Arrange articles in a logical order, put together a table of contents, and illustrate articles with pictures, photographs, and cartoons. Invent a title for the magazine and make photocopies of the first issue for other students.
- Turn your magazine article into a photo essay. Find magazine or newspaper photographs or take your own.
- Read your article to a group of veterans in your community.

STUDENT MODEL

The Causes of World War I
by Andrew Boyer, Ellicott City, Maryland

What were the causes of World War I? World War I was one of the biggest events in world history to date. It had far-reaching effects, changing the political and economic face of Europe. Its outcome would govern events there for several decades. The causes are as follows.

Patriotism was at its peak during the early part of the twentieth century. There was also a great deal of ethnic loyalty as well as bigotry. For instance, Slavic ethnic loyalty was responsible for the strong ties between Serbia, Russia, and Slavic groups within Austria-Hungary.

Europe was divided by many alliances at the beginning of the twentieth century. The two major alliances were the Triple Entente (French for "understanding," "agreement," or "pact"), consisting of England, France, and Russia, and the Triple Alliance, consisting of Germany, Austria-Hungary, and Italy.

Both France and Germany engaged in protectionist trade practices, causing disputes with their economic neighbors. Many minor conflicts between rivals were blown out of proportion, such as the Moroccan crisis between Germany and France in 1911.

At this time, Germany, an industrial giant under the leadership of Wilhelm II, was considered the most powerful country on the mainland of Europe. Germany wanted a political role equal to that of its industrial role. It mainly targeted Great Britain, which then had world supremacy, and France, with which it had fought several wars over the area known as Alsace-Lorraine. Austria was in control of many Slavic lands, which made it the hated neighbor of nearby Serbia, also Slavic. Since Russia was also a Slavic state, Serbia hoped that Russia would come to its aid in case of war.

Britain feared that Germany's fleet of warships might threaten British control of the seas. Russia feared Austria's political presence and motives in the Balkans.

This tension caused a massive arms build-up. Munitions were stockpiled and standing armies raised. Germany had almost two million soldiers, while Britain, France, Russia, and Austria-Hungary had around one million each. Tension was so high that war nearly broke out several times in the years before 1914, but each time, diplomats from the opposing countries managed to preserve peace.

The major event that started the war was the assassination of Austrian Archduke Ferdinand while he was riding through the streets of Sarajevo, capital of Serbia. He was shot, along with his wife, by a young Serbian nationalist.

I found that there were many reasons for World War I. The underlying one, however, was that an area with so many different groups of people is going to be inherently unstable.

Cooperative Learning

FROM PAST TO PRESENT

American writer George Santayana wrote, "Those who cannot remember the past are condemned to repeat it." That is, it's important to learn from the past. This project will give you a chance to find out about the past. With a group, you'll research conflicts during a particular time. Then you'll work with classmates to make a time line.

Research
A TIME PERIOD

As a group, research the following time periods in United States history. Choose a period that most interests members of your group. Appoint a checker, who will make sure you don't use the same time period as another group. Some dates may overlap, but you'll have no problems if you stick to your own heading, such as "Westward Expansion" or "The Last Frontier."

Time Period	Group
Newcomers to the Americas (1492-1700)	
Building a Nation (1700-1800)	
A New Nation (1776-1815)	
Westward Expansion (1800-1855)	
Divided and Reunited (1819-1865)	
The Last Frontier (1860-1900)	

Choose
JOBS

To help with choosing jobs, make a chart like the one on the next page Divide your time period into smaller chunks, so that each group member will have important years to research. For example, if your five-member group picks "Building a Nation," you might divide the

time period as follows: 1700-1730, 1731-1762, 1763-1770, 1771-1780, 1781-1800. On your own, research what conflicts—either wars or other types of disagreement—took place during these years. Use an encyclopedia, almanac, social studies textbook, history book, or other resources. Jot down facts about different conflicts on separate 3" x 5" note cards. Include dates, places, names, and events.

Task	Person
Choose time period	
Check other groups' choices	
Check encyclopedias	

Make YOUR TIME LINE

Share your note cards with your group. Then work together to arrange conflicts in the order in which they happened. Using the format shown on this page, make a time line on butcher paper, oaktag, or construction paper. Since you'll have more dates than are on the sample, use this scale: 1 inch equals 10 years. Work with other groups to make one large class time line. Put all the sections in chronological order and tape them together.

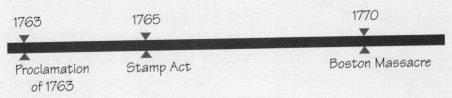

1763	1765	1770
Proclamation of 1763	Stamp Act	Boston Massacre

Present YOUR TIME LINE

Brainstorm for creative ways for your group to present your class time line to other students. For example, hang it in a hallway, the auditorium, a social studies class, a display case, or the library. Trace a map of the United States and use push pins to show where each conflict on the time line happened. Make murals to show what happened in each conflict, or write or collect related newspaper headlines. Your time line will not only help you remember what happened in the past, but it may also encourage you to give peace a chance. Maybe it will encourage other students, too!

Helping Your Community

From the Revolutionary War to the present, Americans have been involved in wars. One of the Big Questions in this unit asks, "How does war affect people's lives?" With this project, you'll have a chance to find out how war has affected people in your community. First, you'll research what happened to one war veteran in your community. Then, with a partner or group, you'll brainstorm to decide on a way to honor local veterans.

Identifying LOCAL VETERANS

Find the names of local war veterans and pick one you'd like to research. You can go back in time to find veterans of the Revolutionary War, the Civil War, or the Spanish-American War. You can also research a veteran of World Wars I and II, the Korean War, the Vietnam War, the Gulf War, or another conflict. Are any of your neighbors or family members veterans? You might like to find out about the military service of someone you know. Here are some ideas to help you identify veterans in your community:

- Call the local post of the Veterans of Foreign Wars or the local American Legion post.
- Call or write local veterans' and military organizations.
- Is there a war memorial in your community? Find a name on the memorial you'd like to research.

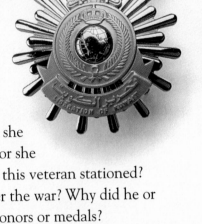

Learning ABOUT A VETERAN

Find biographical information about the veteran you've picked. In which war did he or she serve? To which branch of the military did he or she belong? What was his or her duty? Where was this veteran stationed? What happened to this person during and after the war? Why did he or she go to war? Did he or she win any special honors or medals?

You can get information you need from **secondary sources**—biographies, news clippings, encyclopedia articles, or other documents—found at the local historical society, library, or town hall. You might also be able to use **primary sources**, such as letters, journals, and diary entries written by this veteran.

As you gather information, use a chart like the one on this page to help you organize facts about the veteran. Record as much information as you can. Then use your information to write a short biographical sketch.

Veteran's Name:	Juan Moreno
Military Branch:	Army
Rank:	Lieutenant
Tour of Duty:	Vietnam
Dates Served:	1968-1971
Special Honors:	Bronze Star

Planning A MEMORIAL

With a partner or group, decide how you'd like to honor local war veterans. Use one of the following ideas or devise one of your own.

For example, if your community doesn't have a war memorial, design one, build a scale model, and present it to a local veterans' organization. Turn your biographical sketch into a historical plaque and suggest a spot where you'd place it. Make a class booklet of sketches to present to a local veterans' group. Write a speech about a local war veteran and deliver it at a Memorial Day or Veterans Day ceremony.

War can seriously affect a community, especially through the loss of lives. Your memorial will help demonstrate your appreciation of the sacrifices made by local war veterans.

Putting It All Together

What Have You Learned About Resolving Conflict?

Look back at all the writing you've done for *At Odds* in your journal, in response to your reading, and in the Writing Workshop. Think about how your ideas about conflict have changed now that you've finished this unit. Then write a personal essay about peace. Share your thoughts with classmates in a class peace conference.

GIVE PEACE A CHANCE

Prewriting and Drafting   Is world peace possible? Can global conflict be avoided? Starting with the word *peace*, make a web to help you identify your beliefs and opinions. To get more ideas on paper, use your web to help you freewrite for at least five minutes without stopping.

Now draft a personal essay about peace. Explore your own viewpoint, using an informal tone. Begin with a sentence that states the topic of your essay. Present your ideas clearly, from least to most important.

Include supporting facts, reasons, and examples from what you've read, written, or done as part of the activities and projects in this unit. In your essay, use the first person (*I, me, my, mine*). End with a memorable quotation, a question, or a recommendation.

Revising and Editing   Now exchange personal essays with a partner. Ask your partner to suggest improvements to the content, organization, style, grammar, and spelling of your essay. Make necessary changes and corrections. Then make a publishable copy of your essay. Work together to make an attractive cover for a class booklet.

Publishing   Hold a peace conference in which you and your classmates share your ideas about peace. Sit in a large circle and discuss what you've found out or take turns reading sections from your personal essays. If possible, invite other classes in your school to join your peace conference.

Evaluating Your Work

Think Back About the Big Questions

With a partner, discuss the Big Questions on pages 10—11 and the questions that you generated for **Now Think!** on page 11. Are you easily able to answer all of these questions now? In your journal, write two or three sentences to explain how your responses to the Big Questions have changed after your work in this unit.

Think Back About Your Work

Take a look at your reading, writing, activities, and projects in this unit. How would you honestly evaluate your own work?

Write a letter to a character in this unit. In your letter, explain what you've done during this unit and what you've learned. Use the following questions to help you write your letter:

- Which literature selections affected you most strongly? Why?

- What are the *two* most important things that you learned about conflict?

- What aspects of resolving conflicts would you like to have learned more about? Why?

- If you could choose one activity to do again, which one would you choose? Why?

- How would you rate your work in this unit? Use the following scale and give at least three reasons for your rating.

1 = Outstanding	3 = Fair
2 = Good	4 = Not as good as it could have been

POINT OF VIEW

What Is Point of View?

Point of view is the choice writers make about who will tell their story. *First-person narrative* tells the story from the point of view of a character in the story who uses the first-person pronouns *I* and *we*. The two types of *third-person narrative* use the pronouns *he, she, it,* or *they.* In *limited third-person point of view,* the narrator observes and reports the words and actions of the characters, but not their thoughts and feelings. The narrator in *third-person omniscient point of view* (all-knowing), on the other hand, tells the story by observing and relating not only the words and actions of the story's characters, but also their thoughts and feelings.

Writing from Another Point of View

Find a favorite selection from this unit and rewrite it using a different point of view. Focus on an important incident in a story or a narrative and change the point of view from first to third person or vice versa. You could also, for example, rewrite a poem such as "Thanks, Nurse" from the serviceman's point of view instead of the nurse's. In this case, be sure to keep the first-person point of view.

Changing Perspectives

Think of a real or imaginary person whose life has changed as a result of certain events. Briefly describe the events that changed the life of the character you're writing about. Use either the first person or the third person to write two to four paragraphs that tell how events have changed the perspective of the person. Be certain to show your character both before and after the events that caused the change.

What Is Conflict?

Conflict in literature is a problem or a struggle between opposing forces. The conflict may be *internal*, as when the struggle takes place within a character, or *external*, as when the struggle takes place between the character and nature, the character and another person, or the character and society. In drama and narrative fiction, for example, the plot shows how the conflict builds to a point of high intensity and is eventually resolved. The author holds the reader's interest by showing how the conflict affects the main character and how he or she will resolve the conflict.

Solving a Problem   With a partner, discuss a conflict that you have experienced or that you have heard about or read about. During your discussion, take notes to describe the conflict and the person or persons involved. Next, on your own, think about how the person solved the problem. Then come up with a solution that you think is better. Write your solution on a separate sheet of paper and compare it with your partner's solution. Discuss both solutions and come to a peaceful agreement about who has the better solution. Present your views and your solution to the class.

Writing About Conflict   This unit addresses conflict both as a literary element and as a theme. Each selection is concerned with a serious conflict—often war. Choose one of the selections in the unit and, on a separate sheet of paper, describe the exterior conflict. Then list ways in which conflict changed the perspective of the main character. Write a short essay that describes how the exterior conflict caused a struggle within the character. Tell how the character solved the problem and how he or she was changed because of the interior struggle.

GLOSSARY OF LITERARY TERMS

A

alliteration Repetition of the first sound—usually a consonant sound—in several words of a sentence or a line of poetry.

allusion An author's indirect reference to someone or something that is presumed to be familiar to the reader.

anecdote A short narrative about an interesting or a humorous event, usually in the life of a person.

antagonist The person or force opposing the protagonist, or main character in a literary work. [See also *protagonist*.]

autobiography A person's written account of his or her own life.

B

ballad A poem, often a song, that tells a story in simple verse.

biography An account of a person's life, written by another person.

blank verse Unrhymed poetry.

C

character A person or an animal that participates in the action of a work of literature. A *dynamic character* is one whose thoughts, feelings, and actions are changeable and lifelike; a *static character* always remains the same. [See also *protagonist, antagonist*.]

characterization The creation of characters through the characters' use of language and through descriptions of their appearance, thoughts, emotions, and actions. [See also *character*.]

chronology An arrangement of events in the order in which they happen.

cliché An overused expression that is trite rather than meaningful.

climax The highest point of tension in the plot of a work of literature. [See also *plot*.]

comedy An amusing play that has a happy ending.

conclusion The final part or ending of a piece of literature.

concrete poem A poem arranged on the page so that its punctuation, letters, and lines make the shape of the subject of the poem.

conflict A problem that confronts the characters in a piece of literature. The conflict may be *internal* (a character's struggle within himself or herself) or *external* (a character's struggle against nature, another person, or society). [See also *plot*.]

context The general sense of words that helps readers to understand the meaning of unfamiliar words and phrases in a piece of writing.

D

description An author's use of words to give the reader or listener a mental picture, an impression, or an understanding of a person, place, thing, event, or idea.

dialect A form of speech spoken by people in a particular group or geographical region that differs in vocabulary, grammar, and pronunciation from the standard language.

dialogue The spoken words and conversation of characters in a work of literature.

drama A play that is performed before an audience according to stage directions and using dialogue. Classical drama has two genres: *tragedy* and *comedy*. Modern drama includes *melodrama, satire, theater of the absurd*, and *pantomime*. [See also *comedy, play*, and *tragedy*.]

dramatic poetry A play written in the form of poetry.

E

epic A long narrative poem—written in a formal style and meant to be read aloud—that relates the adventures and

experiences of one or more great heroes or heroines.

essay Personal nonfiction writing about a particular subject that is important to the writer.

excerpt A passage from a larger work that has been taken out of its context to be used for a special purpose.

exposition Writing that explains, analyzes, or defines.

extended metaphor An elaborately drawn out metaphor. [See also *metaphor*.]

F

fable A short, simple story whose purpose is to teach a lesson, usually with animal characters who talk and act like people.

fantasy Imaginative fiction about unrealistic characters, places, and events.

fiction Literature, including the short story and the novel, that tells about imaginary people and events.

figurative language Language used to express ideas through figures of speech: descriptions that aren't meant to be taken literally. Types of figurative language include *simile, metaphor, extended metaphor, hyperbole,* and *personification.*

figure of speech A type of figurative language, not meant to be taken literally, that expresses something in such a way that it brings the thing to life in the reader's or listener's imagination. [See also *figurative language*.]

flashback A break in a story's action that relates a past happening in order to give the reader background information about a present action in the story.

folktale A story that has been passed along from storyteller to storyteller for generations. Kinds of folktales include *tall tales, fairy tales, fables, legends,* and *myths.*

foreshadowing The use of clues to create suspense by giving the reader or audience hints of events to come.

free verse Poetry that has no formal rhyme scheme or metrical pattern.

G

genre A major category of art. The three major literary genres are poetry, prose, and drama.

H

haiku A three-line Japanese verse form. In most haiku, the first and third lines have five syllables, while the second line has seven. The

traditional haiku describes a complicated feeling or thought in simple language through a single image.

hero/heroine The main character in a work of literature. In heroic literature, the hero or heroine is a particularly brave, noble, or clever person whose achievements are unusual and important. [See also *character*.]

heroic age The historical period in western civilization—from about 800 B.C. through A.D. 200—during which most works of heroic literature, such as myths and epics, were created in ancient Greece and Rome.

hubris Arrogance or excessive pride leading to mistakes; the character flaw in a hero of classical tragedy.

hyperbole An obvious exaggeration used for emphasis. [See also *figurative language*.]

I

idiom An expression whose meaning cannot be understood from the ordinary meaning of the words. For example, *It's raining cats and dogs.*

imagery The words and phrases in writing that appeal to the senses of sight, hearing, taste, touch, and smell.

irony   An effect created by a sharp contrast between what is expected and what is real. An *ironic twist* in a plot is an event that is the complete opposite of what the characters have been hoping or expecting will happen. An *ironic statement* declares the opposite of the speaker's literal meaning.

J

jargon   Words and phrases used by a group of people who share the same profession or special interests in order to refer to technical things or processes with which they are familiar. In general, jargon is any terminology that sounds unclear, overused, or pretentious.

L

legend   A famous folktale about heroic actions, passed along by word of mouth from generation to generation. The legend may have begun as a factual account of real people and events but has become mostly or completely fictitious.

limerick   A form of light verse, or humorous poetry, written in one five-line stanza with a regular scheme of rhyme and meter.

literature   The branch of art that is expressed in written language and includes all written genres.

lyric poem   A short poem that expresses personal feelings and thoughts in a musical way. Originally, lyrics were the words of songs that were sung to music played on the lyre, a stringed instrument invented by the ancient Greeks.

M

metamorphosis   The transformation of one thing, or being, into another completely different thing or being, such as a caterpillar's change into a butterfly.

metaphor   Figurative language in which one thing is said to be another thing. [See also *figurative language*.]

meter   The pattern of rhythm in lines of poetry. The most common meter, in poetry written in English, is iambic pentameter, that is, a verse having five metrical feet, each foot of verse having two syllables, an unaccented one followed by an accented one.

mood   The feeling or atmosphere that a reader senses while reading or listening to a work of literature.

motivation   A character's reasons for doing, thinking, feeling, or saying something. Sometimes an author will make a character's motivation obvious from the beginning. In realistic fiction and drama, however, a character's motivation may be so complicated that the reader discovers it gradually, by studying the character's thoughts, feelings, and behavior.

myth   A story, passed along by word of mouth for generations, about the actions of gods and goddesses or superhuman heroes and heroines. Most myths were first told to explain the origins of natural things or to justify the social rules and customs of a particular society.

N

narration   The process of telling a story. For both fiction and nonfiction, there are two main kinds of narration, based on whether the story is told from a first-person or third-person point of view. [See also *point of view*.]

narrative poem   A poem that tells a story containing the basic literary ingredients of fiction: character, setting, and plot.

narrator   The person, or voice, that tells a story. [See also *point of view, voice*.]

nonfiction   Prose that is factually true and is about real people, events, and places.

nonstandard English
Versions of English, such as slang and dialects, that use pronunciation, vocabulary, idiomatic expressions, grammar, and punctuation that differ from the accepted "correct" constructions of English.

novel   A long work of narrative prose fiction. A novel contains narration, a setting or settings, characters, dialogue, and a more complicated plot than a short story.

O

onomatopoeia   The technique of using words that imitate the sounds they describe, such as *hiss*, *buzz*, and *splash*.

oral tradition   Stories, poems, and songs that have been kept alive by being told, recited, and sung by people over many generations. Since the works were not originally written, they often have many different versions.

P

parable   A brief story—similar to a fable, but about people—that describes an ordinary situation and concludes with a short moral or lesson to be learned.

personification   Figurative language in which an animal, an object, or an idea is given human characteristics. [See also *figurative language*.]

persuasion   A type of speech or writing whose purpose is to convince people that something is true or important.

play   A work of dramatic literature written for performance by actors before an audience. In classical or traditional drama, a play is divided into five acts, each containing a number of scenes. Each act represents a distinct phase in the development of the plot. Modern plays often have only one act and one scene.

playwright   The author of a play.

plot   The sequence of actions and events in fiction or drama. A traditional plot has at least three parts: the *rising action*, leading up to a turning point that affects the main character; the *climax*, the turning point or moment of greatest intensity or interest; and the *falling action*, leading away from the conflict, or resolving it.

poetry   Language selected and arranged in order to say something in a compressed or nonliteral way. Modern poetry may or may not use many of the traditional poetic techniques that include *meter, rhyme, alliteration, figurative language, symbolism,* and *specific verse forms*.

point of view   The perspective from which a writer tells a story. *First-person* narrators tell the story from their own point of view, using pronouns such as *I* or *me*. *Third-person* narrators, using pronouns such as *he*, *she*, or *them*, may be *omniscient* (knowing everything about all characters), or *limited* (taking the point of view of one character). [See also *narration*.]

propaganda   Information or ideas that may or may not be true, but are spread as though they are true, in order to persuade people to do or believe something.

prose   The ordinary form of written and spoken language used to create fiction, nonfiction, and most drama.

protagonist   The main character of a literary work. [See also *character* and *characterization*.]

R

refrain   A line or group of lines that is repeated, usually at the end of each verse, in a poem or a song.

repetition   The use of the same formal element more than once in a literary work, for emphasis or in order to achieve another desired effect.

resolution   The falling action in fiction or drama,

including all of the developments that follow the climax and show that the story's conflict is over. [See also *plot*.]

rhyme scheme   A repeated pattern of similar sounds, usually found at the ends of lines of poetry or poetic drama.

rhythm   In poetry, the measured recurrence of accented and unaccented syllables in a particular pattern. [See also *meter*.]

S

scene   The time, place, and circumstances of a play or a story. In a play, a scene is a section of an act. [See also *play*.]

science fiction   Fantasy literature set in an imaginary future, with details and situations that are designed to seem scientifically possible.

setting   The time and place of a work of literature.

short story   Narrative prose fiction that is shorter and has a less complicated plot than a novel. A short story contains narration, at least one setting, at least one character, and usually some dialogue.

simile   Figurative language that compares two unlike things, introduced by the words "like" or "as." [See also *figurative language*.]

soliloquy   In a play, a short speech spoken by a single character when he or she is alone on the stage. A soliloquy usually expresses the character's innermost thoughts and feelings, when he or she thinks no other characters can hear.

sonnet   A poem written in one stanza, using fourteen lines of iambic pentameter. [See also *meter*.]

speaker   In poetry, the individual whose voice seems to be speaking the lines. [See also *narration, voice*.]

stage directions   The directions, written by the playwright, to tell the director, actors, and theater technicians how a play should be dramatized. Stage directions may specify such things as how the setting should appear in each scene, how the actors should deliver their lines, when the stage curtain should rise and fall, how stage lights should be used, where on the stage the actors should be during the action, and when sound effects should be used.

stanza   A group of lines in poetry set apart by blank lines before and after the group; a poetic verse.

style   The distinctive way in which an author composes a work of literature in written or spoken language.

suspense   An effect created by authors of various types of fiction and drama, especially adventure and mystery, to heighten interest in the story.

symbol   An image, person, place, or thing that is used to express the idea of something else.

T

tall tale   A kind of folk tale, or legend, that exaggerates the characteristics of its hero or heroine.

theme   The main idea or underlying subject of a work of literature.

tone   The attitude that a work of literature expresses to the reader through its style.

tragedy   In classical drama, a tragedy depicts a noble hero or heroine who makes a mistake of judgment that has disastrous consequences.

V

verse   A stanza in a poem. Also, a synonym for poetry as a genre. [See also *stanza*.]

voice   The narrator or the person who relates the action of a piece of literature. [See also *speaker*.]

ACKNOWLEDGMENTS

Grateful acknowledgment is made for permission to reprint the following copyrighted material.

"The Two Brothers" by Lloyd Alexander, copyright © 1990 by Lloyd Alexander, is reprinted from *The Big Book for Peace*, Dutton Children's Books, a division of Penguin Books USA, Inc.

"By the Waters of Babylon" by Stephen Vincent Benét, copyright 1937 by Stephen Vincent Benét, copyright renewed 1971 by Rachael Benét Lewis, Thomas C. Benét, and Stephanie Benét Mahin. Reprinted by permission of Brandt & Brandt.

"Where Have All the Flowers Gone?" by Pete Seeger, copyright © 1961 by Fall River Music Company, Inc. All rights reserved. Used by permission.

"The Afternoon" from *April Morning* by Howard Fast. Copyright © 1961 and renewed 1989 by Howard Fast. Reprinted by permission of Crown Publishers, Inc., a subsidiary of Random House, Inc.

"A Woman's Fight" by Pretty Shield from *Spiderwoman's Granddaughter* by Paula Gunn Allen. Copyright © 1986 by Paula Gunn Allen. Reprinted by permission of Beacon Press.

"What a Foolish Boy" by Jim Murphy from *The Boys' War* by Jim Murphy. Text copyright ©1990 by Jim Murphy. Reprinted by permission of Clarion Books/Houghton Mifflin Co. All rights reserved.

"Law of the Great Peace" by John Bierhorst from *The Iroquois Book of the Great Law* is reprinted by permission.

"The Peacekeepers" by Michael Meek is reprinted from Teaching Tolerance, copyright © 1992 by Southern Poverty Law Center.

"Crispus Attucks" by Burke Davis from *Black Heroes of the American Revolution*. Copyright © 1976 by Burke Davis. Used by permission of Harcourt Brace and Company.

"Thanks, Nurse" by Diane Carlson Evans. Copyright © 1991 by Diane Carlson Evans. Reprinted from *Visions of War, Dreams of Peace: Writings of Women in the Vietnam War*, edited by Lynda Van Devanter and Joan A. Furey, Warner Books, Inc.

"A Picture of My Family" by Luis Garcia from *Children of the Maya* by Brent Ashabranner, text copyright © 1986 by Brent Ashabranner. Reprinted by permission.

"Fantasia" by Eve Merriam from *Finding a Poem* by Eve Merriam. Copyright © 1970 by Eve Merriam. Reprinted by permission of Marian Reiner.

ILLUSTRATION

94-99 José Ortega.

PHOTOGRAPHY

4 *l* Julie Bidwell/©D.C. Heath; *r* Sarah Putnam/©D.C. Heath; **5** John Running; **6** Jean-Claude Lejeune; **8-9** Jacques Cournoyer; **10** *t* David Strickler/The Image Works; *b* Julie Bidwell/©D.C. Heath; **11** *t* Sarah Putnam/©D.C. Heath; *c* Jim Whitmer/Stock Boston; *b* John Owens/©D.C. Heath; **12, 13** Erich Lessing/Art Resource, NY; **14** The Metropolitan Museum of Art, The Cloisters Collection, 1954. (54.1.1); **18** Bibliothèque Nationale, Paris; **19** Photo by Alexander Limont. Courtesy of Penguin, USA; **20-34** ©1987 Jay Dunitz; **35** AP/Wide World Photos; **36-37, 38-39** The Andy Warhol Foundation for the Visual Arts, Inc.; **39** The Bettmann Archive; **40-41** Bancroft Collection, Miriam & Ira D. Wallach Division of Art Prints & Photographs. The New York Public Library, Astor, Lenox, & Tilden Foundations; **45, 46, 49, 50** Chicago Historical Society; **55** AP/Wide World Photos; **56, 59** John Running; **60** Gary C. Cole; **61** Eleanor S. Brockenbrough Library, The Museum of the Confederacy. Richmond, VA; **62-63, 64** Gary C. Cole; **65** Cook Collection, Valentine Museum, Richmond, VA; **68-69** Gary C. Cole; **69** *tl* The Library of Congress; *tr* Museum of Fine Arts, Boston; *b* Courtesy of Clarion Books; **70-71** Photo courtesy of Haines Gallery, San Francisco, CA; **72-73** Gayna Hoffman; **73** *t* Photo courtesy of Haines Gallery, San Francisco, CA; *b* Courtesy of John Bierhorst; **74-75, 78, 81** *t* Larry Ford; **81** *b* Courtesy of Michael Meek; **82** Chicago Historical Society; **86** American Antiquarian Society, Worcester, MA; **88** *c* Medford Taylor/Black Star; *b* Christopher Morris/Black Star; **88-89** Medford Taylor/Black Star; **90-91** Christopher Morris/Black Star; **92-93** Claus Guglberger/Black Star; **99** AP/Wide World Photos; **100** Courtesy of the Fogg Art Museum, Harvard University Art Museums. Bequest, Collection of Maurice Wertheim, Class of 1906. ©1995 ARS, NY/SPADEM, Paris; **101** Photo by Bachrach; **105** Nancy Sheehan/©D.C. Heath; **106** *t* Jerry Berndt/Stock Boston; *b* ©The Peace Museum; **107** Ken O'Donoghue/©D.C. Heath; **111** R.R. Donnelley/©D.C. Heath; **112** *t* Sarah Putnam/©D.C. Heath; *bl* North Wind Picture Archive; *br* "Fighting Buffalo" by William Cary. The Thomas Gilcrease Institute of American History and Art, Tulsa, OK; **114** *t* Rhoda Sidney/Stock Boston; *b*, **115** Ken O'Donoghue/©D.C. Heath. **Back cover** *t* Richard Haynes/©D.C. Heath; *c* John Owens/©D.C. Heath; *b* Julie Bidwell/©D.C. Heath.

Full Pronunciation Key for Footnoted Words

(Each pronunciation and definition is adapted from *Scott, Foresman Advanced Dictionary* by E.L. Thorndike and Clarence L. Barnhart.)

The pronunciation of each footnoted word is shown just after the word, in this way: **abbreviate** [ə brē′ vē āt]. The letters and signs used are pronounced as in the words below. The mark ′ is placed after a syllable with primary or heavy accent, as in the example above. The mark ′ after a syllable shows a secondary or lighter accent, as in **abbreviation** [ə brē′ vē ā′ shən].

Some words, taken from foreign languages, are spoken with sounds that do not otherwise occur in English. Symbols for these sounds are given in the key as "foreign sounds."

a	hat, cap	j	jam, enjoy	u	cup, butter	**foreign sounds**
ā	age, face	k	kind, seek	u̇	full, put	
ä	father, far	l	land, coal	ü	rule, move	Y as in French *du*. Pronounce (ē) with the lips rounded as for (ü).
b	bad, rob	m	me, am	v	very, save	
ch	child, much	n	no, in	w	will, woman	à as in French *ami*. Pronounce (ä) with the lips spread and held tense.
d	did, red	ng	long, bring	y	young, yet	
				z	zero, breeze	
e	let, best	o	hot, rock	zh	measure, seizure	œ as in French *peu*. Pronounce (ā) with the lips rounded as for (ō).
ē	equal, be	ō	open, go			
ėr	term, learn	ô	order, all	ə represents:		N as in French *bon*. The N is not pronounced, but shows that the vowel before it is nasal.
		oi	oil, voice	a in about		
f	fat, if	ou	house, out	e in taken		
g	go, bag			i in pencil		
h	he, how	p	paper, cup	o in lemon		H as in German *ach*. Pronounce (k) without closing the breath passage.
		r	run, try	u in circus		
i	it, pin	s	say, yes			
ī	ice, five	sh	she, rush			
		t	tell, it			
		th	thin, both			
		ŦH	then, smooth			

CHANGES
AND
CHOICES

H E A T H
MIDDLE LEVEL
LITERATURE

HEATH
MIDDLE LEVEL
LITERATURE

Changes and Choices

THEME
CHALLENGES AND ACHIEVEMENTS

AUTHORS

Donna Alvermann
Linda Miller Cleary
Kenneth Donelson
Donald Gallo
Alice Haskins
J. Howard Johnston
John Lounsbury
Alleen Pace Nilsen
Robert Pavlik
Jewell Parker Rhodes
Alberto Alvaro Ríos
Sandra Schurr
Lyndon Searfoss
Julia Thomason
Max Thompson
Carl Zon

STAFF CREDITS

EDITORIAL	Barbara A. Brennan, Susan Belt Cogley, DeVona Dors, Christopher Johnson, Rita M. Sullivan, Patricia B. Weiler
	Proofreading: JoAnne B. Sgroi
CONTRIBUTING WRITERS	Kathy Tuchman Glass, Jo Pitkin
SERIES DESIGN	Robin Herr
BOOK DESIGN	Caroline Bowden, Daniel Derdula, Susan Geer, Diana Maloney, Angela Sciaraffa, Bonnie Chayes Yousefian
	Art Editing: Carolyn Langley
PHOTOGRAPHY	*Series Photography Coordinator:* Carmen Johnson
	Photo Research Supervisor: Martha Friedman
	Photo Researchers: Wendy Enright, Linda Finigan, Po-yee McKenna, PhotoSearch, Inc., Gillian Speeth, Denise Theodores
	Assignment Photography Coordinators: Susan Doheny, Gayna Hoffman, Shawna Johnston
COMPUTER PREPRESS	Ricki Pappo, Kathy Meisl
	Richard Curran, Michele Locatelli
PERMISSIONS	Dorothy B. McLeod
PRODUCTION	Patrick Connolly

Cover *collage photos* Top row 1. John Owens/©D.C. Heath; 2. Sarah Putnam/©D.C. Heath; 3. John Owens/©D.C. Heath; 4. Nita Winter/The Image Works; 5,6 Sarah Putnam/©D.C. Heath; Bottom row 1. John Owens/©D.C. Heath; 2. Sarah Putnam/©D.C. Heath; 3. John Owens/©D.C. Heath; 4 *t* Julie Bidwell/©D.C. Heath, *b* Jim Whitmer/Stock Boston; 5 *t* Richard Haynes/©D.C. Heath, *b* Sarah Putnam/©D.C. Heath.
Cover Design: Robin Herr

Acknowledgments for copyrighted material are on page 125 and constitute an extension of this page.

Published simultaneously in Canada

Printed in the United States of America

International Standard Book Number: 0-669-32109-5 (soft cover)
   4 5 6 7 8 9 10-RRD-99 98

International Standard Book Number: 0-669-38178-0 (hard cover)
   5 6 7 8 9 10-RRD-99

Middle Level Authors

Donna Alvermann, University of Georgia
Alice Haskins, Howard County Public Schools, Maryland
J. Howard Johnston, University of South Florida
John Lounsbury, Georgia College
Sandra Schurr, University of South Florida
Julia Thomason, Appalachian State University
Max Thompson, Appalachian State University
Carl Zon, California Assessment Collaborative

Literature and Language Arts Authors

Linda Miller Cleary, University of Minnesota
Kenneth Donelson, Arizona State University
Donald Gallo, Central Connecticut State University
Alleen Pace Nilsen, Arizona State University
Robert Pavlik, Cardinal Stritch College, Milwaukee
Jewell Parker Rhodes, Arizona State University
Alberto Alvaro Ríos, Arizona State University
Lyndon Searfoss, Arizona State University

Teacher Consultants

Suzanne Aubin, Patapsco Middle School, Ellicott City, Maryland
Judy Baxter, Newport News Public Schools, Newport News, Virginia
Saundra Bryn, Director of Research and Development, El Mirage, Arizona
Lorraine Gerhart, Elmbrook Middle School, Elm Grove, Wisconsin
Kathy Tuchman Glass, Burlingame Intermediate School, Burlingame, California
Lucretia Pannozzo, John Jay Middle School, Katonah, New York
Carol Schultz, Jerling Junior High, Orland Park, Illinois
Jeanne Siebenman, Grand Canyon University, Phoenix, Arizona
Gail Thompson, Garey High School, Pomona, California
Rufus Thompson, Grace Yokley School, Ontario, California
Tom Tufts, Conniston Middle School, West Palm Beach, Florida
Edna Turner, Harpers Choice Middle School, Columbia, Maryland
C. Anne Webb, Buerkle Junior High School, St. Louis, Missouri
Geri Yaccino, Thompson Junior High School, St. Charles, Illinois

CONTENTS

THE LITERATURE

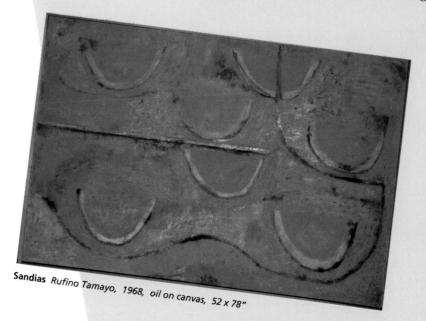

Sandias *Rufino Tamayo, 1968, oil on canvas, 52 x 78"*

ASKING BIG QUESTIONS ABOUT THE LITERATURE

P R O J E C T S

1 WRITING WORKSHOP

WEAR A CRITIC'S HAT 106-111

Choose a book, movie, or piece of literature to evaluate. Then write a review for other students, giving the work a thumbs up or a thumbs down.

2 COOPERATIVE LEARNING

WELCOME TO MIDDLE SCHOOL! 112-113

Do you remember starting middle school? What was your biggest challenge? Create an orientation packet for sixth graders, drawing upon your own prior experiences and past concerns.

3 HELPING YOUR COMMUNITY

VOICES FROM THE PAST 114-115

Interview an adult about changes, choices, and challenges that he or she has experienced in life. Record the interview as part of a class oral history project.

WHAT if...

You and a classmate have been best friends since third grade. But lately you don't talk to each other much. And when you do speak, your friend is cold and abrupt. Then, one day during lunch, you discover that your friend isn't sitting at your customary table. When you scan the lunchroom, you can't believe your eyes. Your friend has abandoned you for another group at school.

Suddenly, your whole world has changed, and you don't know what to do. But help is on the way. In this activity, you'll work with a partner or a group to learn how to make choices when faced with challenges.

START ➤

1 Pick a dilemma.

With your partner or group, pick a dilemma on which to practice. Choose the dilemma in the blue panel above, pick one from the game cards on this page, or use a dilemma from your own life.

When a good friend tells you a secret, you promise not to tell anyone else. Then, by accident, you let the secret slip. You want to regain your friend's trust, but you don't know how.

The kids in your crowd want to make some prank phone calls. "Come on," they tell you, "we'll have fun, and no one will get hurt." When you say you'd rather not, they call you a baby and walk away. You want to stick by your principles, but you also want to keep your friends.

One night, you and your friends sneak into the yard of the neighborhood grouch and cut down a small rose bush. The next day, you're astonished to see him standing in his yard trembling and crying. Suddenly he doesn't appear mean at all but just a lonely old man in need of friendship.

2 Learn how to make a decision.

Some people don't make decisions until they're forced to, and then they decide based on their emotions at the time. Decisions made this way are not the best. A better way is to make decisions based on careful thought and analysis.

Look at the diagram on the right. It lists the five steps of the decision-making process. It will help you as you try to solve your dilemma.

1. Identify the problem.

2. List your options.

3. Evaluate positive and negative outcomes of each option.

4. Decide and act.

5. Review the results of your decision.

3 Solve your dilemma.

Use the five steps in the diagram above to help you reach a solution to the dilemma you selected.

- Choose one person in your group to record ideas and thoughts about each step.
- Work with your group to form a **consensus** about how you would deal with the dilemma. In a consensus, each of you agrees about a course of action. Have the recorder write down your decision.

4 Compare results.

- Choose a spokesperson for your group to share your dilemma and your decision with the rest of the class.
- Compare your decision with groups who chose the same dilemma. How are the decisions similar? Different? What was most difficult about making a decision? What part of the process surprised you?

Asking Big Questions About the Theme

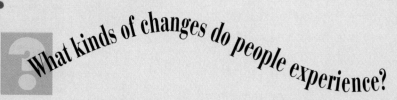

What kinds of changes do people experience?

In your journal, draw two pictures. In the first picture, show the way you looked a year ago. Did you wear braces? Enjoy basketball? Have long hair? Were you short or tall, happy or moody, carefree or worried? In the second picture, show yourself today. In a paragraph, describe how you have changed. Include examples not shown in your drawings, such as changes within your family or among your friends.

What challenges result from these changes?

In your journal, draw a cause-and-effect diagram like the one shown. In the box labeled *Change*, write one change you have experienced during the past year. In each of the boxes labeled *Challenge*, write a challenge you have faced as a result of this change. Finally, beneath your diagram, write several sentences about the challenge that seems most important to you.

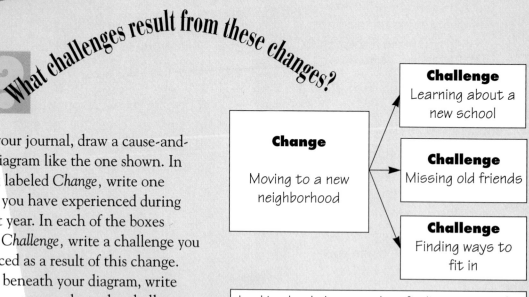

Change

Moving to a new neighborhood

Challenge
Learning about a new school

Challenge
Missing old friends

Challenge
Finding ways to fit in

Looking back, I guess that finding ways to fit in was the most difficult for me...

What choices do people make when faced with challenges?

Imagine that you have moved to a new neighborhood. What would you do to meet each of the following challenges?
- Learn about your new school
- Keep in touch with old friends
- Find ways to fit in

In your journal, write about the choices you might make. Then discuss your choices with a partner or a group.

What qualities help people face change successfully?

What qualities help you deal with changes? In your journal, create a cluster or web like the one that has been started. Include traits or qualities that help you confront change. (It may help to think of specific changes, such as moving to a new community.) Then work with classmates to make a large web or cluster of qualities that you can post in the classroom.

NOW Think!

What is the most important change you have faced in life? How have you handled this change? As you read "Changes and Choices," think about this change. Compare your experiences in facing change with the experiences of the characters in the selections. What do the characters say to you about dealing with changes successfully?

patience

What qualities help me face change?

flexibility

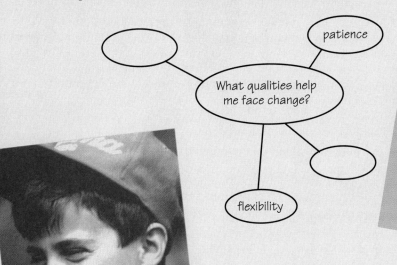

GROWING UP

GARY SOTO

Now that Maria was a tenth-grader, she felt she was too grown-up to have to go on family vacations. Last year, the family had driven three hundred miles to see their uncle in West Covina. There was nothing to do. The days were hot, with a yellow sky thick with smog they could feel on their fingertips. They played cards and watched game shows on television. After the first four days of doing nothing while the grown-ups sat around talking, the kids finally got to go to Disneyland.

Disneyland stood tall with castles and bright flags. The Matterhorn[1] had wild dips and curves that took your breath away if you closed your eyes and screamed. The Pirates of the Caribbean didn't scare anyone but was fun anyway, and so were the teacups and It's a Small World. The parents spoiled the kids, giving each of them five dollars to spend on trinkets. Maria's younger sister, Irma, bought a Pinocchio coloring book and a candy bracelet. Her brothers, Rudy and John, spent their money on candy that made their teeth blue.

1. **Matterhorn** [mat′ ər hôrn]: a ride at Disneyland in California patterned on a mountain peak in the Alps between Switzerland and Italy.

Maria saved her money. She knew everything was overpriced, like the Mickey Mouse balloons you could get for a fraction of the price in Fresno. Of course, the balloon at Hanoian's supermarket didn't have a Mickey Mouse face, but it would bounce and float and eventually pop like any other balloon.

Maria folded her five dollars, tucked it in her red purse, and went on rides until she got sick. After that, she sat on a bench, jealously watching other teenage girls who seemed much better dressed than she was. She felt stricken by poverty. All the screaming kids in nice clothes probably came from homes with swimming pools in their backyards, she thought. Yes, her father was a foreman at a paper mill, and yes, she had a Dough-boy swimming pool in her backyard, but *still*, things were not the same. She had felt poor, and her sun dress, which seemed snappy in Fresno, was out of style at Disneyland, where every other kid was wearing Esprit shirts and Guess jeans.

This year Maria's family planned to visit an uncle in San Jose. Her father promised to take them to Great America,[2] but she knew that the grown-ups would sit around talking for days before they remembered the kids and finally got up and did something. They would have to wait until the last day before they could go to Great America. It wasn't worth the boredom.

"Dad, I'm not going this year," Maria said to her father. He sat at the table with the newspaper in front of him.

"What do you mean?" he asked, slowly looking up. He thought a moment and said, "When I was a kid we didn't have the money for vacations. I would have been happy to go with my father."

"I know, I know. You've said that a hundred times," she snapped.

"What did you say?" he asked, pushing his newspaper aside.

Everything went quiet. Maria could hear the hum of the refrigerator and her brothers out in the front yard arguing over a popsicle

2. **Great America:** an amusement park in California.

stick, and her mother in the backyard watering the strip of grass that ran along the patio.

Her father's eyes locked on her with a dark stare. Maria had seen that stare before. She pleaded in a soft daughterly voice, "We never do anything. It's boring. Don't you understand?"

"No, I don't understand. I work all year, and if I want to go on a vacation, then I go. And my family goes too." He took a swallow of ice water, and glared.

"You have it so easy," he continued. "In Chihuahua,[3] my town, we worked hard. You worked, even *los chavalos!*[4] And you showed respect to your parents, something you haven't learned."

Here it comes, Maria thought, stories about his childhood in Mexico. She wanted to stuff her ears with wads of newspaper to keep from hearing him. She could recite his stories word-for-word. She couldn't wait until she was in college and away from them.

"Do you know my father worked in the mines? That he nearly lost his life? And today his lungs are bad." He pounded his chest with hard, dirt-creased knuckles.

Maria pushed back her hair and looked out the window at her brothers running around in the front yard. She couldn't stand it anymore. She got up and walked away, and when he yelled for her to come back, she ignored him. She locked herself in her bedroom and tried to read *Seventeen*, though she could hear her father complaining to her mother, who had come in when she had heard the yelling.

"*Habla con tu mocosa,*"[5] she heard him say.

She heard the refrigerator door open. He was probably getting a beer, a "cold one," as he would say. She flipped through the pages of her magazine and stopped at a Levi's ad of a girl about her age walking between two

---

3. **Chihuahua** [chi wä′ wä]: a state in northern Mexico; its capital has the same name.
4. *los chavalos* [lōs chä vä′ lōs]: Spanish for "young boys."
5. *Habla con tu mocosa* [ä′ blä con tü mō kō′ sä]: Spanish for "Talk to your brat."

happy-looking guys on a beach. She wished she were that girl, that she had another life. She turned the page and thought, I bet you he gets drunk and drives crazy tomorrow.

Maria's mother was putting away a pitcher of Kool-Aid the boys had left out. She looked at her husband, who was fumbling with a wadded-up napkin. His eyes were dark, and his thoughts were on Mexico, where a father was respected and his word, right or wrong, was final. "Rafael, she's growing up; she's a teenager. She talks like that, but she still loves you."

"Sure, and that's how she shows her love, by talking back to her father." He rubbed the back of his neck and turned his head trying to make the stiffness go away. He knew it was true, but he was the man of the house and no daughter of his was going to tell him what to do.

Instead, it was his wife, Eva, who told him what to do. "Let the girl stay. She's big now. She don't want to go on rides no more. She can stay with her *nina*."[6]

The father drank his beer and argued, but eventually agreed to let his daughter stay.

The family rose just after six the next day and was ready to go by seven-thirty. Maria stayed in her room. She wanted to apologize to her father but couldn't. She knew that if she said, "Dad, I'm sorry," she would break into tears. Her father wanted to come into her room and say, "We'll do something really special this vacation. Come with us, honey." But it was hard for him to show his emotions around his children, especially when he tried to make up to them.

---

6. *nina* [nē′ nä]: Spanish for "godmother."

The mother kissed Maria. "Maria, I want you to clean the house and then walk over to your *nina*'s. I want no monkey business while we're gone, do you hear me?"

"*Sí*, Mama."

"Here's the key. You water the plants inside and turn on the sprinkler every couple of days." She handed Maria the key and hugged her. "You be good. Now, come say goodbye to your father."

Reluctantly, she walked out in her robe to the front yard and, looking down at the ground, said goodbye to her father. The father looked down and said goodbye to the garden hose at his feet.

After they left, Maria lounged in her pajamas listening to the radio and thumbing through magazines. Then she got up, fixed herself a bowl of Cocoa Puffs, and watched "American Bandstand."[7] Her dream was to dance on the show, to look at the camera, smile, and let everyone in Fresno see that she could have a good time, too.

But an ill feeling stirred inside her. She felt awful about arguing with her father. She felt bad for her mother and two brothers, who would have to spend the next three hours in the car with him. Maybe he would do something crazy, like crash the car on purpose to get back at her, or fall asleep and run the car into an irrigation ditch. And it would be her fault.

7. **American Bandstand:** TV program that featured the studio audience dancing to popular music.

She turned the radio to a news station. She listened for half an hour, but most of the news was about warships in the Persian Gulf and a tornado in Texas. There was no mention of her family.

Maria began to calm down because, after all, her father was really nice beneath his gruffness. She dressed slowly, made some swishes with the broom in the kitchen, and let the hose run in a flower bed while she painted her toenails with her mother's polish. Afterward, she called her friend Becky to tell her that her parents had let her stay home, that she was free—for five days at least.

"Great," Becky said. "I wish my mom and dad would go away and let me stay by myself."

"No, I have to stay with my godmother." She made a mental note to give her *nina* a call. "Becky, let's go to the mall and check out the boys."

"All right."

"I'll be over pretty soon."

Maria called her *nina*, who said it was OK for her to go shopping, but to be at her house for dinnertime by six. After hanging up, Maria took off her jeans and T-shirt, and changed into a dress. She went through her mother's closet to borrow a pair of shoes and drenched her wrists in Charlie perfume. She put on coral-pink lipstick and a smudge of blue eyeshadow. She felt beautiful, although a little self-conscious. She took off some of the lipstick and ran water over her wrists to dilute the fragrance.

While she walked the four blocks to Becky's house, she beamed happiness until she passed a man who was on his knees pulling weeds from his flower bed. At his side, a radio was reporting a traffic accident. A big rig had overturned after hitting a car near Salinas, twenty miles from San Jose.

A wave of fear ran through her. Maybe it was *them*. Her smile disappeared, and her shoulders slouched. No, it couldn't be, she thought. Salinas is not that close to San Jose. Then again, maybe her father wanted to travel through Salinas because it was a pretty valley with wide plains and oak trees, and horses and cows that stared as you passed them in your speeding car. But maybe it did happen; maybe they had gotten in an awful wreck.

By the time she got to Becky's house, she was riddled with guilt, since it was she who would have disturbed her father and made him crash.

"Hi," she said to Becky, trying to look cheerful.

"You look terrific, Maria," Becky said. "Mom, look at Maria. Come inside for a bit."

Maria blushed when Becky's mother said she looked gorgeous. She didn't know what to do except stare at the carpet and say, "Thank you, Mrs. Ledesma."

Becky's mother gave them a ride to the mall, but they'd have to take a bus back. The girls first went to Macy's, where they hunted for a sweater, something flashy but not too flashy. Then they left to have a Coke and sit by the fountain under an artificial tree. They watched people walk by, especially the boys, who, they agreed, were dumb but cute nevertheless.

They went to The Gap, where they tried on some skirts, and ventured into The Limited, where they walked up and down the aisles breathing in the rich smells of 100-percent wool and silk. They were about to leave, when Maria heard once again on someone's portable radio that a family had been killed in an auto accident near Salinas. Maria stopped smiling for a moment as she pictured her family's overturned Malibu station wagon.

Becky sensed that something was wrong and asked, "How come you're so quiet?"

Maria forced a smile. "Oh, nothing, I was just thinking."

" 'bout what?"

Maria thought quickly. "Oh, I think I left the water on at home." This could have been true. Maria remembered pulling the hose from the flower bed, but couldn't remember if she had turned the water off.

Afterward they rode the bus home with nothing to show for their three hours of shopping except a small bag of See's candies. But it had been a good day. Two boys had followed them, joking and flirting, and they had flirted back. The girls gave them made-up telephone numbers, then turned away and laughed into their hands.

"They're fools," Becky said, "but cute."

Maria left Becky when they got off the bus, and started off to her *nina*'s house. Then she remembered that the garden hose might still be running at home. She hurried home, clip-clopping clumsily in her mother's shoes.

The garden hose was rolled neatly against the trellis. Maria decided to check the mail and

went inside. When she pushed open the door, the living room gave off a quietness she had never heard before. Usually the TV was on, her younger brothers and sister were playing, and her mother could be heard in the kitchen. When the telephone rang, Maria jumped. She kicked off her shoes, ran to the phone, and picked up the receiver only to hear a distant clicking sound.

"Hello, hello?" Maria's heart began to thump. Her mind went wild with possibilities. An accident, she thought, they're in an accident, and it's all my fault. "Who is it? Dad? Mom?"

She hung up and looked around the room. The clock on the television set glowed 5:15. She gathered the mail, changed into jeans, and left for her *nina*'s house with a shopping bag containing her nightie and a toothbrush.

Her *nina* was happy to see her. She took Maria's head in her hands and gave it a loud kiss.

"Dinner is almost ready," she said, gently pulling her inside.

"Oh, good. Becky and I only had popcorn for lunch."

They had a quiet evening together. After dinner, they sat on the porch watching the stars. Maria wanted to ask her *nina* if she had heard from her parents. She wanted to know if the police had called to report that they had gotten into an accident. But she just sat on the porch swing, letting anxiety eat a hole in her soul.

The family was gone for four days. Maria prayed for them, prayed that she would not wake up to a phone call saying that their car had been found in a ditch. She made a list of the ways she could be nicer to them: doing the dishes without being asked, watering the lawn, hugging her father after work, and playing with her youngest brother, even if it bored her to tears.

At night Maria worried herself sick listening to the radio for news of an accident. She thought of her uncle Shorty and how he fell asleep and crashed his car in the small town of Mendota. He lived confined to a motorized wheelchair and was scarred with burns on the left side of his face.

"Oh, please, don't let anything like that happen to them," she prayed.

In the morning she could barely look at the newspaper. She feared that if she unfolded it, the front page would feature a story about a family from Fresno who had flown off the roller coaster at Great America. Or that a shark had attacked them as they bobbed happily among the white-tipped waves. Something awful is going to happen, she said to herself as she poured Rice Krispies into a bowl.

But nothing happened. Her family returned home, dark from lying on the beach and full of great stories about the Santa Cruz boardwalk and Great America and an Egyptian museum. They had done more this year than in all their previous vacations.

"Oh, we had fun," her mother said, pounding sand from her shoes before entering the house.

Her father gave her a tight hug as her brothers ran by, dark from hours of swimming.

Maria stared at the floor, miffed. How dare they have so much fun? While she worried herself sick about them, they had splashed in the waves, stayed at Great America until nightfall, and eaten at all kinds of restaurants. They even went shopping for fall school clothes.

Feeling resentful as Johnny described a ride that dropped straight down and threw your stomach into your mouth, Maria turned away and went off to her bedroom, where she kicked off her shoes and thumbed through an old *Seventeen*. Her family was alive and as obnoxious as ever. She took back all her promises. From now on she would keep to herself and ignore them. When they asked, "Maria, would you help me," she would pretend not to hear and walk away.

"They're heartless," she muttered. "Here I am worrying about them, and there they are having fun." She thought of the rides they had gone on, the hours of body surfing, the handsome boys she didn't get to see, the restaurants, and the museum. Her eyes filled with tears. For the first time in years, she hugged a doll, the one her grand-mother Lupe had stitched together from rags and old clothes.

"Something's wrong with me," she cried softly. She turned on her radio and heard about a single-engined plane that had crashed in Cupertino, a city not far from San Jose. She thought of the plane and the people inside, how the pilot's family would suffer.

She hugged her doll. Something was happening to her, and it might be that she was growing up. When the news ended, and a song started playing, she got up and washed her face without looking in the mirror.

That night the family went out for Chinese food. Although her brothers fooled around, cracked jokes, and spilled a soda, she was happy. She ate a lot, and when her fortune cookie said, "You are ma-ture and sensible," she had to agree. And her father and mother did too. The family drove home singing the words to "La Bamba" along with the car radio.

GARY SOTO

Gary Soto was born in Fresno, California, in 1952 and grew up in the San Joaquin Valley, where he was a migrant farm worker. When he entered college he planned to study geography, but soon found that he was more interested in literature.

Soto is best known as a poet. His first collection of poetry, *The Elements of San Joaquin*, won the United States Award of the International Poetry Forum. He continues to write poetry and is thought of as one of the country's most important poets. Soto teaches English and Chicano Studies at the University of California, in Berkeley.

Soto did not publish prose until 1985, but since then he has become well known for his autobiographical essays and sketches. Most of these focus on his childhood and his teen years growing up in a Mexican American family. "Growing Up" is from a collection of autobiographical stories titled *Baseball in April and Other Stories*. Other such collections are *A Summer Life* and *Pacific Crossing*.

Curtains Roy Lichtenstein, 1962, oil and magna on canvas, 68$^3/_4$″ x 58$^1/_2$″,
The St. Louis Art Museum

As It Is with Strangers

SUSAN BETH PFEFFER

It wasn't until right before I went to bed on Thursday that Mom bothered to tell me the son she'd given up for adoption twenty years earlier was coming over for supper the next day.

"What son?" I asked.

"I'm sure I've told you about him," Mom said. "You must have forgotten."

I figured I probably had. I'm always forgetting little things like my homework assignments and being elected President of the United States. Having an older brother must have just slipped my mind. "How'd you two find each other?" I asked. Presumably Mom had never told me that.

"I registered with an agency," she said. "Put my name and address in a book, so if he ever wanted to find me, he could. I guess he did. Don't be late for supper tomorrow."

"I won't be," I promised. This was one reunion I had no intention of missing.

School the next day really dragged on. School never goes fast on Fridays, but when your mind is on some newly acquired half brother, it's real hard to care about Julius Caesar. I didn't tell anybody, though. It seemed to me it was Mom's story, not mine, and besides, my friends all think she's crazy anyway. Probably from things I've said over the years.

I went straight home from school, and was surprised, first to find the place spotless, and then to see Mom in the kitchen cooking away.

"I took a sick day," she informed me. "So I could prepare better."

"Everything looks great," I told her. It was true. I hadn't seen the place look so good since Great-Aunt Trudy came with the goat, but that's another story. "You look very pretty too."

"I got my nails done," Mom said, showing them off for me. They were coral colored. "And my hair."

I nodded. Mom had taught me that nothing was unbearable if your hair looked nice.

"Is that what you're planning to wear tonight?" she asked.

"I thought I'd shower and change into my dress," I said. I own a grand total of one dress, but this seemed to be the right kind of occasion for it.

Mom gave me a smile like I'd just been canonized. "Thank you," she said. "Tonight's kind of important for me."

I nodded. I wasn't sure just what to say anymore. Mom and I have been alone for eight years, and you'd figure by now I'd know how to handle her under any circumstances, but this one had me stumped. "What's for supper?" I finally asked.

"Southern fried chicken," Mom said. "At first I thought I'd make a roast, but then what if he doesn't like his meat rare? And turkey seemed too Thanksgivingish, if you know what I mean. Everybody likes fried chicken. And I made mashed potatoes and biscuits and a spinach salad."

"Spinach salad?" I asked. I could picture Mom pouring the spinach out of a can and dousing it with Wishbone.

"From scratch," Mom informed me. "Everything's from scratch.

And I baked an apple pie too. The ice cream is store bought, but I got one of those expensive brands. What do you think?"

I thought that there obviously was something to that Prodigal Son[1] story, since Mom never made anything more elaborate for me than scrambled eggs. "It smells great," I said. It did, too, the way you picture a house in a commercial smelling, all homey and warm. "I'm sure everything will go fine."

"I want it to," Mom said, as though I'd suggested that maybe she didn't.

There were a few things I knew I'd better clear up before Big Brother showed up. "What's his name?" I asked, for starters.

"Jack," Mom said. "That's not what I would have named him. I would have named him Ronald."

"You would have?" I asked. I personally am named Tiffany, and Ronald would not have been my first guess.

"That was my boyfriend's name," Mom said. "Ronny."

"Your boyfriend," I said. "You mean his father?"

Mom nodded. "You think of them as boyfriends, not fathers, when you're sixteen," she said.

Well that answered question number two. It had seemed unlikely to me that my father was responsible, but who knew? I wasn't there. Maybe he and Mom had decided they wanted a girl, and chucked out any boys that came along first.

Speaking of which. "There aren't any other brothers I've forgotten about?" I asked. "Is this going to be the first of many such dinners?"

"Jack's the only one," Mom replied. "I wanted to keep him, but Ronny wasn't about to get married, and Dad said if I gave him up for adoption then I could still go to college. I did the right thing, for him and for me. And I would have gone to college if I hadn't met your father. I don't know. Maybe because I gave up the baby, I was too eager to get married. I never really thought about it."

"Did Dad know?" I asked.

---

1. **Prodigal Son** [prod′ ə gəl]: story in the New Testament of the Bible concerning a reckless son who returns home and asks and receives forgiveness from his father.

Turkey Roy Lichtenstein, 1961, oil on canvas, 26" x 30", ©Roy Lichtenstein, photo by Robert McKeever

"I told him," Mom said. "He said it didn't matter to him. And it didn't. Whatever else was wrong in our marriage, he never threw the baby in my face."

I found myself picturing a baby being thrown in Mom's face, and decided I should take my shower fast. So I sniffed the kitchen appreciatively and scurried out. In the shower I tried to imagine what this Jack would look like, but he kept resembling Dad's high-school graduation picture, which made no sense biologically at all. So I stopped imagining.

When I went to my bedroom to change, though, I was really shocked. Mom had extended her cleaning ways to include my room. All my carefully laid out messes were gone. It would probably take me months to reassemble things. I considered screaming at Mom

Cherry Pie Roy Lichtenstein, 1962, oil on canvas, 20" x 24", Collection of Sydney and Frances Lewis

about the sanctity of one's bedroom, but I decided against it. Mom obviously wanted this guy to think she and I were the perfect American family, and if that meant even my room had to be clean, then nothing was going to stop her. I could live with it, at least for the evening.

Mom and I set the table three times before the doorbell finally rang. When it did, neither one of us knew who should answer it, but Mom finally opened the door. "Hello," this guy said. "I'm Jack."

"I'm Linda," Mom replied. "Come on in. It's nice to . . . well, it's good seeing you."

"Good to see you too," Jack said. He didn't look anything like my father.

"This is Tiffany," Mom said. "She, uh . . ."

"Her daughter," I said. "Your sister." I mean, those words were going to be used at some point during the evening. We might as well get them out of the way fast. Then when we got around to the big tricky words like *mother* and *son,* at least some groundwork would have been laid.

"It's nice to meet you," Jack said, and he gave me his hand to shake, so I shook it. They say you can tell a lot about a man from his handshake, but not when he's your long-lost brother. "I hope my coming like this isn't any kind of a brother. I mean bother."

"Not at all," Mom said. "I'm going to check on dinner. Tiffany, why don't you show Jack the living room? I'll join you in a moment."

"This is the living room," I said, which was pretty easy to show Jack, since we were already standing in it. "Want to sit down?"

"Yeah, sure," Jack said. "Have you lived here long?"

"Since the divorce," I said. "Eight years ago."

"That long," Jack said. "Where's your father?"

"He lives in Oak Ridge," I said. "That's a couple of hundred miles from here. I see him sometimes."

"Is he . . ." Jack began. "I mean, I don't suppose you'd know . . ."

"Is he your father too?" I said. "No. I kind of asked. Your father's name is Ronny. My father's name is Mike. I don't know much else about your father except he didn't want to marry Mom. They were both teenagers, I guess. Do you want to meet him too?"

"Sometime," Jack said. "Not tonight."

I could sure understand that one. "I've always wanted to have a big brother," I told him. "I always had crushes on my friends' big brothers. Did you want that—to have a kid sister, I mean?"

"I have one," Jack said. "No, I guess now I have two. I have a sister back home. Her name is Leigh Ann. She's adopted too. She's Korean."

"Oh," I said. "That's nice. I guess there isn't much of a family resemblance, then."

"Not much," Jack said, but he smiled. "She's twelve. How old are you?"

"Fifteen," I said. "Do you go to college?"

Jack nodded. "I'm a sophomore at Bucknell," he said. "Do you think you'll go to college?"

"I'd like to," I said. "I don't know if we'll have the money, though."

"It's rough," Jack said. "College costs a lot these days. My father's always griping about it. He owns a car dealership. New and used. I work there summers. My mom's a housewife."

I wanted to tell him how hard Mom had worked on supper, how messy the apartment usually was, how I never wore a dress, and Mom's nails were always a deep sinful scarlet. I wanted to tell him that maybe someday I'd be jealous that he'd been given away to a family that could afford to send him to college, but that it was too soon for me to feel much of anything about him. There was a lot I wanted to say, but I didn't say any of it.

"What's she like?" Jack asked me, and he gestured toward the kitchen, as though I might not otherwise know who he was talking about.

"Mom?" I said. "She's terrible. She drinks and she gambles and she beats me black and blue if I even think something wrong."

Jack looked horrified. I realized he had definitely not inherited Mom's sense of humor.

"I'm only kidding," I said. "I haven't even been spanked since I was five. She's fine. She's a good mother. It must have really hurt her to give you away like that."

"Have you known long?" Jack asked. "About me?"

"Not until recently," I said. It didn't seem right to tell him I'd learned less than twenty-four hours before. "I guess Mom was waiting until I was old enough to understand."

"I always knew I was adopted," Jack said. "And for years I've wanted to meet my biological parents. To see what they looked like. I love Mom and Dad, you understand. But I felt this need."

"I can imagine," I said, and I could too. I was starting to develop a real need to see what Jack's parents looked like, and we weren't even related.

"Tiffany, could you come in here for a minute?" Mom called from the kitchen.

"Coming, Mom," I said, and left the living room fast. It takes a lot out of you making small talk with a brother.

"What do you think?" Mom whispered as soon as she saw me. "Does he look like me?"

"He has your eyes," I said. "And I think he has your old hair color."

"I know," Mom said, patting her bottle red hair. "I almost asked them to dye me back to my original shade, but I wasn't sure I could remember it anymore. Do you like him? Does he seem nice?"

"Very nice," I said. "Very good manners."

"He sure didn't inherit those from Ronny," Mom declared. "Come on, let's start taking the food out."

So we did. We carried out platters of chicken and mashed potatoes and biscuits and salad. Jack came to the table as soon as he saw what we were doing.

"Oh, no," he said. "I mean, I'm sorry. I should have told you. I'm a vegetarian."

"You are?" Mom said. She looked as shocked as if he'd told her he was a vampire. Meat is very important to Mom. "You're not sick or anything, are you?"

"No, it's for moral reasons," Jack said. "It drives my mom, my mother, her name's Cathy, it drives Cathy crazy."

"Your mom," my mom said. "It would drive me crazy, too, if Tiffany stopped eating meat just for moral reasons."

"Don't worry about it," I told her. "I'll never be that moral."

"There's plenty for me to eat," Jack said. "Potatoes and biscuits and salad."

"The salad has bacon in it," Mom said. "I crumbled bacon in it."

"We can wash the bacon off, can't we Jack?" I said. "You'll eat it if we wash the bacon off, won't you?"

I thought he hesitated for a moment, but then he said, "Of course I can," and for the first time since we'd met, I kind of liked him. I took the salad into the kitchen and washed it all. The salad dressing went the way of the bacon, but we weren't about to complain. At least there'd be something green on Jack's plate. All his other food was gray-white.

Mom hardly ate her chicken, which I figured was out of deference to the vegetarian, but I had two and a half pieces, figuring it might be years before Mom made it again. Jack ate more potatoes than I'd ever seen another human being eat. No gravy, but lots of potatoes. We talked polite stuff during dinner, what he was studying in college, where Mom worked, the adjustments Leigh Ann had had to make. The real things could only be discussed one on one, so after the pie and ice cream, I excused myself and went to Mom's room to watch TV. Only I couldn't make my eyes focus, so I crossed the hall to my room, and recreated my messes. Once I had everything in proper order, though, I put things back the way Mom had had them. I could hear them talking while I moved piles around, and then I turned on my radio, so I couldn't even hear the occasional stray word, like *father* and *high school* and *lawyer*. That was a trick I'd learned years ago, when Mom and Dad were in their fighting stage. The radio played a lot of old songs that night. It made me feel like I was seven all over again.

After a while Mom knocked on my door and said Jack was leaving, so I went to the living room and shook hands with him again. I still couldn't tell anything about his personality from his handshake, but he did have good manners, and he gave me a little pecking kiss on my cheek, which I thought was sweet of him. Mom kept the door open, and watched as he walked the length of the corridor to the stairs. She didn't close the door until he'd gotten into a car, his I assumed. Maybe it was a loaner from his father.

"You give away a baby," Mom said, "and twenty years later he turns up on your doorstep a vegetarian."

"He turns up a turnip," I said.

But Mom wasn't in the mood for those kinds of jokes. "Don't you ever make that mistake," she said.

"What mistake?" I asked, afraid she meant making jokes. If I couldn't make jokes with Mom, I wouldn't know how to talk with her.

"Don't you ever give up something so important to you that it breathes when you do," Mom said. "It doesn't have to be a kid. It can be a dream, an ambition, or a marriage, or a house. It can be anything

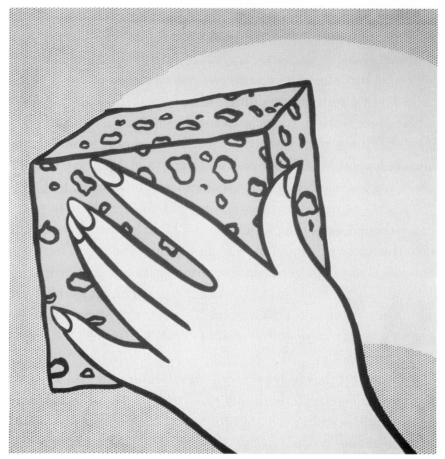

Sponge II Roy Lichtenstein, 1962, oil on canvas, 36"x 36", ©Roy Lichtenstein

you care about as deeply as you care about your own life. Don't ever just give it away, because you'll spend the rest of your life wondering about it, or pretending you don't wonder, which is the same thing, and you'll wake up one morning and realize it truly is gone and a big part of you is gone with it. Do you hear me, Tiffany?"

"I hear you," I said. I'd never seen Mom so intense, and I didn't like being around her. "I'm kind of tired now, Mom. Would you mind if I went to bed early?"

"I'll clean up tomorrow," Mom said. "You can go to bed."

So I did. I left her sitting in the living room and went to my bedroom and closed my door. But this time I didn't turn the radio on, and later, when I'd been lying on my bed for hours, not able to sleep, I could hear her in her room crying. I'd heard her cry in her room a hundred times before, and a hundred times before I'd gotten up and comforted her, and I knew she'd cry a hundred times again, and I'd comfort her then, too, but that night I just stayed in my room, on my bed, staring at the ceiling and listening to her cry. I think I did the right thing, not going in there. That's how it is with strangers. You can never really comfort them.

SUSAN BETH PFEFFER

Susan Beth Pfeffer, who was born in New York City in 1948, has written a number of young-adult novels about important teenage issues concerning home, school, and work. "My interests range from baseball to medieval art," she says, "with stops at movie history, the lives of innumerable writers, and local theater. I've been writing since age six when I completed my first novel, *Dookie the Cookie*." That first novel is still unpublished, but one that is available is called *Better Than All Right*.

THE TORN INVITATION

NORMAN KATKOV

At fifteen, in the spring of his sophomore year at Hamilton High School, Harry Wojick was as big as a college senior, a long, thin, big-boned left-hander, who could anchor a leg in first base and stretch halfway to right field for a bad throw from his shortstop.

Now, in the waning daylight, he turned into Glover Street toward his home, his arms swinging as he moved onto the unpaved road. For a few feet he ran easily, bringing his knees up high, until, without warning, he stopped short and bent low to field the imaginary ball cleanly, beating the runner by a mile. He straightened up, grinning in the half darkness, blushing a little from the applause at the brilliant play he had made.

Harry Wojick came off the street onto the opposite sidewalk. He passed the four-family flat in the middle of the block. He passed the empty lot and beyond it the condemned building with all the windows long since broken, and then he turned into the cement walk which ran the length of his house.

Mother and Child Elizabeth Catlett, 1972, pecan wood, courtesy of the Museum of African-American Art

The windows were raised in the kitchen and he smelled the roast. He smelled the asparagus for the roast and the fried potatoes with onions that nobody made like Ma, and he was suddenly terribly hungry after the three hours of baseball practice.

When he came into the kitchen, Theresa Wojick turned from the stove, smiling at her son, rubbing her hands on her apron as she walked to meet him. She held him at the elbows, examining him carefully, her face warm and her eyes gentle, welcoming him as though he had returned from a long and perilous journey. She was a tall woman with large, capable hands and black, unkempt hair shot through with gray. She held Harry and she said, "Hello, my little son. Will you eat supper?" joking with him as always.

He put his cheek to hers, noticing again the redness of her chapped hands. She could try to do something about it, he said to himself, as she released him, remembering the mothers of his team-mates who lived above the flats on Livingston Drive and Harding Boulevard and scattered through Maple Heights. They were mothers with manicures and they were thin—and their hair was always set just right.

Harry went to the sink to wash and, turning, saw the table set for three. He thought for an instant that his father was home, that Peter Wojick had not gone to his night-watchman's job in the office building downtown. But he saw the hooks on the wall near the door empty of cap and coat.

"For Frankie Thomas," his mother whispered, looking at her son. "His mother is gone again till half the night, and leaves cold cuts. Boy like Frankie to eat cold cuts," she whispered. "You call him, Harry."

"Why can't she learn to speak English?" he asked himself savagely, turning away. "She's been here long enough!"

Harry walked through the short hall and stood under the arch which led into the living room. He saw the frail, black-haired boy with whom he had grown up, sitting in the chair under the lamp. "Hey, Frankie," Harry said. "Come on and eat." Harry whistled shrilly and came back into the kitchen.

He pulled the chair out and held it suspended off the clean, bare floor, his fingers tightening on the wood. There, next to his plate, was the white, square envelope, and atop it, covered by a transparent sheet of thin paper, was the embossed[1] invitation.

Harry looked at his mother, who had her back to him, busy at the stove. He heard Frankie coming through the house and knew it was Frankie's work, *knew* it. He moved the chair at last and sat down and, without touching it, his hands holding his knees, he read the invitation from the faculty of Hamilton High School to an open house in honor of all the students' mothers.

It was for tomorrow.

Harry knew *that*, all right. Had known it for ten days and had kept it secret. He looked up as Frankie sat down across the table.

Harry's mother was sitting between them, and as she handed her son the roast she said, "I asked Frankie maybe he has this invitation, Harry. I heard by Celusik, the grocery man, about this open house. Must be open house for junior, senior mothers." Frankie had skipped a grade.

Harry was busy with the roast. "It's for everyone," he said, watching the roast. "Didn't you get one, Ma?" He turned to his mother. "They mailed them out," Harry said, remembering now that morning when he had waited for the postman on the corner, taken the envelopes from him, searched for the square, white one, and had torn it, scattering the pieces in the empty lot before running home and dropping the rest of the mail in the black metal box beside the door.

"Maybe they make a mistake," his mother said.

She reached for a thick slice of the rye bread she baked herself and held it flat in her left hand. She buttered it completely and thickly and brought it to her mouth, taking a large bite, and Harry wanted to leave the table and this house. He remembered the homes on Maple Heights to which he had been invited, where they called it dinner and ate in a dining room with tablecloths; where George Sidley's mother sat at one end of the table and broke her bread piece by piece, buttering it lightly and eating slowly.

1. **embossed** [em bôsd´]: having letters that are raised to stand out from the surface.

"Frankie's ma got this invitation," Theresa Wojick said, nodding at their guest, who lived with his mother in one of the upstairs apartments of the four-family flat. "How long she got the open house, Frankie?"

"Mother had it," Frankie said. "She—we didn't talk about it."

She turned to Harry, smiling at her son. "You eat, Harry. Big ballplayer must eat good," she said.

Harry ate. The three sat in silence.

Later, while Theresa Wojick set out the dessert plates, Frankie said, "How's practice going, Harry?"

"All right, I guess." He wanted this supper finished.

Theresa Wojick filled the dessert plates with pudding. As she sat down she said to Frankie, "Your ma goes to this open house?"

"I don't know," he answered. "She—well, you know, she's pretty busy. One of my aunts is sick and I think she's going to be with her for a few days. She packed her suitcase when she left today."

"Ma," Harry said.

She set her coffee cup down.

"I wanted to tell you, Ma," he said. "I meant to tell you about it and then I forgot, I guess."

"Easy to forget," she said.

"It wouldn't make any difference anyway, Ma," Harry lied. "We've got that game with Central next week and the coach is worried. He's been working us hard all week. He's got a game for tomorrow. You know, he picks two teams from the squad and we play each other."

"I've got to go," Frankie said. "Thanks very much for supper, Mrs. Wojick."

"You're welcome, Frankie. Here"—she reached across the table—"here is the invitation, Frankie," and she offered it to him.

He held it, shifting it from one hand to the other. "Thanks," he said, moving toward the kitchen door. "Thanks. Thanks." And he was gone.

"I won't be finished until about six o'clock, Ma," Harry said.

She nodded. Harry watched her walking to the sink. "Do you want me to miss practice, Ma?" he asked.

She had her back to him.

Mother and Child Elizabeth Catlett, 1970, cedar, courtesy of the artist

"We'll go next year, Ma. I'll be a regular on the team then. We can go next year," he said, but she didn't turn, nor move, nor did she answer him, and he left the kitchen quickly. He went into the living room and stood before the windows. He tried to blame Frankie and couldn't, and he tried to blame Theresa Wojick and couldn't. He was seldom a liar, but he just didn't want her there with George Sidley's mother and Eric Portland's mother.

Harry heard the water running in the sink and the clatter of dishes, and he went back into the kitchen. He opened the cabinet door, reaching for one of the dish towels his mother had cut from sugar sacks and washed white and soft. She took it from his hand.

"You rest, Harry," his mother said. "Big ball game tomorrow. You must rest up for the ball game." She turned from him to the sink.

"All right," he thought, and now he left the house, going out into the vestibule and then to the rear porch. "Let her wash her own dishes," he thought, and walked out to the sidewalk.

Frankie said, "Hi, Harry." He was leaning against the fence in front of Harry's house. He said, "I didn't want to jam you up, Harry."

"You didn't jam me up."

"That ought to be a pretty good game tomorrow, that intrasquad game," Frankie said. "Think I'll watch it."

"There isn't any intrasquad game," Harry muttered.

"You said—"

"I said. I say a lot of things." He felt the meanness in him. He started to walk away, but Frankie took his arm.

"I've got enough for a movie," Frankie said.

"I'm busy," Harry said, jerking his arm free. He left Frankie there, walking down Glover Street. He passed the corner and went on aimlessly.

When he came home he entered the house through the front door and moved through the living room in darkness, turning into his bedroom. He could see the cracks of light below the bathroom door and heard the water running; he wondered if there was ever a time in this house when the water *wasn't* running. He made it to his bedroom and undressed in the darkness, dropping his clothes on the floor and crawling into the turned-down bed.

"All right," he thought, "this time tomorrow it'll be over." He heard the bathroom door open and his mother moving around the house. He lay still, his eyes closed, his breath coming evenly as he simulated sleep, but the sound of her footsteps faded.

For a bad moment he thought of his ma, saw her again at the kitchen table, but he chased the scene from his mind and went, instead, to baseball, seeing himself leading infield practice, and thus, at last, fell asleep.

The first thing he noticed in the morning was his clothes, arranged neatly on the chair beside the bed, the shoes together on the floor and clean socks across them. He dressed quickly.

The kitchen was deserted. He saw his cornflakes and the orange juice and the milk before his chair, but he stood behind it, gulping the juice. As he set the empty glass on the table his mother came in from the rear porch.

"You didn't eat, Harry," she said.

"I'm late, Ma. I've got a test this morning. I've got to study for the test." He wanted to be out of here now as he turned from the table, saw that her hands were full.

She held the clean, freshly dried sweatshirt and the two pairs of wool socks, and he knew now why the water had been running in the bathroom last night. "For your game today, Harry," she said. "You bring me tonight your dirty stuff."

Harry watched her wrap the bundle and he wanted to kiss her, suddenly. He wanted to put his arms around her and hold her as she tied the bundle carefully with the string she always saved. But he only took the package from her and said thanks, and left.

All the way up to school he promised he'd make it up to her. He'd start tonight. He'd sit in the kitchen with Ma; she liked him there studying while she worked. He'd take her for a walk if she wanted. Saturday and Sunday he was staying home the whole time, that's all.

He came into school on the Livingston Drive side. His locker was on the first floor. He put the package inside, took his books, and slammed the locker shut. The bell sounded for first hour and Harry went to English.

Pete Overholt, the team's catcher, sat behind Harry. As they waited for the tardy bell, he nudged Harry. "Look at the women, man," he whispered. "Look at 'em, Harry!"

Harry looked. Not a girl in the class wore saddle shoes, or blue jeans, or boys' shirts with the sleeves rolled above the elbows. They were in Sunday dresses and suits, and high heels.

"The open house," Pete whispered. "All of them showing off for their mothers."

The tardy bell sounded, and Harry saw Miss Liggett look up from the desk. He wasn't called on during the hour, and afterward, on his way to study hall, he waved to George Sidley, who played third base, and to Bernie Cremmens, the right-fielder. They were both wearing sports jackets and regular shirts, and they wore ties. Harry looked down at his sweater worn over the skivvy shirt. His corduroys were clean, but they were corduroys, and around him, in the study hall, was a sea of gray flannels.

There was only one lunch period today because they had to get the cafeteria ready for the open house. Harry bought a sandwich and a glass of milk. Then he saw that half the guys on the team, sitting at the table they shared every day, were dressed up, too. He sat down in a far corner with two guys he didn't know, ate quickly, and left by the side door so he wouldn't have to pass Sidley and Cremmens and the others.

He went to his locker for his afternoon books. He had only a French class left, because, for today, school was over after fifth hour. He sat half hearing Miss Formanek, gazing out the window until his name was called sharply.

Harry turned to the teacher, his face red, feeling the eyes of the whole class on him as Miss Formanek smiled. "Let's look alive there," said Miss Formanek. "Your mother will find her way, Harry," and she told him the place in the French book.

The bell sounded at last and Harry hurried to his locker. He saw the cafeteria cleared of tables, the floor bare and chairs lining the walls. He saw the huge coffeepots steaming, and then he got his package out and threw his books into the locker and slammed it shut.

He was half running for the door when George Sidley stopped him: "Hey, where you headed for?"

Harry stared at him. "Headed for?" he asked. "Where do you think I'm headed for? Aren't you going to practice?"

"Not me," George grinned. "Coach said anybody who wanted to could be excused. Isn't your mother coming?"

"She had to go downtown," Harry said. "She had to see a doctor. She hasn't been feeling well."

"Hey, that's not good," George said, frowning. Then his face brightened. "Well, hang around anyway. Lots of fun."

Harry shook his head. He swung his left arm. "It feels like it's stiffening up," he said. "Guess I'll work out. See you."

He walked down Livingston Drive toward the baseball field. He crossed the playing area, moving toward the Quonset hut[2] that served as dressing room for the team. There was nobody inside but Art Hughes, the student manager.

"You alone, Harry?" Art asked.

"Yup."

Art turned and opened the doors of the uniform rack. "Anybody that's coming better come quick—that's all I got to say," he announced. "My mother is over at school waiting for me. I'm not keeping her waiting too long."

Harry sat down on the bench before the lockers and unwrapped the package. He pulled his sweater off and he was in his pants and skivvy shirt, standing in his socks on the cement floor when Oscar Anderson walked in. In a few minutes they were joined by Chuck Kellerman, the shortstop, and Mr. Quint, who taught chemistry and was assistant baseball coach.

Mr. Quint came over to the bench. "Look, you fellows; my wife's outside in the car. It seems there are only three of you here. You won't mind if I go back to school, will you?"

---

2. **Quonset hut** [kwon′ sit hut]: prefabricated building made of corrugated metal.

"Go ahead, Mr. Quint," Chuck said.

"I don't want to run out on you," Mr. Quint said. "It's just—well, with only three of you here, there doesn't seem to be much we could do."

"Can I get a ride back?" Art Hughes said. "You guys can check out your own uniforms today."

"Come ahead, Art," Mr. Quint said.

When they were gone, Chuck Kellerman slammed his baseball cap down on the cement floor. "All the way over here for nothing," he said.

He looked at Oscar Anderson. "How about you?" he asked. "Aren't you going to Mamma's Day and eat cookies?"

"Listen; I've got six brothers and sisters and I'm the baby," Oscar said. "My mother's tired of this stuff. I'm going home and get the grass cut, and then I got Saturday for myself."

"How about you, Harry?" Chuck asked.

"How about *you*, wise guy?" Harry said, beginning to tie his shoelaces.

Chuck got up from the bench and reached for a bat. "My mother is dead," he said, and he swung the bat desperately, as though he were hitting a line drive. Then he dropped the bat into the wicker basket. Harry watched him pick up his books and walk to the door and leave without turning to them.

"Will you lock up, Harry?" Oscar asked.

Harry saw his mother in the kitchen, and he reached for his sweater.

"Will you, Harry?"

He remembered the light under the bathroom door and the sound of water as she washed the sweatshirt and the socks.

Mother and Child Jacob Epstein, 1913, marble, 17¼" x 17" x 4", The Museum of Modern Art, New York, gift of A. Conger Goodyear

"HARRY!"

"It isn't too late yet," Harry said. He had his sweater on.

"Are you nuts?" Oscar asked.

He'd call her. He'd use the phone in the principal's office. "See you tomorrow," he said, and he ran out of the Quonset hut. Far off, walking in left-center field, Harry saw Chuck Kellerman, and then he began to run.

He could call her, he thought as he ran, and she could even take a taxi. Just this once a taxi; Pa wouldn't care. Harry knew that. She could get dressed and be up there in half an hour, and he was suddenly breathless with anticipation. He'd wait out in front of the school, on Hamilton Avenue, and help her from the cab and hold her arm and lead her to the front door. He didn't care about the bread any more, or how she talked. She was his ma.

Harry was out of the alley now, running across Livingston Drive. There were cars all around the school, almost like it was graduation night. He cut across the grass, toward the long flight of steps that led up to the second floor. He was gasping for breath when he reached the door.

He stood there a moment, then pulled the heavy door open and stepped into the deserted corridor. There was nobody on the second floor, but from the cafeteria below he heard the muted murmur of a hundred voices.

The principal's door was open. There was a phone in the outer office, an ancient upright that Miss Tibbetts, the principal's secretary, used. Harry took the receiver off the hook, set it on the desk and, holding the upright with his left hand, dialed his home number.

He grinned with excitement thinking of her when she answered. Ma didn't like phones and couldn't hear good on them, but she'd hear this. He could see her listening and her face lighting up, and then, afterward, ordering Pa around to help her, getting the gray dress ready and her coat. She never wore a hat, but let the wind command her hair, and Harry didn't care.

But she didn't answer.

Aloud he said, "Wrong number," but felt the first, tiny stabs of alarm in his chest. He dialed again, slowly now, holding the receiver to his ear, hearing the first ring, the second, the third, the eighth, the ninth, and finally, the operator's voice telling him there was no answer.

He felt the ache in his chest now, and his hands were wet. "Maybe Ma is sick or something," he thought, and he knew who had to take the blame. He dialed the 0 and asked the operator to check the number; maybe the phone was out of order. But all the time he knew it wasn't.

At last he thanked the operator and replaced the receiver and stood listlessly at the desk, wondering what to do. Now he remembered his ma helping him with fractions when he was at Crowley School. He remembered her at graduation, Ma and Pa sitting alone in the back row, and after he had his diploma, when the other guys were bringing their parents up to the front of the auditorium, he had led them out to the hall and home immediately. He remembered her walking over to the skating rink on Inverness Street, standing in a corner beside the fence to watch him skate under the floodlights, careful not to be seen, but he had seen her, all right. Seen her and kept away from that corner.

It seemed to him now, alone in the principal's office, that he had been hiding his ma all his life, and he was sick inside then, with a physical distaste in his mouth. He grimaced with self-hatred, wanting, somehow, to feel a sharper pain, to hurt himself deliberately; and he left the office and almost ran into Mr. Quint and a woman.

"Hello, Harry," Mr. Quint said. "I thought you were practicing."

"I guess not, sir."

"This is my wife, Harry," Mr. Quint said. "Harry Wojick, Emma," he said. "Harry's our first baseman."

Mrs. Quint smiled and shook hands with him.

"Mrs. Quint wants to use the phone," the assistant coach said. "She's worried about our little girl. . . . I'll see you in the cafeteria, dear," he said to his wife.

She nodded, and Mr. Quint took Harry's arm. "Let's get some of those cookies, Harry."

"I can't, sir. My mother isn't there," Harry said.

"Oh, yes. One of the boys told me. She's seeing a doctor. Hasn't been feeling well, eh?"

Harry pulled his arm away. "That's a lie," he said. "I didn't want her to come today."

Mr. Quint started laughing. He put his arm around Harry's shoulders and they walked toward the stairs. "You guys," he said, shaking his head. He looked at Harry. "Do I really look that old, Harry? An old fossil whose leg you all enjoy pulling?"

"What's the difference?" Harry thought. "What difference does it make now?" And his heart leaped as he thought of next year. There'd be an open house next year, but Ma wouldn't go. If she never went anywhere with him, he'd deserve it. If she never talked with him, he had that coming, too. "Just let me get away from Mr. Quint," he thought. Get out of here without trouble and without a fuss. But now they were in the cafeteria, in the midst of mothers and daughters and sons and teachers, and Mr. Quint was pulling him through the mob.

But they got separated and Harry was alone. He wanted to get out quickly now, away from all the laughter and gaiety. He saw Miss Formanek, the French teacher. He saw her wave at him, her finger curved beckoning him. He saw Frankie Thomas standing beside her and the woman between them. He was moving sideways, pushing through the people, and he looked up for Miss Formanek again, and then felt his heart stop. For a long time he remembered his heart stopping dead as he saw the woman in the gray dress.

He thought his legs would give away. His legs were shaking and he was shaking, and he couldn't move until someone pushed him clear and he was standing there before them. He couldn't get his hands free of sweat. He rubbed his hands up and down against the corduroys and looked at his ma.

"I was telling your mother how you were watching for her, Harry. You have a devoted son, Mrs. Wojick," the French teacher said.

Harry saw his ma smile and nod. She was beautiful.

Frankie was wearing a jacket and a tie. How come *he* was dressed up?

"And you're pinch-hitting for Frankie's mother, too," Miss Formanek said. "Frankie was my best student, Mrs. Wojick."

"Frankie's a good boy," Theresa Wojick said.

"They're all good boys," Miss Formanek said, and she excused herself and left them then.

"Ma," Harry said. He had to tell her.

She had her hand in Frankie's arm. She

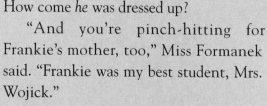

Cochiti figurine
Laurencita Herrera, pre-1930, polychrome ceramic, 6", Blair Clark photographer, Museum of New Mexico, Santa Fe

was smiling, and her hair was pulled back neat, and she was the loveliest woman he had ever seen. "Ma, I tore up the invitation," he said, and he looked right at her.

"I know," she said. "But Frankie has an invitation. We are two orphans: mother without a son, and son without a mother."

"I'm your son, Ma," Harry said, and saw Frankie slipping away, but his mother held the black-haired boy.

She was wearing white gloves and she looked right at him, and he was more afraid than he had ever been in his life.

"Ma." He held her elbows as she had held his and he didn't drop his eyes. He said, "Please, Ma, I'm your son. Please, Ma, let's get something to eat. There's my coach there. I want to introduce you to my coach."

"Yes," she said, and she smiled at him then, and for him. "Yes," she said, and put one hand through his arm and the other through Frankie's. "Introduce, please, to this coach, my little son."

NORMAN KATKOV
....

Soon after Norman Katkov's birth in Russia in 1918, his family emigrated to the United States. After attending the University of Minnesota, he served in the army during World War II, and then decided to become a professional writer. Katkov has written a number of books as well as short stories, serials, and articles. He found his niche, however, in writing movie and television scripts—including "The Virginian" and "Hawaiian Eye."

The Writer

RICHARD WILBUR

In her room at the prow of the house
Where light breaks, and the windows are tossed with linden,
My daughter is writing a story.

I pause in the stairwell, hearing
From her shut door a commotion of typewriter keys   5
Like a chain hauled over a gunwale.[1]

Young as she is, the stuff
Of her life is a great cargo, and some of it heavy:
I wish her a lucky passage.

But now it is she who pauses,   10
As if to reject my thought and its easy figure.
A stillness greatens, in which

The whole house seems to be thinking,
And then she is at it again with a bunched clamor
Of strokes, and again is silent.   15

I remember the dazed starling
Which was trapped in that very room, two years ago;
How we stole in, lifted a sash

And retreated, not to affright it;
And how for a helpless hour, through the crack of the door, 20
We watched the sleek, wild dark

And iridescent creature
Batter against the brilliance, drop like a glove
To the hard floor, or the desk-top,

1. gunwale [gun 'l]: the upper edge of the side of a ship.

And wait then, humped and bloody,   25
For the wits to try it again; and how our spirits
Rose when, suddenly sure,

It lifted off from a chair-back,
Beating a smooth course for the right window
And clearing the sill of the world.   30

It is always a matter, my darling,
Of life or death, as I had forgotten. I wish
What I wished you before, but harder.

RICHARD WILBUR

Richard Wilbur, born in New York City in 1921, grew up
in a rural area of New Jersey, where he spent a "pleasant and
somewhat solitary boyhood." He wrote his first poem, "That's
Where the Nightingales Wake," when he was eight years old.
A prize-winning poet and a professor, Richard Wilbur
has published numerous collections of his poetry, including *The Mind-Reader* from which the poem "The
Writer" is taken.

Carrying the Clouds Dionisio Blanco, acrylic and oil on canvas, 1989, 45" x 72"

NA TREE

JAMES BERRY

In the hours the hurricane stayed, its presence made everybody older. It made Mr. Bass see that not only people and animals and certain valuables were of most importance to be saved.

From its very buildup the hurricane meant to show it was merciless, unstoppable, and, with its might, changed landscapes.

All day the Jamaican sun didn't come out. Then, ten minutes before, there was a swift shower of rain that raced by and was gone like some urgent messenger-rush of wind. And again everything went back to that quiet, that unnatural quiet. It was as if trees crouched quietly in fear. As if, too, birds knew they should shut up. A thick and low black cloud had covered the sky and shadowed everywhere, and made it seem like night was coming on. And the cloud deepened. Its deepening spread more and more over the full stretch of the sea.

The doom-laden afternoon had the atmosphere of Judgment Day for everybody in all the districts about. Everybody knew the hour of disaster was near. Warnings printed in bold lettering had been put up at post offices, police stations, and schoolyard entrances and in clear view on shop walls in village squares.

Carrying children and belongings, people hurried in files and in scattered groups, headed for the big, strong, and safe community buildings. In Canerise Village, we headed for the schoolroom. Loaded with bags and cases, with bundles and lidded baskets, individuals carrying or leading an animal, parents shrieking for children to stay at their heels, we arrived there. And, looking around, anyone would think the whole of Canerise was here in this vast superbarn of a noisy chattering schoolroom.

With violent gusts and squalls the storm broke. Great rushes, huge bulky rushes, of wind struck the building in heavy repeated thuds, shaking it over and over, and carrying on.

Families were huddled together on the floor. People sang, sitting on benches, desks, anywhere there was room. Some people knelt in loud prayer. Among the refugees' noises a goat bleated, a hen fluttered or cackled, a dog whined.

Mr. Jetro Bass was sitting on a soap box. His broad back leaned on the blackboard against the wall. Mrs. Imogene Bass, largely pregnant, looked a midget beside him. Their children were sitting on the floor. The eldest boy, Gustus, sat farthest from his father. Altogether, the children's heads made seven different levels of height around the parents. Mr. Bass forced a reassuring smile. His toothbrush mustache moved about a little as he said, "The storm's bad, chil'run. Really bad. But it'll blow off. It'll spen' itself out. It'll kill itself."

Except for Gustus's, all the faces of the children turned up with subdued fear and looked at their father as he spoke.

"Das true wha' Pappy say," Mrs. Bass said. "The good Lord won' gi' we more than we can bear."

Mr. Bass looked at Gustus. He stretched fully through the sitting children and put a lumpy, blistery hand—though a huge hand—on the boy's head, almost covering it. The boy's clear brown eyes looked straight and unblinkingly into his father's face. "Wha's the matter, bwoy?" his dad asked.

He shook his head. "Nothin', Pappy."

"Wha' mek you say nothin'? I sure somet'ing bodder you, Gustus. You not a bwoy who frighten easy. Is not the hurricane wha' bodder you? Tell Pappy."

"Is nothin'."

"You're a big bwoy now. Gustus—you nearly thirteen. You strong. You very useful fo' you age. You good as mi right han'. I depen' on you. But this afternoon—earlier—in the rush, when we so well push to move befo' storm broke, you couldn' rememba a t'ing! Not one t'ing! Why so? Wha' on you mind? You harborin' t'ings from me, Gustus?"

Gustus opened his mouth to speak, but closed it again. He knew his father was proud of how well he had grown. To strengthen him, he had always given him "last milk" straight from the cow in the mornings. He was thankful. But to him his strength was only proven in the number of innings he could pitch for his cricket team. The boy's lips trembled. What's the good of tellin' when Pappy don' like cricket. He only get vex an' say it's Satan's game for idle hands! He twisted his head and looked away. "I'm harborin' nothin', Pappy."

"Gustus . . ."

At that moment a man called, "Mr. Bass!" He came up quickly. "Got a hymnbook, Mr. Bass? We want you to lead us singing."

The people were sitting with bowed heads, humming a song. As the repressed singing grew louder and louder, it sounded mournful in the room. Mr. Bass shuffled, looking around as if he wished to back out of the suggestion. But his rich voice and singing leadership were too famous. Mrs. Bass already had the hymnbook in her hand, and she pushed it at her husband. He took it and began turning the leaves as he moved toward the center of the room.

Immediately Mr. Bass was surrounded. He started with a resounding chant over the heads of everybody. "Abide[1] wid me; fast fall the eventide. . . ."[2] He joined the singing, but broke off to recite the next line. "The darkness deepen; Lord, wid me, abide. . . ." Again, before the last long-drawn note faded from the deeply stirred voices, Mr. Bass intoned musically, "When odder helpers fail, and comfo'ts flee . . ."

In this manner he fired inspiration into the singing of hymn after hymn. The congregation swelled their throats, and their mixed voices filled the room, pleading to heaven from the depths of their hearts. But the wind outside mocked viciously. It screamed. It whistled. It smashed everywhere up.

1. **abide** [ə bīd′]: stay, remain.
2. **eventide** [ē′ vən tīd]: evening.

Party Time Caribbean Urania Cummings, 1976, oil on canvas, 19" x 25",
Collection of the Cummings Family, photo by M. Lee Fatherree

Mrs. Bass had tightly closed her eyes, singing and swaying in the center of the children who nestled around her. But Gustus was by himself. He had his elbows on his knees and his hands blocking his ears. He had his own worries.

What's the good of Pappy asking all those questions when he treat him so bad? He's the only one in the family without a pair of shoes! Because he's a big boy, he don't need anyt'ing an' must do all the work. He can't stay at school in the evenings an' play cricket because there's work to do at home. He can't have no outings with the other children because he has no shoes. An' now when he was to sell his bunch of bananas an' buy shoes so he can go out with his cricket team, the hurricane is going to blow it down.

It was true: the root of the banana was his "navel string." After his birth the umbilical cord was dressed with castor oil and sprinkled with nutmeg and buried, with the banana tree planted over it for him. When he was nine days old, the nana midwife had taken him out into the open for the first time. She had held the infant proudly, and walked the twenty-five yards that separated the house from the kitchen, and at the back showed him his tree. "'Memba when you grow up," her toothless mouth had said, "it's you nable strings feedin' you tree, the same way it feed you from you mudder."

Refuse from the kitchen made the plant flourish out of all proportion. But the rich soil around it was loose. Each time the tree gave a shoot, the bunch would be too heavy for the soil to support; so it crashed to the ground, crushing the tender fruit. This time, determined that his banana must reach the market, Gustus had supported his tree with eight props. And as he watched it night and morning, it had become very close to him. Often he had seriously thought of moving his bed to its root.

Muffled cries, and the sound of blowing noses, now mixed with the singing. Delayed impact of the disaster was happening. Sobbing was everywhere. Quickly the atmosphere became sodden with the wave of weeping outbursts. Mrs. Bass's pregnant belly heaved. Her younger children were upset and cried, "Mammy, Mammy, Mammy. . . ."

Realizing that his family, too, was overwhelmed by the surrounding calamity, Mr. Bass bustled over to them. Because their respect for him bordered on fear, his presence quieted all immediately. He looked around. "Where's Gustus! Imogene . . . where's Gustus!"

"He was 'ere, Pappy," she replied, drying her eyes. "I dohn know when he get up."

Briskly Mr. Bass began combing the schoolroom to find his boy. He asked; no one had seen Gustus. He called. There was no answer. He tottered, lifting his heavy boots over heads, fighting his way to the jalousie.[3] He opened it and his eyes gleamed up and down the road, but saw nothing of the boy. In despair Mr. Bass gave one last thunderous shout: "Gustus!" Only the wind sneered.

By this time Gustus was halfway on the mile journey to their house. The lone figure in the raging wind and shin-deep road flood was tugging, snapping, and pitching branches out of his path. His shirt was fluttering from his back like a boat sail. And a leaf was fastened to his cheek. But the belligerent wind was merciless. It bellowed into his ears and drummed a deafening commotion. As he grimaced and covered his ears, he was forcefully slapped against a coconut tree trunk that lay across the road.

When his eyes opened, his round face was turned up to a festered sky. Above the tormented trees a zinc sheet[4] writhed, twisted, and somersaulted in the tempestuous flurry. Leaves of all shapes and sizes were whirling and diving like attackers around the zinc sheet. As Gustus turned to get up, a bullet drop of rain struck his temple. He shook his head, held grimly to the tree trunk, and struggled to his feet.

Where the road was clear, he edged along the bank. Once, when the wind staggered him, he recovered with his legs wide apart. Angrily he stretched out his hands with clenched fists and shouted, "I almos' hol' you that time . . . come solid like that again an' we fight like man an' man!"

When Gustus approached the river he had to cross, it was flooded and blocked beyond recognition. Pressing his chest against the gritty road bank, the boy closed his weary eyes on the brink of the spating river. The wrecked footbridge had become the harboring fort for all the debris, branches, and monstrous tree trunks which the river swept along its course. The river was still swelling. More accumulation arrived each moment, ramming and pressing the bridge. Under pressure it was cracking and shifting minutely toward a turbulent forty-foot fall.

---

3. **jalousie** [jalʹ ə zē]: a window shade or shutter that keeps out sun and rain.
4. **zinc sheet**: a sheet of blue-white metal; one of its uses is as roofing material.

Gustus had seen it! A feeling of dismay paralyzed him, reminding him of his foolish venture. He scraped his cheek on the bank looking back. But how can he go back? He has no strength to go back. His house is nearer than the school. An' Pappy will only strap him for nothin' . . . for nothin' . . . no shoes, nothin' when the hurricane is gone.

With trembling fingers he tied up the remnants of his shirt. He made a bold step and the wind half lifted him, ducking him in the muddy flood. He sank to his neck. Floating leaves, sticks, coconut husks, dead ratbats, and all manner of feathered creatures and refuse surrounded him. Forest vines under the water entangled him. But he struggled desperately until he clung to the laden bridge and climbed up among leafless branches.

His legs were bruised and bore deep scratches, but steadily he moved up on the slimy pile. He felt like a man at sea, in the heart of a storm, going up the mast of a ship. He rested his feet on a smooth log that stuck to the water-splashed heap like a black torso. As he strained up for another grip, the torso came to life and leaped from under his feet. Swiftly sliding down, he grimly clutched some brambles.

The urgency of getting across became more frightening, and he gritted his teeth and dug his toes into the debris, climbing with maddened determination. But a hard gust of wind slammed the wreck, pinning him like a motionless lizard. For a minute the boy was stuck there, panting, swelling his naked ribs.

He stirred again and reached the top. He was sliding over a breadfruit limb when a flutter startled him. As he looked and saw the clean-head crow and glassy-eyed owl close together, there was a powerful jolt. Gustus flung himself into the air and fell in the expanding water on the other side. When he surfaced, the river had dumped the entire wreckage into the gurgling gully. For once the wind helped. It blew him to land.

Gustus was in a daze when he reached his house. Mud and rotten leaves covered his head and face, and blood caked around a gash on his chin. He bent down, shielding himself behind a tree stump whose white heart was a needly splinter, murdered by the wind.

He could hardly recognize his yard. The terrorized trees that stood were writhing in turmoil. Their thatched house had collapsed like an open umbrella that was given a heavy blow. He looked the other way and whispered, "Is still there! That's a miracle. . . . That's a miracle."

Dodging the wind, he staggered from tree to tree until he got to his own tormented banana tree. Gustus hugged the tree. "My nable string!" he cried. "My nable string! I know you would stan' up to it, I know you would."

The bones of the tree's stalky leaves were broken, and the wind lifted them and harrassed them. And over Gustus's head the heavy fruit swayed and swayed. The props held the tree, but they were squeaking and slipping. And around the plant the roots stretched and trembled, gradually surfacing under loose earth.

With the rags of his wet shirt flying off his back, Gustus was down busily on his knees, bracing, pushing, tightening the props. One by one he was adjusting them until a heavy rush of wind knocked him to the ground. A prop fell on him, but he scrambled to his feet and looked up at the thirteen-hand bunch of bananas. "My good tree," he bawled, "hol' you fruit. . . . Keep it to you heart like a mudder savin' her baby! Don't let the wicked wind t'row you to the groun' . . . even if it t'row me to the groun'. I will not leave you."

But several attempts to replace the prop were futile. The force of the wind against his weight was too much for him. He thought of a rope to lash the tree to anything, but it was difficult to make his way into the kitchen, which, separate from the house, was still standing. The invisible hand of the wind tugged, pushed, and forcefully restrained him. He got down and crawled on his belly into the earth-floor kitchen. As he showed himself with the rope, the wind tossed him, like washing on the line, against his tree.

The boy was hurt! He looked crucified against the tree. The spike of the wind was slightly withdrawn. He fell, folded on the ground. He lay there unconscious. And the wind had no mercy for him. It shoved him, poked him, and molested his clothes like muddy newspaper against the tree.

Hurricane Julio Larraz, 1985, oil on canvas, 48 1/2" x 79"

As darkness began to move in rapidly, the wind grew more vicious and surged a mighty gust that struck the resisting kitchen. It was heaved to the ground in a rubbled pile. The brave wooden hut had been shielding the banana tree, but in its death fall missed it by inches. The wind charged again and the soft tree gurgled—the fruit was torn from it and plunged to the ground.

The wind was less fierce when Mr. Bass and a searching party arrived with lanterns. Because the bridge was washed away, the hazardous roundabout journey had badly impeded them.

Talks about safety were mockery to the anxious father. Relentlessly he searched. In the darkness his great voice echoed everywhere, calling for his boy. He was wrenching and ripping through the house wreckage

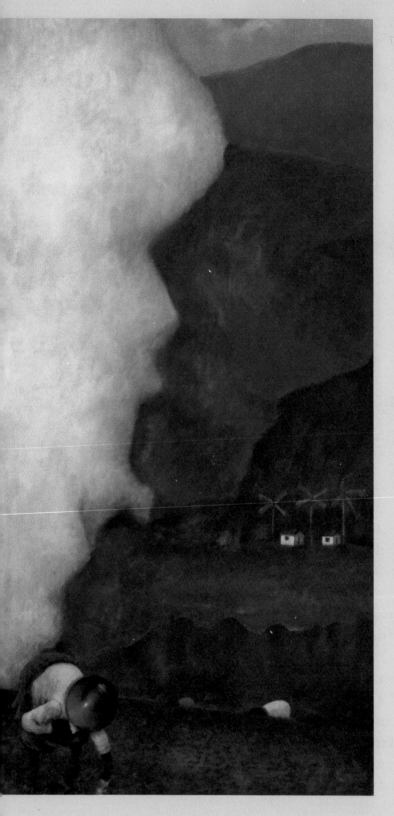

Tropical Landscape Dionisio Blanco,
oil on canvas, 1990, 24 1/2"x 50"

when suddenly he vaguely remembered how the boy had
been fussing with the banana
tree. Desperate, the man struggled from the ruins, flagging the
lantern he carried.

The flickering light above
his head showed Mr. Bass the
forlorn and pitiful banana tree.
There it stood, shivering and
twitching like a propped-up
man with lacerated throat and
dismembered head. Half of the
damaged fruit rested on Gustus.
The father hesitated. But when
he saw a feeble wink of the
boy's eyelids, he flung himself
to the ground. His bristly chin
rubbed the child's face while
his unsteady hand ran all over
his body. "Mi bwoy!" he murmured. "Mi hurricane bwoy!
The Good Lord save you. . . .
Why you do this? Why you do
this?"

"I did want buy mi shoes,
Pappy. I . . . I can't go anywhere
'cause I have no shoes. . . . I didn'

go to school outing at the factory. I didn' go to Government House. I didn' go to Ol' Fort in town."

Mr. Bass sank into the dirt and stripped himself of his heavy boots. He was about to lace them to the boy's feet when the onlooking men prevented him. He tied the boots together and threw them over his shoulder.

Gustus's broken arm was strapped to his side as they carried him away. Mr. Bass stroked his head and asked how he felt. Only then grief swelled inside him and he wept.

JAMES BERRY

James Berry was born in 1925 in Jamaica and moved to England when he was twenty-three years old. While leading writing workshops for children in the British school system, he discovered there were very few books that related to his childhood in Jamaica. "In the Caribbean, we were the last outpost of the British Empire," he noted. "No one had reported our stories or the way we saw things." Berry began to write to fill the gap with stories "straight out of my own childhood."

Berry writes both poetry and prose. He feels that more people of all cultures now accept and enjoy the ethnic differences among them. Two notable books by James Berry are *When I Dance: Poems* and *A Thief in the House and Other Stories.*

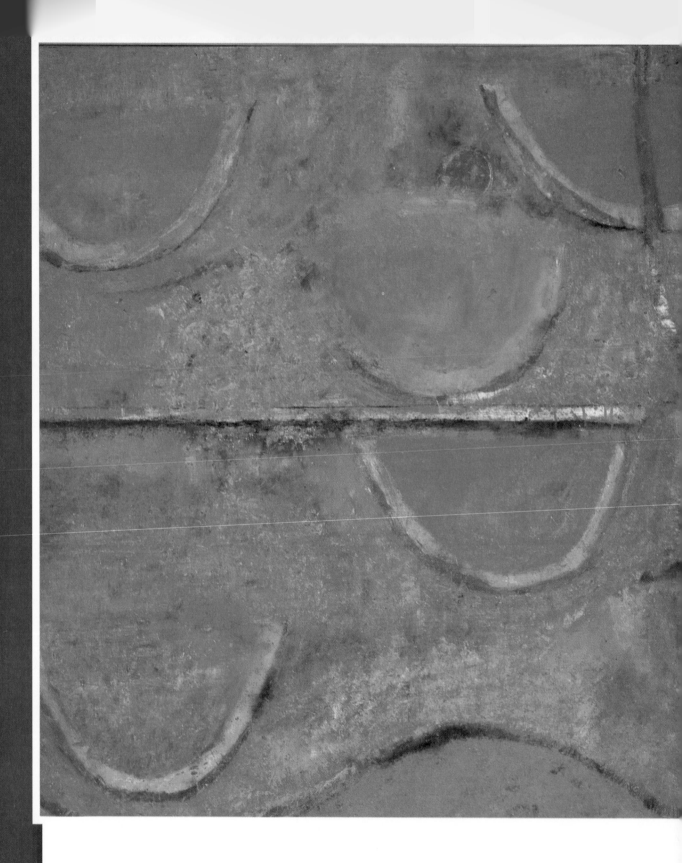

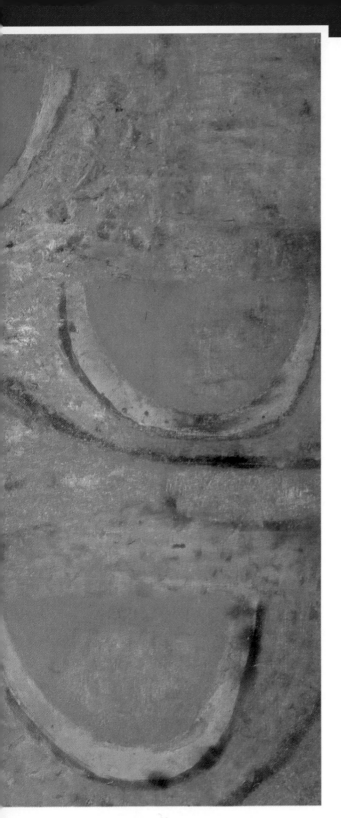

Sandías Rufino Tamayo, 1968,
oil on canvas, 52 x 78",
Collection: Museo Tamayo/INBA

The Taste of Melon

BORDEN DEAL

When I think of the summer I was sixteen, a lot of things come crowding in to be thought about. We had moved just the year before, and sixteen is still young enough that the bunch makes a difference. I had a bunch, all right, but they weren't sure of me yet. I didn't know why. Maybe because I'd lived in town, and my father still worked there instead of farming, like the other fathers did. The boys I knew, even Freddy Gray and J. D., still kept a small distance between us.

Then there was Willadean Wills. I hadn't been much interested in girls before. But I had to admit to myself that I was interested in Willadean. She was my age, nearly as tall as I, and up till the year before, Freddy Gray told me, she had been good at playing Gully Keeper and Ante-Over. But she didn't play such games this year. She was tall and slender, and Freddy Gray and J. D. and I had several discussions about the way she walked. I maintained she was putting it on, but J. D. claimed she couldn't help it. Freddy Gray remarked that she hadn't walked that way last year. He said she'd walked like any other human being. So then I said, put on or not, I liked the way she walked, and then there was a large silence.

It wasn't a comfortable silence, because of Mr. Wills, Willadean's father. We were all afraid of Mr. Wills.

Mr. Wills was a big man. He had bright, fierce eyes under heavy brows and, when he looked down at you, you just withered. The idea of having him angry at one of us was enough to shrivel the soul. All that summer Willadean walked up and down the high road or sat on their front porch in a rocking chair, her dress flared out around her, and not one of us dared do more than say good morning to her.

Mr. Wills was the best farmer in the community. My father said he could drive a stick into the ground and grow a tree out of it. But it wasn't an easy thing with him; Mr. Wills fought the earth when he worked it. When he plowed his fields, you could hear him yelling for a mile. It was as though he dared the earth not to yield him its sustenance.

Above all, Mr. Wills could raise watermelons. Now, watermelons are curious things. Some men can send off for the best watermelon seed, they can plant it in the best ground they own, they can hoe it and tend it with the greatest of care, and they can't raise a melon bigger than your two fists. Other men, like Mr. Wills, can throw seed on the ground, scuff dirt over it, walk off, and leave it and have a crop of the prettiest, biggest melons you ever saw.

Mr. Wills always planted the little field directly behind his barn to watermelons. It ran from the barn to the creek, a good piece of land with just the right sandy soil for melon raising. It seemed as though the melons just bulged up out of the ground for him.

But they were Mr. Wills's melons; he didn't have any idea of sharing them with the boys of the neighborhood. He was fiercer about his melons than anything else; if you just happened to walk close to his melon patch, you'd see Mr. Wills standing and watching you with a glower on his face. And likely as not he'd have his gun under his arm.

Everybody expected to lose a certain quantity of their watermelons to terrapins[1] and a certain quantity to boys. It wasn't considered stealing to sneak into a man's melon patch and judiciously borrow a sample of his raising. You might get a load of salt in the seat of your pants if you were seen, but that was part of the game. You'd be looked down on only if you got malicious and stamped a lot of melons into the ground while you were about it. But Mr. Wills didn't think that way.

That summer I was sixteen Mr. Wills raised the greatest watermelon ever seen in the country. It grew in the very middle of his patch, three times as big as any melon anybody had ever seen. Men came from miles around to look at it. Mr. Wills wouldn't let them go into the melon patch. They had to stand around the edge.

Just like all other daredevil boys in that county, I guess Freddy Gray and J. D. and I had talked idly about stealing that giant watermelon. But we all knew that it was just talk. Not only were we afraid of Mr. Wills and his rages but we knew that Mr. Wills sat in the hayloft window of his barn every night with his shotgun, guarding the melon. It was his seed melon.[2] He meant to plant next year's crop out of that great one, and maybe raise a whole field of them. Mr. Wills was in a frenzy of fear that somebody would steal it. Why, he would rather you stole Willadean than his melon. At least, he didn't guard Willadean with his shotgun.

Every night I could sit on our front porch and see Mr. Wills sitting up there in the window of his hayloft, looking fiercely out over his melon patch. I'd sit there by the hour and watch him, the shotgun cradled in his arm, and feel the tremors of fear and excitement chasing up and down my spine.

"Look at him," my father would say. "Scared to death somebody will steal his seed melon. Wouldn't anybody steal a man's seed melon."

"He ought to be in the house taking care of that wife of his," my mother would say tartly. "She's been poorly all year."

1. **terrapins** [ter′ ə pinz]: edible North American turtles that live in fresh water or tidewater.
2. **seed melon**: a melon whose seeds are planted for the next crop.

You hardly ever saw Mrs. Wills. She was a wraith of a woman, pale as a butter bean. Sometimes she would sit for an hour or two on their porch in the cool of the day. They didn't visit back and forth with anybody, though.

"There's Willadean," my father would say mildly.

My mother would make a funny kind of sound that meant disgust. "He cares more about that seed melon than he does his wife," she'd say. "I wish somebody *would* steal it. Maybe then—"

"Helen," my father would say, chiding, "you shouldn't even think of such a thing."

About the time the great watermelon was due to come ripe, there was a night of a full moon. J. D. and Freddy Gray and I had decided we'd go swimming in the creek, so I left the house when the moon rose and went to meet them. The moon floated up into the sky and made everything almost as bright as day, but at the same time softer and gentler than ever daylight could be. It was the kind of night when you feel as though you can do anything in the world, even boldly ask Willadean Wills for a date. On a night like that, you couldn't help feel she'd gladly accept.

"Boy, what a moon!" J. D. said when I met Freddy Gray and him.

"Wouldn't you like to take old Willadean out on a night like this?" Freddy said.

We scoffed at him, but secretly in our hearts we knew how he felt. We were getting old enough to think that that sort of thing might be a lot more fun than going swimming in the moonlight.

As I said before, I was a part of the bunch. J. D. and Freddy Gray were my good friends. But because I was still new, there were certain things and certain feelings where I was left out. This was one of them; they were afraid, because I was more of a stranger to Willadean, that she might like the idea of dating me better than she did either of them. This was all way down under the surface, because none of us had admitted to ourselves that we wanted to be Willadean's boy friend. But far down though it was, I could feel it, and they could feel it.

"I wish I had a newspaper," I said then. "I'll bet you could read it in this moonlight."

We had reached the swimming hole in the creek, and we began shucking off our clothes. We were all excited by the moonlight, yelling at one another and rushing to be

American Still Life anonymous, c. 1870, oil on canvas, Private Collection,
courtesy Samuel Herrup Antiques

first into the water. Freddy Gray made it first, J.D. and I catapulting in right behind him. The water was cold, and the shock of it struck a chill into us. But we got rid of it by a water fight and then we were all right.

We climbed out finally, to rest, and sat on the bank. That big old moon sailed serenely overhead, climbing higher into the sky, and we lay on our backs to look up at it.

"Old Man Wills won't have to worry about anybody stealing his melon tonight, anyway," Freddy Gray said. "Wouldn't anybody dare try it, bright as day like it is."

"He's not taking any chances," J. D. said. "I saw him sitting up in that hayloft when I came by, his shotgun loaded with buckshot. That melon is as safe as it would be in the First National Bank."

"Shucks," I said in a scoffing voice, "he ain't got buckshot in that gun. He's just got a load of salt, like anybody else guarding a watermelon patch."

Freddy Gray sat upright, looking at me. "Don't kid yourself, son," he said loftily. "He told my daddy that he had it loaded with double-ought buckshot."[3]

"Why," I said, "that would kill a man."

"That's what he's got in mind," Freddy Gray said, "if anybody goes after that seed melon."

It disturbed me more than it should have. After all, I'd never had it in mind to try for the melon, had I? "I don't be-lieve it," I said flatly. "He wouldn't kill anybody over a watermelon. Even a seed melon like that one."

"Old Man Wills would," J. D. said.

Freddy Gray was still watching me. "What's got you into such a swivet?"

he said. "You weren't planning on going after that melon yourself?"

"Well, yes," I said. "As a matter of fact, I was."

There was a moment of respect-ful silence. Even from me. I hadn't known I was going to say those words. To this day I don't know why I said them. It was all mixed up with Willadean and the rumor of Mr. Wills having his gun loaded with double-ought buckshot and the boys still thinking of me as an outsider. It surged up out of me—not the idea of making my name for years to come by such a deed, but the feeling that there was a rightness in defying the world and Mr. Wills.

Mixed up with it all there came into my mouth the taste of water-melon. I could taste the sweet red juices oozing over my tongue, feel the delicate threaded redness of the heart as I squeezed the juices out of it.

I stood up. "As a matter of fact," I said, "I'm going after it right now."

"Wait a minute," J. D. said in alarm. "You can't do it on a moon-light night like this. It's 200 yards from the creek bank to that melon. He'll see you for sure."

"Yeah," Freddy Gray said, "wait until a dark night. Wait until—"

3. **double-ought buckshot** [dubl ôt buk′shot]: small lead ball or shot fired from a shotgun; double-ought (00) refers to the size of the shot.

"Anybody could steal it on a dark night," I said scornfully. "I'm going to take it right out from under his nose. Tonight."

I began putting on my clothes. My heart was thudding in my chest. I didn't taste watermelon any more; I tasted fear. But it was too late to stop now. Besides, I didn't want to stop.

We dressed silently, and I led the way up the creek bank. We came opposite the watermelon patch and ducked down the bank. We pushed through the willows on the other side and looked toward the barn. We could see Mr. Wills very plainly. The gun was cradled in his arms, glinting from the moonlight.

"You'll never make it," J. D. said in a quiet, fateful voice. "He'll see you before you're six steps away from the creek."

"You don't think I mean to walk, do you?" I said.

I pushed myself out away from them, on my belly in the grass that grew up around the watermelon hills. I was absolutely flat, closer to the earth than I thought it was possible to get. I looked back once, to see their white faces watching me out of the willows.

I went on, stopping once in a while to look cautiously up toward the barn. He was still there, still quiet. I met a terrapin taking a bite

out of a small melon. Terrapins love watermelon, better than boys do. I touched him on the shell and whispered, "Hello, brother," but he didn't acknowledge my greeting. He just drew into his shell. I went on, wishing I were equipped like a terrapin for the job, outside as well as inside.

It seemed to take forever to reach the great melon in the middle of the field. With every move, I expected Mr. Wills to see me. Fortunately the grass was high enough to cover me. At last the melon loomed up before me, deep green in the moonlight, and I gasped at the size of it. I'd never seen it so close.

I lay still for a moment, panting. I didn't have the faintest idea how to get it out of the field. Even if I'd stood up, I couldn't have lifted it by myself. A melon is the slipperiest, most cumbersome object in the world. And this was the largest I'd ever seen. It was not a long melon, but a fat round one. Besides, I didn't dare stand up.

For five minutes I didn't move. I lay there, my nostrils breathing up the smell of the earth and the musty smell of the watermelon vines, and I wondered why I was out here in the middle of all that moonlight on such a venture. There was more to it than just bravado. I was proving something to

The Taste of Melon   73

myself—and to Mr. Wills and Willadean.

I thought of a tempting way out then. I would carve my name into the deep greenness of the melon. Mr. Wills would see it the next morning when he inspected the melon, and he would know that I could have stolen it if I'd wanted to. But no—crawling to the melon wasn't the same thing as actually taking it.

I reached one hand around the melon and found the stem. I broke the tough stem off close against the smooth roundness, and I was committed. I looked toward the barn again. All quiet. I saw Mr. Wills stretch and yawn, and his teeth glistened; the moon was that bright and I was that close.

I struggled around behind the melon and shoved at it. It rolled over sluggishly, and I pushed it again. It was hard work, pushing it down the trough my body had made through the grass. Dust rose up around me, and I wanted to sneeze. My spine was crawling, expecting a shot. Surely he'd see that the melon was gone out of its accustomed space.

It took about a hundred years to push that melon out of the field. I say that advisedly because I felt that

much older when I finally reached the edge. With the last of my strength I shoved it into the willows and collapsed. I was still lying on the edge of the field.

"Come on," Freddy Gray said, his voice pleading. "He's—"

I couldn't move. I turned my head. He was standing up to stretch and yawn to his content, and then he sat down again. By then I was rested enough to move again. I snaked into the willows, and they grabbed me.

"You did it!" they said. "By golly, you did it!"

There was no time to bask in their admiration and respect. "Let's get it on out of here," I said. "We're not safe yet."

We struggled the melon across the creek and up the bank. We started toward the swimming hole. It took all three of us to carry it, and it was hard to get a grip. J. D. and Freddy Gray carried the ends, while I walked behind the melon, grasping the middle. We stumbled and thrashed[4] in our hurry, and we nearly dropped it three or four times. It was the most difficult object I'd ever tried to carry in my life.

At last we reached the swimming hole and sank down, panting. But not for long; the excitement was too

4. **thrashed** [thrashed]: moved violently.

strong in us. Freddy Gray reached out a hand and patted the great melon.

"By golly," he said, "there it is. All ours."

"Let's bust it and eat it before somebody comes," J. D. said.

"Wait a minute," I said. "This isn't just any old melon. This is old man Will's seed melon, and it deserves more respect than to be busted open with a fist. I'm going to cut it."

I took out my pocketknife and looked at it. It was small, and the melon was big. We really needed a butcher knife. But when the little knife penetrated the thick green rind, the melon split of itself, perfectly down the middle. There was a ragged, silken, tearing sound, and it lay open before us.

The heart meat, glistening with sweet moisture, was grained with white sugar specks. I tugged at it with two fingers, and a great chunk of the meat came free. I put it into my mouth and closed my eyes. The melon was still warm from the day's sun. Just as in my anticipation, I felt the juice trickle into my throat, sweet and seizing. I had never tasted watermelon so delicious.

The two boys were watching me savor the first bite. I opened my eyes. "Dive in," I said graciously. "Help yourselves."

We gorged ourselves until we were heavy. Even then, we had still only eaten the heart meat, leaving untouched more than we had consumed. We gazed with sated eyes at the leftover melon, still good meat peopled with a multitude of black seeds.

"What are we going to do with it?" I said.

"There's nothing we can do," J. D. said. "I can just see us taking a piece of this melon home for the folks."

"It's eat it or leave it," Freddy Gray said.

We were depressed suddenly. It was such a waste, after all the struggle and danger, that we could not eat every bite. I stood up, not looking at the two boys, not looking at the melon.

"Well," I said. "I guess I'd better get home."

"But what about this?" J. D. said, motioning toward the melon.

I kicked half the melon, splitting it in three parts. I stamped one of the chunks under my foot. Then I set methodically to work, destroying the rest of the melon. The boys watched me silently until I picked up a chunk of rind and threw it at them. Then they swept into the destruction also, and we were laughing again. When we stopped, only the battered rinds

The Taste of Melon   **75**

Cherry Stand Wayne Thiebaud, 1963, oil on canvas, The Collection of Mr. and Mrs. Graham Gund, Cambridge, MA

were left, the meat muddied on the ground, the seed scattered.

We stood silent, looking at one another. "There was nothing else to do," I said. They nodded solemnly.

But the depression went with us toward home. I did not feel triumph or victory, as I had expected, though I knew that tonight's action had brought me closer to my friends than I had ever been before.

"Where have you been?" my

father asked as I stepped up on the porch. He was sitting in his rocker.

"Swimming," I said.

I looked toward Mr. Wills's barn. The moon was still high and bright, but I could not see him. My breath caught in my throat when I saw him in the field, walking toward the middle. I stood stiffly, watching him. He reached the place where the melon should have been. I saw him hesitate, looking around; then he bent, and I knew he was looking at the depression in the earth where the melon had lain. He straightened, a great, strangled cry tearing out of his throat. It chilled me deep down and all the way through, like the cry of a wild animal.

My father, startled by the sound, jerked himself out of the chair. He turned in time to see Mr. Wills lift the shotgun over his head and hurl it from him, his voice crying out again in a terrible, surging yell of pain and anger.

"Lord, what's the matter?" my father said.

Mr. Wills was tearing up and down the melon patch, and I was puzzled by his actions. Then I saw; he was destroying every melon in the patch. He was breaking them open with his feet, silent now, concentrating on his frantic destruction. I was horrified by the awful sight, and my stomach moved sickly.

My father stood for a moment, watching Mr. Wills; then he jumped off the porch and ran toward him. I followed him. I saw Mrs. Wills and Willadean huddled together in the kitchen doorway. My father ran into the melon patch and caught Mr. Wills by the arm.

"What's come over you?" he said. "What's the matter, man?"

Mr. Wills struck his grip away. "They've stolen my seed melon," he yelled. "They took it right out from under me."

My father grabbed him with both arms. He was a brave man, for he was smaller than Mr. Wills, and Mr. Wills looked insane with anger, his teeth gripped over his lower lip, his eyes gleaming furiously. Mr. Wills shoved my father away, and struck him with his fist. My father went down into the dirt. Mr. Wills didn't seem to notice. He went back to his task of destruction, raging up and down the field, stamping melons large and small.

My father got up and began to chase him. But he didn't have a chance. Every time he got close, Mr. Wills would sweep his great arm and knock him away again. At last Mr. Wills stopped of his own accord. He was standing on the place where the great melon had grown. His chest

The Taste of Melon   77

was heaving with great sobs of breath. He gazed about him at the destruction he had wrought, but I don't think that he saw it.

"They stole my seed melon," he said. His voice was quieter now than I had ever heard it. I had not believed such quietness was in him. "They got it away, and now it's gone."

I saw that tears stood on his cheeks, and I couldn't look at him any more. I'd never seen a grown man cry, crying in such strength.

"I had two plans for that melon," he told my father. "Mrs. Wills has been poorly all the spring, and she dearly loves the taste of melon. It was her melon for eating, and my melon for planting. She would eat the meat, and next spring I would plant the seeds for the greatest melon crop in the world. Every day she would ask me if the great seed melon was ready yet."

I looked toward the house. I saw the two women, the mother and the daughter, standing there. I couldn't bear any more. I fled out of the field toward the sanctuary of my house. I ran past my mother, standing on the porch, and went into my room.

I didn't sleep that night. I heard my father come in, heard the low-voiced conversation with my mother, heard them go to bed. I lay wide-eyed and watched the moon through the window as it slid slowly down the sky and at last brought welcome darkness into the world.

I don't know all the things I thought that night. Mostly it was about the terrible thing I had committed so lightly, out of pride and out of being sixteen years old and out of wanting to challenge the older man, the man with the beautiful daughter.

That was the worst of all, that I had done it so lightly, with so little thought of its meaning. In that country and in that time, watermelon stealing was not a crime. It was tolerated, laughed about. The men told great tales of their own watermelon-stealing days, how they'd been set on by dogs and peppered with salt-loaded shotgun shells. Watermelon raiding was a game, a ritual of defiance and rebellion by young males. I could remember my own father saying, "No melon tastes as sweet as a stolen one," and my mother laughing and agreeing.

But stealing this great seed melon from a man like Mr. Wills lay outside the safe magic of the tacit understanding between man and boy. And I knew that it was up to me, at whatever risk, to repair as well as I could the damage I had done.

When it was daylight I rose from my bed and went out into the fresh world. It would be hot later on; but now the air was dew-cool and fragrant. I had found a paper sack in the kitchen, and I carried it in my hand as I walked toward the swimming hole. I stopped there and looked down at the wanton waste we had made of the part of the melon we had not been able to eat. It looked as though Mr. Wills had been stamping here too.

I kneeled down on the ground, opened the paper sack and began picking up the black seeds. They were scattered thickly, still stringy with watermelon pulp, and soon my hands were greasy with them. I kept on doggedly, searching out every seed I could find, until at the end I had to crawl over the ground, seeking for the last ones.

They nearly filled the paper sack. I went back to the house. By the time I reached it, the sun and my father had risen. He was standing on the porch.

"What happened to you last night?" he said. "Did you get so frightened you had to run home? It was frightening to watch him, I'll admit that."

"Father," I said, "I've got to go talk to Mr. Wills. Right now. I wish you would come with me."

He stopped, watching me. "What's the matter?" he said. "Did you steal that seed melon of his?"

"Will you come with me?" I said.

His face was dark and thoughtful. "Why do you want me?"

"Because I'm afraid he'll shoot me," I said. My voice didn't tremble much, but I couldn't keep it all out.

"Then why are you going?" he said.

"Because I've got to," I said.

My father watched me for a moment. "Yes," he said quietly, "I guess you do." He came down the steps and stood beside me. "I'll go with you," he said.

We walked the short distance between our house and his. Though it was so near, I had never been in his yard before. I felt my legs trembling as I went up the brick walk and stood at the bottom of the steps, the paper sack in my hand. I knocked on the porch floor, and Willadean came to the screen door.

I did not look at her. "I want to talk to your father."

She stared at me for a moment,

then she disappeared. In a moment Mr. Wills appeared in the doorway. His face was marked by the night, his cheeks sunken, his mouth bitten in. He stared at me absent-mindedly, as though I were only a speck in his thinking.

"What do you want, boy?" he said.

I felt my teeth grit against the words I had to say. I held out the paper bag. "Mr. Wills," I said, "here are the seeds from your seed melon. That's all I could bring back."

I could feel my father standing quietly behind me. Willadean was standing in the doorway, watching. I couldn't take my eyes away from Mr. Wills's face.

"Did you steal it?"

"Yes, sir," I said.

He advanced to the edge of the porch. The shotgun was standing near the door, and I expected him to reach for it. Instead he came toward me, a great, powerful man, and leaned down to me.

Watermelon in Blue-bordered Dish
anonymous, c. 1840, Abby Aldrich Rockefeller Folk Art Center, Williamsburg, VA

"Why did you steal it?" he said.

"I don't know," I said.

"Didn't you know it was my seed-melon?"

"Yes, sir," I said. "I knew it."

He straightened up again and

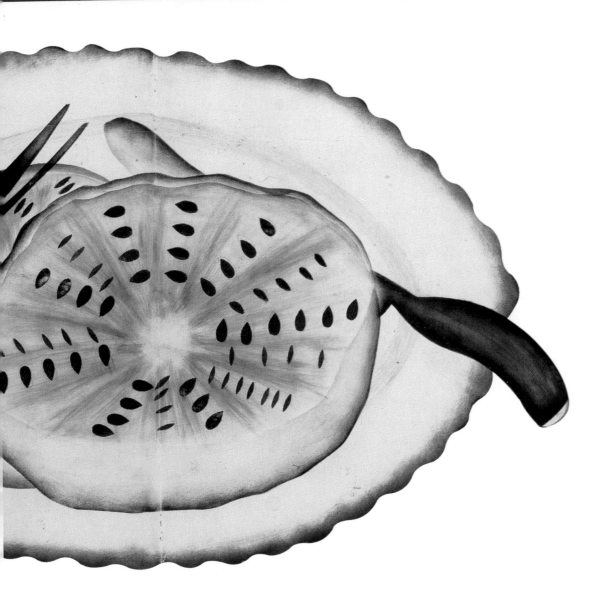

his eyes were beginning to gleam. I wanted to run, but I couldn't move.

"And my sick wife hungered for the taste of that melon," he said. "Not for herself, like I thought. But to invite the whole neighborhood in for a slice of it. She knew I wouldn't ever think of anything like that myself. She hungered for that."

I hung my head. "I'm sorry," I said.

He stopped still then, watching me. "So you brought me the seeds," he said softly. "That's not much, boy."

I lifted my head. "It was all I could think to do," I said. "The melon is gone. But the seeds are next year. That's why I brought them to you."

"But you ruined this year," he said.

"Yes, sir," I said. "I ruined this year."

I couldn't look at him any more. I looked at Willadean standing behind him. Her eyes were a puzzle, watching me, and I couldn't tell what she was thinking or feeling.

"I'm about as ashamed of myself last night as you are of yourself," Mr. Wills said. He frowned at me with his heavy brows. "You ruined the half of it, and I ruined the other. We're both to blame, boy. Both to blame."

It seemed there ought to be something more for me to say. I searched for it in my mind and discovered only the thought that I had found this morning in the gray light of dawning.

"The seeds are next year," I said. I looked at him humbly. "I'll help you plant them, Mr. Wills. I'll work hard."

Mr. Wills looked at my father for the first time. There was a small, hard smile on his face; his eyes didn't look as fierce as before.

"A man with a big farm like mine needs a son," he said. "But Willadean here was all the good Lord saw fit to give me. Sam, I do wish I had me a boy like that."

He came close to me then, put his hand on my shoulder. "We can't do anything about this year," he said. "But we'll grow next year, won't we? We'll grow it together."

"Yes, sir," I said.

I looked past him at Willadean, and her eyes were smiling too. I felt my heart give a great thump in my chest.

"And you don't have to offer the biggest melon in the world to get folks to come visiting," I blurted. "Why, I'll set on the porch with Willadean any time."

Mr. Wills and my father burst out laughing. Willadean was blushing red in the face. But somehow she didn't look mad. Flustered, I began to beat a retreat toward the gate. Then I stopped, and looked back at Mr. Wills. I couldn't leave yet.

"Can I ask you one thing, Mr. Wills?" I said.

He stopped laughing, and there was no fierceness in his voice. "Anything you want to, boy," he said.

"Well, I just wanted to know," I said. "Was there double-ought buckshot in that gun?"

He reached around and picked up the gun. He unbreeched it and took out a shell. He broke the shell in his strong fingers and poured the white salt out into his palm.

"You see?" he said.

"Yes, sir," I said, taking a deep breath. "I see."

I went on then, and the next year started that very day.

BORDEN DEAL

Borden Deal was born in Pontotoc, Mississippi, in 1922. When he was a young man, at the end of the Depression, he "beat around the country," working for a circus, on a showboat, and in the Civilian Conservation Corps. He started writing while working in Washington, D.C., for the United States Department of Labor. He did not publish anything, however, until he left the Navy and entered the University of Alabama.

Deal did graduate work in Mexico and then supported his writing with a series of odd jobs. A popular story that reflects his southern background is "Antaeus," about a farm boy transplanted to a city.

THE
Medicine
Bag

VIRGINIA DRIVING HAWK SNEVE

Detail from
Medicine Pouch,
Sioux

My kid sister Cheryl and I always bragged about our Sioux[1] grandpa, Joe Iron Shell. Our friends, who had always lived in the city and only knew about Indians from movies and TV, were impressed by our stories. Maybe we exaggerated and made Grandpa and the reservation sound glamorous, but when we'd return home to Iowa after our yearly summer visit to Grandpa, we always had some exciting tale to tell.

We always had some authentic Sioux article to show our listeners. One year Cheryl had new moccasins that Grandpa had made. On another visit he gave me a small, round, flat, rawhide drum that was decorated with a

1. **Sioux** [sü]: member of a Native American people of the northern United States and southern Canada.

Brulé Sioux with Travois
John Anderson, c. 1900, black
and white photo, Nebraska
State Historical Society

painting of a warrior riding a horse. He taught me a real Sioux chant to sing while I beat the drum with a leather-covered stick that had a feather on the end. Man, that really made an impression.

We never showed our friends Grandpa's picture. Not that we were ashamed of him, but because we knew that the glamorous tales we told didn't go with the real thing. Our friends would have laughed at the picture, because Grandpa wasn't tall and stately like TV Indians. His hair wasn't in braids, but hung in stringy, gray strands on his neck, and he was old. He was our great-grandfather, and he didn't live in a tipi, but all by himself in a part log, part tar-paper shack on the Rosebud Reservation in South Dakota. So when Grandpa came to visit us, I was so ashamed and embarrassed I could've died.

There are a lot of yippy poodles and other fancy little dogs in our neighborhood, but they usually barked singly at the mailman from the safety of their own yards. Now it sounded as if a whole pack of mutts were barking together in one place.

I got up and walked to the curb to see what the commotion was. About a block away I saw a crowd of little kids yelling, with the dogs yipping and growling around someone who was walking down the middle of the street.

I watched the group as it slowly came closer and saw that in the center of the strange procession was a man wearing a tall black hat. He'd pause now and then to peer at something in his hand and then at the houses on either side of the street. I felt cold and hot at the same time as I recognized the man. "Oh, no!" I whispered. "It's Grandpa!"

I stood on the curb, unable to move even though I wanted to run and hide. Then I got mad when I saw how the yippy dogs were growling and nipping at the old man's baggy pant legs and how wearily he poked them away with his cane. "Stupid mutts," I said as I ran to rescue Grandpa.

When I kicked and hollered at the dogs to get away, they put their tails between their legs and scattered. The kids ran to the curb where they watched me and the old man.

"Grandpa," I said and felt pretty dumb when my voice cracked. I reached for his beat-up old tin suitcase, which was tied shut with a rope. But he set it down right in the street and shook my hand.

"*Hau, Takoza,*[2] Grandchild," he greeted me formally in Sioux.

All I could do was stand there with the whole neighborhood watching and shake the hand of the leather-brown old man. I saw how his gray hair straggled from under his big black hat, which had a drooping feather in its crown. His rumpled black suit hung like a sack over his stooped frame. As he shook my hand, his coat fell open to expose a bright red satin shirt with a beaded bolo tie[3] under the collar. His get-up wasn't out of place on the reservation, but it sure was here, and I wanted to sink right through the pavement.

"Hi," I muttered with my head down. I tried to pull my hand away when I felt his bony hand trembling, and looked up to see

2. **Hau, Takoza** [häü tä kō′ zä]
3. **bolo tie** [bō′ lo tī]: string tie, with decorated slide.

fatigue in his face. I felt like crying. I couldn't think of anything to say so I picked up Grandpa's suitcase, took his arm, and guided him up the driveway to our house.

Mom was standing on the steps. I don't know how long she'd been watching, but her hand was over her mouth and she looked as if she couldn't believe what she saw. Then she ran to us.

"Grandpa," she gasped. "How in the world did you get here?"

She checked her move to embrace Grandpa and I remembered that such a display of affection is unseemly to the Sioux and would embarrass him.

"*Hau*, Marie," he said as he shook Mom's hand. She smiled and took his other arm.

As we supported him up the steps, the door banged open and Cheryl came bursting out of the house. She was all smiles and was so obviously glad to see Grandpa that I was ashamed of how I felt.

"Grandpa!" she yelled happily. "You came to see us!"

Grandpa smiled, and Mom and I let go of him as he stretched out his arms to my ten-year-old sister, who was still young enough to be hugged.

"*Wicincala*,[4] little girl," he greeted her and then collapsed.

He had fainted. Mom and I carried him into her sewing room, where we had a spare bed.

After we had Grandpa on the bed, Mom stood there helplessly patting his shoulder.

"Shouldn't we call the doctor, Mom?" I suggested, since she didn't seem to know what to do.

"Yes," she agreed with a sigh. "You make Grandpa comfortable, Martin."

I reluctantly moved to the bed. I knew Grandpa wouldn't want to have Mom undress him, but I didn't want to, either. He was so skinny and frail that his coat slipped off easily. When I loosened his tie and opened his shirt collar, I felt a small leather pouch that hung from a thong around his neck. I left it alone and moved to remove

4. *Wicincala* [wē chēn′ chä lä]

Beaded Sneakers 1993, made on the Rosebud Reservation, South Dakota

Ceremonial or Dress Mocassins Sioux, 1880s to 1890s, 26 cm, Montclair Art Museum, Rand Collection

his boots. The scuffed old cowboy boots were tight, and he moaned as I put pressure on his legs to jerk them off.

I put the boots on the floor and saw why they fit so tight. Each one was stuffed with money. I looked at the bills that lined the boots and started to ask about them, but Grandpa's eyes were closed again.

Mom came back with a basin of water. "The doctor thinks Grandpa is suffering from heat exhaustion," she explained as she bathed Grandpa's face. Mom gave a big sigh, "Oh, *hinh*,[5] Martin. How do you suppose he got here?"

We found out after the doctor's visit. Grandpa was angrily sitting up in bed while Mom tried to feed him some soup.

"Tonight you let Marie feed you, Grandpa," spoke my dad, who had gotten home from work just as the doctor was leaving. "You're not really sick," he said as he gently pushed Grandpa back against the pillows. "The doctor said you just got too tired and hot after your long trip."

Grandpa relaxed, and between sips of soup, he told us of his journey. Soon after our visit to him, Grandpa decided that he would like to see

5. **Oh, hinh** [ō hēn]

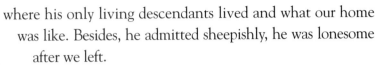

where his only living descendants lived and what our home was like. Besides, he admitted sheepishly, he was lonesome after we left.

I knew everybody felt as guilty as I did—especially Mom. Mom was all Grandpa had left. So even after she married my dad, who's a white man and teaches in the college in our city, and after Cheryl and I were born, Mom made sure that every summer we spent a week with Grandpa.

I never thought that Grandpa would be lonely after our visits, and none of us noticed how old and weak he had become. But Grandpa knew, and so he came to us. He had ridden on buses for two and a half days. When he arrived in the city, tired and stiff from sitting for so long, he set out, walking, to find us.

He had stopped to rest on the steps of some building downtown, and a policeman found him. The cop, according to Grandpa, was a good man who took him to the bus stop and waited until the bus came and told the driver to let Grandpa out at Bell View Drive. After Grandpa got off the bus, he started walking again. But he couldn't see the house numbers on the other side when he walked on the sidewalk, so he walked in the middle of the street. That's when all the little kids and dogs followed him.

I knew everybody felt as bad as I did. Yet I was so proud of this 86-year-old man, who had never been away from the reservation, having the courage to travel so far alone.

"You found the money in my boots?" he asked Mom.

"Martin did," she answered, and roused herself to scold. "Grandpa, you shouldn't have carried so much money. What if someone had stolen it from you?"

Grandpa laughed. "I would've known if anyone tried to take the boots off my feet. The money is what I've saved for a long time—a hundred dollars—for my funeral. But you take it now to buy groceries so that I won't be a burden to you while I am here."

"That won't be necessary, Grandpa," Dad said. "We are honored to have you with us, and you will never be a burden. I am only sorry that we never thought to bring you home with us this summer and spare you the discomfort of a long trip."

Grandpa was pleased. "Thank you," he answered. "But do not feel bad that you didn't bring me with you, for I would not have come then. It was not time." He said this in such a way that no one could argue with him. To Grandpa and the Sioux, he once told me, a thing would be done when it was the right time to do it, and that's the way it was.

"Also," Grandpa went on, looking at me, "I have come because it is soon time for Martin to have the medicine bag."

We all knew what that meant. Grandpa thought he was going to die, and he had to follow the tradition of his family to pass the medicine bag, along with its history, to the oldest male child.

"Even though the boy," he said still looking at me, "bears a white man's name, the medicine bag will be his."

I didn't know what to say. I had the same hot and cold feeling that I had when I first saw Grandpa in the street. The medicine bag was the dirty leather pouch I had found around his neck. "I could never wear such a thing," I almost said aloud. I thought of having my friends see it in gym class, or at the swimming pool, and could imagine the smart things they would say. But I just swallowed hard and took a step toward the bed. I knew I would have to take it.

But Grandpa was tired. "Not now, Martin," he said, waving his hand in dismissal. "It is not time. Now I want sleep."

So that's how Grandpa came to be with us for two months. My friends kept asking to come see the old man, but I put them off. I told myself that I didn't want them laughing at Grandpa. But even as I made excuses, I knew it wasn't Grandpa that I was afraid they'd laugh at.

Nothing bothered Cheryl about bringing her friends to see Grandpa. Every day after school started, there'd be a crew of giggling little girls or round-eyed little boys crowded around the old man on the patio, where he'd gotten in the habit of sitting every afternoon.

Grandpa would smile in his gentle way and patiently answer their questions, or he'd tell them stories of brave warriors, ghosts, animals; and the kids listened in awed silence. Those little guys thought Grandpa was great.

Finally, one day after school, my friends came home with me because nothing I said stopped them. "We're going to see the great Indian of Bell View Drive," said Hank, who was supposed to be my best friend. "My brother has seen him three times so he oughta be well enough to see us."

When we got to my house, Grandpa was sitting on the patio. He had on his red shirt, but today he also wore a fringed leather vest that was decorated with beads. Instead of his usual cowboy boots, he had solidly beaded moccasins on his feet that stuck out of his black trousers. Of course, he had his old black hat on—he was seldom without it. But it had been brushed, and the feather in the beaded headband was proudly erect, its tip a brighter white. His hair lay in silver strands over the red shirt collar.

I stared just as my friends did, and I heard one of them murmur, "Wow!"

Grandpa looked up, and, when his eyes met mine, they twinkled as if he were laughing inside. He nodded to me, and my face got all hot. I could tell that he had known all along I was afraid he'd embarrass me in front of my friends.

"*Hau, hoksilas,*[6] boys," he greeted and held out his hand.

My buddies passed in a single file and shook his hand as I introduced them. They were so polite I almost laughed. "How, there, Grandpa," and even a "How-do-you-do, sir."

"You look fine, Grandpa," I said as the guys sat on the lawn chairs or on the patio floor.

"*Hanh,*[7] yes," he agreed. "When I woke up this morning, it seemed the right time to dress in the good clothes. I knew that my grandson would be bringing his friends."

6. *Hau, hoksilas* [häü hōk sē′ läs]
7. *Hanh* [hän]

"You guys want some lemonade or something?" I offered. No one answered. They were listening to Grandpa as he started telling how he'd killed the deer from which his vest was made.

Grandpa did most of the talking while my friends were there. I was so proud of him and amazed at how respectfully quiet my buddies were. Mom had to chase them home at supper time. As they left, they shook Grandpa's hand again and said to me.

"Martin, he's really great!"

"Yeah, man! Don't blame you for keeping him to yourself."

"Can we come back?"

But after they left, Mom said, "No more visitors for a while, Martin. Grandpa won't admit it, but his strength hasn't returned. He likes having company, but it tires him."

That evening Grandpa called me to his room before he went to sleep. "Tomorrow," he said, "when you come home, it will be time to give you the medicine bag."

I felt a hard squeeze from where my heart is supposed to be and was scared, but I answered, "OK, Grandpa."

All night I had weird dreams about thunder and lightning on a high hill. From a distance I heard the slow beat of a drum. When I woke up in the morning, I felt as if I hadn't slept at all. At school it seemed as if the day would never end and, when it finally did, I ran home.

Grandpa was in his room, sitting on the bed. The shades were down, and the place was dim and cool. I sat on the floor in front of Grandpa, but he didn't even look at me. After what seemed a long time he spoke.

"I sent your mother and sister away. What you will hear today is only for a man's ears. What you will receive is only for a man's hands." He fell silent, and I felt shivers down my back.

"My father in his early manhood," Grandpa began, "made a vision quest to find a spirit guide for his life. You cannot understand how it was in that time, when the great Teton Sioux were first made to stay on the reservation. There was a strong need for guidance from *Wakantanka*,[8] the Great Spirit. But too many of the young men were

8. **Wakantanka** [wä kän′ tänk ä]: Great Spirit, creator of the world.

Medicine Pouch Sioux, late nineteenth century, 6 cm, Robert Hull Fleming Museum at the University of Vermont, Read Collection

Red Cloud Oglala Sioux Edward Curtis, 1905, black-and-white photograph, Philadelphia Museum of Art

filled with despair and hatred. They thought it was hopeless to search for a vision when the glorious life was gone and only the hated confines of a reservation lay ahead. But my father held to the old ways.

"He carefully prepared for his quest with a purifying sweat bath, and then he went alone to a high butte top[9] to fast and pray. After three days he received his sacred dream—in which he found, after long searching, the white man's iron. He did not understand his vision of finding something belonging to the white people, for in that time they were the enemy. When he came down from the butte to cleanse himself at the stream below, he found the remains of a campfire and the broken shell of an iron kettle. This was a sign that reinforced his dream. He took a piece of the iron for his medicine bag, which he had made of elk skin years before, to prepare for his quest.

"He returned to his village, where he told his dream to the wise old men of the tribe. They gave him the name *Iron Shell*, but neither did they understand the meaning of the dream. This first Iron Shell

9. **butte top** [byüt top]: top of a steep, flat-topped hill.

kept the piece of iron with him at all times and believed it gave him protection from the evils of those unhappy days.

"Then a terrible thing happened to Iron Shell. He and several other young men were taken from their homes by the soldiers and sent far away to a white man's boarding school. He was angry and lonesome for his parents and the young girl he had wed before he was taken away. At first Iron Shell resisted the teacher's attempts to change him, and he did not try to learn. One day it was his turn to work in the school's blacksmith shop. As he walked into the place, he knew that his medicine had brought him there to learn and work with the white man's iron.

"Iron Shell became a blacksmith and worked at the trade when he returned to the reservation. All of his life he treasured the medicine bag. When he was old, and I was a man, he gave it to me, for no one made the vision quest any more."

Grandpa quit talking, and I stared in disbelief as he covered his face with his hands. His shoulders were shaking with quiet sobs, and I looked away until he began to speak again.

"I kept the bag until my son, your mother's father, was a man and had to leave us to fight in the war across the ocean. I gave him the bag, for I believed it would protect him in battle, but he did not take it with him. He was afraid that he would lose it. He died in a faraway place."

Again Grandpa was still, and I felt his grief around me.

"My son," he went on after clearing his throat, "had only a daughter, and it is not proper for her to know of these things."

He unbuttoned his shirt, pulled out the leather pouch, and lifted it over his head. He held it in his hand, turning it over and over as if memorizing how it looked.

"In the bag," he said as he opened it and removed two objects, "is the broken shell of the iron kettle, a pebble from the butte, and a piece of the sacred sage."[10] He held the pouch upside down and dust drifted down.

"After the bag is yours you must put a piece of prairie sage within and never open it again until you pass it on to your son." He replaced the pebble and the piece of iron, and tied the bag.

10. **sage** [sāj]: a small shrub whose leaves are used as seasoning and in medicine.

I stood up, somehow knowing I should. Grandpa slowly rose from the bed and stood upright in front of me holding the bag before my face. I closed my eyes and waited for him to slip it over my head. But he spoke.

"No, you need not wear it." He placed the soft leather bag in my right hand and closed my other hand over it. "It would not be right to wear it in this time and place where no one will understand. Put it safely away until you are again on the reservation. Wear it then, when you replace the sacred sage."

Grandpa turned and sat again on the bed. Wearily he leaned his head against the pillow. "Go," he said. "I will sleep now."

"Thank you, Grandpa," I said softly and left with the bag in my hands.

That night Mom and Dad took Grandpa to the hospital. Two weeks later I stood alone on the lonely prairie of the reservation and put the sacred sage in my medicine bag.

VIRGINIA DRIVING HAWK SNEVE

Virginia Driving Hawk Sneve was born in 1933 in Rosebud, South Dakota, and grew up on the Sioux Reservation there. She has spent most of her life in her native state, teaching English and speech, and writing about Sioux life and legends. Sneve has said, "In my writing . . . I try to present an accurate portrayal of American Indian life as I have known it. I also attempt to interpret history from the viewpoint of the American Indian and in so doing I hope to correct many misconceptions and untruths. . . ." "The Medicine Bag" is from her book titled *High Elk's Treasure*. Some of her other books include *Jimmy Yellow Hawk* and *When the Thunder Spoke*.

Randy: My Whole

from Putting It All Together

EDITED BY PAULA McGUIRE

Family Is Women

I have two sisters, and we all have different fathers. My eldest sister's father used to be married to my mother, but unfortunately they got a divorce. My mother had several boyfriends afterward, and two of them happened to be my second eldest sister's father and my father. So we have three different fathers in the family, which isn't such a good situation.

When I was a little kid I didn't really notice it much; my mind was on playing and having fun. Back then, I just had a mother, and I thought that was all I was supposed to have. Mom took care of me and my sisters. Everybody was happy. My mother didn't say much about my father. She didn't explain why there was no one there, and I never really asked. My sisters probably knew, but they never told me, and I never talked to them about it. We were happy, just Mom and my sisters.

Not having a father really struck me during my junior high school years. All of a sudden everybody started talking about my dad this, my dad that. I just sat down one day and said, "Where's my father? What's he doing for me?" I really got a complex about it. I felt depressed and angry. Sometimes my friends would talk about their dads, and I'd just blow up at them. Jealousy, I guess. But it was tough.

Ever since I can remember, my sisters have been going off to see their dads, or their fathers would come to the house and visit them. And that, too, contributed to my jealousy. I'd think, "God, they get to see their pops.

I don't get to see mine." I didn't hate them, but I sure felt they were more lucky than I was. They still see their fathers and go to visit them. But all this time, there has never been any talk about my father or any explanation for the situation.

My sisters are grown up now and married. We came out pretty well, actually, when you think about it. I think a lot of people would be pretty down under without a father, but I came through all right.

But when I first noticed it, it crushed me. It struck me all of a sudden. Other kids would say, my father's a lawyer, my dad goes overseas and does this, my father's a professor at the university. I had to lie about my father. I said he was a car dealer. It was tough. It hurt. I had to work it out. I looked at myself and said, "Hey, I'm talented, I'm attractive, I have the smarts. Some people have fathers but they don't have that, so I'll just make the best of it. If it wasn't supposed to be this way, God would have made it different. But God made it this way, so I'll just have to blossom the way I'm planted."

My whole family is women. I look back in the past, and every lady in my family never really had a man. They were married, but it didn't work out. They're all manless. My grandmother doesn't have a husband, my great-grandmother doesn't have a husband, my aunts don't have husbands. But all the women are great.

My mother is a dietician, so she's got a pretty good job and has been able to carry us along. It's been tough, though, believe me. We've all had to work.

I was always pretty worried about my mother too. My mother didn't show much emotion, but I know down deep inside she was probably hurting. I can look in her eyes every day, I can look in my grandmother's eyes every day, and you can tell it's been tough on them. But they're strong now, and they know they have to make it, so there's no sense really being down about the situation when it's not going to help.

I know my mom missed having a husband, having a partner to help out. She needs companionship. She has boyfriends, and I can see they make her happy. Once she laid down little hints to me that she was thinking about getting married. I objected. I didn't say, "No, Mom, don't get married," but I let her know I wouldn't really approve of it. I got jealous. I'd been the male figure in the family, and for somebody to invade my space—that was terrible. I was selfish, but I was very young then. I didn't cooperate at all. I'm sorry now.

I wouldn't say the same thing now. I would encourage her to get married. In fact she has one good boyfriend now, and he likes me. He's a real nice guy and he's helped me a lot. So whatever she wants to do. As long as she's happy. I want to see my mom happy.

I've seen my father before, but I haven't seen him in a long time. I don't think I will, unless I go to see him. I hope I will. I don't hate him. You might think that's funny, but I don't hate him. Hey, I love him! I'll be honest with you, my father's my father. My life has been tough, but there have been a lot of great things. A lot of great people. If it wasn't for him I wouldn't be here. I'll give him that much credit.

What does really burn me up, however, is that he has another family. Actually I have another brother and sister. I feel kind of jealous, and I feel bad for my mother. He's over in R____ , living it up with a wife and a nice family and stuff, and he leaves me with my mother. Put the burden on my mother. But I put myself where I can look at him and say, "Hey, you're not really a man. You going and leaving my mother like this, you're not really a man. And I want to be better than you." So I will. I'm going to be the man in my family that all the women deserved but never got. I'm going to represent that man!

I used to dream what it would be like to have a father. I had all these funny thoughts; it'd be great, we'd go fishing, play sports and stuff. Every day I looked at my friends and thought, they're probably having all that fun. And I'm not having it. They'd talk about what they did with their dads, and I couldn't do that. I was so jealous. Nobody talks about their mom. [Laughs.] I did though, 'cause I had to!

That's another thing, success is very important in this town. Most of the people around me are in successful families with successful fathers. I used to feel pretty inferior around those people. Wealth is important around here. Compared to those people, I'm not so wealthy. I don't live in such a nice area of town. Other people around here talk about going yachting, going skiing in Vermont, and so forth. My mom goes out and breaks her back so I can have some dinner to eat!

That's why I want to be a father. That's my goal, just to be a *good* father. How could you leave a lady anyway? I mean, if it doesn't work out, okay, but at least come back and visit the children.

When I was going through that bad time in junior high, there were so many changes in my life going on—physical, social—I just got caught up in them. I didn't know what to do and had to rely on my own self to carry through. It would have helped to have someone. I wanted a brother too. I grew up with just girls, girls, girls. I needed a male figure just to talk to, just to be with. On the other hand, being with *ladies* has helped me. Because I'm more sensitive now. I care about other people's feelings. I'm not the macho man who tells a woman what to do. I see the woman's side of things. So that's helped me become a more full person. That's why I'm good with girls now. Because I understand.

But for a while, I couldn't do anything. I didn't play basketball for a couple of years. I didn't have much confidence in myself. And I think all that could be linked to my feeling bad about not having a father, about not having anybody to support me. You know, when you're down you talk to your mom or your pop. And I didn't want to talk to my mom, because I didn't want to put any more burdens on her. So usually I'd solve my problems by myself. But maybe during this time in my life I really needed somebody to turn to. But nobody was there. My sisters were in school, and I couldn't talk to friends about that. At least not then.

I wish I hadn't held it all in, but during that time I was feeling too unsure about a lot of things. And up until that point, my life was great! I was a good athlete, pretty good student, I had good friends, both black and white. Then all of a sudden, I don't know, I just thought that I couldn't do it any more. I didn't have anybody there for me. So I got lost in myself. I wasted away. I just got lazy and didn't do anything for myself.

Anyway, I'm back on the track now. I just seem to have this ability to come through. It's natural. I don't want to go into detail about this, but I think my situation was made to be. God put me on earth for a purpose. Because nobody in my family had a father. At least a man who stays around. So I was put on the earth as a very talented young man, attractive young man, I think, very intelligent, to compensate for what I didn't have. I always had this air about me that attracted people. I could do a lot for myself without even trying. Things came easy. Things besides family life. You put aside all the financial burdens and all the family burdens, things were pretty easy for me. That really never stopped. The only thing that ever stopped me was *me*. And I did stop myself for a while, but that's over with. I've been humbled, and I know now.

Would I want to have had it some other way? No, I'm not going to say that. No, I'm happy. If that's the way it is, that's the way it is. I'm not going to say I wish it had been different.

It hasn't been easy, but I've been able to cope. Other kids have had it worse. I can remember kids coming to school, saying their parents were getting a divorce, and looking really bad, being in really bad shape. Maybe they had lived with their father and mother for ten or fifteen years, and all of a sudden there's a divorce. That can be emotionally very hard. Very depressing. But me, I never had a father to begin with, so you can't miss what you've never had.

But if I was to talk to my father now, I'd let him know something. I wouldn't be *that* friendly with him or anything. I'd just let him know that "Hey, I don't hate you or anything. I don't particularly like you for what you did, but you're still my father, and you have to live with that." I will. I'll go to see him, maybe next year when I get my navy uniform. That'll shock him. "This is ME, man!" I'll say. "I'm your son, man. Mom and I did without you, man!"

Asking Big Questions About the Literature

What kinds of changes do people experience?

MAKE

AN OVERVIEW CHART

Make a chart of the changes experienced by the characters in this unit. In the column headed *Change(s)*, list changes that happen to the character. Label these *E* for *external*. Also include changes that happen within the person. Label these *I* for *internal*. A chart has been begun for you in the right column. When you have finished, compare your chart with others in your class. Notice the different ways classmates interpreted changes.

Write a

GREETING CARD

Create a greeting card for a friend who has recently experienced a change, or do the same for a character in this unit. Identify the change on the outside of the card. On the inside, write a greeting to congratulate this person or to make him or her feel better. Use your imagination and create illustrations for the card.

Literature	Character	Change(s)
"As It Is with Strangers"	Tiffany	1. Discovers she has a half brother. *E* 2. Discovers new inner strengths. *I* 3.

LITERATURE STUDY

Characterization

Sometimes actions speak louder than words. Revealing a character's traits through his or her actions is one aspect of **characterization**—the way in which a writer makes a character come alive.

Write the name of a character in the literature whose actions make him or her seem lifelike. Then write a paragraph describing what character trait a specific action reveals to you. For example, in the beginning of "The Banana Tree," James Berry tells us that "the eldest boy, Gustus, sat farthest from his father." What does this tell you about Gustus's feelings toward his father? (*See "Characterization" on page 118.*)

What challenges result from these changes?

Writing a
SONG

Team up with a classmate to write a song (or poem) about one of the challenges experienced by a character in this unit. Make sure your music and song lyrics convey a strong, positive message that will help other young people deal with a similar challenge.

LITERATURE STUDY
Conflict

Have you ever talked to yourself? If you have, don't worry. You were probably hashing over a challenge or a problem you were facing. In this kind of **conflict**, the forces at odds are within yourself.

When a character in literature talks to himself or herself, that conversation is called a monologue. Write a monologue for one of the characters in this unit. Show the internal conflict that the character is experiencing. (*See "Conflict" on page 119.*)

F.A.C.E.
THE CHALLENGE

As producer of a television program entitled "Face the Challenge," it's up to you to find stories about people and the challenges they face. Write a memo to your supervisor urging that the network do a story about one of the characters in this unit. In your memo, include details that illustrate the character's challenge. A memo has been started for you.

To:

From:

Subject: Proposal for an episode of "Face the Challenge"

Date:

Please consider using Martin from "The Medicine Bag" as the star of an episode of "Face the Challenge." I am convinced that he is a good candidate because . . .

Asking Big Questions About the Literature

What choices do people make when faced with challenges?

Create A RADIO TALK SHOW

With several classmates, create a call-in radio talk show. Some members of your group will portray characters in this unit who call to ask questions about challenges they face. For example, the father in "The Writer" might ask: "How can I protect my daughter from hurt as she gets older?"

Other group members will act as a panel of experts who answer questions. Create a catchy title that reflects the show's content and appeals to the audience most likely to tune in.

Write an
ADVICE COLUMN

Write an advice column to help one character in *Changes and Choices* make a different choice from the one he or she made in the story. Make a cluster or web like the one shown to help you gather ideas. Use advice columns in magazines and newspapers as models.

LITERATURE STUDY

Conflict

Have you ever heard the expression "No pain, no gain"? When people face change, they often experience pain or conflict. In literature, a **conflict** is the struggle between opposing forces.

Conflict is internal when it comes from within a person, such as a conflict of conscience. Conflict is external when it occurs between two people or between a person and the outside world.

Choose a character from this unit and identify the type of conflict he or she faces. Write a paragraph explaining what the conflict is. Use specific examples from the selection to defend your choice. (*See "Conflict" on page 119.*)

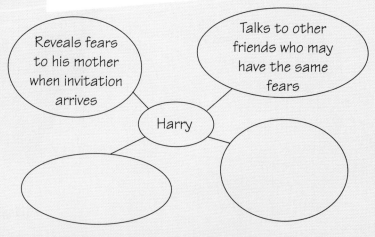

Reveals fears to his mother when invitation arrives

Talks to other friends who may have the same fears

Harry

What qualities help people face change successfully?

COMPARE & CONTRAST

Which two characters from different stories in *Changes and Choices* might be good friends in real life? Draw a Venn diagram, as shown, in which you compare and contrast these two characters. In addition to listing qualities that help these characters face challenge, include details about their lives, such as age, gender, and neighborhood.

Harry from "The Torn Invitation"

Martin from "The Medicine Bag"

Parents born in a foreign country

Lives with mother and father

Loves someone dearly but feels ashamed of that person

Grandfather is Native American

Lives with mother, father, sister, and, eventually, grandfather

LITERATURE STUDY

Characterization

The way in which a writer reveals a character's traits and qualities is called **characterization.**

Suppose a writer wants to let us know that a character is selfish. The writer may reveal this trait directly by saying "Maria is selfish." Or the writer may reveal this trait indirectly by showing us what Maria *does* that shows she is selfish, what Maria or other characters *say* that shows she is selfish, or what Maria *thinks* that shows she is selfish. (*See "Characterization" on page 118.*)

With a partner, agree on a character from this unit to analyze. Write down the character's name and generate a list of traits that describe him or her. Then create trait webs or clusters. In the center of each web, write a trait, such as *selfish.* In the outer portions of the web, show how the writer reveals this trait in the story.

PLAY a Role

Work with a partner to role-play a situation in which you face a personal challenge or crisis, such as the death of a family member or the loss of a good friend. How would you respond? As you role-play, draw upon the qualities that helped characters in this unit successfully face challenge.

NOW Choose a Project!

Three projects involving changes and choices are described on the following pages.

Writing Workshop

WEAR A CRITIC'S HAT

Prewriting
....
**GETTING
STARTED**

Usually people want to see a movie or read a book because they've heard others say how good it is. For this project, *you* will be the reviewer; you'll recommend or pan the work you've chosen. Your **purpose** in this project will be to evaluate or review a movie, a play, a performance, or a book about people who are going through changes and making choices. Your **audience** will be other students or members of your community.

To help you choose a work to evaluate, try freewriting in your journal. Write for three to five minutes without lifting your pen from your paper.

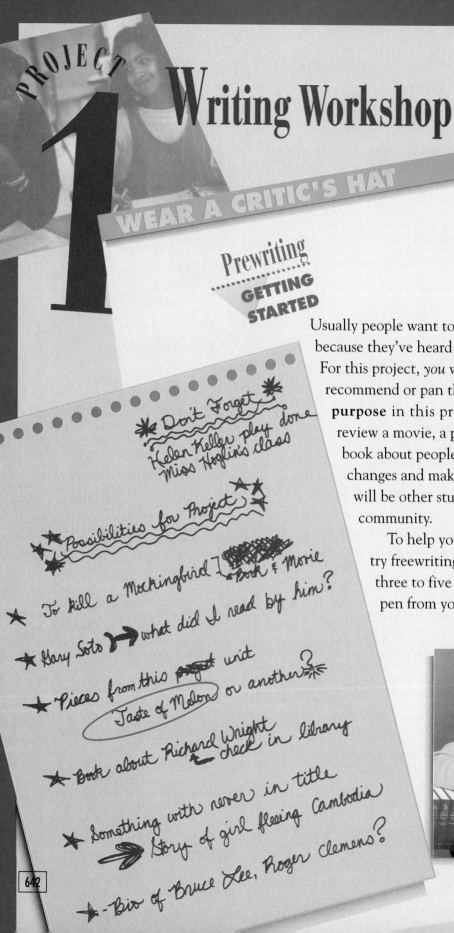

* Don't Forget *
Helen Keller play done
Miss Hoglin's class

* Possibilities for Project *

★ To kill a Mockingbird] Book & Movie

★ Gary Soto → what did I read by him?

★ Pieces from this unit
Taste of Melon or another?

★ Book about Richard Wright → check in library

★ Something with never in title
Story of girl fleeing Cambodia

★ Bio of Bruce Lee, Roger Clemens?

Write down the names of movies or plays you've recently seen, performances you've attended, books or short stories you've read. Choose works that you have strong feelings about, either positive or negative, or works that really affected you. Then circle one work that you'd like to review for classmates or friends.

Prewriting
BEGINNING TO EVALUATE

Look in newspapers or magazines—or even on TV—for reviews done by professional critics. How are these reviews usually set up? Then think about who the audience for your review will be. Will you publish your review in the school or local newspaper? Can you videotape your review, perhaps working with a partner, and show it on your local cable station? Knowing your audience will help you decide what to include in your review and where to present it.

Now consider how you feel about the work you've circled in your journal. Did you like it or not? Why? What changes does the main character experience? What choices does he or she make?

Think about different elements that you noticed. For example, if you review a book, think about elements like plot, setting, and character. If you review a movie, think about elements like plot, acting, music, and special effects.

Judge the strengths and weaknesses of each element. In your journal, rank each element using a chart similar to the one that follows. Give a reason for each rating.

	Poor 1	Fair 2	3	Excellent 4	5	Reason for Rating
Taste of Melon				✓		Exciting! Like struggle between right & wrong
Plot Setting				✓		Mr. Wills is great—like how he changes at end

With both your audience and the strengths and weaknesses of the work you've chosen in mind, you're ready to draft your review.

- To get your audience's attention, write a catchy beginning. For example, Tony Durso, a student writer, asks a question to introduce his review of the short story "The Taste of Melon" on pages 110–111. " How far would <u>you</u> go to gain the acceptance of your friends?" Notice that the rest of Tony's first paragraph includes the title and author of the work and states his judgment of the work.

- Tell why you did or didn't like the work. Make sure to support your judgment with specific details, quotations, and examples from the work. For example, Tony explains that one reason he recommends "The Taste of Melon" is that Mr. Wills is such a strong character. He supports his recommendation by the following quotation about Mr. Wills: "He straightened, a great, strangled cry tearing out of his throat. It chilled me deep down and all the way through, like the cry of a wild animal." You could write a separate paragraph discussing each element from your chart.

- End by summarizing your response to the work. Give it "thumbs up" or "thumbs down" by recommending the work to your audience or telling them why they shouldn't read or see it. Tony ended his review as follows: "Read this story! It proves that good things <u>can</u> grow out of bad experiences."

Keep in mind your purpose—to write a review—and your audience when you write. Use clear, precise language to convey your judgments and opinions. To motivate his audience to read "The Taste of Melon," for instance, Tony wrote comments such as "I really recommend this story" and "Read this story!" Finally, when you write your review, use the present tense.

Revising
YOUR REVIEW

Ask a partner or a group to respond to your review and make suggestions for improving it. Do you state your judgment of the work? Do you tell your audience enough about the work to get them interested? Do you tell them too much? You don't want to give away the ending of a really exciting book, for example. Do you support your judgments with specific details, quotations, and examples from the work that you're reviewing? Have you successfully persuaded your audience either to avoid or to read or see the work you've reviewed?

Look at the model on pages 110–111 for an example of a review.

Editing
YOUR REVIEW

After you've revised your draft, work with a partner to edit your review. Read one another's reviews and check for errors in spelling, grammar, and punctuation. Correct your errors and make a publishable copy of your review.

THE TASTE OF MELON

GROWING UP

Publishing

YOUR REVIEW

Now share your review with your audience. Brainstorm creative ideas for publishing and write your ideas in your journal. Here are some ideas to get you started.

- Create a classroom newsletter called the "Critical I" in which you print your own reviews.
- Invent a rating system like the one shown on this page to rank books, movies, and pieces of literature. For example, use a scale of bookmarks to rate books; a real page turner would rate five bookmarks.

STUDENT MODEL

"The Taste of Melon"

review by Tony Durso, Belmont, Massachusetts

How far would <u>you</u> go to gain the acceptance of your friends? In the short story "The Taste of Melon," Borden Deal tells the story of a sixteen-year-old boy who wants to be liked by his friends and will do anything to gain their admiration—even steal. I really recommend this story. It does a great job of showing what happens when you do something wrong.

"The Taste of Melon" is about stealing and what it does to the person who steals. The boy just wants to impress his friends. He's new in town and doesn't really fit in yet. He and his new friends hear about Mr. Wills's huge seed melon and how carefully Mr. Wills guards it, and suddenly the boy decides to steal it.

At first, the boy thinks stealing is fun, and it is. It's fun to sneak into the tall grass, break the stem off, and roll the melon into the creek to safety. It's a thrill to risk being caught by Mr. Wills, who's so close that the boy can see his teeth glistening. It's fun to break the melon open with his friends and eat the sweet fruit. But by the end, the boy is depressed about what he's done and talks about his let-down in the following words: "I did not feel triumph or victory, as I had expected, though I knew that tonight's action had brought me closer to my friends than I had ever been before."

Mr. Wills is my favorite character. At first, everyone thinks he's a sourpuss. The boy is even afraid that Mr. Wills will hurt him. The scene where Mr. Wills realizes the melon is gone is just great. "He straightened, a great, strangled cry tearing out of his throat. It chilled me deep down and all the way through, like the cry of a wild animal."

In the end, though, Mr. Wills turns out to be a pretty nice guy. He smiles when the boy gives him the bag of seeds and says, "I'm sorry." When the boy also says he'll be willing to help Mr. Wills plant the seeds, Mr. Wills says they can grow the seeds together. Read this story! It proves that good things <u>can</u> grow out of bad experiences.

Cooperative Learning

WELCOME TO MIDDLE SCHOOL!

The PROJECT

Do you remember your first day of middle school? What was your biggest challenge? What worries or questions did you have? This project will give you a chance to think about changes you've experienced and choices you've made. With a partner or a group, you'll create an orientation packet for students beginning middle school next year.

The PROCESS

Put yourself in a sixth grader's shoes. Work with a partner or a group to list questions a new sixth grader might have—about teachers, the building, sports teams, and other issues.

Then select the most important questions. Categorize them by sorting the questions into groups, such as *Questions About the Building* or *Questions About Classes*. Add the answers and other helpful information. Don't be afraid to be funny if it's appropriate. Draw maps or illustrations to help orient sixth graders to your school. If you can, use photographs of teachers, the principal, and other school personnel.

In your journal, make a chart like the one below to keep track of what tasks you must do, which member of your group will do each task, and what materials you and your group will need.

Task	Materials	Person Responsible
Brainstorm questions		
Categorize questions		
Answer questions		
Create graphic aids		

The PACKET

Now organize your materials so that they will really help new students. Arrange them in a pocket folder or a three-ring binder. Write a brief introduction that summarizes what your packet includes. Don't forget maps, photographs, and illustrations.

The PRESENTATION

Now decide how and when to present your orientation packet to sixth graders. You could organize an assembly to welcome the sixth grade and give out your packets there, or you could hand out individual packets to one class.

With the help of your teacher and the elementary school principal or a sixth-grade teacher, schedule a date and time for your presentation. Plan your presentation carefully and make sure you have enough copies of your packets for everyone. Then congratulate yourselves! You've really helped sixth graders make a smooth adjustment to middle school.

Helping Your Community

VOICES FROM THE PAST

Choosing THE PERSON

One of the Big Questions in this unit asks, "What kinds of changes do people experience?" This project will give you a chance to interview an adult—a parent, a neighbor, a family member, or a resident of a nursing home in your community—to find out about changes and choices in his or her life. Your interview will become part of a community oral history project.

Organizing THE INTERVIEW

In your journal, brainstorm a list of people you'd like to interview. Then circle the name of the person you find most interesting. Write a list of questions you'd like to ask your interview subject about changes and choices, using *who? what? where? when? why?* and *how?* to get started.

Now choose a convenient time and place for conducting your interview. Explain the purpose of your project and tell your interview subject that you'll be recording the entire conversation. Before the day of your interview, be sure that you have access to recording equipment—a tape recorder, a microphone, blank cassette tapes—and that you know how to use it.

Recording
THE INTERVIEW

On the day of your interview, be sure that your equipment is working properly and that you have a completed list of questions. When you conduct your interview, speak clearly and slowly. Don't worry if you don't get to ask every question you've prepared. Your interview will be more interesting if you let your subject go where your questions lead him or her. When you're finished with the interview, label and date your tape.

Making
AN ORAL HISTORY

After you've recorded your interview, make a label or a J-card for your tape. Identify the interview subject and summarize the interview. Then work with your classmates to do an oral history project. Categorize all the interviews by grouping them according to the changes and choices your interview subjects discuss. Make an index using the following model.

Tape #	Date	Person	Change/Choice	Length
1	4/2	Emma Tewskbury	moved to a new town	20 min
2	4/6	Geraldo Rodriquez	decided to be a doctor	18 min
3				

Presenting
THE ORAL HISTORY

Brainstorm some ideas for presenting your completed oral history project. For example, make copies for the local historical society or the town library. Provide an attractive container for storing the tapes. Notify your local newspaper that the tapes are available to all citizens in your community.

Putting It All Together
What Have You Learned About Changes and Choices?

Now that you've finished *Changes and Choices*, think about how your ideas about this theme have changed. Look back at the writing you've done for this unit—in your journal, in response to your reading, in the Writing Workshop. Share your thoughts with your classmates by writing an essay, a short story, or a poem about a person who has made a choice when faced with a change. Then create your own *Changes and Choices* magazine by collecting the writing you and your classmates have done.

PEOPLE, CHANGES, CHOICES

Prewriting and Drafting   Brainstorm a list of people you know or have read about—including characters in this unit—who made admirable choices when faced with challenges. For example, in the 1960s, civil rights activist Rosa Parks, an African American woman, protested against racial segregation by refusing to move to the back of a bus. Choose your favorite person from the list.

Now draft an essay, a short story, or a poem about the person you've chosen. Identify the person and what he or she did. Include facts, quotations, or appropriate funny stories, and provide specific details about this person's changes and choices. Use chronological order (*first, next, last*) to tell what happened, and explain why this person interests you. End with an interesting quotation, a question, or an anecdote.

Revising and Editing   It's time to work with a partner. Read your writing aloud to one another. Ask your partner to suggest improvements to the content of your writing. Check the grammar, punctuation, and spelling too.

Publishing   Now put your magazine together. Think of an appropriate title and decide on the order of your essays, short stories, and poems. Then design an exciting cover. Share your magazine by displaying copies in your school or local library.

Evaluating Your Work

Think Back About the Big Questions

With a partner, discuss the Big Questions on pages 10-11 and the questions you generated for **Now Think!** on page 11. Do you have trouble answering any of these questions now? In your journal, write two or three sentences discussing how your responses to the Big Questions have changed after your work in this unit.

Think Back About Your Work

Now think about the unit you've just finished and evaluate your work, including your reading, your writing, your activities, and your projects. Be kind to yourself, but be honest too!

Write a note to your teacher. In your note, explain what you've done during this unit and what you've learned. Use the following questions to help you write your note.

- Which literature selections in this unit affected you most strongly? Why?
- What was your favorite activity in this unit? Why?
- What was your least favorite activity? Why?
- If you were to do your project again, what parts would you do the same way?
- What parts would you do differently?
- What did you learn as you worked on your project?
- What have you learned in this unit about what you like to read?
- How would you rate your work in this unit? Use the following scale and give at least three reasons for your rating.

  1 = Outstanding   3 = Fair
  2 = Good   4 = Not as good as it could have been

What Is Characterization?

Characterization consists of all the methods a writer uses to create a character who seems like a real person. Such characterization may consist of direct description, or it may be an indirect revelation of the character through dialogue, through what other characters say about him or her, or through examples of the character's appearance and actions. A character who seems so real that readers or audiences feel as though they know him or her in the way that they might know a real person is a *rounded character*. A character who seems to represent an idea, or who seems to have only one main quality, is a *two-dimensional* or a *flat character*.

Writing a Word Portrait Try your own hand at the fiction-writer's craft. Find your favorite character in a selection from this unit. Then imagine this character in an ordinary situation, doing something that involves talking, such as talking on the phone or talking to a friend at a party. Write a detailed, convincing characterization of the person doing this activity, without naming him or her. Finally, see whether a classmate can guess what character you have portrayed.

Creating Real People Write a one-act play, or one scene from a longer play, in which you show who two human characters are through their dialogue and actions. The characters may be based on real or imaginary people, but anyone reading or watching the scene should believe they know both characters well. The setting and plot events are up to you. When your play or scene is finished, invite a friend to take the part of one character as you take the other. Then discuss the characterization with your partner. Is it convincing? If not, revise your manuscript. Then ask your friend to help you present your dramatic work as a reader's theater event for your class.

What Is Conflict?

Conflict in a piece of literature is the struggle between opposing forces. Sometimes the conflict is *internal*, as when the struggle takes place within a person. At other times, for example, when a character struggles against nature, another person, or society, the conflict is external. In drama and narrative fiction, the plot shows how this conflict builds to a point of greatest intensity or interest and is eventually resolved. Most of the reader's interest in the story is really an interest in how the story's conflict affects the main character's life, together with a curiosity about how he or she will resolve the conflict.

Rewriting the Ending Alone or with a partner, choose one of the selections in this unit and imagine a different outcome to the conflict. Then role-play or rewrite the conclusion to show your ideas. Which conclusion do you think works best? Which seems most like real life? Write or talk about why you think so.

Working Out a Conflict Think about the different kinds of conflict in the selections in this unit and how each is developed and resolved. Then, with a partner, discuss a challenging real-life conflict you can imagine yourselves in. It could be a misunderstanding between a parent and a teenager, or the experience of two enemies who find themselves together in a dangerous situation, or two friends debating whether to include a new kid in a group event. What would each person be thinking? How would each show his or her inner thoughts and feelings? With your partner, role-play how the two people become aware of the conflict and gradually work through it. Offer to act out your scene in front of the class.

GLOSSARY OF LITERARY TERMS

A

alliteration   Repetition of the first sound—usually a consonant sound—in several words of a sentence or a line of poetry.

allusion   An author's indirect reference to someone or something that is presumed to be familiar to the reader.

anecdote   A short narrative about an interesting or a humorous event, usually in the life of a person.

antagonist   The person or force opposing the protagonist, or main character in a literary work. [See also *protagonist*.]

autobiography   A person's written account of his or her own life.

B

ballad   A poem, often a song, that tells a story in simple verse.

biography   An account of a person's life, written by another person.

blank verse   Unrhymed poetry.

C

character   A person or an animal that participates in the action of a work of literature. A *dynamic character* is one whose thoughts, feelings, and actions are changeable and lifelike; a *static character* always remains the same. [See also *protagonist, antagonist*.]

characterization   The creation of characters through the characters' use of language and through descriptions of their appearance, thoughts, emotions, and actions. [See also *character*.]

chronology   An arrangement of events in the order in which they happen.

cliché   An overused expression that is trite rather than meaningful.

climax   The highest point of tension in the plot of a work of literature. [See also *plot*.]

comedy   An amusing play that has a happy ending.

conclusion   The final part or ending of a piece of literature.

concrete poem   A poem arranged on the page so that its punctuation, letters, and lines make the shape of the subject of the poem.

conflict   A problem that confronts the characters in a piece of literature. The conflict may be *internal* (a character's struggle within himself or herself) or *external* (a character's struggle against nature, another person, or society). [See also *plot*.]

context   The general sense of words that helps readers to understand the meaning of unfamiliar words and phrases in a piece of writing.

D

description   An author's use of words to give the reader or listener a mental picture, an impression, or an understanding of a person, place, thing, event, or idea.

dialect   A form of speech spoken by people in a particular group or geographical region that differs in vocabulary, grammar, and pronunciation from the standard language.

dialogue   The spoken words and conversation of characters in a work of literature.

drama   A play that is performed before an audience according to stage directions and using dialogue. Classical drama has two genres: *tragedy* and *comedy*. Modern drama includes *melodrama, satire, theater of the absurd*, and *pantomime*. [See also *comedy, play*, and *tragedy*.]

dramatic poetry   A play written in the form of poetry.

E

epic   A long narrative poem—written in a formal style and meant to be read aloud—that relates the adventures and

experiences of one or more great heroes or heroines.

essay Personal nonfiction writing about a particular subject that is important to the writer.

excerpt A passage from a larger work that has been taken out of its context to be used for a special purpose.

exposition Writing that explains, analyzes, or defines.

extended metaphor An elaborately drawn out metaphor. [See also *metaphor*.]

F

fable A short, simple story whose purpose is to teach a lesson, usually with animal characters who talk and act like people.

fantasy Imaginative fiction about unrealistic characters, places, and events.

fiction Literature, including the short story and the novel, that tells about imaginary people and events.

figurative language Language used to express ideas through figures of speech: descriptions that aren't meant to be taken literally. Types of figurative language include *simile*, *metaphor*, *extended metaphor*, *hyperbole*, and *personification*.

figure of speech A type of figurative language, not meant to be taken literally, that expresses something in such a way that it brings the thing to life in the reader's or listener's imagination. [See also *figurative language*.]

flashback A break in a story's action that relates a past happening in order to give the reader background information about a present action in the story.

folktale A story that has been passed along from storyteller to storyteller for generations. Kinds of folktales include *tall tales*, *fairy tales*, *fables*, *legends*, and *myths*.

foreshadowing The use of clues to create suspense by giving the reader or audience hints of events to come.

free verse Poetry that has no formal rhyme scheme or metrical pattern.

G

genre A major category of art. The three major literary genres are poetry, prose, and drama.

H

haiku A three-line Japanese verse form. In most haiku, the first and third lines have five syllables, while the second line has seven. The

traditional haiku describes a complicated feeling or thought in simple language through a single image.

hero/heroine The main character in a work of literature. In heroic literature, the hero or heroine is a particularly brave, noble, or clever person whose achievements are unusual and important. [See also *character*.]

heroic age The historical period in western civilization—from about 800 B.C. through A.D. 200—during which most works of heroic literature, such as myths and epics, were created in ancient Greece and Rome.

hubris Arrogance or excessive pride leading to mistakes; the character flaw in a hero of classical tragedy.

hyperbole An obvious exaggeration used for emphasis. [See also *figurative language*.]

I

idiom An expression whose meaning cannot be understood from the ordinary meaning of the words. For example, *It's raining cats and dogs.*

imagery The words and phrases in writing that appeal to the senses of sight, hearing, taste, touch, and smell.

irony An effect created by a sharp contrast between what is expected and what is real. An *ironic twist* in a plot is an event that is the complete opposite of what the characters have been hoping or expecting will happen. An *ironic statement* declares the opposite of the speaker's literal meaning.

J

jargon Words and phrases used by a group of people who share the same profession or special interests in order to refer to technical things or processes with which they are familiar. In general, jargon is any terminology that sounds unclear, overused, or pretentious.

L

legend A famous folktale about heroic actions, passed along by word of mouth from generation to generation. The legend may have begun as a factual account of real people and events but has become mostly or completely fictitious.

limerick A form of light verse, or humorous poetry, written in one five-line stanza with a regular scheme of rhyme and meter.

literature The branch of art that is expressed in written language and includes all written genres.

lyric poem A short poem that expresses personal feelings and thoughts in a musical way. Originally, lyrics were the words of songs that were sung to music played on the lyre, a stringed instrument invented by the ancient Greeks.

M

metamorphosis The transformation of one thing, or being, into another completely different thing or being, such as a caterpillar's change into a butterfly.

metaphor Figurative language in which one thing is said to be another thing. [See also *figurative language*.]

meter The pattern of rhythm in lines of poetry. The most common meter, in poetry written in English, is iambic pentameter, that is, a verse having five metrical feet, each foot of verse having two syllables, an unaccented one followed by an accented one.

mood The feeling or atmosphere that a reader senses while reading or listening to a work of literature.

motivation A character's reasons for doing, thinking, feeling, or saying something. Sometimes an author will make a character's motivation obvious from the beginning. In realistic fiction and drama, however, a character's motivation may be so complicated that the reader discovers it gradually, by studying the character's thoughts, feelings, and behavior.

myth A story, passed along by word of mouth for generations, about the actions of gods and goddesses or superhuman heroes and heroines. Most myths were first told to explain the origins of natural things or to justify the social rules and customs of a particular society.

N

narration The process of telling a story. For both fiction and nonfiction, there are two main kinds of narration, based on whether the story is told from a first-person or third-person point of view. [See also *point of view*.]

narrative poem A poem that tells a story containing the basic literary ingredients of fiction: character, setting, and plot.

narrator The person, or voice, that tells a story. [See also *point of view, voice*.]

nonfiction Prose that is factually true and is about real people, events, and places.

nonstandard English
Versions of English, such as slang and dialects, that use pronunciation, vocabulary, idiomatic expressions, grammar, and punctuation that differ from the accepted "correct" constructions of English.

novel   A long work of narrative prose fiction. A novel contains narration, a setting or settings, characters, dialogue, and a more complicated plot than a short story.

O

onomatopoeia   The technique of using words that imitate the sounds they describe, such as *hiss*, *buzz*, and *splash*.

oral tradition   Stories, poems, and songs that have been kept alive by being told, recited, and sung by people over many generations. Since the works were not originally written, they often have many different versions.

P

parable   A brief story—similar to a fable, but about people—that describes an ordinary situation and concludes with a short moral or lesson to be learned.

personification   Figurative language in which an animal, an object, or an idea is given human characteristics. [See also *figurative language*.]

persuasion   A type of speech or writing whose purpose is to convince people that something is true or important.

play   A work of dramatic literature written for performance by actors before an audience. In classical or traditional drama, a play is divided into five acts, each containing a number of scenes. Each act represents a distinct phase in the development of the plot. Modern plays often have only one act and one scene.

playwright   The author of a play.

plot   The sequence of actions and events in fiction or drama. A traditional plot has at least three parts: the *rising action*, leading up to a turning point that affects the main character; the *climax*, the turning point or moment of greatest intensity or interest; and the *falling action*, leading away from the conflict, or resolving it.

poetry   Language selected and arranged in order to say something in a compressed or nonliteral way. Modern poetry may or may not use many of the traditional poetic techniques that include *meter*, *rhyme*, *alliteration*, *figurative language*, *symbolism*, and *specific verse forms*.

point of view   The perspective from which a writer tells a story. *First-person* narrators tell the story from their own point of view, using pronouns such as *I* or *me*. *Third-person* narrators, using pronouns such as *he*, *she*, or *them*, may be *omniscient* (knowing everything about all characters), or *limited* (taking the point of view of one character). [See also *narration*.]

propaganda   Information or ideas that may or may not be true, but are spread as though they are true, in order to persuade people to do or believe something.

prose   The ordinary form of written and spoken language used to create fiction, nonfiction, and most drama.

protagonist   The main character of a literary work. [See also *character* and *characterization*.]

R

refrain   A line or group of lines that is repeated, usually at the end of each verse, in a poem or a song.

repetition   The use of the same formal element more than once in a literary work, for emphasis or in order to achieve another desired effect.

resolution   The falling action in fiction or drama,

including all of the developments that follow the climax and show that the story's conflict is over. [See also *plot*.]

rhyme scheme   A repeated pattern of similar sounds, usually found at the ends of lines of poetry or poetic drama.

rhythm   In poetry, the measured recurrence of accented and unaccented syllables in a particular pattern. [See also *meter*.]

S

scene   The time, place, and circumstances of a play or a story. In a play, a scene is a section of an act. [See also *play*.]

science fiction   Fantasy literature set in an imaginary future, with details and situations that are designed to seem scientifically possible.

setting   The time and place of a work of literature.

short story   Narrative prose fiction that is shorter and has a less complicated plot than a novel. A short story contains narration, at least one setting, at least one character, and usually some dialogue.

simile   Figurative language that compares two unlike things, introduced by the words "like" or "as." [See also *figurative language*.]

soliloquy   In a play, a short speech spoken by a single character when he or she is alone on the stage. A soliloquy usually expresses the character's innermost thoughts and feelings, when he or she thinks no other characters can hear.

sonnet   A poem written in one stanza, using fourteen lines of iambic pentameter. [See also *meter*.]

speaker   In poetry, the individual whose voice seems to be speaking the lines. [See also *narration*, *voice*.]

stage directions   The directions, written by the playwright, to tell the director, actors, and theater technicians how a play should be dramatized. Stage directions may specify such things as how the setting should appear in each scene, how the actors should deliver their lines, when the stage curtain should rise and fall, how stage lights should be used, where on the stage the actors should be during the action, and when sound effects should be used.

stanza   A group of lines in poetry set apart by blank lines before and after the group; a poetic verse.

style   The distinctive way in which an author composes a work of literature in written or spoken language.

suspense   An effect created by authors of various types of fiction and drama, especially adventure and mystery, to heighten interest in the story.

symbol   An image, person, place, or thing that is used to express the idea of something else.

T

tall tale   A kind of folk tale, or legend, that exaggerates the characteristics of its hero or heroine.

theme   The main idea or underlying subject of a work of literature.

tone   The attitude that a work of literature expresses to the reader through its style.

tragedy   In classical drama, a tragedy depicts a noble hero or heroine who makes a mistake of judgment that has disastrous consequences.

V

verse   A stanza in a poem. Also, a synonym for poetry as a genre. [See also *stanza*.]

voice   The narrator or the person who relates the action of a piece of literature. [See also *speaker*.]

ACKNOWLEDGMENTS

Grateful acknowledgment is made for permission to reprint the following copyrighted material.

"Growing Up" from *Baseball in April and Other Stories* by Gary Soto, copyright ©1990 by Gary Soto, reprinted by permission of Harcourt Brace Jovanovich, Inc., Publishers.

"As It Is with Strangers" by Susan Beth Pfeffer, copyright ©1989 by Susan Beth Pfeffer, is reprinted from *Connections*, edited by Donald Gallo, by permission of Delacorte Press.

"The Torn Invitation" by Norman Katkov, copyright 1952, copyright renewed 1980 by Norman Katkov, reprinted by permission of the Harold Matson Company.

"The Writer" from *The Mind Reader* by Richard Wilbur, copyright ©1971 by Richard Wilbur, reprinted by permission of Harcourt Brace Jovanovich, Inc., Publishers.

"The Banana Tree" from *A Thief In The Village and Other Stories* by James Berry, copyright ©1987 by James Berry, reprinted by permission of Orchard Books, New York.

"The Taste of Melon" by Borden Deal, published in the *Saturday Evening Post*, September 1985, reprinted by permission of the Borden Deal Family Trust.

"The Medicine Bag" by Virginia Driving Hawk Sneve, published in *Boy's Life*, March 1975, reprinted by permission of the author.

"My Whole Family Is Women" by Randy from *Putting It All Together* by Paula McGuire copyright © 1987 by Visual Education Corporation, reprinted by permission of Delacorte Press.

ILLUSTRATION

67-83 Illustration by Dave Shepherd

PHOTOGRAPHY

4 *l* Nita Winter/The Image Works; **4** *t* Jim Whitmer/Stock Boston; **5** *b* Collection: Museo Rufino Tamayo/INBA Foteca Museo Rufino Tamayo; **6** Sarah Putnam/©D.C. Heath; **8-9** Ken O'Donohue/©D.C. Heath and Company; **10** *t* Carol Palmer; **10** *b* David Strickler/The Image Works; **11** *b* Robert Finken/The Picture Cube; *m* Jim Whitmer/Stock Boston, *t* Jim Whitmer/Stock Boston; **12-13** Tony Savino/The Image Works; **14-15** Frank Cezus/Tony Stone Images; **16-17** Tony Savino/The Image Works; **18-19** Rafael Macia/Photo Researchers; **20** Will McIntyre/Photo Researchers; **22** John E. Fogle/The Picture Cube; **23** Carolyn Soto; **24** The St. Louis Art Museum, gift of Mr. and Mrs. Joseph Pulitzer, Jr.; **28** ©Roy Lichtenstein. Photo by Robert McKeever; **29** Collection of Sydney and Frances Lewis © Roy Lichtenstein; **34** ©Roy Lichtenstein; **35** Photography by Christy Emanuel; **36** ©SEMA, courtesy of the artist; **41** Courtesy of the Museum of African-American Art; **46-47** Museum of Modern Art, New York. Gift of A. Conger Goodyear; **50** Museum of Indian Arts & Culture/Laboratory of Anthropology. Museum of New Mexico, Santa Fe. Cat. 53605/12. Photo by Blair Clark; **51** Courtesy of Norman Katkov; **52-53** David F. Hughes/The Picture Cube; **53** *inset* R. Sorensen & J. Olsen/NHPA; **54-55** Carib Art Gallery, New York City; **58** Collection of the Cummings Family. Photo by M. Lee Fatherree; **63** Courtesy Nohra Haime Gallery, New York; **64** Carib Art Gallery, New York City; **65** James Berry photo; **66-67** Collection: Museo Rufino Tamayo/INBA Fototeca Museo Rufino Tamayo; **70-71** Private Collection, courtesy Samuel Herrup Antiques; **76** The Collection of Mr. and Mrs. Graham Gund; **80-81** Abby Aldrich Rockefeller Folk Art Center, Williamsburg, VA; **83** Babs H. Deal/AP/Wide World Photos; **84** Courtesy Robert Hull Fleming Museum at the University of Vermont; Read Collection. 1881.3.83; **84-85** John A. Anderson Collection. Nebraska State Historical Society; **88-89** Kevin Thomas/©D.C. Heath and Company; **88** *l* The Montclair Art Museum Permanent Collection; **93** *l* Courtesy Robert Hull Fleming Museum, University of Vermont, Burlington, VT.; **93** *r* Philadelphia Museum of Art: Purchased with funds from the American Museum of Photography; **95** *b* Courtesy of Virginia Driving Hawk Sneve; **96** *bl* Myrleen Ferguson/PhotoEdit; **96-97** *b* Bob Daemmrich/The Image Works; **96** *c* Dan Bosler/Tony Stone Images; **96** *cb* Rhoda Sidney/Stock Boston; **96** *cl* Larry Lawfer/The Picture Cube; **96** *cr* Lawrence Migdale/Photo Researchers; **96** *tl* Lawrence Migdale/Stock Boston; **96-97** *t* Julie Houck/Stock Boston; **97** *b* David C. Bitters/The Picture Cube; **97** *c* Bob Daemmrich/Stock Boston; **97** *t* Jose L. Pelaez/The Stock Market; **103** Nancy Sheehan/©D.C. Heath; **106** *b* John Stuart/The Image Bank; **107** Alvin Uptis/The Image Bank; **109** The Far Side cartoon by Gary Larson is reprinted by permission of Chronicle Features, San Francisco, CA. All rights reserved; **112** Jeffry Myers/Stock Boston; **113** *all* Ken O'Donohue/©D.C. Heath and Company; **114** *b* Ken O'Donohue/©D.C. Heath and Company; **114** *t* Rhoda Sidney/Stock Boston; **115** *all* Ken O'Donohue/©D.C. Heath and Company.

Back cover *t/* John Owens/© D.C. Heath: *c,b/* Julie Bidwell/© D.C. Heath

Full Pronunciation Key for Footnoted Words

(Each pronunciation and definition is adapted from *Scott, Foresman Advanced Dictionary* by E.L. Thorndike and Clarence L. Barnhart.)

The pronunciation of each footnoted word is shown just after the word, in this way: **abbreviate** [ə brē′ vē āt]. The letters and signs used are pronounced as in the words below. The mark ′ is placed after a syllable with primary or heavy accent, as in the example above. The mark ′ after a syllable shows a secondary or lighter accent, as in **abbreviation** [ə brē′ vē ā′ shən].

Some words, taken from foreign languages, are spoken with sounds that do not otherwise occur in English. Symbols for these sounds are given in the key as "foreign sounds."

a	hat, cap	j	jam, enjoy	u	cup, butter		**foreign sounds**
ā	age, face	k	kind, seek	ù	full, put		
ä	father, far	l	land, coal	ü	rule, move		Y as in French *du*.
		m	me, am	v	very, save		Pronounce (ē) with
b	bad, rob	n	no, in	w	will, woman		the lips rounded as
ch	child, much	ng	long, bring	y	young, yet		for (ü).
d	did, red			z	zero, breeze		
		o	hot, rock	zh	measure, seizure		à as in French *ami*.
e	let, best	ō	open, go				Pronounce (ä) with
ē	equal, be	ô	order, all	ə represents:			the lips spread and
ėr	term, learn	oi	oil, voice		a in about		held tense.
		ou	house, out		e in taken		
f	fat, if				i in pencil		œ as in French *peu*.
g	go, bag	p	paper, cup		o in lemon		Pronounce (ā) with the
h	he, how	r	run, try		u in circus		lips rounded as for (ō).
		s	say, yes				
i	it, pin	sh	she, rush				N as in French *bon*.
ī	ice, five	t	tell, it				The N is not pro-
		th	thin, both				nounced, but shows
		ŦH	then, smooth				that the vowel before
							it is nasal.

H as in German *ach*. Pronounce (k) without closing the breath passage.

VOICES through the AGES

HEATH
MIDDLE LEVEL
LITERATURE

HEATH
MIDDLE LEVEL
LITERATURE

Voices Through the Ages

THEME
MYTHS, LEGENDS, AND FOLKTALES

AUTHORS

Donna Alvermann
Linda Miller Cleary
Kenneth Donelson
Donald Gallo
Alice Haskins
J. Howard Johnston
John Lounsbury
Alleen Pace Nilsen
Robert Pavlik
Jewell Parker Rhodes
Alberto Alvaro Ríos
Sandra Schurr
Lyndon Searfoss
Julia Thomason
Max Thompson
Carl Zon

STAFF CREDITS

EDITORIAL	Barbara A. Brennan, Susan Belt Cogley, DeVona Dors, Christopher Johnson, Rita M. Sullivan, Patricia B. Weiler
	Proofreading: JoAnne B. Sgroi
CONTRIBUTING WRITERS	Kathy Tuchman Glass, Jo Pitkin
SERIES DESIGN	Robin Herr
BOOK DESIGN	Caroline Bowden, Daniel Derdula, Susan Geer, Diana Maloney, Angela Sciaraffa, Bonnie Chayes Yousefian
	Art Editing: Carolyn Langley
PHOTOGRAPHY	*Series Photography Coordinator:* Carmen Johnson
	Photo Research Supervisor: Martha Friedman
	Photo Researchers: Wendy Enright, Linda Finigan, Po-yee McKenna, PhotoSearch, Inc., Gillian Speeth, Denise Theodores
	Assignment Photography Coordinators: Susan Doheny, Gayna Hoffman, Shawna Johnston
COMPUTER PREPRESS	Ricki Pappo, Kathy Meisl, Richard Curran, Michele Locatelli
PERMISSIONS	Dorothy B. McLeod
PRODUCTION	Patrick Connolly

Cover: *Icarus* by Henri Matisse, 1947, gift of Mr. and Mrs. Andrew S. Keck, © National Gallery of Art, Washington, D.C. **Cover Design:** Robin Herr

Acknowledgments for copyrighted material are on page 125 and constitute an extension of this page.

Published simultaneously in Canada

Printed in the United States of America

International Standard Book Number: 0-669-32115-X (soft cover)
3 4 5 6 7 8 9 10-RRD-99 98 97 96

International Standard Book Number: 0-669-38183-7 (hard cover)
3 4 5 6 7 8 9 10-RRD-99 98 97 96 95

Middle Level Authors

Donna Alvermann, University of Georgia
Alice Haskins, Howard County Public Schools, Maryland
J. Howard Johnston, University of South Florida
John Lounsbury, Georgia College
Sandra Schurr, University of South Florida
Julia Thomason, Appalachian State University
Max Thompson, Appalachian State University
Carl Zon, California Assessment Collaborative

Literature and Language Arts Authors

Linda Miller Cleary, University of Minnesota
Kenneth Donelson, Arizona State University
Donald Gallo, Central Connecticut State University
Alleen Pace Nilsen, Arizona State University
Robert Pavlik, Cardinal Stritch College, Milwaukee
Jewell Parker Rhodes, Arizona State University
Alberto Alvaro Ríos, Arizona State University
Lyndon Searfoss, Arizona State University

Teacher Consultants

Suzanne Aubin, Patapsco Middle School, Ellicott City, Maryland
Judy Baxter, Newport News Public Schools, Newport News, Virginia
Saundra Bryn, Director of Research and Development, El Mirage, Arizona
Lorraine Gerhart, Elmbrook Middle School, Elm Grove, Wisconsin
Kathy Tuchman Glass, Burlingame Intermediate School, Burlingame, California
Lucretia Pannozzo, John Jay Middle School, Katonah, New York
Carol Schultz, Jerling Junior High, Orland Park, Illinois
Jeanne Siebenman, Grand Canyon University, Phoenix, Arizona
Gail Thompson, Garey High School, Pomona, California
Rufus Thompson, Grace Yokley School, Ontario, California
Tom Tufts, Conniston Middle School, West Palm Beach, Florida
Edna Turner, Harpers Choice Middle School, Columbia, Maryland
C. Anne Webb, Buerkle Junior High School, St. Louis, Missouri
Geri Yaccino, Thompson Junior High School, St. Charles, Illinois

CONTENTS

ASKING BIG QUESTIONS ABOUT THE LITERATURE

PROJECTS

1 WRITING WORKSHOP

WRITE A FOLKTALE 106-111

What's a good way to be? Select one trait that you think is important and then write a folktale that shows the benefits of that trait.

2 COOPERATIVE LEARNING

CREATE AND PERFORM A PLAY 112-113

Some stories are so good, they bear repeating. Here's your chance to retell a folktale as a play.

3 HELPING YOUR COMMUNITY

RESEARCH PLACE NAMES 114-115

Why are rivers, mountains, and buildings called what they're called? Research the origins of place names in your area and then present your findings to your community.

A Long Time Ago . . .

Long ago, before TV, even before books, people found that their children loved listening to stories told around the campfire, but never listened when their parents told them important things or scolded them for bad behavior. Hummmm.

Wise people figured out that if a message were put in story form, others were much more likely to listen and heed the message. Work with a group of classmates to think of a plot for a story with a message. Then act out your story for another group.

1 Choose a Message

Folktales—myths, legends, and fables—might teach a lesson, make a statement about why some human traits or qualities are good or bad, or explain why things are they way they are. Look at the boxes below. For your group's message, choose a lesson, a trait, or a reason why.

MESSAGE ELEMENTS

LESSONS

- *Shortcuts take more time than they save.*
- *Be yourself.*
- *Virtue is rewarded.*

TRAITS

- *kindness*
- *persistence*
- *greediness*
- *meanness*

REASONS WHY

- *why the sun shines*
- *why the animals don't talk*
- *why people have ear lobes*

2 Create a Story to Deliver the Message

Now that you've chosen a message, how can you present it in story form? As a group, brainstorm for several story ideas. Since you'll only have about ten minutes to act out your story, keep it simple. For example, if you want to show why shortcuts take more time than they save, you'll probably need to limit your story to one shortcut and its consequences.

Keep your characters simple too. Think of the kinds of characters that will be familiar to your audience. A character such as a kind grandmother or an honest young farmer can help to present your message without distracting from it.

Finally, make sure your story entertains your audience. They won't get your message if they're snoring in their seats!

3 Tell Your Story

Decide who will play each role. Then do a quick rehearsal. Use your voices to create character. Improvise a few simple props to create setting. A stick of chalk can be a magic wand, and a yardstick can substitute for a rushing river.

Make sure that you're delivering your message without being preachy or too obvious. You audience will be more likely to accept your message if they're allowed to get the point for themselves.

4 Check Your Success

After you present your role-play, ask your audience to state your message. Did they think you were making a statement about envy when you thought you were explaining the origin of ear lobes? If your audience didn't get the message, ask them why.

Asking Big Questions About the Theme

What do people through the ages have in common?

Have you ever noticed that people have some traits, or ways of being, in common? For instance, people desire freedom. On the other hand, personality traits, such as kindness, are not common to all people. Most people seem to agree though that certain personality traits are good and others are bad.

In your journal, list as many kinds of traits as you can. Use a chart like the one begun here. When you finish, compare your lists with those of your classmates. Why do you think it's important for a storyteller to be aware of these traits?

> **Traits That People Share**
> feel protective of children
> want to survive
>
> **Traits That People Agree Are Bad**
> greediness
> meanness
>
> **Traits That People Agree Are Good**
> kindness
> honesty

Monitoring the Human Species Imagine that you're visiting Earth from another planet. To find out what the inhabitants of Earth are like, you monitor television and radio broadcasts. As you watch and listen, you take notes in your journal. What can you tell about the traits that humans value if you listen to their music and watch their television programs?

In your journal, write a report to your "home planet" and state your findings.

Why do people around the world tell folktales?

Think of a folktale that you remember hearing when you were younger. It might be an Aesop's fable, a Greek myth, or a Native American story. Summarize the story in your journal. Then tell your story to a small group. After everyone tells a story, decide as a group why each story might have been passed down from generation to generation.

What lessons do we learn about people through folktales?

Ask a grandparent, a relative, or a senior citizen in your neighborhood to tell you a story that teaches a lesson. Retell the story to a group of classmates. Agree on what lesson each story teaches. Organize your ideas by using a chart like the one shown. Then work as a class to create a poster that shows the lessons that folktales teach. Include drawings and magazine pictures.

Story Name

Story's Lesson

Way to Illustrate Lesson

NOW Think!

With a partner or small group of classmates, compare your ideas about human traits and folktales. As you read the selections in *Voices Through the Ages*, try to think of answers to the three Big Questions.

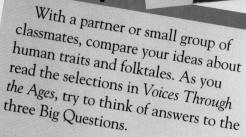

THE
EARTH
GIANT

BERNARD EVSLIN

Untitled Michel Nedjar, 1985, tissue, plaster, glue, 71 x 30 cm

Once again, Hercules[1] had done what he set out to do and was sailing home with three golden apples. Once again, he was sailing on a raft he had made himself with his spear as a mast and his lion skin as a sail. The raft was slow and clumsy, but ever since his fight with the octopus, he considered a raft to be the best platform for fighting sea monsters, and that was more important than speed.

However, he was not allowed to sail peacefully home. Hera[2] whispered to Poseidon,[3] who called a half-gale out of the north, driving the raft southward toward the hot hump of land called Libya, where the giant Anteus[4] ruled. Hercules stood on his raft, studying the coast. He didn't like what he saw. It was a bare scorched-looking stretch of shore. But then he saw something he liked even less. An enormous figure was wading toward him, waist-deep in the sea.

"Can this be that giant Nereus[5] spoke of?" wondered Hercules. "The one I have to fight? I hope not. He's almost as big as Atlas."[6]

He watched, horrified, as the giant reached into the water with a hand as big as a skiff and pulled out a swordfish. This was a terrible creature, as big as a shark; its sword was three feet long, and needle-pointed. But the giant cupped it out of the water like a boy catching a minnow and stood there, waves swirling around his waist, picking his teeth with the swordfish. He cast it back into the water, laughing a great rumbling laugh.

"Ho there," he called. "You, little one, standing on those twigs, who are you?"

"I am Hercules."

"I'm glad to see you, Hercules. You're bringing me three golden apples, aren't you?"

1. **Hercules** [hėr´ kyə lēz´]: in Greek myths, hero who had to perform twelve labors as a punishment.
2. **Hera** [hir´ ə]: in Greek myths, a goddess, wife of Zeus.
3. **Poseidon** [pə sīd´ n]: in Greek myths, god of the sea.
4. **Anteus** [an tā´ əs]: (also *Antaeus*) in Greek myths, an African giant who was invincible only when in direct contact with the earth.
5. **Nereus** [nir´ ús]: in Greek myths, a sea god.
6. **Atlas** [at´ ləs]: in Greek myths, a giant who was punished for revolting against Zeus by having to support the heavens on his shoulders.

"I have three golden apples," said Hercules. "But not for you. One of them I must bring back to the king of Mycenae,[7] for that is my task. Another one is a gift for a girl I know, named Iole.[8] And the third is a gift for a young lady named Dienera."[9]

"Very generous. But I'm afraid you don't understand. I am Anteus. This is my land and my harbor. And I am charging you a docking fee: three golden apples. You must pay or you cannot leave."

"I won't give you these apples. You'll have to take them."

"Do you really want me to use force? You're either very brave or very foolish or perhaps both. Don't you know that I can squash you like an ant?"

"Very well, I challenge you to a wrestling match. But let me come ashore and eat something and sleep a bit. I have sailed a long way."

"I like you, little Hercules," boomed Anteus. "You've not only brought me three beautiful golden apples, but you're going to give me some sport as well. Come ashore, come ashore. We'll dine together. It'll be your last meal, of course, for tomorrow we fight."

When you're not used to the desert, it looks flat and ugly by day. But it can be beautiful at night. If you sleep outdoors, you see stars flaring like torches in black sky, and they sink toward you, spinning like fire wheels. You can weave their threads of light among your thoughts and make pictures that flicker against the velvet sky.

That's what Hercules was doing the night before the fight. He lay out on the sand looking up at the sky. He couldn't sleep. He was trying to puzzle out the verse spoken by Nereus. "To prove the giant's worth,/stretch him flat on earth." Earth was Mother Earth, Nereus had said. And contact with earth robbed Anteus of his strength. But was this the truth or a lie? Should he believe it or do the opposite? Had the verse helped him before or not? A memory picture flared. He was standing in the orchard throwing beehives into Ladon's[10] gullet. Had Nereus told him the truth about that?

---

7. **Mycenae** [mī sē′ nā]: a city in the southern part of ancient Greece.
8. **Iole** [ī′ ə lē′]: the daughter of King Eurytus; Hercules wanted to marry her.
9. **Dienera** [dē ə nā′ rə]: wife of Hercules.
10. **Ladon** [lād′ ən]: in Greek myths, a dragon with one hundred heads, killed by Hercules.

"Honey to the snake," he had said, but hadn't mentioned bees. Yet bees and honey were connected, very much so. So was that line a lie or not? And the next line, "Titan's[11] burden take." Another picture flared, his own hunched shadow being crushed by the heavy rim of the sky. He had shouldered the Titan's burden and had almost been stuck with it forever. Yet, and this was true too, if he hadn't taken the sky from Atlas and frightened him by shaking the stars he would never have been able to get the golden apples away from the orchard. So, were those lines true or not?

Now another picture flickered. Himself fighting the giant, Anteus, who was ten times his own size, strong enough to crush stones in his hands and to pick his teeth with swordfish. "To prove the giant's worth,/stretch him flat on earth." A truth or a lie or something between? Important to know, because when fighting an Anteus, one mistake is all you're allowed.

"Well, maybe it'll get clearer during the fight," he said to himself. "Best thing I can do now is get some sleep." So he chased the pictures and the puzzling verse out of his head, shut his eyes, and went fast asleep.

The next morning, they fought, and everyone in the land came to watch. They wrestled in a natural arena, a level place cupped by worn-down hills. The only rule in this match was that you had to come in without weapons. After the bout started, you could do anything you wanted, use anything you could get. Punching, kicking, gouging, choking—these were what the people wanted to see. But they were also used to being disappointed. No one had ever lasted more than a minute against Anteus.

The wrestlers stripped and oiled themselves. Slaves had to lean ladders against Anteus and climb with sponges and buckets of oil to the great plateau of his shoulders and the huge keg of his chest. The slaves departed. The wrestlers crouched.

"I barely reach to his kneecap," thought Hercules. "What can I possibly do? Well, when in doubt, charge!"

And the audience was amazed to see the man hurtle straight

11. **Titan** [tīt′n]: in Greek myths, one of a family of giants who once ruled the world.

The Earth Gia

toward the giant. Anteus stood, waiting. Then he swung his leg in a terrific kick. His foot, traveling at enormous speed, hit the top of Hercules' head, which was hard as a rock. The small bones of instep and ankle shattered like glass. Anteus hopped in agony. Hercules thrust his shoulder against that leg, pushing it out from under the giant, who went crashing to the ground. People sitting on the slopes felt the hills tremble as Anteus fell full length on the ground, cracking his head on a tree stump.

Hercules heard the ugly dry sound of that head splitting open. He saw the giant's blood soaking into the ground, heard the rattling gasp of his breath. He stood over his enemy, watching him die, and was amazed to see the ashy face flush with life. He saw the giant's eyes snap open, blazing with hatred, and the great chest swell. Before he could dodge away, Anteus shot his arm out, and the huge fingers caught Hercules by the throat and began to strangle him.

The air darkened. The earth tilted. Hercules struggled, trying to tear those baling-hook[12] fingers from his throat. In all his battles he had never felt a force equal to that of Anteus who, lying at ease on the ground, was calmly throttling Hercules to death with one hand. And, as his sight faded, he heard again the thin sneering voice of Nereus: "To prove the giant's worth,/stretch him flat on earth," and he knew suddenly the power of that lie. He knew that he should have done the opposite, for Anteus was the favorite son of Mother Earth and drew new strength from her touch. Felled to earth, the giant must rise again, stronger than before, and destroy the one who had laid him in his mother's lap.

This truth glimmered in the young man's darkening mind; it flared brightly, as truth does ever when things are worst. And the strangling Hercules felt his tortured breathing ease a bit as the new idea cast a light that became strength beyond the strength of muscles.

He swung his arm in a desperate arc, knocking away the hand that was choking him. Taking a huge breath, he stooped swiftly, grasped the giant about the waist, and tried to pull him off the

12. **baling-hook:** a large hook used to lift heavy objects; here the reference is to the great size of Anteus' fingers.

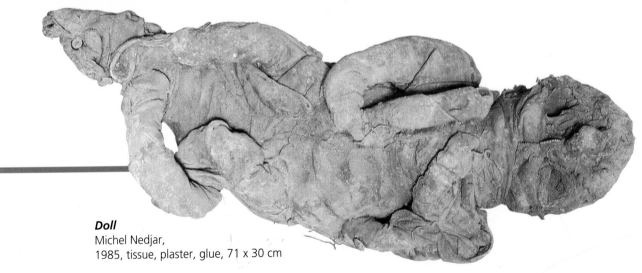

Doll
Michel Nedjar,
1985, tissue, plaster, glue, 71 x 30 cm

ground. But Anteus kicked and flailed and clung to the earth. And his mother, knowing he was in danger, pulled with all her strength—called gravity—trying to hug her son to her and keep him safe. Hercules couldn't pull him up, and he knew that if he couldn't, he was lost. He pulled and tugged. Anteus clung to the earth, which hugged him close.

"Father Zeus, help me now," whispered Hercules. And with those words, he felt the lightning energy that belonged to the Lord of the Sky fill his veins with a voltage of strength that allowed him to tear the struggling giant from the clutch of earth and lift him slowly toward the sky. His split head began to bleed again, and his life drained out as Hercules held him to the brassy sun.

Hercules kept holding the giant even after he was dead. He didn't dare let him touch earth again. He carried the enormous body to the beach and cast it into the sea and watched as the triangular fins of sharks began to cut the water.

BERNARD EVSLIN

Bernard Evslin was born in 1922 in Philadelphia, Pennsylvania, and grew up with a fondness for the heroes, gods, and monsters from Greek mythology. Evslin's popular novels include *Heraclea: A Legend of Warrior Women* and *Jason and the Argonauts*. In addition to writing books, Evslin has also written plays and screenplays for television documentaries.

ANTAEUS

BORDEN DEAL

This was during the wartime,[1] when lots of people were coming North for jobs in factories and war industries, when people moved around a lot more than they do now and sometimes kids were thrown into new groups and new lives that were completely different from anything they had ever known before. I remember this one kid; T. J. his name was, from somewhere down South, whose family moved into our building during that time. They'd come North with everything they owned piled into the back seat of an old-model sedan that you wouldn't expect could make the trip, with T. J. and his three younger sisters riding shakily atop the load of junk.

Our building was just like all the others there, with families crowded into a few rooms, and I guess there were twenty-five or thirty kids about my age in that one building. Of course, there were a few of us who formed a gang and ran together all the time after school, and I was the one who brought T. J. in and started the whole thing.

The building right next door to us was a factory where they made walking dolls. It was a low building with a flat, tarred roof that had a parapet[2] all around it about head-high, and we'd found out a long time before that no one, not even the watchman, paid any attention to the roof because it was higher than any of the other buildings around. So my gang used the roof as a headquarters. We could get up there by crossing over to the fire escape from our own roof on a plank and then going on up. It was a secret place for us, where nobody else could go without our permission.

I remember the day I first took T. J. up there to meet the gang. He was a stocky, robust kid with a shock of hair, nothing sissy about him except his voice—he talked different from any of us and you noticed it right away. But I liked him anyway, so I told him to come on up.

We climbed up over the parapet and dropped down on the roof. The rest of the gang were already there.

"Hi," I said. I jerked my thumb at T. J. "He just moved into the building yesterday."

He just stood there, not scared or anything, just looking, like the

---

1. **wartime:** reference here is to World War II.
2. **parapet** [par′ ə pet]: a low barrier at the edge of a roof.

first time you see somebody you're not sure you're going to like.

"Hi," Blackie said. "Where you from?"

"Marion County," T. J. said.

We laughed. "Marion County?" I said. "Where's that?"

He looked at me like I was a stranger, too. "It's in Alabama," he said, like I ought to know where it was.

"What's your name?" Charley said.

"T. J.," he said, looking back at him. He had pale blue eyes that looked washed-out but he looked directly at Charley, waiting for his reaction. He'll be all right, I thought. No sissy in him . . . except that voice. Who ever talked like that?

"T. J.," Blackie said. "That's just initials. What's your real name? Nobody in the world has just initials."

"I do," he said. "And they're T. J. That's all the name I got."

His voice was resolute[3] with the knowledge of his rightness and for a moment no one had anything to say. T. J. looked around at the rooftop and down at the black tar under his feet. "Down yonder where I come from," he said, "we played out in the woods. Don't you-all have no woods around here?"

"Naw," Blackie said. "There's the park a few blocks over, but it's full of kids and old women. You can't do a thing."

T. J. kept looking at the tar under his feet. "You mean you ain't got no fields to raise nothing in? No watermelons or nothing?"

"Naw," I said scornfully. "What do you want to grow something for? The folks can buy everything they need at the store."

He looked at me again with that strange, unknowing look. "In Marion County," he said, "I had my own acre of cotton and my own acre of corn. It was mine to plant ever' year."

He sounded like it was something to be proud of, and in some obscure way it made the rest of us angry. "Heck!" Blackie said. "Who'd want to have their own acre of cotton and corn? That's just work. What can you do with an acre of cotton and corn?"

T. J. looked at him. "Well, you get part of the bale offen your acre," he said seriously. "And I fed my acre of corn to my calf."

3. **resolute** [rez′ ə lŭt]: bold, determined.

"There's those wholesale seed houses over on Sixth," I said. "We could probably swipe some grass seed over there."

T. J. looked at the earth. "You-all seem mighty set on raising some grass," he said. "I never put no effort into that. I spent all my life trying not to raise grass."

"But it's pretty," Blackie said. "We could play on it and take sun-baths on it. Like having our own lawn."

"Well," T. J. said. He looked at the rest of us, hesitant for the first time. He kept on looking at us for a moment. "I did have it in mind to raise some corn and vegetables. But we'll plant grass."

He was smart. He knew where to give in. And I don't suppose it made any difference to him really. He just wanted to grow something, even if it was grass.

"Of course," he said, "I do think we ought to plant a row of water-melons. They'd be mighty nice to eat while we was a-laying on that grass."

We all laughed. "All right," I said. "We'll plant us a row of water-melons."

Things went very quickly then. Perhaps half the roof was covered with the earth, the half that wasn't broken by ventilators, and we swiped pocketfuls of grass seed from the open bins in the wholesale seed house, mingling among the buyers on Saturdays and during the school lunch hour. T. J. showed us how to prepare the earth, breaking up the clods and smoothing it and sowing[15] the grass seed. It looked rich and black now with moisture, receiving of the seed, and it seemed that the grass sprang up overnight, pale green in the early spring.

We couldn't keep from looking at it, unable to believe that we had created this delicate growth. We looked at T. J. with understanding now, knowing the fulfillment of the plan he had carried alone within his mind. We had worked without full understanding of the task, but he had known all the time.

We found that we couldn't walk or play on the delicate blades, as we had expected to, but we didn't mind. It was enough just to look at

15. **sowing** [sō′ ing]: planting.

it, to realize that it was the work of our own hands, and each evening the whole gang was there, trying to measure the growth that had been achieved.

One time a foot was placed on the plot of ground . . . one time only Blackie stepping onto it with sudden bravado.[16] Then he looked at the crushed blades and there was shame in his face. He did not do it again. This was his grass, too, and not to be desecrated.[17] No one said anything, for it was not necessary.

T. J. had reserved a small section for watermelons and he was still trying to find some seed for it. The wholesale house didn't have any watermelon seed and we didn't know where we could lay our hands on them. T. J. shaped the earth into mounds, ready to receive them, three mounds lying in a straight line along the edge of the grass plot.

We had just about decided that we'd have to buy the seed if we were to get them. It was a violation[18] of our principles but we were anxious to get the watermelons started. Somewhere or other, T. J. got his hands on a seed catalog and brought it one evening to our roof garden.

"We can order them now," he said, showing us the catalog. "Look!"

We all crowded around, looking at the fat, green watermelons pictured in full color on the pages. Some of them were split open, showing the red, tempting meat, making our mouths water.

"Now we got to scrape up some seed money," T. J. said, looking at us. "I got a quarter. How much you-all got?"

We made up a couple of dollars between us and T. J. nodded his head. "That'll be more than enough. Now we got to decide what kind to get. I think them Kleckley Sweets. What do you-all think?"

He was going into matters beyond our reach. We hadn't even known there were different kinds of melons. So we just nodded our heads and agreed that yes, we thought the Kleckley Sweets, too.

---

16. **bravado** [brə vä′ dō]: a show of courage without much real courage.
17. **desecrated** [des′ ə krāt əd]: treated without respect.
18. **violation** [vī′ ə lā′ shən]: a going against.

"I'll order them tonight," T. J. said. "We ought to have them in a few days."

Then an adult voice said behind us: "What are you boys doing up here?"

It startled us for no one had ever come up here before, in all the time we had been using the roof of the factory. We jerked around and saw three men standing near the trap door at the other end of the roof. They weren't policemen, or night watchmen, but three men in business suits, looking at us. They walked toward us.

"What are you boys doing up here?" the one in the middle said again.

We stood still, guilt heavy among us, and looked at the three strangers.

The men stared at the grass flourishing behind us. "What's this?" the man said. "How did this get up here?"

"Sure is growing good, ain't it?" T. J. said conversationally. "We planted it."

The men kept looking at the grass as if they didn't believe it. It was a thick carpet over the earth now, a patch of deep greenness startling in the sterile industrial surroundings.

"Yes, sir," T. J. said proudly. "We toted that earth up here and planted that grass." He fluttered the seed catalog. "And we're just fixing to plant some watermelon."

The man looked at him then, his eyes strange and faraway. "What do you mean, putting this on the roof of my building?" he said. "Do you want to go to jail?"

T. J. looked shaken. The rest of us were silent, frightened by the authority of his voice. We had grown up aware of adult authority, of policemen, night watchmen, teachers, and this man sounded like all the others. But it was a new thing to T. J.

"Well, you wasn't using the roof," T. J. said. He paused a moment and added shrewdly, "So we just thought to pretty it up a little bit."

"And sag it so I'd have to rebuild it," the man said sharply. He turned away, saying to a man beside him, "See that all that junk is shoveled off by tomorrow."

"Yes, sir," the man said.

T. J. started forward. "You can't do that," he said. "We toted it up here and it's our earth. We planted it and raised it and toted it up here."

The man stared at him coldly. "But it's my building," he said. "It's to be shoveled off tomorrow."

"It's our earth," T. J. said desperately. "You got no right!"

The men walked on without listening and descended clumsily through the trap door. T. J. stood looking after them, his body tense with anger, until they had disappeared. They wouldn't even argue with him, wouldn't let him defend his earth-rights.

He turned to us. "We won't let 'em do it," he said fiercely. "We'll stay up here all day tomorrow and the day after that and we won't let 'em do it."

We just looked at him. We knew that there was no stopping it. He saw it in our faces and his face wavered for a moment before he gripped it into determination.

"They got no right," he said. "It's our earth. It's our land. Can't nobody touch a man's own land."

We kept on looking at him, listening to the words but knowing that it was no use. The adult world had descended on us even in our richest dream, and we knew there was no calculating the adult world, no fighting it, no winning against it.

We started moving slowly toward the parapet and the fire escape, avoiding a last look at the green beauty of the earth that T. J. had planted for us . . . had planted deeply in our minds as well as in our experience. We filed slowly over the edge and down the steps to the plank, T. J. coming last, and all of us could feel the weight of his grief behind us.

"Wait a minute," he said suddenly, his voice harsh with the effort of calling. We stopped and turned, held by the tone of his voice, and looked up at him standing above us on the fire escape.

"We can't stop them?" he said, looking down at us, his face strange in the dusky light. "There ain't no way to stop 'em?"

"No," Blackie said with finality. "They own the building."

We stood still for a moment, looking up at T. J., caught into inaction by the decision working in his face. He stared back at us and his face was pale and mean in the poor light, with a bald nakedness in his skin like cripples have sometimes.

"They ain't gonna touch my earth," he said fiercely. "They ain't gonna lay a hand on it! Come on."

He turned around and started up the fire escape again, almost running against the effort of climbing. We followed more slowly, not knowing what he intended. By the time we reached him, he had seized a board and thrust it into the soil, scooping it up and flinging it over the parapet into the areaway below. He straightened and looked us squarely in the face.

"They can't touch it," he said. "I won't let 'em lay a dirty hand on it!"

We saw it then. He stooped to his labor again and we followed, the gusts of his anger moving in frenzied labor among us as we scattered along the edge of earth, scooping it and throwing it over the parapet, destroying with anger the growth we had nurtured with such tender care. The soil carried so laboriously upward to the light and the sun cascaded[19] swiftly into the dark areaway, the green blades of grass crumpled and twisted in the falling.

It took less time than you would imagine . . . the task of destruction is infinitely easier than that of creation. We stopped at the end, leaving only a scattering of loose soil, and when it was finally over a stillness stood among the group and over the factory building. We looked down at the bare sterility[20] of black tar, felt the harsh texture of it under the soles of our shoes, and the anger had gone out of us, leaving only a sore aching in our minds like overstretched muscles.

T. J. stooped for a moment, his breathing slowing from anger and effort, caught into the same contemplation of destruction as all of us. He stooped slowly, finally, and picked up a lonely blade of grass left trampled under our feet and put it between his teeth, tasting it, sucking the greenness out of it into his mouth. Then he started

19. **cascaded** [ka skād′ əd]: flowed.
20. **sterility** [stə ril′ ə tē]: lifelessness.

walking toward the fire escape, moving before any of us were ready to move, and disappeared over the edge while we stared after him.

We followed him but he was already halfway down to the ground, going on past the board where we crossed over, climbing down into the areaway. We saw the last section swing down with his weight and then he stood on the concrete below us, looking at the small pile of earth scattered by our throwing. Then he walked across the place where we could see him and disappeared toward the street without glancing back, without looking up to see us watching him.

They did not find him for two weeks. Then the Nashville police caught him just outside the Nashville freight yards. He was walking along the railroad track; still heading in a southerly direction, still heading home.

As for us, who had no remembered home to call us . . . none of us ever again climbed the escape-way to the roof.

BORDEN DEAL

Borden Deal was born in 1922 in Pontotoc, Mississippi, and grew up knowing the world from which the hero of "Antaeus" came. After graduating from college, Deal spent years wandering around the United States, supporting himself by taking odd jobs with a circus, a showboat, and a federal work project. Deal settled down in Washington, D.C., and worked for the U.S. Department of Labor. He began writing then and published his first story in 1948. By 1955, he had decided to become a full-time writer. Deal's short stories have appeared in many magazines and anthologies.

Dream Girl Qiu Tao, oil on canvas, Pacific Asia Museum, Pasadena

FOX HUNT

LENSEY NAMIOKA

Andy Liang[1] watched the kids from his school bus walk home with their friends. He could hear them talking together and laughing. He always got off the bus alone and walked home by himself.

But this time it was different. A girl got off the bus just behind him and started walking in the same direction. He wondered why he hadn't seen her before. She was also Asian-American, which made it all the more surprising that he hadn't noticed her earlier.

As he tried to take a better look, she went into the neighborhood convenience store and disappeared behind a shelf of canned soup. He peered into the store, hoping for another glimpse of her. All he saw were some of the kids from the bus getting bags of potato chips and soft drinks.

Andy sighed. He was used to being a loner, and usually it didn't bother him—not much, anyway. But today, the loneliness was heavy. He overheard the other kids talking, and knew they were planning to

1. **Liang** [lyäng]

study together for the PSAT.[2] From the looks of the snacks, they were expecting a long session.

Andy would be practicing for the test, too, but he would be doing it by himself. *I'm better off doing it alone, anyway,* he thought. *Studying with somebody else would just slow me down.*

The truth was that none of the others had invited him to study with them. *So all right,* he said to himself, *they think I'm a grind. What's wrong with that? I'll be getting better scores on the PSAT than any of them, even if there's nobody to coach me.*

He finally found the girl standing in front of a case of barbecued chicken. She was staring so hungrily at the chickens that his own mouth began watering, and he would have bought a piece on the spot if he had the money. But with the change in his pocket, he had to be satisfied with a candy bar.

Leaving the store, he reached his street and passed the corner house with the moody German shepherd. As usual, it snapped at him, and he automatically retreated to the far side of the sidewalk. Although the dog was on a chain, Andy didn't like the way it looked at him. Besides, a chain could always break.

Today, the dog not only snapped, it began to bark furiously and strained against its chain. Andy jumped back, and bumped against the girl he had seen earlier. Somehow she had appeared behind him without making any noise.

He apologized. "I didn't mean to crash into you. That dog always growls at me, but today he's really barking like crazy."

The girl shivered. "The dog doesn't seem to like me very much, either." Before he had a chance to say anything more, she turned and walked away.

Again Andy sighed. He didn't even get a chance to find out what her name was or where she lived. Was she Chinese-American, like him? What grade was she in? At least she went on the same school bus, so there was a chance of seeing her again.

But he didn't have much hope that she would be interested in him. Girls didn't go for the quiet, studious type. Last year, one of the

2. **PSAT:** Preliminary Scholastic Aptitude Test.

girls in his geometry class had asked him to give her some help after school. That went pretty well, and for a while he thought they might have something going. But after she passed the geometry test, she didn't look at him again.

Maybe if he studied less and went in for sports, girls would get interested in him. But then his grades might slip, and his parents would never let him hear the end of it. He had to keep his grades up, study hard, be the dutiful son.

His brother had managed to get a math score of 800 in the PSAT, and now he was at Yale[3] with a full scholarship. Andy had to try and do as well.

More than once he had asked his parents why it was so important to get into a good college. "Lots of people get rich in this country without going to college at all," he told them.

His father would draw himself up stiffly. "The Liangs belonged to the mandarin[4] class in China. I've told you again and again that to become a mandarin, one had to pass the official examinations. Only outstanding scholars passed, and only they had the qualifications to govern the country."

Andy's father always got worked up about the subject. He might be only a minor clerk in America, he said, but he was descended from a family of high-ranking officials in China.

Another thing Andy noticed was that when his father went on at length about the illustrious[5] Liang family, his mother always listened with a faint smile. She seemed to be amused for some reason.

But that didn't stop her from also putting pressure on Andy to study hard. Every night, she would ask him whether he had done his homework, and she double-checked his papers to make sure everything was correct.

Normally Andy didn't mind doing his homework. He liked the satisfaction of a job well done when he finished a hard problem in

3. **Yale:** university in New Haven, Connecticut.
4. **mandarin** [man′dər ən]: member of one of the nine ranks of public officials of the Chinese Empire.
5. **illustrious** [i lus′ trē əs]: very famous and important.

math. But lately, all the extra work preparing for the exam was beginning to get him down. His mind wandered and he began to daydream. He had visions of becoming a snake charmer, making a balloon trip over the Andes,[6] or practicing kung fu[7] in Shaolin[8] Temple. He saw himself in the English countryside, riding a galloping horse in a fox hunt.

He tried to stop wasting time on these stupid daydreams. Maybe his mind wouldn't wander if he had someone to study with. But nobody wanted to study with him. Nobody wanted to spend time with a nerd.

Next day the girl got off the bus again with Andy, and this time, instead of going into the convenience store, she began to walk with him. When they reached the yard with the German shepherd, they both automatically backed away from the fence.

Andy and the girl looked at each other and grinned. He was encouraged. "I'm Andy Liang. Are you new in the neighborhood?"

"We moved here last week," she replied. "My name is Leona Hu.[9] But Leona is a silly name, and my friends call me Lee."

She was inviting him to call her Lee and including him among her friends! Andy could hardly believe his luck. An attractive girl was actually ready to be friends. He was grateful to the German shepherd.

The girl had big, almond-shaped eyes. Andy had overheard Americans saying that Chinese had slanty eyes, although his own eyes did not slant. Lee's eyes, on the other hand, definitely slanted upward at the corners.

Her hair had a slightly reddish tint, instead of being blue-black like his own. She wasn't exactly beautiful, but with her hair and her slanting eyes, she looked exotic[10] and fascinating.

When they came to his house, Andy wished he could keep Lee

---

6. **Andes** [an′dēz]: mountains in western South America.
7. **kung fu** [kung′ fu′]: ancient Chinese method of self-defense that uses the hands and legs as weapons.
8. **Shaolin** [shäw lin′]
9. **Hu** [hü]
10. **exotic** [eg zot′ ik]: interesting because strange or different.

talking with him. But she smiled at him briefly and went on. He had to stop himself from running after her to find out where she lived. He didn't want her to think that he was pestering her.

Was she going to take the PSAT this year? If she was, maybe they could study together!

At dinner that night, his father went on as usual about how important it was to do well on the PSAT. "We immigrants start at the bottom here in America, and the only way we can pull ourselves up is to get a good education. Never forget that you're descended from illustrious ancestors, Andy."

Again, Andy noticed his mother's faint smile. Later, he went into the kitchen where he found her washing the dishes. "Why do you always smile when Father gives me his pep talk about education? Don't you agree with him?"

"Oh, I agree with him about the importance of education," his mother said. "I'm just amused by all that talk about *illustrious ancestors*."

"You mean Father wasn't telling the truth about Liangs being mandarins?" asked Andy. He took up a bunch of chopsticks and began to wipe them dry. Usually, his mother refused his help with the chores. She wanted him to spend all his time on his homework.

But tonight she didn't immediately send him upstairs to his desk. She rinsed a rice bowl and put it in the dish rack. "Well, the Liangs haven't always been mandarins," she said finally. "They used to be quite poor, until one of them achieved success by passing the official examinations and raising the status of the whole Liang family."

"Hey, that's great!" Andy liked the idea of a poor boy making good. It was more interesting than coming from a long line of decadent aristocrats.[11] "Tell me more about this ancestor."

"His name was Fujin[12] Liang," replied his mother. "Or I should say Liang Fujin, since in China, last names come first." Again she smiled faintly. "Very well. You should really be studying, but it's good for you to know about your ancestors."

11. **decadent aristocrats** [dek′ ə dənt ə ris′ tə kratz]: immoral people of noble birth.
12. **Fujin** [fü jin′]

Liang Fujin lived with his widowed mother in a small thatched cottage and earned money by looking after a neighbor's water buffalo. His mother added to their meager income by weaving and selling cotton cloth. It was a hard struggle to put rice in their bowls.

But Fujin's mother was ambitious for him. She knew he was smart, and she decided that he should try for the official examinations. In theory, any poor boy could take the examinations, and if he passed, he could raise his family to mandarin status. But rich boys could afford tutors to help them study. For Fujin, even buying a book was a luxury.

He was so eager to learn that he crouched under the window of the nearby school and tried to eavesdrop on the lessons. Whenever he saved enough money to buy books, he would read them while seated on the back of the water buffalo. Once he was so absorbed that he walked the buffalo into a rice paddy. But he managed to read the precious books until he knew them all by heart.

Through hard work he grew up to be a fine scholar. His mother thought he was finally ready to take the examinations, but he himself wasn't so confident. The other competitors were the sons of rich families, who could afford the very best tutors.

He continued to study late every night, until his head began to nod. So he tied the end of his pigtail to a nail in the ceiling, and whenever his head fell forward, the pigtail jerked him awake.

One night, while he was struggling to stay awake over his book, he heard a soft voice behind him. "A fine, hardworking young man like you deserves to pass the examination."

Fujin whirled around and saw a beautiful girl standing behind him. Somehow she had appeared without making any noise. She had huge, bewitching eyes which slanted sharply. Could he be dreaming?

"Let me help you," continued the girl. "I can act as a tutor and coach you."

"And that was how your ancestor, Liang Fujin, got the coaching he needed to pass the examinations," said Andy's mother.

Andy blinked. "But . . . but who was this mysterious girl? And how come she was such a great scholar? I thought women didn't get much education in the old days."

His mother laughed. "Nobody in the Liang family would say. But I'll give you a hint: When the girl lifted her skirt to sit down, Fujin caught a flash of something swishing. It looked like a long, bushy tail!"

It took Andy a moment to get it. Then he remembered the Chinese stories his mother used to tell him, stories about the *huli jing*,[13] or "fox spirit." The mischievous fox, or *huli*, often appeared in the form of a beautiful girl and played tricks on people. But in some of the stories, the fox fell in love with a handsome young man and did him a great service. She expected a reward for her service, of course, and the reward was marriage.

"So my ancestor passed the examinations because he was coached by a fox?" asked Andy.

"That story is a lie!" cried Andy's father, stomping into the kitchen. "It was made up by malicious neighbors who were jealous of the Liangs!"

Andy's mother shrugged and began to pack the dishes away. His father continued. "Liang Fujin passed the examinations because he was smart and worked hard! Don't you forget it, Andy! So now you can go up to your room and start working!"

His father was right, of course. Fox spirits belonged in fairy tales. He, Andy Liang, would have to study for the PSAT the hard way.

Andy was delighted when Lee told him that she was also planning to take the PSAT. She agreed that it would be a good idea to study together. He was eager to begin that very evening. "How about coming over to my house? I'm sure my parents would love to meet you."

Actually, he wasn't sure just how delighted his parents would be.

13. *huli jing* [hü lē′ jing]

He suspected that they would be glad to see him with a Chinese-American girl, but they'd probably think that a girl—any girl—would distract him from his studies.

He was half sorry and half relieved when she said, "I'm going to be busy tonight. Maybe we can go to the public library tomorrow afternoon and get some sample tests and study guides."

That night he had a dream about fox hunting. Only this time, he found himself running on the ground trying to get away from the mounted horsemen and howling dogs. There was somebody running with him—another fox, with reddish hair and a bushy tail. It flashed a look at him with its slanting eyes.

Andy and Lee began studying sample SAT tests at the library. Working with someone else certainly made studying less of a drudgery.[14] Andy felt relaxed with Lee. He didn't suffer the paralyzing shyness that seized him when he was with other girls.

She was really good at finding out what his weaknesses were. English grammar was his worst subject, and Lee fed him the right questions so that the fuzzy points of grammar got cleared up. As the days went by, Andy became confident that he was going to do really well on the PSAT. At this rate, he might get a scholarship to some famous university.

He began to worry that the help was one-sided. *He* was getting first rate coaching, but what was Lee getting out of this? "You're helping me so much," he told her. "But I don't see how I'm helping you at all."

She smiled at him. "I'll get my reward someday."

Something about her glance looked familiar. Where had he seen it before?

They had an extra long study session the day before the exam. When they passed the corner house on their way home, the German shepherd went into a frenzy of barking and scrabbled[15] to climb the

14. **drudgery** [druj′ ər ē]: hard, tiresome work.
15. **scrabbled** [skrab′ əld]: struggled.

cyclone fence. Both the chain and the fence held, fortunately. Lee looked shaken and backed away from the fence.

At Andy's house she recovered her color. "Well, good luck on the exam tomorrow." She looked at him for a moment with her slanting eyes, and then she was gone.

Again, he thought he remembered that look from somewhere. All during supper, he was tantalized[16] by the memory, which was just out of reach.

That night he dreamed about fox hunting again. It was more vivid than usual, and he could see the scarlet coats of the riders chasing him. The howling of the dogs sounded just like the German shepherd. Again, he was running with another fox. It had huge slanting eyes, bright with mischief.

He woke up, and as he sat in his bed, he finally remembered where he had seen those huge, slanting eyes. They were Lee's eyes.

Next day Andy met Lee at the entrance to the examination hall. He suddenly realized that if he said her name in the Chinese order,

Dream Girl
Qiu Tao,
detail

it would be Hu Lee, which sounded the same as *huli*, or "fox."

She smiled. "So you know?"

Andy found his voice. "Why did you pick me, particularly?"

Her smile widened. "We foxes hunt out our own kind."

That was when Andy knew why the German shepherd always snapped at him. He himself must be part fox. His ancestor, Liang Fujin, had accepted help from the fox spirit after all, and she had collected her reward.

16. **tantalized** [tan′ tl īzd]: bothered, distracted from trying to remember.

LENSEY NAMIOKA

Lensey Namioka was born in 1929 in Beijing, China, and came to the United States with her parents when she was nine years old. Namioka studied mathematics at college and married a Japanese American mathematician. In her writing, Namioka draws on her own Chinese heritage. For instance, the stories about a fox spirit that Namioka heard as a child became the background for "Fox Hunt." Namioka says, "I thought it would be fun to write about the fox spirit in America." Namioka explored her husband's Japanese heritage for her series about two young Samurai warriors in feudal Japan. The first book in that series is *White Serpent Castle*.

Namioka and her family live in Seattle, Washington. One of her most recent books, *Yang the Youngest and His Terrible Ear*, tells the story of an immigrant Chinese family living in Seattle.

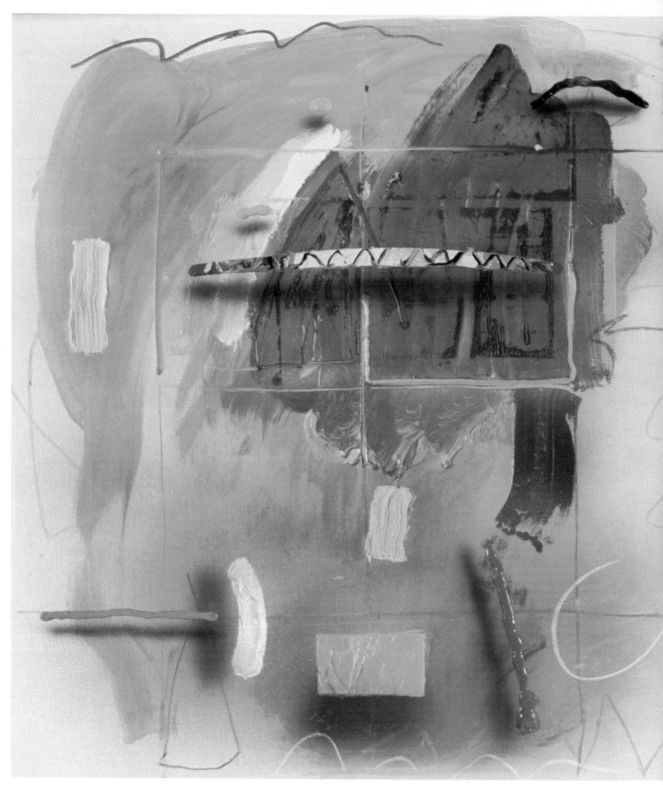

Chippewa James Havard, 1976, acrylics on canvas, 48" x 48"

ALMOST A WHOLE TRICKSTER

GERALD VIZENOR

Uncle Clement told me last night that he knows *almost* everything. Almost, that's his nickname and favorite word in stories, lives with me and my mother in a narrow house on the Leech Lake Chippewa[1] Indian Reservation in northern Minnesota.

Last night, just before dark, we drove into town to meet my cousin at the bus depot[2] and to buy rainbow ice cream in thick brown cones. Almost sat in the backseat of our old car and started his stories the minute we were on the dirt road around the north side of the lake to town. The wheels bounced and the car doors shuddered and raised thick clouds of dust. He told me about the time he almost started an ice cream store when he came back from the army. My mother laughed and turned to the side. The car rattled on the washboard road. She shouted, "I heard that one before!"

"Almost!" he shouted back.

"What almost happened?" I asked. My voice bounced with the car.

1. **Chippewa** [chip′ ə wȧ]
2. **depot** [dē′ pō]: station.

"Well, it was winter then," he said. Fine brown dust settled on his head and the shoulders of his overcoat. "Too cold for ice cream in the woods, but the idea came to mind in the summer, almost."

"Almost, you know almost everything about nothing," my mother shouted and then laughed, "or almost nothing about almost everything."

"Pincher, we're almost to the ice cream," he said, and brushed me on the head with his hard right hand. He did that to ignore what my mother said about what he knows. Clouds of dust covered the trees behind us on both sides of the road.

Almost is my great-uncle and he decides on our nicknames, even the nicknames for my cousins who live in the cities and visit the reservation in the summer. Pincher, the name he gave me, was natural because I pinched my way through childhood. I learned about the world between two fingers. I pinched everything, or *almost* everything as my uncle would say. I pinched animals, insects, leaves, water, fish, ice cream, the moist night air, winter breath, snow, and even words, the words I could see, or almost see. I pinched the words and learned how to speak sooner than my cousins. Pinched words are easier to remember. Some words, like *government* and *grammar*, are unnatural, never seen and never pinched. Who could pinch a word like grammar?

Almost named me last winter when my grandmother was sick with pneumonia and died on the way to the public health hospital. She had no teeth and covered her mouth when she smiled, almost a child. I sat in the backseat of the car and held her thin brown hand. Even her veins were hidden, it was so cold that night. On the road we pinched summer words over the hard snow and ice. She smiled and said *papakine*,[3] *papakine*, over and over. That means cricket or grasshopper in our tribal language and we pinched that word together. We pinched *papakine* in the backseat of our cold car on the way to the hospital. Later she whispered *bisanagami sibi*,[4] the river is still, and then she died. My mother straightened my grandmother's

3. *papakine* [pä pä′ kēn ā]
4. *bisanagami sibi* [bē sä′ nä gä mē si′ bē]

fingers, but later, at the wake in our house, she'd pinched a summer word and we could see that. She was buried in the cold earth with a warm word between her fingers. That's when my uncle gave me my nickname.

Almost never told lies, but he used the word *almost* to stretch the truth like a tribal trickster, my mother told me. The trickster is a character in stories, an animal, or person, even a tree at times, *who pretends the world can be stopped with words,* and he frees the world in stories. Almost said the trickster is almost a man and almost a woman, and almost a child, a clown, who laughs and plays games with words in stories. The trickster is almost a free spirit. Almost told me about the trickster many times, and I think I almost understand his stories. He brushed my head with his hand and said, "The *almost* world is a better world, a sweeter dream than the world we are taught to understand in school."

"I understand, almost," I told my uncle.

"People are almost stories, and stories tell almost the whole truth," Almost told me last winter when he gave me my nickname. "Pincher is your nickname and names are stories too, *gega.*"[5] The word *gega* means almost in the Anishinaabe[6] or Chippewa language.

"Pincher *gega,*" I said, and then tried to pinch a tribal word I could not yet see clear enough to hold between my fingers. I could almost see *gega.*

Almost, no matter the season, wore a long dark overcoat. He bounced when he walked, and the thick bottom of the overcoat hit the ground. The sleeves were too short but he never minded that because he could eat and deal cards with no problems. So there he was in line for a rainbow ice cream cone dressed for winter, or almost winter he would say. My mother wonders if he wears that overcoat for the attention.

"*Gega, gega,*" an old woman called from the end of the line. "You spending some claims money on ice cream or a new coat?" No one ignored his overcoat.

5. **gega** [gā´ gä]
6. **Anishinaabe** [ä ne´ shin ä ä bā]

"What's that?" answered Almost. He cupped his ear to listen because he knew the old woman wanted to move closer, ahead in the line. The claims money she mentioned is a measure of everything in the reservation. The federal government promised to settle a treaty over land with tribal people. Almost and thousands of others had been waiting for more than a century to be paid for land that was taken from them. There were rumors at least once a week that federal checks were in the mail, final payment for the broken treaties. When white people talk about a rain dance, tribal people remember the claims dancers who promised a federal check in every mailbox.

"Claims money," she whispered in the front of the line.

"Almost got a check this week," Almost said and smiled.

"Almost is as good as nothing," she said back.

"Pincher gets a bicycle when the claims money comes."

"My husband died waiting for the claims settlement," my mother said. She looked at me and then turned toward the ice cream counter to order. I held back my excitement about a new bicycle because the claims money might never come; no one was ever sure. Almost believed in rumors and he waited for a check to appear one morning in his mailbox on the reservation. Finally, my mother scolded him for wasting his time on promises made by the government. "You grow old too fast on government promises," she said. "Anyway, the government has nothing to do with bicycles." He smiled at me and we ate our rainbow ice cream cones at the bus depot. That was a joke because the depot is nothing more than a park bench in front of a restaurant. On the back of the bench there was a sign that announced an ice sculpture contest to be held in the town park on July Fourth.

"Ice cube sculpture?" asked my mother.

"No blocks big enough around here in summer," I said, thinking about the ice sold to tourists, cubes and small blocks for camp coolers.

"Pig Foot, he cuts ice from the lake in winter and stores it in a cave, buried in straw," my uncle whispered. He looked around, concerned that someone might hear about the ice cave. "Secret *mikwam*,[7] huge blocks, enough for a great sculpture." The word *mikwam* means ice.

"Never mind," my mother said as she licked the ice cream on her fingers. The rainbow turned pink when it melted. The pink ran over her hand and under her rings.

We were going to pick up my cousin, Black Ice, from the bus station.

Black Ice was late but that never bothered her because she liked to ride in the back of buses at night. She sat in the dark and pretended that she could see the people who lived under the distant lights. She lived in a dark apartment building in Saint Paul[8] with her mother and older brother and made the world come alive with light more than from sound or taste. She was on the reservation for more than a month last summer and we thought her nickname would be *light* or *candle* or something like that, even though she wore black clothes. Not so. Almost avoided one obvious name and chose another when she attended our grandmother's funeral. Black Ice had never been on the reservation in winter. She slipped and fell seven times on black ice near the church and so she got that as a nickname.

Black Ice was the last person to leave the bus. She held back, behind the darkened windows, as long as she could. Yes, she was shy, worried about being embarrassed in public. I might be that way too, if we lived in an apartment in the cities, but the only public on the reservation are the summer tourists. She was happier when we bought her a rainbow ice cream cone. She was dressed in black, black everything, even black canvas shoes, no almost black. The latest television style in the cities. Little did my uncle know that her reservation nickname would describe a modern style of clothes. We sat in the backseat on the way back to our house. We could smell the dust in the dark, in the tunnel of light through the trees. The moon was new that night.

7. **mikwam** [mē′ kwäm]
8. **Saint Paul:** city in Minnesota.

"Almost said he would buy me my first bicycle when he gets his claims money," I told Black Ice. She brushed her clothes, there was too much dust.

"I should've brought my new mountain bike," she said. "I don't use it much though—too much traffic and you have to worry about it being stolen."

"Should we go canoeing? We have a canoe."

"Did you get television yet?" asked Black Ice.

"Yes," I boasted, "my mother won a big screen with a dish[9] and everything at a bingo game on the reservation." We never watched much television though.

"Really?"

"Yes, we can get more than a hundred channels."

"On the reservation?"

"Yes, and bingo too."

"Well, here we are, paradise at the end of a dust cloud," my mother announced as she turned down the trail to our house on the lake. The headlights held the eyes of animals, a raccoon, and we could smell a skunk in the distance. Low branches brushed the side of the car and whipped through the open windows. The dogs barked and ran ahead of the car; we were home. We sat in the car for a few minutes and listened to the night. The dogs were panting. Mosquitoes, so big we called them the state bird, landed on our arms, bare knuckles, and warm shoulder blades. The water was calm and seemed to hold back a secret dark blue light from the bottom of the lake. One loon[10] called and another answered. One thin wave rippled over the stones on the shore. We ducked mosquitoes and went into the house. We were tired, and too tired in the morning to appreciate the plan to carve a trickster from a block of ice.

Pig Foot lived alone on an island. He came down to the wooden dock to meet us in the morning. We were out on the lake before dawn, my uncle at the back of the canoe in his overcoat. We paddled

9. **dish:** satellite dish for TV.
10. **loon** [lün]: large, fish-eating, web-footed bird that has a loud cry and lives in northern regions.

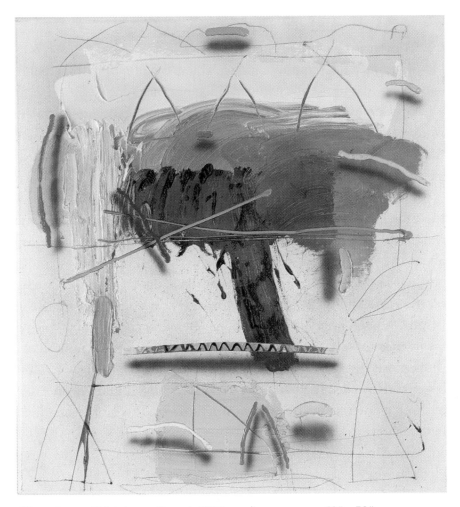

Ghost Dance Shirt James Havard, 1976, acrylics on canvas, 62" x 58"

and he steered us around the point of the island where bald eagles nested.

"Pig Foot?" questioned Black Ice.

"Almost gave him that nickname," I whispered to my cousin as we came closer to the dock. "Watch his little feet—he prances like a pig when he talks. The people in town swear his feet are hard and cloven."[11]

"Are they?"

11. **cloven** [klō′ vən]: split or divided into two parts, as in the hoof of a goat.

"No," I whispered as the canoe touched the dock.

"Almost," shouted Pig Foot.

"Almost," said Almost. "Pincher, you know him from the funeral, and this lady is from the city; we named her Black Ice."

"*Makate Mikwam*,"[12] said Pig Foot. "Black ice comes with the white man and roads. No black ice on the island." He tied the canoe to the dock and patted his thighs with his open hands. The words *makate mikwam* mean black ice.

Black Ice looked down at Pig Foot's feet when she stepped out of the canoe. He wore black overshoes. The toes were turned out. She watched him prance on the rough wooden dock when he talked about the weather and mosquitoes. The black flies and mosquitoes on the island, a special breed, were more vicious than anywhere else on the reservation. Pig Foot was pleased that no one camped on the island because of the black flies. Some people accused him of raising mean flies to keep the tourists away. "Not a bad idea, now that I think about it," said Pig Foot. He had a small bunch of black hair on his chin. He pulled the hair when he was nervous and revealed a row of short stained teeth. Black Ice turned toward the sunrise and held her laughter.

"We come to see the ice cave," said Almost. "We need a large block to win the ice sculpture contest in four days."

"What ice cave is that?" questioned Pig Foot.

"The almost secret one!" shouted Almost.

"That one, sure enough," said Pig Foot. He mocked[13] my uncle and touched the lapel of his overcoat. "I was wondering about that contest—what does ice have to do with July Fourth?" He walked ahead as he talked and then every eight steps he would stop and turn to wait for us. But if you were too close you would bump into him when he stopped. Black Ice counted his steps and when we were near the entrance to the ice cave she imitated his prance, toes turned outward. She pranced seven steps and then waited for him to turn on the eighth.

12. **Makate Mikwam** [mä käʹ tā mēʹ kwäm]
13. **mocked** [mokd]: made fun of.

Pig Foot stopped in silence on the shore, where the bank was higher and where several trees leaned over the water. There, in the vines and boulders we could feel the cool air. A cool breath on the shore.

Pig Foot told us we could never reveal the location of the ice cave, but he said we could tell stories about ice and the great spirit of winter in summer. He said this because most tribal stories should be told in winter, not in summer when evil spirits could be about to listen and do harm to words and names. We agreed to the conditions and followed him over the boulders into the wide, cold cave. We could hear our breath, even a heartbeat. Whispers were too loud in the cave.

"Almost the scent of winter on July Fourth," whispered Almost. "In winter we overturn the ice in shallow creeks to smell the rich blue earth, and then in summer we taste the winter in this ice cave, almost."

"Almost, you're a poet, sure enough, but that's straw, not the smell of winter," said Pig Foot. He was hunched over where the cave narrowed at the back. Beneath the mounds of straw were huge blocks of ice, lake ice, blue and silent in the cave. Was that thunder, or the crack of winter ice on the lake? "Just me, dropped a block over the side." In winter he sawed blocks of ice in the bay where it was the thickest and towed the blocks into the cave on an aluminum slide. Pig Foot used the ice to cool his cabin in summer, but Almost warned us that there were other reasons. Pig Foot believes that the world is becoming colder and colder, the ice thicker and thicker. Too much summer in the blood would weaken him, so he rests on a block of ice in the cave several hours a week to stay in condition for the coming of the ice age on the reservation.

"Black Ice, come over here," said Almost. "Stretch out on this block." My cousin brushed the straw from the ice and leaned back on the block. "Almost, almost, now try this one, no this one, almost."

"Almost what?" asked Black Ice.

"Almost a whole trickster," whispered Almost. Then he told us what he had in mind. A trickster, Almost wanted us to carve a tribal trickster to enter in the ice sculpture contest.

"What does a trickster look like?" I asked. The trickster was a word I could not see, there was nothing to pinch. How could I know a trickster between my fingers?

"Almost like a person," he said, and brushed the straw from a block as large as me. "Almost in there, we have three days to find the trickster in the ice."

Early the next morning we paddled across the lake to the ice cave to begin our work on the ice trickster. We were dressed for winter. I don't think my mother believed us

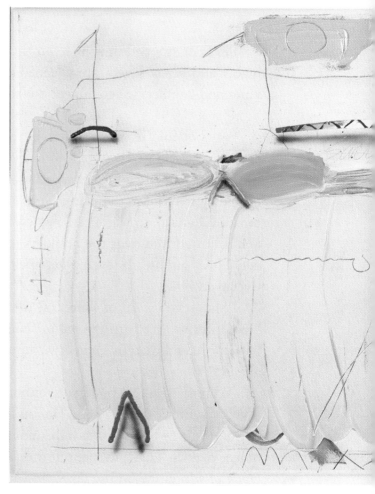

Ghost Dance Shirt James Havard, 1977, acrylics on canvas, 60"x 96"

when we told her about the ice cave. "Almost," she said with a smile, "finally found the right place to wear his overcoat in the summer."

Pig Foot was perched on a block of ice when we arrived. We slid the block that held the trickster to the center of the cave and set to work with an axe and chisels. We rounded out a huge head, moved down the shoulders, and on the second day we freed the nose, ears, and hands of the trickster. I could see him in the dark blue ice, the trickster was almost free. I could almost pinch the word "trickster."

Almost directed us to carve the ice on the first and second days, but on the third and final day he surprised us. We were in the cave, dressed in winter coats and hats, ready to work when he told us to

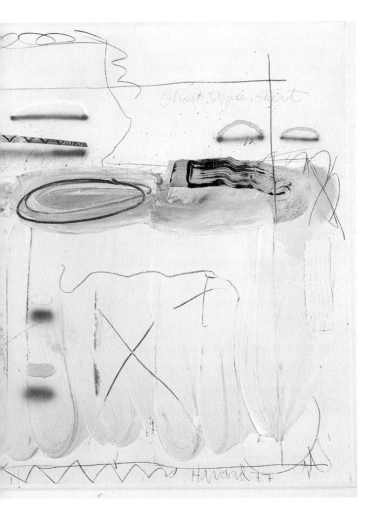

make the final touches on our own, to liberate[14] the face of the trickster. That last morning he leaned back on a block of ice with Pig Foot; we were in charge of who the trickster would become in ice.

Black Ice wanted the trickster to look like a woman. I wanted the ice sculpture to look like a man. The trickster, we decided, would be both, one side a man and the other side a woman. The true trickster, almost a man and almost a woman.

It took us a few hours but in the end the ice trickster had features that looked like our uncle, our grandmother, and other members of our families. The trickster had small feet turned outward, he wore an overcoat, and she pinched her fingers on her female hand. He was ready for the contest—she was the ice trickster on the Fourth of July.

That same night we tied sheets around the ice trickster and towed her behind the canoe to the park on the other side of the lake. The ice floated and the trickster melted slower in the water. We rounded the south end of the island and headed to the park near the town, slow and measured like traders on a distant sea. The park lights reflected on the calm water. We tied the ice trickster to the end of the town dock and beached our canoe. We were very excited, but

14. **liberate** [lib′ ə rāt]: set free.

soon we were tired and slept on the grass in the park near the dock. The trickster was a liberator,[15] she would win on Independence Day. Almost anyway.

"The trickster almost melted," shouted Almost the next morning. He stood on the end of the dock, a sad uncle in his overcoat, holding the rope and empty sheets. At first we thought he had tricked us, we thought the whole thing was a joke, from the beginning, so we laughed. We rolled around on the grass and laughed. Almost was not amused at first, he turned toward the lake to hide his face, but then he broke into wild laughter. He laughed so hard he almost lost his balance in that heavy overcoat. He almost fell into the lake.

"The ice trickster won the ice sculpture contest at last," said Black Ice.

"No, wait, she almost won. No ice trickster would melt that fast into the lake," he said, and ordered us to launch the canoe for a search. Overnight the trickster had slipped from the sheets and floated free from the dock, somewhere out in the lake. The ice trickster was free on July Fourth.

We paddled the canoe in circles and searched for hours and hours but we could not find the ice trickster. Later, my mother rented a motorboat and we searched in two circles.

Almost was worried about the time that the registration would close, so he abandoned the search and appealed to the people who organized the ice sculpture competition. They agreed to extend the time and they even invited other contestants to search for the ice trickster. The lake was crowded with motorboats.

"There she floats," a woman shouted from a fishing boat. The trickster was almost submerged, only a shoulder was above water. We paddled out and towed the trickster back to the dock. Then we hauled her up the bank to the park and a pedestal. We circled the pedestal and admired the ice trickster.

"Almost a trickster," said Almost. We looked over the other entries. There were more birds than animals, more heads than hips or hands, and

15. **liberator** [lib′ ə rāt ər]: one who sets others free.

the other ice sculptures were much smaller. Dwarfs next to the ice trickster. She had melted some overnight in the lake, but he was still head and shoulders above the other entries. The competition was about to close when we learned that there was a height restriction. Almost never read the rules. No entries over three feet and six inches in any direction. The other entries were much smaller, no one found large blocks of ice in town, so they were all within the restrictions. Our trickster was four feet tall, or at least she was that tall when we started out in the ice cave.

"No trickster that started out almost he or she can be too much of either," said Almost. We nodded in agreement but we were not certain what he meant.

"What now?" asked Black Ice.

"Get a saw," my mother ordered. "We can cut the trickster down a notch or two on the bottom." She held her hand about four inches from the base to see what a shorter trickster would look like.

"Almost short enough," said Almost. "He melted some, she needs to lose four more inches by my calculations. We should have left her in the lake for another hour."

Pig Foot turned the trickster on his side, but when we measured four inches from the bottom he protested. "Not the feet, not my feet, those are my feet on the trickster."

"Not my ear either."

"Not the hands," I pleaded.

"The shins," shouted Black Ice. No one had claimed the shins on the ice trickster so we measured and sawed four inches from his shins and then carved the knees to fit the little pig feet.

"Almost whole," announced Almost.

"What's a trickster?" asked the three judges who hurried down the line of pedestals before the ice sculptures melted beyond recognition.

"Almost a person," said Black Ice.

"What person?"

"My grandmother," I told the judges. "See how she pinched her fingers, she was a trickster, she pinched a cricket there." Pig Foot was nervous; he pranced around the pedestal.

Shoshoni James Havard, 1977, acrylics on canvas, 96"x 72"

The judges prowled back and forth, whispered here and there between two pedestals, and then they decided that there would be two winners because they could not decide on one. "The winners are the Boy and His Dog, and that ice trickster, Almost a Person," the judges announced.

The ice trickster won a bicycle, a large camp cooler, a dictionary, and twelve double rainbow cones. The other ice cave sculptors gave me the bicycle because I had never owned one before, and because the claims payment might be a bad promise. We divided the cones as best we could between five people, Almost, Pig Foot, Black Ice, me, and my mother.

Later, we packed what remained of the ice trickster, including the shin part, and took him back to the ice cave, where she lasted for more than a year. She stood in the back of the cave without straw and melted down to the last drop of a trickster. She was almost a whole trickster, almost.

GERALD VIZENOR

Gerald Vizenor, born in 1934 in Minneapolis, Minnesota, is a member of the Ojibwa people. After college graduation, Vizenor launched into a wide-ranging life that included working with the Minnesota Department of Corrections, newspaper reporting, and instructing in Native American studies.

Vizenor's earliest books were poetry, much of it in the form of haiku. His love of haiku began during his Army service in occupied Japan after World War II. When he began writing short stories, such as "Almost a Whole Trickster," Vizenor drew on his Native American heritage for inspiration. One such collection of stories is called *Summer in the Spring: Ojibwa Songs and Stories.*

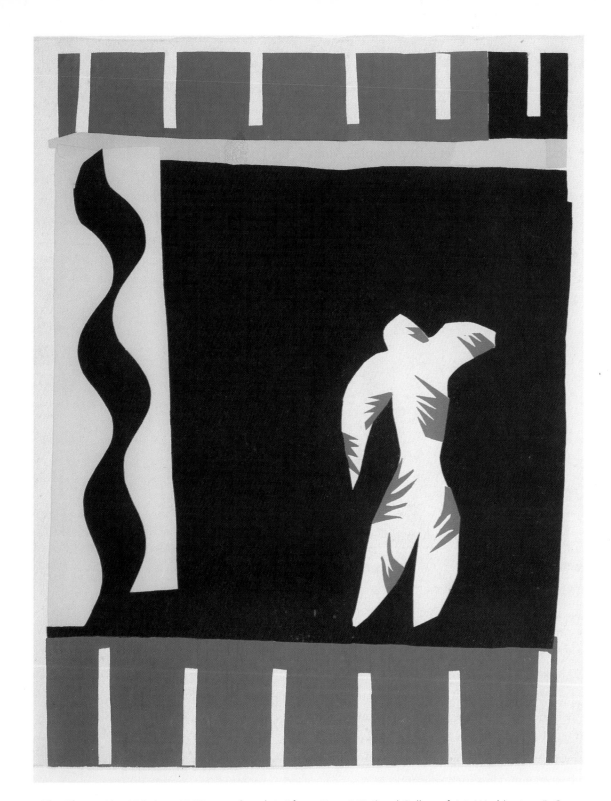

The Clown Henri Matisse, 1947, gouache, plate I from "Jazz," National Gallery of Art, Washington, D.C.

DAEDALUS

OLIVIA COOLIDGE

In the very early days it was not the mainland of Greece that was the most important, but the island of Crete, which lies below the Aegean sea, south of most of the other islands. In it there are still ruins of a great palace, almost more a city than a palace, with so many rooms and passages that it must have had many people dwelling in it. These people were evidently traders and powerful on the sea. They must have been skilled shipbuilders, and from the remains we have found, we know they were also great architects, craftsmen, and artists. In later times the island sank into unimportance, and its former prominence was forgotten. Nevertheless the story of its greatness lingers on and is associated with the skills for which we know it was famous.

In legend the king of the island of Crete was called Minos. He had a great fleet and power that extended far and wide, dominating, among other places, the city of Athens. He seems to have been a fierce tyrant, for he forced the Athenians to send him a yearly tribute of seven youths and seven maidens, whom he fed to a horrible monster that he owned. This animal was called the Minotaur[1] and was a creature with the head of a bull and the body of a man. To keep him safe and to prevent his victims from escaping, it was necessary to build him some special dwelling. For this purpose Minos hired a famous architect whose name was Daedalus.[2]

1. **Minotaur** [min′ ə tôr]
2. **Daedalus** [ded′ l əs]: in Greek legends, a skilled workman who, with his son Icarus, escaped imprisonment by flying wings of feathers fastened to their bodies with wax.

Daedalus, the Greeks used to say, was the first great artist, craftsman, and engineer. It was he who invented many of the tools of carpentry: the saw, the gimlet,[3] and an efficient glue. He also was the first to make statues more lifelike than a roughly carved pillar. Before this time statues had held their legs stiffly together and their arms down by their sides. Daedalus made them stepping forward and holding something in front of them. He is said to have built a great reservoir, fortified a city, and done many other engineering works. But the most famous of all the things he made was the house he built for Minos to keep the Minotaur in. This house was a labyrinth[4] or maze, with countless winding passages, so that it was hard to find the way in or out. Perhaps the idea got into the story from a vague memory of the countless confusing passages in the Cretan palace. In any case Daedalus is supposed to have built a maze for Minos, so elaborate in its windings that no man without a clue could possibly escape from it.

Minos was delighted with his labyrinth and held the architect in great honor. Unfortunately when the wandering artist wished to take his fee and go, the king had other ideas. There were many things that could well be made for him by the greatest craftsman in the world, and he saw no reason why he should let the man build things for someone else. Being king over an island, Minos found it easy to keep Daedalus where he was. He simply forbade all ships to give the artist passage, provided him with an elaborate workshop, and suggested that he might as well settle down and be happy.

Thus Minos gained the services of Daedalus, but the great craftsman was not content. Beyond anything else he loved freedom to wander as he pleased, seeing the world and picking up new ideas. He was not the kind of man who could easily settle down. Therefore when he saw that he could not possibly get away by ship, he turned his talents to working out something else. Minos did not visit the fine workshop he had given his artist, but if he had, he would have

3. **gimlet** [gim′ lit]: a small tool for boring holes.
4. **labyrinth** [lab′ ə rinth′]

seen a curious sight. The whole place was deep in feathers. There were feathers of all shapes and sizes, some just thrown down anyhow as they had been brought in, and some neatly sorted into heaps. A young boy, Icarus, Daedalus' only son and companion, was doing the sorting, while Daedalus himself was busy with twine, wax, and glue, fixing the feathers together in orderly rows on a wooden framework.

Daedalus was making wings. He had seen that it would be impossible to cross the sea by boat because of Minos' order, so he had determined to fly across it. After studying the wings of birds for a long time, he designed some which he thought would support a man, and now he was working on them. Icarus was terribly excited and was helping eagerly. He did not so much dislike living in Crete, but he wanted to fly as the gods do. Think of being the first man to have wings!

The wings took a long time to finish, but at last they were done, a mighty pair for Daedalus, and a smaller one for his son. The workshop being in the top of a lofty tower, Daedalus planned that they should simply launch themselves into the air from it. As they stood there, fastening the wings onto their shoulders, Daedalus gave his excited son some last instructions.

"I shall go first," he said, "to show the way. We must go straight across the sea by the shortest route, lest we become tired and drown before we can reach land. Follow me, and remember the wings on your shoulders are not natural wings, like those of Cupid.[5] We are men and must use tools to do what the gods can do for themselves. Even with our tools we must always fall short of them. If you fly too near the sea, the feathers will become wet and heavy, and you will drown; if you fly up into the air as the gods do, the wax will melt in the sun long before you reach Olympus.[6] Then your wings will fall off and you will perish. Follow me as I go through the middle of the air, neither too high nor too low. So you will be safe."

5. **Cupid** [kyü′ pid]: in Roman myths, the god of love, usually in the form of a winged child with bow and arrows. The Greeks called him Eros.
6. **Olympus** [ō lim′ pəs]: a mountain in northeast Greece. Mount Olympus was believed to be the home of the Greek gods.

Icarus Henri Matisse, 1947, gouache, plate VIII from "Jazz," National Gallery of Art, Washington, D.C.

He spoke and jumped, falling like a stone till the wind caught him and he steadied. Then he began to rise again as the wings beat steadily from his shoulders. He turned and beckoned Icarus to come on. Icarus jumped. The fall was terrible; so was the sudden stop as his spread wings caught the air. Still, he had the presence of mind to work his arms as he had seen his father do, and pretty soon he was sailing ahead in long swoops over the sea.

Presently the boy began to play tricks in the air. His father flew steadily on, but it would be easy, Icarus thought, to catch up with him. Father was too old to enjoy this properly. The swoops were rather sickening, but climbing was wonderful. Up, up he went, like the lark, like the eagle, like the gods. His father called something, but the wind whistled the sound away. Icarus realized he ought to come down, but nobody had ever been up there before, except the gods. Perhaps the real difference between gods and men was that gods could fly. If he wanted to reach Olympus, he would have to take some risk.

Up, up Icarus went, soaring into the bright sun. In vain Daedalus called to him. He was only a black speck by now. At last he was coming down. He was coming very fast, much too fast. In another second Daedalus caught sight of the boy, whirling headlong. The framework was still on his shoulders, but the feathers had all fallen off, as the hot sun had melted the wax. One moment he saw him; then with a mighty splash Icarus hit the water and was gone. Daedalus circled round over the sea, not daring to go too low lest his own wings become soaked. There was no point in both being drowned. But not even a clutching hand broke the surface. The white foam hung on the water for a space; then it too disappeared.

Daedalus flew on. He reached the land at last, white-faced and exhausted, but he would neither use his wings nor teach others how to make them. He had learned man's limitations. It is not right for him to soar like the gods.

OLIVIA COOLIDGE

Olivia Coolidge was born in 1908 in London, England, and grew up in a family fond of "classics and politics." After studying at Oxford University in England, Coolidge taught English in Germany. Next, she taught Latin and Greek in England. Coolidge then decided to come to the United States to teach English. She published her first book, *Greek Myths*, in 1949. Since the publication of her first book, she has divided her writing energies between writing about literary classics and writing biographies of modern heroes, including Mahatma Gandhi.

Coolidge enjoys doing research for both types of writing. She also enjoys the challenge of making both ancient and modern heroes come alive for her readers.

SUMMERTIME ON ICARUS

ARTHUR C. CLARKE

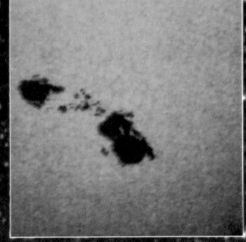

When Colin Sherrard opened his eyes after the crash, he could not imagine where he was. He seemed to be lying, trapped in some kind of vehicle, on the summit of a rounded hill which sloped steeply away in all directions. Its surface was seared and blackened, as if a great fire had swept over it. Above him was a jet-black sky crowded with stars; one of them hung like a tiny, brilliant sun, low down on the horizon.

Could it be the sun? Was he so far from Earth? No—that was impossible. Some nagging memory told him that the sun was very close—hideously close—not so distant that it had shrunk to a star. And with that thought, full consciousness returned. Sherrard knew exactly where he was, and the knowledge was so terrible that he almost fainted again.

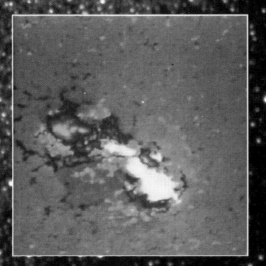
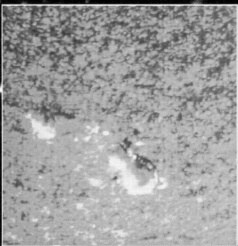

He was nearer to the sun than any man had ever been. His damaged space-pod—a miniature spaceship, only ten feet long—was lying on no hill, but the steeply-curving surface of a world only two miles in diameter. That brilliant star sinking swiftly in the west was the light of "Prometheus,"[1] the ship that had brought him here across so many millions of miles of space. She was hanging up there among the stars, wondering why his pod had not returned like a homing pigeon to its roost. In a few minutes she would have passed from sight, dropping

1. **"Prometheus"** [prə mē′ thē əs]: in Greek myths, Prometheus was a Titan who stole fire from heaven and taught people its use. Zeus was so enraged that he chained Prometheus to a rock for punishment.

below the horizon in her perpetual game of hide-and-seek with the sun.

That was a game that he had lost. He was still on the night side of the asteroid,[2] in the cool safety of its shadow, but the short night would be ending soon. The four-hour day of Icarus[3] was spinning him swiftly towards that dreadful dawn, when a sun thirty times larger than ever shone upon Earth would blast these rocks with fire. Sherrard knew all too well why everything around him was burned and blackened. Icarus was still a week from perihelion[4] but the temperature at noon had already reached a thousand degrees Fahrenheit.

Though this was no time for humor, he suddenly remembered Captain McClellan's description of Icarus: "The hottest piece of real estate in the solar system." The truth of that jest had been proved, only a few days before, by one of those simple and unscientific experiments that are so much more impressive than any number of graphs and instrument readings.

Just before daybreak, someone had propped a piece of wood on the summit of one of the tiny hills. Sherrard had been watching, from the safety of the night-side, when the first rays of the rising sun had touched the hilltop. When his eyes had adjusted to the sudden detonation of light, he saw that the wood was already beginning to blacken and char. Had there been an atmosphere here, the stick would have burst into flames; such was dawn upon Icarus.

Yet it had not been impossibly hot at the time of their first landing when they were passing the orbit of Venus five weeks ago. "Prometheus" had overtaken the asteroid as it was beginning its plunge towards the sun, had matched speed with the little world and had touched down upon its surface as lightly as a snowflake. (A snowflake on Icarus—*that* was quite a thought.) Then the scientists had fanned out across the fifteen square miles of jagged nickel-iron that covered most of the asteroid's surface, setting up their instruments and check points, collecting samples and making endless observations.

2. **asteroid** [as′ tə roid′]: any of the thousands of very small planets that revolve about the sun.
3. **Icarus** [ik′ ər əs]: the asteroid (or small planet) in Clarke's story is named after the son of Daedalus in Greek myths. Icarus and his father escaped from the island of Crete with wings that Daedalus made. Icarus flew so close to the sun that his waxen wings melted.
4. **perihelion** [per′ ə hē′ lyən]: the point closest to the sun in the orbit of a planet or comet.

Everything had been carefully planned, years in advance, as part of the International Astrophysical[5] Decade. Here was a unique opportunity for a research ship to get within a mere seventeen million miles of the sun, protected from its fury by a two-mile-thick shield of rock and iron. In the shadow of Icarus, the ship could ride safely round the central fire which warmed all the planets, and upon which the existence of all life depended. As the Prometheus of legend had brought the gift of fire to mankind, so the ship that bore his name would return to Earth with other unimagined secrets from the heavens.

There had been plenty of time to set up the instruments and make the surveys before "Prometheus" had to take off and seek the permanent shade of night. Even then, it was still possible for men in the tiny self-propelled space-pods to work on the night-side for an hour or so, as long as they were not overtaken by the advancing line of sunrise. That had seemed a simple enough condition to meet, on a world where dawn marched forward at only a mile an hour; but Sherrard had failed to meet it, and the penalty was death.

He was still not quite sure what had happened. He had been replacing a seismograph[6] transmitter at Station 145, unofficially known as *Mount Everest* because it was a full ninety feet above the surrounding territory. The job had been a perfectly straightforward one, even though he had to do it by remote control through the mechanical arms of his pod. Sherrard was an expert at manipulating these; he could tie knots with his metal fingers almost as quickly as with his flesh-and-bone ones. That task had taken little more than twenty minutes, and then the radio-seismograph was on air

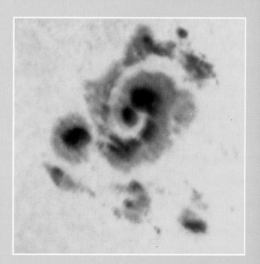

5. **astrophysical** [as′ trō fiz′ ə kəl]: concerns the branch of astronomy dealing with the physical and chemical characteristics of heavenly bodies.
6. **seismograph** [sīz′ mə graf]: an instrument used for recording the direction, intensity, and duration of an earthquake.

again, monitoring the tiny quakes and shudders that racked Icarus in ever-increasing numbers as the asteroid approached the sun. It was small satisfaction to know that he had now made a king-sized addition to the record.

When he had checked the signals, he had carefully replaced the sun-screens around the instrument. It was hard to believe that two flimsy sheets of polished metal foil, no thicker than paper, could turn aside a flood of radiation that would melt lead or tin within seconds. But the first screen reflected more than ninety per cent of the sunlight falling upon its mirror-surface and the second turned back most of the rest, so that only a harmless fraction of the heat passed through.

He had reported completion of the job, received an acknowledgment from the ship, and prepared to head for home. The brilliant floodlights hanging from "Prometheus"—without which the night-side of the asteroid would have been in utter darkness—had been an unmistakable target in the sky. The ship was only two miles up, and in this feeble gravity he could have jumped that distance, had he been wearing a planetary-type spacesuit with flexible legs. As it was, the low-powered micro-rockets of his pod would get him there in a leisurely five minutes.

He had aimed the pod with its gyros,[7] set the rear jets at Strength Two and pressed the firing button. There had been a violent explosion somewhere in the vicinity of his feet and he had soared away from Icarus but not towards the ship. Something was horribly wrong; he was tossed to one side of the vehicle, unable to reach the controls. Only one of the jets was firing, and he was pinwheeling across the sky, spinning faster and faster under the off-balanced drive. He tried to find the cutoff, but the spin had completely disorientated him. When he was able to locate the controls, his first reaction made matters worse—he pushed the throttle over to full, like a nervous driver stepping on the accelerator instead of the brake. It took only a second to correct the mistake and kill the jet, but by then he was spinning so rapidly that the stars were wheeling round in circles.

Everything had happened so quickly that there was no time for fear, no time even to call the ship and report what was happening. He

---

7. **gyros** [jī′ rōs]: short for gyroscopes; instruments consisting of rotating wheels so mounted that the axis can turn freely in one or more directions. Gyroscopes keep vehicles steady.

took his hands away from the controls; to touch them now would only make matters worse. It would take two or three minutes of cautious jockeying to unravel his spin, and from the flickering glimpses of the approaching rocks it was obvious that he did not have as many seconds. Sherrard remembered a piece of advice at the front of the *Spaceman's Manual*: "When you don't know what to do, *do nothing*." He was still doing it when Icarus fell upon him, and the stars went out.

It had been a miracle that the pod was unbroken, and that he was not breathing space. (Thirty minutes from now he might be glad to do so, when the capsule's heat insulation began to fail.) There had been some damage, of course. The rear-view mirrors, just outside the dome of transparent plastic that enclosed his head, were both snapped off so that he could no longer see what lay behind him without twisting his neck. This was a trivial mishap; far more serious was the fact that his radio antennae had been torn away by the impact. He could not call the ship, and the ship could not call him. All that came over the radio was a faint crackling, probably produced inside the set itself. He was absolutely alone, cut off from the rest of the human race.

It was a desperate situation, but there was one faint ray of hope. He was not, after all, completely helpless. Even if he could not use the pod's rockets—he guessed that the starboard motor had blown back and ruptured a fuel line, something the designers said was impossible—he was still able to move. He had his arms.

But which way should he crawl? He had lost all sense of location, for though he had taken off from Mount Everest, he might now be thousands of feet away from it. There were no recognizable landmarks in his tiny world; the rapidly sinking star of "Prometheus" was his best guide, and if he could keep the ship in view he would be safe. It would be only a matter of minutes before his absence was noted, if indeed it had not been discovered already. Yet without radio, it might take his colleagues a long time to find him; small though Icarus was, its fifteen square miles of fantastically rugged no man's land could provide an effective hiding-place for a ten-foot cylinder. It might take an hour to locate him—which meant that he would have to keep ahead of the murderous sunrise.

He slipped his fingers into the controls that worked his mechanical limbs. Outside the pod, in the

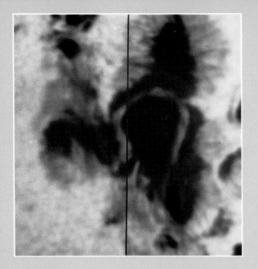

hostile vacuum that surrounded him, his substitute arms came to life. They reached down, thrust against the iron surface of the asteroid, and levered the pod from the ground. Sherrard flexed them and the capsule jerked forward, like some weird, two-legged insect . . . first the right arm, then the left, then the right.

It was less difficult than he had feared, and for the first time he felt his confidence return. Though his mechanical arms had been designed for light precision work, very little pull was needed to set the capsule moving in this weightless environment. The gravity of Icarus was ten thousand times weaker than Earth's: Sherrard and his space-pod weighed less than an ounce here, and once he had set himself in motion he floated forward with an effortless, dreamlike ease.

Yet that very effortlessness had its dangers. He had travelled several hundred yards, and was rapidly overhauling the sinking star of the "Prometheus," when overconfidence betrayed him. (Strange how quickly the mind could switch from one extreme to the other; a few minutes ago he had been steeling himself to face death—now he was wondering if he would be late for dinner.) Perhaps the novelty of the movement, so unlike anything he had ever attempted before, was responsible for the catastrophe; or perhaps he was still suffering from the after-effects of the crash.

Like all astronauts, Sherrard had learned to orientate himself in space, and had grown accustomed to living and working when the Earthly conceptions of Up and Down were meaningless. On a world such as Icarus, it was necessary to pretend that there was a real honest-to-goodness planet "beneath" your feet, and that when you moved you were traveling over a horizontal plane. If this innocent self-deception failed, you were heading for space-vertigo.

The attack came without warning, as it usually did. Quite suddenly, Icarus no longer seemed to be beneath him, the stars no longer above. The universe tilted through a right angle; he was moving straight *up* a vertical cliff, like a mountaineer scaling a rock-face, and though Sherrard's reason told him that this was pure illusion, all his senses screamed that it was true. In a moment gravity must drag him off this sheer wall, and he would drop down mile upon endless mile until he smashed into oblivion.

Worse was to come; the false vertical was still swinging like a compass needle that had lost the pole. Now he was on the *underside* of an immense rocky roof, like a fly clinging to a ceiling; in another moment it would have become a wall again— but this time he would be moving straight down it, instead of up.

He had lost all control over the pod, and the clammy sweat that had begun to dew his brow warned him that he would soon lose control over his body. There was only one thing to do; he clenched his eyes tightly shut, squeezed as far back as possible into the tiny closed world of the capsule, and pretended with all his might that the universe outside did not exist. He did not even allow the slow, gentle crunch of his second crash to interfere with his self-hypnosis.

When he again dared to look outside, he found that the pod had come to rest against a large boulder. Its mechanical arms had broken the force of the impact, but at a cost that was more than he could afford to pay. Though the capsule was virtually weightless here, it still possessed its normal five hundred pounds of inertia,[8] and it had been moving at perhaps four miles an hour. The momentum had been too much for the metal arms to absorb; one had snapped, and the other was hopelessly bent.

When he saw what had happened, Sherrard's first reaction was not despair, but anger. He had been so certain of success, when the pod had started its glide across the barren face of Icarus. And now this, all through a moment of physical weakness. But Space made no allowance for human frailties or emotions, and a man who did not accept that fact had no right to be here.

At least he had gained precious time in his pursuit of the ship; he had put an extra ten minutes, if not more, between himself and dawn. Whether that ten minutes would merely prolong the agony, or

---

8. **inertia** [in ėr′ shə]: a tendency for all objects and matter to stay still or move in the same direction unless acted upon by an outside force.

whether it would give his shipmates the extra time they needed to find him, he would soon know.

Where were they? Surely they had started the search by now. He strained his eyes towards the brilliant star of the ship, hoping to pick out the fainter lights of space-pods moving towards him—but nothing else was visible against the slowly turning vault of heaven.

He had better look to his own resources, slender though they were. Only a few minutes were left before the "Prometheus" and her trailing lights would sink below the edge of the asteroid and leave him in darkness. It was true that the darkness would be all too brief, but before it fell upon him he might find some shelter against the coming day. This rock into which he had crashed, for example.

Yes, it would give some shade, until the sun was halfway up the sky. Nothing could protect him if it passed right overhead, but it was just possible that he might be in a latitude where the sun never rose far above the horizon at this season of Icarus' four-hundred-and-nine-day year. Then he might survive the brief period of daylight; that was his only hope, if the rescuers did not find him before dawn.

There went "Prometheus" and her lights, below the edge of the world. With her going, the now unchallenged stars blazed forth with redoubled brilliance. More glorious than any of them—so lovely that even to look upon it almost brought tears to his eyes—was the blazing beacon of Earth, with its companion moon beside it. He had been born on one, and had walked on the other; would he see either again?

Strange that until now he had given no thought to his wife and children, and to all that he loved in the life that now seemed so far away. He felt a spasm of guilt, but it passed swiftly. The ties of affection were not weakened, even across the hundred million miles of space that now sundered him from his family. At this moment, they were simply irrelevant. He was now a primitive, self-centered animal fighting for his life, and his only weapon was his brain. In this conflict, there was no place for the heart; it would merely be a hindrance, spoiling his judgment and weakening his resolution.

And then he saw something that banished all thoughts of his distant home. Reaching up above the horizon behind him, spreading across the stars like a milky mist, was a faint and ghostly cone of phosphorescence.[9] It was the herald of the sun—the beautiful, pearly phantom of the corona,[10] visible on Earth only during the rare moments of a total eclipse. When the corona was rising, the sun would not be far behind, to smite[11] this little land with fury.

Sherrard made good use of the warning. Now he could judge, with some accuracy, the exact point where the sun would rise. Crawling slowly and clumsily on the broken stumps of his metal arms, he dragged the capsule round to the side of the boulder that should give the greatest shade. He had barely reached it when the sun was upon him like a beast of prey, and his tiny world exploded into light.

He raised the dark filters inside his helmet, one thickness after another, until he could endure the glare. Except where the broad shadow of the boulder lay across the asteroid, it was like looking into a furnace. Every detail of the desolate land around him was revealed by that merciless light; there were no greys, only blinding whites and impenetrable blacks. All the shadowed cracks and hollows were pools of ink, while the higher ground already seemed to be on fire. Yet it was only a minute after dawn.

Now Sherrard could understand how the scorching heat of a billion summers had turned Icarus into a cosmic cinder, baking the rocks until the last traces of gas had bubbled out of them. Why should men travel, he asked himself bitterly, across the gulf of stars at such expense and risk— merely to land on a spinning slag[12] heap? For the same reason, he knew, that they had once struggled to reach Everest and the Poles and the far places of the Earth—for the excitement of the body that was adventure, and the more enduring excitement of the mind that was discovery. It was an answer that gave him little consolation, now that he was about to be grilled like a joint on the turning spit of Icarus.

Already he could feel the first breath of heat upon his face. The boulder against which he was lying gave him protection from direct sunlight, but the glare reflected back at him from those blazing rocks only a few yards away was striking through

---

9. **phosphorescence** [fos′ fə res′ ns]: a light given out without apparent heat or burning.
10. **corona** [kə rō′ nə]: a ring of light around the sun, seen only during an eclipse.
11. **smite** [smīt]: strike hard.
12. **slag** [slag]: the rough waste left after a metal is separated from ore by melting.

the transparent plastic of the dome. It would grow swiftly more intense as the sun rose higher; he had even less time than he had thought, and with the knowledge came a kind of numb resignation that was beyond fear. He would wait—if he could—until the sunrise engulfed him, and the capsule's cooling unit gave up the unequal struggle; then he would crack the pod and let the air gush out into the vacuum of space.

Nothing to do but to sit and think in the minutes that were left to him before his pool of shadow contracted. He did not try to direct his thoughts, but let them wander where they willed. How strange that he should be dying now, because back in the 1940's—years before he was born—a man at Palomar[13] had spotted a streak of light on a photographic plate, and had named it so appropriately after the boy who flew too near the sun.

One day, he supposed, they would build a monument here for him on this blistered plain. What would they inscribe upon it? "Here died Colin Sherrard, astronics[14] engineer, in the cause of science."

That would be funny, for he had never understood half the things that the scientists were trying to do.

Yet some of the excitement of their discoveries had communicated itself to him. He remembered how the geologists had scraped away the charred skin of the asteroid, and had polished the metallic surface that lay beneath. It had been covered with a curious pattern of lines and scratches. They wrote the history of Icarus, though only a geologist could read it. They revealed, so Sherrard had been told, that this lump of iron and rock had not always floated alone in space. At some remote time in the past, it had been under enormous pressure— and that could mean only one thing. Billions of years ago it had been part of a much larger body, perhaps a planet like Earth. For some reason that planet had blown up, and Icarus and all the thousands of other asteroids were the fragments of that cosmic explosion.

Even at this moment, as the incandescent[15] line of sunlight came closer, this was a thought that stirred his mind. What Sherrard was lying upon was the core of a world—perhaps

---

13. **Palomar** [pal′ ə mär′]: a mountain in San Diego, California where an astronomical observatory with a giant 200-inch telescope is located.
14. **astronics**: a word invented by Clarke, probably close in meaning to astronautics [as′ trə nô′ tiks], a science having to do with space travel.
15. **incandescent** [in′ kən des′ nt]: glowing with heat and light.

a world that had once known life. In a strange, irrational way it comforted him to know that his might not be the only ghost to haunt Icarus until the end of time.

The helmet was misting up; that could only mean that the cooling unit was about to fail. It had done its work well: even now, though the rocks only a few yards away must be glowing a sullen red, the heat inside the capsule was not unendurable. When failure came, it would be sudden and catastrophic.

He reached for the red lever that would rob the sun of its prey—but before he pulled it, he would look for the last time upon Earth. Cautiously, he lowered the dark filters, adjusting them so that they still cut out the glare from the rocks, but no longer blocked his view of space.

The stars were faint now, dimmed by the advancing glow of the corona. And just visible over the boulder whose shield would soon fail him was a stub of crimson flame, a crooked finger of fire jutting from the edge of the sun itself. He had only seconds left.

There was the Earth, there was the Moon. Good-by to them both, and to his friends and loved ones on each of them. While he was looking at the sky, the sunlight had begun to lick the base of the capsule, and he felt the first touch of fire. In a reflex as automatic as it was useless, he drew up his legs, trying to escape the advancing wave of heat.

What was that? A brilliant flash of light, infinitely brighter than any of the stars, had suddenly exploded overhead. Miles above him, a huge mirror was sailing across the sky, reflecting the sunlight as it slowly turned through space. Such a thing was utterly impossible; he was beginning to suffer from hallucinations, and it was time he took his leave. Already the sweat was pouring from his body, and in a few seconds the capsule would be a furnace.

He waited no longer, but pulled on the emergency release with all his waning strength, bracing himself at the same moment to face the end.

Nothing happened; the lever would not move. He tugged it again and again before he realized that it was hopelessly jammed. There was no easy way out for him, no merciful death as the air gushed from his lungs. It was then, as the true terror of his situation struck home to him, that his nerve finally broke and he began to scream like a trapped animal.

When he heard Captain McClellan's voice speaking to him,

thin but clear, he knew that it must be another hallucination. Yet some last remnant of discipline and self-control checked his screaming; he clenched his teeth and listened to that familiar commanding voice.

"Sherrard! Hold on, man. We've got a fix on you—but keep shouting."

"Here I am," he cried, "but hurry, for God's sake. I'm burning."

Deep down in what was left of his rational mind he realized what had happened. Some feeble ghost of a signal was leaking through the broken stubs of his antennae, and the searchers had heard his screams—as he was hearing their voices. That meant they must be very close indeed, and the knowledge gave him sudden strength.

He stared through the streaming plastic of the dome, looking once more for that impossible mirror in the sky. There it was again—and now he realized that the baffling perspectives of space had tricked his senses. The mirror was not miles away, nor was it huge. It was almost on top of him, and it was moving fast.

He was still shouting when it slid across the face of the rising sun, and its blessed shadow fell upon him like a cool wind that had blown out of the heart of winter, over leagues of snow and ice. Now that it was so close he recognized it at once; it was merely a large metal-foil radiation screen, no doubt hastily snatched from one of the instrument sites. In the safety of its shadow, his friends had been searching for him.

A heavy-duty, two-man capsule was hovering overhead, holding the glittering shield in one set of arms and reaching for him with the other. Even through the misty dome and the haze of heat that still sapped his senses, he recognized Captain McClellan's anxious face, looking down at him from the other pod.

So this was what birth was like, for truly he had been reborn. He was too exhausted for gratitude—that would come later—but as he rose from the burning rocks his eyes sought and found the bright star of Earth. "Here I am," he said silently. "I'm coming back."

Back to enjoy and cherish all the beauties of the world he had thought was lost forever. No—not all of them.

He would never enjoy summer again.

Arthur C. Clarke was born in 1917 in Minehead on the coast of England and grew up on his family's farm there. Clarke's interest in science began at the age of ten when his father gave him a picture of a dinosaur. When he was twelve, he built a telescope from cardboard tubes and old lenses and fell in love with outer space. Then, in his teens, he discovered American science-fiction magazines and began writing.

Clarke was an active member, and for several years president, of the British Interplanetary Society. His first nonfiction book, *Interplanetary Flight*, an account of the dawn of the space age, was published in 1950. His second book had a very direct title: *The Exploration of Space*. Clarke then turned to novels. *Islands in the Sky*, a story about community life in space stations, has been read by young people everywhere.

Clarke wrote of people traveling to the moon long before it was a reality. He has faith in the future. As he once said, "Anything that is theoretically possible will be achieved in practice."

THE CASE OF THE
UNCOOKED
EGGS

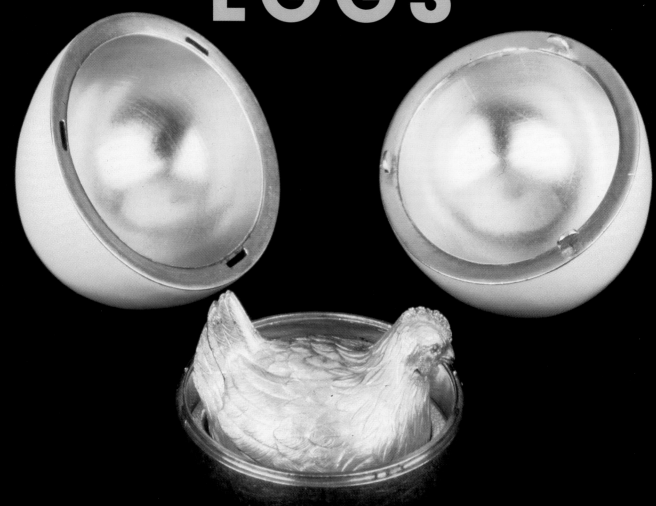

DIANE WOLKSTEIN

Dadi, a Haitian storyteller, told this familiar story of the uncooked eggs in such a way that her hearers, including Diane Wolkstein who published the story, felt that they were hearing a brand new tale.

A poor woman in Kenscoff[1] once offered lodging to a soldier, and before he left he gave her a gift of three eggs. She looked at the eggs. They were longer on one end. She decided not to cook them but to put them under the hen to hatch.

Soon three fat red roosters peeped out of the shells. The woman raised the roosters and took them to market and sold them for five dollars. With the money, she bought two small pigs. She nourished the pigs on banana peels and corn and sold them for a goat. She sold the goat for a calf, and when the calf had grown into a strong ox, she sold it and bought land.

Some years later, the same soldier was again passing through Kenscoff and asked for lodging at the woman's house.

"Oh, don't you recognize me?" she cried. "When you were here last you gave me three eggs. I never forget when someone does me a good turn."

She was so happy to see him she made him a large meal, and as they ate together, she told him what she had done with the three eggs. After they had finished their coffee, she took him around her property and showed him her fields of carrots, tomatoes, leeks, and radishes; her cattle; even her flowers. He stayed with her for five days. She treated him royally and then he left.

Eight days later she received a summons to appear in court. As she had never done any harm to anyone in her life, she did not go. A week later, she received a second summons. She ignored this one as well. But when the third summons came, she woke at two in the morning and walked five hours to town.

Waiting for her in the courthouse was the soldier. He declared that because of his gift to her of three eggs, she was able to buy

---

1. **Kenscoff:** a town in Haiti, a country in the western part of the island of Hispaniola, near the Dominican Republic.

livestock, fields, and even roses and violets. Now it was only correct that she share her goods with him.

"But the soldier did not give me roosters," she told the judge, "he only gave me eggs!"

"Yes, and those eggs, did they not give you all that you have?" the soldier insisted.

The woman left the courthouse. She hired a lawyer. The soldier hired a lawyer. The case went on and on; the two lawyers deliberating endlessly. As the case came to a close the woman was so exhausted, she was nearly willing to divide her property with the soldier.

Then, on the Thursday evening before the final decision was to be made on Monday, an old ragged beggar knocked on her door.

"Charity for a poor man," he said. "A little something to eat."

"Not at this moment," she said. "I am not giving out charity. I do not even know what I will have tomorrow." And she explained the case to him.

"Madame, don't you worry; nothing serious will happen!"

"Nothing serious! It's almost all over!" But she relented and offered him some bread and rice and beans.

Then he said, "Madame, here is some advice. Eat well on Saturday and Sunday. Get up early Monday, make yourself coffee, walk to town, and I will be waiting for you in the court."

The woman looked at him. "*You* will be waiting for me. But what can you do?"

"You shall see."

Sunday, just before midnight, the woman woke up. She prepared coffee for herself and started down to Port-au-Prince.[2] The beggar was already seated on one of the benches. The woman sat down. The lawyers arrived and the final speeches were made. They talked and talked and talked. The woman felt so tired she was certain that if someone dropped a handkerchief on her, she would fall to the floor and not be able to get up.

2. **Port-au-Prince** [pōrt′ ō prins′]

Just then the old beggar called out: "Judge!"

"What is it, old vagabond?"

"I have come to hear the verdict."

"Why should an old beggar like you concern yourself with the verdict of this case?"

"Several days ago, this good woman gave me as charity some of her dinner of rice and beans. I ate the rice but brought the beans home to plant. I told my friend I have seven beans to plant and he offered me space in his fields. He is at this moment in the fields waiting for me. And now I am waiting for you, for your decision. I want to know whether it is worth the effort for me to plant my beans."

The people in the courthouse laughed and shouted. The lawyers stood up to look at the man.

The judge said, "Whoever heard of cooked beans being planted?"

"Thank you, judge," said the beggar. "When this good woman told me it was believed in court that eggs could provide flowers and pigs and goats, I thought, perhaps I, too, should make the effort. After all, if the laws have been changed, and eggs can give all that, what can beans do?"

Everyone shouted, "Bravo!"

The case was dismissed. The woman had won.

DIANE WOLKSTEIN

Diane Wolkstein, who was born in 1942, remembers that her mother used to tell her stories at night. These stories, and books that she loved, gave Wolkstein the idea of making stories come alive for other people. It was several years before she found a way to do it.

After college, Wolkstein traveled in Europe and studied pantomime in Paris. She returned to the United States to teach the fifth grade, reading part of *The Odyssey* to her class every morning. Then, in the summer of 1967, Wolkstein got a job as a storyteller in the parks of New York City. From that time on, she says, "I understood that telling stories combined the many things I loved and what I had wanted most to do: to feel and share with others the incredibleness of being alive."

MUFARO'S BEAUTIFUL DAUGHTERS

JOHN STEPTOE

Face Mask African, Gabon, 19th-20th cent., wood, pigment, $11^{3}/_{8}$" x $7^{1}/_{4}$", Metropolitan Museum of Art

Staff of Office African,
Luba, wood, beads, 11 1/2",
The Field Museum, Chicago,
detail

A LONG TIME AGO, IN A CERTAIN PLACE IN AFRICA, A SMALL VILLAGE LAY ACROSS A RIVER AND HALF A DAY'S JOURNEY FROM A CITY WHERE A GREAT KING LIVED.

A MAN NAMED MUFARO LIVED IN THIS VILLAGE WITH HIS TWO DAUGHTERS, WHO WERE CALLED MANYARA AND NYASHA. EVERYONE AGREED THAT MANYARA AND NYASHA WERE VERY BEAUTIFUL.

Manyara[1] was almost always in a bad temper. She teased her sister whenever their father's back was turned, and she had been heard to say, "Someday, Nyasha,[2] I will be a queen, and you will be a servant in my household."

"If that should come to pass," Nyasha responded, "I will be pleased to serve you. But why do you say such things? You are clever and strong and beautiful. Why are you so unhappy?"

"Because everyone talks about how kind *you* are, and they praise everything you do," Manyara replied. "I'm certain that Father loves you best. But when I am a queen, everyone will know that your silly kindness is only weakness."

Nyasha was sad that Manyara felt this way, but she ignored her sister's words and went about her chores. Nyasha kept a small plot of land, on which she grew millet,[3] sunflowers, yams, and vegetables. She always sang as she worked, and some said it was her singing that made her crops more bountiful than anyone else's.

One day, Nyasha noticed a small garden snake resting beneath a yam vine. "Good day, little Nyoka,"[4] she called to him. "You are welcome here. You will keep away any creatures who might spoil my vegetables." She bent forward, gave the little snake a loving pat on the head, and then returned to her work.

From that day on, Nyoka was always at Nyasha's side when she tended her garden. It was said that she sang all the more sweetly when he was there.

Mufaro[5] knew nothing of how Manyara treated Nyasha. Nyasha was too considerate of her father's feelings to complain, and Manyara was always careful to behave herself when Mufaro was around.

Early one morning, a messenger from the city arrived. The Great King wanted a wife. "The Most Worthy and Beautiful Daughters in the Land are invited to appear before the King, and he will choose one to become Queen!" the messenger proclaimed.

1. **Manyara** [män yä′ rä]
2. **Nyasha** [nə yä′ shä]
3. **millet** [mil′ it]: a cereal grass used as a food grain.
4. **Nyoka** [nə yō′ kä]
5. **Mufaro** [mü fä′ rō]

Mufaro called Manyara and Nyasha to him. "It would be a great honor to have one of you chosen," he said. "Prepare yourselves to journey to the city. I will call together all our friends to make a wedding party. We will leave tomorrow as the sun rises."

"But, my father," Manyara said sweetly, "it would be painful for either of us to leave you, even to be wife to the king. I know Nyasha would grieve to death if she were parted from you. I am strong. Send me to the city, and let poor Nyasha be happy here with you."

Mufaro beamed with pride. "The king has asked for the most worthy and the most beautiful. No, Manyara, I cannot send you alone. Only a king can choose between two such worthy daughters. Both of you must go!"

That night, when everyone was asleep, Manyara stole quietly out of the village. She had never been in the forest at night before, and she was frightened, but her greed to be the first to appear before the king drove her on. In her hurry, she almost stumbled over a small boy who suddenly appeared, standing in the path.

"Please," said the boy. "I am hungry. Will you give me something to eat?"

"I have brought only enough for myself," Manyara replied.

"But, please!" said the boy. "I am so *very* hungry."

"Out of my way, boy! Tomorrow I will become your queen. How dare you stand in my path?"

After traveling for what seemed to be a great distance, Manyara came to a small clearing. There, silhouetted against the moonlight, was an old woman seated on a large stone.

The old woman spoke. "I will give you some advice, Manyara. Soon after you pass the place where two paths cross, you will see a grove of trees. They will laugh at you. You must not laugh in return. Later, you will meet a man with his head under his arm. You must be polite to him."

"How do you know my name? How dare you advise your future queen? Stand aside, you ugly old woman!" Manyara scolded, and then rushed on her way without looking back.

Just as the old woman had foretold, Manyara came to a grove of trees, and they did indeed seem to be laughing at her.

"I must be calm," Manyara thought. "I will *not* be frightened." She looked up at the trees and laughed out loud. "I laugh at you, trees!" she shouted, and she hurried on.

It was not yet dawn when Manyara heard the sound of rushing water. "The river must be up ahead," she thought. "The great city is just on the other side."

But there, on the rise, she saw a man with his head tucked under his arm. Manyara ran past him without speaking. "A queen acknowledges only those who please her," she said to herself. "I will be queen. I will be queen," she chanted, as she hurried on toward the city.

Nyasha woke at the first light of dawn. As she put on her finest garments, she thought how her life might be changed forever beyond this day. "I'd much prefer to live here," she admitted to herself. "I'd hate to leave this village and never see my father or sing to little Nyoka again."

Her thoughts were interrupted by loud shouts and a commotion from the wedding party assembled outside. Manyara was missing! Everyone bustled about, searching and calling for her. When they found her footprints on the path that led to the city, they decided to go on as planned.

As the wedding party moved through the forest, brightly plumed birds darted about in the cool green shadows beneath the trees. Though anxious about her sister, Nyasha was soon filled with excitement about all there was to see.

They were deep in the forest when she saw the small boy standing by the side of the path.

"You must be hungry," she said, and handed him a yam she had brought for her lunch. The boy smiled and disappeared as quietly as he had come.

Later, as they were approaching the place where the two paths crossed, the old woman appeared and silently pointed the way to the city. Nyasha thanked her and gave her a small pouch filled with sunflower seeds.

The sun was high in the sky when the party came to the grove of towering trees. Their uppermost branches seemed to bow down to

Nyasha as she passed beneath them.

At last, someone announced that they were near their destination.

Nyasha ran ahead and topped the rise before the others could catch up with her. She stood transfixed[6] at her first sight of the city. "Oh, my father," she called. "A great spirit must stand guard here! Just look at what lies before us. I never in all my life dreamed there could be anything so beautiful!"

Arm in arm, Nyasha and her father descended the hill, crossed the river, and approached the city gate. Just as they entered through the great doors, the air was rent[7] by piercing cries, and Manyara ran wildly out of a chamber at the center of the enclosure. When she saw Nyasha, she fell upon her, sobbing.

"Do not go to the king, my sister. Oh, please, Father, do not let her go!" she cried hysterically. "There's a great monster there, a snake with five heads! He said that he knew all my faults and that I displeased him. He would have swallowed me alive if I had not run. Oh, my sister, please do not go inside that place."

It frightened Nyasha to see her sister so upset. But, leaving her father to comfort Manyara, she bravely made her way to the chamber and opened the door.

On the seat of the great chief's stool lay the little garden snake. Nyasha laughed with relief and joy.

"My little friend!" she exclaimed. "It's such a pleasure to see you, but why are you here?"

"I am the king," Nyoka replied.

And there, before Nyasha's eyes, the garden snake changed shape.

"I am the king. I am also the hungry boy with whom you shared a yam in the forest and the old woman to whom you made a gift of sunflower seeds. But you know me best as Nyoka. Because I have been all of these, I know you to be the Most Worthy and Most Beautiful Daughter in the Land. It would make me very happy if you would be my wife."

6. **transfixed** [trans fiksd´]: made still with amazement.
7. **rent:** penetrated with sound.

AND SO IT WAS THAT, A LONG TIME AGO, NYASHA AGREED TO BE MARRIED. THE KING'S MOTHER AND SISTERS TOOK NYASHA TO THEIR HOUSE, AND THE WEDDING PREPARATIONS BEGAN. THE BEST WEAVERS IN THE LAND LAID OUT THEIR FINEST CLOTH FOR HER WEDDING GARMENTS. VILLAGERS FROM ALL AROUND WERE INVITED TO THE CELEBRATION, AND A GREAT FEAST WAS HELD. NYASHA PREPARED THE BREAD FOR THE WEDDING FEAST FROM MILLET THAT HAD BEEN BROUGHT FROM HER VILLAGE.

MUFARO PROCLAIMED TO ALL WHO WOULD HEAR HIM THAT HE WAS THE HAPPIEST FATHER IN ALL THE LAND, FOR HE WAS BLESSED WITH TWO BEAUTIFUL AND WORTHY DAUGHTERS—NYASHA, THE QUEEN; AND MANYARA, A SERVANT IN THE QUEEN'S HOUSEHOLD.

Female Figure African, Chad, Bagirmi, 19th-20th cent., wood, paint, metal bands, nails, 11$^7/_8$" x 14$^3/_8$", Metropolitan Museum of Art

J O H N
S T E P T O E

John Steptoe [1950-1989] was an author and illustrator of books for children and young adults. A native of Brooklyn, New York, Steptoe was just sixteen when he wrote and illustrated his first book, *Stevie*. Originally published in a 1969 *Life* magazine, *Stevie* is one of the first stories ever written that speaks from the perspective of a young African American child living in the ghetto. The author commented, "I wanted it to be something black children could read without translating the language, something real which would relate to what a black child would know."

Steptoe's later works are innovative retellings of legends. *The Story of Jumping Mouse: A Native American Legend* revises the beautiful tale of a humble mouse who becomes a noble eagle. *Mufaro's Beautiful Daughters*, a legend from South Africa, also explores the timeless themes of humility and pride. Frequently inspired by native culture and art, Steptoe said, "I owe a debt of gratitude to the original storytellers. I think they would have understood me as much as I hope I have understood them."

The Piece of Straw

YOSHIKO UCHIDA

Long ago, in the land of Yamato,[1] there was a poor young man who lived all alone. He had no family to care for him, and no friends to whom he might go for help. Each day he watched his purse grow slimmer and slimmer, for there was no one who would give him work. Finally, one day, he saw that his money was almost gone.

"Alas, what am I to do?" he sighed. "The only one who can help me now is the Goddess of Mercy at the Hase[2] Temple."

So the poor young man hurried to the temple and knelt before the shrine of the Goddess of Mercy.

"Oh, Kannon-Sama,"[3] he said. "I am without food or money, and I cannot find work to keep myself alive. I shall kneel here before your shrine until you show me some way in which I can save myself."

The young man sat very still and waited for some sign from the Goddess of Mercy. "Show me in a dream just what I am to do," he

1. **Yamato** [yä mä tō]: a province in legendary Japan, the location of the original settlement of the imperial clan.
2. **Hase** [hä sä]
3. **Kannon-Sama** [kä non sä mä]

Three Sparrows and Bamboo
Nagasawa Rosetsu,
Japan, 1754-99,
Los Angeles County Art Museum

The Piece of Straw   93

pleaded. And the young man did not move from his place before the shrine. He sat there through the long night and all the next day, and still he had no dream. He sat there for many more days and nights, but still the goddess did not help him.

At last the priests of the temple noticed the young man who neither ate nor slept, but sat quietly in front of the shrine. "He will surely starve to death if he stays there much longer," they said to each other.

Then one of the priests went to question the young man.

"Who are you, my good fellow?" he asked. "And why do you sit here for so many days and nights?"

"Alas, I have no friends nor family," said the young man sadly. "And since no one will give me work, I am also without food and money. I have come here to ask the help of the Goddess of Mercy, but if she does not help me soon, I know that I shall die here before her shrine."

Now the good priests of the temple felt great pity for the poor young man, and decided they would take turns bringing him food and water so he would not starve to death. So with their help, the young man continued to sit before the shrine for many more days and nights. He was growing sad and weary, and began to

think perhaps the kind goddess would not help him after all.

At last, on the twenty-first day, as his head nodded with weariness and sleep, he thought he saw a faint dream. An old, old man with a long flowing beard seemed to be coming out of the goddess' shrine. The old man stood before him and told him to leave the temple quickly. "The very first thing that your hand touches after you leave the temple will bring you much good fortune," the old man said to him. "So keep safely whatever it is, no matter how small it may be." And then the old man faded away just as quickly as he had appeared. The young man rubbed his eyes and looked around. The Goddess of Mercy was smiling down at him, just as she had for the last twenty-one days.

"Ah, that dream was her message to me," thought the young man, and he quickly prepared to leave the temple. The priests gave him some food to take along, and the young man hurried out through the temple gates. Just as he was about to turn onto the road, he tripped over a stone and fell flat on the dirt road. As he hastened to pick himself up, he saw that he was grasping a single piece of straw in his right hand. He started to throw it away, but he suddenly remembered what the old man had said to him in his dream— "The first thing that your hand touches after you leave the temple will bring you much good fortune."

"But surely this little piece of straw can bring me no great fortune," thought the young man, and he was about to toss it on the roadside. Then he thought again, "No, I had better do exactly as the Kannon-Sama instructed me," so he carried the piece of straw carefully in his hand.

As he walked along the road, a horsefly began to buzz about his head. The young man picked up a stick and tried to shoo the fly away, but it would not stop bothering him. It buzzed and it buzzed, and it flew in little circles about his head. Finally the young man could bear it no longer. He cupped his hand, and with one big swoop, he caught the little horsefly. Then he strung it on the end of his stick with his piece of straw, and walked on.

Before long, a carriage carrying a noblewoman and her son to the temple came rolling toward him. The little boy was weary and hot, and was tired of sitting quietly in his carriage. He was fretting and crying, but he spied the horsefly buzzing on the end of the young man's stick.

"I want the little fly that's buzzing on the stick!" the little boy cried to his servant.

The servant approached the young man and said politely, "I wonder if you would be kind enough to give your stick to the little boy? He has grown weary from the long, hot ride, and this would make him very happy."

"Well, the fly is tied to the stick with a piece of straw which the goddess of the temple told me I must keep, but if it will make the little boy happy, I shall give it to him," said the young man.

"How very, very kind of you," the noblewoman said, as she leaned out of the carriage. "I'm afraid I have nothing with which I can repay you, except these three oranges." And she held out three large oranges on a beautiful white napkin.

The young man thanked the noblewoman, wrapped up the three oranges carefully, and walked on down the road. The sun was hot as it beat down on the dusty road. Before long, he saw a procession of men and women coming toward him. They were walking on either side of a beautiful carriage, and appeared to be the handmaidens and guards of the noblewoman inside. As the group walked by the young man, one of the young women suddenly grew faint and collapsed at the side of the road.

"Oh, I am so thirsty," she said weakly, and held her hand out for some water.

"Quickly, find some water," the guards shouted, but there was no water to be seen anywhere.

They called to the young man and asked if he could tell them where there might be some water.

"I fear there are no wells or streams nearby," said the young man. "But I have three oranges here. Give her the juice from these oranges to quench her thirst," and he handed his oranges to the guards. They quickly gave the young maiden the juice from the three oranges, and before long, she felt well enough to go on.

"If you had not come by and given me your oranges, I might have died here on this hot and dusty road," the maiden said to the young man. "I would give you anything to thank you, but I have only these three rolls of white silk. Take them and accept my thanks," she said, as she gave the rolls of silk to the young man.

The young man thanked her for the gift, and with the rolls of silk under his arm, he walked on down the road. "My goodness, one piece of straw brought me three oranges, and now my oranges have brought me three rolls of silk," thought the young man happily.

That night he found an inn where he could spend the night, and he gave the innkeeper one of the rolls of silk to pay for his room. Early the next morning, he started off down the road again. Toward noon, he saw a group of men on horseback cantering[4] toward him. The horses held their heads up proudly, and whisked their long, shiny tails. The young man thought he had never seen such beautiful horses before, and looked at them longingly, for he had always wanted a horse for himself. Then, just as one of the noblemen rode past the young man, his horse suddenly faltered and fell to the ground. The men gathered about the animal and stroked its side and gave it water, but the horse would not move or raise its head.

"I'm afraid it's dead," said the nobleman sadly, and he took the saddle from the horse's back and the bit from its mouth. He then left one of his servants to care for the horse's remains, and rode off on another horse with his men.

4. **cantering** [kan′ tər ing]: galloping gently.

The young man went up to the servant who was left to care for the horse. "He must have been a very fine horse," said the young man, as he looked down at the dead animal.

"Oh, yes, indeed he was," answered the servant. "He was such a valuable animal that even though many people offered large sums of money, the master would not think of selling him. It certainly is strange that he died so suddenly," he added, shaking his head.

"What are you going to do now?" the young man asked.

"I can't let the horse just lie here beside the road. I really don't know what to do," answered the servant sadly.

"Well, if you like, I'll give you a roll of silk for the horse. Then you can return home and I shall take care of the horse," said the young man.

"What a strange person to want a dead horse," thought the servant, but he was happy to be on his way. "Why, that is a fine bargain, my friend," he said out loud, and he quickly took the roll of silk and hurried away before the young man should change his mind.

The young man then knelt down before the horse and prayed to the Goddess of Mercy that he might come to life again. "Oh, Kannon-Sama," he pleaded. "Please give life to this beautiful horse once more." Then, as he watched, the horse slowly opened its eyes. Then it slowly got to its feet, and before long, began to drink water and eat some oats. It shook its head, whisked its long, silky tail, and looked as good as new once again. The young man was so happy, he quickly climbed up on the horse's back and rode into the next village. There he spent the night at another inn, and used his last roll of silk to pay for his room.

The next day, he rode on his fine horse until he came to the town of Toba.[5] He knew it wasn't far from the big city of Kyoto[6] when, suddenly, the young man thought of a problem. The nobleman was very well known in Kyoto, and many people probably knew his beautiful chestnut-colored horse. "It would never do if I should be accused of stealing the nobleman's horse," he thought, "for no one would believe the strange story of how the horse came to be mine."

So the young man decided he would sell the horse. Just then, he passed by the home of a family who

5. **Toba** [tō bə]
6. **Kyoto** [kē ō tō]

appeared to be getting ready to leave on a journey. A wagon piled high with bags and boxes stood by the front gate. The young man called out to the man of the house, "Good sir, would you like to buy this horse from me?"

"My, what a beautiful horse. I certainly would like to buy it from you, but alas, I have no money," he answered.

Then the man came closer to look at the horse. It was more beautiful than any he had ever seen.

"Ah, what a pity I cannot buy such a fine animal," he said. "But wait, I know what I can do. I can give you three rice fields in exchange for your horse," said the man happily.

The young man thought for a moment. "Well—" he began.

"What's more, since we are going away, I shall leave you the house, and you may live in it until we return," continued the man.

"That's a fair bargain indeed," said the young man. "The horse is yours!"

"In case we decide not to return, the house will be yours too," called the man, and soon he and his family rode off down the road with their wagon rumbling after them.

Now the young man found that one field of rice was plenty to keep

Grapevines Ito Jakuchu, Japan, 1716-1800, Los Angeles County Art Museum

himself well fed, so he rented out his other fields. As if by magic, the rice in his field grew and grew, until he had so much rice, he could sell many, many sacks each day. He grew richer and richer, and his purse grew fatter and fatter, and his luck seemed to grow with the years.

Many years went by, and still no one returned to the house, so the young man continued to live there and to raise fine crops of rice. His wealth increased tenfold, and he became an important man in the town. He married a beautiful young maiden of the village, and they had many lovely children. And there they lived happily for many years with their children, and their children's children in the little town of Toba.

So the one little piece of straw which the young man picked up so many years ago outside the temple gate had truly brought him great fortune and happiness, just as the old man in his dream had said it would.

YOSHIKO UCHIDA

Yoshiko Uchida [1921-1992] was born in Alameda, California, and grew up in Berkeley in a house full of books. She has said, "I've been interested in books and writing for as long as I can remember. I was writing stories when I was ten." Uchida also kept a journal of important events, starting on the day she graduated from elementary school.

Besides rewriting folktales, such as "The Piece of Straw," Uchida also wrote about the experiences of Japanese Americans who were confined to internment camps during World War II.

RISING VOICES

CARLA WILLETTO

Way out in the heart of the reservation,
sand always blowing, tumbleweeds rolling,
the Navajos are gaining control of their destination.

Sheltered by Black Mountain,
whites and Navajos are striving to educate   5
with understanding and appreciation,
not defiance, scorn, or hate.

Trying to teach and learn side by side.
Bilingual and bicultural.
Will it work? Is it working?   10
Maybe . . . and maybe not.

But we people are giving it a try,
Trying to learn both ways,
Trying to be in harmony with both ways —
If only those outside will let us.   15

Our traditions survive;
Our heroes of legends and tribal history
are alive in what we learn.
So we can continue to tell our story.

Our cherished medicine men   20
have young trainees, so that when
the old ones are dead and gone,
the ceremonies for another generation
will live on.

What will be the result of this attempted peace?   25
I'll tell you this—listen!
From the silent, windswept land a voice can be
    heard.

Rising from the monolithic monuments,
purple mountains and rolling grasslands,
The moaning winds carry a soft   30
but steadily rising voice . . .

A voice made of many voices
of proud men and women
with a hope and a question . . .
Will we make it? . . . Listen?   35

The Voice—our Voice—is getting
    stronger
Rising to the turquoise sky—
Listen! You will hear it soon . . .
very soon . . .

CARLA WILLETTO

Carla Willetto grew up on a Navajo reservation and went
to school at Rough Rock Community High School in Arizona.
She wrote "Rising Voices" during her 1977-1978 school year.

Asking Big Questions About the Literature

What do people through the ages have in common?

Identifying Common Traits

As you read the selections in this unit, you probably noticed that the characters have traits you've encountered before in real life or in literature.

Skim the selections you've read, and identify each main character's traits. Also jot down the evidence from the selection that supports your judgment. Use a chart like the one begun here.

When you're finished, work with a small group and compare your chart with theirs. Which traits do people through the ages have in common?

Plot

The arrangement of events that make up a story is called the **plot**. The plots of most works of literature begin by explaining the setting and a character's problem or conflict. Most of the story then involves resolving something about this problem. For example, in "Daedalus" the main character must find a way to escape from Crete. (*See "Plot" on page 118.*)

Think of a story, a TV show, or a movie with a plot like that of a story in this unit. How are the plots alike and different? Which traits do the characters share? Write a short paper in which you describe similarities and differences.

Character	Traits	Evidence from story
Daedalus	desire for freedom	willing to die for freedom
	creative thinker	could design original things

Write a "Way of Being"
POEM

In the poem "Rising Voices," the speaker states that Navajos want to get along and to retain their freedom and identity—desires that most other people share. Think of wishes that other characters in this unit have that might be shared by others. Choose one wish and write a poem about that wish. Share your poem with a small group of students.

Writing About the Bad Guys

Think of the characters in this unit who are presented as *not the way to be*, for example, Manyara in "Mufaro's Beautiful Daughters" or Minos in "Daedalus." If the story were continued, would the character learn a lesson or remain the same?

Choose a story with one bad character and write the next chapter in that character's life. See the flowchart below for ideas.

Folktales

Folktale is a catch-all term that includes the following:

- *fairy tales*, such as "Cinderella"
- *myths*, such as "Hercules"
- *legends*, such as "Davy Crockett"
- *fables*, such as "The Tortoise and the Hare"

In many folktales, the success of the main character hinges on one or two key personality traits. For example, Hercules in "The Earth Giant" and Colin in "Summertime on Icarus" are both successful because of their courage and cleverness. (*See "Folktales" on page 119.*)

Choose one character from this unit who is successful because of certain personality traits. Write a revised version of the story in which the character's key traits are the same—but the character is a member of the opposite sex *and* lives in another time and place. Tell your story to a partner, focusing on the traits that lead to the character's success.

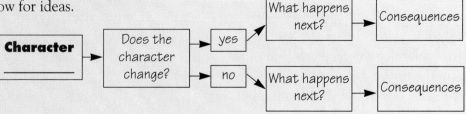

Asking Big Questions About the Literature 103

Asking Big Questions About the Literature

Why do people around the world tell folktales?

LITERATURE STUDY

Folktales

A **folktale** is often a simple story with a message or a moral. The point of the message may be to explain why things are the way they are—for example, why the stars shine—or to teach a lesson, such as "virtue is rewarded." (*See "Folktales" on page 119.*)

Folk songs like "John Henry" are folktales set to music. Rewrite a favorite story from this unit as a song. (You can use an existing tune.) Keep the point of the original story. Record your song and share it with classmates.

Write a Galactic

FOLKTALE

Imagine that you're a member of a future society, like the one in *Star Trek*. Write a folktale that people will want to read in the future. Base your folktale on a story in this unit. Bind your class stories in a *Cosmic Folktale Anthology*.

MAPPING

Story Locations

Work in a small group and use a world map to locate the approximate settings of some of the selections in this unit. Put a "quick stick" note on each location. If no location is given ("a kingdom"), theorize about where the story *could* be set based on the details in the story. (Show outer-space locations beyond the world's boundaries.)

On each note, jot a few words to identify the story's name and what you feel is the purpose of the story.

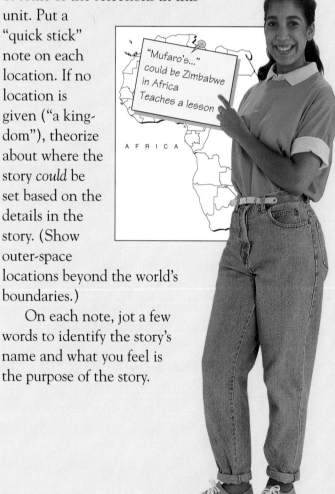

"Mufaro's..."
could be Zimbabwe
in Africa
Teaches a lesson

AFRICA

What lessons do we learn about people through folktales?

Write a "Hip" FOLKTALE

Some of the updated folktales in this unit, such as "Antaeus" and "Summertime on Icarus," retell old myths, but because of their modern settings, they seem new. Take a message from a folktale in this unit and retell it as a "hip" folktale for urban students. Put the major events in boxes as shown, and decide how you'll change them.

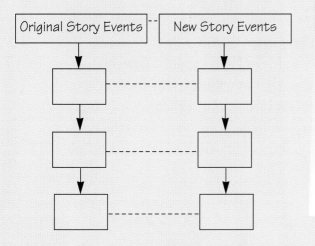

Create A BUMPER STICKER

Think of the ideas and opinions that the characters in this unit might have. Turn one of those ideas into a bumper sticker. Post your bumper sticker in the classroom.

LITERATURE STUDY

Plot

The **plot** of a work of literature is a situation that, after a series of events, reaches a final resolution. People read literature because they're curious about what will happen next, but folktales that teach lessons about "good" behavior often have more predictable plots than other pieces of literature. For example, readers expect the good princess will be rewarded for her virtue and the evil princess will be punished. (*See* "Plot" *on page 118.*)

Work with a small group and choose a story from this unit with an ending you could predict when you read it. At what point in the story did you know how it was going to end? Was it at the same point that you guessed what the story's lesson about people was going to be? Perform a skit of the story. Use the story as a guide to reveal the plot and the story's lesson.

NOW Choose a Project!

Three projects involving folktales are described on the following pages.

Writing Workshop

WRITE A FOLKTALE

Many of the stories in this unit feature characters who possess the qualities we most admire, such as courage or kindness. Readers identify what those qualities are and why those qualities are important through description. Without good description, Hercules would seem like just another guy having a bad day. Your **purpose** in this project is to create a folktale that describes a character with an important quality or trait. Then you'll develop a story that clearly shows the value of that trait. Your **audience** is students in your school.

Prewriting

GIVE YOUR IMAGINATION WINGS

Think of people you admire. What important qualities do they have? Kindness? High ideals? Loyalty? Choose one trait or quality as the focus of your story. Next brainstorm for instances in which you've observed that trait in action. For example, if you've chosen the trait of kindness, think of all instances in which you've seen people displaying kindness.

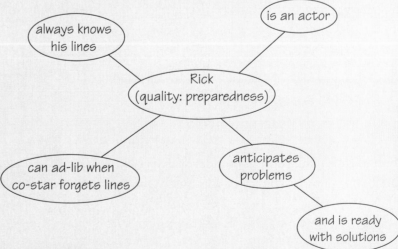

always knows his lines

is an actor

Rick
(quality: preparedness)

can ad-lib when co-star forgets lines

anticipates problems

and is ready with solutions

Now choose a character, real or imaginary, to display the trait you've chosen. (Your character might, in fact, be a combination of several different people and their actions.) Create a web like the one shown for the story by student writer Steve Johnston on pages 110-111. Use these questions as guides: Who is my character? What does my character do on a day-to-day basis? What problems might the character face?

Prewriting
MAP THE STORY

Now that you have a character, think of possible plots. Review your web and look for a problem that might set the plot in motion. Your character, like the characters in this unit, should encounter a problem and use his or her key personality trait to overcome the problem. For example, in "Daedalus," Daedalus is held prisoner and uses his creativity to escape from Crete.

Create a story map like the one started here to organize your ideas. As you map your story, remind yourself to select those elements that will have the most appeal to your audience and effectively show your character's important quality or trait.

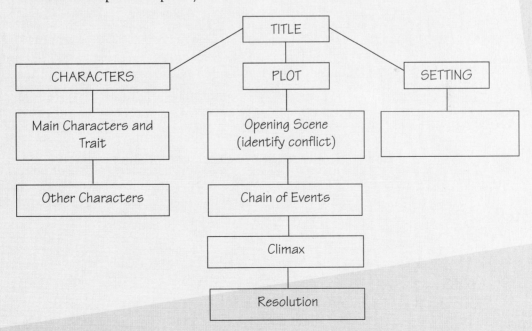

Drafting YOUR FOLKTALE

Using your story map as a guide, begin drafting your folk-tale. You may open your story with the setting, a description of a character, or a situation. Notice that on page 110, student writer Steve Johnston begins his modern folktale by vividly describing the scene of an empty theater before a performance. After giving his readers a general orientation to the scene, "The theater was empty," he fills in the specific sensory details: "the echoing openness of the theater" and the "padded seats seemed to wait expectantly in the darkness."

Grab your readers' interest in the first paragraph. Make sure that you introduce the conflict near the beginning of the story because the conflict is what sets the story in motion. The story introduces the conflict in the second paragraph by de-scribing the co-star who is "habitually late and unprepared for nearly everything."

After you establish the scene and the conflict, provide an example of the personality trait that you will develop. Early on, Steve describes his character, Rick, as the kind of guy who's prepared—he even takes his costume to the cleaners himself. If your folktale is more of the super-hero variety, you have artistic freedom to make the trait "larger than life." For example, Hercules in "The Earth Giant" has the sort of courage that few people ever witness.

When you conclude your folktale, make sure the ending leaves your audience feeling satisfied. They should feel that the characters "got what they deserved" and that all loose ends are tied up.

Revising
YOUR FOLKTALE

Ask a small group to read your folktale and make suggestions for improvement. Begin by asking them to name your character's personality trait. If they don't "get it," you've got a problem. Check your use of description. Notice that on pages 110-111, Steve Johnston uses specific details to show the hero's quality of being prepared: the hero takes charge of his own dry cleaning and insists on rehearsing scenes until he knows them perfectly.

Notice also the description of the cast backstage "chattering and bustling about, putting on their costumes and make-up" and Rick's co-star who is "wringing her hands and frantically reciting her lines." Such description helps readers feel as if they are on the scene. Ask your readers for suggestions about where you could add more descriptive detail.

Editing
YOUR FOLKTALE

Work with a partner to edit your revision. Read one another's folktales, checking for errors in spelling, grammar, and punctuation. Correct your errors and make a publishable copy of your folktale. You won't want to end up as the "Legend of the Student Who Couldn't Spell."

~~Night at the Theater~~
Be Prepared for Anything

~~There wasn't anyone in the theater when Rick came in.~~ Standing
in the ~~void~~ emptiness on stage made Rick feel small in comparison to the
echoing openness of the ~~stage~~ theater. The padded seats seemed to wait
expectantly in the darkness. It was ~~thrilling~~ exciting but
almost ~~frightening~~ sickening to think that in about an hour all of the
seats would be filled with people waiting to see him perform.
He ~~glanced~~ looked at his watch and ~~walked~~ quickly walked off stage, ~~(knowing he~~
~~was prepared.)~~ confident in the knowledge that he was
prepared.
The theater was empty when Rick arrived.

Publishing
YOUR FOLKTALE

Bind your folktale with those of your fellow students into a classroom anthology. Choose a title. Volunteers might design a cover, prepare a table of contents and author biographies, and create a few choice illustrations. Donate your anthology to the school library. The beginning of Steve Johnston's folktale follows.

STUDENT MODEL

Be Prepared for Anything
by Steve Johnston of Elburn, Illinois

The theater was empty when Rick arrived. Standing in the emptiness on stage made Rick feel small in comparison to the echoing openness of the theater. The padded seats seemed to wait expectantly in the darkness. It was exciting, but almost sickening, to think that in about an hour all of the seats would be filled with squirming people, eagerly waiting to see him perform. He looked at his watch and quickly walked off stage, confident in the knowledge that he was prepared.

In the dressing room, Rick discovered that most of the cast had already arrived and were chattering and bustling about, putting on their costumes and make-up. Unfortunately, his co-star, who seemed habitually late and unprepared for nearly everything, was not among them.

Rick walked to the costume rack and pulled out the hanger with his butler outfit. He'd personally taken it to the cleaners himself to make sure that it was perfect for tonight's performance. Rick's tall, straight body was perfect for his role as a butler, and his natural English accent added the perfect touch to the part. After putting on his costume and making sure all the buttons were fastened, he grabbed his towel and made his way to the area that was set aside for the make-up crew.

As the make-up man blotted his face with color, Rick thought of the long rehearsals and the many scenes that he'd insisted on rehearsing until they were perfect. He'd tried to anticipate every disaster and have a solution for it. The fifteen-minute call snapped him out of his memories.

His make-up job finished, he went to see whether his co-star had arrived. She played the role of a maid, and in most of the scenes, the maid tries to win over the butler's heart, and in the end, does. His co-star was wringing her hands and frantically reciting her lines, trying to learn them at the last moment. Rick groaned inwardly. He'd made all possible preparations so that if she muddled her lines, he could quickly ad-lib his lines to cover for her. It looked as if his preparation would soon be put to the test.

Cooperative Learning

CREATE AND PERFORM A PLAY

For this project, you'll work with a small group of students to choose a folktale and then write a script to revise it as a play. You'll perform your play for other students in your grade.

Choose A FOLKTALE

Your group's first step is to choose a folktale to revise as a play. Choose one from this unit, or go to a library and research other folktales. Cast a wide net. African folklore and Native American fables are often overlooked but are especially rich sources of interesting stories. When you have about six folktales, discuss which one could best be rewritten and staged as a play. Choose one folktale on which to base your play.

Create A SCRIPT

As a group, reread your folktale paragraph by paragraph. Decide which scenes and characters should be dropped and which scenes need to be revised. When you've developed the major ideas for the beginning, climax, and end of the play, stop brainstorming. At this point, divide up jobs using the categories shown in the chart on the next page.

The Lead Playwright will take charge and assign group members portions of the script to write. When the script is written, the Lead Playwright will lead a meeting in which group members read aloud what they've written. After each person reads, group members will offer feedback.

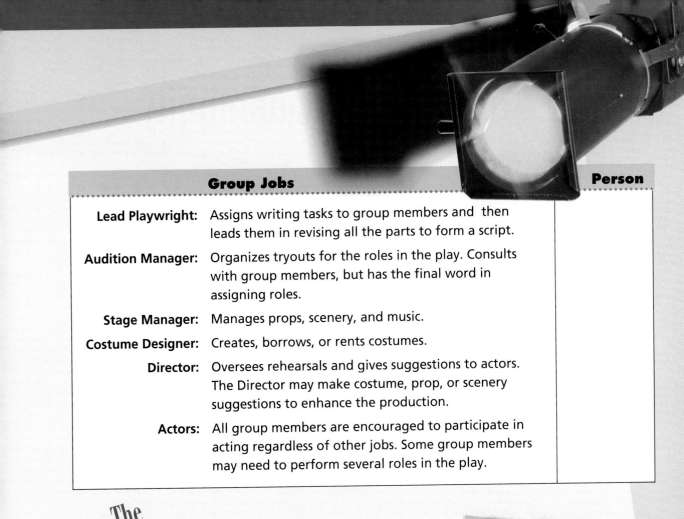

Group Jobs		Person
Lead Playwright:	Assigns writing tasks to group members and then leads them in revising all the parts to form a script.	
Audition Manager:	Organizes tryouts for the roles in the play. Consults with group members, but has the final word in assigning roles.	
Stage Manager:	Manages props, scenery, and music.	
Costume Designer:	Creates, borrows, or rents costumes.	
Director:	Oversees rehearsals and gives suggestions to actors. The Director may make costume, prop, or scenery suggestions to enhance the production.	
Actors:	All group members are encouraged to participate in acting regardless of other jobs. Some group members may need to perform several roles in the play.	

The REHEARSAL

Once roles in the play are chosen, rehearsals begin. The Director is in charge. He or she needs to make sure that all costumes, props, scenery, rehearsals, and so on are ready for the day of production. The Director also needs to find a suitable place for the production.

The PERFORMANCE

Perform your play for another class—or several classes. You may want to post notices or send out invitations a week or so prior to the production. Then on with the show!

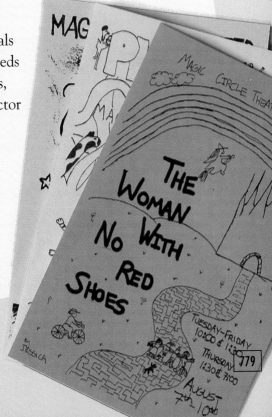

Helping Your Community

RESEARCH PLACE NAMES

The names of places can link us to the past, just as folktales do. For example, Jump Off Joe Lake in Washington is named for an accident in which an out-of-control horse-drawn wagon hurtled down a mountain. Just before the wagon tipped over the edge of a ravine, the driver yelled to his partner, "Jump off, Joe!" For this project, work with a group of students to research the origins of the names of places and buildings in your community. Prepare a written report of your findings to give to the town library or city hall.

Making A LIST OF NAMES

Brainstorm for a list of names of the mountains, lakes, buildings, and streets in your community. Use a map and a city directory as references. List places, buildings, and streets that have odd names, but include those with common names too. Their name origins might surprise you.

Doing RESEARCH

Divide up the research task so that some group members conduct interviews with senior citizens, historians, and historical societies, while others do library research. Or each person might research one category, such as buildings or rivers.

Use a chart like the one begun here to record your research findings. If you discover other place names as you do research, add them to your chart.

How a Place Got Its Name

Name	Origin	Information Source
Nome (Alaska)	It's short for "ka-no-me," meaning "I don't know," which is what the original inhabitants replied when asked the name of the region by white explorers whose language they didn't understand.	interview with Jane Konlit
Buildings		
Streets		
Other		

Organizing YOUR FINDINGS

After everyone has completed researching, organize your findings into categories and subcategories. To prepare the report, write a brief introduction for each major category. Then list each place name alphabetically and provide an explanation (a sentence or a paragraph) for each entry.

Assembling YOUR REPORT

After you've revised, edited, and proofread your report, prepare it for readers. To give your report pizzazz, add maps, photographs, and photocopies of historical records. Design an attractive cover, and bind the report. Don't be shy about presenting your report in person to the mayor or city librarian. You've added to your community's knowledge and you deserve a pat on the back!

Putting It All Together

What Roles Do Folktales Play in Your Life?

How has this unit helped you understand folktales and their messages? Look back on the writing you've done for this unit—in your journal, in response to your reading, and for the Projects.

Use what you've learned to write an essay about the role of folktales in your life—how they connect you to your cultural heritage, your community, and your personal values. Share your essay with classmates and people you care about. You may wish to save a copy to share with your own children someday.

MAKING CONNECTIONS WITH THE PAST

Prewriting and Drafting   Brainstorm for folktales that you've grown up hearing. Some may have been told at holiday times. (Remember George Washington and the cherry tree?) Other folktales might have been told to you as "just fun" stories that actually had a lesson. (Does Br'er Rabbit ring a bell?) Some folktales might even be about a family ancestor who is remembered as a real character.

Also think about folktales you've heard in song form, such as "The Wreck of the Edmund Fitzgerald." Make a web to record your thoughts about your favorite folktales. When you finish, organize your ideas into a rough outline of reasons why folktales are important to you. Use your outline to guide your drafting.

Revising and Editing   Work with a partner to revise and edit your essay. Ask your partner to make suggestions for improvement and to check your usage, punctuation, and spelling. No one wants to read an essay that's messy and filled with errors.

Publishing   Your first audience will be classmates. You might be surprised at the number of similar connections you have with them.

Because your essay is personal, you'll probably also want to share it with people closest to you—your family, good friends, and special teachers or clergy members.

Evaluating Your Work

Think Back About the Big Questions

With a partner, discuss the Big Questions on pages 10-11 and the questions you generated for **Now Think!** on page 11. Do you have trouble answering any of the questions now? In your journal, create a "before and after" chart to show how your responses to the Big Questions have changed after your work in *Voices Through the Ages*.

Think Back About Your Work

Think about the unit you've just finished—including your reading, writing, and activities. How would you evaluate your efforts?

Write a note to your teacher, explaining what you've done during this unit and what you've learned. Use the following questions to guide your thinking.

- Which selection in this unit did you like the most? The least? Why?
- Generally, which kind of folktale do you like best? Stories of long ago and far away? Modern updated folktales?
- What is the most surprising thing that you learned about folktales?
- Which activities helped you learn more about the value of folktales? Why?
- What did you learn about yourself as you read the selections and worked through the activities?
- If you could do one activity again, which one would you choose? What would you do differently?
- How would you rate your work in this unit? Use the following scale and give at least three reasons for your rating.

  1 = Outstanding   3 = Fair
  2 = Good   4 = Not as good as it could have been

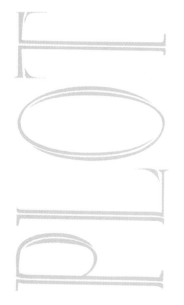

PLOT

What Is Plot?   A **plot** is the series of events that happen in a story. Most plots follow this pattern: The *exposition*, the beginning of a story, introduces the setting, the characters, and the conflict—the problems—that the characters will try to overcome. Next, in the *rising action* of the story, complications set in. After a series of events, the action reaches a peak, called the *climax* of the action. The conflict is resolved. Finally, in the *falling action*, the suspense is over and all the loose ends are wrapped up.

Graphing the Action   Choose one selection from this unit and decide what the plot is. Then use graph paper to plot each event in the selection. Label each event *exposition*, *rising action*, *climax*, or *falling action*. When you finish, compare your graph with that of someone else who chose the same selection. Are your graphs the same? Why or why not?

Writing a Heroic Poem   Many folktales in ancient Greece told of the deeds of mythical super heroes, such as Hercules, but these folktales were in the form of poems and were always told by professional storytellers. Try your hand at writing a poem with a plot of a super hero who does great deeds. (You may want to deal with only one great deed in your poem.) Base your folktale on an ancient tale or think up your own hero—a man or woman of today or yesterday. In the tradition of ancient storytellers, read your poem aloud to the class or to a small group of students.

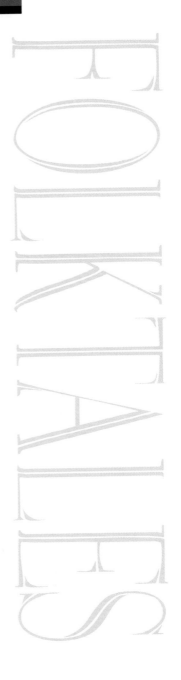

What Are Folktales?

The term **folktale** includes the simple stories that most people grow up hearing, such as, fairy tales, myths, legends, and fables. People may tell folktales to remember past events, to explain reasons for events, and to teach lessons or cultural values. For example, the African folktale "Mufaro's Beautiful Daughters" stresses the value of kindness and teaches that kindness will be rewarded.

Older folktales, such as "Daedalus" and "The Case of the Uncooked Eggs," usually have simple plots and little description other than "a beautiful princess" or "a busy market place." The pace of the action may be very quick and the passing of years explained in a sentence or two. However, when old folktales are updated and retold, as is the case with "Summertime on Icarus" and "Antaeus," the action drifts along at a more leisurely pace, slowed down by description and character development.

Giving the Author a Hand with Description   Choose a folktale that contains little descriptive detail. Retell the folktale, but add lavish description of the scenes, characters, and events. When you finish, add your folktale and those of your classmates to a classroom anthology, *Folktales: The Full Treatment.*

Picturing the "Pow!" and the "Wow!"   Choose a folktale from this unit that uses very little description. As you read the story, you probably pictured some of the scenes in your mind's eye. Think about your favorite scene and draw it the way you see it in your imagination. Post your picture on your class bulletin board and challenge your classmates to identify the scene.

GLOSSARY OF LITERARY TERMS

A

alliteration Repetition of the first sound—usually a consonant sound—in several words of a sentence or a line of poetry.

allusion An author's indirect reference to someone or something that is presumed to be familiar to the reader.

anecdote A short narrative about an interesting or a humorous event, usually in the life of a person.

antagonist The person or force opposing the protagonist, or main character in a literary work. [See also *protagonist*.]

autobiography A person's written account of his or her own life.

B

ballad A poem, often a song, that tells a story in simple verse.

biography An account of a person's life, written by another person.

blank verse Unrhymed poetry.

C

character A person or an animal that participates in the action of a work of literature. A *dynamic character* is one whose thoughts, feelings, and actions are changeable and lifelike; a *static character* always remains the same. [See also *protagonist, antagonist*.]

characterization The creation of characters through the characters' use of language and through descriptions of their appearance, thoughts, emotions, and actions. [See also *character*.]

chronology An arrangement of events in the order in which they happen.

cliché An overused expression that is trite rather than meaningful.

climax The highest point of tension in the plot of a work of literature. [See also *plot*.]

comedy An amusing play that has a happy ending.

conclusion The final part or ending of a piece of literature.

concrete poem A poem arranged on the page so that its punctuation, letters, and lines make the shape of the subject of the poem.

conflict A problem that confronts the characters in a piece of literature. The conflict may be *internal* (a character's struggle within himself or herself) or *external* (a character's struggle against nature, another person, or society). [See also *plot*.]

context The general sense of words that helps readers to understand the meaning of unfamiliar words and phrases in a piece of writing.

D

description An author's use of words to give the reader or listener a mental picture, an impression, or an understanding of a person, place, thing, event, or idea.

dialect A form of speech spoken by people in a particular group or geographical region that differs in vocabulary, grammar, and pronunciation from the standard language.

dialogue The spoken words and conversation of characters in a work of literature.

drama A play that is performed before an audience according to stage directions and using dialogue. Classical drama has two genres: *tragedy* and *comedy*. Modern drama includes *melodrama, satire, theater of the absurd*, and *pantomime*. [See also *comedy, play*, and *tragedy*.]

dramatic poetry A play written in the form of poetry.

E

epic A long narrative poem—written in a formal style and meant to be read aloud—that relates the adventures and

experiences of one or more great heroes or heroines.

essay   Personal nonfiction writing about a particular subject that is important to the writer.

excerpt   A passage from a larger work that has been taken out of its context to be used for a special purpose.

exposition   Writing that explains, analyzes, or defines.

extended metaphor   An elaborately drawn out metaphor. [See also *metaphor*.]

F

fable   A short, simple story whose purpose is to teach a lesson, usually with animal characters who talk and act like people.

fantasy   Imaginative fiction about unrealistic characters, places, and events.

fiction   Literature, including the short story and the novel, that tells about imaginary people and events.

figurative language   Language used to express ideas through figures of speech: descriptions that aren't meant to be taken literally. Types of figurative language include *simile, metaphor, extended metaphor, hyperbole,* and *personification*.

figure of speech   A type of figurative language, not meant to be taken literally, that expresses something in such a way that it brings the thing to life in the reader's or listener's imagination. [See also *figurative language*.]

flashback   A break in a story's action that relates a past happening in order to give the reader background information about a present action in the story.

folktale   A story that has been passed along from storyteller to storyteller for generations. Kinds of folktales include *tall tales, fairy tales, fables, legends,* and *myths*.

foreshadowing   The use of clues to create suspense by giving the reader or audience hints of events to come.

free verse   Poetry that has no formal rhyme scheme or metrical pattern.

G

genre   A major category of art. The three major literary genres are poetry, prose, and drama.

H

haiku   A three-line Japanese verse form. In most haiku, the first and third lines have five syllables, while the second line has seven. The traditional haiku describes a complicated feeling or thought in simple language through a single image.

hero/heroine   The main character in a work of literature. In heroic literature, the hero or heroine is a particularly brave, noble, or clever person whose achievements are unusual and important. [See also *character*.]

heroic age   The historical period in western civilization—from about 800 B.C. through A.D. 200—during which most works of heroic literature, such as myths and epics, were created in ancient Greece and Rome.

hubris   Arrogance or excessive pride leading to mistakes; the character flaw in a hero of classical tragedy.

hyperbole   An obvious exaggeration used for emphasis. [See also *figurative language*.]

I

idiom   An expression whose meaning cannot be understood from the ordinary meaning of the words. For example, *It's raining cats and dogs*.

imagery   The words and phrases in writing that appeal to the senses of sight, hearing, taste, touch, and smell.

irony An effect created by a sharp contrast between what is expected and what is real. An *ironic twist* in a plot is an event that is the complete opposite of what the characters have been hoping or expecting will happen. An *ironic statement* declares the opposite of the speaker's literal meaning.

J

jargon Words and phrases used by a group of people who share the same profession or special interests in order to refer to technical things or processes with which they are familiar. In general, jargon is any terminology that sounds unclear, overused, or pretentious.

L

legend A famous folktale about heroic actions, passed along by word of mouth from generation to generation. The legend may have begun as a factual account of real people and events but has become mostly or completely fictitious.

limerick A form of light verse, or humorous poetry, written in one five-line stanza with a regular scheme of rhyme and meter.

literature The branch of art that is expressed in written language and includes all written genres.

lyric poem A short poem that expresses personal feelings and thoughts in a musical way. Originally, lyrics were the words of songs that were sung to music played on the lyre, a stringed instrument invented by the ancient Greeks.

M

metamorphosis The transformation of one thing, or being, into another completely different thing or being, such as a caterpillar's change into a butterfly.

metaphor Figurative language in which one thing is said to be another thing. [See also *figurative language.*]

meter The pattern of rhythm in lines of poetry. The most common meter, in poetry written in English, is iambic pentameter, that is, a verse having five metrical feet, each foot of verse having two syllables, an unaccented one followed by an accented one.

mood The feeling or atmosphere that a reader senses while reading or listening to a work of literature.

motivation A character's reasons for doing, thinking, feeling, or saying something. Sometimes an author will make a character's motivation obvious from the beginning. In realistic fiction and drama, however, a character's motivation may be so complicated that the reader discovers it gradually, by studying the character's thoughts, feelings, and behavior.

myth A story, passed along by word of mouth for generations, about the actions of gods and goddesses or superhuman heroes and heroines. Most myths were first told to explain the origins of natural things or to justify the social rules and customs of a particular society.

N

narration The process of telling a story. For both fiction and nonfiction, there are two main kinds of narration, based on whether the story is told from a first-person or third-person point of view. [See also *point of view.*]

narrative poem A poem that tells a story containing the basic literary ingredients of fiction: character, setting, and plot.

narrator The person, or voice, that tells a story. [See also *point of view, voice.*]

nonfiction Prose that is factually true and is about real people, events, and places.

nonstandard English
Versions of English, such as slang and dialects, that use pronunciation, vocabulary, idiomatic expressions, grammar, and punctuation that differ from the accepted "correct" constructions of English.

novel   A long work of narrative prose fiction. A novel contains narration, a setting or settings, characters, dialogue, and a more complicated plot than a short story.

O

onomatopoeia   The technique of using words that imitate the sounds they describe, such as *hiss*, *buzz*, and *splash*.

oral tradition   Stories, poems, and songs that have been kept alive by being told, recited, and sung by people over many generations. Since the works were not originally written, they often have many different versions.

P

parable   A brief story—similar to a fable, but about people—that describes an ordinary situation and concludes with a short moral or lesson to be learned.

personification   Figurative language in which an animal, an object, or an idea is given human characteristics. [See also *figurative language*.]

persuasion   A type of speech or writing whose purpose is to convince people that something is true or important.

play   A work of dramatic literature written for performance by actors before an audience. In classical or traditional drama, a play is divided into five acts, each containing a number of scenes. Each act represents a distinct phase in the development of the plot. Modern plays often have only one act and one scene.

playwright   The author of a play.

plot   The sequence of actions and events in fiction or drama. A traditional plot has at least three parts: the *rising action*, leading up to a turning point that affects the main character; the *climax*, the turning point or moment of greatest intensity or interest; and the *falling action*, leading away from the conflict, or resolving it.

poetry   Language selected and arranged in order to say something in a compressed or nonliteral way. Modern poetry may or may not use many of the traditional poetic techniques that include *meter*, *rhyme*, *alliteration*, *figurative language*, *symbolism*, and *specific verse forms*.

point of view   The perspective from which a writer tells a story. *First-person* narrators tell the story from their own point of view, using pronouns such as *I* or *me*. *Third-person* narrators, using pronouns such as *he*, *she*, or *them*, may be *omniscient* (knowing everything about all characters), or *limited* (taking the point of view of one character). [See also *narration*.]

propaganda   Information or ideas that may or may not be true, but are spread as though they are true, in order to persuade people to do or believe something.

prose   The ordinary form of written and spoken language used to create fiction, nonfiction, and most drama.

protagonist   The main character of a literary work. [See also *character* and *characterization*.]

R

refrain   A line or group of lines that is repeated, usually at the end of each verse, in a poem or a song.

repetition   The use of the same formal element more than once in a literary work, for emphasis or in order to achieve another desired effect.

resolution   The falling action in fiction or drama,

including all of the developments that follow the climax and show that the story's conflict is over. [See also *plot*.]

rhyme scheme A repeated pattern of similar sounds, usually found at the ends of lines of poetry or poetic drama.

rhythm In poetry, the measured recurrence of accented and unaccented syllables in a particular pattern. [See also *meter*.]

S

scene The time, place, and circumstances of a play or a story. In a play, a scene is a section of an act. [See also *play*.]

science fiction Fantasy literature set in an imaginary future, with details and situations that are designed to seem scientifically possible.

setting The time and place of a work of literature.

short story Narrative prose fiction that is shorter and has a less complicated plot than a novel. A short story contains narration, at least one setting, at least one character, and usually some dialogue.

simile Figurative language that compares two unlike things, introduced by the words "like" or "as." [See also *figurative language*.]

soliloquy In a play, a short speech spoken by a single character when he or she is alone on the stage. A soliloquy usually expresses the character's innermost thoughts and feelings, when he or she thinks no other characters can hear.

sonnet A poem written in one stanza, using fourteen lines of iambic pentameter. [See also *meter*.]

speaker In poetry, the individual whose voice seems to be speaking the lines. [See also *narration, voice*.]

stage directions The directions, written by the playwright, to tell the director, actors, and theater technicians how a play should be dramatized. Stage directions may specify such things as how the setting should appear in each scene, how the actors should deliver their lines, when the stage curtain should rise and fall, how stage lights should be used, where on the stage the actors should be during the action, and when sound effects should be used.

stanza A group of lines in poetry set apart by blank lines before and after the group; a poetic verse.

style The distinctive way in which an author composes a

work of literature in written or spoken language.

suspense An effect created by authors of various types of fiction and drama, especially adventure and mystery, to heighten interest in the story.

symbol An image, person, place, or thing that is used to express the idea of something else.

T

tall tale A kind of folk tale, or legend, that exaggerates the characteristics of its hero or heroine.

theme The main idea or underlying subject of a work of literature.

tone The attitude that a work of literature expresses to the reader through its style.

tragedy In classical drama, a tragedy depicts a noble hero or heroine who makes a mistake of judgment that has disastrous consequences.

V

verse A stanza in a poem. Also, a synonym for poetry as a genre. [See also *stanza*.]

voice The narrator or the person who relates the action of a piece of literature. [See also *speaker*.]

ACKNOWLEDGMENTS

Grateful acknowledgment is made for permission to reprint the following copyrighted material.

"The Earth Giant" by Bernard Evslin from *Hercules*, copyright © 1984 by Bernard Evslin. Reprinted by permission of William Morrow and Company.

"Antaeus" by Borden Deal, copyright ©1961 by Southern Methodist University. By permission of The Borden Deal Family Trust.

"Fox Hunt" by Lensey Namioka, copyright © 1992 by Lensey Namioka, is reprinted by permission of the author and the Ruth Cohen Literary Agency.

"Almost a Whole Trickster" by Gerald Vizenor is used by permission of HarperCollins Publishers from *A Gathering of Flowers: Stories About Being Young in America*, edited by Joyce Carol Thomas.

"Daedalus" by Olivia Coolidge from *Greek Myths* by Olivia Coolidge. Copyright 1949, copyright renewed 1977 by Olivia E. Coolidge. Reprinted with permission of Houghton Mifflin Co. All rights reserved.

"Summertime on Icarus" by Arthur C. Clarke is reprinted by permission of the author and the author's agents, Scott Meredith Literary Agency, Inc., 845 Third Avenue, New York, New York 10022.

"The Case of the Uncooked Eggs" told by Dadi from *The Magic Orange Tree and Other Haitian Folk Tales* by Diane Wolkstein, illustrated by Elsa Henriquez. Text copyright © 1978 by Diane Wolkstein. Reprinted by permission of Alfred A. Knopf, Inc.

Mufaro's Beautiful Daughters by John Steptoe. Copyright © 1987 by John Steptoe by permission of Lothrop, Lee & Shepard Books, a division of William Morrow & Co., Inc., with the approval of the Estate of John Steptoe.

"The Piece of Straw" by Yoshiko Uchida is reprinted by permission of the Estate of Yoshiko Uchida.

"Rising Voices" by Carla Willetto is reprinted from *Rough Stones Are Precious Too*, Vol.2, a publication of the Navajo Curriculum Center, copyright © 1982.

ILLUSTRATION

18-31 Richard Downs.

PHOTOGRAPHY

4 *l* Sarah Putnam/©D.C. Heath; *r* John Owens/©D.C. Heath; 5 The *Forbes* Magazine Collection, New York. Photo by H. Peter Curran; 6 Julie Bidwell/©D.C. Heath; 8-9 Craig Aurness/Westlight; 10 *t* Jim Whitmer/Stock Boston; *b* Julie Bidwell/©D.C. Heath; 11 *all* Sarah Putnam/©D.C. Heath; 12 *background* Nancy Sheehan/©D.C. Heath; *inset,* 17 *t* Outsider Archive, London; 17 *b* Courtesy of Dorothy Evslin; 31 Babs H. Deal/AP/Wide World Photos; 32 Pacific Asia Museum, Pasadena, CA; 38-39 Harvard Theatre Collection; 42 Pacific Asia Museum, Pasadena, CA; 43 Harvard Theatre Collection; 43 Photo by Don Perkins; 44, 51, 54-55, 58 Louis K. Meisel Gallery, New York; 59 University of California; 60 ©National Gallery of Art, Washington, D.C. Gift of Mr. and Mrs. Andrew S. Keck, 1980.8.1; 64 ©National Gallery of Art, Washington, D.C. Gift of Mr. and Mrs. Andrew S. Keck, 1980.8.8; 65 Courtesy of Russell & Volkening, Inc.; 66-67 *all* National Optical Astronomical Observatories; 68-69 NASA; 69 *inset* National Optical Astronomical Observatories; 70-71 NASA; 72 *inset* National Optical Astronomical Observatories; 72-73, 74-75, 76-77 NASA; 78-79 National Optical Astronomical Observatories; 80 The *Forbes* Magazine Collection, New York. Photo by H. Peter Curran; 84 The Metropolitan Museum of Art, acc. no. 1978.412.300; 85 ©The Field Museum, Neg. no. A109443c, Chicago; 91 *l* The Metropolitan Museum of Art, acc. no. 1979.206.28; *r* Photo by James Ropiequet Schmidt. Courtesy of William Morrow & Co.; 92, 93 ©1993 Los Angeles County Museum of Art; 98 ©Los Angeles County Museum of Art; 100, 101 John Running; 104 Nancy Sheehan; 106 *t* Jerry Berndt/Stock Boston; *b* Photofest; 111 The Far Side cartoon by Gary Larson is reprinted by permission of Chronicle Features, San Francisco, CA. All rights reserved; 112 *t* Sarah Putnam/©D.C. Heath; *b,* 113 Ken O'Donoghue/©D.C. Heath; 114 *t* Rhoda Sidney/Stock Boston; *b* Ken O'Donoghue/©D.C. Heath.
Back cover *t* John Owens/©D.C. Heath; *c* Sarah Putnam/©D.C. Heath; *b* John Owens/©D.C. Heath.

Full Pronunciation Key for Footnoted Words

(Each pronunciation and definition is adapted from *Scott, Foresman Advanced Dictionary* by E.L. Thorndike and Clarence L. Barnhart.)

The pronunciation of each footnoted word is shown just after the word, in this way: **abbreviate** [ə brē′ vē āt]. The letters and signs used are pronounced as in the words below. The mark ′ is placed after a syllable with primary or heavy accent, as in the example above. The mark ′ after a syllable shows a secondary or lighter accent, as in **abbreviation** [ə brē′ vē ā′ shən].

Some words, taken from foreign languages, are spoken with sounds that do not otherwise occur in English. Symbols for these sounds are given in the key as "foreign sounds."

a	hat, cap	j	jam, enjoy	u	cup, butter	**foreign sounds**
ā	age, face	k	kind, seek	u̇	full, put	Y as in French *du*.
ä	father, far	l	land, coal	ü	rule, move	Pronounce (ē) with
		m	me, am	v	very, save	the lips rounded as
b	bad, rob	n	no, in	w	will, woman	for (ü).
ch	child, much	ng	long, bring	y	young, yet	
d	did, red			z	zero, breeze	à as in French *ami*.
		o	hot, rock	zh	measure, seizure	Pronounce (ä) with
e	let, best	ō	open, go			the lips spread and
ē	equal, be	ô	order, all	ə represents:		held tense.
ėr	term, learn	oi	oil, voice		a in about	
		ou	house, out		e in taken	œ as in French *peu*.
f	fat, if				i in pencil	Pronounce (ā) with the
g	go, bag	p	paper, cup		o in lemon	lips rounded as for (ō).
h	he, how	r	run, try		u in circus	
		s	say, yes			N as in French *bon*.
i	it, pin	sh	she, rush			The N is not pro-
ī	ice, five	t	tell, it			nounced, but shows
		th	thin, both			that the vowel before
		ŦH	then, smooth			it is nasal.

H as in German *ach*. Pronounce (k) without closing the breath passage.

A Dark and Stormy Night

HEATH
MIDDLE LEVEL
LITERATURE

HEATH

MIDDLE LEVEL

LITERATURE

A Dark and Stormy Night

THEME

MYSTERY AND THE IMAGINATION

AUTHORS

Donna Alvermann
Linda Miller Cleary
Kenneth Donelson
Donald Gallo
Alice Haskins
J. Howard Johnston
John Lounsbury
Alleen Pace Nilsen
Robert Pavlik
Jewell Parker Rhodes
Alberto Alvaro Ríos
Sandra Schurr
Lyndon Searfoss
Julia Thomason
Max Thompson
Carl Zon

STAFF CREDITS

EDITORIAL Barbara A. Brennan, Susan Belt Cogley, DeVona Dors,
Christopher Johnson, Rita M. Sullivan, Patricia B. Weiler
Proofreading: JoAnne B. Sgroi

CONTRIBUTING WRITERS Kathy Tuchman Glass, Jo Pitkin

SERIES DESIGN Robin Herr

BOOK DESIGN Caroline Bowden, Daniel Derdula, Susan Geer, Diana Maloney,
Angela Sciaraffa, Bonnie Chayes Yousefian
Art Editing: Carolyn Langley

PHOTOGRAPHY *Series Photography Coordinator:* Carmen Johnson
Photo Research Supervisor: Martha Friedman
Photo Researchers: Wendy Enright, Linda Finigan, Po-yee McKenna,
PhotoSearch, Inc., Gillian Speeth, Denise Theodores
Assignment Photography Coordinators: Susan Doheny,
Gayna Hoffman, Shawna Johnston

COMPUTER PREPRESS Ricki Pappo, Kathy Meisl,
Richard Curran, Michele Locatelli

PERMISSIONS Dorothy B. McLeod

PRODUCTION Patrick Finbarr Connolly

Cover Photograph: top, middle, Tom Ives/The Stock Market;
bottom, Ken O'Donoghue/© D. C. Heath. **Cover Design:** Robin Herr

Acknowledgments for copyrighted material are on page 125 and constitute an extension
of this page.

Published simultaneously in Canada

Printed in the United States of America

International Standard Book Number: 0-669-32107-9 (soft cover)
5 6 7 8 9 10-RRD-99

International Standard Book Number: 0-669-38176-4 (hard cover)
4 5 6 7 8 9 10-RRD-99 98 97

CONTENTS

THE LITERATURE

Ships Setting Sail Paul Klee

ASKING BIG QUESTIONS ABOUT THE LITERATURE

P R O J E C T S

1 WRITING WORKSHOP

WRITE A SUSPENSE STORY   106-111

Write a suspense story of your own that keeps readers on the edge of their seats.

2 COOPERATIVE LEARNING

AT THE STROKE OF MIDNIGHT. . .   112-113

Lights! Camera! Action! You and your team will create a script and then star in your own video.

3 HELPING YOUR COMMUNITY

LOCAL MYSTERIES   114-115

Research a local mystery or unexplained event. Look for clues, develop theories to explain the mysteries, and share your findings with the community.

Cliff-hanger!

"It was a dark and stormy night. . . " So, what happens next? A good suspense story keeps a reader racing through the pages, eagerly anticipating what will happen next. Tension grows as the story unfolds. Will the hero escape? Who is at the door?

Working in a group of three or four classmates, use your imagination to think of a suspense story. Then act out just the first part of the suspense story—and challenge the class to guess the ending.

1 What are your story elements?

For your group's story, choose a setting, a conflict, and a character and brainstorm to create several beginnings to a story. Use the material in the boxes on the right or make up your own. As a group, decide what might happen next after each beginning. Which story seems most likely to keep your audience on the edge of their seats? Choose your favorite story. Discuss how the story will end, but focus just on developing an exciting first scene—the scene you'll present to the class.

A locked box with strange markings

Lee Davis, a lost motorist

An unexplained noise

Corisha Brown, a new bank employee

A roadside diner out in the middle of nowhere

A long, dark hallway in a bank office after regular work hours

Manuel Ortiz, a famous archaeologist

A rare coin mailed in an envelope without a return address

A leather briefcase that contains forged financial papers

How **2** do you create suspense?

- Create at least one *sympathetic character*—a character that your audience will care about. (Nobody cheers for the bad guys!)
- Present a *conflict* that grabs your audience's interest; for instance, a mounting fear of danger or injustice.
- Choose a *setting* that adds to the suspense and fuels the plot of the story. For example, how can the time of day and the location of the action add to the tension in your story?

How **3** do you prepare to present your story?

Decide who will play each role. Then do a quick rehearsal. To create a character, you might wear a hat, carry a briefcase, or turn up your collar. Use your imagination to invent costumes!

To help create a setting, improvise simple props. For example, a group of chairs can become a lobby, and a box covered with doodled-on paper can become a mysterious antique. To create mood, you might dim the lights or close the classroom blinds.

How **4** will the cliff-hanger end?

After you present the beginning of your suspense story, stop. Challenge the audience—your classmates—to guess the ending. You might want to act out two endings, one the class suggests and the one your group chose. Which do you prefer? Why?

Asking Big Questions About the Theme

How do you respond to suspense stories?

Think about the kinds of spine-tingling, nail-biting suspense stories you've either read, seen, or heard. List three or four of these stories in your journal. How do you respond, physically and emotionally, to suspense stories? Do you respond differently to other kinds of stories? Why or why not? Record your ideas in your journal.

Why do people find suspense stories fascinating?

Work with a group or the whole class to create a survey about suspense stories. First, write five questions that can be answered *yes* or *no*. Ask questions about both physical and emotional responses to suspense stories. Then write five questions that can be answered in complete sentences. Distribute your survey to students in your class or school. Have them complete and return their surveys. Compile survey results in chart form.

SUSPENSE STORY SURVEY		
Part A		
1. Do you get goosebumps when you read a suspense story?	yes	no
2. Do suspense stories make you feel anxious or frightened?	yes	no
Part B		
1. What do you like best about suspense stories?		
2. What do you like least about suspense stories?		

What makes a good suspense story?

Think again about the suspense stories you've either read, seen on video, or heard. What keeps you riveted to each story—even when your heart is pounding with fear? For each story, draw a web in your journal. Write the specific details that add to the story's suspense. Then create a final web, like the one started here, that summarizes the similarities in all the stories.

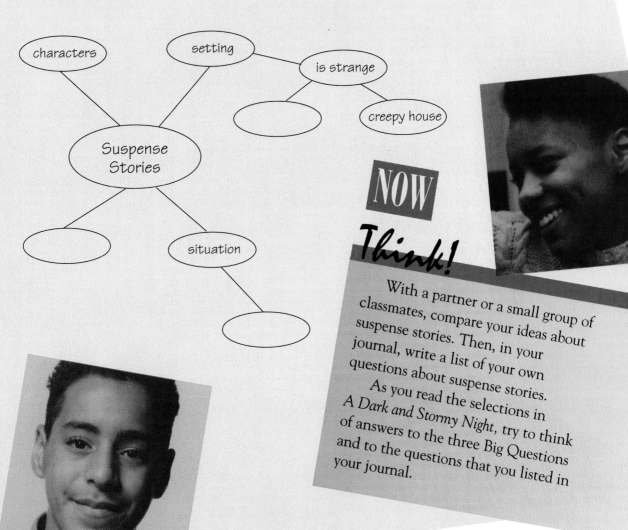

characters

setting — is strange

creepy house

Suspense Stories

situation

NOW Think!

With a partner or a small group of classmates, compare your ideas about suspense stories. Then, in your journal, write a list of your own questions about suspense stories.

As you read the selections in *A Dark and Stormy Night*, try to think of answers to the three Big Questions and to the questions that you listed in your journal.

THE **TELL-TALE**

EDGAR ALLAN POE

HEART

True!—nervous—very, very dreadfully nervous I had been and am; but why will you say that I am mad? The disease had sharpened my senses —not destroyed—not dulled them. Above all was the sense of hearing acute. I heard all things in the heaven and in the earth. I heard many things in hell. How, then, am I mad? Hearken! and observe how healthily —how calmly I can tell you the whole story.

It is impossible to say how first the idea entered my brain; but once conceived, it haunted me day and night. Object there was none. Passion there was none. I loved the old man. He had never wronged me. He had never given me insult. For his gold I had no desire. I think it was his eye! yes, it was this! He had the eye of a vulture—a pale blue eye, with a film over it. Whenever it fell upon me, my blood ran cold; and so by degrees—very gradually—I made up my mind to take the life of the old man, and thus rid myself of the eye forever.

Now this is the point. You fancy me mad. Madmen know nothing. But you should have seen *me*. You should have seen how wisely I proceeded—with what caution—with what foresight—with what dissimulation I went to work! I was never kinder to the old man than during the whole week before I killed him. And every night, about midnight, I turned the latch of his door and opened it—oh, so gently! And then, when I had made an opening sufficient for my head, I put in a dark lantern, all closed, closed, so that no light shone out, and then I thrust in my head. Oh, you would have laughed to see how cunningly I thrust it in! I moved it slowly—very, very slowly, so that I might not disturb the old man's sleep. It took me an hour to place my whole head within the opening so far that I could see him as he lay upon his bed. Ha!—would a madman have been so wise as this? And then, when my head was well in the room, I undid the lantern cautiously—oh, so cautiously—cautiously (for the hinges creaked)— I undid it just so much that a single thin ray fell upon the vulture eye. And this I did for seven long nights—every night just at midnight— but I found the eye always closed; and so it was impossible to do the work; for it was not the old man who vexed me, but his Evil Eye. And every morning, when the day broke, I went boldly into the chamber, and spoke courageously to him, calling him by name in a hearty tone, and inquiring how he had passed the night. So you see he would have been a very profound old man, indeed, to suspect that every night, just at twelve, I looked in upon him while he slept.

Upon the eighth night I was more than usually cautious in opening the door. A watch's minute hand moves more quickly than did

mine. Never before that night, had I *felt* the extent of my own powers—
of my sagacity.[1] I could scarcely contain my feelings of triumph. To
think that there I was, opening the door, little by little, and he not
even to dream of my secret deeds or thoughts. I fairly chuckled at the
idea; and perhaps he heard me; for he moved on the bed suddenly, as
if startled. Now you may think that I drew back—but no. His room
was as black as pitch with the thick darkness, (for the shutters were
close fastened, through fear of robbers,) and so I knew that he could
not see the opening of the door, and I kept pushing it on steadily,
steadily.

I had my head in, and was about to open the lantern, when my
thumb slipped upon the tin fastening, and the old man sprang up in
the bed, crying out—"Who's there?"

I kept quite still and said nothing. For a whole hour I did not
move a muscle, and in the meantime I did not hear him lie down. He
was still sitting up in the bed, listening;—just as I have done, night
after night, hearkening to the deathwatches[2] in the wall.

Presently I heard a slight groan, and I knew it was the groan of
mortal terror. It was not a groan of pain or of grief—oh, no!—it was
the low stifled sound that arises from the bottom of the soul when
overcharged with awe. I knew the sound well. Many a night, just at
midnight, when all the world slept, it has welled up from my own
bosom, deepening, with its dreadful echo, the terrors that distracted
me. I say I knew it well. I knew what the old man felt, and pitied him,
although I chuckled at heart. I knew that he had been lying awake
ever since the first slight noise, when he had turned in the bed. His
fears had been ever since growing upon him. He had been trying to
fancy them causeless, but could not. He had been saying to himself—
"It is nothing but the wind in the chimney—it is only a mouse crossing the floor," or "it is merely a cricket which has made a single
chirp." Yes, he has been trying to comfort himself with these supposi-
tions: but he had found all in vain. *All in vain*; because Death, in

1. **sagacity** [sə gas′ ə tē]: sound judgment, shrewdness.
2. **deathwatches** [deth′ woch əz]: insects that make a ticking sound; they were
   once believed to predict death.

approaching him had stalked with his black shadow before him, and enveloped the victim. And it was the mournful influence of the unperceived shadow that caused him to feel—although he neither saw nor heard—to *feel* the presence of my head within the room.

When I had waited a long time, very patiently, without hearing him lie down, I resolved to open a little—a very, very little crevice in the lantern. So I opened it—you cannot imagine how stealthily, stealthily—until, at length a single dim ray, like the thread of the spider, shot from out the crevice and fell full upon the vulture eye.

It was open—wide, wide open—and I grew furious as I gazed upon it. I saw it with perfect distinctness—all a dull blue, with a hideous veil over it that chilled the very marrow in my bones; but I could see nothing else of the old man's face or person: for I had directed the ray as if by instinct, precisely upon the damned spot.

And have I not told you that what you mistake for madness is but over-acuteness of the senses?—now, I say, there came to my ears a low, dull, quick sound, such as a watch makes when enveloped in cotton. I knew *that* sound well, too. It was the beating of the old man's heart. It increased my fury, as the beating of a drum stimulates the soldier into courage.

But even yet I refrained and kept still. I scarcely breathed. I held the lantern motionless. I tried how steadily I could maintain the ray upon the eye. Meantime the hellish tattoo of the heart increased. It grew quicker and quicker, and louder and louder every instant. The old man's terror *must* have been extreme! It grew louder, I say, louder every moment!—do you mark me well? I have told you that I am nervous: so I am. And now at the dead hour of the night, amid the dreadful silence of that old house, so strange a noise as this excited me to uncontrollable terror. Yet, for some minutes longer I refrained and stood still. But the beating grew louder, louder! I thought the heart must burst. And now a new anxiety seized me—the sound would be heard by a neighbour! The old man's hour had come! With a loud yell, I threw open the lantern and leaped into the room. He shrieked once—once only. In an instant I dragged him to the floor, and pulled the heavy bed over him. I then smiled gaily, to find the deed so far done. But, for many minutes, the heart beat on with a muffled sound. This, however, did not vex me; it would not be heard through the wall. At length it ceased. The old man was dead. I removed the bed and examined the corpse. Yes, he was stone, stone dead. I placed my hand upon the heart and held it there many minutes. There was no pulsation. He was stone dead. His eye would trouble me no more.

If still you think me mad, you will think so no longer when I describe the wise precautions I took for the concealment of the body. The night waned, and I worked hastily, but in silence. First of all I dismembered the corpse. I cut off the head and the arms and the legs.

I then took up three planks from the flooring of the chamber, and deposited all between the scantlings. I then replaced the boards so cleverly, so cunningly, that no human eye—not even *his*—could have detected anything wrong. There was nothing to wash out—no stain of any kind—no blood-spot whatever. I had been too wary for that. A tub had caught all—ha! ha!

When I had made an end of these labors, it was four o'clock—still dark as midnight. As the bell sounded the hour, there came a knocking at the street door. I went down to open it with a light heart—for what had I *now* to fear? There entered three men, who introduced themselves, with perfect suavity, as officers of the police. A shriek had been heard by a neighbour during the night; suspicion of foul play had been aroused; information had been lodged at the police office, and they (the officers) had been deputed to search the premises.

I smiled,—for *what* had I to fear? I bade the gentlemen welcome. The shriek, I said, was my own in a dream. The old man, I mentioned, was absent in the country. I took my visitors all over the house. I bade them search—search *well*. I led them, at length, to *his* chamber. I showed them his treasures, secure, undisturbed. In the enthusiasm of my confidence, I brought chairs into the room, and desired them *here* to rest from their fatigues, while I myself, in the wild audacity of my perfect triumph, placed my own seat upon the very spot beneath which reposed the corpse of the victim.

The officers were satisfied. My *manner* had convinced them. I was singularly at ease. They sat, and while I answered cheerily, they chatted of familiar things. But, ere long, I felt myself getting pale and wished them gone. My head ached, and I fancied a ringing in my ears: but still they sat and still chatted. The ringing became more distinct:—it continued and became more distinct: I talked more freely to get rid of the feeling: but it continued and gained definiteness—until, at length, I found that the noise was *not* within my ears.

No doubt I now grew *very* pale;—but I talked more fluently, and with a heightened voice. Yet the sound increased—and what could I do? It was *a low, dull, quick sound—much such a sound as a watch makes when enveloped in cotton.* I gasped for breath—and yet the officers heard it not. I talked more quickly—more vehemently; but the noise steadily increased. I arose and argued about trifles, in a high key and with violent gesticulations; but the noise steadily increased. Why *would* they not be gone? I paced the floor to and fro with heavy strides, as if excited to fury by the observations of the men—but the noise steadily increased. Oh God! what *could* I do? I foamed—I raved—I swore! I swung the chair upon which I had been sitting, and grated it upon the boards, but the noise arose over all and continually increased. It grew louder—louder—*louder!* And still the men chatted pleasantly, and smiled. Was it possible they heard not? Almighty God!—no, no! They heard!—they suspected!—they *knew!*—they were making a mockery of my horror!—this I thought, and this I think. But anything was better than this agony! Anything was more tolerable than this derision! I could bear those hypocritical smiles no longer! I felt that I must scream or die! and now—again!—hark! louder! louder! louder! *louder!*—

"Villains!" I shrieked, "dissemble no more! I admit the deed!—tear up the planks! here, here!—it is the beating of his hideous heart!"

EDGAR ALLAN POE

Edgar Allan Poe (1809-1849) was born in Boston and grew up in Virginia. He attended the University of Virginia for a short time, and then, in 1827, he enlisted in the army. Within two years, Poe was a sergeant-major and had managed to write and publish two books of poems. His foster father helped him get into the military academy at West Point, but Poe soon dropped out and for the rest of his life tried to live by his writing. "With me," Poe said, "poetry has not been a purpose, but a passion."

Poe became famous in Europe long before he found fame at home. His morbid and colorful imagination created weird tales of mystery, horror, and crime that foreshadowed the modern detective story. Unfortunately, his addiction to alcohol kept him poor and ill. His greatest tragedy was the death of his wife in 1847. In 1849, Poe was found unconscious in Baltimore; he died four days later at the age of forty.

Other Edgar Allan Poe tales of horror include "The Cask of Amontillado" and "The Fall of the House of Usher." Two of Poe's most famous poems are "The Raven" and "The Bells."

THE
MONKEY'S PAW

W.W. JACOBS

I

Without, the night was cold and wet, but in the small parlor of Laburnam Villa the blinds were drawn and the fire burned brightly. Father and son were at chess, the former, who possessed ideas about the game involving radical changes, putting his king into such sharp and unnecessary perils that it even provoked comment from the white haired old lady knitting placidly by the fire.

"Hark at the wind," said Mr. White, who, having seen a fatal mistake after it was too late, was amiably desirous of preventing his son from seeing it.

"I'm listening," said the latter, grimly surveying the board as he stretched out his hand. "Check."

"I should hardly think that he'd come tonight," said his father, with his hand poised over the board.

"Mate," replied the son.

"That's the worst of living so far out," bawled Mr. White, with sudden and unlooked-for violence; "of all the beastly, slushy, out-of-the-way places to live in, this is the worst. Pathway's a bog, and the road's a torrent. I don't know what people are thinking about. I suppose because only two houses on the road are let, they think it doesn't matter."

"Never mind, dear," said his wife soothingly; "perhaps you'll win the next one."

Mr. White looked up sharply, just in time to intercept a knowing glance between mother and son. The words died away on his lips, and he hid a guilty grin in his thin gray beard.

"There he is," said Herbert White, as the gate banged to loudly and heavy footsteps came toward the door.

The Monkey's Paw 21

The old man rose with hospitable haste, and opening the door, was heard condoling with the new arrival. The new arrival also condoled with himself, so that Mrs. White said, "Tut, tut!" and coughed gently as her husband entered the room, followed by a tall burly man, beady of eye and rubicund[1] of visage.

"Sergeant-Major Morris," he said, introducing him.

The sergeant-major shook hands, and taking the proffered seat by the fire, watched contentedly while his host got out whisky and tumblers and stood a small copper kettle on the fire.

At the third glass his eyes got brighter, and he began to talk, the little family circle regarding with eager interest this visitor from distant parts, as he squared his broad shoulders in the chair and spoke of wild scenes and doughty[2] deeds; of wars and plagues and strange peoples.

"Twenty-one years of it," said Mr. White, nodding at his wife and son. "When he went away he was a slip of a youth in the warehouse. Now look at him."

"He don't look to have taken much harm," said Mrs. White, politely.

"I'd like to go to India myself," said the old man, "just to look round a bit, you know."

"Better where you are," said the sergeant-major, shaking his head. He put down the empty glass, and sighing softly, shook it again.

"I should like to see those old temples and fakirs[3] and jugglers," said the old man. "What was that you started telling me the other day about a monkey's paw or something, Morris?"

"Nothing," said the soldier hastily. "Leastways nothing worth hearing."

"Monkey's paw?" said Mrs. White, curiously.

"Well, it's just a bit of what you might call magic, perhaps," said the sergeant-major off-handedly.

His three listeners leaned forward eagerly. The visitor absent-mindedly put his empty glass to his lips and then set it down again. His host filled it for him.

"To look at," said the sergeant-major, fumbling in his pocket, "it's

---

1. **rubicund** [rü′ bə kund]: reddish, ruddy.
2. **doughty** [dou′ tē]: brave, strong.
3. **fakirs** [fə kirz′]: members of religious group in India who often walk on coals or charm snakes.

just an ordinary little paw, dried to a mummy."

He took something out of his pocket and proffered it. Mrs. White drew back with a grimace, but her son, taking it, examined it curiously.

"And what is there special about it?" inquired Mr. White, as he took it from his son, and having examined it, placed it upon the table.

"It had a spell put on it by an old fakir," said the sergeant-major, "a very holy man. He wanted to show that fate ruled people's lives, and that those who interfered with it did so to their sorrow. He put a spell on it so that three separate men could each have three wishes from it."

His manner was so impressive that his hearers were conscious that their light laughter jarred somewhat.

"Well, why don't you have three, sir?" said Herbert White cleverly.

The soldier regarded him in the way that middle age is wont to regard presumptuous youth. "I have," he said quietly, and his blotchy face whitened.

"And did you really have the three wishes granted?" asked Mrs. White.

"I did," said the sergeant-major, and his glass tapped against his strong teeth.

"And has anybody else wished?" persisted the old lady.

"The first man had his three wishes. Yes," was the reply; "I don't know what the first two were, but the third was for death. That's how I got the paw."

His tones were so grave that a hush fell upon the group.

"If you've had your three wishes, it's no good to you now, then, Morris," said the old man at last. "What do you keep it for?"

The soldier shook his head. "Fancy, I suppose," he said slowly. "I did have some idea of selling it, but I don't think I will. It has caused enough mischief already. Besides, people won't buy. They think it's a fairy tale; some of them, and those who do think anything of it want to try it first and pay me afterward."

"If you could have another three wishes," said the old man, eyeing him keenly, "would you have them?"

"I don't know," said the other. "I don't know."

He took the paw, and dangling it between his forefinger and thumb, suddenly threw it upon the fire.

White, with a slight cry, stooped down and snatched it off.

"Better let it burn," said the soldier solemnly.

"If you don't want it, Morris," said the other, "give it to me."

"I won't," said his friend doggedly. "I threw it on the fire. If you keep it, don't blame me for what happens. Pitch it on the fire again like a sensible man."

The other shook his head and examined his new possession closely. "How do you do it?" he inquired.

"Hold it up in your right hand and wish aloud," said the sergeant-major, "but I warn you of the consequences."

"Sounds like the *Arabian Nights*," said Mrs. White, as she rose and began to set the supper. "Don't you think you might wish for four pairs of hands for me?"

Her husband drew the talisman from his pocket, and then all three burst into laughter as the sergeant-major, with a look of alarm on his face, caught him by the arm.

"If you must wish," he said gruffly, "wish for something sensible."

Mr. White dropped it back into his pocket, and placing chairs, motioned his friend to the table. In the business of supper the talisman was partly forgotten, and afterward the three sat listening in an enthralled fashion to a second installment of the soldier's adventures in India.

"If the tale about the monkey's paw is not more truthful than those he has been telling us," said Herbert, as the door closed behind their guest, just in time for him to catch the last train, "we shan't make much out of it."

"Did you give him anything for it, father?" inquired Mrs. White, regarding her husband closely.

"A trifle," said he, coloring slightly. "He didn't want it, but I made him take it. And he pressed me again to throw it away."

"Likely," said Herbert, with pretended horror. "Why, we're going to be rich, and famous and happy. Wish to be an emperor, father, to begin with; then you can't be henpecked."

He darted round the table, pursued by the maligned Mrs. White armed with an antimacassar.[4]

---

4. **antimacassar** [an´ ti mə kas´ ər]: a covering that prevents the arms and back of a chair or sofa from being soiled.

Mr. White took the paw from his pocket and eyed it dubiously. "I don't know what to wish for, and that's a fact," he said slowly. "It seems to me I've got all I want."

"If you only cleared the house, you'd be quite happy, wouldn't you?" said Herbert, with his hand on his shoulder. "Well, wish for two hundred pounds, then; that'll just do it."

His father, smiling shamefacedly at his own credulity, held up the talisman, as his son, with a solemn face, somewhat marred by a wink at his mother, sat down at the piano and struck a few impressive chords.

"I wish for two hundred pounds," said the old man distinctly.

A fine crash from the piano greeted the words, interrupted by a shuddering cry from the old man. His wife and son ran toward him.

"It moved," he cried, with a glance of disgust at the object as it lay on the floor. "As I wished, it twisted in my hands like a snake."

"Well, I don't see the money," said his son as he picked it up and placed it on the table, "and I bet I never shall."

"It must have been your fancy, father," said his wife, regarding him anxiously.

He shook his head. "Never mind, though; there's no harm done, but it gave me a shock all the same."

They sat down by the fire again while the two men finished their pipes. Outside, the wind was higher than ever, and the old man started nervously at the sound of a door banging upstairs. A silence unusual and depressing settled upon all three, which lasted until the old couple rose to retire for the night.

"I expect you'll find the cash tied up in a big bag in the middle of your bed," said Herbert, as he bade them good night, "and something horrible squatting up on top of the wardrobe watching you as you pocket your ill-gotten gains."

He sat alone in the darkness, gazing at the dying fire, and seeing faces in it. The last face was so horrible and so simian that he gazed at it in amazement. It got so vivid that, with a little uneasy laugh, he felt on the table for a glass containing a little water to throw over it. His hand grasped the monkey's paw, and with a little shiver he wiped his hand on his coat and went up to bed.

II

In the brightness of the wintry sun next morning as it streamed over the breakfast table he laughed at his fears. There was an air of prosaic[5] wholesomeness about the room which it had lacked on the previous night, and the dirty, shriveled little paw was pitched on the sideboard with a carelessness which betokened no great belief in its virtues.

"I suppose all old soldiers are the same," said Mrs. White. "The idea of our listening to such nonsense! How could wishes be granted in these days? And if they could, how could two hundred pounds hurt you, father?"

"Might drop on his head from the sky," said the frivolous Herbert.

"Morris said the things happened so naturally," said his father, "that you might if you so wished attribute it to coincidence."

"Well, don't break into the money before I come back," said Herbert as he rose from the table. "I'm afraid it'll turn you into a mean, avaricious man, and we shall have to disown you."

His mother laughed, and following him to the door, watched him down the road; and returning to the breakfast table, was very happy at the expense of her hus-

5. **prosaic** [prō zā′ ik]: ordinary.

band's credulity. All of which did not prevent her from scurrying to the door at the postman's knock, nor prevent her from referring somewhat shortly to retired sergeant-majors of bibulous[6] habits when she found that the post brought a tailor's bill.

"Herbert will have some more of his funny remarks, I expect, when he comes home," she said, as they sat at dinner.

"I dare say," said Mr. White, pouring himself out some beer; "but for all that, the thing moved in my hand; that I'll swear to."

"You thought it did," said the old lady soothingly.

"I say it did," replied the other. "There was no thought about it; I had just—What's the matter?"

His wife made no reply. She was watching the mysterious movements of a man outside, who, peering in an undecided fashion at the house, appeared to be trying to make up his mind to enter. In mental connection with the two hundred pounds, she noticed that the stranger was well dressed, and wore a silk hat of glossy newness. Three times he paused at the gate, and then walked on again. The fourth time he stood with his hand upon it, and then with sudden resolution flung it open and walked up the path. Mrs. White at the same moment placed her hands behind her, and hurriedly unfastening the strings of her apron, put that useful article of apparel beneath the cushion of her chair.

She brought the stranger, who seemed ill at ease, into the room. He gazed at her furtively, and listened in a preoccupied fashion as the old lady apologized for the appearance of the room, and her husband's coat, a garment which he usually reserved for the garden. She then waited as patiently as her sex would permit for him to broach his business, but he was at first strangely silent.

"I—was asked to call," he said at last, and stooped and picked a piece of cotton from his trousers. "I come from Maw and Meggins."

The old lady started. "Is anything the matter?" she asked breathlessly. "Has anything happened to Herbert? What is it? What is it?"

Her husband interposed. "There, there, mother," he said hastily. "Sit down, and don't jump to conclusions. You've not brought

6. **bibulous** [bib′ yə ləs]: fond of drinking alcoholic drinks.

bad news, I'm sure, sir;" and he eyed the other wistfully.

"I'm sorry—sir," began the visitor.

"Is he hurt?" demanded the mother wildly.

The visitor bowed in assent. "Badly hurt," he said quietly, "but he is not in any pain."

"Oh, thank God!" said the old woman, clasping her hands. "Thank God for that! Thank—"

She broke off suddenly as the sinister meaning of the assurance dawned upon her and she saw the awful confirmation of her fears in the other's averted face. She caught her breath, and turning to her slower-witted husband, laid her trembling old hand upon his. There was a long silence.

"He was caught in the machinery," said the visitor at length in a low voice.

"Caught in the machinery," repeated Mr. White, in a dazed fashion, "yes."

He sat staring blankly out at the window, and taking his wife's hand between his own, pressed it as he had been wont to do in their old courting-days nearly forty years before.

"He was the only one left to us," he said, turning gently to the visitor. "It is hard."

The other coughed, and rising, walked slowly to the window. "The firm wished me to convey their sincere sympathy with you in your great loss," he said, without looking round. "I beg that you will understand I am only their servant and merely obeying orders."

There was no reply; the old woman's face was white, her eyes staring, and her breath inaudible; on the husband's face was a look such as his friend the sergeant-major might have carried into his first action.

"I was to say that Maw and Meggins disclaim all responsibility," continued the other. "They admit no liability at all, but in consideration of your son's services, they wish to present you with a certain sum as compensation."

Mr. White dropped his wife's hand, and rising to his feet, gazed with a look of horror at his visitor. His dry lips shaped the words, "How much?"

"Two hundred pounds," was the answer.

Unconscious of his wife's shriek, the old man smiled faintly, put out his hands like a sightless man, and dropped, a senseless heap, to the floor.

III

In the huge new cemetery, some two miles distant, the old people buried their dead, and came back to a house steeped in shadow and silence. It was all over so quickly that at first they could hardly realize it, and remained in a state of expectation as though of something else to happen—something else which was to lighten this load, too heavy for old hearts to bear. But the days passed, and expectation gave place to resignation—the hopeless resignation of the old, sometimes miscalled apathy. Sometimes they hardly exchanged a word, for now they had nothing to talk about, and their days were long to weariness.

It was about a week after that the old man, waking suddenly in the night, stretched out his hand and found himself alone. The room was in darkness, and the sound of subdued weeping came from the window. He raised himself in bed and listened.

"Come back," he said tenderly. "You will be cold."

"It is colder for my son," said the old woman, and wept afresh.

The sound of her sobs died away on his ears. The bed was warm, and his eyes heavy with sleep. He dozed fitfully, and then slept until a sudden wild cry from his wife awoke him with a start.

"The paw!" she cried wildly. "The monkey's paw!"

He started up in alarm. "Where? Where is it? What's the matter?"

She came stumbling across the room toward him. "I want it," she said quietly. "You've not destroyed it?"

"It's in the parlor, on the bracket," he replied, marveling. "Why?"

She cried and laughed together, and bending over, kissed his cheek.

"I only just thought of it," she said hysterically. "Why didn't I think of it before? Why didn't *you* think of it?"

"Think of what?" he questioned.

"The other two wishes," she replied rapidly. "We've only had one."

"Was not that enough?" he demanded fiercely.

"No," she cried triumphantly. "We'll have one more. Go down and get it quickly, and wish our boy alive again."

The man sat up in bed and flung the bedclothes from his quaking limbs. "Good God, you are mad!" he cried, aghast.

"Get it," she panted; "get it quickly, and wish—Oh, my boy, my boy!"

Her husband struck a match and lit the candle. "Get back to bed," he said unsteadily. "You don't know what you are saying."

"We had the first wish granted," said the old woman feverishly; "why not the second?"

"A coincidence," stammered the old man.

"Go and get it and wish," cried his wife, quivering with excitement.

The old man turned and regarded her, and his voice shook. "He has been dead ten days, and besides he—I would not tell you else, but—I could only recognize him by his clothing. If he was too terrible for you to see then, how now?"

"Bring him back," cried the old woman, and dragged him toward the door. "Do you think I fear the child I have nursed?"

He went down in the darkness, and felt his way to the parlor, and then to the mantelpiece. The talisman was in its place, and a horrible fear that the unspoken wish might bring his mutilated son before him ere he could escape from the room seized upon him, and he caught his breath as he found that he had lost the direction of the door. His brow cold with sweat, he felt his way round the table, and groped along the wall until he found himself in the small passage with the unwholesome thing in his hand.

Even his wife's face seemed changed as he entered the room. It was white and expectant, and to his fears seemed to have an unnatural look upon it. He was afraid of her.

"*Wish!*" she cried, in a strong voice.

"It is foolish and wicked," he faltered.

"*Wish!*" repeated his wife.

He raised his hand. "I wish my son alive again."

The talisman fell to the floor, and he regarded it fearfully. Then he sank trembling into a chair as the old woman, with burning eyes, walked to the window and raised the blind.

He sat until he was chilled with the cold, glancing occasionally at the figure of the old woman peering through the window. The candle-end, which had burnt below the rim of the china candlestick, was throwing pulsating shadows on the ceiling and walls, until, with a flicker larger than the rest, it expired. The old man, with an unspeakable sense of relief at the failure of the talisman, crept back to his bed, and a minute or two afterward the old woman came silently and apathetically beside him.

Neither spoke, but both lay silently listening to the ticking of the clock. A stair creaked, and a squeaky mouse scurried noisily through the wall. The darkness was oppressive, and after lying for some time screwing up his courage, he took the box of matches, and striking one, went downstairs for a candle.

At the foot of the stairs the match went out, and he paused to strike another; and at the same moment a knock, so quiet and stealthy as to be scarcely audible, sounded on the front door.

The matches fell from his hand and spilled in the passage. He stood motionless, his breath suspended until the knock was repeated. Then he turned and fled swiftly back to his room, and closed the door behind him. A

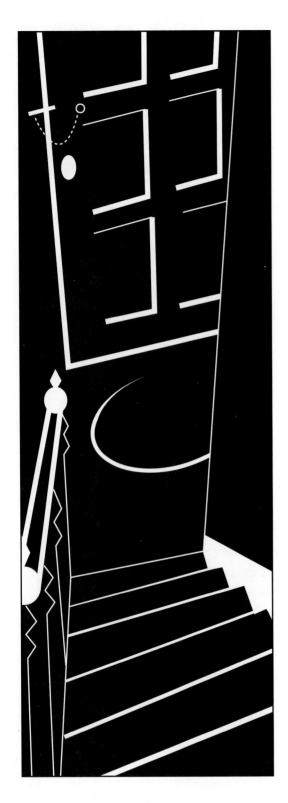

third knock sounded through the house.

"*What's that?*" cried the old woman, starting up.

"A rat," said the old man in shaking tones, "a rat. It passed me on the stairs."

His wife sat up in bed listening. A loud knock resounded through the house.

"It's Herbert!" she screamed. "It's Herbert!"

She ran to the door, but her husband was before her, and catching her by the arm, held her tightly.

"What are you going to do?" he whispered hoarsely.

"It's my boy; it's Herbert!" she cried, struggling mechanically. "I forgot it was two miles away. What are you holding me for? Let go. I must open the door."

"For God's sake don't let it in," cried the old man, trembling.

"You're afraid of your own son," she cried, struggling. "Let me go. I'm coming, Herbert; I'm coming."

There was another knock, and another. The old woman with a sudden wrench broke free and ran from the room. Her husband followed to the landing, and called after her appealingly as she hurried downstairs. He heard the chain rattle back and the bottom bolt drawn slowly and stiffly from the socket. Then the old woman's voice, strained and panting.

"The bolt," she cried loudly. "Come down. I can't reach it."

But her husband was on his hands and knees groping wildly on the floor in search of the paw. If he could only find it before the thing outside got in. A perfect fusillade[7] of knocks reverberated through the house, and he heard the scraping of a chair as his wife put it down in the passage against the door. He heard the creaking of the bolt as it came slowly back, and at the same moment he found the monkey's paw, and frantically breathed his third and last wish.

The knocking ceased suddenly, although the echoes of it were still in the house. He heard the chair drawn back and the door opened. A cold wind rushed up the staircase, and a long loud wail of disappointment and misery from his wife gave him courage to run down to her side, and then to the gate beyond. The street lamp flickering opposite shone on a quiet and deserted road.

7. **fusillade** [fyü′ zə lād′]: rapid and continuous sound.

W . W . J A C O B S

William Wymark Jacobs (1863-1943) grew up in England with a love for the sea and its legends. His father managed a wharf in the London dockyard district. As an adult, Jacobs's own life was an ordinary one. He held unexciting small jobs in a bank and in a post office. However, Jacobs found adventure—and material for stories—by prowling the London waterfront and shipyards along the Thames River. There he picked up more sailor's yarns, full of mystery and superstition. With his first writing success he quit his job and began to earn his living by his pen.

Besides a number of plays, Jacobs wrote humorous tales of the sea and of seafarers ashore. His sea stories can be found in a collection called *Snug Harbor*. His only tale of horror, "The Monkey's Paw," is one of the most well known short stories in the English language.

Ships Setting Sail Paul Klee, 1927, oil, 19$\frac{11}{16}$" x 23$\frac{5}{8}$"

THE MOST DANGEROUS GAME

RICHARD CONNELL

"Off there to the right—somewhere—is a large island," said Whitney. "It's rather a mystery—"

"What island is it?" Rainsford asked.

"The old charts call it 'Ship-Trap Island,'" Whitney replied. "A suggestive name, isn't it? Sailors have a curious dread of the place. I don't know why. Some superstition—"

"Can't see it," remarked Rainsford, trying to peer through the dank tropical night that was palpable as it pressed its thick, warm blackness in upon the yacht.

"You've good eyes," said Whitney, with a laugh, "and I've seen you pick off a moose moving in the brown fall bush at four hundred yards, but even you can't see four miles or so through a moonless Caribbean night."

"Not four yards," admitted Rainsford. "Ugh! It's like moist black velvet."

"It will be light enough where we're going," promised Whitney. "We should make it in a few days. I hope the jaguar guns have come. We'll have good hunting up the Amazon. Great sport, hunting."

"The best sport in the world," agreed Rainsford.

"For the hunter," amended Whitney. "Not for the jaguar."

"Don't talk rot, Whitney," said Rainsford. "You're a big-game hunter, not a philosopher. Who cares how a jaguar feels?"

"Perhaps the jaguar does," observed Whitney.

"Bah! They've no understanding."

"Even so, I rather think they understand one thing—fear. The fear of pain and the fear of death."

"Nonsense," laughed Rainsford. "This hot weather is making you soft, Whitney. Be a realist. The world is made up of two classes—the hunters and the hunted. Luckily, you and I are hunters. Do you think we've passed that island yet?"

"I can't tell in the dark. I hope so."

"Why?" asked Rainsford.

"The place has a reputation—a bad one."

"Cannibals?" suggested Rainsford.

"Hardly. Even cannibals wouldn't live in such a God-forsaken place. But it's got into sailor lore, somehow. Didn't you notice that the crew's nerves seemed a bit jumpy today?"

"They were a bit strange, now that you mention it. Even Captain Nielsen—"

"Yes, even that tough-minded old Swede, who'd go up to the devil himself and ask him for a light. Those fishy blue eyes held a look I never saw there before. All I could get out of him was: 'This place has an evil name among seafaring men, sir.' Then he said to me, very gravely: 'Don't you feel anything?'—as if the air about us was actually poisonous. Now, you mustn't laugh when I tell you this—I did feel something like a sudden chill.

"There was no breeze. The sea was as flat as a plate-glass window. We were drawing near the island then. What I felt was a—a mental chill; a sort of sudden dread."

"Pure imagination," said Rainsford. "One superstitious sailor can taint the whole ship's company with his fear."

"Maybe. But sometimes I think sailors have an extra sense that tells them when they are in danger. Sometimes I think evil is a tangible thing—with wave lengths, just as sound and light have. An evil place can, so to speak, broadcast vibrations of evil. Anyhow, I'm glad we're getting out of this zone. Well, I think I'll turn in now, Rainsford."

"I'm not sleepy," said Rainsford. "I'm going to smoke another pipe up on the afterdeck."

"Good night, then, Rainsford. See you at breakfast."

"Right. Good night, Whitney."

There was no sound in the night as Rainsford sat there, but the muffled throb of the engine that drove the yacht swiftly through the darkness, and the swish and ripple of the wash of the propeller.

Rainsford, reclining in a steamer chair, indolently puffed on his favorite briar. The sensuous drowsiness of the night was on him. "It's so dark," he thought, "that I could sleep without closing my eyes; the night would be my eyelids—"

An abrupt sound startled him. Off to the right he heard it, and his ears, expert in such matters, could not be mistaken. Again he heard the sound, and again. Somewhere, off in the blackness, someone had fired a gun three times.

Rainsford sprang up and moved quickly to the rail, mystified. He strained his eyes in the direction from

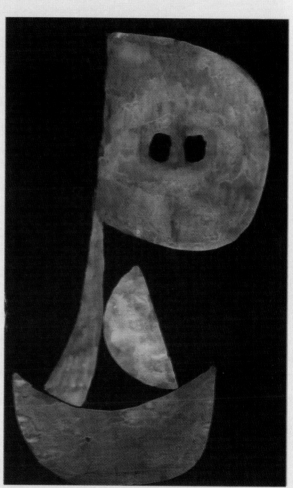

Stern Visage Paul Klee, 1939, watercolor and tempera on newspaper, 39.9 cm x 20.9 cm, Kunstmuseum, Bern, Switzerland

which the reports had come, but it was like trying to see through a blanket. He leaped upon the rail and balanced himself there, to get greater elevation; his pipe, striking a rope, was knocked from his mouth. He lunged for it; a short, hoarse cry came from his lips as he realized he had reached too far and had lost his balance. The cry was pinched off short as the blood-warm waters of the Caribbean Sea closed over his head.

He struggled up to the surface and tried to cry out, but the wash from the speeding yacht slapped him in the face and the salt water in his open mouth made him gag and strangle. Desperately he struck out with strong strokes after the receding lights of the yacht, but he stopped before he had swum fifty feet. A certain cool-headedness had come to him; it was not the first time he had been in a tight place. There was a chance that his cries could be heard by someone aboard the yacht, but that chance was slender, and grew more slender as the yacht raced on. He wrestled himself out of his clothes, and shouted with all his power. The lights of the yacht became faint and ever-vanishing fireflies; then they were blotted out entirely by the night.

Rainsford remembered the shots. They had come from the right, and doggedly he swam in that direction, swimming with slow, deliberate strokes, conserving his strength. For a seemingly endless time he fought the sea. He began to count his strokes; he could do possibly a hundred more and then—

Rainsford heard a sound. It came out of the darkness, a high screaming sound, the sound of an animal in an extremity of anguish and terror.

He did not recognize the animal that made the sound—he did not try to; with fresh vitality he swam toward the sound. He heard it again; then it was cut short by another noise, crisp, staccato.

"Pistol shot," muttered Rainsford, swimming on.

Ten minutes of determined effort brought another sound to his ears—the most welcome he had ever heard—the muttering and growling of the sea breaking on a rocky shore. He was almost on the rocks before he saw them; on a night less calm he would have been shattered against them. With his remaining strength he dragged himself from the swirling waters. Jagged crags appeared to jut into the opaqueness; he forced himself upward, hand over hand. Gasping, his hands raw, he reached a flat place at the top. Dense jungle came down to the very edge of the cliffs. What perils that tangle of trees and underbrush might hold for him did not concern Rainsford just then. All he knew was that he was safe from his enemy, the sea, and that utter weariness was on him. He flung himself down at the jungle edge and tumbled headlong into the deepest sleep of his life.

When he opened his eyes he knew from the position of the sun that it was late in the afternoon. Sleep had given him new vigor; a sharp hunger was picking at him. He looked about him, almost cheerfully.

"Where there are pistol shots, there are men. Where there are men, there is food," he thought. But what kind of men, he wondered, in so forbidding a place? An unbroken front of snarled and jagged jungle fringed the shore.

He saw no sign of a trail through the closely knit web of weeds and trees; it was easier to go along the shore, and Rainsford floundered along by the water. Not far from where he had landed, he stopped.

Some wounded thing, by the evidence a large animal, had thrashed about in the underbrush; the jungle weeds were crushed down and the moss was lacerated; one patch of weeds was stained crimson. A small, glittering object not far away caught Rainsford's eye and he picked it up. It was an empty cartridge.

"A twenty-two," he remarked. "That's odd. It must have been a fairly large animal too. The hunter had his nerve with him to tackle it with such a light gun. It's clear that the brute put up a good fight. I suppose the first three shots I heard were when the hunter flushed his quarry and wounded it. The last shot was when he trailed it here and finished it."

He examined the ground closely and found what he had hoped to find—the print of hunting-boots. They pointed along the cliff in the direction he had been going. Eagerly he hurried along, now slipping on a rotten log or a loose stone, but making headway; night was beginning to settle down on the island.

Bleak darkness was blacking out the sea and jungle when Rainsford sighted the lights. He came upon them as he turned a crook in the coast line, and his first thought was that he had come upon a village, for there were many lights. But as he forged along he saw to his great astonishment that all the lights were in one enormous building—a lofty structure with pointed towers plunging upward into the gloom. His eyes made out the shadowy outlines of a palatial château;[1] it was set on a high bluff, and on three sides of it cliffs dived down to where the sea licked greedy lips in the shadows.

"Mirage," thought Rainsford. But it was no mirage, he found, when he opened the tall spiked iron gate. The stone steps were real enough; the massive door with a leering gargoyle[2] for a knocker was real enough; yet about it all hung an air of unreality.

He lifted the knocker, and it creaked up stiffly, as if it had never before been used. He let it fall, and it startled him with its booming loudness. He thought he heard steps within; the door remained closed. Again Rainsford lifted the heavy knocker, and let it fall. The door opened then, opened as suddenly as if it were on a spring, and Rainsford stood blinking in the river of glaring gold light that poured out. The first thing Rainsford's eyes discerned was the largest man Rainsford had ever seen—a gigantic creature, solidly made and black-bearded to the waist. In his hand the man held a long-barrelled revolver, and he was pointing it straight at Rainsford's heart.

Out of the snarl of beard two small eyes regarded Rainsford.

"Don't be alarmed," said Rainsford, with a smile which he hoped was disarming. "I'm no robber. I fell off a yacht. My name is Sanger Rainsford of New York City."

The menacing look in the eyes did not change. The revolver pointed as rigidly as if the giant were a statue. He gave no sign that he understood Rainsford's words, or that he had even heard them. He was dressed in uniform, a black uniform trimmed with gray astrakhan.

1. **château** [shä tō′]: French for "castle."
2. **gargoyle** [gär′ goil]: a strange-looking carved head of an animal.

Nocturnal Flowers Paul Klee, 1918, 7" x 6¼", Museum Folkwang, Essen, Germany

"I'm Sanger Rainsford of New York," Rainsford began again. "I fell off a yacht. I am hungry."

The man's only answer was to raise with his thumb the hammer of his revolver. Then Rainsford saw the man's free hand go to his forehead in a military salute, and he saw him click his heels together and stand at attention. Another man was coming down the broad marble steps, an erect, slender man in evening clothes. He advanced and held out his hand.

In a cultivated voice marked by a slight accent that gave it added precision and deliberateness, he said: "It is a very great pleasure and honor to welcome Mr. Sanger Rainsford, the celebrated hunter, to my home." Automatically Rainsford shook the man's hand.

"I've read your book about hunting snow leopards in Tibet, you see," explained the man. "I am General Zaroff."

Rainsford's first impression was that the man was singularly handsome; his second was that there was an original, almost bizarre quality about the general's face. He was a tall man past middle age, for his hair was a vivid white; but his thick eyebrows and pointed military mustache were as black as the night from which Rainsford had come. His eyes, too, were black and very bright. He had high cheekbones, a sharp-cut nose, a spare, dark face, the face of a man used to giving orders, the face of an aristocrat. Turning to the giant in uniform, the general made a sign. The giant put away his pistol, saluted, withdrew.

"Ivan is an incredibly strong fellow," remarked the general, "but he has the misfortune to be deaf and dumb. A simple fellow, but, I'm afraid, like all his race, a bit of a savage."

"Is he Russian?"

"He is a Cossack,"[3] said the general, and his smile showed red lips and pointed teeth. "So am I."

"Come," he said, "we shouldn't be chatting here. We can talk later. Now you want clothes, food, rest. You shall have them. This is a most restful spot."

Ivan had reappeared, and the general spoke to him with lips that moved but gave forth no sound.

"Follow Ivan, if you please, Mr. Rainsford," said the general. "I was about to have my dinner when you came. I'll wait for you. You'll find that my clothes will fit you, I think."

It was to a huge, beam-ceilinged bedroom with a canopied bed big enough for six men that Rainsford followed the silent giant. Ivan laid out an evening suit, and Rainsford, as he put it on, noticed that

3. **Cossack** [kos´ ak]: a member of an elite group of adventurous, warlike horsemen from the southwestern section of the former Soviet Union.

it came from a London tailor who ordinarily cut and sewed for none below the rank of duke.

The dining room to which Ivan conducted him was in many ways remarkable. There was a medieval magnificence about it; it suggested a baronial hall of feudal times with its oaken panels, its high ceiling, its vast refectory table where twoscore men could sit down to eat. About the hall were the mounted heads of many animals—lions, tigers, elephants, moose, bears; larger or more perfect specimens Rainsford had never seen. At the great table the general was sitting alone.

"You'll have a cocktail, Mr. Rainsford," he suggested. The cocktail was surpassingly good; and, Rainsford noted, the table appointments were of the finest—the linen, the crystal, the silver, the china.

They were eating *borsch*, the rich, red soup with whipped cream so dear to Russian palates. Half apologetically General Zaroff said: "We do our best to preserve the amenities of civilization here. Please forgive any lapses. We are well off the beaten track, you know. Do you think the champagne has suffered from its long ocean trip?"

"Not in the least," declared Rainsford. He was finding the general a most thoughtful and affable host, a true cosmopolite. But there was one trait of the general's that made Rainsford uncomfortable. Whenever he looked up he found the general studying him, appraising him narrowly.

"Perhaps," said General Zaroff, "you were surprised that I recognized your name. You see, I read all books on hunting published in English, French, and Russian. I have but one passion in my life, Mr. Rainsford, and it is the hunt."

"You have some wonderful heads here," said Rainsford as he ate a particularly well-cooked filet mignon. "That Cape buffalo is the largest I ever saw."

"Oh, that fellow. Yes, he was a monster."

"Did he charge you?"

"Hurled me against a tree," said the general. "Fractured my skull. But I got the brute."

"I've always thought," said Rainsford, "that the Cape buffalo is the most dangerous of all big game."

Room Perspective with Occupants Paul Klee, watercolor over a drawing in oil, 1921, 19$\frac{1}{16}$" x 21$\frac{1}{2}$", Kunstmuseum, Bern, Switzerland

For a moment the general did not reply; he was smiling his curious red-lipped smile. Then he said slowly: "No. You are wrong, sir. The Cape buffalo is not the most dangerous big game." He sipped his wine. "Here in my preserve on this island," he said in the same slow tone, "I hunt more dangerous game."

Rainsford expressed his surprise. "Is there big game on this island?"

The general nodded. "The biggest."

"Really?"

"Oh, it isn't here naturally, of course. I have to stock the island."

"What have you imported, General?" Rainsford asked. "Tigers?"

The general smiled. "No," he said. "Hunting tigers ceased to interest me some years ago. I exhausted their possibilities, you see. No thrill left in tigers, no real danger. I live for danger, Mr. Rainsford."

The general took from his pocket a gold cigarette case and offered his guest a long black cigarette with a silver tip; it was perfumed and gave off a smell like incense.

"We will have some capital hunting, you and I," said the general. "I shall be most glad to have your society."

"But what game—" began Rainsford.

"I'll tell you," said the general. "You will be amused, I know. I think I may say, in all modesty, that I have done a rare thing. I have invented a new sensation. May I pour you another glass of port, Mr. Rainsford?"

"Thank you, General."

The general filled both glasses, and said: "God makes some men poets. Some He makes kings, some beggars. Me He made a hunter. My hand was made for the trigger, my father said. He was a very rich man with a quarter of a million acres in the Crimea,[4] and he was an ardent sportsman. When I was only five years old he gave me a little gun, specially made in Moscow for me, to shoot sparrows with. When I shot some of his prize turkeys with it, he did not punish me;

4. **Crimea** [krī mē′ ə]: a peninsula in the former Soviet Union on the north coast of the Black Sea.

he complimented me on my marksmanship. I killed my first bear in the Caucasus[5] when I was ten. My whole life had been one prolonged hunt. I went into the army—it was expected of noblemen's sons—and for a time commanded a division of Cossack cavalry, but my real interest was always the hunt. I have hunted every kind of game in every land. It would be impossible for me to tell you how many animals I have killed."

The general puffed at his cigarette.

"After the debacle in Russia I left the country, for it was imprudent for an officer of the Czar to stay there. Many noble Russians lost everything. I, luckily, had invested heavily in American securities, so I shall never have to open a tearoom in Monte Carlo or drive a taxi in Paris. Naturally, I continued to hunt—grizzlies in your Rockies, crocodiles in the Ganges,[6] rhinoceroses in East Africa. It was in Africa that the Cape buffalo hit me and laid me up for six months. As soon as I recovered I started for the Amazon to hunt jaguars, for I had heard they were unusually cunning. They weren't." The Cossack sighed. "They were no match at all for a hunter with his wits about him, and a high-powered rifle. I was bitterly disappointed. I was lying in my tent with a splitting headache one night when a terrible thought pushed its way into my mind. Hunting was beginning to bore me! And hunting, remember, had been my life. I have heard that in America businessmen often go to pieces when they give up the business that has been their life."

"Yes, that's so," said Rainsford.

The general smiled. "I had no wish to go to pieces," he said. "I must do something. Now, mine is an analytical mind, Mr. Rainsford. Doubtless that is why I enjoy the problems of the chase."

"No doubt, General Zaroff."

"So," continued the general, "I asked myself why the hunt no longer fascinated me. You are much younger than I am, Mr. Rainsford, and have not hunted as much, but you perhaps can guess the answer."

5. **Caucasus** [kô′ kə səs]: a mountain range that extends from the Black Sea to the Caspian Sea.
6. **Ganges** [gan′ jēz′]: a river in India and Bangladesh.

"What was it?"

"Simply this: hunting had ceased to be what you call 'a sporting proposition.' It had become too easy. I always got my quarry. Always. There is no greater bore than perfection."

The general lit a fresh cigarette.

"No animal had a chance with me any more. That is no boast; it is a mathematical certainty. The animal had nothing but his legs and his instinct. Instinct is no match for reason. When I thought of this it was a tragic moment for me, I can tell you."

Rainsford leaned across the table, absorbed in what his host was saying.

"It came to me as an inspiration what I must do," the general went on.

"And that was?"

The general smiled the quiet smile of one who has faced an obstacle and surmounted it with success. "I had to invent a new animal to hunt," he said.

"A new animal? You're joking."

"Not at all," said the general. "I never joke about hunting. I needed a new animal. I found one. So I bought this island, built this house, and here I do my hunting. The island is perfect for my purposes—there are jungles with a maze of trails in them, hills, swamps—"

"But the animal, General Zaroff?"

"Oh," said the general, "it supplies me with the most exciting hunting in the world. No other hunting compares with it for an instant. Every day I hunt, and I never grow bored now, for I have a quarry with which I can match my wits."

Rainsford's bewilderment showed in his face.

"I wanted the ideal animal to hunt," explained the general. "So I said: 'What are the attributes of an ideal quarry?' And the answer was, of course: 'It must have courage, cunning, and, above all, it must be able to reason.'"

"But no animal can reason," objected Rainsford.

"My dear fellow," said the general, "there is one that can."

"But you can't mean—" gasped Rainsford.

"And why not?"

"I can't believe you are serious, General Zaroff. This is a grisly joke."

"Why should I not be serious? I am speaking of hunting."

"Hunting? Good God, General Zaroff, what you speak of is murder."

The general laughed with entire good nature. He regarded Rainsford quizzically. "I refuse to believe that so modern and civilized a young man as you harbors romantic ideas about the value of human life. Surely your experiences in the war—"

"Did not make me condone cold-blooded murder," finished Rainsford stiffly.

Laughter shook the general. "How extraordinarily droll you are!" he said. "One does not expect nowadays to find a young man of the educated class, even in America, with such a naïve and, if I may say so, mid-Victorian point of view. It's like finding a snuffbox[7] in a limousine. Ah, well, doubtless you had Puritan ancestors. So many Americans appear to have had. I'll wager you'll forget your notions when you go hunting with me. You've a genuine thrill in store for you, Mr. Rainsford."

"Thank you, I'm a hunter, not a murderer."

"Dear me," said the general, quite unruffled, "again that unpleasant word. But I think I can show you that your scruples are quite unfounded."

"Yes?"

"Life is for the strong, to be lived by the strong, and, if needs be, taken by the strong. The weak of the world were put here to give the strong pleasure. I am strong. Why should I not use my gift? If I wish to hunt, why should I not? I hunt the scum of the earth—sailors from tramp ships—lascars,[8] blacks, Chinese, whites, mongrels[9]—

7. **snuffbox** [snuf′boks]: a small box for holding snuff, a powdered tobacco that is inhaled.
8. **lascars** [las′kərz]: sailors, artillery men, or army servants.
9. **mongrels** [mung′grəlz]: in this context, people of mixed race.

a thoroughbred horse or hound is worth more than a score of them."

"But they are men," said Rainsford hotly.

"Precisely," said the general. "That is why I use them. It gives me pleasure. They can reason, after a fashion. So they are dangerous."

"But where do you get them?"

Intention Paul Klee, 1938, paint mixed with glue on newspaper, 29½" x 44", Kunstmuseum, Bern, Switzerland

The general's eyelid fluttered down in a wink. "This island is called Ship-Trap," he answered. "Sometimes an angry god of the high seas sends them to me. Sometimes, when Providence is not so kind, I help Providence a bit. Come to the window with me."

Rainsford went to the window and looked out toward the sea.

"Watch! Out there!" exclaimed the general, pointing into the night. Rainsford's eyes saw only blackness, and then, as the general pressed a button, far out to sea Rainsford saw the flash of lights.

The general chuckled. "They indicate a channel," he said, "where there's none: giant rocks with razor edges crouch like a sea monster with wide-open jaws. They can crush a ship as easily as I crush this nut." He dropped a walnut on the hardwood floor and brought his heel grinding down on it. "Oh, yes," he said, casually, as if in answer to a question, "I have electricity. We try to be civilized here."

"Civilized? And you shoot down men?"

A trace of anger was in the general's black eyes, but it was there for but a second, and he said, in his most pleasant manner: "Dear me, what a righteous young man you are! I assure you I do not do the thing you suggest. That would be barbarous. I treat these visitors with every consideration. They get plenty of good food and exercise. They get into splendid physical condition. You shall see for yourself tomorrow."

"What do you mean?"

"We'll visit my training school," smiled the general. "It's in the cellar. I have about a dozen pupils down there now. They're from the Spanish bark, 'San Lucar,' that had the bad luck to go on the rocks out there. A very inferior lot, I regret to say. Poor specimens and more accustomed to the deck than to the jungle."

He raised his hand, and Ivan, who served as waiter, brought thick Turkish coffee. Rainsford, with an effort, held his tongue in check.

"It's a game, you see," pursued the general blandly. "I suggest to one of them that we go hunting. I give him a supply of food and an excellent hunting knife. I give him three hours' start. I am to follow, armed only with a pistol of the smallest caliber and range. If my quarry eludes me for three whole days, he wins the game. If I find him," the general smiled, "he loses."

"Suppose he refuses to be hunted?"

"Oh," said the general, "I give him his option, of course. He need not play that game if he doesn't wish to. If he does not wish to hunt I turn him over to Ivan. Ivan once had the honor of serving as official knouter[10] to the Great White Czar, and he has his own ideas of sport. Invariably, Mr. Rainsford, invariably they choose the hunt."

"And if they win?"

The smile on the general's face widened. "To date I have not lost," he said.

Then he added, hastily: "I don't wish you to think me a braggart, Mr. Rainsford. Many of them afford only the most elementary sort of problem. Occasionally I strike a tartar.[11] One almost did win. I eventually had to use the dogs."

"The dogs?"

"This way, please. I'll show you."

The general steered Rainsford to a window. The lights from the window sent a flickering illumination that made grotesque patterns on the courtyard below, and Rainsford could see moving about there a dozen or so huge black shapes; as they turned toward him, their eyes glittered greenly.

"A rather good lot, I think," observed the general. "They are let out at seven every night. If anyone should try to get into my house—or out of it—something extremely regrettable would occur to him." He hummed a snatch of song from the Folies Bergères.[12]

"And now," said the general, "I want to show you my new collection of heads. Will you come with me to the library?"

"I hope," said Rainsford, "that you will excuse me tonight, General Zaroff. I'm really not feeling at all well."

"Ah, indeed?" the general inquired solicitously. "Well, I suppose that's only natural, after your long swim. You need a good, restful night's sleep. Tomorrow you'll feel like a new man, I'll wager. Then we'll hunt, eh? I've one rather promising prospect—"

Rainsford was hurrying from the room.

"Sorry you can't go with me tonight," called the general. "I expect rather fair sport—a big, strong black. He looks resourceful—Well, good

10. **knouter** [nout′ ər]: one who flogs others with a knout (whip).
11. **tartar** [tär′ tər]: a person with a bad temper; the Tartars were Mongolians and Turks who invaded Asia and eastern Europe during the Middle Ages.
12. **Folies Bergères** [fô lē′ ber zher′]: a nightclub in Paris.

Captive Paul Klee, 1940, colored paste on burlap mounted canvas, 18 $^7/_8$" x 17 $^3/_8$", Beyeler Collection, Basel, Switzerland

night, Mr. Rainsford; I hope you have a good night's rest."

The bed was good and the pajamas of the softest silk, and he was tired in every fiber of his being, but nevertheless Rainsford could not quiet his brain with the opiate of sleep. He lay, eyes wide open. Once he thought he heard stealthy steps in the corridor outside his room. He sought to throw open the door; it would not open. He went to the window and looked out. His room was high up in one of the towers. The lights of the château were out now, and it was dark and silent, but there was a fragment of sallow moon, and by its wan light he could see, dimly, the courtyard; there, weaving, in and out in the pattern of shadow, were black, noiseless forms; the hounds heard him at the window and looked up, expectantly, with their green eyes. Rainsford went back to the bed and lay down. By many methods he tried to put himself to sleep. He had achieved a doze when, just as morning began to come, he heard, far off in the jungle, the faint report of a pistol.

General Zaroff did not appear until luncheon. He was dressed faultlessly in the tweeds of a country squire. He was solicitous about the state of Rainsford's health.

"As for me," sighed the general, "I do not feel so well. I am worried, Mr. Rainsford. Last night I detected traces of my old complaint."

To Rainsford's questioning glance the general said: "Ennui.[13] Boredom."

Then, taking a second helping of crêpe suzette, the general explained: "The hunting was not good last night. The fellow lost his head. He made a straight trail that offered no problems at all. That's the trouble with these sailors; they have dull brains to begin with, and they do not know how to get about in the woods. They do excessively stupid and obvious things. It's most annoying. Will you have another glass of Chablis, Mr. Rainsford?"

"General," said Rainsford firmly, "I wish to leave this island at once."

The general raised his thickets of eyebrows; he seemed hurt. "But, my dear fellow," the general protested, "you've only just come. You've had no hunting—"

"I wish to go today," said Rainsford. He saw the dead black eyes of the general on him, studying him. General Zaroff's face suddenly brightened.

He filled Rainsford's glass with venerable Chablis from a dusty bottle.

"Tonight," said the general, "we will hunt—you and I."

Rainsford shook his head. "No, General," he said. "I will not hunt."

---

13. **ennui** [än wē′]: weariness, boredom.

The general shrugged his shoulders and nibbled delicately at a hothouse grape. "As you wish, my friend," he said. "The choice rests entirely with you. But may I not venture to suggest that you will find my idea of sport more diverting than Ivan's?"

He nodded toward the corner where the giant stood, scowling, his thick arms crossed on his hogshead of chest.

"You don't mean—" cried Rainsford.

"My dear fellow," said the general, "have I not told you I always mean what I say about hunting? This is really an inspiration. I drink to a foeman worthy of my steel—at last."

The general raised his glass, but Rainsford sat staring at him.

"You'll find this game worth playing," the general said enthusiastically. "Your brain against mine. Your woodcraft against mine. Your strength and stamina against mine. Outdoor chess. And the stake is not without value, eh?"

"And if I win—" began Rainsford huskily.

"I'll cheerfully admit myself defeated if I do not find you by midnight of the third day," said General Zaroff. "My sloop will place you on the mainland near a town."

The general read what Rainsford was thinking.

"Oh, you can trust me," said the Cossack. "I will give you my word as a gentleman and a sportsman. Of course, you, in turn, must agree to say nothing of your visit here."

"I'll agree to nothing of the kind," said Rainsford.

"Oh," said the general, "in that case—but why discuss that now? Three days hence we can discuss it over a bottle of Veuve Cliquot, unless—"

The general sipped his wine.

Then a businesslike air animated him. "Ivan," he said to Rainsford, "will supply you with hunting clothes, food, a knife. I suggest you wear moccasins; they leave a poorer trail. I should suggest too that you avoid the big swamp in the southeast corner of the island. We call it Death Swamp. There's quicksand there. One foolish fellow tried it. The deplorable part of it was that Lazarus followed him. You can imagine my feelings, Mr. Rainsford. I loved Lazarus; he was the finest hound in my pack. Well, I must beg you to excuse me now. I always take a siesta after lunch. You'll hardly have time for a nap, I fear. You'll want to start, no doubt. I shall not follow till dusk. Hunting at night is so much more exciting than by day, don't you think? Au revoir, Mr. Rainsford, au revoir."

General Zaroff, with a deep, courtly bow, strolled from the room.

From another door came Ivan. Under one arm he carried khaki hunting clothes, a haversack of food, a leather sheath containing a long-bladed hunting knife; his right hand rested on a cocked revolver thrust in the crimson sash around his waist. . . .

Rainsford had fought his way through the bush for two hours.

"I must keep my nerve. I must keep my nerve," he said through tight teeth.

He had not been entirely clear-headed when the château gates snapped shut behind him. His whole idea at first was to put distance between himself and General Zaroff, and, to this end, he had plunged along, spurred on by the sharp rowels of something very like panic. Now he had got a grip on himself, had stopped, and was taking stock of himself and the situation.

He saw that straight flight was futile; inevitably it would bring him face to face with the sea. He was in a picture with a frame of water, and his operations, clearly, must take place within that frame.

"I'll give him a trail to follow," muttered Rainsford, and he struck off from the rude path he had been following into the trackless wilderness. He executed a series of intricate loops; he doubled on his trail again and again, recalling all the lore of the fox hunt, and all the dodges of the fox. Night found him leg-weary, with hands and face lashed by the branches, on a thickly wooded ridge. He knew it would be insane to blunder on through the dark, even if he had the strength. His need for rest was imperative and he thought: "I have played the fox, now I must play the cat of the fable." A big tree with a thick trunk and outspread branches was near by, and, taking care to leave not the slightest mark, he climbed up into the crotch, and stretching out on one of the broad limbs, after a fashion, rested.

Rest brought him new confidence and almost a feeling of security. Even so zealous a hunter as General Zaroff could not trace him there, he told himself; only the devil himself could follow that complicated trail through the jungle after dark. But, perhaps, the general was a devil—

An apprehensive night crawled slowly by like a wounded snake, and sleep did not visit Rainsford, although the silence of a dead world was on the jungle. Toward morning when a dingy gray was varnishing the sky, the cry of some startled bird focused Rainsford's attention in that direction. Something was coming through the bush, coming slowly, carefully, coming by the same winding way Rainsford had come. He flattened himself down on the limb, and through a screen of leaves almost as thick as tapestry, he watched. The thing that was approaching was a man.

It was General Zaroff. He made his way along with his eyes fixed in utmost concentration on the ground before him. He paused almost beneath the tree, dropped to his knees, and studied the ground before him. Rainsford's impulse was to hurl himself down like a panther, but he saw that the general's right hand held something small and metallic—an automatic pistol.

The hunter shook his head several times as if he were puzzled. Then he straightened up and took from his case one of his black cigarettes; its pungent incenselike smoke floated up to Rainsford's nostrils.

Rainsford held his breath. The general's eyes had left the ground and were traveling inch by inch up the tree. Rainsford froze there, every muscle tensed for a spring. But the sharp eyes of the hunter stopped before they reached the limb where Rainsford lay; a smile spread over his brown face. Very deliberately he blew a smoke ring into the air; then he turned his back on the tree and walked carelessly away, back along the trail he had come. The swirls of the underbrush against his hunting boots grew fainter and fainter.

The pent-up air burst hotly from Rainsford's lungs. His first thought made him feel sick and numb. The general could follow a trail through the woods at night; he could follow an extremely

Hot Pursuit Paul Klee, 1939, colored paste and oil on paper on jute, 19" x 25 ½", the Fogg Art Museum, Harvard University, Cambridge, Massachusetts

difficult trail; he must have uncanny powers; only by the merest chance had the Cossack failed to see his quarry.

Rainsford's second thought was even more terrible. It sent a shudder of cold horror through his whole being. Why had the general smiled? Why had he turned back?

Rainsford did not want to believe what his reason told him was true, but the truth was as evident as the sun that had by now pushed through the morning mists. The general was playing with him. The general was saving him for another day's sport! The Cossack was the cat; he was the mouse. Then it was that Rainsford knew the full meaning of terror.

"I will not lose my nerve. I will not."

He slid down from the tree, and struck off again into the woods. His face was set and he forced the machinery of his mind to function. Three hundred yards from his hiding place he stopped where a huge dead tree leaned precariously on a smaller living one. Throwing off his sack of food, Rainsford took his knife from its sheath and began to work with all his energy.

The job was finished at last, and he threw himself down behind a fallen log a hundred feet away. He did not have to wait long. The cat was coming again to play with the mouse.

Following the trail with the sureness of a bloodhound came General Zaroff. Nothing escaped those searching black eyes, no crushed blade of grass, no bent twig, no mark, no matter how faint, in the moss. So intent was the Cossack on his stalking that he was upon the thing Rainsford had made before he saw it. His foot touched the protruding bough that was the trigger. Even as he touched it, the general sensed his danger and leaped back with the agility of an ape. But he was not quite quick enough; the dead tree, delicately adjusted to rest on the cut living one, crashed down and struck the general a glancing blow on the shoulder as it fell; but for his alertness, he must have been smashed beneath it. He staggered, but he did not fall; nor did he drop his revolver. He stood there rubbing his injured shoulder, and Rainsford, with fear again gripping his heart, heard the general's mocking laugh ring through the jungle.

"Rainsford," called the general, "if you are within sound of my voice, as I suppose you are, let me congratulate you. Not many men know how to make a Malay man-catcher.[14] Luckily, for me, I too have hunted in Malacca.[15] You are proving interesting, Mr. Rainsford. I am going now to have my wound dressed; it's only a slight one. But I shall be back. I shall be back."

When the general, nursing his bruised shoulder, had gone, Rainsford took up his flight again. It was flight now, a desperate, hopeless flight, that carried him on for some hours. Dusk came, then darkness, and still he pressed on. The ground grew softer under his moccasins; the vegetation grew ranker, denser; insects bit him savagely. Then, as he stepped forward, his foot sank into the ooze. He tried to wrench it back, but the muck sucked viciously at his foot as if it were a giant leech. With a violent effort, he tore his foot loose. He knew where he was now. Death Swamp and its quicksand.

His hands were tight closed as if his nerve were something tangible that someone in the darkness was trying to tear from his grip. The softness of the earth had given him an idea. He stepped back from the quicksand a dozen feet or so and, like some huge prehistoric beaver, he began to dig.

Rainsford had dug himself in in France when a second's delay meant death. That had been a placid pastime compared to his digging now. The pit grew deeper; when it was above his shoulders, he climbed out and from some hard saplings cut stakes and sharpened them to a fine point. These stakes he planted in the bottom of the pit with the points sticking up. With flying fingers he wove a rough carpet of weeds and branches and with it he covered the mouth of the pit. Then, wet with sweat and aching with tiredness, he crouched behind the stump of a lightning-charred tree.

He knew his pursuer was coming; he heard the padding sound of feet on the soft earth, and the night breeze brought him the perfume of the general's cigarette. It seemed to Rainsford that the general was

14. **Malay man-catcher** [mā′ lā]: trap made in the Malay Peninsula in Southeast Asia.
15. **Malacca** [mə läk′ ə]: a city of the Malay Peninsula.

coming with unusual swiftness; he was not feeling his way along, foot by foot. Rainsford, crouching there, could not see the general, nor could he see the pit. He lived a year in a minute. Then he felt an impulse to cry aloud with joy, for he heard the sharp crackle of the breaking branches as the cover of the pit gave way; he heard the sharp scream of pain as the pointed stakes found their mark. He leaped up from his place of concealment. Then he cowered back. Three feet from the pit a man was standing, with an electric torch in his hand.

"You've done well, Rainsford," the voice of the general called. "Your Burmese tiger pit[16] has claimed one of my best dogs. Again you score. I think, Mr. Rainsford, I'll see what you can do against my whole pack. I'm going home for a rest now. Thank you for a most amusing evening."

At daybreak Rainsford, lying near the swamp, was awakened by a sound that made him know that he had new things to learn about fear. It was a distant sound, faint and wavering, but he knew it. It was the baying of a pack of hounds.

Rainsford knew he could do one of two things. He could stay where he was and wait. That was suicide. He could flee. That was postponing the inevitable. For a moment he stood there, thinking. An idea that held a wild chance came to him, and, tightening his belt, he headed away from the swamp. The baying of the hounds drew nearer, then still nearer, nearer, ever nearer. On a ridge Rainsford climbed a tree. Down a watercourse, not a quarter of a mile away, he could see the bush moving. Straining his eyes, he saw the lean figure of General Zaroff; just ahead of him Rainsford made out another figure whose wide shoulders surged through the tall jungle weeds; it was the giant Ivan, and he seemed pulled forward by some unseen force; Rainsford knew that Ivan must be holding the pack in leash.

They would be on him any minute now. His mind worked frantically. He thought of a native trick he had learned in Uganda. He slid down the tree. He caught hold of a springy young sapling and to it he fastened his hunting knife, with the blade pointing down the trail; with a bit of wild grapevine he tied back the sapling. Then he ran for

16. **Burmese tiger pit** [bėr′ mēz′]: pit made to catch a Burmese tiger.

his life. The hounds raised their voices as they hit the fresh scent. Rainsford knew now how an animal at bay feels.

He had to stop to get his breath. The baying of the hounds stopped abruptly, and Rainsford's heart stopped too. They must have reached the knife.

He shinned excitedly up a tree and looked back. His pursuers had stopped. But the hope that was in Rainsford's brain when he climbed died, for he saw in the shallow valley that General Zaroff was still on his feet. But Ivan was not. The knife, driven by the recoil of the springing tree, had not wholly failed.

Rainsford had hardly tumbled to the ground when the pack resumed the chase.

"Nerve, nerve, nerve!" he panted, as he dashed along. A blue gap showed between the trees dead ahead. Ever nearer drew the hounds. Rainsford forced himself on toward that gap. He reached it. It was the shore of the sea. Across a cove he could see the gloomy gray stone of the château. Twenty feet below him the sea rumbled and hissed. Rainsford hesitated. He heard the hounds. Then he leaped far out into the sea. . . .

When the general and his pack reached the place by the sea, the Cossack stopped. For some minutes he stood regarding the blue-green expanse of water. He shrugged his shoulders. Then he sat down, took a drink of brandy from a silver flask, lit a perfumed cigarette, and hummed a bit from *Madame Butterfly*.[17]

General Zaroff had an exceedingly good dinner in his great paneled dining hall that evening. With it he had a bottle of Pol Roger and a half bottle of Chambertin. Two slight annoyances kept him from perfect enjoyment. One was the thought that it would be difficult to replace Ivan; the other was that his quarry had escaped him; of course, the American hadn't played the game—so thought the general as he tasted his after-dinner liqueur. In his library he read, to soothe himself, from the works of Marcus Aurelius.[18] At ten he went up to his bedroom. He

17. **Madame Butterfly** [mad′ əm but′ ər flī]: an opera by the Italian composer Giacomo Puccini.
18. **Marcus Aurelius** [mär′ kəs ô rē′ lē əs]: Roman emperor (A.D. 161-180) and philosopher.

Harmonized Combat Paul Klee, 1937, pastel on cotton and hemp, Kunstmuseum, Bern, Switzerland

was deliciously tired, he said to himself, as he locked himself in. There was a little moonlight, so, before turning on his light, he went to the window and looked down at the courtyard. To the great hounds he called: "Better luck another time!" Then he switched on the light.

A man, who had been hiding in the curtains of the bed, was standing there.

"Rainsford!" screamed the general. "How in God's name did you get here?"

"Swam," said Rainsford. "I found it quicker than walking through the jungle."

The general sucked in his breath and smiled. "I congratulate you," he said. "You have won the game."

Rainsford did not smile. "I am still a beast at bay," he said, in a low, hoarse voice. "Get ready, General Zaroff."

The general made one of his deepest bows. "I see," he said. "Splendid! One of us is to furnish a repast for the hounds. The other will sleep in this very excellent bed. On guard, Rainsford." . . .

He had never slept in a better bed, Rainsford decided.

RICHARD EDWARD CONNELL

Richard Edward Connell (1893-1949) was born in Duchess County, New York, and while still in high school worked at the Poughkeepsie *News-Press*. "My first writing was done for the daily newspaper my father edited in Poughkeepsie, New York. I covered baseball games. I was ten years old and got ten cents a game. I have been a professional writer ever since."

Connell graduated from Harvard in 1915, and then served in the United States Army during World War I. He resumed his writing and eventually moved to California in 1925. There he wrote screen plays, including the one for his story "The Most Dangerous Game."

Untitled goblet Sultan Rogers,
1985, wood, 6$\frac{1}{4}$" x 2$\frac{3}{4}$", The University
of Mississippi Cultural Center

THE DINNER PARTY

MONA GARDNER

The country is India. A large dinner party is being given in an up-country station by a colonial official and his wife. The guests are army officers and government attachés[1] and their wives, and an American naturalist.

At one side of the long table a spirited discussion springs up between a young girl and a colonel. The girl insists women have long outgrown the jumping-on-a-chair-at-the-sight-of-a-mouse era, that they are not as fluttery as their grandmothers. The colonel says they are, explaining that women haven't the actual nerve control of men. The other men at the table agree with him.

"A woman's unfailing reaction in any crisis," the colonel says, "is to scream. And while a man may feel like it, yet he has that ounce more of control than a woman has. And that last ounce is what counts!"

---

1. **attachés** [at′ ə shās′]: members of the diplomatic staff of an ambassador or minister to a foreign country.

The American scientist does not join in the argument, but sits watching the faces of the other guests. As he looks, he sees a strange expression come over the face of the hostess. She is staring straight ahead, the muscles of her face contracting slightly. With a small gesture she summons the native boy standing behind her chair. She whispers to him. The boy's eyes widen: he turns quickly and leaves the room. No one else sees this, nor the boy when he puts a bowl of milk on the verandah outside the glass doors.

The American comes to with a start. In India, milk in a bowl means only one thing. It is bait for a snake. He realizes there is a cobra in the room.

He looks up at the rafters—the likeliest place—and sees they are bare. Three corners of the room, which he can see by shifting only slightly, are empty. In the fourth corner a group of servants stand, waiting until the next course can be served. The American realizes there is only one place left—under the table.

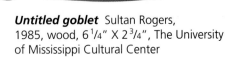

Untitled goblet Sultan Rogers, 1985, wood, 6¼" X 2¾", The University of Mississippi Cultural Center

His first impulse is to jump back and warn the others. But he knows the commotion will frighten the cobra and it will strike. He speaks quickly, the quality of his voice so arresting that it sobers everyone.

"I want to know just what control everyone at this table has. I will count three hundred—that's five minutes—and not one of you is to move a single muscle. The persons who move will forfeit 50 rupees.[2] Now! Ready!"

The 20 people sit like stone images while he counts. He is saying ". . . two-hundred and eighty . . ." when, out of the corner of his eye, he sees the cobra emerge and make for the bowl of milk. Four or five screams ring out as he jumps to slam shut the verandah doors.

"You certainly were right, Colonel!" the host says. "A man has just shown us an example of real control."

"Just a minute," the American says, turning to his hostess, "there's one thing I'd like to know. Mrs. Wynnes, how did you know that cobra was in the room?"

A faint smile lights up the woman's face as she replies: "Because it was lying across my foot."

2. **rupees** [rü pēz´]: Indian coins.

MONA GARDNER

Mona Gardner (1900-1981) was born in Seattle, Washington, but spent a number of years in Hong Kong, South Africa, and California. Many of her novels and short stories are set in Asia. Of all her stories, "The Dinner Party," is best known. Its setting is India, its time the early 1900s, when India was still a British colony.

A Running Brook of Horror

DANIEL P. MANNIX

I had first heard of Grace Wiley some years before when Dr. William Mann, then director of the National Zoological Park in Washington, D.C., handed me a picture of a tiny woman with a gigantic king cobra draped over her shoulders like a garden hose. The snake had partly spread his hood and was looking intently into the camera while his mistress stroked his head to quiet him. Dr. Mann told me: "Grace lives in a little house full of poisonous snakes, imported from all over the world. She lets them wander around like cats. There's been more nonsense written about 'snake charming' than nearly any other subject. Grace is probably the only non-Oriental who knows the real secrets of this curious business."

Looking at the picture of that deadly creature I knew what Ruskin[1] meant when he described a snake as a "running brook of horror." Still, I like snakes and when Jule and I moved into our Malibu house, I made it a point to call on Grace Wiley.

Grace wasn't at the address Dr. Mann had given me. The neighbors had seen some of her pets in the yard and called the police. Grace finally settled outside Los Angeles near the little town of Cypress. After a phone call, I drove out to see her. She was living in a small three-room cottage, surrounded by open fields. Behind the cottage was a big, ramshackle barn where the snakes were kept. Grace was cleaning snake boxes with a hose when I arrived.

1. **Ruskin, John** [rus′ kin]: nineteenth-century English author, art critic, and social reformer.

She was a surprisingly little lady, scarcely over five feet, and probably weighed less than a hundred pounds. Although Grace was sixty-four years old, she was as active as a boy and worked with smooth dexterity. When she saw me, she hurriedly picked up the four-foot rattlesnake who had been sunning himself while his box was cleaned and poured him into his cage. The snake raised his head but made no attempt to strike or even to rattle. I was impressed but not astonished. In captivity, rattlers often grow sluggish and can be handled with comparative impunity.

Grace came forward, drying her hands on her apron. "Oh dear, I meant to get dressed up for you," she said, trying to smooth down her thatch of brown hair. "But I haven't anybody here to help me with the snakes, except Mother—and she's eighty-four years old. Don't trip over an alligator," she added as I came forward. I noticed for the first time in the high grass a dozen or so alligators and crocodiles. They ranged from a three-foot Chinese croc to a big Florida 'gator more than twelve feet long. I threaded my way among them without mishap, although several opened their huge jaws to hiss at me.

"They don't mean anything by that, any more than a dog barking," Grace explained fondly. "They're very tame and most of them know their names. Now come in and meet my little family of snakes."

We entered the barn. The walls were lined with cages of all sizes and shapes containing snakes. Grace stopped at each cage, casually lifting the occupant and pointing out his fine points while she stroked and examined him. Grace unquestionably had one of the world's finest collections of reptiles. I watched her handle diamondback rattlesnakes from Texas, vipers from Italy, fer-de-lance[2] from the West Indies, a little Egyptian cobra (the "asp" that killed Cleopatra),[3] and the deadly karait from India. Then I saw Grace perform a feat I would have believed impossible.

We had stopped in front of a large, glass-fronted cage containing apparently nothing but newspaper. "These little fellows arrived only

2. **fer-de-lance** [fer′ də läns′]: a poisonous pit viper.
3. **Cleopatra** [klē′ ə pat′ rə]: the last queen of ancient Egypt.

a short time ago, so they're very wild," explained Grace indulgently. She quietly lifted the paper. Instantly a forest of heads sprang up in the cage. Grace moved the paper slightly. At the movement, the heads seemed to spread and flatten. Then I saw that they were not heads but hoods. I was looking at the world's most deadly creature—the Indian cobra.

Man-eating tigers are said to kill 600 natives a year but cobras kill 25,000 people a year in India alone. Hunters have been mauled by wounded elephants and lived to tell about it, but no one survives a body bite from a big cobra. I have caught rattlesnakes with a forked stick and my bare hands, but I'm not ashamed to say I jumped back from that cage as though the devil were inside—as indeed he was.

Grace advanced her hand toward the nearest cobra. The snake swayed like a reed in the wind, feinting for the strike. Grace raised her hand above the snake's head, the reptile twisting around to watch her. As the woman slowly lowered her hand, the snake gave that most terrible of all animal noises—the unearthly hiss of a deadly snake. I have seen children laugh with excitement at the roar of a lion, but I have never seen anyone who did not cringe at that cold, uncanny sound. Grace deliberately tried to touch the rigid, quivering hood. The cobra struck at her hand. He missed. Quietly, Grace presented her open palm. The cobra hesitated a split second, his reared body quivering like a plucked banjo string. Then he struck.

I felt sick as I saw his head hit Grace's hand, but the cobra did not bite. He struck with his mouth closed. As rapidly as an expert boxer drumming on a punching bag, the snake struck three times against Grace's palm, always for some incredible reason with his mouth shut. Then Grace slid her open hand over his head and stroked his hood. The snake hissed again and struggled violently under her touch.

Grace continued to caress him. Suddenly the snake went limp and his hood began to close. Grace slipped her other hand under the snake's body and lifted him out of the cage. She held the reptile in her arms as though he were a baby. The cobra raised his head to look Grace in the face; his dancing tongue was less than a foot from her mouth. Grace braced her hand against the curve of his body and talked calmly to him until he folded his hood. He curled up in her arms quietly until I made a slight movement; then he instantly reared up again, threatening me.

I had never seen anything to match this performance. Later, Grace opened the cobra's mouth to show me that the fangs were still intact. The yellow venom was slowly oozing over their tips.

If Grace Wiley had wished to make a mystery out of her amazing ability I am certain she could have made a fortune by posing as a woman with supernatural power. There isn't a zoologist alive who could have debunked her. But Grace was a perfectly honest person who was happy to explain in detail exactly how she could handle these terrible creatures. I spent several weeks with her studying her technique and now that I understand it I'm even more impressed than I was before.

Although I had kept snakes for many years, I was probably more astonished by Grace's performance than someone who knew nothing about reptiles. My mistake lay in supposing that all snakes are more or less alike. I knew rattlesnakes but I knew nothing about cobras. Although the cobra is intrinsically a far more dangerous snake than the rattlesnake, Grace would never have attempted to handle a diamondback rattler in the manner she handled this cobra. To understand why, you have to know the physical and psychological differences between the two reptiles.

A rattler has two "coils." When he is resting, he lies coiled up like a length of rope with his head lying on the topmost coil and his rattle sticking up in the center of the heap. When he is angry, he rears the upper third of his body a foot or more off the ground, coiling it into an S-shaped design and sounding his rattle continuously. Snake men call this position the "business coil." The rattler is like a coiled spring. He can strike out the full length of the S, inject his venom, and return into position for another strike literally faster than the eye can follow. He cannot strike farther than the raised S, nor will he attack. To attack, he would have to come out of coil and lose his advantageous position. He is like a boxer with his bent arm drawn back for a haymaker.[4] As soon as his opponent comes close enough, he can let him have it.

A cobra, on the other hand, rears straight upward. If you put your elbow on a table, cup your hand to represent the open hood, and sway your forearm back and forth, you will have a good idea of the fighting stance of a cobra. Your index finger represents the tiny, mouselike head that does the business. You will see at once that you cannot strike out as far as you could with your arm drawn back. Your range is limited to the length of your forearm. Here is a large part of the secret in handling cobras.

Because of the deceptively coiled S, no one can tell exactly how far a rattler can strike. But with a little practice, you can tell a cobra's range to the inch. Also, the blow of a cobra is comparatively slow. A man with steady nerves can jerk away in time to avoid being bitten. This is exactly what a mongoose[5] does. The mongoose keeps just outside the cobra's range and when he does dart in for a bite, he can jump clear of the blow. A mongoose would stand no chance at all against a rattlesnake.

4. **haymaker**: a hard, upward punch with the fist.
5. **mongoose** [mong´güs]: an animal of Asia and Africa; the Asian mongoose is noted for being able to kill cobras.

Another vital difference lies in the method of striking. The rattler does not bite. He stabs with his fangs. A rattler's fangs are very long, so long that they would pierce his lower jaw if he did not keep them folded back against the roof of his mouth. When he strikes, the rattler opens his mouth to its fullest extent, the fangs snap down into place, and the snake stabs. The fangs are hollow and connect directly with the poison glands in either side of the snake's head. When the snake feels his fangs go home, he instantly discharges his venom deep into the wound. The fangs operate like miniature hypodermic needles and are extremely efficient.

The cobra has no such elaborate apparatus. His fangs are short and do not fold back. Instead of stabbing like the rattler, he must actually bite. He grabs his victims and then deliberately chews while the venom runs down into the wound he is making. These apparently minor distinctions mean the difference between life and death to anyone working with snakes.

When Grace approached a wild cobra, she moved her hand back and forth just outside the snake's range. The cobra would then strike angrily until he became tired. Then he was reluctant to strike again. Grace's next move was to raise her hand over the snake's hood and bring it down slowly. Because of his method of rearing, a cobra cannot strike directly upward (a rattler can strike up as easily as in any other direction), and Grace could actually touch the top of the snake's head. The snake became puzzled and frustrated. He felt that he was fighting an invulnerable opponent who, after all, didn't seem to mean him any harm. Then came the final touch. Grace would put her open palm toward the snake. At last the cobra was able to hit her. But he had to bite and he could not get a grip on the flat surface of the palm. If he could get a finger or a loose fold of skin he could fasten his teeth in it and start chewing. But his strike is sufficiently slow that Grace could meet each blow with the flat of her palm. At last Grace would be able to get her hand over the snake's head and stroke his hood. This seemed to relax the reptile and from then on Grace could handle him with some degree of confidence.

I don't mean to suggest that this is a cut-and-dried procedure. Grace knew snakes perfectly and could tell by tiny, subtle indications what the reptile would probably do next. She had been bitten many times—she would never tell me just how many—but never by a cobra. You're only bitten once by a cobra.

"Now I'll show you what I know you're waiting to see," said Grace as she put the snake away. "My mated pair of king cobras." Dropping her voice reverently, she added, "I call the big male 'the King of Kings.' " She led the way to a large enclosure and for the first time in my life I was looking into the eyes of that dread reptile, the king cobra—or hamadryad.[6]

The common cobra is rarely more than five feet long. Even so, he has enough venom in his poison glands to kill fifty men. Grace's king cobras were more than fifteen feet long—longer than a boa constrictor. The two hamadryads contained enough venom, if injected drop by drop, to kill nearly a thousand human beings. That wasn't all. The hamadryad is the only snake known to attack without any provocation. These fearful creatures have been reported to trail a man through a jungle for the express purpose of biting him. They are so aggressive that they have closed roads in India by driving away all traffic. This is probably because the hamadryads, unlike other snakes, guard their eggs and young, and if a pair sets up housekeeping in a district, every other living thing must get out—including elephants. When a king cobra rears up, he stands higher than the head of a kneeling man. They are unquestionably the most dangerous animal in the world today.

6. **hamadryad** [ham′ ə drī′ əd]: one who lives in a tree; the king cobra is a tree-dweller.

When Grace first got these monsters, she was unable to handle them as she would ordinary cobras; so she had to devise an entirely new method of working with them. When the kings first arrived, they were completely unapproachable. They reared up more than four feet, snorting and hissing, their lower jaws open to expose the poison fangs. "A very threatening look, indeed," Grace called it. She put them in a large cage with a sliding partition. Unlike other snakes, hamadryads are knowing enough to notice that when their keeper opens the door in the side of the cage to put in fresh water, he must expose his hand for a fraction of a second. These cobras soon learned to lie against the side of the cage and wait for Grace to open the door. She outwitted them by waiting until both of the hamadryads were on one side of the cage and then sliding in the partition before changing water pans. She did not dare to go near them with her bare hands; she used a padded stick to stroke them. Yet she was able to touch them four days after their arrival. "I petted the kings on their tails when their heads were far away," she told me. "Later in the day I had a little visit with them and told them how perfectly lovely they were; that I liked them and was sure we were going to be good friends."

A few weeks later, the King of Kings began shedding his skin. Snakes are irritable and nervous while shedding and the hamadryad had trouble sloughing off the thin membrane covering his eyes. Grace wrote in her diary: "I stroked his head and then pulled off the eyelids with eyebrow forceps. He flinched a little but was unafraid. He put out his tongue in such a knowing manner! I mounted the eyelids and they looked just like pearls. What a pity that there have been nothing but unfriendly, aggressive accounts about this sweet snake. Really, the intelligence of these creatures is unbelievable."

The King of Kings was so heavy that Grace was unable to lift him by herself. Jule offered to help her carry the snake outside for a picture. While Jule and Grace were staggering out the door with the monster reptile between them, the king suddenly reared and rapped Jule several times on her forehead with his closed mouth. "He's trying to tell you something!" exclaimed Grace. He was indeed. I saw that the Chinese crocodile had rushed out from under a table and grabbed the hamadryad by the tail. Jule relaxed her grip and the king dropped his head and gave a single hiss. The croc promptly let go and the ladies bore the cobra out into the sunlight. I was the only person who seemed upset by the incident.

Out of curiosity, I asked Grace if she ever used music in taming her snakes. She laughed and told me what I already knew: all snakes are deaf. Grace assured me that the Hindu fakir uses his flute only to attract a crowd and by swaying his own body back and forth the fakir keeps the snake swaying as the cobra is feinting to strike. The man times his music to correspond to the snake's movements and it appears to dance to the tune. The fakir naturally keeps well outside of the cobra's striking range. Years later when I was in India, I discovered that this is exactly what happens. I never saw any Oriental snake charmer even approximate Grace's marvelous powers over reptiles.

Grace's only source of income was to exhibit her snakes to tourists, although she was occasionally able to rent a snake to a studio (she always went along to make sure the reptile wasn't frightened or injured) and sometimes she bought ailing snakes from dealers, cured them, and resold them for a small profit to zoos. While I was with her, a dusty car stopped and discharged a plump couple with three noisy children who had seen her modest sign: *Grace Wiley—Reptiles*. Grace explained that she would show them her collection, handle the poisonous snakes, call over the tame alligators, and let the children play with Rocky, an eighteen-foot Indian Rock python[7] which she had raised from a baby. The charge was twenty-five cents. "That's too much," the woman said to her husband, and they went back to the car. Grace sighed. "No one seems interested in my snakes. No one really cares about them. And they're so wonderful."

7. **python** [pī′thon]: a large, nonpoisonous snake of Asia, Africa, and Australia that kills by squeezing.

One day Grace telephoned me to say that she had gotten in a new shipment of snakes, including some Indian cobras from Siam. "One of them has markings that form a complete G on the back of his hood," she told me. "Isn't it curious that the snake and I have the same initial! I call him 'my snake.'" We laughed about this, and then Jule and I went out to Cypress to take a last set of pictures of Grace and her snakes for an article I was doing about this remarkable woman.

When we arrived Grace was talking to a couple of kids who had brought a pet turtle to show her. We set up our photographic apparatus and after a while I began to grow restless. "Couldn't we go ahead with our pictures?" I hinted. Grace replied gently, "These boys have come for miles on their bicycles to show me this turtle. They really seem to love reptiles and I can't send them away." We waited for more than an hour before the boys departed with their remarkable turtle.

We took several pictures and then I asked Grace to let me get a picture of the cobra with the G on the hood. "I didn't look very well in those other pictures," said Grace anxiously. "I'll comb my hair and put on another blouse." She was back in a few minutes. Jule and I had set up our cameras in the yard behind the barn, first removing several alligators and a big monitor lizard[8] named Slinky to avoid any possibility of accidents. I wanted a shot of the cobra with spread hood, and Grace brought him out cradled in her arms. Before allowing me to take the picture, she removed her glasses, as she felt that she looked better without them. The cobra refused to spread and Grace put him down on the ground and extended her flat palm toward him to make him rear—something I had often seen her do before, but never without her glasses.

I was watching through the finder of my camera. I saw the cobra spread and strike as I clicked the shutter. As the image disappeared from the ground glass of my Graflex,[9] I looked up and saw the snake

8. **monitor lizard** [mon′ ə tər liz′ ərd]: a large lizard of Africa, Asia, and Australia.
9. **Graflex** [graf′ lex]: single-lens reflex camera; first made in the United States in 1898.

had seized Grace by the middle finger. She said in her usual quiet voice, "Oh, he's bitten me."

I dropped the camera and ran toward her, feeling an almost paralyzing sense of shock, for I knew that Grace Wiley was a dead woman. At the same time I thought, "Good Lord, it's just like the book," for the cobra was behaving exactly as textbooks on cobras say they behave; he was deliberately chewing on the wound to make the venom run out of his glands. It was a terrible sight.

Quietly and expertly, Grace took hold of the snake on either side of his jaws and gently forced his mouth open. I knew that her only chance for life was to put a tourniquet around the finger instantly and slash open the wound to allow the venom to run out. Seconds counted. I reached out my hand to take the snake above the hood so she could immediately start squeezing out the venom, but Grace motioned me away. She stood up, still holding the cobra, and walked into the barn. Carefully, she put the snake into his cage and closed the door.

This must have taken a couple of minutes and I knew that the venom was spreading through her system each moment. "Jule," said Grace, "call Wesley Dickinson. He's a herpetologist[10] and a friend of mine. He'll know what to do." Calmly and distinctly she gave Jule the telephone number and Jule ran to the phone. Then Grace turned to me. Suddenly she said, "He didn't really bite me, did he?" It was the only emotion I saw her show. I could only say, "Grace, where's your snake-bite kit?" We both knew that nothing except immediate amputation of her arm could save her, but anything was worth a chance.

She pointed to a cabinet. There was a tremendous collection of the surgical aids used for snake bite but I don't believe any of the stuff had been touched for twenty years. I pulled out a rubber tourniquet and tried to twist it around her finger. The old rubber snapped in my hands. Grace didn't seem to notice. I pulled out my handkerchief

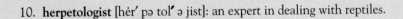

10. **herpetologist** [hėr′ pə tol′ ə jist]: an expert in dealing with reptiles.

and tried that. It was too thick to go around her finger and I twisted it around her wrist. "I'll faint in a few minutes," said Grace. "I want to show you where everything is before I lose consciousness."

Cobra venom, unlike rattlesnake, affects the nervous system. In a few minutes the victim becomes paralyzed and the heart stops beating. I knew Grace was thinking of this. She said, "You must give me strychnine[11] injections to keep my heart going when I begin to pass out. I'll show you where the strychnine is kept. You may have to give me caffeine also."

She walked to the other end of the room and I ran alongside trying to keep the tourniquet in place. She got out the tiny glass vials of strychnine and caffeine and also a hypodermic syringe with several needles. I saw some razor blades with the outfit and picked one up, intending to make a deep incision to let out as much of the venom as possible. Grace shook her head. "That won't do any good," she told me. Cobra venom travels along the nerves, so making the wound bleed wouldn't be very effective; but it was all I could think of to do.

Jule came back with a Mr. Tanner, Grace's cousin who lived next door. Tanner immediately got out his jackknife, intending to cut open the wound, but Grace stopped him. "Wait until Wesley comes," she said. Tanner told me afterward that he was convinced that if he had amputated the finger Grace might have lived. This is doubtful. Probably nothing except amputation of her arm would have saved her then, and we had nothing but a jackknife. She probably would have died of shock and loss of blood.

Grace lay on the floor to keep as quiet as possible and slow the absorption of the venom. "You'd better give me the strychnine now, dear," she told Jule. Jule snapped off the tip of one of the glass vials but the cylinder broke in her hands. She opened another tube and tried to fill the syringe; the needle was rusted shut. Jule selected another needle, tested it, and filled the syringe. "I'm afraid it will hurt," she told Grace. "Now don't worry, dear," said Grace comfortingly. "I know you'll do it very well."

11. **strychnine** [strik′ nən]: a poison that is a stimulant for the heart when used in small doses.

After the injection, Grace asked Jule to put a newspaper under her head to keep her hair from getting dirty. A few minutes later, the ambulance, with Wesley Dickinson following in his own car, arrived. Wesley had telephoned the hospital and arranged for blood transfusions and an iron lung.[12]

As Grace was lifted into the ambulance, she called back to Tanner, "Remember to cut up the meat for my frogs very fine and take good care of my snakes." That was the last we ever saw of her.

Grace died in the hospital half an hour later. She lived about ninety minutes after being bitten. In the hospital, Wesley directed the doctors to drain the blood out of her arm and pump in fresh blood. When her heart began to fail she was put into the lung. She had become unconscious. Then her heart stopped. Stimulants were given. The slow beating began again but grew steadily weaker. Each time stimulants were given, the heart responded less strongly, and finally stopped forever.

We waited with Mr. and Mrs. Tanner at the snake barn, calling the hospital at intervals. When we heard that Grace was dead, Mrs. Tanner burst into tears. "Grace was such a beautiful young girl—and so talented," she moaned. "There wasn't anything she couldn't do. Why did she ever want to mess around with those awful snakes?"

"I guess that's something none of us will ever understand," said her husband sadly.

Grace was born in Kansas in 1884. She studied entomology[13] at the University of Kansas and during field trips to collect insects it was a great joke among Grace's fellow students that she was terrified of even harmless garter snakes. Grace turned with a passionate interest to the creatures she had so long feared. In 1923 she became curator of the Museum of Natural History at the Minneapolis Public Library but quarreled with the directors, who felt that her reckless handling

12. **iron lung:** a device used to help the breathing of people whose chest muscles are paralyzed.
13. **entomology** [en′ tə mol′ ə jē]: the study of insects.

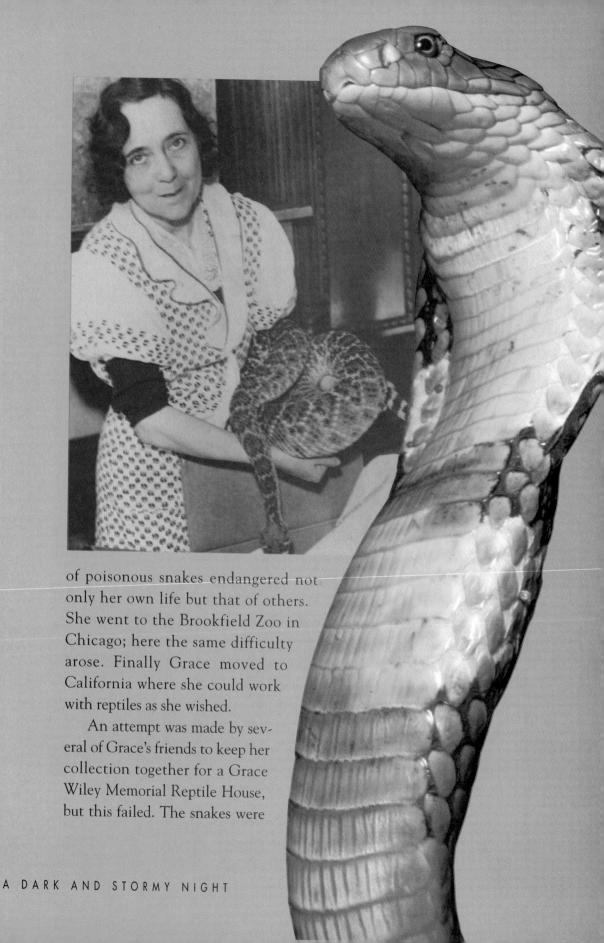

of poisonous snakes endangered not only her own life but that of others. She went to the Brookfield Zoo in Chicago; here the same difficulty arose. Finally Grace moved to California where she could work with reptiles as she wished.

An attempt was made by several of Grace's friends to keep her collection together for a Grace Wiley Memorial Reptile House, but this failed. The snakes were auctioned off and the snake that had killed Grace was purchased by a roadside zoo in Arizona; huge signboards bearing an artist's conception of the incident were erected for miles along the highways. So passed one of the most remarkable people I have ever known.

DANIEL P. MANNIX

Daniel P. Mannix, born in 1911, had a zoo in his own backyard when he was a child, but his pets were not the everyday kind of guinea pigs and rabbits. Young Mannix had foxes and skunks—and tarantulas, an alligator, and a vulture as well. When he went to the University of Pennsylvania to study writing, he sold zoo stories to the *Saturday Evening Post*. Before finishing college, Mannix decided to join a carnival. He spent the next three years as a sword-swallower and fire-eater called "The Great Zadma." This experience provided material for a book called *The Spangled Road*.

Mannix and his wife Jule have traveled to many places, finding background material for film scripts, television specials, and magazine articles. For a home base, they chose a Pennsylvania farm—and created a zoo in the backyard.

Mannix is best known as a nature writer. One most enjoyable book, *The Fox and the Hound*, has appeared as a movie. His nonfiction article, "Bat Quest," gives a compelling look at a misunderstood creature.

THE HIGHWAYMAN

ALFRED NOYES

Moonlight Ralph Albert Blakelock, c. 1885-1890,
oil on board, 12" X 16", Columbus Museum of Art, Ohio

PART ONE

The wind was a torrent of darkness among the gusty trees.
The moon was a ghostly galleon[1] tossed upon cloudy seas.
The road was a ribbon of moonlight over the purple moor,
And the highwayman came riding—
    Riding—riding—
The highwayman came riding, up to the old inn-door.

He'd a French cocked-hat on his forehead, a bunch of lace at his chin,
A coat of the claret[2] velvet, and breeches of brown doe-skin.
They fitted with never a wrinkle. His boots were up to the thigh.
And he rode with a jewelled twinkle,
    His pistol butts a-twinkle,
His rapier hilt[3] a-twinkle, under the jewelled sky.

Over the cobbles he clattered and clashed in the dark inn-yard.
He tapped with his whip on the shutters, but all was locked and barred.
He whistled a tune to the window, and who should be waiting there
But the landlord's black-eyed daughter,
    Bess, the landlord's daughter,
Plaiting a dark red love-knot into her long black hair.

And dark in the dark old inn-yard a stable-wicket[4] creaked
Where Tim the ostler[5] listened. His face was white and peaked.
His eyes were hollows of madness, his hair like mouldy hay,
But he loved the landlord's daughter,
    The landlord's red-lipped daughter.
Dumb as a dog he listened, and he heard the robber say—

1. **galleon** [gal′ ē ən]: a large sailing ship with three or four decks.
2. **claret** [klar′ ət]: dark purplish red.
3. **rapier hilt** [rā′ pē ər hilt]: handle of a long, light sword.
4. **stable-wicket** [stā′ bəl wik′ it]: a small door or gate in a horse stable.
5. **ostler** [os′ lər]: a person who cares for horses at an inn or stable.

"One kiss, my bonny sweetheart, I'm after a prize to-night,
But I shall be back with the yellow gold before the morning light;
Yet, if they press me sharply, and harry me through the day,
Then look for me by moonlight,
  Watch for me by moonlight,
I'll come to thee by moonlight, though hell should bar the way."

He rose upright in the stirrups. He scarce could reach her hand,
But she loosened her hair in the casement.[6] His face burnt like a brand
As the black cascade of perfume came tumbling over his breast;
And he kissed its waves in the moonlight,
  (O, sweet black waves in the moonlight!)
Then he tugged at his reins in the moonlight, and galloped away to the west.

PART TWO

He did not come in the dawning. He did not come at noon;
And out of the tawny sunset, before the rise of the moon,
When the road was a gypsy's ribbon, looping the purple moor,
A red-coat troop came marching—
  Marching—marching—
King George's men came marching, up to the old inn-door.

They said no word to the landlord. They drank his ale instead.
But they gagged his daughter, and bound her, to the foot of her narrow bed.
Two of them knelt at her casement, with muskets at their side!
There was death at every window;
  And hell at one dark window;
For Bess could see, through her casement, the road that *he* would ride.

6. **casement** [kās′ mənt]: a window that opens on hinges as a door does.

They had tied her up to attention, with many a sniggering jest.
They had bound a musket beside her, with the muzzle beneath her breast!
"Now, keep good watch!" and they kissed her. She heard the doomed man say—
Look for me by moonlight;
    Watch for me by moonlight;
I'll come to thee by moonlight, though hell should bar the way!

She twisted her hands behind her; but all the knots held good!
She writhed her hands till her fingers were wet with sweat or blood!
They stretched and strained in the darkness, and the hours crawled by like years,
Till, now, on the stroke of midnight,
    Cold, on the stroke of midnight,
The tip of one finger touched it! The trigger at least was hers!

The tip of one finger touched it. She strove no more for the rest.
Up, she stood up to attention, with the muzzle beneath her breast.
She would not risk their hearing; she would not strive again;
For the road lay bare in the moonlight;
    Blank and bare in the moonlight;
And the blood of her veins, in the moonlight, throbbed to her love's refrain.

Tlot-tlot; tlot-tlot! Had they heard it? The horsehoofs ringing clear;
Tlot-tlot, tlot-tlot, in the distance? Were they deaf that they did not hear?
Down the ribbon of moonlight, over the brow of the hill,
The highwayman came riding—
    Riding—riding—
The red-coats looked to their priming![7] She stood up, straight and still.

Tlot-tlot, in the frosty silence! *Tlot-tlot,* in the echoing night!
Nearer he came and nearer. Her face was like a light.
Her eyes grew wide for a moment; she drew one last deep breath,
Then her finger moved in the moonlight,
    Her musket shattered the moonlight,
Shattered her breast in the moonlight and warned him—with her death.

7. **priming** [prī′ ming]: powder used in guns and explosives.

He turned. He spurred to the west; he did not know who stood
Bowed, with her head o'er the musket, drenched with her own blood!
Not till the dawn he heard it, and his face grew gray to hear
How Bess, the landlord's daughter,
   The landlord's black-eyed daughter,
Had watched for her love in the moonlight, and died in the darkness there.

Back, he spurred like a madman, shouting a curse to the sky,
With the white road smoking behind him and his rapier brandished high.
Blood-red were his spurs in the golden noon; wine-red was his velvet coat;
When they shot him down on the highway,
   Down like a dog on the highway,
And he lay in his blood on the highway, with a bunch of lace at his throat.

And still of a winter's night, they say, when the wind is in the trees,
When the moon is a ghostly galleon tossed upon cloudy seas,
When the road is a ribbon of moonlight over the purple moor,
A highwayman comes riding—
   Riding—riding—
A highwayman comes riding, up to the old inn-door.

Over the cobbles he clatters and clangs in the dark inn-yard.
He taps with his whip on the shutters, but all is locked and barred.
He whistles a tune to the window, and who should be waiting there
But the landlord's black-eyed daughter,
   Bess, the landlord's daughter,
Plaiting a dark red love-knot into her long black hair.

ALFRED NOYES

Alfred Noyes (1880-1958) was born in Staffordshire, England. In his school days, he was active in athletics but also developed a great inter-est in writing. After his college years at Oxford, he settled down in London and devoted himself to writing.

Besides "The Highwayman," the other most well-known poem of Alfred Noyes is "Drake," an epic poem about the British naval hero, Sir Francis Drake. He also wrote *Tales of the Mermaid Tavern* and a novel, *No Other Man*, that was made into a Frank Capra movie in the 1940s.

DUFFY'S JACKET

BRUCE COVILLE

IF my cousin Duffy had the brains of a turnip it never would have happened. But as far as I'm concerned, Duffy makes a turnip look bright. My mother disagrees. According to her, Duffy is actually very bright. She claims the reason he's so scatterbrained is that he's too busy being brilliant inside his own head to remember everyday things. Maybe. But hanging around with Duffy means you spend a lot of time saying, "Your glasses, Duffy," or "Your coat, Duffy," or—well, you get the idea: a lot of three-word sentences that start with "Your," end with "Duffy," and have words like "book," "radio," "wallet," or whatever it is he's just put down and left behind, stuck in the middle.

Me, I think turnips are brighter.

But since Duffy's my cousin, and since my mother and her sister are both single parents, we tend to do a lot of things together—like camping, which is how we got into the mess I want to tell you about.

Personally, I thought camping was a big mistake. But since Mom and Aunt Elise are raising the three of us—me, Duffy, and my little sister, Marie—on their own, they're convinced they have to do man-stuff with us every once in a while. I think they read some kind of book that said me and Duffy would come out weird if they don't. You can take him camping all you want. It ain't gonna make Duffy normal.

Anyway, the fact that our mothers were getting wound up to do something fatherly, combined with the fact that Aunt Elise's boss had a friend who had a friend who said we could use his cabin, added up to the five of us bouncing along this horrible dirt road late one Friday in October.

It was late because we had lost an hour going back to get Duffy's suitcase. I suppose it wasn't actually Duffy's fault. No one remembered to say, "Your suitcase, Duffy," so he couldn't really have been expected to remember it.

"Oh, Elise," cried my mother, as we got deeper into the woods. "Aren't the leaves beautiful?"

That's why it doesn't make sense for them to try to do man-stuff with us. If it had been our fathers, they would have been drinking beer and burping and maybe telling dirty stories, instead of talking about the leaves. So why try to fake it?

Anyway, we get to this cabin, which is about eighteen million miles from nowhere, and to my surprise, it's not a cabin at all. It's a house. A big house.

"Oh, my," said my mother as we pulled into the driveway.

"Isn't it great?" chirped Aunt Elise. "It's almost a hundred years old, back from the time when they used to build big hunting lodges up here. It's the only one in the area still standing. Horace said he hasn't been able to get up here in some time. That's why he was glad to let us use it. He said it would be good to have someone go in and air the place out."

Leave it to Aunt Elise. This place didn't need airing out—it needed fumigating. I never saw so many spider webs in my life. From the sounds we heard coming from the walls, the mice seemed to have made it a population center. We found a total of two working light bulbs: one in the kitchen, and one in the dining room, which was paneled with dark wood and had a big stone fireplace at one end.

"Oh, my," said my mother again.

Duffy, who's allergic to about fifteen different things, started to sneeze.

"Isn't it charming?" said Aunt Elise hopefully.

No one answered her.

Four hours later we had managed to get three bedrooms clean enough to sleep in without getting the heebie-jeebies—one for Mom and Aunt Elise, one for Marie, and one for me and Duffy. After a supper of beans and franks we hit the hay, which I think is what our mattresses were stuffed with. As I was drifting off, which took about thirty seconds, it occurred to me that four hours of housework wasn't all that much of a man-thing, something it might be useful to remember the next time Mom got one of these plans into her head.

Things looked better in the morning when we went outside and found a stream where we could go wading. ("Your sneakers, Duffy.")

Later we went back and started poking around the house, which really was enormous.

That was when things started getting a little spooky. In the room next to ours I found a message scrawled on the wall. BEWARE THE SENTINEL,[1] it said in big black letters.

When I showed Mom and Aunt Elise, they said it was just a joke, and got mad at me for frightening Marie.

Marie wasn't the only one who was frightened.

We decided to go out for another walk. ("Your lunch, Duffy.") We went deep into the woods, following a faint trail that kept

1. **sentinel** [sen′ tə nəl]: a person who keeps watch and guards against surprise attacks.

threatening to disappear, but never actually faded away altogether. It was a hot day, even in the deep woods, and after a while we decided to take off our coats.

When we got back and Duffy didn't have his jacket, did they get mad at him? My mother actually had the nerve to say, "Why didn't you remind him? You know he forgets things like that."

What do I look like, a walking memo pad?

Anyway, I had other things on my mind—like the fact that I was convinced someone had been following us out of the woods.

I tried to tell my mother about it, but first she said I was being ridiculous, and then she accused me of trying to sabotage the trip.

So I shut up. But I was pretty nervous, especially when Mom and Elise announced that they were going into town—which was twenty miles away—to pick up some supplies (like light bulbs).

"You kids will be fine on your own," said Mom cheerfully. "You can make popcorn and play Monopoly. And there's enough soda here for you to make yourselves sick on."

And with that they were gone.

It got dark.

We played Monopoly.

They didn't come back. That didn't surprise me. Since Duffy and I were both fifteen they felt it was okay to leave us on our own, and Mom had warned us they might decide to have dinner at the little inn we had seen on the way up.

But I would have been happier if they had been there.

Especially when something started scratching on the door.

"What was that?" said Marie.

"What was what?" asked Duffy.

"That!" she said, and this time I heard it too. My stomach rolled over and the skin at the back of my neck started to prickle.

"Maybe it's the Sentinel!" I hissed.

"Andrew!" yelled Marie. "Mom told you not to say that."

"She said not to try to scare you," I said. "I'm not. *I'm scared!* I told you I heard something following us in the woods today."

Scratch, scratch.

"But you said it stopped," said Duffy. "So how would it know where we are now?"

"I don't know. I don't know what it is. Maybe it tracked us, like a bloodhound."

Scratch, scratch.

"Don't bloodhounds have to have something to give them a scent?" asked Marie. "Like a piece of clothing, or—"

We both looked at Duffy.

"Your jacket, Duffy!"

Duffy turned white.

"That's silly," he said after a moment.

"There's something at the door," I said frantically. "Maybe it's been lurking around all day, waiting for our mothers to leave. Maybe it's been waiting for years for someone to come back here."

Scratch, scratch.

"I don't believe it," said Duffy. "It's just the wind moving a branch. I'll prove it."

He got up and headed for the door. But he didn't open it. Instead he peeked through the window next to it. When he turned back, his eyes looked as big as the hard-boiled eggs we had eaten for supper.

"There's something out there!" he hissed. *"Something big!"*

"I told you," I cried. "Oh, I knew there was something there."

"Andrew, are you doing this just to scare me?" said Marie. "Because if you are—"

Scratch, scratch.

"Come on," I said, grabbing her by the hand. "Let's get out of here."

I started to lead her up the stairs.

"Not there!" said Duffy. "If we go up there we'll be trapped."

"You're right," I said. "Let's go out the back way!"

The thought of going outside scared the daylights out of me. But at least out there we would have somewhere to run. Inside—well, who knew what might happen if the thing found us inside.

We went into the kitchen.

I heard the front door open.

"Let's get out of here!" I hissed.

We scooted out the back door. "What now?" I wondered, looking around frantically.

"The barn," whispered Duffy. "We can hide in the barn."

"Good idea," I said. Holding Marie by the hand, I led the way to the barn. But the door was held shut by a huge padlock.

The wind was blowing harder, but not hard enough to hide the sound of the back door of the house opening, and then slamming shut.

"Quick!" I whispered. "It knows we're out here. Let's sneak around front. It will never expect us to go back into the house."

Duffy and Marie followed me as I led them behind a hedge. I caught a glimpse of something heading toward the barn and swallowed nervously. It was big. Very big.

"I'm scared," whispered Marie.

"Shhhh!" I hissed. "We can't let it know where we are."

We slipped through the front door. We locked it, just like people always do in the movies, though what good that would do I couldn't figure, since if something really wanted to get at us it would just break the window and come in.

"Upstairs," I whispered.

We tiptoed up the stairs. Once we were in our bedroom, I thought we were safe. Crawling over the floor, I raised my head just enough to peek out the window. My heart almost stopped. Standing in the moonlight was an enormous, manlike creature. It had a scrap of cloth in its hands. It was looking around—looking for us. I saw it lift its head and sniff the wind. To my horror, it started back toward the house.

"It's coming back!" I yelped, more frightened than ever.

"How does it know where we are?" said Marie.

But I knew how. It had Duffy's jacket. It was tracking us down, like some giant bloodhound.

We huddled together in the middle of the room, trying to think of what to do.

A minute later we heard it.

Scratch, scratch.

None of us moved.

Scratch, scratch.

We stopped breathing, then jumped up in alarm at a terrible crashing sound.

The door was down.

We hunched back against the wall as heavy footsteps came clomping up the stairs.

I wondered what our mothers would think when they got back. Would they find our bodies? Or would there be nothing left of us at all?

Thump. Thump. Thump.

It was getting closer.

Thump. Thump. Thump.

It was outside the door.

Knock, knock.

"Don't answer!" hissed Duffy.

Like I said, he doesn't have the brains of a turnip.

It didn't matter. The door wasn't locked. It came swinging open. In the shaft of light I saw a huge figure. The Sentinel of the Woods! It had to be. I thought I was going to die.

The figure stepped into the room. Its head nearly touched the ceiling.

Marie squeezed against my side tighter than a tick in a dog's ear.

The huge creature sniffed the air. It turned in our direction. Its eyes seemed to glow. Moonlight glittered on its fangs.

Slowly the Sentinel raised its arm. I could see Duffy's jacket dangling from its fingertips.

And then it spoke.

"You forgot your jacket, stupid."

It threw the jacket at Duffy, turned around, and stomped down the stairs.

Which is why, I suppose, no one has had to remind Duffy to remember his jacket, or his glasses, or his math book, for at least a year now.

After all, when you leave stuff lying around, you never can be sure just who might bring it back.

BRUCE COVILLE

Bruce Coville was born in Syracuse, New York, in 1950 and is married to Katherine Dietz, who has illustrated a number of his books. After attending Duke University, he returned to New York.

Growing up, Coville worked as a camp counselor, gravedigger, and toy maker, but when he settled down to writing, it was for life. Most of his work, both for children and young adults, is fantasy. Myth is very important to him, but, says Coville, "the first and foremost job in writing is to tell a whacking good story."

Among his creations are several musical plays. One, co-authored with Barbara Russell, is called *It's Midnight: Do You Know Where Your Toys Are?*

MONSTER

THEY DID THE MASH. THEY DID THE MONSTER MASH. THE MONSTER MASH. IT WAS A

WORDS AND MUSIC BY

BOBBY PICKETT AND LEONARD CAPIZZI

Spoken: I was

working in the lab late one night, when my eyes beheld an eerie sight, for my monster from his slab

began to rise, and suddenly, to my surprise (sung:) He/They did the

Copyright © 1962, 1973 Gary S. Paxton Music, Inc., Acoustic Music, Inc. and Capizzi Music Co.
1962 Copyright Renewed. All rights administered by Acoustic Music, Inc. P.O. Box 210317, Nashville, Tenn. 37221-0317.
International Copyright Secured. Made in U.S.A. All Rights Reserved.

1. *I was working in the lab late one night,*

When my eyes beheld an eerie sight,

For my monster from his slab began to rise,

And suddenly to my surprise

(to Chorus: He did the mash)

2. *From my laboratory in the castle east.*

To the master bedroom where the vampires feast.

The ghouls all came from their humble abodes

To catch a jolt from my electrodes.

(to Chorus: They did the mash)

Bridge (Spoken)

The zombies were having fun,

The party had just begun.

The guests included Wolf-man,

Dracula, and his son.

THEY DID THE MASH. THEY

3. The scene was rockin'; all were digging the sounds,

Igor on chains, backed by his baying hounds.

The coffin-bangers were about to arrive

With their vocal group "The Crypt-Kicker Five"

(to Chorus: They played the mash)

4. Out from his coffin, Drac's voice did ring;

Seems he was troubled by just one thing.

He opened the lid and shook his fist,

And said, "Whatever happened to my Transylvanian twist?"

(to Chorus: It's now the mash)

5. Now everything's cool, Drac's a part of the band

And my monster mash is the hit of the land.

For you, the living, this mash was meant too,

When you get to my door, tell them Boris sent you. (till fade)

(to Chorus: And you can mash)

DID THE MONSTER MASH.

Asking Big Questions About the Literature

How do you respond to suspense stories?

COMPARE & CONTRAST

Hair-Raising Experiences Have you had experiences that gave you physical responses similar to those you felt when reading selections in this unit? For example, do riding on roller coasters and speaking before large groups create the same tension as reading "The Monkey's Paw"?

Choose one or two selections that caused a strong reaction in you. Then write an essay in which you compare and contrast your reactions during hair-raising experiences with your feelings while reading the selections.

RANK the Stories

In your journal, make a chart to rank the suspense of each selection that you read in this unit. Use the following categories: *Absolutely gripping, Suspenseful, Mildly suspenseful,* and *Not very suspenseful.* Then give a reason for your evaluation. Compare your rankings with those of your classmates.

LITERATURE STUDY

Plot

The arrangement of events that make up a story is called the **plot**. A series of events leads to the high point in the story, called the *climax*. Events that occur before the climax make up the *rising action*. Events that occur after the climax make up the *falling action*. (*See "Plot" on page 118.*)

In your journal, draw a diagram as shown below. Then choose one suspense story from this unit and identify the rising action, the climax, and the falling action by adding important events from the story to the diagram.

climax

falling action

rising action

Literature	"The Monkey's Paw"
Evaluation	Absolutely gripping
Reason for Evaluation	Herbert's corpse at the front door was creepy; I didn't want to see it, yet I had to know what was going to happen.

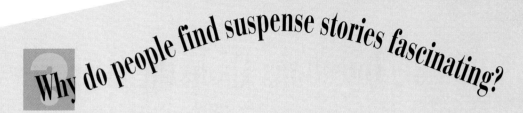

Why do people find suspense stories fascinating?

Understanding Emotions

Find the most suspenseful point in two of the selections that you read in this unit. At that point, did the suspense make you feel frightened? Queasy? Tense? Why did you keep reading, even though you might have been feeling emotions that people usually avoid?

Now write a suspense scene that will create those same emotions in your classmates. Read your scene aloud in class.

Illustrating

SUSPENSE...

Working with four or five other students, compile a list of thirty or so suspenseful story plots. In your list include films, short stories, novels, poems, legends, and campfire stories. Next, as a group, determine why each plot is suspenseful. Then work together to create a movie poster for one of these plots. Make sure your poster shows that your choice is a suspenseful movie. Ask the school library to display your poster.

Irony

Irony is a contrast between what characters seem to be and what they are—or between what is expected to happen and what happens. (See "Irony" on page 119.) Examples of irony include the following:

- characters who think they are kind but act cruelly,
- evil characters who become the victims of their own plots,
- characters whose petty greed backfires and robs them of something of value.

Work with a partner or a group of classmates to find irony in the stories that you read. Then make a chart like the one on this page

Title	Examples of Irony
"The Dinner Party"	Colonel says women have less nerve control; yet in a tense moment, a woman shows greater control.

Asking Big Questions About the Literature

What makes a good suspense story?

Irony

The **irony** of some stories is revealed in the justice that the characters get at the story's end. For example, a character may experience the bitter justice of getting a dose of his own medicine, like General Zaroff in "The Most Dangerous Game." (*See "Irony" on page 119.*)

Working with a group of students, choose a suspense story from this unit and list the fate of each main character. Then discuss whether each character deserved his or her fate. Did the characters get what they deserved? More than they deserved? Why? Summarize your conclusions in an oral classroom presentation.

Be an Armchair Explorer

Some suspense stories, such as "The Most Dangerous Game," contain references to colorful foreign locations, exotic creatures, and lifestyles of the very wealthy. These references help to create the mood or setting of the story.

Explore an exotic location of your own choosing or from one of the unit selections by doing library research, reading travel brochures, or watching travel videos. Photocopy or draw a map, pinpointing the location. Then write a story into which you weave the location.

THINKING Through Decisions

Part of what keeps readers on the edges of their seats is wondering what a character will do next—and what will happen as a result. Choose a main character from one suspense story in this unit. Then make a flowchart that shows the decisions that the character made, the decisions that the character could have made, and the results from each. Use your imagination to speculate on the results of decisions that the character could have made but didn't. Use the flowchart begun here as a model.

Share your completed flowchart in a small group. What general conclusions can you draw about characters' choices in suspense stories?

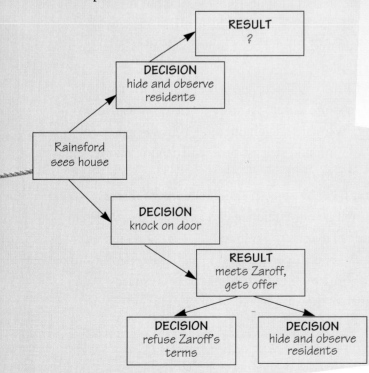

LITERATURE STUDY

Plot

Plot is the arrangement of events in a story. Writers might arrange events in chronological order—from first to last—or they may use foreshadowing and flashback.

Foreshadowing is the use of clues about what will happen next. For example, in "The Most Dangerous Game," gunshots in the story's beginning foreshadow later events. A *flashback* is a look back in time to what has happened before the story began. "A Running Brook of Horror" ends with a flashback about Grace Wiley's life. (*See "Plot" on page 118.*)

In your journal, list three examples of foreshadowing or flashback from this unit. Then write a paragraph explaining how each did—or didn't—affect your enjoyment of the story.

NOW *Choose a Project!*
Three projects involving suspense stories are described on the following pages.

Writing Workshop

WRITE A SUSPENSE STORY

One of the Big Questions in this unit asks, "What makes a good suspense story?" Your **purpose** in this project will be to answer that question by writing your own suspense story. You'll publish your story in a classroom anthology of suspense stories for an **audience** of other students in your school.

Prewriting

GETTING STARTED

Brainstorm for unusual events that might provide ideas for your story. List the ideas in your journal and think about how you could develop each one.

Once you've chosen a rough idea for your suspense story, develop a story plan. What is the setting? Who are the characters? Your suspense story should include at least one sympathetic character. What sort of life-or-death situation does the character face? Who is the audience for your story? Knowing your audience can help you decide what kinds of events to include.

A good suspense story puts characters in a situation in which readers hope for their success, yet fear that they might fail as time runs out. To increase the story's tension, the solutions the

Unusual Events

☆ Strange messages on answering machine ? ?

... new neighbors

🐕 dog—howls for no reason!

🏠 Antique watches... mom finds a box of watches in the attic.

??? Mystery in the mall

character tries shouldn't work right away. For example, in "The Most Dangerous Game," you hope that Rainsford can escape. Yet you also fear that Rainsford will be caught before the three days are up as he keeps trying—and failing—to escape.

In your journal, organize your ideas by making a story map as shown.

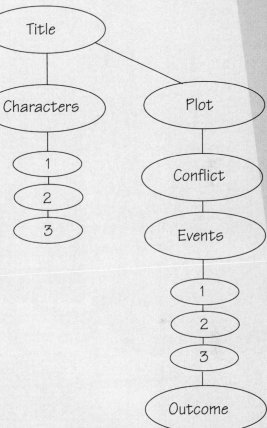

Drafting
YOUR STORY

Once you've identified story elements, you're ready to draft your story. You might follow these steps:

Draft a catchy beginning. To get readers interested in your story, introduce the main character, setting, and conflict.

Look at the beginning of a suspense story by student writer Sana Krasikov on page 111. In the first paragraph, she sets the stage for her story by describing an unusual, violent storm. The setting creates an atmosphere ripe for suspense. Most readers will be curious about the situation and will read on.

Then, in the second paragraph, Sana gets a tighter grip on her readers' interest when she introduces the character's dilemma with the sentence, "No use trying to sleep, knowing what I've done." Ah, ha! Readers know the character has done something bad, and there's no way they'll stop reading until they find out what it is. The remaining portion of Sana's suspense story (which isn't printed) is a flashback to the dark deed.

Build to the climax of the story. As you tell your story, use dialogue, description, and narration to build the action. Each event in the story should make the reader race to the climax.

As your story unfolds, you may withhold some information from readers. On the other hand, you might provide clues to lead readers down a trail of false expectations. Be sure not to give too much away; a good suspense story keeps readers on the edge of their seats.

Bring your story to a close. After the conflict is resolved, write an ending that will satisfy your readers. You might write a surprise ending, as in "The Most Dangerous Game."

Revising
YOUR STORY

Work with a group of peers to revise your story. Take turns reading your stories aloud. Begin by telling your group what you need help with. Ask yourselves questions such as the following:

- Will the beginning grab readers' interest? Why or why not?
- When are the characters' actions or dialogue not believable? (Read the dialogue aloud to check and see whether it sounds natural.)
- Where could the connections between events be clearer?
- How does the setting add to the suspense?
- What will the audience need or want to know that isn't stated?

If you want to speed up the pace of the action, try using short sentences. They'll make the action seem faster because readers are reading faster.

Editing
YOUR STORY

After you've finished revising, work with a partner to edit your story. Check for errors in spelling, usage, and punctuation. You don't want the mystery to be your punctuation! Correct your errors and make a publishable copy of your story.

Publishing
YOUR STORY

Share your story by creating a classroom anthology of suspense stories. With classmates you can design a cover, choose a title, and add illustrations or photographs. If your stories aren't too frightening, you could read them to fourth or fifth grade classes. If you do read them to these classes, be sure to read with expression and in a suspenseful way. Donate your anthology to the school library so that other students can check it out.

When Opportunity Knocks

by Sana Krasikov of Katonah, New York

The rain is pelting down my window pane. Crazy zig-zags of lightning stab through the darkness, illuminating my room in quick, violent flashes. Boom! Boom! Close thunder rattles the window, then fades in a low rolling rumble. My room turns phosphorous.

I cannot sleep. Every time that I shut my eyes, they open as if theirs is a force stronger than my own. Oh, it is no use. No use trying to sleep, knowing what I've done.

An hour ago I begged myself to sleep, thinking that dreamland might offer me a solution, a way out. But there is no solution. There is no way out. I've done something horrible, and I'm going to have to pay for it.

I knew what I was getting into and predicted the inevitable reactions, but I didn't imagine it being quite so dreadful.

Remorse. The dull life, the small little shame—they would have been better than this agony and anticipation. I remember how it all started. It plays over and over in my mind, like a movie I can't walk out on. The film is rolling.

Cooperative Learning

AT THE STROKE OF MIDNIGHT...

Have you ever wished that you could write, produce, and star in your own video? Here's your chance. This project will give you and a group of classmates a chance to choose a suspense story, create a script, and then star in your own video. Throughout the process of creating your video, remember your **purpose**—to create fist-clenching suspense—for an **audience** of fellow students.

Preparing THE SCRIPT

First, your group will need to choose a story. Consider these as possible sources: the stories in this unit, stories you've read, and your own writing. Next prepare a script that organizes the story into scenes. For each scene, determine the action, write dialogue, and choose sound effects. Everyone should take part in script preparation. Your script might look like the one below.

Next choose a director or two. Then decide who will play each character and perform each task. Use a chart like the one begun on page 113 to organize your efforts. Everyone will have more than one job.

SCENE: a basement	
ACTION: three girls walk around, one shines flashlight on ceiling pipes	**SOUND EFFECTS**
	(a screechy groaning)
DIALOGUE	
Miko: So, where's that sound coming from?	
Sandy: I'm looking! I'm looking!	
Juanita: (Yawns) It's probably just a giant, woman-killing rodent.	(a "clunk")
(All jump)	

Task	Persons
filming directors	DeWayne, Tishia
costume director	DeWayne
lighting director	Chivi
camera persons	Melissa, Jason
sound-effects creators	Melissa, Tishia
role of Miko	Chivi

Rehearsing YOUR VIDEO

Read through the dialogue and tighten the script where needed. Then shoot a complete rehearsal. As the group watches the tape of the rehearsal, everyone should offer suggestions for improvement. Look for places where the action lags, where the dialogue seems unnatural, or where the scenes don't naturally flow into one another.

Filming YOUR VIDEO

Before shooting the final video, film a title and credits. (Print the credits on large sheets of white paper and tape them on a wall. Film the paper.) As you film the story, improvise to avoid glitches. Also, remember that if something goes wrong, you can always stop the camera and film the scene again.

Presenting YOUR VIDEO

When filming is complete, the group can edit the film before sharing it. You might decide that certain segments should be cut or that music should be added. Show your video to friends and students in your school. You might even donate your video to the school library.

PROJECT 3

Helping Your Community

LOCAL MYSTERIES

Every community seems to have its unsolved mysteries and un-explained events. This project gives you an opportunity to research one of those mysteries in your community. You'll share your information—and possible solutions to the mystery—by going on the road with your classmates. You'll give oral presentations of your mystery to adults in your community.

Interviewing SOURCES

Your first step is to think of local unexplained events and unsolved mysteries. To get ideas, explore these sources:

- your grandparents and senior citizens in your community
- members of the local historical society and librarians
- local newspaper editors and reporters
- police detectives

As you speak with your sources, it's a good idea to take notes. For accuracy, you might even want to use a tape recorder. After you develop a list of mysteries, choose one that you want to research.

Who? - Grandma
      - Mrs Toby

What? - about town characters

- old houses
- weird storms

where to find ?
      - library

      - old newspapers
      - town hall

Researching
A MYSTERY

Talk to and interview as many people as possible about your mystery or unexplained event. Go back to the people with whom you originally spoke. Interview them in depth. Each source can lead you to other sources. As you gather information, keep looking for possible solutions to the mystery. As you speak to new sources, ask them to comment on your evolving ideas and explanations.

Also do library research, taking notes on your sources. Look for the *who, what, when, where,* and *why* of what you learn. Keep an ongoing log that summarizes each source of information and your theories. You can use the following as an example.

Person	Comments	Possible Explanation
Mrs. Toby	She said there were flashing	Could be an electrical
	lights in the sky. There was	thing . . . St. Elmo's Fire?
	a storm that night.	

Sharing
YOUR FINDINGS

After you've thoroughly explored your mystery, you're ready to share your findings. Team up with other students in your class. Contact local civic groups, fraternal organizations, retirement homes, and any other groups that would enjoy having guest speakers. You may want to take visual aids, such as photographs, strange rocks, or fossils, but remember, anything that you take must be portable. Don't be surprised if local television stations want to feature your findings—mysteries fascinate everyone!

Putting It All Together

What Have You Learned About Creating Suspense?

Now that you've finished *A Dark and Stormy Night*, think about what you've learned about how writers create suspense—and how you've created suspense in the activities in this unit. You might have noticed that suspense stories often begin with a scene from ordinary life that takes a sharp turn into the unexpected.

Imagine a scene from your daily life that could be the start of a mystery and then write a script for an audiotape drama. Your classmates can help you produce and record your audiotape. Share your audiotape with other students in your school.

MYSTERY AND SUSPENSE

Prewriting and Drafting   To begin, brainstorm for ordinary events that could provide the seeds for a good suspense story. Freewrite to develop the plot of each story idea. Which story idea seems most likely to interest your audience? Will that story lend itself to taping?

After choosing a story, draft a script. Your opening scene should establish the characters and the setting and then quickly move on to develop the conflict. Remember, you'll need to use dialogue to describe settings, to bridge any changes of location, and to explain any jumps in time. As you write, check to make sure that each scene flows naturally into the one that follows.

Revising and Editing   As you revise and edit, consider your audience. Will they think that the characters and situations are believable? Will your audience be able to follow the action? Will the action keep them on the edge of their seats?

After your teacher approves your script, classmates can help you to produce and record an audiotape of it. Tape your rehearsal, and use it as a guide for any further revising and editing of your script.

Presenting Your Audiotape Story   Play your audiotape for the class. You and your classmates may even want to present your tapes to the rest of the school as a Lunch-Hour Mystery series. You could also donate a copy of your audiotape to your local library.

Evaluating Your Work

Think Back About The Big Questions

With a partner, discuss the three Big Questions on pages 10-11 and the questions that you generated for **Now Think!** on page 11. Do you have trouble answering any of these questions now? In your journal, write several paragraphs discussing how your responses to the Big Questions and to your own questions have changed after your work in this unit.

Think Back About Your Work

Now think about your work in this unit. Include your reading, writing, activities, and projects. Evaluate your work by writing answers to the following questions. When you finish your self-evaluation, give it to your teacher.

- Which selections in the unit did you like the least? The most? Why?

- What are the *two* most important things that you learned about suspense stories as you worked on this unit?

- What did you learn about yourself as a reader—and as a writer— as a result of the readings and activities in this unit?

- If you could choose one activity to do again, which one would you choose? What would you do differently? Why?

- How would you rate your work in this unit? Use the following scale and give at least three reasons for the rating.

  1 = Outstanding   3 = Fair
  2 = Good   4 = Not as good as it could have been

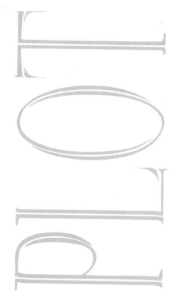

PLOT

What Is Plot?   A story's **plot** is the series of events that happen in the story. Most plots have the following pattern: The *exposition*, the beginning of a story, introduces the setting, the characters, and the conflict—the problems—that the characters will try to overcome. Next, in the *rising action* of the story, complications set in. Suspense builds as the characters struggle. Then, in the *climax*, the high point of the action, the conflict is resolved. Finally, in the *falling action*, the suspense is over and the results of the characters' actions are known to the reader. To speed up the plot, suspense stories often use vivid action verbs, short sentences, brief scenes, and concise descriptions.

Writing an Outscene   To speed up a story's plot, writers often refer to past events but don't fully describe them. These references are called outscenes. For example, in "The Most Dangerous Game" the general says, "I killed my first bear in the Caucasus when I was ten." This event itself could have been a suspense story. Choose an outscene from one of the stories that you've read. Then develop it into a separate story.

Telling a Suspense Story Through Poetry   You might think that it's a special challenge to tell a suspense story and make it rhyme, but "The Highwayman" does just that. Poetry, after all, makes use of brief scenes, concise language, and vivid verbs. In addition, poets can use language itself to create mood and a setting. For example, in "The Highwayman," repeating the "c" sound in the line "Over the cobbles he clattered and clashed" suggests the sound of a horse's hoofbeats. Try telling your own story through rhyming poetry. With a partner, brainstorm for story ideas. Try out different rhyme patterns by experimenting with those of existing poems or songs. Then write your own poem. Read it to your partner and then share it with classmates by reading it aloud.

What Is Irony?

Irony is the contrast between what things seem to be and what they are. In *irony of speech*, a speaker says one thing but means the opposite. For example, a speaker who says, "Let children eat candy—dentists need the money" actually wants readers to do the opposite. *Irony of character* contrasts what a character seems to be and what he or she truly is. Take, for example, the character who proclaims his honesty, yet never passes up the opportunity for a small dishonesty. *Irony of situation* contrasts what is expected to happen with what does happen. For example, a grandmother promises her grandson the best dog in the world—and gives him her sickly poodle. Irony is often subtle and requires an alert reader to spot it.

Dramatizing Irony in Ordinary Life   One of the reasons irony is so common in fiction is that it's so common in ordinary life. People often have plans and expectations that backfire. For example, you try to get a friend on your sports team—and your friend ends up taking your place on the team. With a small group of peers, brainstorm for real events that show irony of situation. Begin by thinking of events that have happened to you and to people you know. As a group, choose one event to dramatize in a skit. Then draft a chain of events. Decide how to develop the characters. Next, choose roles. After a brief rehearsal, dramatize the event for the class.

Looking for Irony of Character   The physical appearance of fictional characters may intentionally create irony. For instance, in "The Most Dangerous Game," General Zaroff first appears as "a slender man in evening clothes" who speaks in "a cultivated voice." Readers expect Zaroff to be a refined and cultured gentleman—the opposite of what he truly is. Draw a sketch of a character from this unit whose outward appearance implies some irony of character. Then, working in pairs, challenge your partner to find the irony in your sketch.

GLOSSARY OF LITERARY TERMS

A

alliteration   Repetition of the first sound—usually a consonant sound—in several words of a sentence or a line of poetry.

allusion   An author's indirect reference to someone or something that is presumed to be familiar to the reader.

anecdote   A short narrative about an interesting or a humorous event, usually in the life of a person.

antagonist   The person or force opposing the protagonist, or main character in a literary work. [See also *protagonist*.]

autobiography   A person's written account of his or her own life.

B

ballad   A poem, often a song, that tells a story in simple verse.

biography   An account of a person's life, written by another person.

blank verse   Unrhymed poetry.

C

character   A person or an animal that participates in the action of a work of literature. A *dynamic character* is one whose thoughts, feelings, and actions are changeable and lifelike; a *static character* always remains the same. [See also *protagonist, antagonist*.]

characterization   The creation of characters through the characters' use of language and through descriptions of their appearance, thoughts, emotions, and actions. [See also *character*.]

chronology   An arrangement of events in the order in which they happen.

cliché   An overused expression that is trite rather than meaningful.

climax   The highest point of tension in the plot of a work of literature. [See also *plot*.]

comedy   An amusing play that has a happy ending.

conclusion   The final part or ending of a piece of literature.

concrete poem   A poem arranged on the page so that its punctuation, letters, and lines make the shape of the subject of the poem.

conflict   A problem that confronts the characters in a piece of literature. The conflict may be *internal* (a character's struggle within himself or herself) or *external* (a character's struggle against nature, another person, or society). [See also *plot*.]

context   The general sense of words that helps readers to understand the meaning of unfamiliar words and phrases in a piece of writing.

D

description   An author's use of words to give the reader or listener a mental picture, an impression, or an understanding of a person, place, thing, event, or idea.

dialect   A form of speech spoken by people in a particular group or geographical region that differs in vocabulary, grammar, and pronunciation from the standard language.

dialogue   The spoken words and conversation of characters in a work of literature.

drama   A play that is performed before an audience according to stage directions and using dialogue. Classical drama has two genres: *tragedy* and *comedy*. Modern drama includes *melodrama, satire, theater of the absurd,* and *pantomime*. [See also *comedy, play,* and *tragedy*.]

dramatic poetry   A play written in the form of poetry.

E

epic   A long narrative poem—written in a formal style and meant to be read aloud—that relates the adventures and

experiences of one or more great heroes or heroines.

essay   Personal nonfiction writing about a particular subject that is important to the writer.

excerpt   A passage from a larger work that has been taken out of its context to be used for a special purpose.

exposition   Writing that explains, analyzes, or defines.

extended metaphor   An elaborately drawn out metaphor. [See also *metaphor*.]

F

fable   A short, simple story whose purpose is to teach a lesson, usually with animal characters who talk and act like people.

fantasy   Imaginative fiction about unrealistic characters, places, and events.

fiction   Literature, including the short story and the novel, that tells about imaginary people and events.

figurative language Language used to express ideas through figures of speech: descriptions that aren't meant to be taken literally. Types of figurative language include *simile, metaphor, extended metaphor, hyperbole,* and *personification.*

figure of speech   A type of figurative language, not meant to be taken literally, that expresses something in such a way that it brings the thing to life in the reader's or listener's imagination. [See also *figurative language.*]

flashback   A break in a story's action that relates a past happening in order to give the reader background information about a present action in the story.

folktale   A story that has been passed along from storyteller to storyteller for generations. Kinds of folktales include *tall tales, fairy tales, fables, legends,* and *myths.*

foreshadowing   The use of clues to create suspense by giving the reader or audience hints of events to come.

free verse   Poetry that has no formal rhyme scheme or metrical pattern.

G

genre   A major category of art. The three major literary genres are poetry, prose, and drama.

H

haiku   A three-line Japanese verse form. In most haiku, the first and third lines have five syllables, while the second line has seven. The traditional haiku describes a complicated feeling or thought in simple language through a single image.

hero/heroine   The main character in a work of literature. In heroic literature, the hero or heroine is a particularly brave, noble, or clever person whose achievements are unusual and important. [See also *character.*]

heroic age   The historical period in western civilization—from about 800 B.C. through A.D. 200—during which most works of heroic literature, such as myths and epics, were created in ancient Greece and Rome.

hubris   Arrogance or excessive pride leading to mistakes; the character flaw in a hero of classical tragedy.

hyperbole   An obvious exaggeration used for emphasis. [See also *figurative language.*]

I

idiom   An expression whose meaning cannot be understood from the ordinary meaning of the words. For example, *It's raining cats and dogs.*

imagery   The words and phrases in writing that appeal to the senses of sight, hearing, taste, touch, and smell.

irony An effect created by a sharp contrast between what is expected and what is real. An *ironic twist* in a plot is an event that is the complete opposite of what the characters have been hoping or expecting will happen. An *ironic statement* declares the opposite of the speaker's literal meaning.

J

jargon Words and phrases used by a group of people who share the same profession or special interests in order to refer to technical things or processes with which they are familiar. In general, jargon is any terminology that sounds unclear, overused, or pretentious.

L

legend A famous folktale about heroic actions, passed along by word of mouth from generation to generation. The legend may have begun as a factual account of real people and events but has become mostly or completely fictitious.

limerick A form of light verse, or humorous poetry, written in one five-line stanza with a regular scheme of rhyme and meter.

literature The branch of art that is expressed in written language and includes all written genres.

lyric poem A short poem that expresses personal feelings and thoughts in a musical way. Originally, lyrics were the words of songs that were sung to music played on the lyre, a stringed instrument invented by the ancient Greeks.

M

metamorphosis The transformation of one thing, or being, into another completely different thing or being, such as a caterpillar's change into a butterfly.

metaphor Figurative language in which one thing is said to be another thing. [See also *figurative language*.]

meter The pattern of rhythm in lines of poetry. The most common meter, in poetry written in English, is iambic pentameter, that is, a verse having five metrical feet, each foot of verse having two syllables, an unaccented one followed by an accented one.

mood The feeling or atmosphere that a reader senses while reading or listening to a work of literature.

motivation A character's reasons for doing, thinking, feeling, or saying something. Sometimes an author will make a character's motivation obvious from the beginning. In realistic fiction and drama, however, a character's motivation may be so complicated that the reader discovers it gradually, by studying the character's thoughts, feelings, and behavior.

myth A story, passed along by word of mouth for generations, about the actions of gods and goddesses or superhuman heroes and heroines. Most myths were first told to explain the origins of natural things or to justify the social rules and customs of a particular society.

N

narration The process of telling a story. For both fiction and nonfiction, there are two main kinds of narration, based on whether the story is told from a first-person or third-person point of view. [See also *point of view*.]

narrative poem A poem that tells a story containing the basic literary ingredients of fiction: character, setting, and plot.

narrator The person, or voice, that tells a story. [See also *point of view, voice*.]

nonfiction Prose that is factually true and is about real people, events, and places.

nonstandard English
Versions of English, such as slang and dialects, that use pronunciation, vocabulary, idiomatic expressions, grammar, and punctuation that differ from the accepted "correct" constructions of English.

novel   A long work of narrative prose fiction. A novel contains narration, a setting or settings, characters, dialogue, and a more complicated plot than a short story.

O

onomatopoeia   The technique of using words that imitate the sounds they describe, such as *hiss*, *buzz*, and *splash*.

oral tradition   Stories, poems, and songs that have been kept alive by being told, recited, and sung by people over many generations. Since the works were not originally written, they often have many different versions.

P

parable   A brief story—similar to a fable, but about people—that describes an ordinary situation and concludes with a short moral or lesson to be learned.

personification   Figurative language in which an animal, an object, or an idea is given human characteristics. [See also *figurative language*.]

persuasion   A type of speech or writing whose purpose is to convince people that something is true or important.

play   A work of dramatic literature written for performance by actors before an audience. In classical or traditional drama, a play is divided into five acts, each containing a number of scenes. Each act represents a distinct phase in the development of the plot. Modern plays often have only one act and one scene.

playwright   The author of a play.

plot   The sequence of actions and events in fiction or drama. A traditional plot has at least three parts: the *rising action*, leading up to a turning point that affects the main character; the *climax*, the turning point or moment of greatest intensity or interest; and the *falling action*, leading away from the conflict, or resolving it.

poetry   Language selected and arranged in order to say something in a compressed or nonliteral way. Modern poetry may or may not use many of the traditional poetic techniques that include *meter*, *rhyme*, *alliteration*, *figurative language*, *symbolism*, and *specific verse forms*.

point of view   The perspective from which a writer tells a story. *First-person* narrators tell the story from their own point of view, using pronouns such as *I* or *me*. *Third-person* narrators, using pronouns such as *he*, *she*, or *them*, may be *omniscient* (knowing everything about all characters), or *limited* (taking the point of view of one character). [See also *narration*.]

propaganda   Information or ideas that may or may not be true, but are spread as though they are true, in order to persuade people to do or believe something.

prose   The ordinary form of written and spoken language used to create fiction, nonfiction, and most drama.

protagonist   The main character of a literary work. [See also *character* and *characterization*.]

R

refrain   A line or group of lines that is repeated, usually at the end of each verse, in a poem or a song.

repetition   The use of the same formal element more than once in a literary work, for emphasis or in order to achieve another desired effect.

resolution   The falling action in fiction or drama,

including all of the developments that follow the climax and show that the story's conflict is over. [See also *plot*.]

rhyme scheme A repeated pattern of similar sounds, usually found at the ends of lines of poetry or poetic drama.

rhythm In poetry, the measured recurrence of accented and unaccented syllables in a particular pattern. [See also *meter*.]

S

scene The time, place, and circumstances of a play or a story. In a play, a scene is a section of an act. [See also *play*.]

science fiction Fantasy literature set in an imaginary future, with details and situations that are designed to seem scientifically possible.

setting The time and place of a work of literature.

short story Narrative prose fiction that is shorter and has a less complicated plot than a novel. A short story contains narration, at least one setting, at least one character, and usually some dialogue.

simile Figurative language that compares two unlike things, introduced by the words "like" or "as." [See also *figurative language*.]

soliloquy In a play, a short speech spoken by a single character when he or she is alone on the stage. A soliloquy usually expresses the character's innermost thoughts and feelings, when he or she thinks no other characters can hear.

sonnet A poem written in one stanza, using fourteen lines of iambic pentameter. [See also *meter*.]

speaker In poetry, the individual whose voice seems to be speaking the lines. [See also *narration*, *voice*.]

stage directions The directions, written by the playwright, to tell the director, actors, and theater technicians how a play should be dramatized. Stage directions may specify such things as how the setting should appear in each scene, how the actors should deliver their lines, when the stage curtain should rise and fall, how stage lights should be used, where on the stage the actors should be during the action, and when sound effects should be used.

stanza A group of lines in poetry set apart by blank lines before and after the group; a poetic verse.

style The distinctive way in which an author composes a work of literature in written or spoken language.

suspense An effect created by authors of various types of fiction and drama, especially adventure and mystery, to heighten interest in the story.

symbol An image, person, place, or thing that is used to express the idea of something else.

T

tall tale A kind of folk tale, or legend, that exaggerates the characteristics of its hero or heroine.

theme The main idea or underlying subject of a work of literature.

tone The attitude that a work of literature expresses to the reader through its style.

tragedy In classical drama, a tragedy depicts a noble hero or heroine who makes a mistake of judgment that has disastrous consequences.

V

verse A stanza in a poem. Also, a synonym for poetry as a genre. [See also *stanza*.]

voice The narrator or the person who relates the action of a piece of literature. [See also *speaker*.]

ACKNOWLEDGMENTS

Grateful acknowledgment is made for permission to reprint the following copyrighted material.

"The Tell-Tale Heart" by Edgar Allan Poe is reprinted from *The Complete Works of Edgar Allan Poe*, edited by James A. Harrison, New York, 1902.

"The Monkey's Paw" by W.W. Jacobs is reprinted from *Classic Ghost Stories* by W. W. Jacobs, Dover Publications, Inc., New York, 1975.

"The Most Dangerous Game" by Richard Connell. Copyright 1924 by Richard Connell. Renewed 1952 by Louise Fox Connell. Reprinted by permission of Brandt & Brandt Literary Agents, Inc.

"The Dinner Party" by Mona Gardner, copyright 1942, ©1970 by SATURDAY REVIEW, reprinted by permission of Bill Berger Associates, Inc.

"A Running Brook of Horror," from *All Creatures Great and Small* by Daniel P. Mannix, copyright © 1963, renewed ©1991 by Daniel P. Mannix, is reprinted by permission of Harold Matson Company, Inc.

"The Highwayman" by Alfred Noyes is reprinted from *Collected Poems by Alfred Noyes* by permission of Hugh Noyes, England.

"Duffy's Jacket" by Bruce Coville, copyright © 1989 by Bruce Coville. First published in *Things That Go Bump in The Night*, edited by Jane Yolen and Martin H. Greenberg.

ILLUSTRATION

20 Alex Cervany; 26-32 Daniel Derdula.

PHOTOGRAPHY

4 *t* Jim Whitmer/Stock Boston; *b* Jean-Claude Lejeune; 5 Private Collection, Switzerland; 6 Nancy Sheehan; 8 J.A. Kraulis/Masterfile; 10 *t* Nancy Sheehan; *b* David Strickler/The Image Works; 11 *t* Robert Finken/The Picture Cube; *m* Jim Whitmer/Stock Boston; *b* Julie Bidwell/©D.C. Heath; 12-19 *t* Scott M. Morgan; 19 inset Bettman Archive; 33 UPI/Bettmann; 34-35 Private Collection, Switzerland. Colorfoto: Hans Hinz. ©Paul Klee/VAGA, NY 1995; 37 Paul-Klee-Stiftung, Kunstmuseum, Bern. ©Paul Klee/VAGA, NY 1995; 41 Museum Folkwang, Essen; 44, 49 ©1993 by VG Bild-Kunst Bonn. Paul-Klee-Stiftung, Kunstmuseum, Bern; 52 Beyeler Collection, Basel. ©Paul Klee/VAGA, NY 1995; 57 Courtesy of The Fogg Art Museum, Harvard University Art Museums. Gift of Mr. and Mrs. Alfred Jaretzki, Jr.; 62 Paul-Klee-Stiftung, Kunstmuseum, Bern. ©Paul Klee/VAGA, NY 1995; 63 Courtesy of Brandt and Brandt Literary Agents, Inc.; 64, 66 Courtesy of the University Museums, University of Mississippi Cultural Center; 68 AP/Wide World Photos; 69 *l* Michael Fogden/Animals Animals/Earth Scenes; *r* Joe McDonald/Animals Animals/Earth Scenes; 71 Paul Freed/Animals Animals/Earth Scenes; 72 Phil A. Dotson/Photo Researchers; 73 Brownie Harris/The Stock Market; 75 Zig Leszczynski/Animals Animals/Earth Scenes; 77 Andrew Rakoczy/Photo Researchers; 78 Robert Zappalorti/Photo Researchers; 79 Zig Leszczynski/Animals Animals/Earth Scenes; 80-81 Michael Fogden/Animals Animals/Earth Scenes; 82 *l* Courtesy of Minneapolis Public Library Archives; 82 *r* Zig Leszczynski/Animals Animals/Earth Scenes; 83 Courtesy of Harold Mason Company, Inc.; 84 Columbus Museum of Art, Ohio. Bequest of John R. and Louise Lersch Gobey; 89 AP/Wide World Photos; 90 *l* Jon Nickson; 90-91 Alvin Upitus/The Image Bank; 92-93 Robert Farber/The Image Bank; 94-95 Tim Bieber/The Image Bank; 96-97 Hans Neleman/The Image Bank; 97 David Revette/Courtesy of Harper Collins Publishers; 104 Nancy Sheehan/©D.C. Heath; 106 J. Berndt/Stock Boston; 107 Mark Daniels; 109 PEANUTS reprinted by permission of UFS, Inc.; 110 Tom Ives/The Stock Market; 110-111 Ken O'Donoghue/©D.C. Heath; 112 *t* Sarah Putnam/©D.C. Heath; *b* Nancy Sheehan/©D.C. Heath; 113 Nancy Sheehan/©D.C. Heath; 114 Rhoda Sidney/Stock Boston.
Back cover *t* Jim Whitmer/Stock Boston; *c* Sarah Putnam/©D.C. Heath; *b* John Owens/©D.C. Heath.

Full Pronunciation Key for Footnoted Words

(Each pronunciation and definition is adapted from *Scott, Foresman Advanced Dictionary* by E.L. Thorndike and Clarence L. Barnhart.)

The pronunciation of each footnoted word is shown just after the word, in this way: **abbreviate** [ə brē′ vē āt]. The letters and signs used are pronounced as in the words below. The mark ′ is placed after a syllable with primary or heavy accent, as in the example above. The mark ′ after a syllable shows a secondary or lighter accent, as in **abbreviation** [ə brē′ vē ā′ shən].

Some words, taken from foreign languages, are spoken with sounds that do not otherwise occur in English. Symbols for these sounds are given in the key as "foreign sounds."

						foreign sounds
a	hat, cap	j	jam, enjoy	u	cup, butter	
ā	age, face	k	kind, seek	ù	full, put	Y as in French *du*.
ä	father, far	l	land, coal	ü	rule, move	Pronounce (ē) with
		m	me, am	v	very, save	the lips rounded as
b	bad, rob	n	no, in	w	will, woman	for (ü).
ch	child, much	ng	long, bring	y	young, yet	
d	did, red			z	zero, breeze	å as in French *ami*.
		o	hot, rock	zh	measure, seizure	Pronounce (ä) with
e	let, best	ō	open, go			the lips spread and
ē	equal, be	ô	order, all	ə represents:		held tense.
ėr	term, learn	oi	oil, voice		a in about	
		ou	house, out		e in taken	œ as in French *peu*.
f	fat, if				i in pencil	Pronounce (ā) with the
g	go, bag	p	paper, cup		o in lemon	lips rounded as for (ō).
h	he, how	r	run, try		u in circus	
		s	say, yes			N as in French *bon*.
i	it, pin	sh	she, rush			The N is not pro-
ī	ice, five	t	tell, it			nounced, but shows
		th	thin, both			that the vowel before
		ᴛʜ	then, smooth			it is nasal.

H as in German *ach*. Pronounce (k) without closing the breath passage.

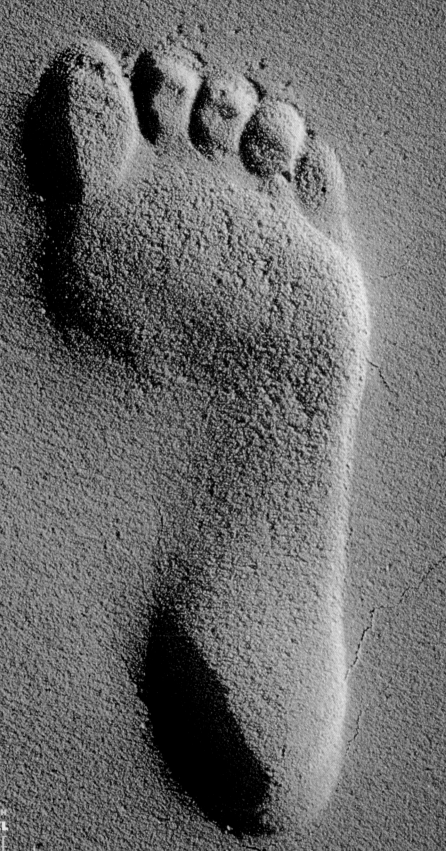

To be Somebody

To Be Somebody

▼
T H E M E
IDENTITY AND SELF-ESTEEM

A U T H O R S

Donna Alvermann
Linda Miller Cleary
Kenneth Donelson
Donald Gallo
Alice Haskins
J. Howard Johnston
John Lounsbury
Alleen Pace Nilsen
Robert Pavlik
Jewell Parker Rhodes
Alberto Alvaro Ríos
Sandra Schurr
Lyndon Searfoss
Julia Thomason
Max Thompson
Carl Zon

STAFF CREDITS

EDITORIAL	Barbara A. Brennan, Susan Belt Cogley, DeVona Dors, Christopher Johnson, Rita M. Sullivan, Patricia B. Weiler
	Proofreading: JoAnne B. Sgroi
CONTRIBUTING WRITERS	Kathy Tuchman Glass, Jo Pitkin
SERIES DESIGN	Robin Herr
BOOK DESIGN	Caroline Bowden, Daniel Derdula, Susan Geer, Diana Maloney, Angela Sciaraffa, Bonnie Chayes Yousefian
	Art Editing: Carolyn Langley
PHOTOGRAPHY	*Series Photography Coordinator:* Carmen Johnson
	Photo Research Supervisor: Martha Friedman
	Photo Researchers: Wendy Enright, Linda Finigan, Po-yee McKenna, PhotoSearch, Inc., Gillian Speeth, Denise Theodores
	Assignment Photography Coordinators: Susan Doheny, Gayna Hoffman, Shawna Johnston
COMPUTER PREPRESS	Ricki Pappo, Kathy Meisl
	Richard Curran, Michele Locatelli
PERMISSIONS	Dorothy B. McLeod
PRODUCTION	Patrick Connolly

Cover Photograph: © Photonica/Sigeru Ueki. **Cover Design:** Caroline Bowden

Acknowledgments for copyrighted material are on page 127 and constitute an extension of this page.

Published simultaneously in Canada

Printed in the United States of America

International Standard Book Number: 0-669-32108-7 (soft cover)
    6 7 8 9 10-RRD-99

International Standard Book Number: 0-669-38177-2 (hard cover)
    5 6 7 8 9 10-RRD-99

Middle Level Authors

Donna Alvermann, University of Georgia
Alice Haskins, Howard County Public Schools, Maryland
J. Howard Johnston, University of South Florida
John Lounsbury, Georgia College
Sandra Schurr, University of South Florida
Julia Thomason, Appalachian State University
Max Thompson, Appalachian State University
Carl Zon, California Assessment Collaborative

Literature and Language Arts Authors

Linda Miller Cleary, University of Minnesota
Kenneth Donelson, Arizona State University
Donald Gallo, Central Connecticut State University
Alleen Pace Nilsen, Arizona State University
Robert Pavlik, Cardinal Stritch College, Milwaukee
Jewell Parker Rhodes, Arizona State University
Alberto Alvaro Ríos, Arizona State University
Lyndon Searfoss, Arizona State University

Teacher Consultants

Suzanne Aubin, Patapsco Middle School, Ellicott City, Maryland
Judy Baxter, Newport News Public Schools, Newport News, Virginia
Saundra Bryn, Director of Research and Development, El Mirage, Arizona
Lorraine Gerhart, Elmbrook Middle School, Elm Grove, Wisconsin
Kathy Tuchman Glass, Burlingame Intermediate School, Burlingame, California
Lucretia Pannozzo, John Jay Middle School, Katonah, New York
Carol Schultz, Jerling Junior High, Orland Park, Illinois
Jeanne Siebenman, Grand Canyon University, Phoenix, Arizona
Gail Thompson, Garey High School, Pomona, California
Rufus Thompson, Grace Yokley School, Ontario, California
Tom Tufts, Conniston Middle School, West Palm Beach, Florida
Edna Turner, Harpers Choice Middle School, Columbia, Maryland
C. Anne Webb, Buerkle Junior High School, St. Louis, Missouri
Geri Yaccino, Thompson Junior High School, St. Charles, Illinois

CONTENTS

THE LITERATURE

Maine Painting, Summer Cycle#1 Anne Neely

ASKING BIG QUESTIONS ABOUT
THE LITERATURE

PROJECTS

ALL ABOUT
PEOPLE

What makes you unique and interesting? What's fascinating about your classmates? To find out, pair up with a classmate and interview one another to find out what makes each of you an individual. Then introduce your partner to a small group. Use your introductions to make the audience want to know your partner better.

1 Ask Good Questions

If you ask your partner good questions, you'll be more likely to get good answers. So take a few minutes to create a list of about fifteen questions that require more than a *yes* or a *no* answer. Remember to respect your partner's privacy. Use questions like the ones shown in the box.

Questions to Start Your Interview

1. Where did you grow up?
2. Who are your family members and pets?
3. Which of your relatives is most interesting? Why?
4. What are your hobbies and interests?
5. What are some of your most memorable experiences?

Get the 2 Facts Straight

As you interview your partner, take notes. Don't worry if your partner doesn't answer every question. Sometimes other interesting questions will come up as you talk. When you've finished your interview, read your notes to your partner. Did you get the facts straight? Make corrections as needed.

Introduce 3 an Interesting Person

Plan to spend three to five minutes introducing your partner to a small group. Keep the tips below in mind as you prepare to speak.

Guidelines for Your Introduction

- Begin by stating your partner's name.
- Focus on things about your partner that are positive and interesting.
- As you speak, you'll probably want to refer to your notes, but try to keep eye contact with your audience members. You'll want them to feel as if you're talking to them, not at them.
- Remember that the audience doesn't know what you know about your partner. Be sure to give complete explanations and descriptions.

After you listen to other people's introductions, don't be shy about applauding. After all, you've just been introduced to an interesting person!

Asking Big Questions About the Theme

What makes each person unique?

What makes you . . . *you*? Where does your sense of identity come from? Your activities and hobbies? Your special talents? Your friends? Your ethnic heritage and family? Create a web of your ideas like the one begun here. Then write in your journal to develop your ideas.

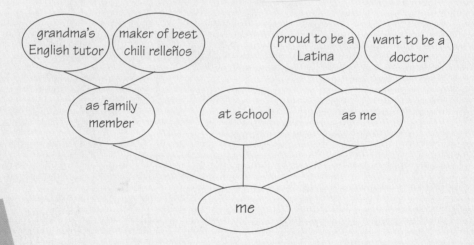

If you had to choose only four words to describe yourself, which four would you choose? Think of your positive qualities, the ones that make you unique. Then, in your journal, write the four words that best capture who you are. Tell why you chose those words and why those words are better than any others.

How do people express their individuality?

What do people express about their individuality through their choice of clothing and hairstyle? Make a collage or a drawing that shows people expressing their individuality through their outward appearance. Use images from magazines and newspapers—or take photographs. Choose a title for your collage that sums up the ideas that your collage illustrates.

What do people care about?

age 6	age 7	age 9
First day of school	Grandma moves in.	Mom changes jobs.

Think about the last seven years of your life. What were the most important events, the ones you cared about most? Draw a time line of those events and label them. Then imagine what your future will be like. Plot possible important future events on your time line. See the beginning of a sample time line shown above.

When you finish, share your time line with a small group of peers. Are there any similarities in what you and your classmates care about?

NOW

Think!

In your journal, list your own questions about what shapes you as a person. As you read the literature and complete the activities and projects, consider the Big Questions and your own questions.

TREE

ALDEN R. CARTER

"We are planning an amicable divorce," Mom said. Dad smiled lovingly at her, as if they hadn't spent the last year at each other's throats.

"Amicable means friendly," Sonia whispered, not looking up from her book.

I glared at her. "I know what it means."

"Mmmm . . ." she said, turning page about six hundred and

HOUSE

starting to study a diagram of the human circulatory system. I could make out the title atop the page: *Gray's Anatomy*.[1] Well, at least I could understand the name of this one.

"Better not drop that book on your foot," I said. "You'll be on crutches for a month."

"I'm trying to read, Phil. Please shut up."

1. *Gray's Anatomy* [grāz ə nat′ ə mē]: a well-known book on the science of the structure of the body by nineteenth-century English doctor, Henry Gray.

Mom paused in the middle of something about her and Dad being mature people who could rise above their differences long enough to "deconstruct" their marriage. She stared at me icily. Dad cleared his throat and said, "Phillip, I would think you'd be interested in hearing about something that is going to deeply affect your life."

"*To deeply affect* is a split infinitive, Dad," Sonia said, and turned a page.

Dad gazed at her admiringly, then turned to Mom. "She never misses a trick does she? Go on, dear."

After another two minutes of congratulating herself and Dad on their maturity, Mom got down to it. "Now the most difficult matter is how we are going to divide the family. We talked to Richard this morning before he left for the chess tournament. He's decided to graduate a year early and move to Minneapolis with your father as soon as school's out. That way he'll be able to take some classes at the U this summer and—"

"But, Mom," I blurted. "How about football and basketball? I mean, heck, the teams are going to fall—"

"Moseburg High will have to take care of itself without Richard. Now, since he is going to Minneapolis, you'll be staying here with me. That leaves Sonia. What do you want to do, dear?"

Sonia closed her book, keeping her place with a skinny forefinger. She gazed at them levelly. "According to virtually all psychological theories, roots are particularly important to preadolescents. I am eleven and prepubescent, hence preadolescent. Therefore, it will be healthier for me to remain here. Besides, I'll be going to the U in a few years, anyway." She opened her book, and they smiled at her. I felt my hands twitch with the desire to throttle her.

Dad got up. "Well, that about does it." He glanced at his watch. "I'll come down on Wednesday to pick up the rest of my stuff."

"Stuff," Sonia murmured, "from the Old French verb *estoffer*,[2] to equip, stock, by way of the Middle French and the Middle English, becoming a noun in the fifteenth century."

2. *estoffer* [es to fā′]

I lunged for her with a scream, the sharp edge of my hand slashing at her windpipe. "So, we'll see you kids soon," Dad said. "Walk me to the car, Margaret."

"Good-bye, Dad," Sonia said, and turned a page.

"Ya," I said, "so long."

Rick—Richard, that is—flopped on the chair by my littered desk. "So, did the folks get everything worked out?" He picked up the three hard-rubber balls on my desk and started juggling them.

"When did you learn how to do that?"

"Just now. Watching you try last night must have gotten me thinking about it. It doesn't seem so tough. You got another ball? I want to see if I can do four."

Four! I'd been trying for weeks to get the hang of three. "No."

He caught the balls in one hand. "Oh, well. So, how'd the meeting go?"

"Okay. But, Rick, do you have to leave? I mean, all the teams are really going to miss—"

"Aw, I'm bored with that stuff. Let some other guys have a chance to play. Besides, I don't want to play college ball. I'm going to try drama, chorus, and some other stuff I haven't had time for."

"Uh, do you know that the word *stuff* comes—"

"From the Old French verb *estoffer?* Ya, I knew that. Hey, it's still light. Want to go throw a ball around?"

"No, thanks."

"Suit yourself. But you ought to work on that gut of yours." He breezed out. Sonia was coming up the stairs, her nose still stuck in *Gray's Anatomy.* "Hey, Sone," Rick yelled. "Aren't you done with that yet? God, you've been at it almost a week. It only took me three days."

"Patience, eldest brother. It takes ordinary mortals longer to scale the Olympian heights."

"Want to go play a duet? I'm out of practice."

Sonia snapped the book shut. "Sure."

A couple of minutes later I heard them rip into some four-handed ragtime on the baby grand in the living room. Ordinary mortals, my butt. I was the only ordinary, common, average, everyday person in this house. I got off the bed, closed the door to a crack, then dug a Snickers bar out of my hiding place behind the bookshelf. I hesitated a second before unwrapping it; I was already one over my daily limit and I'd need at least two more to get through the evening. But it had been a trying day. Tomorrow I'd do better. And maybe if I made this one last, I'd only need one tonight. I sat by the window, munching slowly and watching the last of the early-spring afternoon.

Downstairs Rick and Sonia wrapped up their ragtime performance with a fit of laughter. Maybe I should go down and try to join them. I'd never made it much beyond "Chopsticks" in two years of lessons, but maybe they wouldn't mind if I tapped my foot quietly. Sonia started playing the Chopin sonata[3] she'd been practicing for the competition. They'd be serious now, Rick listening carefully for the slightest flaw in her playing. Fat, dumb Phillip would be a distraction, tapping foot or not.

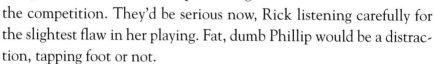

I looked down at the empty candy wrapper in my fingers; somehow the Snickers had disappeared. I rose and got a Milky Way from behind my books. To heck with my genius brother and sister. And my mature, brilliant parents. Come to think of it, to heck with everything.

Right then I decided to build a tree house. I'd build it so high that no one could see me among the leaves. And once I was up there with the wind and the clouds and the birds, I'd pull up the ladder behind me. Now all I needed was the darn tree.

All the rest of that week I doodled with plans for my tree house. It was going to be my secret, but as usual, I screwed that up too.

3. **Chopin sonata** [shō′ pan sə nä′ tə]: a piece of music for one or two instruments by Frederic Chopin, a Polish composer who lived in France.

The day after I flunked a unit exam in geometry, Mr. Bernstein caught me fiddling with my plans rather than doing my homework. He gave me the disgusted look that most of the teachers give the great Rick O'Dell's younger brother.

Bernstein called Mom that night. Mom listened, thanked him, described the situation to Sonia as if I wasn't there, then turned to me with a slight variation of that disgusted look. She devoted the next hour to giving me the usual going-over with the verbal wire brush. She's always more confused than angry, and I guess she figures that if she scrubs hard enough she may finally uncover the reason why two brilliant, mature parents with two brilliant, perfect kids somehow blew it on the middle one.

Sonia's book must have been particularly fascinating that evening, because she didn't contribute her usual theories about switched babies on the maternity ward, vitamin deficiencies in infancy, or her recent favorite: "middle-child syndrome." She only sniggered now and then. The third time she let out a "Ha," I whipped the blowpipe from my back pocket and stuck a poison dart right between her eyes. She lurched forward, her eyes already glassy, and pitched across . . . "I don't know, Phillip," Mom said. "I think it's about time we started thinking about a private military academy for you. Somehow, you're going to have to learn the discipline to . . ." I stared at her. Her mouth was still moving, but I didn't hear the words. Military academy? Discipline? I dived through the window, my eyes shut tight against the spray of shattering glass. She paused. "Anyway, I'm going to talk to your father about it when he comes to pick up Rick this weekend."

"He'll look funny in uniform," Sonia said. "Philly is getting positively corpulent these days." She looked at me. "*Corpulent* means fat. Interesting synonyms are *swag bellied* and *pussle gutted*."

This time I really was going to kill her. Mom said, "Oh, calm down, Phillip. Your sister is just trying to help. Now, stand up and let me look at you. Have you been sneaking candy bars again?"

Rat poison, I thought. They're both so busy reading at supper that they'll never notice a few little crunchies in their salads.

As it turned out, it was a good thing that I didn't poison them. Sonia won a scholarship to study piano in Boston that summer. Mom decided to go along: "I can do some interesting research at the Harvard Medical School. You can spend the summer with your father and Richard." But Dad and Rick had already made plans to spend June rock climbing in Colorado, and pussle-gutted Phil wasn't exactly rock-climbing material. "Well," Sonia said, "there's always Great-Uncle Sean."

Great-Uncle Sean lived in a cabin twenty miles out of town. I suppose you imagine that the ancient O'Dell spent his time translating Sanskrit[4] and meditating on the subtle workings of the cosmos. Wrong. Great-Uncle Sean didn't do much of anything, and—as far as anyone could recall—never had. Somewhere way back he'd lucked into some money, and ever since he'd lived on the interest, his garden, and

---

4. **Sanskrit** [san′ skrit]: the ancient language of India.

whiskey. He didn't own a TV and he didn't read. He just sat on the front porch with the radio playing and a bottle close enough at hand so that periodic sips kept the world in a sort of constant haze.

He didn't object when I moved in. I don't think he really noticed me after the first couple of days. I cleaned out a storeroom and made a bed. Then I relaxed. Completely. I deserved it after busting my tail for six weeks to get my grades up to passing, so I wouldn't get sent to a military academy. And I'd come prepared. I'd secretly replaced all the enlightening books Mom had packed—with Sonia's suggestions—with a gross of candy bars and a dozen sword and sorcery books. Add the case of Pepsi they'd grudgingly let me haul along, and I was set for at least a couple of weeks.

My peace only lasted three days. I heard loud knocking on the screen door and opened it to find this skinny blond girl about my age, eyeing me with laser-beam blue eyes. "Uh, ya. Can I help you?"

"I'm Morgan from down the road. Mom sent a pie for Mr. O'Dell." She shoved it at me.

"Thanks. I'm his nephew, Phil. Great-nephew."

"Ya, we heard you were here. You've got chocolate on your face."

"Oh, sorry." I rubbed at the corners of my mouth.

"Nothing to be sorry about. Just a fact. So, do you sit in the house all the time, or do you go for walks and stuff?"

"I, uh, mostly stay around here."

"You ought to get out; the exercise would do you good. Exercise is good for everybody."

"Thanks for telling me."

"You're welcome. See you around."

Another one! Just once in my life I'd like to meet someone who didn't inform me what a slob I was thirty seconds after meeting me. I went back to my room and slam-dunked a Milky Way. Darn it, one of these days, I was going to build that tree house. I'd sit up there and drop rocks and candy wrappers on everybody who passed.

The next afternoon I saw her turn in at the gate with a paper sack of something. I wasn't about to risk any more judgments on the cleanliness of my face or the girth of my gut. (Well, she hadn't exactly mentioned the latter, but I knew what she'd meant by that crack about exercise.) I grabbed my book, shoved an emergency candy bar in my pocket, and beat it out the back door.

That's how I got started going to the hill behind the cabin every afternoon. I'd read and munch in the shade of the biggest tree for miles around. It was an elm, I think, very straight for a long way up, branching out only when it was already high above all the other trees. I was no woodsman, but I knew the tree was dying, its crown of leaves thin like an old man's hair. And it groaned every once in a while, a sound so faint that I wasn't sure if I'd heard it with my ears or only sensed it when the great trunk swayed ever so slightly against my back.

I'd imagined needing nothing but my stack of fantasy novels and my supply of candy bars and Pepsi. But after a week they let me down. I was *bored*. Worse, I missed my family. Ridiculous. After all the garbage I'd put up with, couldn't I forget them for a while?

I'm not a brooder. I mean, I really don't think I spend a whole lot of time feeling sorry for myself. But I sat a whole afternoon with a perfectly good fantasy novel unread at my side while I tried to figure out where I fit in life. Fate or a vitamin deficiency or a careless nurse or something had stuck me in a situation where I couldn't possibly compete. Not that I couldn't get decent grades if I tried; or even learn to juggle if I kept at it. But I could never really compete with Sonia or Rick or Mom or Dad. They just weren't ordinary people. And I was.

For about the two hundredth time I caught myself staring up at the high crown of the elm. Just once in my life . . .

The next day I started tearing boards off a tumbledown shack out behind the cabin. Great-Uncle Sean caned his

way over to watch me for a few minutes. He gave me a toothless grin. "Do it faster with kerosene and a match, boy."

I wiped sweat from my face. "I'm going to build something with the boards and spikes, Uncle Sean."

"Well, the exercise'll do ya good, boy. You got kind of a gut on you." He started back for the porch and the whiskey bottle.

It took me three days and about a dozen gallons of sweat to make a stack of more or less sound boards in the clearing below the big elm. I'd already begun to have some serious doubts about my sanity, but I kept thinking: just once in your life . . .

Lucky I didn't think any further than that, because the whole thing got a lot harder than I'd ever imagined. The idea of a ladder that I could pull up behind me didn't work. It'd have to be a permanent ladder—or at least as permanent as rickety boards and rusty spikes could make it. I nailed steps as high as I could reach, then looped a rope around my waist and the trunk of the tree. I edged the rope up until I was level with the top rung, then pulled up the next board with a second rope.

I dropped a lot of boards and nails the first couple of days, but slowly my ladder rose. By the fourth day I was halfway to the fork where I'd build my tree house. I had a system by then. After I nailed each board in place, I'd slip the loop over my shoulders, climb down, tie the next board to my hauling rope, take a slug of Pepsi or a bite of candy bar, then climb back up. I also had two black-and-blue fingernails from poorly aimed hammer blows, a considerably increased fear of heights, and the definite opinion that I was completely out of my mind.

"How you doing up there?"

I looked down, the ground starting to spin then rush toward me in a flash of vertigo. Morgan was aiming her laser eyes at me from the foot of the tree. "Right now I'm about to throw up. Better get away from there."

She moved back a few paces and watched as I made my shaky way down to earth. "I brought you some lemonade."

"Why?"

"I thought you'd be thirsty. Why else?"

"How'd you know I was here?"

"Oh, I saw you here yesterday. Just followed the sound of the hammer. I got here just when you hit your thumb. You know a lot of words. What's a pussle gut?"

"A fat person." I hesitated for a second, then accepted the tin cup of lemonade she was offering me. "Thanks."

"Mind if I ask why you're doing this?"

"You wouldn't understand."

"Try me." She sat down at the foot of the ladder, scratched a mosquito bite on a bare ankle, then stared at me expectantly.

"It's kind of personal," I said.

"I don't mind."

Well, suppose I do! I looked down at the lemonade. "Just once in my life I want to be higher than anyone else."

"Wouldn't that take a plane or a space shuttle or something?"

"Well, I don't have one of those! All I've got is this stupid tree and some old boards. But it's kind of a metaphor, you see. Uh, a metaphor is a kind of a comparison."

"I know what a metaphor is. And a simile too."

I groaned. "Oh, God, another bright one."

"I'm not that smart. We just had it in English this spring, that's all. English is my best subject. What's yours?"

I gazed at her. "Nothing. I'm not good at anything. Now excuse me, I've got to get back to work."

She shrugged and stood. "Want some help? I could tie the boards to the rope for you, so you wouldn't have to come down every time."

"No! I mean, uh . . . Hey, look, I've got to do this myself. Thanks for the lemonade. I'll see you."

"Okay. Be careful."

The board broke under my foot and I fell, my fingernails clawing for the fork just inches out of my reach. My weight tore the next rung from the trunk. I was going to slide through the loop of my safety rope and somersault backward away from the trunk. Two or three seconds of tumbling and screaming, then splat. Somehow I managed to catch the loop around my shoulders. I was leaning back as far as I could, my hands gripping either side of the rope and my legs curled as far around the trunk as they could reach.

"Hold on!" Morgan came bounding across the clearing. She got to the foot of the tree. "Are you okay?" I managed to nod. "Just hold on. I'll run get my dad."

"No! Don't you move!" I took a deep breath and pulled my body in toward the trunk. Grunting, I wiggled the loop down an eighth of an inch at a time until it was across the small of my back. I felt for the first solid rung, found it, and started down.

The pain didn't hit until I finally dropped to the ground and collapsed at the foot of the tree. Both my hands had rope burns across the palms, and my legs, arms, and chest had been scraped raw in the few desperate seconds I'd fought for a hold on the bark.

"You've got blood on your forehead," Morgan said quietly.

I felt. Just a little bit. "Ya, but I don't have chocolate on my face."

"You've got to stop this," she said. "It's dangerous. I'm worried all the time about you." She paused, then suddenly her voice got almost shrill. "Look, why don't you just come for a walk with me? Or we could go swimming or horseback riding. I've been waiting almost two weeks for you to come around."

I stared at her. The laser look was gone from her eyes. She looked almost scared. I closed my eyes. "I've got to replace some boards and put extra nails in all of them. It'll be safe."

"Why do you have to do this? Hey, I'll take you to a fire tower. You can climb that and be higher than anybody. I'll stay on the ground if you want to be alone. But forget this. It's crazy." I shrugged. "Look, just forget it for today, okay? Let me take you home and fix those scrapes."

I went with her. I ate supper at her house, and we went for a long walk in the evening. "What's this business about waiting for me to come around?" I asked.

"Well, I just figured you would. I mean, you're all alone with Mr. O'Dell, and I figured you'd come down to see whether the neighbor girl might be a little bored and lonely too."

"You can't be that bored and lonely."

"Try me."

When we said good-night on her porch, she said, "Why don't we go horseback riding tomorrow? I've got Big Ben and my brother won't mind if you ride Soupy."

I hesitated. "Maybe the day after tomorrow."

"You're not going back there, are you?"

"I still want to be higher than anyone else just one time. And don't lurk in the bushes tomorrow. I'll be all right."

She didn't say anything for a long moment. "Well, if you break your darn neck it'll be your funeral!"

I laughed, the sound unfamiliar in my ears. "Well, I think that's usually how it works." She shut the door in my face.

I was sore from my toes to my hairline. But I didn't care; I could make it. I started in early morning, driving extra nails in every rung. Several boards were on the point of breaking. I replaced them, amazed that a day before I hadn't noticed. By late afternoon I'd reached the broken boards high on the trunk. I pulled up a board, nailed it in place, climbed down, tied the next one to the rope, and started up again. By then I knew that I'd never build the tree house, never hide among the leaves where no one could see me. All I wanted was a ladder reaching up out of the forest.

I nailed the last board in place, retied the safety rope around the biggest limb, and hoisted myself into the fork. I stood there, looking over the woods and the farmland into the late-afternoon distance. Far away I could see a twisting line of trees tracing a river flowing southwest toward the Mississippi. Somewhere beyond the haze on the horizon the waters met to flow south across the heart of the continent.

When the light started to fade, I untied the safety rope and climbed down. I walked home in the dusk. Morgan was sitting on the fence near the front gate. "How was it?" she asked.

"Nice. Everything was in its place."

"Did everything look small?"

"No, the world looked real big. Big enough for all sorts of people."

She thought about that a second. "Well, I guess that's good. Here, I made chocolate-chip cookies." She held out a napkin holding three large cookies.

I took one and handed the others back. "Just one. I'm starting a diet."

"Horseback riding bounces the weight off. That's why I'm so thin . . . So, is that it, or are you going up there again?"

"No, once was enough." I took a chance and put my arm around her. She didn't object but slid close. "It was nice," I said, "but kind of lonely too."

ALDEN R. CARTER

Alden R. Carter was born in 1947 in Eau Claire, Wisconsin, and grew up doing the activities he most enjoys today: canoeing, camping, hiking, and reading.

After graduating from the University of Kansas in 1969, Carter served as a lieutenant in the United States Navy during the latter part of the Vietnam War. When he finished his Navy service, Carter attended Montana State University, and then went back to Wisconsin. He taught high school English and journalism for four years and now devotes himself to writing. Most of his work is historical nonfiction for young adults, but he has written novels as well, both for adults and young adults.

IDENTITY

JULIO NOBOA, JR.

Maine Painting, Summer Cycle #1 Anne Neely, 1992, oil on linen, 14"x 11", courtesy of Alpha Gallery

Let them be as flowers,
always watered, fed, guarded, admired,
but harnessed to a pot of dirt.

I'd rather be a tall, ugly weed,
clinging on cliffs, like an eagle   5
wind-wavering above high, jagged rocks.

To have broken through the surface of stone,
to live, to feel exposed to the madness
of the vast, eternal sky.
To be swayed by the breezes of an ancient sea,   10
carrying my soul, my seed, beyond the mountains of time
or into the abyss[1] of the bizarre.

I'd rather be unseen, and if
then shunned by everyone,
than to be a pleasant-smelling flower,   15
growing in clusters in the fertile valley,
where they're praised, handled, and plucked
by greedy, human hands.

I'd rather smell of musty, green stench
than of sweet, fragrant lilac.   20
If I could stand alone, strong and free,
I'd rather be a tall, ugly weed.

1. **abyss** [ə bis´]: a bottomless depth or chasm.

JULIO NOBOA, JR.

Julio Noboa, Jr., was born in 1949 in the Bronx, New
York City. When he began writing poetry, he decided to
write in both Spanish and English. Thus, many of his poems
have been published in both languages. About his poem
"Identity," Noboa has said, "The whole poem is essentially a search for my individuality—finding myself as a person, as opposed to being one of the crowd."

Noboa lives in Chicago and has worked as a leadership trainer with the
Latino Institute.

IT WAS A LONG TIME BEFORE

LESLIE MARMON SILKO

It was a long time before
I learned that my Grandma A'mooh's
real name was Marie Anaya Marmon.
I thought her name really was "A'mooh."
I realize now it had happened when I was a baby   5
and she cared for me while my mother worked.
I had been hearing her say
            "a'moo'ooh"
which is the Laguna[1] expression of endearment
for a young child   10
spoken with great feeling and love.

Her house was next to ours
and as I grew up
I spent a lot of time with her
because she was in her eighties   15
and they worried about her falling.
So I would go check up on her—which was really
an excuse to visit her.
After I had to go to school
I went to carry in the coal bucket   20
which she still insisted on filling.
I slept with her
in case she fell getting up in the night.

She still washed her hair with yucca roots
or "soap weed" as she called it. She said   25
it kept white hair like hers from yellowing.
She kept these yucca roots on her windowsill
and I remember I was afraid of them for a long time
because they looked like hairy twisted claws.

1. **Laguna** [lä gü′ nä]: name of Native American people and their language, from New Mexico.

I watched her make red chili on the grinding stone   30
the old way, even though it had gotten difficult for her
to get down on her knees.
She used to tell me and my sisters
about the old days when they didn't have toothpaste
and cleaned their teeth with juniper ash,   35
and how, instead of corn flakes, in the old days they ate
"maaht'zini" crushed up with milk poured over it.

Her last years they took her away to Albuquerque
to live with her daughter, Aunt Bessie.
But there was no fire to start in the morning   40
and nobody dropping by.
She didn't have anyone to talk to all day
because Bessie worked.
She might have lived without watering morning glories
and without kids running through her kitchen   45
but she did not last long
without someone to talk to.

LESLIE MARMON SILKO

Leslie Marmon Silko was born in 1948 and grew up in the Southwest. After graduating from the University of New Mexico, she taught English at the University of Arizona while getting started as a writer.

Silko is mainly a poet, but she has also written a number of short stories and a popular novel. The novel, *Ceremony*, tells of a World War II veteran, half Native American, who succeeds in readjusting to life on a New Mexico reservation and finds peace and understanding through tribal ceremonies. One of her books, *Storyteller*, includes both short stories and poems.

Great grandparents and grandfather of Leslie Marmon Silko, black and white photograph

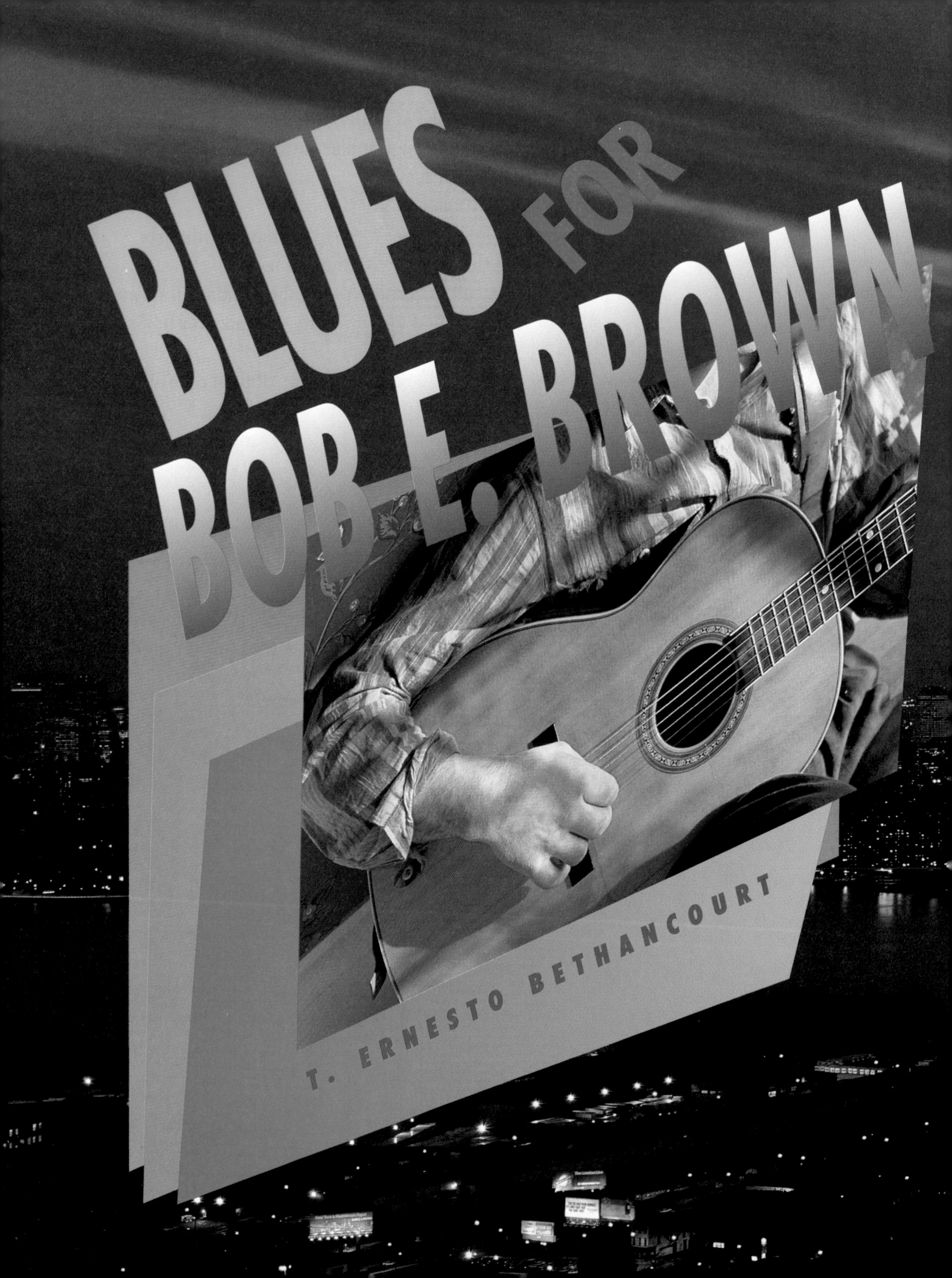
BLUES FOR
BOB E. BROWN
T. ERNESTO BETHANCOURT

I was just getting home from my after school delivery job at the Big Apple Market. It was about eight thirty. I heard Mama and Papa going at it right through our apartment door. I stood outside in the hall of our second floor walkup and tried to make out what was going on inside.

No sense in walking into an argument unless you already know whose side you're supposed to be on. That's the trouble when you're the last kid left at home. They always want you to take sides. Ever since my older brother, Lou, left to join the Navy it's been this way. My married sister, Margie, lives in Queens now. She's too far from West 88th Street in Manhattan, where we live, for Mama to get her involved in her hassles with Papa.

"I don't care!" I heard Papa say. "I won't have him in my house."

"But Juanillo,"[1] I heard Mama counter, "he's your own father. Your flesh and blood . . ."

I knew Mama was trying the soft approach with Papa. When she's really pleased with him or wants something, she calls him *Juanillo*. Any other time, it's plain old Jack. But actually, my father's name *is* Juan—meaning "John" and *Juanillo* means "Johnny" or "Johnny-boy."

All us kids have traditional Latino names, too. My brother Lou is really Luis Alfredo, my sister Margie is Margarita Dolores and I'm Roberto Ernesto, although everyone calls me Bobby. I couldn't imagine anyone calling me by my middle name. Or, worse yet, *Ernie!*

1. **Juanillo** [hwä nē´ yō]

My dad speaks some Spanish; so does my mom. But us kids only know a few words—me least of all, being the youngest. To give you an idea how little, I almost failed Spanish in my junior year at Brandeiss High School.

The hassle was still going on inside the apartment. "My mind's made up, Helen," I heard Papa say. "If he's so interested in seeing his grandchildren after all these years, that's tough. I want nothing to do with him."

Now I knew what was going on. We had heard from my grandfather. I didn't even know he was still alive. My dad never talks about him. Seeing as how my parents' fight wasn't about me, I put my key in the door and went inside.

The hall door opens right into the kitchen of our apartment. Then comes the living room and two bedrooms. But most of the time if we aren't watching TV in the living room, most of our family life is in the kitchen.

Mama was seated at the table with her ever-present cup of *Café Bustelo*[2] coffee with milk. Papa, still wearing his Transit Authority uniform, was having one of his two daily bottles of Coke. I kissed Mama and got a hug from Papa. "Hi, guys," I said. "What's happening?" As if I didn't know.

"Nothing . . . Nothing at all, Bobby," Papa said.

"Pretty loud nothing," I said. "I heard you two down the hall."

"Oh, *that*," my dad said with a wave of a hand. "Just between your mama and me. A family matter."

"Jack!" said Mama, "You mean you aren't going to mention it?"

"Mention what?" I said, still not letting on.

My dad shook his head in a funny mix of disgust and dismay. "You might as well know, Bobby. Your grandfather has decided he's still part of our family. After all these years. We got a letter from him today."

"Grandpa's here in New York? Last time I heard you mention him, he was in California."

"He's still out there," Mama said. "But his letter says he's coming here this week. He says he wants to see us . . . all of us." Mama looked pointedly at Papa, who looked away.

"How did he even know where to find us?" I asked.

"It was from your brother, Lou. He's stationed in Oakland now . . ."

2. **Café Bustelo** [kä fē′ bü stā′ lō]

"I know. But . . . ?"

"Let me finish," put in Papa. "Your brother took it on himself to track the old man down. He had some family records of my mother's that *someone* gave him." Papa looked angrily across the table at Mama. "So Lou found him—a man he'd never seen in his life—a man who didn't even come to his son's wedding . . ."

"We know, Juanillo," Mama said softly.

"Then why should you care about a man you've never met?" my dad demanded of my mom.

"Because no matter what you say, he's your father. Yes, I know. He left when you were ten years old. But that was thirty five years ago, Juanillo. In a way, *you* don't know him, either."

"I know all I need to know. My mother told me, God rest her soul."

I could see they were going to be at this for a while. I opened the fridge and took out a frozen dinner and popped it in the microwave. Then I walked down the hall to my bedroom.

I took my guitar off the chair and sat down to practice. I had an audition on Saturday night, downtown in the SoHo³ section of town.

I started with some simple Blues changes and scales. That's my thing: Traditional Blues and Jazz. No amplifiers—just straight acoustic.⁴ I was really getting into my solo on *Beale Street Mamma*, when I heard the microwave beeping.

When I came into the kitchen Mama and Papa weren't quite so upset. Papa looked at me and said, "Well, what about it, Bobby? Do you want to meet the old man?"

"We decided it's up to you kids," Mama said. "Your father has his mind made up. He won't see your grandpa. But if you want to meet him, that's okay with us."

"What does Margie say?" I asked.

"I'm going to call her in a little while and ask."

"That's not the point," my dad said. "It's what *you* say about meeting him."

I looked at both my parents. Here I was, on the hook again. If I said yes, probably Papa would feel I was letting him down. If I said no, Mama would think I was cold.

---

3. **SoHo** [sō′ hō]: a section of New York City where many artists live and work.
4. **acoustic** [ə kü′ stik]: having to do with the science of sound; here it refers to playing a regular guitar without amplifiers.

After all, I see *her* father and mother every month when they come in from Long Island. And we always have Thanksgiving dinner at their place in Oceanside. Now what was I going to say? They were looking at me, expecting some answer.

"Can I think about it?" I asked.

"Sure, honey," Mama said, ignoring Papa's look. "Take your time. He won't be coming to town until next Monday."

I took my tv dinner out of the microwave and brought it to my room. While it was cooling, I put on an old album of Blues artists that I had found in a second hand store downtown. It was made in the 1960s. The record company doesn't even exist anymore. But there sure was some good stuff on it. That record was where I learned *Beale Street Mamma* from.

The guy who played and sang it was terrific. His name was Ivan Dark. I tried to find out more about him, but it seemed like this was the only recording the guy ever made. Too bad. They didn't even have a picture of him on the album cover. All it said about him was he came from New York.

But I kind of liked the idea. Almost all the great acoustic Blues players came from down South or from the south side of Chicago. But here was a New York Blues man. I had played his album track so many times, it was old and scratchy.

I ate my *Budget Gourmet* sirloin tips while I listened to Ivan Dark. Then I practiced until ten o'clock and went to bed. I had a full day of pedaling the delivery cart for *Big Apple* the next day, Saturday. And eleven thirty that night, at *Mary's Grill* in SoHo, was my live audition.

Saturday at ten, I checked myself out in the bathroom mirror. I was wearing my all-black outfit: suit, shirt, tie, and shades. I debated with myself whether I should wear the black fedora hat. Then I decided I'd look too much like one of the Blues Brothers.

But I did want to look older than eighteen. My brother Lou is lucky that way. He was fifteen when he grew a mustache. I could get away with shaving twice a week. I think it's because Lou is like my dad: dark curly hair, medium complexion and build. Papa has always had a mustache, far as I can remember.

To look at me, you wouldn't think we were related. I'm tall, thin, with straight, light brown hair and hazel eyes. I took a lot of heat from kids in school about that. "Some Puerto Rican *you* are," they'd say. Called me *huero*,[5] and a lot of other names not too choice. A lot of them just couldn't get next to a guy named Roberto Moreno who looks like I do. Mama says there's blondes on her side of the family. Maybe that's where I get my looks.

I looked at myself in the mirror and shrugged. "You are who you are, man," I told my reflection.

Then I went to my room and packed up my guitar. It's an old Gibson arch top acoustic. The pawn shop guy I bought it from said it was made in the 1930s. I can believe it. But man, does that ax have a tone—a full bass and a treble that could cut glass. Just right for Blues.

Mama and Papa were watching the ten o'clock news on Channel 5 as I left. We did the usual going out late stuff. *Yeah, I'll be careful, Mama. Yeah, Papa, I know it's dangerous out there. I'll walk near the curb and away from dark doorways. Yeah, Mama, I'll call if I'm gonna be late . . .* I finally got out the door. Jeez, you'd think I was still a kid!

I hailed a cab at Amsterdam and 79th Street. I'd been saving my tips so I could cab it both ways. You get on the subway at a late hour and you're just asking for it. And if you're wearing a suit and carrying an instrument . . . Well, you might as well wear a sign saying "Take me."

Mary's was in full cry when I got there. It started out years ago as a neighborhood place that served lunches and drinks to the factory workers. But now all the factory lofts are full of artists and sculptors. The little luncheonettes

and neighborhood bars changed with the times. Now they got sidewalk tables, hanging plants inside and serve fancy food.

5. *huero* [wē′ rō]: Spanish for "blond," "fair."

Mary's is a little different, though. They kept the old crummy plastic covered booths and the big, long bar. About all they changed was they put in a little stage and a sound system. And behind the bar, they got a bunch of autographed pictures of Jazz and Blues musicians who played there. Some names you might know, if you're into my kind of music.

Brutus, the guy at the door, knew me and passed me in without checking any ID. Just as well. I was using Lou's old driver's license. He gave it to me when he went into the Navy.

The place was heavy with smoke and the smell of stale beer. It's one of the few places in SoHo where they don't put the cigarette smokers in some kind of sinner's jail room. But by the late hours, the air gets so you can chew each lungfull before you inhale it.

The trio onstage was tearing up a Jazz number I recognized—an old Dave Brubeck tune called *Take Five*—on account of it's in 5/4 time. It's the house policy at *Mary's* that they don't play anything there newer than Be-Bop. I spotted Mary behind the bar, right away.

She's hard to miss. Five four and easy two hundred pounds with a flaming red wig that was probably new when the Beatles were big. She gave me a huge grin and waved me over. "Bob E. Brown, you rascal!" she hollered over the trio and the crowd noise. "I was wondering if you was gonna show. You're on in fifteen minutes."

Maybe I ought to explain about that *Bob E. Brown*. See, when I decided to be a Blues man, Roberto Moreno didn't sound right for that line of work. I was already Bobby, and Moreno means brown in Spanish. And because there's already a rock singer named Bobby Brown, I came up with Bob E. Brown—the "E" being for Ernesto. It sounds the same as Bobby. It's just spelled different. It's no sin or anything to change your name. After all, Muddy Waters' real name was McKinley Morganfield.

I took the empty stool at the end of the long bar. Mary drew me a Coke with a piece of lime in it. "Try and act like it's a *Cuba Libre*,[6] rascal," Mary said. "Don't want to give the customers the wrong idea." Mary knew I was under-age and I don't drink, anyway. But she's in the business of selling drinks.

6. **Cuba Libre** [kü′ bä lē′ brä]: a drink made with rum and Coke.

She leaned across the bar, and a lot of Mary rested on the hardwood. "Best you tune up in the kitchen, rascal," she said. "The group will want the downstairs dressing room when they get off. You ready?"

"As I'll ever get." I didn't want to admit I felt shaky. Sure, I had played at neighborhood places and at assemblies in school. But this was different. This was *professional*.

Even when I had auditioned for Mary, it was in the daytime. And Mary's easy to be with and play for. It's like she's everyone's mama. I took a quick sip of my drink, then went into the kitchen to tune up.

When I came out, the trio was just finishing up. There was a light dusting of applause. It seemed like the crowd was more interested in each other than in what was happening onstage. Mary got up and announced, "Let's have a nice hand for the Milt Lewis Trio, folks." A little more clapping was all that got her.

"Tonight," Mary went on, "we have a special treat for you. A young man who's making his first appearance here at *Mary's*, the home of good Jazz and Blues. Please welcome a new generation Blues man—Bob E. Brown!"

I swallowed a lump in my throat the size of a baseball and got onstage to some indifferent applause. "Go get 'em, rascal," Mary whispered to me. I adjusted the mike in front of the chair on the stage—I work sitting down—and went right into a Bessie Smith tune, *Gimme a Pig's Foot*.

Half way through, I realized I was making as much impression as a snowball on a brick wall. I started to feel dribbles of sweat creep down my back. *What am I doing here?* I thought. *I must have been crazy to try this!* I finished the chorus and went into my vocal.

That's when it happened. Something clicked in my mind. If these people didn't want to listen, that was okay. What I was doing was between me and my guitar. If they liked it—swell. If they didn't, I still had my music.

I thought of what an old Blues man said in an interview I once read: "Making music is like life itself. Even when it's bad, it's good."

I threw back my head, not caring and sang, *Gimme a pig's foot and a bottle of beer. Send me gate, 'cause I don't care . . .* The darndest thing happened. The house got quieter. Every now and then, when I looked up from the fingerboard of my ax, I could see heads turning and faces looking at me. The sweat on my back and on the palms of my hands started to dry out.

When I got to the last line, *Slay me 'cause I'm in my sin . . .* they began clapping. They applauded all the way through the last four bars I played solo to finish the tune. I couldn't believe it. They liked me!

The next two tunes were a blur in my mind. Oh, I know what songs I did. I just don't remember paying attention to *how* I did them. All the hours and years of practice took over. I didn't watch my hands, like I usually do. I watched the faces of those people watching me. I sang *to* them, not at them.

The great Blues man, Josh White, said that he didn't sing songs, he told stories. And every song is a story. I told those folks my story—but in the words of the Blues I sang.

I glanced over and saw Mary. She had come out from behind the

Josh White

Muddy Waters

Mississippi John Hurt

bar and was standing only a few feet away. She was smiling like it would bust her face. She waved and put one index finger across the tip of the other to form a letter "T." That meant it was time for me to do my last number. I finished the tune I was playing and the house really came apart.

For the first time, I spoke directly to the crowd. "Thank you very much," I said, my voice a little shaky. "I'd like to finish up with a tune I learned from a recording by

Dave Brubeck

Bessie Smith

a New York Blues man, Ivan Dark. It's called *Beale Street Mamma*."

I went into the intro, and they were already clapping. I played the first chorus and went into the vocal: *Beale Street Mamma, won't you come on home* . . . As I did, I was startled by the sound of the upright bass from behind me. I almost missed a chord change. Out of the corner of my eye, I saw that the Milt Lewis Trio had come onstage behind me.

Then we really started to cook. Milt Lewis plays alto sax and with the bass and a drummer added, we did I don't know how many choruses. I dropped into rhythm playing while everyone took his solo, then we all finished together.

In my entire life, I never felt anything like that. Nothing compared. Not even the night I kissed Angela Ruiz in the hall outside her folks' apartment. When we played the last note, there was a moment of silence, like the crowd wanted to make sure we were finished. Then the place blew up with clapping, hollers, and whistles.

Suddenly, Mary was at my side. "Let's hear it for Bob E. Brown!" she shouted over the din.

"Let's hear more!" somebody in the house hollered. "Yeah, more!" another voice said.

"We got all night, folks," Mary said. She put a huge meaty arm around my waist. "We gotta let this rascal get some rest. Don't worry. He'll be back . . . Bob E. Brown, ladies and gentlemen. Remember that name!"

I got off-stage on a cloud. As Mary led the way to the bar, people applauded as I went by. Some of them reached out and shook my hand. Lots of them said nice things as I went by.

Back at the bar, Mary drew a Coke with lime and set it in front of me. "Well, rascal, seems like you got the stuff," she said. "And if you want a gig, you got one here. Milt and the guys start a road tour in two more weeks.

"But I like the sound you made together. Can you pick up a trio to work with?"

I almost fell off the bar stool. "I don't know any other musicians," I admitted, my face feeling warm.

Mary frowned. "Bet you don't have a union card, either," she said. I shook my head. Then she smiled that five hundred watt grin. "Then you gotta get busy, rascal. You get your little butt up to the Union Hall. Tell them you got a contract here. They can call me to check it out.

"Pay them the fee. You'll have your card fast enough, if I know that local. And believe me, I know that local. You start in two weeks. I'll book a trio to back you."

It wasn't until I was in a cab headed home after one more show, that Mary's words sank in. A fee? How much did it cost to join the musician's union, anyway? But I was too tired and too happy to think about it that night. I was somebody. I was Bob E. Brown—a real Blues man!

I nearly died when I found out on Monday what the union initiation fee was. I called Local 802 and spent about twenty minutes on the phone. If I drew every cent from my savings account, I was still five hundred dollars short. Half a thousand: all the money in the world!

I put down the phone and stared at the kitchen walls. Mama and Papa were still at work. I had thirty minutes to get over to the Big Apple Market, and I still hadn't eaten a thing. I went to the fridge and saw the note from Mama on the door.

Bobby,

Your grandfather called. He wants you to call him at his hotel. He's in Room 1620. The decision is yours.

I took some spiced ham from the fridge and made myself a quick sandwich. There was no Pepsi left, so I got a glass of water to wash it down with. As I ate, I thought, So he's in town, huh? Guess I gotta make up my mind.

But to tell the truth, all that was on my mind was that five hundred bucks. How in the name of anything was I going to raise that in two weeks? I finally got a professional gig and I was in danger of losing it. It was driving me nuts.

More to get my mind off it than anything else, I dialed the number on Mom's note. After two rings a woman's voice said, "Waldorf Astoria Hotel. How may we help you?"

I couldn't believe it. I'd only walked past the Waldorf. My grandfather was actually staying there, at one of the ritziest places in town. I gave the switchboard operator the room number. It rang for a while before anyone picked up and a man's voice said hello.

"Mr. Moreno, please," I said.

"Which Mr. Moreno?"

All of a sudden, I had to think of what my grandfather's first name was. Then it came to me: same as Papa—Juan. That's who I asked for. "Just a moment," the voice said.

"This is Juan Moreno," a new voice said.

"This is Bobby, your grandson, I think. My mother left me this number."

The voice warmed. "Bobby! How are you, kid? Yeah, this is your grandpa. Where are you? When can we get together?"

"Uh . . . I don't know. I'm home right now, but I got to go to work in a few minutes."

"I thought you were still in school, kid."

"I am. I work afterwards."

"Until when?"

"Eight o'clock."

"Good enough. We'll have dinner. Get a cab. I'll leave money with the doorman. You know where I am?"

"The Waldorf Astoria?"

"That's right. But I'm in the Waldorf *Towers*. That's the side entrance, not the Park Avenue one. Tell the cabbie; he'll know. See you about eight thirty, okay?"

"I ought to clean up and change, right?"

"Okay, then. Nine o'clock. I'll be waiting, Bobby."

When I arrived at the hotel, I was wearing the same outfit I did at the *Mary's* audition, but with a white tie. I figured if I was going to have dinner at a place like this, I'd need one.

My grandfather was taking care of business. The doorman had money for my cab and even tipped the driver for me. And when he showed me into the lobby and what elevator to take, he called me Mister Moreno! I'd been having quite a different kind of life, lately. I first was Bob E. Brown, the Blues man. Now I was *Mister* Moreno.

I rang the bell at 1620 and a guy about twenty opened the door. He was my size and build, with dark hair and eyes. He was wearing a designer shirt and slacks, with a pair of shoes that would cost me a month's pay at the Big Apple. "Come in," the guy said, extending a hand for me to shake. "You must be Bobby. I'm your Uncle Jim."

It wasn't a hotel room he led me into. It was an apartment like I never saw, even in a movie. "Dad," my "Uncle Jim" called out, "Bobby's here."

A man came out of the next room, and I went into shock. If someone had given me a magic mirror to show me what I'd look like in fifty-five years, here I was!

He had a full head of straight white hair. He was thin and over six feet tall and had a deep sun tan that made his hair look silver. His eyes were the same color as mine, too. He was wearing a lightweight suit that screamed money and a conservative tie.

As he extended his arms to give me an *abrazo*,[7] I saw from beneath the white cuff of his shirt, the glint of a gold *Rolex*. This was my grandpa?

He threw a bear hug around me and then stepped back and held me at arms' length. "So you're Bobby, huh?" he said. "I'd have known you anywhere, kid. Same as I'd know myself.

"Here, sit down," he said, waving me to a chair. "You want something to drink? Jimmy, get Bobby what he wants," he told my 'uncle.' "You've already met Jimmy, right?"

I just nodded. I was numb. Finally, I said, "He's my uncle?"

My grandpa laughed. "Yeah, he is. Not much older than you, though." He looked at me and laughed again. "I've been married a few times since your grandma, kid. Jimmy's from the latest edition. What can he give you?"

"A Coke would be fine, sir."

"Sir? What is that? Call me Grandpa. I kind of like it." Jimmy came over and handed me the soda. I thanked him.

"What about I leave you two alone, Dad?" Jimmy asked. "I have to get downtown, anyway."

"Have a good time, Jimmy," Grandpa said. "You got enough money?"

"I'm fine, Dad."

"And don't forget. If they won't let you tape the group, I want a full report on what you think."

Jimmy had put on a leather jacket from a closet near the door. I know guys on West 88th that would kill for one like it. "Come on, Dad," he said. "If I don't know the business by now . . ."

"How do you run it when I step down," Grandpa finished. "Okay, boy. Have a good time."

Jimmy left and Grandpa focused in on me. He sat down on the sofa facing my chair and leaned forward.

7. *abrazo* [ä bräʹ sō]: Spanish for "a hug."

"But tell me about yourself, kid," he said, "and about your family.

"I know a lot from your brother, Lou. Your sister isn't going to see me. And your mom has to side with your father. That, I can understand. You're the only family I got here that's talking to me, it seems."

I thought I saw a far off look of sadness in the old man's eyes. I don't know why, but I started to talk. He was a good listener. He didn't break in and I could tell from the expression on his face he was interested in what I had to say.

I told him everything: my dreams, the gig at *Mary's* coming up, my feeling about being a Blues man. All except the money for the musician's union. I could see the old man was rich, but I didn't want him to think that was why I had come to see him.

When I'd finished talking, he went over to the bar in the corner and poured himself a tall glass of tonic water with ice. He saw me watching him and smiled. "I don't drink any more," he said. "Not my idea. It's the doctors. I stopped smoking, drinking and eating Caribbean cooking.

"I may not live a long time," he said, taking a sip of the tonic water,

"but it sure as heck will *feel* like it." He set the glass down by the bar. "Stay here," he said. "I'll be right back." He went into the other room.

I sat there trying to digest all that had happened. My grandpa was something else. He had to be almost seventy—sixty-five the youngest. Yet, he was so *alive*. Not like my mama's dad, who really looks tired.

And what really knocked me out was that this guy didn't have a trace of an accent. My other grandpa talks like Ricky Ricardo on *I Love Lucy*. He didn't even have a New York accent like Mama and Papa. He came back into the room with a flat top acoustic guitar and I nearly fell off the chair.

It wasn't a nylon strung, either. It was a *Martin*, model D-28. I knew it right away. That's how come I bought the *Gibson*. I couldn't afford one like this. He held it out to me and said, "It's already in tune, kid."

He went over to the bar and brought me one of the stools. "No straight back chairs here," he said. "This will have to do. Okay, play for me."

"Play what?"

"Whatever you think I'd like best. Or better yet, what you like best. Please yourself enough, you'll please your audience." He sat down on the couch.

I played *Beale Street Mamma*, naturally. I'd already told him how good it went down when I played at *Mary's*. When I finished, he reached inside his back pocket and took out a hankie that looked like it was silk. He blew his nose like a trumpet playing an A natural. He gave me a look that had no name on it and said, "You got the stuff, kid."

"That's what Mary said," I replied.

"She would. Mary and me go back thirty-five years. When her husband was still alive and ran the *Jazz Stop* on Hudson Street."

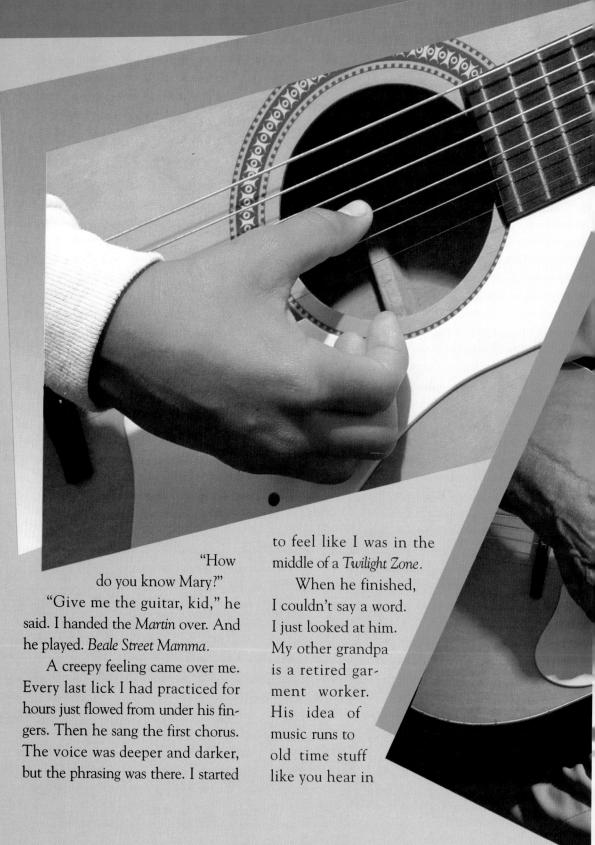

"How do you know Mary?"

"Give me the guitar, kid," he said. I handed the *Martin* over. And he played. *Beale Street Mamma*.

A creepy feeling came over me. Every last lick I had practiced for hours just flowed from under his fingers. Then he sang the first chorus. The voice was deeper and darker, but the phrasing was there. I started to feel like I was in the middle of a *Twilight Zone*.

When he finished, I couldn't say a word. I just looked at him. My other grandpa is a retired garment worker. His idea of music runs to old time stuff like you hear in the black and white musicals on *Televisa*, the Spanish language network on UHF.

"You know the record, too!" I finally got out.

"Kid, I *made* the record," Grandpa said. "If your Spanish was better, you could have figured that out. Moreno doesn't mean brown, like you think. It means *dark*. In Russian, Juan is *Ivan*. That's how I became Ivan Dark. Who ever heard of a Blues man from New York named Juan Moreno?"

"But how come you never made any more records?"

"I did. Lots of them. Just not as Ivan Dark. Got into Latino Jazz. It's where I really belonged to begin with."

"But you were . . . are so good."

"Doesn't matter, Bobby. Sure I was good. I learned from the best. They were still alive in the late '50s and early '60s. Josh White, the Reverend Gary Davis, Mississippi John Hurt, Muddy Waters. I worked with all of them and learned by watching and listening.

"But good isn't great. And those men were great. There were other young guys who hung around and played Blues. They're all gone, most of them.

"A guy I knew in 1957 is still at it. His name's Dave Van Ronk. He had his thirty year anniversary in the music business this weekend. That's part of what brought me to town. They had a big blowout at *The Village Gate*. I was there on Sunday."

"But why did you stop playing Blues?" I insisted.

"I finally figured it out, Bobby. Even though my folks learned their English from Black people—that's the neighborhoods we lived in when they came here from San Juan—and that's the first 'American' music I heard, it's not our culture.

"I could play rings around lots of Black kids my age. That didn't matter. I wasn't accepted, really.

"Dave Van Ronk is a white man from Astoria, Queens. I don't know if Dave was too dumb or too stubborn to quit. But I heard him last night. And he's a Blues man down to his toenails."

"And so you quit?"

"I never quit!" said the old man, sitting up straight. "I went into my Latino roots. I found a way to meld Latino and Jazz music. And I did well. I've got a club in Oakland, my own record label and I do just fine."

"I'm sorry," I said. "I didn't mean to make you mad, Grandpa." But I knew I had said the wrong thing. I got up. "Well, I guess I have to go now."

"Why? We didn't even have dinner. I can call room service. Look kid. I don't want to lose touch with you. We hardly started to know each other."

I came out and said what was on my mind. "Look, Grandpa. Maybe it was different when you were coming up. But there's lots of kids of all backgrounds who play Blues, Jazz, even Soul.

"That's the great thing about music. It cuts across all lines today. The Milt Lewis Trio is Black; they never said anything but how much they liked what I did. Mary is Black and she's gonna give me a job at her club. And are you gonna tell me that Joe Cocker, a white Englishman, has no soul?

"What brings us all together is the music. And it don't matter where you come from or where you're at. You're Juan Moreno. I'm gonna be Bob E. Brown."

The old man stood up and smiled. "Maybe your Uncle Jimmy is right, kid," he said. "It's time for me to step down. Us *viejos* [8] think we know it all. Maybe we can learn a lot from you kids. If we're smart enough to listen. I wish you well."

I got up and headed for the door. "It's getting late, Grandpa," I said. "And I got school tomorrow."

"I'll give you cab fare," he said.

"That's okay," I replied. "The subway's still running." I knew I was taking a chance wearing a suit, but I didn't want to ask the old man for anything more.

"You sure?" he asked.

"You already gave me *Beale*

8. **viejos** [vyā ′hōs]: Spanish for "old people."

Street Mamma," I answered. "Thanks, *abuelo*."[9] I took an *abrazo* from him and left.

I get regular letters from him now. I write when I can. The first letter I wrote was a thank-you. He got in touch with Mary the next day. He also paid my whole initiation fee to Local 802. When I got my union card, it was already made out. In the space that reads *Member's Name* it said Roberto Moreno. But there's another space on the card for the name you play under: your stage name. In that space, Grandpa had the clerk put in *Ivan Dark II*.

I really was grateful for what Grandpa did. And I love the old man for it. But later for that *Ivan Dark II*. I'm Bob E. Brown and I'll show the world I am.

9. **abuelo** [ä bwā′ lō]: Spanish for "grandfather."

T. ERNESTO BETHANCOURT

T. Ernesto Bethancourt was born in 1932 in Brooklyn, New York. He started out as a singer and composer as well as a writer and changed his name from Thomas E. Passailaigue to Tom Paisley. As Tom Paisley, he has written books on music and has also written television scripts, including a series called "The New Americans." Most of his writing, however, has been for young adults, under the name of T. Ernesto Bethancourt.

Bethancourt wrote his first novel when he was forty years old. As a "Brooklyn-born Puerto Rican ex-shoeshine boy-turned-entertainer," he could not see, at first, that a career in writing was possible. He has always loved reading. "The Brooklyn Public Library was a place of refuge from street gangs. There was adventure, travel, and escape to be found on the shelves." However, he never tried to write a book. "I thought it wasn't allowed for kids of my background. . . . No one was more surprised than I when my first attempt was. . . published," he says. "I've been at it ever since, and I owe it to the public library system."

A HAIRCUT

I. S. NAKATA

People have trouble deciding what I am. Indians mistake me for one of their own; in Chinatown they give me a menu written in Chinese; and once even a Japanese kid asked me if I was Korean. My ancestors are full-blooded Japanese, but I have had to get used to people thinking I'm something else.

Like that time I went to the barber college on North Clark Street for my cut-rate haircut. It's a place where student-barbers get on-the-job training, and that's where I met this guy. He was last in line, and he kept staring at me as I walked in. I just stared back.

Finally he smiled and said with a southern drawl straight out of Alabama, "Say, you're Indian, aren't you?"

I looked into the long mirror on the opposite wall. "No," I told the guy, "I'm not an Indian."

"Not an Indian?" Alabama said. "I would have sworn you were."

"I'm not."

Alabama shook his head and said, "You can't fool me. I've been all over the country. Seen all kinds of Indians. Cherokees in the Carolinas and Georgia and Alabama. Navajos in Arizona and New Mexico. Winnebagos in Wisconsin, and even some Shastas once in the mountains of California. I know you're some kind of Indian."

I shook my head, crossed my arms in front of my chest, and took a deep breath. "No."

"Cherokee?"

"No, not Cherokee."

"Not Sioux, are you?"

"Never been in North or South Dakota," I said.

"Winnebago?"

I didn't answer. I knew a lot about the Winnebagos. After World War II at an army post just outside Paris, I had met a Winnebago Indian from Black River Falls, Wisconsin. Jameson, I think his name was. A medic. And in the week or so that we were at the army post we spent a lot of time talking and eating. Every night we would go and buy a couple of long loaves of bread fresh from the baker's oven, and we would eat and talk for hours. He made me promise to visit him in Wisconsin when I got back to the States.

"That's God's country—where the Winnebagos live," I told Alabama. "Plenty of hunting and fishing, especially for muskellunge."[1]

"Muskellunge, huh?" Alabama said. He looked impressed.

"Yeah, muskellunge. Most people call them muskies. Good eating, too. Salted, fried, or broiled in the ashes of hickory wood."

"Wish you was there, huh, Chief?"

"Yeah, nice place," I said.

"So you're a Winnebago?" he said with a happy nod.

"I never said that. I am not a Winnebago." I turned away.

"Now, now, Chief. Don't get mad," Alabama said. "I'm your friend. Yes, sir, I'm truly your friend. I've worked with Indians and helped lots of them working for Standard Oil. The reason

---

1. **muskellunge** [mus′ kə lunj]: North American pike, a large fish.

I thought you were Winnebago is because you know so much about them."

"I don't know so much."

"You do. You sure do, Chief." He looked slyly around and then lowered his voice. "You running away from there, Chief? Maybe from the police?"

"I AM NOT RUNNING AWAY FROM THE POLICE," I told him.

"OK, Chief," he said quickly. "I didn't mean no harm."

For a long time Alabama didn't say anything. Some of the guys ahead of us moved up in line and we moved along, too. Soon Alabama had a choice of sitting or standing. He sat down on the bench and slid over to make room for me. Then he began again.

"So you're not a Winnebago, huh?"

I didn't answer him.

"Crow?"

"No, I am not a Crow," I said very sharply, although I had nothing against that tribe.

He rubbed his chin with his left hand and thought hard. "Arapaho?"

I shook my head.

"Navajo, then?"

I smiled. The Navajos were a tribe that I'd be proud to be part of. Great weavers, great in handicrafts, and among the best when it came to farming. I'd once gone to an art school in Kansas City with Custer Begay—a Navajo and a fine artist. I started thinking about Custer and his beautiful drawings of Indians on horseback. Then I remembered some of the great times we'd had and I began to laugh.

Alabama slapped his knee and said, "You're a Navajo! From Arizona."

This guy would not give up!

"Well," I said with a sigh, "I *was* once on a reservation in Arizona."

I really had been, too. I'd been sent to Arizona to live in a relocation camp[2] for Japanese-Americans during World War II, before I volunteered for the army.

Alabama's eyes lit up. "I knew it! You couldn't fool me. What reservation was it, Chief?"

"Poston, Arizona," I said, remembering the wartime internment camp. "On the Colorado River."

"I mean," Alabama moaned, "what tribe was it?"

"Nipponese. We were scattered a bit until Uncle Sam gathered us up and put us all together again."

Alabama nodded a couple of times. "Well, I sure do think that was the best thing to do, having the government look after you all. Nipponese, eh? That must be a very small tribe. Never heard of it, Chief."

I had enjoyed my joke. Alabama wanted me to be something else, but I wasn't going to be anyone else but myself.

"A Nipponese is a Japanese. I am Japanese." I spoke slowly, feeling a little self-conscious as I wondered how I am supposed to say I am what I am.

Alabama rubbed his chin and looked puzzled. "Jap, eh? Wouldn't think it to look at you. You could pass for Indian any day."

---

2. **relocation camp** [rē lō kā′ shun]: one of several inland detention camps established by the United States government during World War II for all Japanese Americans living on the West Coast.

"Japanese," I said.

"Sure, sure, Jap-a-nees. Japanese. But you were born in the USA, weren't you? You can't talk American like that without your being born here."

"I was born in Hawaii."

"Well, you're American like the rest of us, then. A man should be proud of what he is. Aren't you?"

Did I sense a threatening tone in his voice?

"I am pleased that I am who I am, Alabama," I told him. "It's good to be alive."

"Sure is, all right," he said. "But you're wrong about me. I don't come from Alabama."

"No?"

"No!" He stood up because it was finally his turn to get a haircut. "I'm from Georgia," he said in a loud voice, "and proud of it."

"Sorry I made the mistake," I told him. Then I shrugged. For the life of me I couldn't see what difference it made if he came from Georgia or Alabama.

LETTER FROM A CONCENTRATION CAMP

YOSHIKO UCHIDA

Mailing Address: Barrack 16, Apartment 40
Tanforan Assembly Center
San Bruno, California

Actual Address: Stable 16, Horse stall 40
Tanforan Racetrack

May 6, 1942

Dear Hermie:

Here I am sitting on an army cot in a smelly old horse stall, where Mama, Bud, and I have to live for who knows how long. It's pouring rain, the wind's blowing in through all the cracks, and Mama looks like she wants to cry. I guess she misses Papa. Or maybe what got her down was that long, muddy walk along the racetrack to get to the mess hall for supper.

Anyway, now I know how it feels to stand in line at a soup kitchen with hundreds of hungry people. And that cold potato and weiner they gave me sure didn't make me feel much better. I'm still hungry, and I'd give you my last nickel if you appeared this minute with a big fat hamburger and a bagful of cookies.

You know what? It's like being in jail here—not being free to live in your own house, do what you want, or eat what you

background: Japanese Internment Camp

want. They've got barbed wire all around this racetrack and guard towers at each corner to make sure we can't get out. Doesn't that sound like a prison? It sure feels like one!

What I want to know is, What am I doing here anyway? <u>Me</u>—a genuine born-in-California citizen of the United States of America stuck behind barbed wire, just because I <u>look</u> like the enemy in Japan. And how come you're not in here too, with that German blood in your veins and a name like Herman Schnabel. We're at war with Germany too, aren't we? And with Italy? What about the people at Napoli Grocers?

My brother, Bud, says the US government made a terrible mistake that they'll regret someday. He says our leaders betrayed us and ignored the Constitution. But you know what I think? I think war makes people crazy. Why else would a

smart man like President Franklin D. Roosevelt sign an executive order to force us Japanese Americans out of our homes and lock us up in concentration camps? Why else would the FBI take Papa off to a POW camp just because he worked for a Japanese company? Papa—who loves America just as much as they do.

Hey, ask Mrs. Wilford what that was all about. I mean that stuff she taught us in sixth grade about the Bill of Rights and due process of law. If that means everybody can have a hearing before being thrown in prison, how come nobody gave us a hearing? I guess President Roosevelt forgot about the Constitution when he ordered us into concentration camps. I told you war makes people crazy!

Well, Hermie, I gotta go now. Mama says we should get to the showers before the hot water runs out like it did when she went to do the laundry. Tomorrow she's getting up at 4:00 A.M. to beat the crowd. Can you imagine having to get up in the middle of the night and stand in line to wash your sheets and towels? By hand too! No luxuries like washing machines in this dump!

Hey, do me a favor? Go pet my dog, Rascal, for me. He's probably wondering why I had to leave him with Mrs. Harper next door. Tell him I'll be back to get him for sure. It's

Japanese Internment Camp

just that I don't know when. There's a rumor we're getting shipped to some desert—probably in Utah. But don't worry, when this stupid war is over, I'm coming home to California and nobody's ever going to kick me out again! You just wait and see! So long, Hermie.

Your pal,
Jimbo Kurasaki

YOSHIKO UCHIDA

Yoshiko Uchida [1921-1992] was born in Alameda, California, and grew up in Berkeley in a house full of books. She has said, "I've been interested in books and writing for as long as I can remember. I was writing stories when I was ten." Uchida also kept a journal of important events, starting on the day she graduated from elementary school.

She was in her senior year at the University of California, Berkeley, in 1941 when the attack on Pearl Harbor brought the United States into World War II. Only a few months after she graduated, a second terrible event occurred. The fear and suspicion of wartime focused on Japanese Americans—loyal as any Americans. Suddenly, with little warning, the government rounded up all Americans of Japanese descent and interned them in camps secretly built in desolate areas.

Of all the many books Yoshiko Uchida wrote, this painful experience in wartime is the subject of her most important work. As she often said, "the story of the wartime incarceration of the Japanese Americans. . . needs to be told and retold and never forgotten." Two of these books were written for young adults: *Journey to Topaz* and *Journey Home*.

I, TOO

LANGSTON HUGHES

I, too, sing America.

I am the darker brother.
They send me to eat in the kitchen
When company comes,
But I laugh,   5
And eat well,
And grow strong.

Tomorrow,
I'll be at the table
When company comes.   10
Nobody'll dare
Say to me,
"Eat in the kitchen,"
Then.

Besides,   15
They'll see how beautiful I am
And be ashamed—

I, too, am America.

Untitled Romare Bearden, 1975, collage, 20 1/4"x15 1/4",
The New York Public Library

LANGSTON HUGHES

James Langston Hughes [1902-1967] was born in Joplin, Missouri. In 1926, Hughes published his first book of poems, titled *The Weary Blues*, which won him a college scholarship to Lincoln University in Pennsylvania.

Hughes graduated in 1929 just as the Depression began. He had to make a living writing, as he said, to "turn poetry into bread. It was a question of writing or starving." His work was "largely concerned with the depicting of the Negro life in America." Besides poetry, Hughes wrote short stories, novels, essays, movie scripts, and plays. One of his best-known books of poetry is *The Dream Keeper*.

I'm Nobody

EMILY DICKINSON

I'm nobody! Who are you?
Are you—Nobody Too?
Then there's a pair of us?—
Don't tell! they'd advertise—you know!

How dreary—to be—Somebody!
How public—like a Frog—
To tell one's name—the livelong June—
To an admiring Bog!

EMILY DICKINSON

Emily Dickinson [1830-1886] was born in Amherst, Massachusetts, grew up there, and returned to her parents' home after two years of study at Mount Holyoke College.

Dickinson, who wrote for herself, not for publication, was an unknown poet in her lifetime. After her death, however, 1,775 poems were discovered and she was soon recognized as one of our finest poets. There are many collections of Dickinson's poems, including *A Letter to the World: Poems for Young Readers.*

The Moustache

ROBERT CORMIER

At the last minute Annie couldn't go. She was invaded by one of those twenty-four-hour flu bugs that sent her to bed with a fever, moaning about the fact that she'd also have to break her date with Handsome Harry Arnold that night. We call him Handsome Harry because he's actually handsome, but he's also a nice guy, cool, and he doesn't treat me like Annie's kid brother, which I am, but like a regular person. Anyway, I had to go to Lawnrest alone that afternoon. But first of all I had to stand inspection. My mother lined me up against the wall. She stood there like a one-man firing squad, which is kind of funny because she's not like a man at all, she's very feminine, and we have this great relationship—I mean, I feel as if she really likes me. I realize that sounds strange, but I know guys whose mothers love them and cook special stuff for them and worry about them and all but there's something missing in their relationship.

Anyway. She frowned and started the routine.

"That hair," she said. Then admitted: "Well, at least you combed it."

I sighed. I have discovered that it's better to sigh than argue.

"And that moustache." She shook her head. "I still say a seventeen-year-old has no business wearing a moustache."

"It's an experiment," I said. "I just wanted to see if I could grow one." To tell the truth, I had proved my point about being able to grow a decent moustache, but I also had learned to like it.

"It's costing you money, Mike," she said.

"I know, I know."

The money was a reference to the movies. The Downtown Cinema has a special Friday night offer—half-price admission for high school couples, seventeen or younger. But the woman in the box office took one look at my moustache and charged me full price. Even when I showed her my driver's license. She charged full admission for Cindy's ticket, too, which left me practically broke and unable to take Cindy out for a hamburger with the crowd afterward. That didn't help matters, because Cindy has been getting impatient recently about things like the fact that I don't own my own car and have to concentrate on my studies if I want to win that college scholarship, for instance. Cindy wasn't exactly crazy about the moustache, either.

Now it was my mother's turn to sigh.

"Look," I said, to cheer her up. "I'm thinking about shaving it off." Even though I wasn't. Another discovery: You can build a way of life on postponement.

"Your grandmother probably won't even recognize you," she said. And I saw the shadow fall across her face.

Let me tell you what the visit to Lawnrest was all about. My grandmother is seventy-three years old. She is a resident—which is supposed to be a better word than *patient*—at the Lawnrest Nursing Home. She used to make the greatest turkey dressing in the world and was a nut about baseball and could even quote batting averages, for crying out loud. She always rooted for the losers. She was in love with the Mets until they started to win. Now she has arteriosclerosis, which the dictionary says is "a chronic disease characterized by abnormal thickening and hardening of the arterial walls." Which really means that she can't live at home anymore or even with us, and her memory has betrayed her as well as her body. She used to wander off and sometimes didn't recognize people. My mother visits her all the time, driving the thirty miles to Lawnrest almost every day. Because Annie was home for semester break from college, we had decided to make a special Saturday visit. Now Annie was in bed, groaning theatrically—she's a drama major—but I told my mother I'd go, anyway. I hadn't seen my grandmother since she'd been admitted to Lawnrest. Besides, the place is located on the Southwest Turnpike, which meant I could barrel along in my father's new Le Mans. My ambition was to see the speedometer hit seventy-five. Ordinarily, I used the old station wagon, which can barely stagger up to fifty.

Frankly, I wasn't too crazy about visiting a nursing home. They reminded me of hospitals and hospitals turn me off. I mean, the smell of ether makes me nauseous, and I feel faint at the sight of blood. And  as I approached Lawnrest—which is a terrible cemetery kind of name, to begin with—I was sorry I hadn't avoided the trip. Then I felt guilty about it. I'm loaded with guilt complexes. Like driving like a madman after promising my father to be careful. Like sitting in the parking lot, looking at the nursing home with dread and thinking how I'd rather be with Cindy. Then I thought of all the Christmas and birthday gifts my grandmother had given me and I got out of the car, guilty, as usual.

Inside, I was surprised by the lack of hospital smell, although there was another odor or maybe the absence of an odor. The air was antiseptic, sterile. As if there was no atmosphere at all or I'd caught a cold suddenly and couldn't taste or smell.

A nurse at the reception desk gave me directions—my grandmother was in East Three. I made my way down the tiled corridor and was glad to see that the walls were painted with cheerful colors like yellow and pink. A wheelchair suddenly shot around a corner, self-propelled by an old man, white-haired and toothless, who cackled merrily as he barely missed me. I jumped aside—here I was, almost getting wiped out by a two-mile-an-hour wheelchair after doing seventy-five on the pike. As I walked through the corridor seeking East Three, I couldn't help glancing into the rooms, and it was like some kind of wax museum—all these figures in various stances and attitudes, sitting in beds or chairs, standing at windows, as if they were frozen forever in these postures. To tell the truth, I began to hurry because I was getting depressed. Finally, I

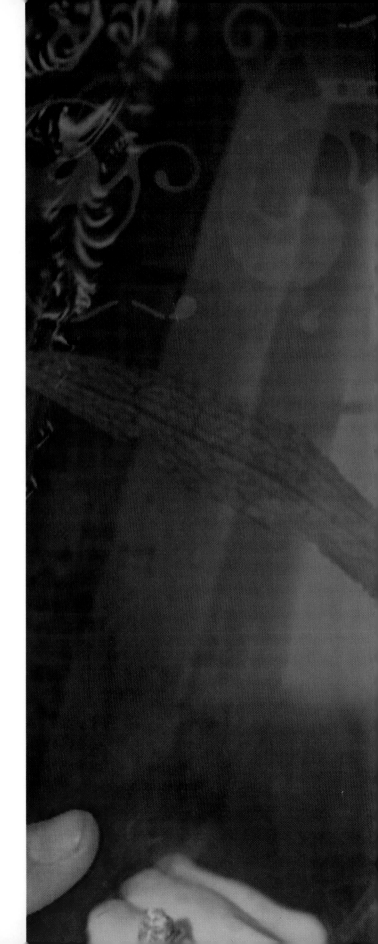

saw a beautiful girl approaching, dressed in white, a nurse or an attendant, and I was so happy to see someone young, someone walking and acting normally, that I gave her a wide smile and a big hello and I must have looked like a kind of nut. Anyway, she looked right through me as if I were a window, which is about par for the course whenever I meet beautiful girls.

I finally found the room and saw my grandmother in bed. My grandmother looks like Ethel Barrymore. I never knew who Ethel Barrymore was until I saw a terrific movie, *None But the Lonely Heart*, on TV, starring Ethel Barrymore and Cary Grant. Both my grandmother and Ethel Barrymore have these great craggy faces like the side of a mountain and wonderful voices like syrup being poured. Slowly. She was propped up in bed, pillows puffed behind her. Her hair had been combed out and fell upon her shoulders. For some reason, this flowing hair gave her an almost girlish appearance, despite its whiteness.

She saw me and smiled. Her eyes lit up and her eyebrows arched and she reached out her hands to me in greeting. "Mike,

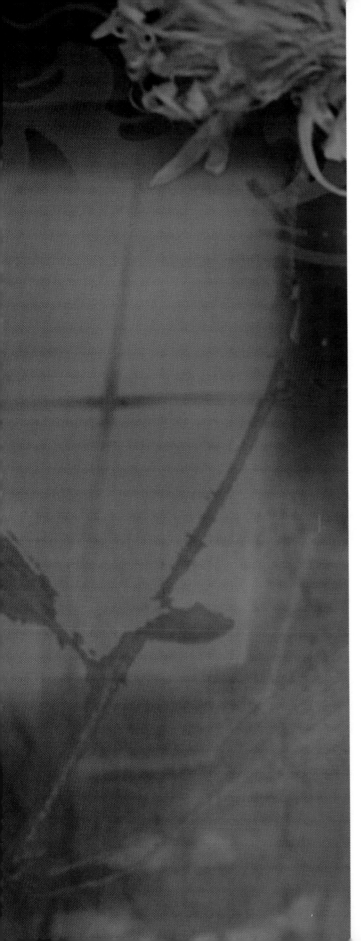

Mike," she said. And I breathed a sigh of relief. This was one of her good days. My mother had warned me that she might not know who I was at first.

I took her hands in mine. They were fragile. I could actually feel her bones, and it seemed as if they would break if I pressed too hard. Her skin was smooth, almost slippery, as if the years had worn away all the roughness the way the wind wears away the surfaces of stones.

"Mike, Mike, I didn't think you'd come," she said, so happy, and she was still Ethel Barrymore, that voice like a caress. "I've been waiting all this time." Before I could reply, she looked away, out the window. "See the birds? I've been watching them at the feeder. I love to see them come. Even the blue jays. The blue jays are like hawks—they take the food that the small birds should have. But the small birds, the chickadees, watch the blue jays and at least learn where the feeder is."

She lapsed into silence, and I looked out the window. There was no feeder. No birds. There was only the parking lot and the sun glinting on car windshields.

She turned to me again, eyes bright. Radiant, really. Or was it a medicine brightness? "Ah, Mike. You look so grand, so grand. Is that a new coat?"

"Not really," I said. I'd been wearing my uncle Jerry's old army-fatigue jacket for months, practically living in it, my mother said. But she insisted that I wear my raincoat for the visit. It was about a year old but looked new because I didn't wear it much. Nobody was wearing raincoats lately.

"You always loved clothes, didn't you, Mike?" she said.

I was beginning to feel uneasy because she regarded me with such intensity. Those bright eyes. I wondered—are old people in places like this so lonesome, so abandoned that they go wild when someone visits? Or was she so happy because she was suddenly lucid and everything was sharp and clear? My mother had described those moments when my grandmother suddenly emerged from the fog that so often obscured her mind. I didn't know the answers, but it felt kind of spooky, getting such an emotional welcome from her.

"I remember the time you bought the new coat—the Chesterfield," she said, looking away again, as if watching the birds that weren't there. "That lovely coat with the velvet collar. Black, it was. Stylish. Remember that, Mike? It was hard times, but you could never resist the glitter."

I was about to protest—I had never heard of a Chesterfield, for crying out loud. But I stopped. Be patient with her, my mother had said. Humor her. Be gentle.

We were interrupted by an attendant who pushed a wheeled cart into the room. "Time for juices, dear," the woman said. She was the standard forty- or fifty-year-old woman: glasses, nothing hair, plump cheeks. Her manner was cheerful but a businesslike kind of cheerfulness. I'd hate to be called "dear" by someone getting paid to do it. "Orange or grape or cranberry, dear? Cranberry is good for the bones, you know."

My grandmother ignored the interruption. She didn't even bother to answer, having turned away at the woman's arrival, as if angry about her appearance.

The woman looked at me and winked. A conspiratorial kind of wink. It was kind of horrible. I didn't think people winked like that anymore. In fact, I hadn't seen a wink in years.

"She doesn't care much for juices," the woman said, talking to me as if my grandmother weren't even there. "But she loves her coffee. With lots of cream and two lumps of sugar. But this is juice time, not coffee time." Addressing my grandmother again, she said, "Orange or grape or cranberry, dear?"

"Tell her I want no juices, Mike," my grandmother commanded regally, her eyes still watching invisible birds.

The woman smiled, patience like a label on her face. "That's all right, dear. I'll just leave some cranberry for you. Drink it at your leisure. It's good for the bones."

She wheeled herself out of the room. My grandmother was still absorbed in the view. Somewhere a toilet flushed. A wheelchair passed the doorway—probably that same old driver fleeing a hit-run accident. A television set exploded with sound somewhere, soap-opera voices filling the air. You can always tell soap-opera voices.

I turned back to find my grandmother staring at me. Her hands cupped her face, her index fingers curled around her cheeks like parenthesis marks.

"But you know, Mike, looking back, I think you were right," she said, continuing our conversation as if there had been no interruption. "You always said, 'It's the things of the spirit that count, Meg.' The spirit! And so you bought the baby grand piano—a baby grand in the middle of the Depression. A knock came on the door and it was the deliveryman. It took five of them to get it into the house." She leaned back, closing her eyes. "How I loved that piano, Mike. I was never that fine a player, but you loved to sit there in the parlor, on Sunday evenings, Ellie on your lap, listening to me play and sing." She hummed a bit, a fragment of melody I didn't recognize. Then she drifted into silence. Maybe she'd fallen asleep. My mother's name is Ellen, but everyone always calls her Ellie. "Take my hand, Mike," my grandmother said suddenly. Then I remembered—my grandfather's name was Michael. I had been named for him.

"Ah, Mike," she said, pressing my hands with all her feeble strength. "I thought I'd lost you forever. And here you are, back with me again. . . ."

Her expression scared me. I don't mean scared as if I were in

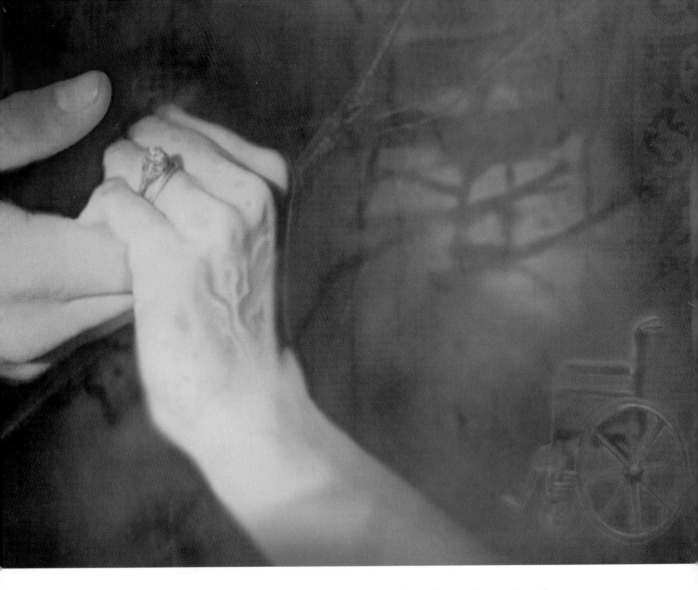

danger but scared because of what could happen to her when she realized the mistake she had made. My mother always said I favored her side of the family. Thinking back to the pictures in the old family albums, I recalled my grandfather as tall and thin. Like me. But the resemblance ended there. He was thirty-five when he died, almost forty years ago. And he wore a

moustache. I brought my hand to my face. I also wore a moustache now, of course.

"I sit here these days, Mike," she said, her voice a lullaby, her hand still holding mine, "and I drift and dream. The days are fuzzy sometimes, merging together. Sometimes it's like I'm not here at all but somewhere else altogether. And I always think of you. Those years we had. Not enough years, Mike, not enough. . . ."

Her voice was so sad, so mournful that I made sounds of sympathy, not words exactly but the kind of soothings that mothers murmur to their children when they awaken from bad dreams.

"And I think of that terrible night, Mike, that terrible night. Have you ever really forgiven me for that night?"

"Listen . . ." I began. I wanted to say: "Nana, this is Mike your grandson, not Mike your husband."

"Sh . . . sh . . ." she whispered, placing a finger as long and cold as a candle against my lips. "Don't say anything. I've waited so long for this moment. To be here. With you. I wondered what I would say if suddenly you walked in that door like other people have done. I've thought and thought about it. And I finally made up my mind—I'd ask you to forgive me. I was too proud to ask before." Her fingers tried to mask her face. "But I'm not proud anymore, Mike." That great voice quivered and then grew strong again. "I hate you to see me this way—you always said I was beautiful. I didn't believe it. The Charity Ball when we led the grand march and you said I was the most beautiful girl there . . ."

"Nana," I said. I couldn't keep up the pretense any longer, adding one more burden to my load of guilt, leading her on this way, playing a pathetic game of make-believe with an old woman clinging to memories. She didn't seem to hear me.

"But that other night, Mike. The terrible one. The terrible accusations I made. Even Ellie woke up and began to cry. I went to her and rocked her in my arms and you came into the room and said I was wrong. You were whispering, an awful whisper, not wanting to upset little Ellie but wanting to make me see the truth. And I didn't answer you, Mike. I was too proud. I've even forgotten the name of the girl. I sit here, wondering now—was it Laura or Evelyn? I can't remember. Later, I learned that you were telling the truth all the time, Mike. That I'd been wrong . . ." Her eyes were brighter than ever as she looked at me now, but tear-bright, the tears gathering. "It was never the same after that night, was it, Mike? The glitter was gone. From you. From us. And then the accident . . . and I never had the chance to ask you to forgive me . . ."

My grandmother. My poor, poor grandmother. Old people aren't supposed to have those kinds of memories. You see their pictures in the family albums and that's what they are: pictures. They're not supposed to come to life. You drive out in your father's Le Mans doing seventy-five on the pike and all you're doing is visiting an old lady in a nursing home. A duty call. And then you find out that she's a person. She's *somebody*. She's my grandmother, all right, but she's also herself. Like my own mother and father. They exist outside of their relationship to me. I was scared again. I wanted to get out of there.

"Mike, Mike," my grandmother said. "Say it, Mike."

.   I felt as if my cheeks would crack if I uttered a word.

"Say you forgive me, Mike. I've waited all these years . . ."

I was surprised at how strong her fingers were.

"Say, '*I forgive you, Meg.*' "

I said it. My voice sounded funny, as if I were talking in a huge tunnel. "I forgive you, Meg."

Her eyes studied me. Her hands pressed mine. For the first time in my life, I saw love at work. Not movie love. Not Cindy's sparkling eyes when I tell her that we're going to the beach on a Sunday afternoon. But love like something alive and tender, asking nothing in return. She raised her face, and I knew what she wanted me to do. I bent and brushed my lips against her cheek. Her flesh was like a leaf in autumn, crisp and dry.

She closed her eyes and I stood up. The sun wasn't glinting on the cars any longer. Somebody had turned on another television set, and the voices were the show-off voices of the panel shows. At the same time you could still hear the soap-opera dialogue on the other television set.

I waited awhile. She seemed to be sleeping, her breathing serene and regular. I buttoned my raincoat. Suddenly she opened her eyes again and looked at me. Her eyes were still bright, but they merely stared at me. Without recognition or curiosity. Empty eyes. I smiled at her, but she didn't smile back. She made a kind of moaning sound and turned away on the bed, pulling the blankets around her.

I counted to twenty-five and then to fifty and did it all over again. I cleared my throat and coughed tentatively. She didn't move; she didn't respond. I wanted to say, "Nana, it's me." But I didn't. I thought of saying, "Meg, it's me." But I couldn't.

Finally I left. Just like that. I didn't say goodbye or anything. I stalked through the corridors, looking neither to the right nor the left, not caring whether that wild old man with the wheelchair ran me down or not.

On the Southwest Turnpike I did seventy-five—no, eighty—most of the way. I turned the radio up as loud as it could go. Rock music—anything to fill the air. When I got home, my mother was vacuuming the living-room rug. She shut off the cleaner, and the silence was deafening. "Well, how was your grandmother?" she asked.

I told her she was fine. I told her a lot of things. How great Nana looked and how she seemed happy and had called me Mike. I wanted to ask her—hey, Mom, you and Dad really love each other, don't you? I mean—there's nothing to forgive between you, is there? But I didn't.

Instead I went upstairs and took out the electric razor Annie had given me for Christmas and shaved off my moustache.

ROBERT CORMIER

Robert Cormier was born in 1925 in Leominster, Massachusetts. In addition to a career in journalism and radio, he has managed to write a number of well-known novels and short stories. He draws on his own life experience for many of his themes. He says, however, that in addition, he is "always writing, going to the movies, reading books."

Turmoil in a Blue and Beige Bedroom

Judie Angell

Please let John call.

Please let John call before two o'clock.

If John calls before two o'clock I promise I'll baby-sit Stewie for three Friday nights in a row without arguing.

Now, what will I wear?

I haven't worn my powder blue sweater with the fluffy collar to school yet . . . I could wear that with my tan slacks. Or my black slacks. Or my white wool ones? Maybe I'll wear a dress. . . .

If Claudia goes with Tim, maybe we could double, since Tim drives. . . . Yes! That's a great idea, I'll call Claudia. No, I'll wait until I hear from John.

Please let John call soon! If he calls soon I'll try not to argue about *anything* for two whole weeks. Unless they tell me I have to be home by eleven or something. . . . But I promise, that would be the only argument.

Can I wear my hair a new way? How can I wear my hair a new way when it's so *short!* Maybe I could stick combs in the sides or something, and pull it up over my ears like this. . . . Yuck, too many pictures stuck in the frame of my mirror, I can't even see myself in it anymore. . . .

Mmmm, I should get rid of *this* picture, anyway. Billy and me. Billy's such a creep, how could I ever have liked him? Look at that, he's wearing Bermuda *shorts,* for Lord's sake, what a stupid picture. And there's stupid Kenny Rappoport in the background, holding up two fingers over Billy's head. Why did I even bother to keep such a stupid picture? And look at *me,* with two dumb ponytails sticking out of the sides of my head . . . I look like a cocker spaniel, for Lord's sake! This picture goes *out,* that's it!

Billy. I bet he wasn't even invited to Nancy's party. And if he was invited I bet he goes with *Marcia!* They really deserve each other.

Oh! The phone! It's ringing, it's ring-ing! I'll let it ring again. Four times, so I won't look anxious. Three . . . four . . .

Hel-low?

Oh. Hi, Mom. What do you mean you're surprised you got through? I've hardly been on the phone at *all* today! Are you calling from the dentist's? Did Stewie have any cavities? Well, good. Listen, Mom, I'm kind of waiting for a call, so—What? Did I do the dishes? Well, not yet, but—The what? The kitty litter? I *will*, Mom, but I haven't had a minute—My *bedroom*? It looks *fine*, it doesn't need any cleaning. It does not, Mom! Okay, okay, I will. I *will*. I said I *would*, Mom—*Please* stop say-ing "all you teen-agers." We are *not* all alike, Mom, in spite of what you parents think! I am not sighing heavily, Mom, and I'll do the stuff, okay? Okay. Bye.

Par-ents!

Now. Where was I?

The party. Clothes.

Maybe I shouldn't wear the powder blue. Practically every-thing I own is powder blue. I'm almost totally *associated* with powder blue, like a trademark or something. Who needs *that!*

Maybe green. No, green makes my skin look yellow. Maybe *yellow!*

Oooooh, there's the phone again. Two . . . threee. . . .

Hel-low?

Oh, it's you, Susan.

No, I'm not disappointed, I thought you were somebody else, that's all. Never *mind* who else. *Nobody* else, I just didn't expect *you*. No, not Roger. No, not Peter, either. *Nobody*, Susan!

Of *course* not *Allen*, Susan, why would you ever think of Allen? Like gross, Susan! Did anyone say anything to you about me and Allen? Did they? You *swear*?

I am *not* overreacting, I just don't know why you would even imagine I might be expecting a call from Allen, he's so wimpy! And he has that awful growth on his cheek. Well, you can call it a beauty mark, I call it a growth!

Listen, I really can't stand Allen Mitchell and let's change the—John? John Carraro? I am not blushing, Susan, how can you tell, anyway, over the phone?

Okay. Maybe John, but just maybe *maybe*, not really *really*.

Stop laughing, Susan, I just thought that *maybe* if John asked me I might go with him, *maybe*. But I don't know and I'm not counting on it. Who are you going with? You're going *stag*? You're kidding! You *are*? But Nancy said *couples*! She did, I swear, I was standing right there when she invited both of us!

She did say couples, Susan. How could you show up there all by yourself when everyone else will be paired off? Susan, I *heard* her say couples.

Well, I think that's pretty gutsy of you, I really do.

The geometry? No, I haven't looked at it yet, why? Trapezoids?[1] What's a trapezoid, I thought that was an order of monks. No, I must have been absent for that. You will? Oh, Susan, you're a doll, you'll really help me? Thanks, you're the best friend I ever had. Phyllis? She is not my best friend. Well, maybe I did, but not anymore. She told Mary Ann I was a snob, do you believe that? Me, a snob! She's the one who's a snob. Just because she had two dates with a boy from Princeton she wouldn't speak to any high school boy for weeks, practically.

Listen, Susan, Phyllis is the type who doesn't even know the meaning of the word *friendship*. She'll just turn on you for no reason and start saying things behind your back.

Oh, boy, what time is it? It is? Say, I'd better hang up. Stop giggling, Susan, it is not because I'm expecting a call from John. I promised my mother I'd help her. Never mind with *what*, Susan, I have to hang up.

Okay, bye.

---

1. **trapezoids** [trap′ ə zoidz]: four-sided plane figures with two sides parallel and two sides not parallel.

I cannot believe Susan would show up at Nancy's party alone! I bet she has a date, she's just not telling me who yet, that's all. Some best friend *she* is. . . .

I am absolutely getting claustrophobic[2] in this room.

I wonder what the other kids are doing?

Are they staying home on a perfectly gorgeous Saturday afternoon waiting for a date for Nancy's party or are they going out?

What I'd really like to do is call Liz or Mary Ann or somebody but I just can't tie up the phone anymore. . .

If John would just call *now*, then I could get out of this room and get on with my *life*! I am just stagnating and withering away in this *room*!

Call, John, call. Call, John, call. One, two, three, ring!

If John calls now I'll know I was right all along. I am special. I am different. I am leading a charmed life. I will get everything I desperately want because I was born under a lucky star and everything will be perfect and beautiful forever.

Oh, I know *some* bad things will happen, but not really tragic and I will rise above them and be a better person afterward. And the things I really want, the really important things in life, will all be there like a dream come true because I am magic. If I close my eyes and will it strongly enough—

I'll lie flat on my back and close my eyes. Not too tightly. I'll take a deep breath. . . .

Maybe I will actually have an out-of-body experience. Wouldn't that be terrific? You leave your body and soar above it . . . but you're still attached to it by a beautiful silver cord. . . .

Deep breath, dee—eep breath.

Ouch, what's that?

Oh, my nightgown is caught under me. I should have

2. **claustrophobic** [klô′ strə fō′ bik]: having an abnormal fear of enclosed places.

made my bed, it's so uncomfortable on your back when stuff is wrinkled up underneath you. . . .

There. That's better.

Breathe deeply, deeply.

I am living a charmed life. Everything is perfect. John will call and I will go with him to Nancy's party and I will wear powder blue and everything will be perfect. . . .

Inhale, exhale.

Inhale, exhale.

Mmmm. . . .

Thephoneisringing. . . . The *phone?*

Hello?

Oh. Hi, Mary Ann.

My voice sounds as if what? Oh. Well . . . maybe I did doze off for a minute, I've been *so* exhausted lately. You too? I know, isn't it awful?

Nancy's party? I guess so, but I'm not sure. Are you? You

are? Who with? By *yourself?* But you're supposed to go with a date. Nancy said so! *She's* going with Bob Reifschneider.

Well, Susan said she's going stag, too, maybe she could be your date.

Oh, I don't know. I'd really feel funny walking in there without a date. Are you really going alone? No, nothing's *wrong* with it. I'd just feel funny, that's all. I mean, I *heard* Nancy say *couples.*

Mary Ann, remember those dumb parties back in junior high where we all went by ourselves and the girls were always on one side of the room and the boys were on the other and how gross and immature it all was?

Yes, I know we're all older now, but still, it would probably end up the same way, don't you think so? That's why Nancy said "couples" to show we've gotten past those kid games and things.

You really think it would be different now? Oh, I don't know. . . .

Go where? Down to the arcade? Oh . . . gee, I'd really like to . . . but I got behind on my geometry and I have to spend the afternoon grinding away on that. You know, trapezoids and stuff. . . .

Okay, thanks anyway. Have a good time. . . . Bye.

Oh, Mary Ann? Call me when you get back and tell me who you saw there, okay? Good. Bye.

Oooooh, that makes me so mad! I *want* to go to the arcade with Mary Ann, I *want* to!

John Carraro, you are ruining my whole afternoon! Will you please just call me so I can unchain myself from this room before my entire life passes by and my hair turns white and falls out?

If Mary Ann is going to the arcade she'll probably see Claudia and maybe Susan and probably Liz and . . . And everyone will be having a perfectly terrific afternoon while I sit here waiting for my date to call!

Of course, it would be okay if he called and I wasn't here and then he'd wonder where I was and all that. . . . Except there isn't a soul in this entire house right now and so I wouldn't get the message. And who knows when and *if* he'd ever call back. Maybe he'd even try someone *else* if he couldn't get me, so no.

No arcade. No terrific afternoon.

Just me and my room.

Wonderful.

Please let John call. Now.

I'm probably going to flunk geometry. Not flunk . . . maybe a D. Mom will die if I get a D. She'll just die. I can't get a D, I just can't. I won't. Susan will help me and I'll get a C. A C isn't so bad. And maybe if I will it strongly enough I'll get a B, especially if I really am living a charmed life.

Maybe I'll put on some records. Good idea! Records will take my mind off everything!

Let's see . . . oh, I'm tired of this one.

This one is boring.

I'm not in the mood for this one. . . .

This one is scratched. I'll *kill* Stewie for coming into this room without permission and touching my things! I'll just kill him! Little brat. . . .

This one I always hated. . . .

There's nothing here! This whole record collection is worth squat!

I'd better lie down and close my eyes again and take deep breaths.

I really hate myself when I get like this.

If John would just call I could finally relax.

I mustn't go to sleep, I mustn't go to sleep. I sounded all muzzy before when Mary Ann called and I can't sound like I've been sleeping on a perfectly gorgeous Saturday afternoon. I mean, what would he think, that I had nothing to do on a perfectly gorgeous Saturday afternoon except sleep?

I will not sleep. I'll just concentrate on relaxing.

Call, John, hurry up.

Breathe in, breathe out.

I can't relax, I can't.

I think I'll call Phyllis.

Just for a minute. Just to see what's happening.

Five-five-five, nine-one-eight . . . three. There.

Hello, Mrs. Atwater? Is Phyllis there? This is June. She went to the arcade? Oh. Well, thanks. Uh, no, no message. Bye.

Phyllis is at the arcade, too! Rats! The whole world is down there having the time of their happy little lives and here I sit in this ROOM!

Maybe even *John* is at the arcade!

No, he never goes there. He's so sweet, he always helps out his father on weekends.

Maybe he's too busy with his father to call.

No, if he's home helping his father, he'll call when he takes his break. I know he will, it will be a perfect time to call.

He's so cute.

He has a beauty mark, too, but it's a nice one. . . .

Aha! The phone! This time I'll give it two rings. Okay.

Hel-low?

Oh, hi, Liz.

No, just geometry, what about you?

Mmmm, Mary Ann called me too, but I told her I was going to hang around here. Thanks, anyway.

Nancy's party? Gee, I've hardly even thought about it, why?

Uh. Well, I thought slacks. I mean, it's not formal or anything.

Do I have a date? Well, I don't want to say yet. No, I'm not keeping secrets, honest. I'm just . . . not sure yet. How about you?

Stag? Really, Liz?

Why do you think couples are a dumb idea?

Well, no, I don't think being paired off "inhibits" anybody, I thought it sounded more mature to go with dates for a change. I mean, we've all been in "groups" since first grade, for Lord's sake.

Oh, well, if you think most kids feel more comfortable going stag, then go stag, I mean—you have to feel comfortable.

Okay, have fun. Bye.

Well.

Nancy will certainly be surprised. I mean, it's *her* party and she should have the right to say how people go to it, after all!

Gosh, why does everything have to get so *complicated?* I mean, I really can't stand it!

Susan is going stag. *Liz* is going stag. Mary *Ann* is going stag. They're going to start an epidemic! I bet now *everyone* will go stag!

Oh, barf *city!* If everyone goes stag, *I'm* sure not going to be the only one with a date, not *me!*

Oh, can you just see how *that* would come off? Everyone laughing and carrying on in cute little groups and I walk in with a date?

Ohhh, no!

Ohmygosh, but what if *John* calls?

What—if—John Carraro calls and asks me to this party that the whole entire *world* is going to *stag!*

I absolutely can't talk to him, I'll have to avoid him!

The first thing to do is get out of this room right now!

Where's my comb?

Here I've been sitting around this positively claustrophobic room all afternoon like the biggest fool who ever grew ears while the entire world is downtown at the arcade—

Where *is* my comb?

Oh, no! The phone.

I won't answer it.

I won't.

But what if it's an emergency or something?

Okay, I'll answer it.

H'lo?

Who?

Ohhh!

Hi, John . . .

Me? Well, I just finished *tons* of geometry and I thought I'd treat myself to a trip downtown, you just caught me. . . . I'm on my way out the door. Right now.

No, you're not keeping me, but what? Just one question? Oh, okay. . . .

Oh, wow, Nancy's party? Oh, wow, this is really a surprise. . . . Hmmm. . . Wow . . . Well, gee, John, it's awfully nice of you to ask me, I mean, I'm really flattered. . . . But the thing is. . . . Well, I was thinking that it could be so much more fun if we all went in a big group, you know, and so no one would feel, you know, inhibited or anything if they didn't have a date, know what I mean? I really do think big groups are so much more congenial, don't you? But, really, John, thanks a lot for asking me, I honestly think it was so nice. Bye, John.

Oh, boy!

Boy!

Now where's that comb?

What—is—*that?* Is that the beginning of a *zit?*

Oh, *please*, don't let me be starting a zit! Please, please, just let my face stay clear and I *promise* I'll catch up on geometry!

JUDIE ANGELL

Judie Angell was born in 1937 in New York City and later taught in Brooklyn. She is well known for her young adult novels. As the best of writers do, she writes from her own experience. As she says, "My background is incredibly useful to me . . . childhood imaginings, diaries, summers at camp . . . and always the music for the mood. But most important to me are the feelings I recall so well."

Angell thinks growing up "heads the list of *The Hardest Things to Do in Life.*" Her hope for her books is to present them "with an invisible card that says, maybe this'll help a little—make you laugh—make you feel you're not alone."

META VAUX WARRICK

WALTER DEAN MYERS

Illiam Edward Burghardt Du Bois, the African American author, editor, and educator, noted that after the Civil War people of African descent were often caught in a dilemma: On the one hand they were Americans, with the same ideas, ambitions, and dreams as other Americans; on the other hand they were trapped in an ethnic identity by American racial attitudes. African Americans could be as gifted, as accomplished, and as wealthy as their white neighbors but found that they would still be regarded differently, would often be judged not by their talents but by color.

The problem was in the minds and hearts of those who were willing to reduce the human adventure to something as superficial as skin color. The answer for African Americans was not to deny their heritage but to embrace it, and in so doing to discover those unique qualities of the black experience that define it as the rich and vital cultural substance from which can grow all the possibilities of life.

Ethiopia Awakening (Right) Meta Warrick Fuller,
Collection Solomon Fuller, Bourne, MA
Exposition of 1889 (Left)
Meta Vaux Warrick Fuller (Inset)

William Warrick wasn't worried about supporting a third child. The Warricks owned a catering business and a hair dressing salon, and had made money in real estate. African Americans had lived in freedom in Philadelphia since colonial times, when James Forten had made a fortune manufacturing sails. Black abolitionists, clergymen, political leaders, and businessmen had made the city the most important one for African Americans in the United States. There were many middle-class and upper-middle-class African American families living in and around Philadelphia when Meta Vaux Warrick was born on June 6, 1877.

Meta was different from most children in America, white or black, in that her family could afford to give her almost anything she wanted. The children she played with most as a young girl were the sons and daughters of prominent merchants. She went to private schools and was trained to be a "lady" as well as to read and write well. Both white and black children attended the schools, and Meta liked being with all of them.

Meta was closer to her father than to her older sister and brother, and William Warrick enjoyed taking his daughter to museums, to the ballet, and for long walks through Philadelphia's Fairmount Park. Meta's ideas of what she wanted to do with her life were influenced to a great extent by her father's love of culture. Like many children, after seeing a ballet she wanted to be a dancer, and she persuaded her family to give her dancing lessons.

The "big-footed fairy" was what her brother, William, called her as she danced from room to room of their large home. Meta ignored her older brother. She didn't mind his racing up and down the block practicing for his track team, she thought, so why should he mind her dancing? She was interested in what her sister, Blanche, was doing with charcoals and paints. There was always an extra piece of paper about that she could draw on, and she did whenever she had a chance.

The Warricks expected their son to go to college. The girls, they thought, would help their mother in the beauty salon. When Meta was ten, she saw that Blanche was already helping her mother wash and set the hair of the women who came to their salon. Meta didn't have any interest in being a hairdresser or in shaping anyone's nails.

Meta enjoyed growing up in Philadelphia. She liked the fancy parties that her parents gave and the elegantly dressed people who came to them. She knew that her family was doing well and that life was clearly more comfortable for them than for many other African Americans she saw.

The Warricks had white friends as well as black, and many of Meta's playmates were white. It was with some of her white girl friends that Meta experienced racism for the first time. A carousel was brought to one of the parks in Philadelphia. It was a small carousel, with brightly colored horses that went up and down on gold and silver bars as it turned to a merry tune.

When the owner said she couldn't ride on the carousel because she was black, she walked away and sat on a bench until her friends returned. She tried not to think about the incident, but in years to come just the sound of the melody she heard that day would upset her.

William Warrick had met a young black painter, Henry Ossawa Tanner, whose work he liked, and had invited him to his home. Tanner, known for his delicate treatment of light, was born in Pittsburgh in 1859 and was the best-known African American artist in the world at the time. Warrick took Meta to see some of Tanner's work, which was on display at the Philadelphia Academy of Fine Arts.

In her last year of high school Meta won a scholarship to the Pennsylvania School of Industrial Art in Philadelphia. The honor of the scholarship was recognized with pride among her family's friends. Now the Warrick family knew that they had reached their comfortable position through hard work. William Warrick was a man who sometimes worked twelve to fourteen hours a day and had little patience with those who did not work hard. He didn't consider art a way of making a living, especially for a woman, but he consented to allow Meta to attend art school.

Meta began both to study art and to help in the family businesses. Her teachers at the School of Industrial Art recognized her talent, and

The Banjo Lesson Henry Tanner, oil on canvas, 49" x 35 1/2",
Hampton University Museum, Hampton, VA

by the time she was graduated, she had won several honors.

She continued to paint and experiment with sculpture and read about art. What she read convinced her that if she were to advance in art, it would have to be in Paris.

Most African Americans couldn't afford a trip across the country, and here Meta wanted to go clear across the Atlantic to Paris. There was a difficult decision to be made in the Warrick household.

Meta had the same problem that any other young woman at the time would have had: She needed to convince her parents that they should invest in her study in Paris when neither of them could see how she could use her art to make a living. An aunt spoke up for Meta. She would be delighted to sponsor the girl's studies. After all, that other African American painter, Tanner, had gone to Paris, and they hadn't heard anything bad about him. If Meta thought her future lay in art, then she was entitled to the chance.

Meta Vaux Warrick was twenty-two when she left for France on the ship *Belgianland* in October 1899. Arriving in Calais,[1] she was tired from the long trip across the ocean but still checked each bag as it was put into the taxi for the train station. There was a short wait for the train, but she was soon settled into a compartment and was absolutely

---

1. **Calais** [kä lē′]: seaport in France.

delighted as the train to Paris pulled out of the busy station on schedule.

When Tanner didn't show up at the train station, she picked herself up and went as planned to the American Girls' Club by taxi. The American manager of the club was shocked to see that Meta was an African American. Her letters had been well composed and her references excellent. The manager had expected her to be white.

The manager explained to Meta that she had nothing against her personally, it was just that her presence might offend the other girls staying at the club or their parents. She refused to let her stay.

Meta was crushed. She had come to Paris filled with excitement and the dreams of an art career. Her first experience there was tainted with the racism she thought she had left behind.

Tanner, having missed Meta at the train station, hurried to the American

Self-Portrait with Palette Pablo Picasso, oil on canvas, 36 1/4″ x 28 3/4″, Philadelphia Museum of Art

Girls' Club, where he found her in heated discussion with the manager. He wasn't surprised to find out that she wasn't welcome at the American Girls' Club. The manager and Tanner began looking for other living arrangements for Meta.

Paris was an exciting place for the young American. Monet, Toulouse-Lautrec, and Cézanne were all working or exhibiting their works in Paris. Young artists such as Picasso, Braque, and Utrillo[2]

2. **Monet, Claude** [mō nā′]: French artist.
   Toulouse-Lautrec, Henri [tü lüz′ lō trek′]: French artist.
   Cézanne, Paul [sē zän′]: French artist.
   Picasso, Pablo [pē kä′ sō]: Spanish artist who lived in France.
   Braque, Georges [bräk]: French artist.
   Utrillo, Maurice [ü trēl′ ō]: French artist.

were discussing their works in the bistros. Once she reached the art community, Meta experienced almost no racial prejudice.

She studied drawing techniques in the formal, classical manner, even though she felt her interests going more and more toward sculpture. On her own she worked on sculpture.

In Paris she met some other African Americans as well as Parisians. She attended the Paris Exposition[3] in 1900 as the guest of W.E.B. Du Bois,[4] who at the time was just beginning to discuss the idea that all people of African descent should identify themselves as one people instead of as different African nationalities. Meta was impressed with Du Bois and his philosophy, and started looking more toward African subject matter for her art.

During her last year in Paris, Meta Vaux Warrick had the opportunity to meet Auguste Rodin,[5] already recognized as one of the greatest sculptors of all time. His works, from the familiar *The Thinker* to his larger, more powerful pieces, were known throughout the world. Meta was nervous as she approached Rodin's studio. But the master sculptor greeted her warmly and carefully examined her sketches and the plaster forms she had brought with her. He was impressed with her talents but wondered why she had not chosen more pleasant subjects.

Warrick explained to Rodin that she did not deliberately choose unattractive subjects, although the piece that had impressed Rodin the most, *A Man Eating His Heart Out*, was certainly not a happy one. She sculpted, she said, what captured her imagination at the moment.

Rodin admired the power in Meta's work, told her so, and encouraged her to use his name as a reference. Rodin, whose own pieces were monuments of power, showed Meta some of his work and some of the anatomical studies he was working on.

3. **Paris Exposition** [paʹris ekʹspə zishʹən]: an international exposition, similar to a world's fair.
4. **W.E.B. Du Bois** [dü boisʹ]: African American sociologist and author.
5. **Auguste Rodin** [ō gɤstʹ rô daNʹ]

Meeting Rodin, having him discuss her work and call her a "true sculptor," reinforced Meta's confidence in her art. Art dealers, partly because of Rodin's praise for the young sculptor, began to take note of Meta Warrick's work. It wasn't long before her work was selling in L'Art Nouveau,[6] one of the best of the Paris galleries.

When Meta Warrick finished her studies, she had to decide whether to stay in France or return to the United States. In 1902 she returned to Philadelphia.

In Paris her talents had been celebrated; her work had been accepted by the European art community and so had she. She was recognized as a very talented sculptor without regard to her color. Her work was good, and people accepted her for that work.

In the United States things were different. African American artists were often discouraged from entering competitions, and few galleries would display their work. Meta Warrick found she was being rejected because she was black.

Meta Warrick had been raised by her parents in Philadelphia to be "different." An African American who was well educated in a time when few of her people had the opportunity to go to any school, she had traveled and studied in Paris. She was determined to be an artist at a time when most women of color were working as domestics or service workers. The response to her in Philadelphia made her color assume an importance that diminished her talent.

More and more she turned to sculpture to express her pain. She depicted an African slave ship on the way to America, showing the Africans crowded belowdecks. *Mary Turner (A Silent Protest Against Mob Violence)*, done in plaster, was painted after the lynching of several African Americans, among them the woman Mary Turner.

6. **L'Art Nouveau** [lär nü vō´]

Rodin with Mlle. Cladel

Art critic David Driskell said about her work:

> [She] introduced America to the power of Black American and
> African subjects long before the Harlem Renaissance[7] was under
> way. Until Meta Warrick, the esthetics[8] of the Black visual artist
> seemed inextricably[9] tied to the taste of White America. . . .
> At a time when Picasso and followers of the modernist tradition
> gleaned[10] design elements from the art of non-Western societies
> without being responsible for the cultural context out of which the
> work came, [her] art evidenced a hereditary union between Black
> Africa and Black America.

7. **Harlem Renaissance** [här′ ləm ren′ ə säns]: a period from 1920 to 1930 when African American art and literature flourished in the Harlem section of New York City.
8. **esthetics** [es thet′ iks]: having or showing an appreciation of beauty in art or nature.
9. **inextricably** [in ek′ strə kə blē]: unable to be disentangled.
10. **gleaned** [glēnd]: gathered little by little

One of her most effective pieces is *Talking Skull*, a bronze statue of an African boy communicating with a skull, making a connection between his present and the past.

While visiting a hospital in Massachusetts, Meta Vaux Warrick met Dr. Solomon C. Fuller. As she commented in her notes:

> *He says he fell in love with me at that visit*
> *at Westboro State Hospital. That's what he claims.*
> *I had a mass of hair, then. I wouldn't call him a*
> *handsome man. Depends on what you call*
> *handsome. He was fairly tall*
> *and thin.*

Solomon proposed, and after some thought Meta accepted. Dr. Fuller started building a home in Framingham, Massachusetts.

The neighbors didn't learn that the doctor was black until the builders had started the excavation for the cellar. Then they circulated a petition to keep him out of the neighborhood. A friend offered them a lot in another area, but Meta would have none of it. She insisted on not giving in to the neighbors. The house went up slowly, but it went up where Meta wanted it.

> *He didn't*
> *carry me across*
> *the threshold. That was too*
> *folderol for him. I had to walk!*

Mother and Child Meta Warrick Fuller, c. 1914-1920, bronze, 5$\frac{1}{2}$" x 4$\frac{3}{4}$" x 4$\frac{3}{4}$", Danforth Museum of Art Collection, Framingham, MA

Solomon C. Fuller was born in Monrovia, Liberia,[11] on August 11, 1872. Earlier we read that his grandfather, John Lewis Fuller, and his father, Solomon—then sixteen—had emigrated to Liberia from Norfolk, Virginia, a decade before the Civil War. John Fuller, born into captivity in Petersburg, Virginia, had been a highly skilled boot and shoemaker. His skills were such that he was able to strike a deal with the man who held him to keep part of his earnings. Fuller saved enough money to buy his own freedom and that of a white indentured servant[12] named Nancy who later became his wife.

The Fuller family prospered in Liberia, growing coffee for export and serving as government officials. When Solomon C. Fuller—the son of the young man who had emigrated to Africa—wanted to become a doctor, he had to go to the United States. He first attended Livingston College, in Salisbury, North Carolina. Livingston, a black college, was founded in 1879 by the African Methodist Episcopal Zion Church.

After receiving his bachelor's degree from Livingston, he attended Long Island College Hospital and Boston University, where he received his medical degree in 1897. In 1904, after years of working as a pathologist[13] at Boston University, Dr. Fuller went to Germany to work with Alois Alzheimer[14] at the University of Munich in the study of the degenerative nerve disease which later became known as Alzheimer's disease. He returned to the United States to teach and practice neurology[15] and to become one of the

---

11. **Liberia** [lī bir′ ē ə]: country in West Africa settled by freed African American slaves in 1822.
12. **indentured servant** [in den′ chərd]: servant bound by a contract to work for someone else, usually for seven years.
13. **pathologist** [pa thol′ ə jist]: a doctor who is an expert in the study of the causes and nature of diseases.
14. **Alois Alzheimer** [äl′ ō ēz älts′ hī mər]: German doctor for whom Alzheimer's disease was named; the disease causes brain deterioration, usually in the elderly.
15. **neurology** [nů rol′ ə jē]: the study of the nervous system and its diseases.

first psychiatrists in America. The *Journal of the National Medical Association* in a tribute published in September 1954 noted that Dr. Fuller was best known for his studies in Alzheimer's disease and dementia.

Where Meta Warrick Fuller was playful and outgoing, Solomon Fuller was scholarly and studious, seeing even the most casual acquaintance as a possible source of knowledge. W.E.B. Du Bois was a frequent visitor to the Fuller household, as was Harry Thacker Burleigh, the famed singer and composer. Solomon's son remembers that his father spent long hours listening to a man they occasionally hired to cart garbage away from their Framingham house. He liked to comb through old bookstores in Massachusetts and find good but damaged copies of books, which he would then carefully repair.

Used to the Liberian way of life, he had fully expected Meta to give up her sculpting when they married, but once it was clear that she did not wish to do so, he became one of her staunchest supporters. Dr. Fuller died in January 1953.

In New York's Harlem community there was an active arts movement which would become known as the Harlem Renaissance, but in Framingham there were very few African Americans, and Meta found herself isolated. Her work was being exhibited less and less frequently, and in 1910 she had much of it stored in a warehouse. A fire that destroyed the warehouse, and most of her work, put her in a deep depression.

Even so, Meta Warrick continued with her art. Most often the commissions she received were small ones, either from the government, when they specifically wanted an African American sculptor, or from a black school or organization.

Her work *Awakening Ethiopia* was displayed at the Making of America Exposition in New York in 1922, and has been displayed in the Framingham library, the San Francisco Museum of Fine Arts, the Fine Arts Department of the Boston Public Library, and the Schomburg Library in New York City.

In her later life Meta Vaux Warrick Fuller turned increasingly to the poetry she loved.

> *I like Tennyson,*[16] *Longfellow,*[17] *I love Rossetti. . . .*[18]
> *I have to dramatize everything I read. I get into the book.*
> *I'm one of the characters. It takes much longer to read if*
> *you do that. But the enjoyment is far greater than if you*
> *just read, read, read.*

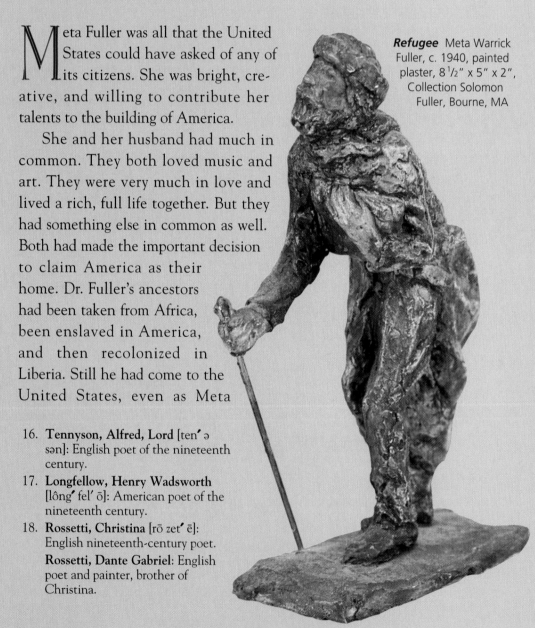

Refugee Meta Warrick Fuller, c. 1940, painted plaster, 8 1/2" x 5" x 2", Collection Solomon Fuller, Bourne, MA

Meta Fuller was all that the United States could have asked of any of its citizens. She was bright, creative, and willing to contribute her talents to the building of America.

She and her husband had much in common. They both loved music and art. They were very much in love and lived a rich, full life together. But they had something else in common as well. Both had made the important decision to claim America as their home. Dr. Fuller's ancestors had been taken from Africa, been enslaved in America, and then recolonized in Liberia. Still he had come to the United States, even as Meta

16. **Tennyson, Alfred, Lord** [ten′ ə sən]: English poet of the nineteenth century.
17. **Longfellow, Henry Wadsworth** [lông′ fel′ ō]: American poet of the nineteenth century.
18. **Rossetti, Christina** [rō zet′ ē]: English nineteenth-century poet.
    Rossetti, Dante Gabriel: English poet and painter, brother of Christina.

Warrick had returned from Paris, and both had given much of themselves to this country. Still, there were places where they could not sit down and eat a meal, or even drink a sip of water. *Plessy vs. Ferguson* [19] had decided that issue for them. Nevertheless, they accomplished much by refusing to accept the limitations placed on them by racism.

Solomon C. Fuller, Jr., presently living on Cape Cod, Massachusetts, has fond memories of his childhood with Dr. Fuller and Meta Vaux Warrick Fuller. His mother, besides being a marvelous sculptor, was a wonderful parent. He still remembers their daily family suppers, the competition to spot the first robin of spring, the first sleigh of winter, and every sign of beauty that nature offered. He read me a poem that she had written, a poem that followed her resolve to accept the end of her life with as much grace as she had accepted the living.

Meta Vaux Warrick Fuller died March 13, 1968.

19. ***Plessy vs. Ferguson*** [ples′ ē věr′ səs fěr gə sən]: a Supreme court decision of 1896 that made it legal to separate persons in public places according to their skin color.

WALTER DEAN MYERS

Walter Dean Myers was born in 1937 in Martinsburg, West Virginia, but grew up in Harlem. He learned to read early, but his education, as Myers says, just "bumped along."

A day in the fifth grade was a turning point, he says. "An already annoyed teacher caught me reading a comic book under the desk. Of course, she tore it up, but the next day she came in with a pile of books." She told young Walter that if he was going to spend so much time reading, he should read something good. He did—and was "hooked" on reading ever after.

Myers began to write stories and poems while in high school as a way to make a "connection with things and events that I was not a part of in 'real' life. . . . I was on my way to becoming a writer. I just didn't know it yet." After serving in the army, he held a series of jobs, but he had decided to be a writer. "I can reach people through my writing," Myers says.

ALMOST PERFECT

SHEL SILVERSTEIN

"Almost perfect . . . but not quite."
Those were the words of Mary Hume
At her seventh birthday party,
Looking 'round the ribboned room.
"This tablecloth is *pink* not *white*—   5
Almost perfect . . . but not quite."

"Almost perfect . . . but not quite."
Those were the words of grown-up Mary
Talking about her handsome beau,
The one she wasn't gonna marry.   10
"Squeezes me a bit too tight—
Almost perfect . . . but not quite."

"Almost perfect . . . but not quite."
Those were the words of ol' Miss Hume
Teaching in the seventh grade,   15
Grading papers in the gloom
Late at night up in her room.
"They never cross their t's just right—
Almost perfect . . . but not quite."

Ninety-eight the day she died   20
Complainin' 'bout the spotless floor.
People shook their heads and sighed.
"Guess that she'll like heaven more."
Up went her soul on feathered wings,
Out the door, up out of sight.   25
Another voice from heaven came—
"Almost perfect . . . but not quite."

SHEL SILVERSTEIN

Shel Silverstein was born in 1932 in Chicago, Illinois. A cartoonist, composer, and folksinger (he wrote the hit song "A Boy Named Sue"), Silverstein puts all his talents together to create imaginative poems illustrated by wonderful sketches. Silverstein has been writing poems for thirty years, but he remains young in outlook. *Where the Sidewalk Ends* and *A Light in the Attic* are two favorite collections of his poems.

Asking Big Questions About the Literature

What makes each person unique?

LITERATURE STUDY

Point of View

Point of view is the perspective from which a story is told. A *first-person point of view* is one in which a story is told by one character, "I." (All short stories in this unit are told from a first-person point of view.) A *third-person point of view* is one in which the story is told by a narrator using pronouns like *he*, *she*, *them*. The poem "Almost Perfect" is told using the third person. (*See "Point of View" on page 121.*)

With a partner, choose a story from this unit. Take turns reading portions of it aloud, changing the point of view to third person. (You'll use the character's name and "he" or "she" instead of "I.") Record yourselves and then share your readings in small groups.

Write a
ONE-ACT PLAY

Choose several characters that you like in this unit and list the qualities that make each character unique. Consider the characters' attitudes, interests, backgrounds, values, and beliefs.

Now choose your favorite character. Explore how you and this character are alike and different by creating a Venn diagram like the one on this page.

Use the information from your Venn diagram to write dialogue for a one-act play in which you and the character meet and talk. Share your one-act play with the class.

Grandma A'mooh in "It Was a Long Time Before"   Me

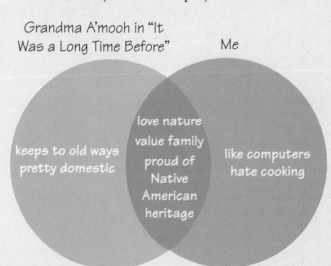

keeps to old ways
pretty domestic

love nature
value family
proud of Native American heritage

like computers
hate cooking

Write a
SONG

Write rap or other song lyrics about one of the characters in this unit. In the song, describe what makes that character unique. You may use the tune from an existing song. Record your song or perform it live for the class.

Characterization

Characterization is the art of developing characters. With *direct characterization*, a writer describes a character: "Juan is shy." With *indirect characterization*, characters speak for themselves—through their words, thoughts, and actions: "I stared at my shoes, tongue-tied." (*See "Characterization" on page 120.*)

Reread your favorite selections from this unit, looking for examples of indirect characterization. For one character, make a chart like the one begun here. What can you infer about a character's personality from what he or she says, does, and thinks? Share your finished chart with a partner or small group.

Literature Title	Speech	Thoughts	What Is Revealed

Asking Big Questions About the Literature

How do people express their individuality?

Characterization

Character interactions and conflicts are a key element of one type of **characterization**, known as *indirect characterization*. For instance, in "The Moustache," readers find out what Mike looks like through his mother's complaints about his hair and moustache. We also learn more about Mike's character from the way in which he deals with her complaints. (*See "Characterization" on page 120.*)

Choose one character whose individuality creates conflict with other characters. Clearly define the problems and then write a letter offering advice to the character. Organize your ideas by using a chart like the one shown. Share your letter with a small group or the class.

Role-Play AN INTERVIEW

With a partner, choose a character from this unit. Then role-play an interview between that character and a TV talk-show host. Before the interview, both of you should think of interview questions and answers that will reveal the character's unique personality. Perform your interview for a small group or the class.

Performing Dramatic Readings

Work in a small group to choose one poem in this unit for a dramatic reading. Take turns reading the poem aloud, using your voice to create the speaker's character. How does each person's reading affect your interpretation of the poet's words?

Character	Problem	Solution
Phil in "Tree House"	He's hostile because his brother and sister act smart and superior.	They are smart—but they aren't mean. Accept them for who they are. Realize that your anger stems from jealousy.

LITERATURE STUDY

Point of View

A writer's choice of narrator determines how readers view the events of a story. In first-person **point of view**, the narrator tells the story, using the pronouns *I* or *we* and describing people and events through his or her own eyes. You'll notice that all of the stories in this unit are written from the first-person point of view. (*See "Point of View" on page 121.*)

Choose one story in this unit and imagine that you're a character who isn't the narrator. As that character, write a first-person diary entry, describing the story's events and revealing what you care about. To help you get started, use a diagram like the one on this page about Phil in "The Tree House." Your diary entry should show how a change in point of view changes the story. Share your writing with the class.

Creating a
CHARACTER

Choose a character from one of the literature selections in this unit and visually represent what is important to that character. Draw a cartoon, paint a watercolor, make a clay sculpture—be creative. Display your art in class, and challenge your classmates to match your art with the character it represents.

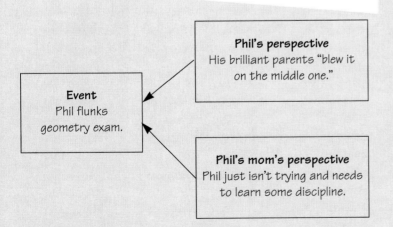

Phil's perspective
His brilliant parents "blew it on the middle one."

Event
Phil flunks geometry exam.

Phil's mom's perspective
Phil just isn't trying and needs to learn some discipline.

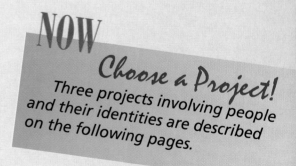

NOW Choose a Project!
Three projects involving people and their identities are described on the following pages.

Writing Workshop

WRITING A PERSONAL-HERO BIOGRAPHY

What kind of people do you admire? For this project, you'll choose someone you admire—someone you either know or know of. Your **purpose** is to write a *biography*, an account of that person's life. Then you'll share with your **audience**—your classmates—the special qualities of that person that make him or her your own personal hero.

Prewriting
CHOOSING A HERO

The first step is to brainstorm for names of people you admire. Begin with people you know personally —a relative, a coach, or a family friend. Then consider other people you may have seen on television or read about. Identify the qualities that you admire in each person. Steer away from persons whose main quality is good looks—you won't want your classmates to think that you're shallow! In your journal, analyze each of your heroes by completing a chart like the one begun here.

Person	Qualities I Admire	Examples of Qualities
Dad	sense of humor, kindness	When I ran over a branch with the lawn mower, Dad didn't yell, and he jokingly called me "Log Mower."
E.O. Wilson	very intelligent	Curiosity led him to become the world's expert on ants and other things.

Prewriting
INTERVIEWING AND RESEARCHING

To discover more about the special qualities of your personal hero, you'll need either to interview the person or do library research. If you interview someone, prepare a list of general and specific questions beforehand. Some examples are shown. Take notes or record the interview.

Interview Questions

What were you like as a child?
What is especially important to you?
How does your cultural heritage affect who you are?
What events, people, and problems helped to shape you?
Who is your personal hero?

If you do library research, inspect a variety of sources: encyclopedias, books, biographical dictionaries, and magazines. (A tip—reference librarians know where everything is. Ask them for help!)

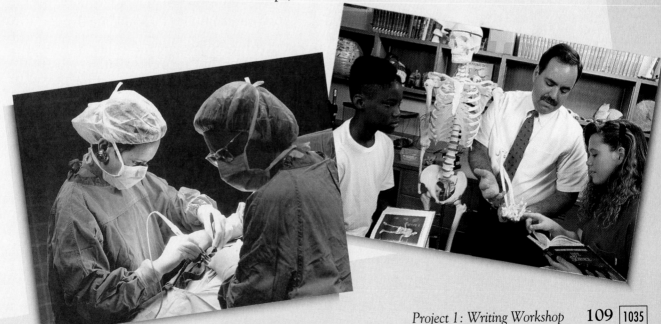

Drafting
YOUR BIOGRAPHY

Use the following steps for drafting:

- Write a beginning that clearly identifies your hero and perks up readers' interest. Notice that student writer Debra Slutak does this in her biography on page 112 by asking a question: "Have you ever wondered how some people can face hardship and tragedy—and still be happy and never complain?" Debra then goes on to state her main idea: "She has been through so much in her life and has always made the best of everything."

- Use chronological order to tell your hero's life story and use transitions to connect events. Debra uses phrases such as "At the age of eighteen" to create a chronology and employs transitions such as "not long after that" and "for the next ten years" to connect events.

- Include examples and details so readers can see why your hero is worthy of their admiration too. Notice how Debra supports her main idea by including details about her grandmother growing up in an orphanage, having a child with cerebral palsy, enduring deaths of loved ones, and having cancer.

- Write a conclusion, such as the one Debra wrote, that summarizes your feelings and admiration about your personal hero: " . . . I wish they [people who complain about how bad things are] could have the same outlook on life as my grandmother does."

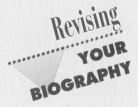

Revising YOUR BIOGRAPHY

Work with a group of peers to revise your draft. Read your draft aloud and ask for suggestions for improvement. For each biography, peer editors might make their comments on a form like the one shown.

What to Look for	Suggestions
• Why will—or won't—the beginning interest readers? • Where could details be added to reveal the hero's personality, accomplishments, and appearance? • What information needs to be added or clarified? • Why does the writer admire the hero? Why do you—or don't you—feel the same toward the hero?	

On pages 112–113 you'll see an example of student Debra Slutak's complete personal-hero biography.

Editing YOUR BIOGRAPHY

After you've finished revising, work with a partner to edit your biography. Check for errors in spelling, usage, and punctuation. You do want to show off your hero, don't you? Correct your errors and make a final copy of your biography.

Publishing YOUR BIOGRAPHY

Now you're ready to share your hero. Choose a title for your work, design a cover, and maybe even add a photograph. If your hero is living, send him or her a copy of your biography!

STUDENT MODEL

My Hero
by Debra Slutak from West Palm Beach, Florida

Have you ever wondered how some people can face hardship and tragedy—and still be happy and never complain? My hero, my grandmother Louise Gasparri, is one of those people. She has been through so much in her life and has always made the best of everything.

My grandmother was born Louise Ottmer in the Bronx, New York, on February 22, 1920. Her parents were poor immigrants from Germany and Hungary. When Louise was twelve years old, her mother died from a brain tumor. Since Louise's father couldn't support and care for her and her three siblings, they were put into an orphanage. Louise and her siblings lived in a cottage at the orphanage. Louise became like a second mother to her brothers and sisters. She cooked and cleaned, did chores, and still managed to graduate from high school.

At the age of eighteen, Louise found a job in a factory, and not long after that, she married a young man named

Sam Gasparri. Within ten years' time, she bore four children. Her last child was born with cerebral palsy. For the next ten years, Louise took constant care of him. Every day she exercised his left hand and arm at home. Every week she took him to New York City for treatment.

In 1959, Louise's oldest child died in a fire. Six weeks later, her mother-in-law died from a stroke. Louise loved her mother-in-law so much, it was as if Louise had lost another mother. Throughout these tragedies, Louise put her family and friends first. She always took time to give lessons in knitting, crocheting, and sewing to anyone who expressed an interest in learning.

In addition to having many surgeries, Louise has recently received radiation treatment after the removal of a cancerous growth. She refused to let it get her down. Louise accepts all the hardships that are dealt to her and always tries to make the best of things. Today, in her seventies, she still enjoys various crafts, bingo, and most of all, being surrounded by her loving family and friends.

When I hear others complain about how bad things are for them, I wish they could have the same outlook on life as my grandmother does.

Cooperative Learning

PRODUCING A BOX MOBILE

For this project, you and four classmates will create a box mobile. Each person will create a panel that will decorate a side—or the bottom—of the box. (A hanger and string occupy the box's top.) Each panel will show two things: a self-portrait of its creator and an illustration of some element that is common to all group members.

When you're finished, you'll hang your mobile in the classroom for other students to enjoy. Then your group will cooperatively prepare a set of guidelines for another class, instructing them how to make a box mobile.

Choose **A JOB**

The first step is to choose jobs and responsibilities as shown.

Job	Person
Facilitator: Makes sure everyone in the group is "on task" and will meet the project deadline.	
Liaison: Reports questions to the teacher that can't be answered within the group. Reports answers to the group.	
Materials Manager: Gets supplies—a plain cube-shaped gift box, glue, yarn, paper, markers, and so on—from the school or gets group members to bring supplies from home.	
Scribe: Takes notes during meetings. Maintains a daily log of comments, insights, and suggestions.	
Presenter: Assembles the mobile, hangs it up, then presents it to the class.	

Find a
COMMON ELEMENT

What is something common among group members that can be featured on each side of the box? Each group member should brainstorm for an answer. (Use the Big Questions as guides.) Then meet as a group and share your ideas. The Facilitator should conduct the meeting; the Scribe should take notes. Agree on the common element and design a representative symbol or picture. That symbol or picture will be featured—in some form—on each group member's panel.

Create a
SELF-PORTRAIT

Make a panel that totally covers your side of the box. The Materials Manager will have the cube-shaped gift box on which you'll glue your panel. Measure it carefully. To express who you are, use symbols, pictures, words, magazine cutouts, paper figures, yarn, or other materials. Remember to include the group symbol or picture.

Present
YOUR PRODUCT

The Presenter assembles the box and punches holes for hanging it up. After interviewing group members about their self-portraits, the presenter explains the box to the class.

Now that you're experienced box-mobile makers, create guidelines that will help another group to make a box mobile. As a group, determine how you want to present your finished product. You might want the guidelines to look like a recipe—beginning with the materials needed, then providing a sequential list of the steps to take. You might also include diagrams for assembly, pitfalls to avoid, and "expert" tips. Present your guidelines to your teacher.

3 Helping Your Community

CREATING A CHILDREN'S BOOK

This unit has given you many chances to think about what it means to be an individual. With this project, you'll work with a partner or a group to share some of what you've learned. Your **purpose** is to create an illustrated book that teaches your **audience**—children—something about individuality.

Targeting AN AUDIENCE

Your first step is to decide who your audience will be. Ask yourselves these questions:

- What age level will we choose for our audience?
- What other children's books can we use as models? (Models will help you to gauge your audience's vocabulary level.)
- What does your audience need to know and want to know about being an individual—or dealing with individuals?

Picking A TOPIC

In your group or with a partner, brainstorm for ideas. List your ideas, and discuss how you might develop each idea. Choose just one idea to develop into a story—for example, write about a child who learns to appreciate new neighbors' cultural differences. Remember your audience's age—you'll confuse them if you flood them with ideas.

Creating A BOOK

Determine the length of your story. (If your audience is small children, your story will probably consist mostly of pictures.) Then follow these steps to create your book.

Write the story.	Use simple language!
Revise and edit the story.	Will children like and understand it?
Type or print the story.	Use big letters and heavy paper.
Illustrate the story.	Bright colors will appeal.
Design and make a cover.	Show off your imagination!
Bind the book.	Try yarn, string, or sturdy plastic.

Presenting YOUR BOOK

Practice reading the story aloud. Then offer to read it aloud to your audience. There's nothing like instant audience feedback! If your audience is in a classroom or a day-care center, you'll probably want to donate your book to them. But don't be surprised if you get requests for more!

Putting It All Together

What Have You Learned About Identity?

Now that you've finished *To Be Somebody*, think about how your ideas about identity have changed. Review the writing you've done in this unit—in your journal, in response to your reading, and in the projects. How has what you've learned affected your ideas about who you are and your goals for the future? Now imagine that it *is* the future, and you've accomplished an important goal. Write a newspaper article that reports your accomplishment. Add your article to those of your classmates to create a *World of Tomorrow* newspaper.

NEWS FOR TOMORROW

Prewriting and Drafting First, think about what you want to accomplish within the next ten years. List your ideas in your journal. Choose the most important goal for your news article of the future.

Next, develop the details of your accomplishment. In your journal, write these one-word questions: *Who? What? When? Where? Why? How?* Then answer the questions in detail.

To draft your article, use a newspaper format: summarize the *who*, *what*, *when*, and *where* in the first paragraph. For example, "Yesterday María Martinez revealed to scientists in Washington, D.C., her device for eliminating pollutants from vehicle exhaust." Subsequent paragraphs should develop the *why* and *how* of your accomplishment.

Revising and Editing Work with a partner to revise and edit your article. Ask your partner to identify places where details need to be added, clarified, or deleted. First, choose a title that puts your accomplishment in a nutshell. Then carefully edit your article, checking grammar, punctuation, and spelling. In the future, people will *still* be critical of errors.

Publishing As a class, compile your articles into a *World of Tomorrow* newspaper. Display your newspaper in the classroom. Save a copy of your article for yourself so that you can read it in ten years!

Evaluating Your Work

Think Back About the Big Questions

With a partner, discuss the three Big Questions on pages 10-11 and the questions that you generated for **Now Think!** on page 11. In your journal, write several paragraphs in which you describe how your ideas have changed after your work in this unit.

Think Back About Your Work

Now think about your work in this unit—your reading, writing, activities, and projects. Evaluate your work by writing answers to the following questions. When you finish your self-evaluation, give it to your teacher.

- Which selections in the unit did you like the most? The least? Why?

- What are the *two* most important things that you learned about identity?

- What aspects of identity would you like to learn more about? Why?

- What did you learn about yourself as a result of the readings and activities in this unit?

- If you could choose one activity to do again, which one would you choose? What would you do differently? Why?

- How would you rate your work in this unit? Use the following scale and give at least three reasons for the rating.

  1 = Outstanding   3 = Fair
  2 = Good   4 = Not as good as it could have been

CHARACTERIZATION

What Is Characterization?   **Characterization** refers to the methods by which writers develop their characters so that they seem real to their readers. When they use *direct characterization*, writers simply describe a character's physical appearance and personality traits.

With *indirect characterization*, writers let characters reveal themselves. Readers see characters through the characters' own actions, feelings, and words. The truth about some characters may be revealed through their interaction with other characters. For example, in "Tree House," the narrator, Phil, tells readers that people treat him cruelly but that he doesn't feel sorry for himself. When other characters treat Phil with kindness and concern, however, they reveal that Phil is envious of his siblings and that he does feel sorry for himself.

Writing a Scene   Main characters usually change—often their lifestyle or attitude—by a story's end. Choose a story in this unit. How is the main character different by the story's end? Reread the story, noting in your journal the clues that the main character provides. If the story were continued, how might the character continue to change? Write a brief scene in which you show that character at some point in the future. Use direct or indirect characterization, based on the way the author presented the character.

Performing a Telephone Conversation   Imagine two characters having a telephone conversation. They may be characters from a selection in this unit, another favorite selection, or ones that you make up. Draft a script for their conversation. You will create characterization through dialogue, so try to write dialogue that is both revealing and realistic. Then pair up with another student and record your dialogue. Play your dialogue for the class or for a small group.

What Is Point of View?

A story's **point of view** is the perspective from which it is told. In *first-person point of view*, the narrator tells the story using the pronoun *I*. This narrator is often intended to be a friendly, sympathetic character who speaks directly to readers. *Third-person point of view* uses the pronouns *she, he,* or *they* and can be of two kinds. The narrator in *third-person limited point of view* reveals characters' words and actions. In *third-person omniscient* ("all knowing") *point of view,* the narrator tells the story from the perspective of one person who is removed from the action yet knows the thoughts and feelings of the characters.

Seeing the Scene Visualize a scene from one of the selections that's described in the first person or the third person. Now imagine how the scene might look from an omniscient point of view. (You might take a bird's eye view of the scene.) Draw a sketch of the scene that you've chosen. Your sketch should reveal a more distanced, objective scene than the one the narrator describes in the selection. Challenge the class to guess the story and the scene that you have depicted in your sketch.

Writing from Another Point of View Choose a selection from this unit and rewrite one scene from a different point of view. Elaborate on the scene, adding details and descriptions to make it believable to a reading audience. Read your scene to small groups or to the class. Ask those who have read the original version which one they prefer and why.

GLOSSARY OF LITERARY TERMS

A

alliteration   Repetition of the first sound—usually a consonant sound—in several words of a sentence or a line of poetry.

allusion   An author's indirect reference to someone or something that is presumed to be familiar to the reader.

anecdote   A short narrative about an interesting or a humorous event, usually in the life of a person.

antagonist   The person or force opposing the protagonist, or main character in a literary work. [See also *protagonist*.]

autobiography   A person's written account of his or her own life.

B

ballad   A poem, often a song, that tells a story in simple verse.

biography   An account of a person's life, written by another person.

blank verse   Unrhymed poetry.

C

character   A person or an animal that participates in the action of a work of literature. A *dynamic character* is one whose thoughts, feelings, and actions are changeable and lifelike; a *static character* always remains the same. [See also *protagonist, antagonist.*]

characterization   The creation of characters through the characters' use of language and through descriptions of their appearance, thoughts, emotions, and actions. [See also *character.*]

chronology   An arrangement of events in the order in which they happen.

cliché   An overused expression that is trite rather than meaningful.

climax   The highest point of tension in the plot of a work of literature. [See also *plot.*]

comedy   An amusing play that has a happy ending.

conclusion   The final part or ending of a piece of literature.

concrete poem   A poem arranged on the page so that its punctuation, letters, and lines make the shape of the subject of the poem.

conflict   A problem that confronts the characters in a piece of literature. The conflict may be *internal* (a character's struggle within himself or herself) or *external* (a character's struggle against nature, another person, or society). [See also *plot.*]

context   The general sense of words that helps readers to understand the meaning of unfamiliar words and phrases in a piece of writing.

D

description   An author's use of words to give the reader or listener a mental picture, an impression, or an understanding of a person, place, thing, event, or idea.

dialect   A form of speech spoken by people in a particular group or geographical region that differs in vocabulary, grammar, and pronunciation from the standard language.

dialogue   The spoken words and conversation of characters in a work of literature.

drama   A play that is performed before an audience according to stage directions and using dialogue. Classical drama has two genres: *tragedy* and *comedy*. Modern drama includes *melodrama, satire, theater of the absurd,* and *pantomime*. [See also *comedy, play,* and *tragedy.*]

dramatic poetry   A play written in the form of poetry.

E

epic   A long narrative poem—written in a formal style and meant to be read aloud—that relates the adventures and

experiences of one or more great heroes or heroines.

essay   Personal nonfiction writing about a particular subject that is important to the writer.

excerpt   A passage from a larger work that has been taken out of its context to be used for a special purpose.

exposition   Writing that explains, analyzes, or defines.

extended metaphor   An elaborately drawn out metaphor. [See also *metaphor*.]

F

fable   A short, simple story whose purpose is to teach a lesson, usually with animal characters who talk and act like people.

fantasy   Imaginative fiction about unrealistic characters, places, and events.

fiction   Literature, including the short story and the novel, that tells about imaginary people and events.

figurative language
Language used to express ideas through figures of speech: descriptions that aren't meant to be taken literally. Types of figurative language include *simile, metaphor, extended metaphor, hyperbole,* and *personification.*

figure of speech   A type of figurative language, not meant to be taken literally, that expresses something in such a way that it brings the thing to life in the reader's or listener's imagination. [See also *figurative language.*]

flashback   A break in a story's action that relates a past happening in order to give the reader background information about a present action in the story.

folktale   A story that has been passed along from storyteller to storyteller for generations. Kinds of folktales include *tall tales, fairy tales, fables, legends,* and *myths.*

foreshadowing   The use of clues to create suspense by giving the reader or audience hints of events to come.

free verse   Poetry that has no formal rhyme scheme or metrical pattern.

G

genre   A major category of art. The three major literary genres are poetry, prose, and drama.

H

haiku   A three-line Japanese verse form. In most haiku, the first and third lines have five syllables, while the second line has seven. The

traditional haiku describes a complicated feeling or thought in simple language through a single image.

hero/heroine   The main character in a work of literature. In heroic literature, the hero or heroine is a particularly brave, noble, or clever person whose achievements are unusual and important. [See also *character.*]

heroic age   The historical period in western civilization—from about 800 B.C. through A.D. 200—during which most works of heroic literature, such as myths and epics, were created in ancient Greece and Rome.

hubris   Arrogance or excessive pride leading to mistakes; the character flaw in a hero of classical tragedy.

hyperbole   An obvious exaggeration used for emphasis. [See also *figurative language.*]

I

idiom   An expression whose meaning cannot be understood from the ordinary meaning of the words. For example, *It's raining cats and dogs.*

imagery   The words and phrases in writing that appeal to the senses of sight, hearing, taste, touch, and smell.

irony   An effect created by a sharp contrast between what is expected and what is real. An *ironic twist* in a plot is an event that is the complete opposite of what the characters have been hoping or expecting will happen. An *ironic statement* declares the opposite of the speaker's literal meaning.

J

jargon   Words and phrases used by a group of people who share the same profession or special interests in order to refer to technical things or processes with which they are familiar. In general, jargon is any terminology that sounds unclear, overused, or pretentious.

L

legend   A famous folktale about heroic actions, passed along by word of mouth from generation to generation. The legend may have begun as a factual account of real people and events but has become mostly or completely fictitious.

limerick   A form of light verse, or humorous poetry, written in one five-line stanza with a regular scheme of rhyme and meter.

literature   The branch of art that is expressed in written language and includes all written genres.

lyric poem   A short poem that expresses personal feelings and thoughts in a musical way. Originally, lyrics were the words of songs that were sung to music played on the lyre, a stringed instrument invented by the ancient Greeks.

M

metamorphosis   The transformation of one thing, or being, into another completely different thing or being, such as a caterpillar's change into a butterfly.

metaphor   Figurative language in which one thing is said to be another thing. [See also *figurative language*.]

meter   The pattern of rhythm in lines of poetry. The most common meter, in poetry written in English, is iambic pentameter, that is, a verse having five metrical feet, each foot of verse having two syllables, an unaccented one followed by an accented one.

mood   The feeling or atmosphere that a reader senses while reading or listening to a work of literature.

motivation   A character's reasons for doing, thinking, feeling, or saying something. Sometimes an author will make a character's motivation obvious from the beginning. In realistic fiction and drama, however, a character's motivation may be so complicated that the reader discovers it gradually, by studying the character's thoughts, feelings, and behavior.

myth   A story, passed along by word of mouth for generations, about the actions of gods and goddesses or superhuman heroes and heroines. Most myths were first told to explain the origins of natural things or to justify the social rules and customs of a particular society.

N

narration   The process of telling a story. For both fiction and nonfiction, there are two main kinds of narration, based on whether the story is told from a first-person or third-person point of view. [See also *point of view*.]

narrative poem   A poem that tells a story containing the basic literary ingredients of fiction: character, setting, and plot.

narrator   The person, or voice, that tells a story. [See also *point of view, voice*.]

nonfiction   Prose that is factually true and is about real people, events, and places.

nonstandard English
Versions of English, such as slang and dialects, that use pronunciation, vocabulary, idiomatic expressions, grammar, and punctuation that differ from the accepted "correct" constructions of English.

novel   A long work of narrative prose fiction. A novel contains narration, a setting or settings, characters, dialogue, and a more complicated plot than a short story.

O

onomatopoeia   The technique of using words that imitate the sounds they describe, such as *hiss, buzz,* and *splash.*

oral tradition   Stories, poems, and songs that have been kept alive by being told, recited, and sung by people over many generations. Since the works were not originally written, they often have many different versions.

P

parable   A brief story—similar to a fable, but about people—that describes an ordinary situation and concludes with a short moral or lesson to be learned.

personification   Figurative language in which an animal, an object, or an idea is given human characteristics. [See also *figurative language*.]

persuasion   A type of speech or writing whose purpose is to convince people that something is true or important.

play   A work of dramatic literature written for performance by actors before an audience. In classical or traditional drama, a play is divided into five acts, each containing a number of scenes. Each act represents a distinct phase in the development of the plot. Modern plays often have only one act and one scene.

playwright   The author of a play.

plot   The sequence of actions and events in fiction or drama. A traditional plot has at least three parts: the *rising action*, leading up to a turning point that affects the main character; the *climax*, the turning point or moment of greatest intensity or interest; and the *falling action*, leading away from the conflict, or resolving it.

poetry   Language selected and arranged in order to say something in a compressed or nonliteral way. Modern poetry may or may not use many of the traditional poetic techniques that include *meter, rhyme, alliteration, figurative language, symbolism,* and *specific verse forms.*

point of view   The perspective from which a writer tells a story. *First-person* narrators tell the story from their own point of view, using pronouns such as *I* or *me*. *Third-person* narrators, using pronouns such as *he, she,* or *them*, may be *omniscient* (knowing everything about all characters), or *limited* (taking the point of view of one character). [See also *narration*.]

propaganda   Information or ideas that may or may not be true, but are spread as though they are true, in order to persuade people to do or believe something.

prose   The ordinary form of written and spoken language used to create fiction, nonfiction, and most drama.

protagonist   The main character of a literary work. [See also *character* and *characterization*.]

R

refrain   A line or group of lines that is repeated, usually at the end of each verse, in a poem or a song.

repetition   The use of the same formal element more than once in a literary work, for emphasis or in order to achieve another desired effect.

resolution   The falling action in fiction or drama,

including all of the developments that follow the climax and show that the story's conflict is over. [See also *plot*.]

rhyme scheme   A repeated pattern of similar sounds, usually found at the ends of lines of poetry or poetic drama.

rhythm   In poetry, the measured recurrence of accented and unaccented syllables in a particular pattern. [See also *meter*.]

S

scene   The time, place, and circumstances of a play or a story. In a play, a scene is a section of an act. [See also *play*.]

science fiction   Fantasy literature set in an imaginary future, with details and situations that are designed to seem scientifically possible.

setting   The time and place of a work of literature.

short story   Narrative prose fiction that is shorter and has a less complicated plot than a novel. A short story contains narration, at least one setting, at least one character, and usually some dialogue.

simile   Figurative language that compares two unlike things, introduced by the words "like" or "as." [See also *figurative language*.]

soliloquy   In a play, a short speech spoken by a single character when he or she is alone on the stage. A soliloquy usually expresses the character's innermost thoughts and feelings, when he or she thinks no other characters can hear.

sonnet   A poem written in one stanza, using fourteen lines of iambic pentameter. [See also *meter*.]

speaker   In poetry, the individual whose voice seems to be speaking the lines. [See also *narration*, *voice*.]

stage directions   The directions, written by the playwright, to tell the director, actors, and theater technicians how a play should be dramatized. Stage directions may specify such things as how the setting should appear in each scene, how the actors should deliver their lines, when the stage curtain should rise and fall, how stage lights should be used, where on the stage the actors should be during the action, and when sound effects should be used.

stanza   A group of lines in poetry set apart by blank lines before and after the group; a poetic verse.

style   The distinctive way in which an author composes a

work of literature in written or spoken language.

suspense   An effect created by authors of various types of fiction and drama, especially adventure and mystery, to heighten interest in the story.

symbol   An image, person, place, or thing that is used to express the idea of something else.

T

tall tale   A kind of folk tale, or legend, that exaggerates the characteristics of its hero or heroine.

theme   The main idea or underlying subject of a work of literature.

tone   The attitude that a work of literature expresses to the reader through its style.

tragedy   In classical drama, a tragedy depicts a noble hero or heroine who makes a mistake of judgment that has disastrous consequences.

V

verse   A stanza in a poem. Also, a synonym for poetry as a genre. [See also *stanza*.]

voice   The narrator or the person who relates the action of a piece of literature. [See also *speaker*.]

ACKNOWLEDGMENTS

Grateful acknowledgment is made for permission to reprint the following copyrighted material.

"Tree House" by Alden R. Carter, copyright © 1989 by Alden R. Carter from *Connnections: Short Stories* by Donald R. Gallo, ed. Used by permission of Delacorte Press, a division of Bantam Doubleday Dell Publishing Group, Inc.

"Identity" by Julio Noboa Jr. is reprinted by permission of the author from *The Rican, Journal of Contemporary Puerto Rican Thought*, Spring 1993.

"It Was a Long Time Before" by Leslie Marmon Silko, copyright © 1981 by Leslie Marmon Silko. Reprinted from *Storyteller* by Leslie Marmon Silko, published by Seaver Books, New York, NY.

"Blues for Bob E. Brown" by T. Ernesto Bethancourt, copyright © 1993 by T. Ernesto Bethancourt, from *Join In, Multiethnic Short Stories* by Donald R. Gallo, ed. Used by permission of Delacorte Press, a division of Bantam Doubleday Dell Publishing Group, Inc.

"A Haircut" by I.S. Nakata is reprinted by permission from *The Husk* (March 29966), Vol. XLV, No. 3.

"Letter from a Concentration Camp" by Yoshiko Uchida is printed by permission of the Estate of Yoshiko Uchida.

"I, Too" by Langston Hughes from *Selected Poems* by Langston Hughes. Copyright 1926 by Alfred A Knopf, Inc. and renewed 1954 by Langston Hughes. Reprinted by permission of the publisher.

"I'm Nobody" by Emily Dickinson is reprinted by permission of the publishers and the Trustees of Amherst College from *The Poems of Emily Dickinson*, Thomas H. Johnson, ed., Cambridge, MA: The Belknap Press of Harvard University Press, copyright 1951, © 1955, 1979, 1983 by the President and Fellows of Harvard College.

"The Moustache" by Robert Cormier, from *Eight Plus One* by Robert Cormier, copyright © 1975 by Robert Cormier, is reprinted by permission of Pantheon Books, a division of Random House, Inc.

"Turmoil in a Blue and Beige Bedroom" by Judie Angell, copyright © 1984 by Judie Angell, from *Sixteen: Short Stories*, Donald Gallo, ed., used by permission of Dell Books, a division of Bantam Doubleday Dell Publishing Group. Inc.

"Meta Vaux Warrick" by Walter Dean Myers from *Now Is Your Time! The African-American Struggle for Freedom*, copyright © 1991 by Walter Dean Myers. Used by permission of HarperCollins Publishers.

"Almost Perfect" by Shel Silverstein from *A Light in the Attic* by Shel Silverstein. Copyright © 1981 by Shel Silverstein. Reprinted by permission of HarperCollins Publishers, Inc. and Jonathan Cape Ltd., Publishers.

ILLUSTRATION

76-87 Susan Pizzo

PHOTOGRAPHY

4 *t* John Owens/©D.C. Heath; *b* Courtesy of Alpha Gallery; **5** Lawrence Migdale; **6** John Owens/©D.C. Heath; **8** *t* D & l MacDonald/PhotoEdit; *c* David Young-Wolff/PhotoEdit; *b* Skjold/The Image Works; **9** Nancy Sheehan/©D.C. Heath; **10** *t* Sarah Putnam/©D.C. Heath; *b* Nancy Sheehan/©D.C. Heath; **11** *t* Jim Whitmer/Stock Boston; *bl* John Owens/©D.C. Heath; *br* David Strickler/The Image Works; **12-21** Computer Imagery by Lois Schlowsky; **25** Photo by Robert Pue; **26** Courtesy of Alpha Gallery; **27** Courtesy of Julio Noboa; **28-29** Copyright ©1981 by Leslie Marmon Silko. Reprinted from *Storyteller* by Leslie Marmon Silko, published by Seaver Books, New York, NY; **29** *r* Photo by Gus Nitsche; **30** Tom Stewart/The Stock Market; **30-31** *background* Berenholtz/The Stock Market; **34, 35** Tom Stewart/The Stock Market; **38** *l* AP/Wide World; *r* Tony Rankin/Globe Photos; **39** *c* The Bettmann Archive; *l* UPI/Bettmann; *r* Sydney Byrd/Globe Photos; **41** Tom Stewart/The Stock Market; **44-45** *background* Joseph Pobereskin/Tony Stone Images; *inset* Tony Freeman/PhotoEdit; **46-47** Tony Freeman/PhotoEdit; **49** Photo by Tom Tondee; **50-55** Julie Bidwell/©D.C. Heath; **56-57, 58-59** U.S. Department of Agriculture, Farm Security Administration: Library of Congress; **57-58** *inset* Library of Congress; **59** Photo by Deborah Storms/Courtesy of Macmillan Children's Book Group; **60** Courtesy Estate of Romare Bearden/Art & Artifacts Division, Schomburg Center for Research in Black Culture, The New York Public Library, Astor, Lenox and Tilden Foundations; **61** AP/Wide World Photos; **62-63** *t* Lawrence Migdale; **63** *b* Historical Pictures/Stock Montage, Inc.; **64-74** Computer Photo Illustration by Jim Carroll; **75** AP/Wide World Photos; **87** Courtesy of Macmillan Children's Book Group; **88-89** Collection Viollet, Paris; **88** *inset*, **89** Collection Solomon Fuller, Bourne, MA; **92** Hampton University Museum, Hampton, VA; **93** Philadelphia Museum of Art: A.E. Gallatin Collection. ©1995 ARS, NY/SPADEM, Paris; **96** Harlingue-Viollet; **97** Danforth Museum of Art Collection, Framingham, MA; **100** Collection Solomon Fuller, Bourne, MA; **101** Courtesy of Harper Collins Publishers; **103** AP/Wide World Photos; **105** Bob Daemmrich/Tony Stone Images; **108** J. Berndt/Stock Boston; **109** *l* Photo by Jean Claude LeJeune; *r* Bachmann/The Image Works; **110** Michael Schroeder; **113** Robert Brenner/ PhotoEdit; **114** *t* Sarah Putnam/©D.C. Heath; **114** *b*, **115** Ken O'Donoghue/©D.C. Heath; **116** Rhoda Sidney/Stock Boston; **117** Photo by Jean Claude LeJeune.
Back cover *t* Sarah Putnam/© D.C. Heath; *c.* John Owens/© D.C. Heath; *b* Julie Bidwell/© D.C. Heath

Full Pronunciation Key for Footnoted Words

(Each pronunciation and definition is adapted from *Scott, Foresman Advanced Dictionary* by E.L. Thorndike and Clarence L. Barnhart.)

The pronunciation of each footnoted word is shown just after the word, in this way: **abbreviate** [ə brē′ vē āt]. The letters and signs used are pronounced as in the words below. The mark ′ is placed after a syllable with primary or heavy accent, as in the example above. The mark ′ after a syllable shows a secondary or lighter accent, as in **abbreviation** [ə brē′ vē ā′ shən].

Some words, taken from foreign languages, are spoken with sounds that do not otherwise occur in English. Symbols for these sounds are given in the key as "foreign sounds."

a	hat, cap	j	jam, enjoy	u	cup, butter	**foreign sounds**
ā	age, face	k	kind, seek	ù	full, put	
ä	father, far	l	land, coal	ü	rule, move	Y as in French *du*.
		m	me, am	v	very, save	Pronounce (ē) with
b	bad, rob	n	no, in	w	will, woman	the lips rounded as
ch	child, much	ng	long, bring	y	young, yet	for (ü).
d	did, red			z	zero, breeze	
		o	hot, rock	zh	measure, seizure	à as in French *ami*.
e	let, best	ō	open, go			Pronounce (ä) with
ē	equal, be	ô	order, all	ə represents:		the lips spread and
ėr	term, learn	oi	oil, voice		a in about	held tense.
		ou	house, out		e in taken	
f	fat, if				i in pencil	œ as in French *peu*.
g	go, bag	p	paper, cup		o in lemon	Pronounce (ā) with the
h	he, how	r	run, try		u in circus	lips rounded as for (ō).
		s	say, yes			
i	it, pin	sh	she, rush			N as in French *bon*.
ī	ice, five	t	tell, it			The N is not pro-
		th	thin, both			nounced, but shows
		ᵺH	then, smooth			that the vowel before
						it is nasal.

H as in German *ach*. Pronounce (k) without closing the breath passage.

GLOSSARY

This glossary is an alphabetical list of words found in the literature selections in this book. Most of the words in the glossary are also defined in footnotes on the pages where they appear. A few foreign words, proper nouns, and words with meanings that are very specific to the literature selection are not listed here but are defined in footnotes on the pages where they appear.

Many English words have several different meanings. This glossary gives you the meanings that apply to the words as they are used in the literature selections in this book.

Unless a word is very easy to pronounce, its pronunciation is given in brackets. A key to the pronunciation symbols appears on the previous page (page 128).

A

abide [ə bīd′]: stay, remain.

abyss [ə bis′]: a bottomless depth or chasm.

acoustic [ə kü′ stik]: having to do with the science of sound.

airlock: an airtight compartment between places where there is a difference in air pressure.

allay [ə lā′]: put at rest, relieve.

altimeters [al tim′ ə tərz]: instruments that measure altitude.

amass [ə mas′]: gather together.

anachronism [ə nak′ rə niz′ əm]: out of keeping with the time in which a person is living.

antimacassar [an′ ti mə kas′ ər]: a covering that prevents the arms and back of a chair or sofa from being soiled.

archaeologist [är′ kē ol′ ə jist]: an expert in the study of people and customs of ancient times.

archerfish: small fresh-water fish of Southeast Asia that preys upon spiders and insects on shore by spitting drops of water at them to knock them into the water.

archers [är′ chərz]: people who shoot with bows and arrows.

asteroid [as′ tə roid′]: any of the thousands of very small planets that revolve about the sun.

astrodome [as′ trə dōm]: transparent dome on the fuselage of an aircraft through which observations are made for navigating through the sky.

astrophysical [as′ trō fiz′ ə kəl]: a branch of astronomy that deals with the physical and chemical characteristics of heavenly bodies.

athwartships [ə thwôrt′ shipz]: placed across from side to side of the ship.

attaches [at′ ə shās′]: members of the diplomatic staff of an ambassador or minister to a foreign country.

augmented [ôg ment′ əd]: increased.

aura [ōr′ ə]: something unseen that surrounds a person or thing.

B

baling-hook: a large hook used to lift heavy objects.

ball peen hammer: hammer that has a rounded or wedged head.

barrio [bä′ ryō]: a neighborhood in which Spanish-speaking people live.

batons: light sticks used by the leader of an orchestra, chorus, or band to indicate the beat and to direct.

bayonets [bā′ ə nets]: knives often attached to the muzzle of rifles.

became: suited, looked good on.

befuddled [bi fud′ ld]: stupified, confused.

begonias [bi gō′ nyəz]: tropical plants with large leaves and waxy flowers.

bougainvillea [bú′ gən vil′ yä]: tropical American vine with bright flowers.

beset [bi set′]: attacked from all sides.

bibulous [bib′ yə ləs]: fond of drinking alcoholic drinks.

biennial [bī en′ ē əl]: every two years.

bingo: game of chance using numbers.

bird shot: small lead pellets usually used in shooting birds.

bolo tie [bō′ lō tī]: string tie, with decorated slide.

boonie hat: camouflaged floppy hat with a brim all around it.

bravado [brə vä′ dō]: a show of courage without much real courage.

bungalow [bung′ gə lō]: small house.

butte top [byüt top]: top of a steep, flat-topped hill.

cairn [kern]: a pile of stones heaped up for a memorial or landmark.

calculated [kal′ kyə lāt əd]: thought about carefully.

calibrated [kal′ ə brāt əd]: checked or adjusted by comparing to a standard instrument.

camouflage [kam′ ə fläzh]: uniform that helps the wearer to blend in with the surroundings.

cantering [kan′ tər ing]: galloping gently.

carbon: a nonmetallic element found in plants and animals.

careened [kə rēnd′]: tipped and swayed very quickly.

cartwrighting [kärt′ rīt ing]: making carts.

cascaded [ka skād′ əd]: flowed.

cascading: flowing like a waterfall.

casement [kās′ mənt]: a window that opens on hinges as a door does.

celestial [sə les′ chəl]: of the sky.

château [shä tō′]: French for "castle."

chifforobe [shif′ ə rōb]: furniture with drawers and a place for hanging clothes.

chimes: set of bells, usually in church towers, tuned to a musical scale.

claret [klar′ ət]: dark purplish red.

claustrophobic [klô′ strə fō′ bik]: having an abnormal fear of enclosed places.

climes: countries or regions.

clods: lumps of earth.

cloven [klō′ vən]: a hoof that is divided into two parts, similar to that of a goat.

coalition [kō′ ə lish′ ən]: group working for a common purpose.

common: land used by everyone in the town; the first battle of the Revolutionary War was fought on the Lexington common or green.

contemplate [kon′ təm plāt]: look at and study for a long time.

convivial [kən viv′ ē əl]: sociable, jovial.

coopering [kü′ pər ing]: making or repairing barrels.

coral [kôr′ əl]: stony substance formed from the skeletons of tropical sea animals called polyps.

corona [kə rō′ nə]: a ring of light around the sun, seen only during an eclipse.

council: group of people called together to settle questions and problems.

crepitation [krep ə tā′ shən]: a crackling sound.

criteria [krī tir′ ē ə]: rules or standards for making a judgment.

crossbreed: make new crops by interbreeding different varieties of plants.

crumpets: round, flat cakes.

culminating [kul′ mə nāt ing]: ending.

D

dead-reckoning: calculation of the position of a ship or aircraft by using a compass and the navigator's record, without observing the sun and the stars.

deathwatches [deth′ woch əz]: insects that make a ticking sound; they were once believed to predict death.

decadent aristocrats [dek′ ə dənt ə ris′ tə kratz]: immoral people of noble birth.

depot [dē pō′]: station.

desecrated [des′ ə krāt əd]: treated without respect.

devastated [dev′ ə stāt əd]: destroyed.

devise [di vīz′]: think out, plan.

dilating [dī lāt′ ing]: becoming wider.

domain [dō mān']: place that is all their own.

doozy [dü' zē]: something outstanding or unusual.

double-ought buckshot [dubl ôt buk' shot]: small lead ball or shot fired from a shotgun; double-ought (00) refers to the size of the shot.

doughty [dou' tē]: brave, strong.

dragoons [drə günz']: soldiers who ride a horse and are trained to fight on foot or on horseback.

drudgery [druj' ər ē]: hard, tiresome work.

E

ecstasy [ek' stə sē]: condition of great joy.

embossed [em bôsd']: having letters that are raised to stand out from the surface.

emerald: green.

empathize [em' pə thīz]: enter, through the imagination, into another's feelings or motives.

ennui [än wē']: weariness, boredom.

entomology [en' tə mol' ə jē]: the study of insects.

essence: that which makes something what it is; necessary part of something.

esthetics [es thėt' iks]: having or showing an appreciation of beauty in art or nature.

eventide [ē' vən tīd]: evening.

evinced [i vinsd']: showed clearly.

exhilarating [eg zil' ə rāt' ing]: extremely energizing.

exotic [eg zot' ik]: interesting because strange or different.

F

fakirs [fə kirz']: members of religious group in India who often walk on coals or charm snakes.

familiar: close friend.

fatigues [fə tēgz']: military uniform usually worn while doing nonmilitary work.

fer-de-lance [fer' də läns']: a poisonous pit viper.

fiesta [fē es' tə]: a religious festival honoring a saint.

fix: the determining of the position of a ship or plane by using mathematical, electronic, or other means.

folly [fol' ē]: foolishness, unwise conduct.

forbearance: patient endurance.

fowling piece: lightweight shotgun, usually used for shooting wild birds.

fretful: unhappy

fusillade [fyü´ zə läd']: rapid and continuous sound.

G

gait: way of walking.

galaxy [gal' ek sē]: system of stars, cosmic dust, and gas held together by gravitation.

galleon [gal' ē ən]: a large sailing ship with three or four decks.

gamboled [gam' bəld]: ran and jumped about.

gargoyle [gär' goil]: a strange-looking carved head of an animal.

geologist [jē ol' ə jist]: an expert in the study of the earth's crust.

gimlet [gim' lit]: a small tool for boring holes.

glancing: flashing, gleaming.

glaucoma [glô kō' mə]: a disease of the eye in which internal pressure results in gradual loss of sight.

gleaned [glēnd]: gathered little by little.

glimmeringly: with a dim perception or a faint idea.

globe thistle: plant with prickly stalks and leaves, usually with purple flowers.

grackle squawk: the harsh sound made by a large blackbird with shiny feathers.

grape shot: cluster of small iron balls used in a cannon.

gravity [grav' ə tē]: the natural force that causes objects to move toward the center of the planet.

grubs: soft, thick, wormlike larva of an insect, especially that of a beetle.

grueling [grü' ə ling]: tiring.

guerrillas [gə ril' əz]: members of a band of fighters who harass the enemy by sudden raids and ambushes.

gunwale [gun 'l]: the upper edge of the side of a ship.

gyros [jī' rōs]: short for gyroscopes; instruments consisting of rotating wheels so mounted that the axis can turn freely in one or more directions. Gyroscopes keep vehicles steady.

H

hallucinations [hə lü' sn ā' shənz]: the state of seeing or hearing things that exist only in a person's imagination.

hamadryad [ham′ ə drī′ əd]: one who lives in a tree; the king cobra is a tree-dweller.

handicapper: reference to the custom in games of giving less skilled people advantages and more skilled people disadvantages so that all have an equal chance to win.

haversacks [hav′ ər sakz]: bags used by soldiers and hikers for carrying food or supplies on a march or hike.

haymaker: a hard, upward punch with the fist.

hearth [härth]: fireside, home.

heath: open land with bushes, but few trees.

heathen [he′ ŦHən]: people who do not believe in the God of the Bible or the Koran.

hereditary: passed down genetically from parent to child.

herpetologist [hėr′ pə tol′ ə jist]: an expert in dealing with reptiles.

hibiscus [hī bis′ kəs]: herb, shrub, or tree of the mallow family, with large red, pink, or white bell-shaped flowers.

hindrances [hin′ drəns əz]: things that hold someone back from accomplishing a goal.

horsehair: hair from the mane or tail of a horse used on the bow of a fiddle, violin, or cello.

I

illustrious [i lus′ trē əs]: very famous and important.

impassioned [im pash′ ənd]: full of strong feeling.

incandescent [in′ kən des′ nt]: glowing with heat and light.

indentured servant [in den′ chərd]: servant bound by a contract to work for someone else, usually for seven years.

inert [in ėrt′]: lacking the power to move.

inertia [in ėr′ shə]: a tendency for all objects and matter to stay still or move in the same direction unless acted upon by an outside force.

inextricably [in ek′ strə kə blē]: unable to be disentangled.

infuse: fill.

intangible [in tan′ jə bəl]: not able to be touched or seen.

interstellar [in′ tər stel′ ər]: situated in the region of the stars.

iron lung: a device used to help the breathing of people whose chest muscles are paralyzed.

irrelevant [i rel′ ə vənt]: not applicable.

J

jalousie [jal′ ə zē]: a window shade or shutter that keeps out sun and rain.

jasmine [jas′ mən]: shrub or vine of the olive family with clusters of fragrant yellow, white, or reddish flowers.

K

keen: sharp, acute.

kimono [kə mō′ nə]: loose robe held in place by a wide sash.

knouter [nout′ ər]: one who flogs others with a knout (whip).

kung fu [kùng′ fü′]: ancient Chinese method of self-defense that uses the hands and legs as weapons.

L

lascars [las′ kərz]: sailors, artillery men, or army servants.

laying out: preparing a body for burial.

liberate [lib′ ə rāt]: set free.

liberator [lib′ ə rāt ər]: one who sets others free.

lodges: small houses.

loon [lün]: large, fish-eating, web-footed bird that has a loud cry and lives in northern regions.

luminous [lü′ mə nəs]: clear.

lump alum [al′ əm]: white mineral salt used in medicine and in preserving such items as pickles.

M

mandarin [man′ dər ən]: member of one of the nine ranks of public officials of the Chinese Empire.

mandolin [man′ də lin′]: a musical instrument with a pear-shaped body, having four to six pairs of strings.

manual dexterity [dek ster′ ə tē]: skill in using the hands.

marine biology: study of animals and plants that live in the ocean.

marrow [mar′ ō]: soft tissue in bones.

mead [mēd]: an ancient English drink made from honey.

mediation: the arranging of an agreement by someone outside a group.

melee [mā′ lā]: hand-to-hand fighting among a number of people.

memorabilia [mem′ ər ə bil′ ē ə]: items saved as a remembrance of someone or something.

meningitis [men′ in jī tis]: an illness that is often fatal.

millet [mil′ it]: a cereal grass used as a food grain.

minnow [min′ ō]: a small fish.

misdemeanor [mis′ di mē′ nər]: misbehavior.

mocked [mokd]: made fun of.

module [moj′ ůl]: a part, component.

molatto: old form of mulatto [mə lat′ ō]; a person of mixed racial descent.

molten [mōlt′ n]: made liquid by heat.

mongoose [mong′ güs]: an animal of Asia and Africa; the Asian mongoose is noted for being able to kill cobras.

monitor lizard [mon′ ə tər liz′ ərd]: a large lizard of Africa, Asia, and Australia.

monsoon [mon sün′]: the rainy season during which the wind of the same name blows from the southwest.

moon-festival celebrations: special festival for children.

mooring cables [můr′ ing]: cables that attach an object to the ground.

moors: open land, with low bushes or swamps.

morocco-bound: reference to an old-fashioned book cover made of leather.

mosaic [mō zā′ ik]: decoration made of small colored pieces of stone, glass, or wood inlaid to form a picture or design.

mouth harp: a harmonica.

muskellunge [mus′ kə lunj]: North American pike, a large fish.

N

neurology [nů rol′ ə jē]: the study of the nervous system and its diseases.

neutralizing [nü′ trə līz ing]: cancelling.

nitro [nī′ trō]: medicine that dilates blood vessels (nitroglycerine).

O

oasis [ō ā′ sis]: a pleasant place.

observatory [əb zėr′ və tôr′ ē]: place for observing the stars and other heavenly bodies.

octant [ok′ tənt]: navigation instrument used to measure the altitude of heavenly bodies in order to determine latitude and longitude.

octogenarians [ok′ tə jə ner′ ē ənz]: people who are between eighty and ninety years old.

offset: make up for.

oleanders [ō′ lē an′ dərz]: fragrant evergreen shrubs with brightly colored flowers.

orchids [ôr′ kidz]: colorful perrenial plants with many petals.

ostler [os′ lər]: a person who cares for horses at an inn or stable.

outfit: provide uniforms and equipment for.

ozone [ō′ zōn]: form of oxygen with a sharp odor, usually present in the air, especially after a thunderstorm.

P

parapet [par′ ə pet]: a low barrier at the edge of a roof.

parfleches [pär flesh′]: pouches made of rawhide, used for carrying arrows.

parley [pär′ lē]: conference, informal talk.

partisans [pär′ tə zenz]: members of the underground.

pathologist [pa thol′ ə jist]: a doctor who is an expert in the study of the causes and nature of diseases.

peaked [pē′ kid]: sick looking.

perennial [pə ren′ ē əl]: lasting for a very long time.

perihelion [per′ ə hē′ lyən]: the point closest to the sun in the orbit of a planet or comet.

perseverance [pėr′ sə vir′ əns]: tenacity, act of sticking to a purpose.

pest: destructive or harmful insect.

phosphorescence [fos′ fə res′ ns]: a light given out without apparent heat or burning.

pilgrimage [pil′ grə mij]: a journey to a special place.

pinch glasses: eyeglasses that clip onto the bridge of the nose and have no bows to go over the ears.

pirouettes [pir′ ü etz′]: act of spinning in circles.

plague [plāg]: highly contagious, often fatal, disease that spreads quickly and affects large numbers of people.

platitudes [plat′ ə tüdz]: dull or ordinary remarks said as if they were new or fresh.

pompadour [pom′ pə dôr]: a hair style in which the front of the hair is puffed high up and back from the forehead.

prance: proud way of walking, similar to a dance.

pre-primer [prē prim′ ər]: very first reading book.

priming [prī′ ming]: powder used in guns and explosives.

prosaic [prō zā′ ik]: ordinary.

python [pī′ thon]: a large, nonpoisonous snake of Asia, Africa, and Australia that kills by squeezing.

Q

quicklime: calcium oxide, a water-soluble solid; it can destroy a body.

R

ramparts [ram′ pärtz]: wide banks of earth, often with walls, built to defend a fort or a building.

ranks: rows or lines of soldiers, placed side by side.

rapier hilt [rā′ pē ər hilt]: handle of a long, light sword.

reckoned [rek′ ənd]: thought.

redcoats: British soldiers during the Revolutionary War.

relocation camp [rē lō kā′ shun]: one of several inland detention camps established by the United States government during World War II for all Japanese Americans living on the West Coast.

resolute [rez′ ə lüt]: bold, determined.

resolutely [rez′ ə lüt lē]: firmly.

reticence [ret′ ə səns]: habit of being silent and reserved, or shy.

riveting gun: gun that drives rivets—metal bolts—into heavy material.

rubicund [rü′ bə kund]: reddish, ruddy.

rupees [rü pēz′]: Indian coins.

S

sabotage [sab′ ə täzh]: damage done deliberately.

saffron [saf′ rən]: an orange-yellow color.

sagacity [sə gas′ ə tē]: sound judgment, shrewdness.

sage [sāj]: a small shrub whose leaves are used as seasoning and in medicine.

sampans [sam′ panz]: small boats with oars, a single sail, and a cabin made of mats.

sapling: a young tree.

sash-weights: metal weights in windows that allow them to be raised and lowered.

scones: thick, flat, round, bread-like cakes.

scrabbled [skrab′ əld]: struggled.

seed melon: a melon whose seeds are planted for the next crop.

seismograph [sīz′ mə graf]: an instrument used for recording the direction, intensity, and duration of an earthquake.

sentinel [sen′ tə nəl]: a person who keeps watch and guards against surprise attacks.

sentry [sen′ trē]: a soldier stationed to keep watch and guard against surprise attacks.

severance [sev′ ər əns]: a separation, breaking off.

shindigs: happy, noisy dances or parties.

shooting a star: aiming the altimeter toward a star.

shrewd [shrüd]: very smart, clever.

shrouding: wrapping a body in a cloth or shroud for burial.

skiff [skif]: a small rowboat, sometimes having a single sail.

slag [slag]: the rough waste left after a metal is separated from ore by melting.

slide guitar: a regular guitar on which the guitarist uses a hollow steel tube or a piece of glass on a finger of the left hand; the tube slides up and down the strings to create a smooth sound, while the right hand plucks the strings.

sloop [slüp]: a sailboat with one mast and several sails.

sluices [slüs′ əz]: gates for holding back the flow of water or other substances.

smite [smīt]: strike hard.

snuffbox [snuf′ boks]: a small box for holding snuff, a powdered tobacco that is inhaled.

something the cat drug in: idiom that means someone looks terrible.

sowing [sō′ ing]: planting.

speech impediment [im ped′ ə mənt]: a problem that interferes with clear speech.

stable-wicket [stā′ bəl wik′ it]: a small door or gate in a horse stable.

stereotyping [ster′ ē ə tīp′ ing]: judging an entire group by the actions of a few.

sterility [stə ril′ ə tē]: lifelessness.

stolid [stol′ id]: showing no emotion.

stringent [strin′ jənt]: strict, severe.

strychnine [strik′ nən]: a poison that is a stimulant for the heart when used in small doses.

surly [sėr′ lē]: bad-tempered and unfriendly, rude.

symmetry [sim′ ə trē]: a regular, balanced arrangement that is the same on each side.

synchronizing [sing′ krə nīz ing]: causing to occur at the same time; agreeing in musical time.

T

tantalized [tan′ tl īzd]: bothered, distracted from trying to remember.

tapir [tā′ pər]: large, piglike mammal of the topics having hooves and a flexible snout.

tartar [tär′ tər]: a person with a bad temper; the Tartars were Mongolians and Turks who invaded Asia and eastern Europe during the Middle Ages.

temples: the flattened part on each side of the forehead.

terrapins [ter′ ə pinz]: edible North American turtles that live in fresh water or tidewater.

thrashed [thrashed]: moved violently.

toilsome [toil′ səm]: requiring hard work.

traits [trātz]: characteristics, distinguishing features.

transfixed [trans sfiksd′]: made still with amazement.

trapezoids [trap′ ə zoids]: four-sided plane figures with two sides parallel and two sides not parallel.

triglycerides [trī glis′ ə rīdz]: fatty acids, blood fats.

turgid [tėr′ jid]: puffed up with big words.

twenty-one-gun salute: usually, firing of cannons as a sign of respect for a famous person.

typhoon [tī fün′]: a violent storm.

U

underground: movement in which people worked in secret against the Nazis.

unorthodox [un ôr′ thə dox]: not having the same opinions as most people.

unscintillating [un sin′ tl āt ing]: not sparkling.

V

vermilion [vər mil′ yən]: bright red.

villa: large elegant house.

violation [vī′ ə lā′ shən]: a going against.

voile [voil]: thin cloth of silk, wool, or cotton.

volleys: showers of stones, bullets, or arrows.

W

wallabies [wol′ ə bēz]: small or medium-sized kangaroos.

whippoorwill: North American bird whose call sounds somewhat like its name; it is active at night or at twilight.

white flag: traditional sign of surrender.

winced: drew back suddenly.

Z

zinc sheet: a sheet of blue-white metal; one of its uses is as roofing material.

INDEX OF FINE ART

INDEX OF SKILLS

LITERATURE STUDY

WRITING

SPEAKING AND LISTENING

CRITICAL THINKING

Applying: 128-129, 130-131, 132, 258-259, 260-261, 262, 390-391, 392, 511, 522, 650-651, 652, 782-783

Classifying: 249, 648-649, 650-651, 676, 780-781, 936

Comparing and Contrasting: 120, 121, 395, 544-545, 638, 641, 676, 677, 768, 898, 1030

Defining: 252-256, 284-285, 286, 378, 1032

Drawing Conclusions: 26, 27, 120, 122-125, 249, 251, 252-256, 382-386, 414-415, 510, 511, 512-515, 522, 544-545, 642-646, 900, 910-911

Evaluating: 118, 132-133, 262-263, 390-391, 392-393, 522-523, 544-545, 642-646, 652-653, 676, 782-783, 806, 898, 912-913, 934-935, 1044-1045

Extending: 118, 120, 121, 135, 248, 250, 251, 260-261, 264, 265, 378, 379, 380, 381, 508, 509, 510, 638, 639, 640, 654, 769, 770, 771, 785, 908-909, 914, 1030, 1031, 1032, 1046, 1047

Generalizing: 26, 251, 252-256, 260-261, 287, 381, 512-515

Imagining: 118, 119, 120, 121, 134, 135, 154-155, 156, 157, 248, 250, 258-259, 262, 264, 265, 284-285, 379, 380, 394, 395, 414-415, 417, 508, 510, 524, 544-545, 638, 639, 641, 654, 655, 674-675, 676, 769, 770, 771, 772-776, 784, 804-805, 902-906, 914, 1030, 1032, 1033, 1044, 1046, 1047

Inferring: 252-256, 414-415, 416, 1031

Interpreting: 119, 120, 249, 250, 508, 525, 638, 677, 910-911, 1032

Organizing: 24-25, 26, 27, 118, 119, 121, 122-125, 128-129, 130-131, 154-155, 157, 248, 251, 252-255, 258-259, 260-261, 286, 287, 378, 380, 382-386, 388-389, 390-391, 416, 508, 509, 510, 512-515, 520-521, 546, 547, 638, 640, 641, 648-649, 768, 769, 772-776, 778-779, 780-781, 807, 901, 902-906, 936, 1030, 1031, 1032, 1033, 1034-1037, 1040-1041

Predicting Outcomes: 154-155, 249, 414-415, 508, 512-515, 641, 655, 769, 771, 804-805

Summarizing: 119, 122-125, 250, 251, 252-256, 260-261, 286, 381, 382-386, 642-646, 807

Synthesizing: 132-133, 262-263, 392-393, 522-523, 652-653, 782-783, 912-913, 1044-1045

Understanding Relationships Between Characters: 134, 248, 249, 250, 264, 265, 378, 380, 394, 509, 510, 511, 524, 654, 769, 772-776, 778-779, 804-805, 902-906, 908-909, 912, 914, 915, 1030, 1033, 1042-1043, 1046, 1047

Understanding Relationships Between Events: 132, 134, 248, 249, 250, 258-259, 265, 382-386, 394, 414-415, 510, 511, 512-515, 524, 546, 652, 769, 771, 772-776, 778-779, 784, 804-805, 898, 900, 902-906, 908-909, 912, 914, 915, 1033, 1042-1043

Understanding Relationships Between Ideas: 122-125, 134, 156, 248, 249, 250, 264, 265, 284-285, 287, 382-386, 512-515, 544-545, 642-646, 652, 674-675, 899

Understanding Causal Relationships: 119, 122-125, 128-129, 134, 156, 157, 249, 250, 252-255, 260-261, 265, 287, 382-386, 392, 414-415, 416, 508, 509, 510, 511, 512-515, 524, 546, 769, 771, 901, 910-911, 1033

Understanding Chronological Relationships (Sequencing): 132, 134, 248, 249, 250, 265, 382-386, 510, 511, 518-519, 524, 652, 769, 771, 772-776, 778-779, 804-805, 902-906, 908-909, 912, 914, 915, 937, 1034-1037, 1042-1043

COLLABORATIVE LEARNING

24-25, 26, 27, 118, 119, 120, 121, 125, 128-129, 132, 133, 154-155, 156, 157, 250, 251, 256, 258-

259, 260-261, 262, 263, 264, 285, 287, 381, 388-389, 390-391, 393, 414-415, 417, 508, 510, 511, 515, 518-519, 520-521, 522, 523, 525, 544-545, 547, 639, 640, 641, 645, 648-649, 652, 653, 655, 674-675, 677, 770, 771, 775, 778-779, 780-781, 782, 783, 804-805, 806, 807, 899, 900, 905, 908-909, 913, 914, 915, 934-935, 1032, 1037, 1040-1041, 1042-1043, 1044, 1045

COMMUNITY SERVICE

130-131, 260-261, 390-391, 520-521, 650-651, 780-781, 910-911, 1042-1043

INDEX OF GENRES

N O N F I C T I O N

D R A M A

INDEX OF AUTHORS AND TITLES